DUMBARTON OAKS
MEDIEVAL LIBRARY

THE WORKS OF HROTSVIT OF GANDERSHEIM

DOML 90

The Works of Hrotsvit of Gandersheim

Edited and Translated by

ROBERT GARY BABCOCK

DUMBARTON OAKS
MEDIEVAL LIBRARY

HARVARD UNIVERSITY PRESS
CAMBRIDGE, MASSACHUSETTS
LONDON, ENGLAND
2025

Printed in the United States of America

First Printing

EU GPSR Authorised Representative
LOGOS EUROPE, 9 rue Nicolas Poussin, 17000, La Rochelle, France
E-mail: Contact@logoseurope.eu

Library of Congress Cataloging-in-Publication Data

Names: Hrotsvitha, approximately 935–approximately 975 author | Babcock, Robert Gary, 1958– editor | Hrotsvitha, approximately 935–approximately 975. Works | Hrotsvitha, approximately 935–approximately 975 Works. English

Title: The works of Hrotsvit of Gandersheim / Hrotsvit of Gandersheim ; edited and translated by Robert Gary Babcock.

Description: Cambridge, Massachusetts : Harvard University Press, 2025. | Series: Dumbarton Oaks Medieval Library ; 90 | Includes bibliographical references and index. | This is a facing-page volume: Latin on the versos; English translation on the rectos. Introduction and notes in English.

Identifiers: LCCN 2025007581 | ISBN 9780674290891 cloth

Subjects: LCGFT: Poetry | Drama | Prefatory works | Personal correspondence

Classification: LCC PA8340 .A2 2025 | DDC 872/.03—dc23/eng/20250519

LC record available at https://lccn.loc.gov/2025007581

Contents

Book 2

Book 3

Introduction

Hrotsvit of Gandersheim, a tenth-century Saxon poet and playwright, is today among the most widely read and studied of Medieval Latin writers.[1] Her surviving works include a series of dramatic compositions that were intended, as she says, to replace the plays of Terence; a collection of hagiographical poems about Christian saints and martyrs; and two epic poems, one on the emperor Otto the Great, the other on the founders and benefactors of her own abbey, Gandersheim. In the quantity of her output, the diversity of genres in which she worked, and the intrinsic interest of her compositions, she ranks among the most important Latin writers of any period. Hrotsvit's plays have been translated several times into English and, since the twentieth century, rather widely performed; but her other works are less readily available in print.[2] This is the first English translation of all her works in a single volume.

Nothing is known of Hrotsvit's life, family, acquaintances, or circumstances beyond what we can extract from the few personal remarks she makes in the prefaces and prologues to her various works. She is not mentioned by any of her contemporaries. The salient points are these: she lived and worked at Gandersheim, about fifty miles south of Hannover, while Gerberga II was abbess (956–1001); her teachers included a woman named Rikkardis, otherwise unknown, and Abbess Gerberga herself, and the latter encouraged her to write; she was older than Gerberga, the date of whose birth is not known but is inferred to be around 940, so Hrotsvit was probably born before 940; she dedicates works to Gerberga, to Emperor Otto I (r. 962–973), and to his coruler and successor Emperor Otto II (r. 967–983), so she was writing in the 960s, but probably also earlier and later than that decade; and her acquaintances included members of the Ottonian dynasty and court, and members of the royal and ducal families of Germany and Saxony as well, so she moved in some of the most important political and cultural circles of her time.[3]

Gandersheim Abbey was a house of secular canonesses, that is to say, a religious community of women who were committed to living chaste lives of religious service, but who did not necessarily take lifelong vows of poverty or celibacy, as Benedictines do.[4] Canonesses might leave their communities to marry or for other reasons, and they were allowed to own private property. Also unlike the Benedictines, who usually lived far from population centers, and whose members were shut off from contact with outsiders, secular canons and canonesses often lived in cities; and the members of such communities might have more extensive interactions with the outside world, their service activities often focusing on nursing or teaching, as opposed to the Benedictines' orientation toward farming. Gandersheim, being the first monastic foundation of the Liudolfing family, held a place of prestige among Saxon houses, especially in the Ottonian period, and the canonesses were generally aristocratic women, many of them with considerable power and resources. The patronage Gandersheim enjoyed from the emperors brought with it the obligation to host the emperor and his retinue, providing accommodation as well as banquets to them when they passed through Gandersheim in their travels around the empire; the canonesses at Gandersheim were thus not cut off from the social world of the highest aristocracy.

Communities like the one at Gandersheim had schools for their novices, and some of these schools also served as educational centers for the daughters of aristocratic families, including daughters who did not take religious vows of any sort or intend to become nuns. Since Gandersheim was patronized by members of the Ottonian dynasty—Gerberga herself was a niece of Otto the Great's, and her successor, Sophia, was the daughter of Otto II—it would have been an attractive place for noble Saxon families to send their girls for schooling. It is a reasonable surmise that Hrotsvit was sent there for that reason by her family and that her family was Saxon and noble. We do not know how old Hrotsvit was when she entered Gandersheim, whether she belonged to other religious communities before or after she was at Gandersheim, nor whether she ever left the religious life, for marriage or for other reasons. We also have no indication of what her daily routine was like while she lived at Gandersheim. That she spent some of her time writing is clear. Given the extent of her reading and the breadth of her knowledge, which included advanced subjects such as dialectic, music, and mathematics, it is possible she was a teacher at Gandersheim. She was certainly one of the most learned women of the Middle Ages; it is not likely she had many intellectual superiors at Gandersheim, or elsewhere, however modest she herself is about her abilities. That she had the academic background to be a teacher is beyond question; whether she was one, we do not know. Her learning in many areas, however, does not mean she was well informed on all topics, and her complete ignorance, for instance, of Judaism (demonstrated in *Theophilus* and *Basil*) and of Islam *(Pelagius),* whose practitioners and practices she does not distinguish from those of pagans, reflects the restrictions on her sources of knowledge and the prejudices of her day.

The lion's share of Hrotsvit's work survives in a single manuscript, produced at Gandersheim around 980.[5] It was preserved during the Middle Ages at Saint Emmeram's Abbey in Regensburg, but it is unclear how it got there from Gandersheim. Since the nineteenth century it has been in Munich (Bayerische Staatsbibliothek, CLM 14485). Given its date and origin, it is not impossible that it was prepared under the eyes of Hrotsvit herself, and it may reflect her own selection and arrangement of her works. The Munich manuscript divides Hrotsvit's writings into three books. The first book contains eight major poems—the shortest being 150 lines, the longest 903—most of them relating the lives and passions of Christian saints or martyrs, but including as well a poem on the Ascension; these are frequently referred to as the "Legends" or the "Sacred Stories" in modern scholarship.[6] The second book consists of six dramas. The third has the epic on Otto the Great, and perhaps originally included the epic on the founding of Gandersheim (and maybe other works as well). Distributed throughout the three books are various prose prefaces, letters, and a variety of shorter poems (mostly prayers, dedications, and prologues). All of her extant work is included and translated in the present volume.

Most of Hrotsvit's poems and plays are based on earlier prose works, a circumstance that she mentions with pride, and one which she often highlights in the titles to the individual poems. That she chose authoritative works as her models is one of her defenses of the veracity and orthodoxy of her work, but by turning her models from dry prose into colorful verse or into dramatic dialogue, she felt she was improving upon them, honoring the saints at the same time that she was demonstrating her own superiority as a writer by competing with learned male writers of the past. Her models provided her with much of the content of her writings, as well as with logical arrangements of the narratives, but in her rewriting of her sources, she makes them her own. She expands or contracts to suit her own purposes, and emphasizes the points that she thinks most interesting and relevant for her readers. The prose sources, since they were so important to her, are identified in the Notes to the Translations for each of the texts. Readers who want fully to appreciate her writing, her genius, and her creativity, should read her sources and compare each of her works with its source text, examining what she left out as well as what she included, how she changed the emphasis and focus of the narratives, how she altered the vocabulary and diction, and in particular how she enlarged the roles of the women she wrote about.

The idea of versifying existing prose works may strike modern readers as peculiar, or even as pointless or undesirable. But versified saints' lives, miracles, and passions were a cherished literary form in Late Antiquity and in the Middle Ages, one practiced by the most learned writers: Prudentius, Venantius Fortunatus, Bede, and Alcuin, among many others. Such poems were widely circulated and read, but many were originally written for individual communities that venerated the saint in question, either because the community was dedicated to that saint, had altars or chapels so dedicated, or held relics of the saint. The hagiographical accounts of local saints might be read on their feast days during divine offices, in refectory, or in chapter meetings; and they were read privately by interested members of the community. *The Conversion of Gallicanus 1* and *2*, were later incorporated into legendaries, collections of saints' lives intended for public reading,[7] but her poems are not known to have been so used. Versified saints' lives were also reworked and recycled in the Middle Ages for liturgical chants, so parts of them were sung as well. Since the poems about the patron saint of a monastery (or church or altar or chapel) were studied with special attention in the schools of that community, they were integrated into its life in a multiplicity of contexts (school, choir, meals, offices, etc.) and so became part of its shared cultural experience—part of what defined it as a community as well as what distinguished it as a community of worshippers. Such works were central to the lives of the community and were highly valued.

Among Hrotsvit's lost works are poems on Gandersheim's original patron saints, Popes Anastasius and Innocent. The Virgin Mary, the subject of the first and longest of the sacred stories, but also a major figure in many of Hrotsvit's other works, was particularly venerated at Gandersheim, as at most female communities of the period. So, it is clear that Hrotsvit wrote poems about figures specifically connected to or important at Gandersheim. Although we lack concrete evidence that her sacred stories were written for Gandersheim, it is likely that the saints she celebrated had some special relevance to the local community because of chapels, altars, or relics. That does not, of course, mean that Hrotsvit did not intend them for a much wider audience as well. The lives and the deaths of virtuous women and men had been popular reading matter in many periods, providing inspiring models of appropriate behavior. When versified, such biographies were all the more attractive to educated medieval readers.

Hrotsvit's second book, by far the best known and most widely read and translated of her writings, is comprised of six dramas. In modern scholarship, these plays are often called comedies, but she never used that term. In an Aristotelian sense—that the fortunes of the main characters improve by the end of the plays—they are indeed comedies, for the protagonists end up in heaven. They are also comedies in the sense that they drew from Terence some of the themes of ancient New Comedy, especially an emphasis on love affairs and marriage (here often marriage to God). There are also humorous scenes in some of the plays, most famously the "rape of the pots" in *The Passion of the Holy Virgins Agape, Chionia, and Hirena,* but also the scene of the anxiety of the lovesick Gallicanus, waiting to hear Constance's response to his proposal of marriage; the dealings of Callimachus with his deceitful servant; and the hesitation of Thais about giving up her toilet, to name just a few. But Hrotsvit's plays are not primarily intended to be funny; they aim to entertain while they teach, and occasionally employ humor to that end.

Hrotsvit is the first Latin dramatist since Late Antiquity whose work survives, and she explains in the *Preface* to her book of plays her motivation for writing them. Terence's comedies, she says, are widely read in her day because of the enticing elegance of their language, but their regrettable content corrupts his readers.[8] A fascinating example of the sort of corruption Hrotsvit has in mind is provided by a manuscript of Terence's plays from Hrotsvit's lifetime. It was written and annotated at the nunnery of Essen, a house closely connected to Gandersheim in the tenth century and, like Gandersheim, especially favored by aristocratic families with ties to the Ottonian court. The early annotators of the manuscript, nuns of the late tenth or early eleventh century, are particularly attuned to the sexual content of Terence's plays, unabashedly supplying various forms of the verb *serten* (a vulgar Old High German word for sexual intercourse, equivalent to Latin *futuere*) to gloss a variety of euphemisms and circumlocutions in Terence.[9] They are, in other words, more enticed by the content of Terence's plays than by his elegant language, which they are eager to render in the most explicit, and least elegant, fashion, leaving little to the imagination.

Hrotsvit felt she could provide her fellow nuns a morally superior alternative, elegant in language *and* content—instead of lascivious women, chaste virgins; instead of misbehaving young men defying their strict though well-intentioned fathers, well-behaved young women obeying their mothers and defying evil-minded male superiors; instead of erotic love, the love of Christ. Hrotsvit's plays are preeminently women's plays. They were not just written by a woman, they were written for an audience of women, and they are principally about women. Women are the main characters, and unlike most of the women in Terence's plays,

Hrotsvit's women normally have extensive speaking parts; they are active, assertive, and self-directed.

Although Hrotsvit's heroes and heroines are, or become, chaste, she does not avoid the subjects of love, nudity, and sex. Two of her leading characters are prostitutes, plying their trade successfully before their conversion, and mocking their male lovers; and even Hrotsvit's chaste virgins are threatened with being stripped and sexually violated by their lustful tormenters. One play includes a scene about necrophilia. Hrotsvit was clearly aware that it was not only Terence's language that attracted his readers but also the sexual content of his plays; she accordingly uses sex and love in her plays,[10] though a morally pure form of love. She states that if she did not incorporate such content because it made her blush, she would not be able to achieve her purpose: supplanting Terence, championing chaste women, and subverting male authority. In order truly to compete with Terence, she had to do so on his playing field. What attracted readers to his works must also attract them to hers. Sex was not a problem for Hrotsvit in and of itself; the problem was the sexual misbehavior of Terence's characters.

It is not only the subject matter of Hrotsvit's plays that deals with sex: some of her language is also erotic, more of it than will be apparent to someone reading only the English translation. It seems likely that Hrotsvit wrote, at least in part, for her fellow nuns, perhaps especially for young ones learning Latin, so her language must be considered in the context of an audience of young women.[11] Words have a multiplicity of meanings and can be understood and translated in a variety of different ways. For instance, when

Hrotsvit writes *sponsus/sponsa,* terms which are here generally translated, according to context, by "spouse," "betrothed," or "groom/bride," Hrotsvit's adolescent female readers are just as likely to have understood something more like the equivalent of our "fiancé/fiancée," a word with the same basic meaning, but a more sexually charged tone; the words *amicus/amica,* here usually translated by "friend," are just as likely to have been understood by the young women as "boyfriend/girlfriend" or "lover." These more erotic renderings, which are equally viable for the Latin terms, would lend a different coloring to the passages. It is not impossible that at least some of Hrotsvit's early readers will have found more sensual language in her texts than others do, just as the nuns at Essen read Terence's language in a more explicitly sexual way than many of us would. In making a translation, one meaning must be chosen over the others; but rendering even a few terms in any poem more erotically would alter its tone. I do not think she was unaware of the potential meanings of the Latin words she chose to use, or unaware that some of her readers would read them in more sexually explicit ways than I have rendered them. In short, there is probably more eroticism in Hrotsvit's work than the reader of the English alone will appreciate.

One of the first questions posed by many modern readers of Hrotsvit's plays is whether they were performed, or, at least, intended to be performed. Many scholars of the nineteenth and early twentieth centuries rejected the possibility out of hand, declaring that the rapidly changing settings and the lack of temporal unity make them impossible to stage.[12] Today there is a broader understanding of what performance means. The simple act of reading aloud is a performance; reading with emphasis or enthusiasm is more of one; dividing the speaking parts between different readers goes a step further. Most reading in the Middle Ages was reading aloud, and there can be no question that Hrotsvit's plays were performed in that sense. There is no reason that a group of students, or nuns, or courtiers could not have divided up the parts, with different people reading the dialogue of each character. The argument that the plays were impossible to stage could no longer be made with any plausibility once they began to be staged in the nineteenth century, and with increasing frequency in the twentieth.[13] While it is true that Hrotsvit herself talks of Terence's plays being widely read, not staged, it is also true that, for her, reading was reading aloud, an oral performance. In that sense at least, her intention was that her plays be performed.

It has recently been demonstrated that Hrotsvit's works enjoyed a modest popularity in the century or so after their composition.[14] A more widespread and celebrated fame, however, first came when the German humanist Conrad Celtis discovered the Saint Emmeram manuscript in the 1490s and produced the first printed edition of Hrotsvit (Nuremberg, 1501). He saw in Hrotsvit an answer to the dismissive attitude of the Italian humanists toward German culture. For Celtis, her writing demonstrated the superiority of the German intellectual tradition: in Germany in the Middle Ages even women were poets![15] Celtis, however, was no feminist. His attitude toward her work was paternalistic, and his goal was to co-opt her efforts in the service of his nationalist, male contemporaries. His edition, although it was fairly careful and accurate by the standards of its day and provided her work with a wider circulation, took outrageous liberties in other respects as he refashioned Hrotsvit to suit his own agenda. For instance, he rewrote many of the titles he found in the Saint Emmeram manuscript, titles that highlight the female characters and their paramount importance in the works. He substituted for the authentic titles new ones of his own invention that shifted the focus to male authority figures. For example, the play entitled *The Passion of the Holy Virgins Agape, Chionia, and Hirena* he renamed *Dulcitius,* after the male buffoon in the play; in Celtis's hands, *The Raising from the Dead of Drusiana and Callimachus* became simply *Callimachus;* while *The Fall and Conversion of Mary, Niece of Abraham* was reduced to *Abraham;* and *The Conversion of Thais* was renamed *Paphnutius,* after the monk who "reformed" her.[16] The titles assigned by Celtis became standard in the modern world, and appear not only in editions and translations but also in almost all the scholarship on the works.[17] Notwithstanding the considerable confusion that the reintroduction of Hrotsvit's titles is likely to have on scholarly discourse, they have, in all instances in which they exist in the Munich manuscript, been restored in the present edition. These titles better and more appropriately describe the works, and they are Hrotsvit's words and embody her understanding of the important themes and characters in her works, not someone else's.

Translation

The present translation is quite literal, in keeping with the philosophy of the Dumbarton Oaks Medieval Library to reflect the original closely, for the benefit of the reader who reads both the Latin and the English. The constraint of being literal means that the rendering is at times rather wooden; and I have, no doubt, exacerbated this tendency—with an eye to the reader of the Latin—by making a particular effort not only to translate every word but also to represent in some fashion every diminutive, prefix, and suffix. This includes comparative and superlative forms of adjectives and adverbs. My goal was to leave nothing she wrote untranslated.

It will strike any reader of the Latin as peculiar how often Hrotsvit uses particles such as *autem, certe, denique, ergo, etenim, forte, iam, immo, nam, namque, nempe, quidem, quidni, scilicet, utpote* (but, certainly, at last, so, and indeed, perhaps, now, rather, for, since, surely, indeed, no doubt, that is, namely);[18] even odder that they are so randomly placed, not always appearing where one would expect them (which would normally be immediately before or after the word or phrase they explain or intensify); and, perhaps most peculiar of all, that a single verse might have several such words. Critics of Hrotsvit's work regularly refer to these as "filler words" and assume they have no meaning, having been introduced solely for the sake of filling out a line of verse or for creating rhyme. So they have been regularly omitted in previous translations of Hrotsvit (English or otherwise). They are all translated here. Leaving them out changes the flavor of her work. The inclusion of all these particles often makes for peculiar English, but it reflects peculiar Latin. We have no way of knowing whether she also employed such a superfluity of these words in speaking Latin; perhaps they were an idiosyncrasy of her speech as well (a verbal tic). Perhaps they are a reflection of the way her community spoke Latin, for any spoken language is likely to have more particles, which can serve as nothing more than pauses in speaking, such as "um," "hmm," and the like in English. While I do not deny that many of Hrotsvit's particles do indeed serve metrical purposes, they are so abundant in her work that they constitute a distinctive feature of her writing: Hrotsvit without all the particles no longer sounds like Hrotsvit. So I have kept them. In contemporary terms, if we think about English speakers who sprinkle phrases such as "you know," "for sure," and "like" in virtually every sentence, sometimes multiple times in a sentence, we can perhaps appreciate better how forcefully such language defines for us the character of the speaker: without these additions, their speech might strike us very differently.

Latin was Hrotsvit's second language, learned through reading, not primarily by speaking (or singing). Her abundant use of particles may reflect her struggles to render a specific register, nuance, or tone in a foreign tongue. Hrotsvit frequently writes dialogue, and not just in her plays. She has many speaking characters in her poetic works as well. One of her principal stylistic models, especially for dialogue, was Terence, whose language was at the same time both archaic and colloquial. She also blends into her texts—poetic as well as dramatic—epic themes, incorporating content and language from works as different as the Latin Bible, the heroic adventures of early Christian saints, and Virgil. This is a complicated mix of Latin periods, genres, styles, and levels, and the particles may be her way of imparting emphasis, enthusiasm, reserve, modesty, aggression, or other qualities.

It would be useful to study Hrotsvit's use of particles more carefully, for instance, examining which words appear in dialogue and which in narrative; which are used by speakers of varying ages, sexes, professions, and levels of authority and education; whether particular words are associated with particular emotions or attitudes; whether some appear more in one genre of her writing than in another. The abundance of particles in her writings suggests that they meant something to her, and we should attempt to discover their shades or gradations of meaning, not simply dismiss them as undifferentiated filler. I hope that including them all in the translation will inspire such investigations. That their inclusion results in some very stilted passages is undeniable.

Another conspicuous aspect of Hrotsvit's Latin is her fondness for diminutives. These are often assumed—or declared—to be employed for metrical purposes (to add an additional syllable or two), or solely for the sake of the rhyme.[19] Hrotsvit uses diminutives to indicate both size (smallness) and affection (dear, precious), and some of her diminutives are her own coinages, unparalleled, or nearly unparalleled, in other Latin writers. These are often ignored in translating Hrotsvit, but they are a distinctive feature of her style, and an effort has been made here to preserve them. If a great many things in the translation seem to be "small" and "dear," that is because Hrotsvit made them small and dear.

A further noticeable feature of her writing is the abundance of comparative and superlative degrees of adjectives and adverbs. These are a feature of vulgar Latin (that is, popular Latin, the Latin of the common people), and of spoken languages in general, especially at lower educational levels. They may reflect enthusiastic or naïve exaggeration on the part of the speakers, who in their zeal make almost everything "greater" or "the greatest." To cite just one example in Hrotsvit's work, very little happens "quickly"; almost everything happens "more quickly" or "very quickly." There is a tendency for translators of Medieval Latin texts—not only of Hrotsvit—to dampen this inflation of emphasis by downgrading many of these forms of comparison to the positive degree. I have generally not done that, but rendered the form she wrote. Already in the Middle Ages, Germans sometimes referred to vulgar Latin as *Küchenlatein,* the Latin of the kitchen. That is, in effect, the Latin of women or servants. Her abundance of comparatives and superlatives—and the same might be true of her excessive use of diminutives and particles—may reflect the spoken Latin of her circle. It is not impossible that Hrotsvit was intentionally trying to reproduce what she understood to be women's latinity, or the way women she knew spoke Latin, so that it would be easier for the women in her circle to understand it. Stilted English often results from rendering all her comparative and superlative forms; but it seemed to me that something valuable might be lost if her excessive use of these forms were eliminated.

Hrotsvit's Latin

The Latin text is based on Walter Berschin's Teubner edition, *Opera omnia* (Munich, 2001); I am grateful to Professor Berschin and to the publisher for permission to use it. I have recorded in the Notes to the Text the rare instances in which I have deviated from his text. Spelling and punctuation, however, have been silently adapted to conform with the series guidelines of the Dumbarton Oaks Medieval Library (see below).

Hrotsvit's Latin is, as a general rule, relatively straightforward and usually easy to follow. But her writing still presents distinctive features, and an awareness of these will enhance the pleasure of reading it. No reader of Hrotsvit's Latin will fail to notice that she often writes *very* long sentences, sometimes drawn out to twenty or more verses.[20] These have at times been broken up in the present translation, since English usage does not easily accommodate sentences with so many subordinate clauses. Since, according to series guidelines, the punctuation of the facing Latin text has been made to reflect, as closely as possible, that of the English translation, this will not be so noticeable to readers of the English alone; readers of the Latin, however, will find shorter sentences here than in most editions of Hrotsvit's works.

Unlike Classical Latin authors, Hrotsvit regularly employs rhyme, almost all of her verses having internal rhyme in which the final syllable before the caesura rhymes with the final syllable in the line (for example, the first line of her first poem: "Unica spes mund*i*, dominatrix inclita cael*i*"). Her prose as well is marked by rhyme (or *homeoteleuton*), with most clauses ending in the same syllable as the preceding or following clause. This is a standard feature of tenth-century Latin prose and verse, and for that reason would not have struck her contemporaries as unusual or strange—though certainly as desirable.[21] I have not attempted to reproduce any sort of rhyme in my translation, since it would have been impossible to do so without sacrificing some of the meaning. I would, however, recommend to readers of Hrotsvit that they compare some of the rhyming translations of Katharina Wilson, to get some feel for the effect.[22] Unlike their medieval counterparts, modern readers are not accustomed to so much rhyme, and it can quickly become cloying in abundance. Hrotsvit's Latin is unlikely to have struck her contemporaries as annoyingly singsong, but that effect is hard to avoid in a modern rhyming English translation—especially in large doses.

A further peculiarity of Hrotsvit's Latin is her freedom with verbal tenses and moods. Since her writing is predominantly about the past, it is hardly surprising—or anomalous—that she frequently employs the historic present; less expected is how unsystematic she is about distinguishing between the various Latin past tenses and how frequently she employs the future in reference to the present (or even on a couple of occasions in reference to the past). The translation here renders such anomalous tenses to make clear sense in English, not to mirror the Latin forms. As for moods, Hrotsvit frequently uses the indicative mood in result clauses, and she sometimes uses present subjunctives instead of imperfect subjunctives in secondary sequence. Readers of the Latin will also be struck by how often she uses deponent verbs with a passive meaning. These anomalies occur often enough—and are paralleled in other writers of her period—that they seem to be intentional traits, not faults (either of her own knowledge of Latin, or of later scribes').[23] They are, rather, reflections of the Latin of her day.

Even readers with a wide experience of Medieval Latin will be puzzled by Hrotsvit's frequent use of the words *mis* and *tis*. Outside of grammatical treatises, they are rarely to be found. She knew these words as alternative forms of the pronouns *ego* and *tu* ("I" and "you") in the possessive (genitive) case; that is to say, they are equivalent to *mei* and *tui* ("of me" and "of you").[24] Additionally she uses possessive pronouns (these and others) where we would expect possessive adjectives in Classical Latin, for example, *mis filia* (literally, "the daughter of me") for *mea filia* (my daughter). Equally puzzling to most Latin readers will be Hrotsvit's frequent use of *si* (if) to mean *non* (not), a usage found in the Vulgate,[25] and one that is paralleled in other medieval writers but unusually common in Hrotsvit.

Hrotsvit's spelling is typical for Latin writers of her day. As a general rule, the preferences in the guidelines of the Dumbarton Oaks Medieval Library have been followed here as regards orthography, and that means that a Classical Latin spelling has generally been imposed on the text, to make it easier for the majority of modern readers who require a translation. But it is not possible to do this in every instance without causing considerable confusion. For example, Hrotsvit generally wrote *e* or *ę* for Classical Latin *ae*. This has been standardized to *ae*, following DOML practice, except when she scanned the vowel as short in her poetry; there *e* has been retained. Also in her verse, she sometimes syncopates words (writing, for example, *domna* for *domina, seclum* for *seculum/saeculum, vinclum* for *vinculum*); though such words are generally spelled out in full here, they remain in their syncopated forms in the verses where the additional syllable would upset the metrical pattern.[26]

Readers of Hrotsvit's Latin will find it easier to scan her verses if they keep in mind the following aspects of her prosody that differ from Classical usage: she often shortens the final *-o* in the ablative case, especially when the word is a gerund; she likewise shortens the final *-o* in imperatives (the future, plural forms) and even sometimes in adverbs; similarly, she at times shortens the final *e* of adverbs. Other vowels are occasionally shortened or lengthened, perhaps because of her pronunciation of them; and these are not mentioned in the Notes to the Translations if the irregular form is cited for other authors by one of the dictionaries in the Database of Latin Dictionaries, or if it is treated by Paul von Winterfeld in the *Index metricus* or the *Index verborum* to his edition, which anyone studying Hrotsvit's metrics should keep at hand.[27]

I am indebted to many people for helping bring this volume to fruition. First, to my friend and colleague Ron Pepin, who tirelessly translated along with me, frequently providing corrections, improvements, and encouragement, and also to Francis Newton, who has been discussing the text and the translation with me almost weekly for more than a decade, always to my advantage. I owe a particular debt to Tino Licht and Walter Berschin, who gave me quiet refuge at the Seminar für Lateinische Philologie des Mittelalters in Heidelberg in the spring of 2015 to work on Hrotsvit, and who answered specific queries about problem passages with their unparalleled expertise. That visit was supported by the Alexander von Humboldt-Stiftung, which has so generously assisted me throughout my career. A number of students over the years have read Hrotsvit in my classes, and I have always learned from their responses and critiques. It is reckless to single out only a few, but I benefitted especially from the input of Amelia Kennedy, Sara Malone, Paul Stapleton, and Burt Westermeier; and I want especially to mention the members of my graduate seminar in Medieval Latin in the fall of 2018 at the University of North Carolina at Chapel Hill, who read through the entire corpus of Hrotsvit's work with me: Evan Colby, Mia Collins, Claudia Epley, Angus Gorman, Katherine Hager, David Harris, Caroline Herman, Leah Hinshaw, India Watkins Nattermann, and Spencer Scott. I am indebted to the Department of Classics and the College of Arts and Sciences at UNC for financial support, including a research leave in the spring of 2018 to work on this volume. And I had a great deal of help with keyboarding and proofreading from Hannelore Segers and Ned Sanger, who worked on the volume as interns at Dumbarton Oaks in the summer of 2018 and also spent a couple of days there that summer reading and discussing Hrotsvit with me. John Beeby provided careful proofreading and produced the Index. I owe a special debt to Jan Ziolkowski for years of support and endless enthusiasm as I worked on Hrotsvit, and to my editors Gregory Hays, then on the editorial board, and Danuta Shanzer, who performed a Herculean labor in working through my translations, and who eliminated many errors, smoothed out countless infelicities, and made the final product much better through their efforts than it would have been otherwise.

My greatest debt is to my wife Elizabeth, to whom this volume is dedicated, 'cause you're the best thing that ever happened to me.

Notes

1 An extensive bibliography is included in Phyllis R. Brown and Stephen L. Wailes, eds., *A Companion to Hrotsvit of Ganderheim (fl. 960): Contextual and Interpretive Approaches* (Leiden, 2013), 363–79. A general account of her life and writings is provided by Fidel Rädle, "Hrotsvit von Gandersheim," in *Die deutsche Literatur des Mittelalters: Verfasserlexikon,* 2nd ed., ed. Kurt

Ruh et al. (Berlin, 1978–2008), vol. 4, pp. 196–210. Hrotsvit's name is spelled in a multiplicity of ways in modern scholarship (also Hrotsvitha, Hrotswitha, Roswitha, Rosvita, etc.). In the principal manuscript of her work (see below, note 4), her name is consistently spelled Hrotsvitha, with Latin inflections, in the first book; but in the second and third books—which were written later—it is spelled Hrotsvit. It seems that as she became a more mature writer, she began using the German (Old Saxon) version of her name. I follow Walter Berschin and the editors of *A Companion to Hrotsvit* in calling her Hrotsvit.

2 English translations of the plays are listed below in the Bibliography. The only previous English translations of the sacred legends or epics are those of Gonsalva Wiegand and Mary Bernadine Bergman, respectively, cited in the Bibliography—both are excellent (though now somewhat dated), but as they were produced originally as PhD dissertations at Saint Louis University, they are not readily available to all.

3 A succinct and judicious account of what is actually known about Hrotsvit's life appears in Fidel Rädle, "Hrotsvit von Gandersheim: Von der poetischen Salvierung einer unheiligen Welt," in *Ambivalenzen des geistlichen Spiels: Revisionen von Texten und Methoden,* ed. Jörn Bockmann and Regina Toepfer (Gottingen, 2018), 259–60.

4 Our information about medieval canonesses comes mostly from other places and periods, and the practices in tenth-century Saxony may not be precisely the same; there is no certainty about specific practices at Gandersheim in Hrotsvit's lifetime. Useful discussion and bibliography on this topic is in Katrinette Bodarwé, "Hrotsvit and her Avatars," in Brown and Wailes, *A Companion to Hrotsvit,* 329–64, especially 358–60; and in greater depth in the same author's *Sanctimoniales Litteratae: Schriftlichkeit und Bildung in den Ottonischen Frauenkommunitäten Gandersheim, Essen und Quedlinburg* (Münster, 2004), 15–86. A good introduction is in Jane Stevenson, "Hrotsvit in Context," in Brown and Wailes, *A Companion to Hrotsvit,* 35–62.

5 On the Munich manuscript, see Bodarwé, *Sanctimoniales Litteratae,* 98–104 (it was Bodarwé who first identified the Munich manuscript, M, as a product of the Gandersheim scriptorium); Hartmut Hoffmann, *Schreibschulen und Buchmalerei: Handschriften und Texte des 9.–11. Jahrhunderts,* MGH, Schriften 65 (Hannover, 2012), pp. 73–74 and plates 35, 37, and 41

(the caption to the last is mislabeled as a Berlin manuscript but is fol. 114r of M); and Walter Berschin, who discusses also the other surviving manuscripts and their interrelations in his edition, *Opera omnia* (Munich, 2001), x–xxviii.

6 Excellent introductions to and summaries of Hrotsvit's sacred stories and plays are provided by Stephen L. Wailes, "The Sacred Stories in Verse," and "Hrotsvit's Plays," in Brown and Wailes, *A Companion to Hrotsvit,* 85–120 and 121–45.

7 References in Berschin, *Opera omnia,* xvii–xviii.

8 Some earlier scholars wrongly rejected Hrotsvit's claim that Terence was widely read in her day, but this view is no longer tenable; see Stephen L. Wailes and Phyllis R. Brown, "Hrotsvit and Her World," in Brown and Wailes, *A Companion to Hrotsvit,* 4–5.

9 The manuscript is Leipzig, Universitätsbibliothek, Rep. I 37. Examples of the glosses are at *Eunuchus* 149, where Terence's polite, if ambiguous, *aliquos parere amicos beneficio meo,* rendered in the Loeb translation of John Barsby, *Terence* (Cambridge, MA, 2001), vol. 1, p. 329, as "gain some friends by doing a good turn of my own," is glossed *bit serdene minen* (by my f**king them); or where Terence's *vitiavit* (*Eunuchus* 654, "violated") is glossed by *sart* (f**ked). The Latin glossing can be just as direct; for example, at *Eunuchus* 180: *quam ioco rem voluisti a me tandem quin perfeceris?* (Barsby, *Terence,* vol. 1, p. 333: "what have you asked from me even in jest, which you haven't obtained?") is glossed *voluisti umquam futuere quando non perfeceris?* (did you ever want to f**k me and not get to?). On the Leipzig manuscript and its glosses, see Robert Kauer, "Bericht über die Terenzlitertur in den Jahren 1898–1908," *Jahresbericht über die Fortschritte der klassischen Altertumswissenschaft* 37 (1909): 177n2; and Hartmut Hoffmann, "Das Skriptorium von Essen in ottonischer und frühsalischer Zeit," in *Kunst im Zeitalter der Kaiserin Theophanu,* ed. Anton von Euw and Perter Shreiner (Cologne, 1993), 113–53, at 127.

10 I employ the term "uses" in the sense discussed by C. Gnilka, *Chrêsis: Die Methode der Kirchenväter im Umgang mit der antiken Kultur,* 2 vols. (Basel, 1984–1993): that is, as a Christian appropriation of pagan culture that aimed at transformation through correction and purification.

11 See Linda A. McMillin, "The Audiences of Hrotsvit," in Brown and Wailes, *A Companion to Hrotsvit,* 311–27.

12 The older scholarship is discussed by Edwin H. Zeydel, "Were Hrotsvitha's Dramas Performed during Her Lifetime?" *Speculum* 20 (1945): 443–56.
13 Discussions of aspects of staging can be found in "Conducting Performances," section 4 in *Hrotsvit of Gandersheim: Contexts, Identities, Affinities, and Performances,* ed. Phyllis R. Brown, Linda A. McMillin, and Katharina Wilson (Toronto, 2004), 213–82, especially the contributions of Jane Snyder (pp. 235–50) and Michael Zampelli (pp. 265–82).
14 See Tino Licht, "Hrotsvitspuren in ottonischer Dichtung (nebst einem neuen Hrotsvitgedicht)," *Mittellateinisches Jahrbuch* 43 (2008): 347–53.
15 On Celtis and his promotion of Hrotsvit, see Bodarwé, "Hrotsvit and Her Avatars," 331–36.
16 Latin works, when not otherwise titled, generally take their titles from their opening words, and such is the case with Hrotsvit's plays. At the end of the fifteenth century and the beginning of the sixteenth, titles for the plays were inserted into the Munich manuscript by Celtis and others, but these titles are not Hrotsvit's.
17 The first steps toward restoring her titles—or at least more appropriate titles—were made by Berschin, *Opera omnia,* who used the Latin incipits for the titles, and by the editors of Brown and Wailes, *A Companion to Hrotsvit,* xv–xix; but even in that latter pioneering volume, not all of the authors avoid Celtis's paternalistic titles.
18 The translations listed here are only examples; each of the terms can be, and is, rendered in my translation in a variety of ways, depending on the immediate context. I use the term "particle" as defined by J. H. Allen and J. B. Greenough, *New Latin Grammar,* rev. ed., ed. J. B. Greenough, G. L. Kittredge, A. A. Howard, Benjamin L. D'Ooge (Boston, 1931), section 213: "Adverbs, prepositions, conjunctions, and interjections are called particles." A list is provided by Paul von Winterfeld, ed., *Hrotsvithae opera,* MGH Scriptores rerum Germanicarum in usum scholarum 34 (Berlin, 1902), 546.
19 Putting third-declension nouns in the diminutive form makes them into first- or second-declension nouns, so they will have the same inflectional endings as, and therefore rhyme with, any first/second-declension adjectives that modify them. (First/second-declension adjectives are the most numerous in Latin, but third-declension nouns are the most numerous, so normally the two do not have the same inflections.)

20 So, for example, the opening twenty-four lines of *On the Ascension of the Lord,* which syntactically form a single sentence.

21 See, for instance, Karl Polheim, *Die lateinische Reimprosa* (Berlin, 1925).

22 For example, the selection of works in her *Hrotsvit of Gandersheim: A Florilegium of Her Works* (Cambridge, 1998).

23 For fuller details, one may consult the *Index grammaticus* in von Winterfeld, *Hrotsvithae opera,* 512–42 (on deponents used passively, p. 525; on verb tenses and moods in particular, pp. 526–29). A further peculiarity of Hrotsvit's treatment of verbs is her use of archaic forms for infinitives of the third conjugation: the present passive (and also deponent) infinitives sometimes end in *-ier* instead of *-i.* Details of Medieval Latin practice regarding all these grammatical and syntactical topics will be found in Peter Stotz, *Handbuch zur lateinischen Sprache des Mittelalters,* 5 vols. (Munich, 1996–2004).

24 See, for example, Donatus, *Ars minor,* ed. H. Keil, *Grammatici Latini* (Leipzig, 1864), vol. 4, p. 357, where he states, *pronomen . . . declinabitur sic* (the pronoun will be declined this way): *ego, mei vel mis, mihi, me, a me . . . tu, tui vel tis, tibi, te, a te.*

25 W. W. Plater and H. J. White, *A Grammar of the Vulgate* (Oxford, 1926), 27.

26 A list of these is in von Winterfeld, *Hrotsvithae opera,* 548.

27 Database of Latin Dictionaries, ed. Toon Van Hal and Paul Tombeur, updated January 9, 2024, https://www.brepolis.net/; von Winterfeld, *Hrotsvithae opera,* 543–48.

BOOK ONE

LIBER PRIMUS

Praefatio

Hunc libellum, parvo ullius decoris cultu ornatum, sed non
parva diligentia illaboratum, omnium sapientium benigni-
tati offero expurgandum, eorum dumtaxat qui erranti non
2 delectantur derogare, sed magis errata corrigere. Fateor
namque me haud mediocriter errasse non solum in dinos-
cendis syllabarum naturis, verum etiam in dictionibus com-
ponendis; pluraque sub hac serie reprehensione digna lati-
tare. Sed errores fatenti facilis venia, vitiisque debetur pia
correctio.

3 Si autem obicitur quod quaedam huius operis, iuxta quo-
rumdam aestimationem, sumpta sint ex apocryphis, non est
crimen praesumptionis iniquae, sed error ignorantiae, quia
quando huius stamen seriei ceperam ordiri, ignoravi dubia
4 esse in quibus disposui laborare. At ubi recognovi, pessum-
dare detrectavi, quia quod videtur falsitas, forsan probabitur
5 esse veritas. Cum res sese ita habeant, tanto ad perfecti
defensionem opusculi permultorum iuvamine egeo, quanto
in ipsa inceptione minus ulla proprii vigoris fulciebar suf-
ficientia; quia nec matura adhuc aetate vigens, nec scientia
fui proficiens. Sed nec alicui sapientium affectum meae

BOOK I

Preface

This little book, distinguished by little concern for any sort of elegance, but labored over with no small care, I offer to the benevolence of all persons of wisdom so it may be improved, so long as they delight not in ridiculing someone
who errs, but in correcting errors. For I acknowledge that I 2
have erred to some degree, not only in determining the quantities of syllables, but also in arranging words; and there are many things deserving of censure lurking in this collection. But it is easy to pardon one who confesses her errors, and kindly correction is owed to shortcomings.

If, however, anyone finds fault with me on the grounds 3
that some portions of this work, in the opinion of certain men, were derived from apocryphal writings, this is not a crime of ill willed presumption, but a mistake of ignorance, because when I first began to spin the thread of this collection, I was ignorant that the things I planned to work on
were questionable. Moreover, when I found out that this 4
was the case, I decided not to discard them, because what appears to be false in the present, perhaps in the future will
prove to be true. Given these circumstances, all the more do 5
I need the aid of a great many people to defend this little work now that it is finished, since I was so little supported by any adequate amount of inner strength when I started it; for I was not yet of mature age, nor was I proficient in learning. Furthermore, I did not presume to reveal to any learned

intentionis consulendo praesumpsi enucleare, ne prohibe-
rer pro rusticitate.

6 Unde clam cunctis et quasi furtim, nunc in componendis
sola desudando, nunc male composita destruendo, satage-
bam iuxta meum posse, licet minime necessarium, aliquem
tamen conficere textum ex sententiis scripturarum quas
intra aream nostri Gandeshemensis collegeram coenobii;
7 primo sapientissimae atque benignissimae Rikkardis ma-
gistrae aliarumque suae vicis instruente magisterio, deinde
prona favente clementia regiae indolis Gerbergae cuius
nunc subdor dominio abbatissae. Quae aetate minor, sed
ut imperialem decebat neptem, scientia provectior, aliquot
auctores quos ipsa prior a sapientissimis didicit me admo-
dum pie erudivit.

8 Quamvis etiam metrica modulatio femineae fragilitati
difficilis videatur et ardua, solo tamen semper miserentis
supernae gratiae auxilio non propriis viribus confisa, huius
carmina opusculi dactylicis modulis succinere apposui, ne
crediti talentum ingenioli, sub obscuro torpens pectoris
<antro>, rubigine neglegentiae exterminaretur, sed sedulae
malleo devotionis percussum aliquantulum divinae lauda-
tionis referret tinnitum, quo si occasio non daretur nego-
tiando aliud lucrari, ipsum tamen in aliquod saltim extremae
utilitatis transformaretur instrumentum.

9 Unde quicumque lector, si recte et secundum Deum
sapias, egenti paginae, quae nullius praeceptoris munitur

persons the progress of my plan by seeking their advice, lest I be prevented from carrying it out because of my rusticity.

For these reasons, hiding from everyone and more or less 6
on the sly, now sweating in solitude over constructions, now obliterating what had been badly composed, I did the best I could according to my ability, inadequate though it is, to put together something woven from the statements in the writings which I had gathered together within the environs of our cloister at Gandersheim. I gathered them, first through 7
the instructive teaching of the most learned and gentle teacher Rikkardis and of her successors, and secondly through the favorably inclined indulgence of the regal nature of Gerberga, the abbess to whose authority I am now subject. Younger in age but, as befits an imperial niece, more advanced in learning, she most generously taught me some of the authors whom she herself had earlier learned from the greatest scholars.

Even though metrical cadences may seem difficult and 8
arduous for the frailty of a woman, nevertheless, trusting solely in the aid of the ever-merciful grace of heaven, not in my own powers, I have applied myself to sing the poems of this little work in dactylic meters so that the talent of slight intelligence entrusted to me, lying idle in the dark recess of my heart, not be destroyed by the rust of neglect, but rather, struck by the hammer of eager devotion, might sound some peal of divine praise, so that, if no opportunity should be given to me to profit otherwise from using that talent, still it might at least be transformed into some instrument of minimal value.

And so, reader, whoever you are, if you are properly 9
wise according to God, do not hesitate in offering to my

auctoritate, opem tuae rectitudinis ne pigriteris adhibere, Deo videlicet si quid forte probetur recte compositum, meaeque neglegentiae designando universale vitiorum; nec tamen vituperando sed indulgendo, quia vis frangitur obiurgationis ubi intervenit humilitas confessionis.

impoverished page, which is not protected by the authority of any master, the aid of your correction, attributing, of course, to God anything that fortuitously happens to be well written, and attributing to my failure the totality of the faults; yet do this not by reproaching, but by making allowances, because the violence of a rebuke is shattered when the humility of acknowledgment intercedes.

<Historia nativitatis Mariae>

<Prologus 1. Ad Gerbergam abbatissam>

Salve, regalis proles clarissima stirpis,
Gerbirg, illustris moribus et studiis.
Accipe fronticula, dominatrix alma, serena,
quae tibi purganda offero carminula.
Eius et incultos dignanter dirige stichos,
quam doctrina tua instruit egregia,
et, cum sis certe vario lassata labore,
ludens dignare hos modulos legere.
Hanc quoque sordidolam tempta purgare Camenam
ac fulcire tui flore magisterii,
quo laudem dominae studium supportet alumnae,
doctricique piae carmina discipulae.

Historia nativitatis laudibilisque conversationis intactae Dei Genetrics, quam scriptam repperi sub nomine sancti Iacobi, fratris Domini

Unica spes mundi, dominatrix inclita caeli,
sancta parens Regis, lucida stella maris,
quae parens mundo restaurasti, pia Virgo,
vitam, quam virgo perdiderat vetula,
tu dignare tuae famulae clementer adesse

History of the Birth of Mary

Prologue 1. To Abbess Gerberga

Hail, most celebrated progeny of a royal line, Gerberga, brilliant in character and learning. Receive with a calm demeanor, gracious mistress, these little songs I offer you, which are in need of refinement. Straighten out as you see fit the inelegant verses of a woman whom your exceptional wisdom guides, and, even though you are undoubtedly exhausted by your many labors, consent to read these poems in your leisure. Attempt, additionally, to refine this slightly shabby muse of mine, and support her with the flower of your magisterial authority, so that the effort of a schoolgirl may bring glory to a schoolmistress, and the songs of her disciple bring glory to her devoted teacher.

The History of the Birth and Praiseworthy Way of Life of the Virgin Mother of God, Which I Found Written under the Name of Saint James, the Brother of the Lord

Singular hope of the world, celebrated mistress of heaven, holy mother of the King, shining star of the sea, merciful Virgin, who by obedience restored to the world the life which Eve, the virgin of olden times, had destroyed, I ask that you indulgently consent to attend to the prayers and

Hrotsvithae votis carminulisque novis.
Quae tibi femineae studio famulante camenae
iam supplex modulis succino dactylicis,
exoptans vel summatim attingere saltem
laudis particulam, Virgo, tuae minimam
ortus atque tui primordia clara beati
necnon regalem pangere progeniem.
Hoc tamen agnosco fragiles excedere vires,
ut temptem laude te merita canere.
Digne pro meritis quam totus non canit orbis,
quaeque super laudes angelicas renites,
hunc quia virgineo portasti ventre puella
inclusum, cuncta qui regit imperio.
Olim sed stultum fari qui iussit asellum
in laudem sancti nominis ille sui
teque per angelicum fecit, Virguncula, verbum
de sancto digne Flamine concipere
atque suae prolis matrem sine sorde pudoris
effecit cunctis dissimilem meritis—
si placet, ipse meam potis est dissolvere linguam
et cor rore suae tangere gratiolae.
Quo praestante suae mitis dono pietatis
grata sibi pangam. Te quoque, Virgo, canam,
ne comes ingratis condamner iure pigellis,
quos piget Altithrono psallere pro modulo,
sed mage purpureum laudare perenniter agnum
promerear turmis addita virgineis.

Mundi labentis lustris nam mille peractis,
incepit quando felix aetatula sexta,
qua deus impleri iussit pietate fideli

the new little songs of your servant Hrotsvit. Through my efforts in the service of my womanly muse, I now humbly sing to you in dactylic meters, hoping at least superficially, O Virgin, to touch upon even the tiniest bit of your praise and to write about the illustrious beginnings of your own blessed birth and also about your royal progeny. Yet I acknowledge that it is beyond my delicate powers to attempt singing of you with due praise. The whole world does not sing of you as your merits deserve, and you shine beyond the praises of angels, because you, a girl, carried enclosed in your virgin womb the one who rules the world with supreme authority. But he, who once ordered a dumb donkey to speak in praise of his holy name, and who, through the angel's word, made you, dear Virgin, honorably conceive through the Holy Spirit, and who brought it about that you, with no stain on your purity and unparalleled in rewards, would be the mother of his son—he, if he wishes, can loosen my tongue and touch my heart with the dew of his precious grace. With him by my side, by the gift of his gentle kindness, I will write things that please him. I will sing of you too, Virgin, so that I not be justly condemned as partner to those lazy ingrates, who were slow in singing suitably to the One enthroned on high, but rather so that I, joined to the virgin choirs, earn the right to praise forever the regal lamb.

When five thousand years of the fleeting world were finished, when that happy sixth age began, in which with faithful kindness God ordered that everything be fulfilled which

quicquid veraces iam praecinuere prophetae
(qui mundo Iesum mox praedixere futurum),
germine de Iuda quidam surrexerat ergo
Israel in terra senior sub lege vetusta,
ortus regali David de germine magni,
quem tradunt etenim nomen tenuisse Ioachim.
Hic in mandatis genitricis ab ubere legis
exstiterat iustus necnon digne studiosus.
Hoc quoque continuo fuerat sua maxima cura
ut gregis ipse sui bene pasceret agmina magni,
designans veri sese pastoris haberi
dignum quandoquidem terrestri carne parentem,
qui portare suos umeris non distulit agnos
in propriis, vitae ducens ad gaudia laetae,
passurus mortem magnum nostri per amorem,
empturusque reos animae pretio sibi carae.
    Hic heros etenim, de quo narrabo, Ioachim—
tali percerte felix patriarcha nepote—
toto se placidis ornans conamine factis.
Quicquid possedit, per tres partes resecavit,
partem dans viduis, peregrinis, atque pupillis,
saepius in templo partem famulantibus ergo,
particulamque suae domui servaverat omni.
Hoc quoque non raro faciens pietate benigna,
digne mercedem suscepit denique talem
ut propria substantiola bene multiplicata
ipsius gentis proceres praecelleret omnes.
Nec sibi consimilem portaret terra potentem,
quem sic cunctarum fulciret copia rerum.
    Quattuor hic certe cum iam feliciter ipse
volveret in summa fortuna lustra rotata,

true prophets had already predicted (they had foretold that Jesus would soon be in the world), from the tribe of Judah, then, a certain old man had arisen in the land of Israel, still under the old law, born from the royal line of the mighty David, who, they say, in fact had the name Joachim. From the time he was at his mother's breast, this man had lived according to the mandates of the law, a just man and duly zealous. Additionally, it had always been his greatest concern to keep the multitude of his great flock well fed, signifying that he was worthy to be considered the earthly forefather of that true shepherd, who did not hesitate to carry his own lambs on his own shoulders, leading them to the joys of a happy life, willing to suffer death because of his great love for us, and willing to redeem sinners at the cost to himself of his own precious life.

Now, this hero Joachim, whose story I will recount—a fortunate patriarch indeed with such a grandson!—distinguished himself to the utmost by his kindly actions. He divided everything he possessed into three parts. Giving one part to widows, pilgrims, and orphans, then one part to those who frequently served in the temple, he reserved one small portion for his entire household. And by doing this regularly and with gentle kindness, in due time he rightly received such a reward that he surpassed all the leaders of his tribe, his own small property being richly multiplied. And the land did not produce any man as powerful as him, for so did the abundance of his possessions sustain him.

In truth, when he had already happily lived in the greatest fortune through twenty successive years, he engaged

vultu praepulchram sibi desponsavit amicam
necnon praenitidam laudandis moribus Annam,
Acharis natam, David de stirpe creatam;
foedere legali proprio quam iunxit amori.
Hanc autem memorant sterilem non tempore parvo
spem partus homini nullam conferre fideli.
Tandem digestis bis denis scilicet annis
contigit in templo Ioachim sub tempore festo
inter sacratos altaris stare ministros
incensum digni fuerant qui ponere visi.
Quem Ruben templi dum vidit scriba sacrati
exosus factum dictis affatur amaris:
"Non licet incensum," dixit, "te tangere sanctum,
munera nec domino praestat dare sacrificando,
te quia despexit, subolis cum dona negavit."
    Non dedit econtra verbum vir nobilis ullum,
sed maerens abiit silvas tristisque petivit,
in quis saepe gregem consuevit pascere pridem.
Ac in longinquam pergens per devia terram
ipsum cum propriis secum ducendo magistris,
hic in secretis latitat pascendo latebris.
Nec post ad patriam placuit remeare relictam
passus namque gravem secreta mente pudorem
ex Ruben verbis, qui se causatur, amaris.
    Cuius percerte post menses inclita quinque
coniux desperans illum iam vivere salvum,
in soles flevit nec solamen sibi scivit.
Hasque preces domino profudit triste dolendo:
"Israelis rector solus quoque gentis amator,
qui semper refoves miti pietate dolentes,
cur mihimet socium voluisti tollere carum,

himself to his beloved Anna, who was most beautiful in appearance and resplendent and praiseworthy in character, a daughter of Achar, born from the line of David; he joined her to himself by lawful accord to be his particular love. They say, however, that being infertile for a long time, she offered no hope of offspring to her faithful husband. At length—that is, after twenty years had gone by—it happened that Joachim was standing in the temple on a feast day among the sacred ministers who had been reckoned worthy to offer incense. When Ruben, a scribe of the sacred temple, saw Joachim, he was disgusted by the situation and addressed him with bitter words: "It is not right for you to touch the holy incense," he said, "and it is better that you not offer gifts by sacrificing to God, because he rejected you, when he denied you the gift of progeny."

The noble man spoke not a word in return, but went away grieving and sadly headed for the woods, where often in former days he used to pasture his flock. Continuing through the wilds into a land far away, leading with him his flock, each with its own shepherds, he hid here in secluded retreats pasturing his herds. And it did not please him afterward to return to the fatherland he had left behind, for he had suffered profound shame deep in his heart because of the bitter words of Ruben, who had denounced him.

His illustrious wife, quite rightly despairing after five months that he was still alive and well, wept every day and knew no solace within her. She sadly poured forth these prayers to the Lord, in her pain: "Sole ruler of Israel and lover of its people, you who with gentle kindness always comfort those in pain, why have you chosen to take away my

addens maerorem tristi semperque dolenti,
quae semper sterilis mansi sine germine ventris?
Sed nunc maioris vulnus suspiro doloris,
hoc quia nec penitus, quid conferret, scio, casus
legali domino, devoto legis amico.
O me felicem, si saltem noscere possem,
utrum mors illum subito sorberet amara,
an frueretur adhuc calida vitaliter aura.
Certe si scirem, non ius maeroris haberem
tantum; cum tenebris leti succumberet atris,
funus sed summa colerem praenobile pompa
inclita condigno committens membra sepulcro."
His ita finitis sublatis cernit ocellis
in ramis lauri resonantes murmure dulci
pullos plumigeris volucres circumdare pennis.
Hoc ubi cernebat, subtristi voce canebat:
"Rex caeli fortis, cui subiacet astriger axis,
omnia qui certe potis es disponere recte,
semper cunctarum tibi laus exstet pietatum,
quod clemens cunctos pietatis munere vivos,
pisciculos, pecudes, serpentes, atque volucres
congaudere suis donasti sedulo pullis.
Sed meme solam sterilem remanere, misellam,
causa iudicii iussisti denique recti.
Te tamen Omnipatrem constanti pectore testem
invoco, coniugii primo quod tempore vovi,
si ventris fructum mihi praestares pius ullum,
hunc mox in templo sisti tibi rite sacrato,
obsequioque tui legali more sacrari."
Talia dum mundis formaret verbula labris,

dear companion, adding grief to one who is sad and always in pain, I who have always remained sterile, with no fruit of my womb? But now I sigh over a wound of greater pain because of this, that I do not know deep in my heart what disaster has befallen my lawful master, a devoted lover of the law. Oh, I would be happy if at least I could know whether a bitter death suddenly swallowed him up, or if he is still alive, enjoying the warm breezes. For if I knew for certain, I would have no right to grieve so much; even if he were lying in the dark shadows of death, still I would honor his noble corpse with the greatest solemnity, entrusting his illustrious limbs to a worthy tomb."

When she had completed her prayers in this way, she raised up her eyes and noticed in the branches of a laurel tree birds chirping sweetly and enfolding their chicks in their feathery wings. When she noticed this, she sang in a very sad voice: "Brave King of heaven, to whom the starry firmament is subject, you who assuredly have the power to arrange everything properly, may there always be praise for all your mercies, for you have indulgently granted as a gift of mercy that all living things, little fishes, flocks, reptiles, and birds, eagerly delight in their young. But me alone, poor little me, you have ordered, in short, to remain sterile because of your righteous judgment. It is you, nevertheless, Father of everything, whom with a constant heart I call to be my witness that at the beginning of my marriage I made a vow, that if in your mercy you should grant me any fruit of my womb, I would directly offer it to you in the holy temple in accordance with ritual, and I would consecrate it lawfully to your service."

While she was forming this little speech with her pure

angelus astrigero subito descendit ab alto
maxima tristitiae portans solamina tantae,
et stans sub facie dictis haec fatur amicis:
“Exue maerorem, cordis depone dolorem,
consilioque Dei germen tibi credito summi;
hoc, quod ventre tuo procedet tempore certo,
vere fiet idem populis mirabile cunctis.”
Dixit et aurivagis revolans secat aethera pennis.
Anna sed angelicis nimium perterrita verbis
maesta domum petiit sese lectoque locavit,
et tremefacta diem Psalmorum lege †perorat†
effusis noctem precibus ducendo sequentem.
Post haec ergo suam praecepit adesse puellam
astantem rogitans propriis illam sub ocellis,
cur se despiceret vel cur tam sero veniret,
cum sibi sentiret fieri quid forte stupendi.

Reddidit econtra dominae lasciva famella
opprobriis iactum servili murmure verbum:
“Si te despexit sterilem faciens Deus,” inquit,
“dic, rogo, divinae causae quid pertinet ad me?”
Anna sed opprobrium patienter pertulit istud
effundens tantum lacrimas subtristis amaras.

Scilicet hac ipsa Ioachim praedictus in hora
angelus apparens inter montana refulgens,
in quis tunc pascendo gregem latitaverat autem,
iusserat ad sociam citius remeare relictam.
Qui dixit monitis animo permotus ab illis:
“Haec iam bis denis mecum permanserat annis,
ex illa Dominus subolem mihi nec dedit ullam.
Insuper opprobriis discessi plenus amaris

lips, an angel suddenly descended from the starry heights bringing the greatest consolations for such sadness, and standing before her in person he spoke with friendly words as follows: "Strip off your grief, put aside the pain of your heart, and trust in the plan of God the highest that you will have a child; this same child, who will come forth from your womb in due time, truly will be a source of wonder to all peoples." He said this and cut through the air, flying back to heaven on wings which journey through the breezes. Anna, however, thoroughly frightened by the angel's words, went home sadly and took to her bed, and trembling she prayed the entire day on the law of the Psalms, continuing into the following night with effusive prayers. After this, then, she ordered her servant girl to come to her, asking the girl standing before her very eyes why she looked down on her, or why she came so reluctantly, when she was aware that something overwhelming was, perchance, happening to her mistress.

The impudent little servant in return gave back to her mistress a reply tossed out insultingly in a servile grumble: "If God has looked down on you, making you sterile," she said, "tell me, please, what has God's reason to do with me?" Anna, however, bore that insult patiently, only pouring out bitter tears in her great sadness.

In fact, at that very same hour, the aforementioned angel appeared radiantly to Joachim among the mountains in which he, for his part, was then hiding, pasturing his flock; and the angel ordered him to return very speedily to the companion he had abandoned. Disturbed in his heart by these admonitions, he replied: "This woman has now lived with me for twice ten years, and the Lord has given me no offspring from her. In addition, fed up with bitter insults, I

nuper de templo causa confusus ab ipsa.
Et me despectum tantisque malis saturatum
hortaris regredi subdi primoque pudori?"
Ad quem mansuetis caelestis nuntius orsis:
"Me fore caelestem," dicebat, "credito civem
custodemque tui factum pietate superni
Regis, qui iustam consolari dedit Annam
per me, dum preculas flendo profunderet almas.
At nunc ergo tui causa de cardine caeli
aequa ferens veni permagni gaudia doni,
hocque tibi dico, quod mox praenobilis Anna
concipiet natam cunctis saeclis venerandam.
Haec inter natas hominum fiet sacra cunctas,
Spiritus et merito sanctus requiescet in illa.
Ac per quam veniet mundo benedictio summa,
nec primam similem nec fertur habere sequentem.
At nunc ad sociam tempta remeare beatam,
quae gaudens omni tantum pariet decus orbi.
Et semper grates Factori reddite dulces,
cui placuit stirpem vobis concedere talem,
qualem percerte numquam tenuere prophetae,
omnes electi post haec non sunt habituri."
   Ad quem promissis Ioachim laetatus in illis,
"Si mihi certa tuo maneat tua gratia servo,
ad tempus dignare meo requiescere tecto
et gustare cibum non dedignere paratum."
   Angelus econtra dicebat voce decora,
"Desine, posco, meum post haec te dicere servum,
esse sed angelicae consortem credito turmae.
Nam mihi terrenis opus est non vescier escis,
quem pascit Domini semper praesentia summi;

recently departed from the temple, shamed for this very reason. And you encourage me, despised and glutted with such ill treatments, to return and be subjected to my former shame?" To him the heavenly messenger spoke in gentle terms: "Believe that I am a citizen of heaven and that I have been made your guardian through the mercy of the King on high, who granted that the righteous Anna be consoled by me when she was in tears pouring out holy prayers. But now, therefore, I have come for your sake from the vault of heaven, bringing to you the agreeable joys of an exceptional gift, and I tell you this, that soon noble Anna will conceive a daughter who shall be venerated by all ages. She will become holy among all the daughters of men, and the Holy Spirit will rightly come to rest in her. And through her the greatest blessing will come upon the world, and she is said to have no equal in the past, and will have none in the future. But now, strive to return to your blessed companion, who rejoices that she will give birth to so great a glory for the whole world. And both of you should always give sweet thanks to the Creator, who took pleasure in granting to you such a child as the prophets certainly never had, and such as all the chosen people in the future will not have."

Gladdened by these promises, Joachim said to the angel, "If your regard for me, your servant, is assured, deign to stay awhile under my roof and do not disdain to taste the food which has been prepared."

In reply, the angel said in a respectful tone, "From now on, I ask you, do not say that you are my servant, but believe that you are an equal member of the heavenly host. There is no need, however, for me to eat earthly foods, since the presence of the supreme Lord nourishes me; therefore,

quapropter moneo Domino libamine sacro
hoc te ferre, meis satagis quod ponere mensis."
Qui citus anniculum gregibus subtraxerat agnum,
sperans opprobrium Ruben cessasse vetustum,
immolat et Domino gavisus pectore laeto
ignibus appositis, ut habet praeceptio legis.
Angelus his votis, ut iussit, rite peractis
altaris fumo sublatus pergit ad astra.

Iam tunc clementis paulatim gratia Patris
incoepit radiis mundo lucescere claris,
atque prior stabilem discordia sumere finem.
Cum sua caelestes primum consortia cives
olim terrigenas promittebant habituros,
quos prius e meritis Adam sprevere parentis.
Nec latuit tunc angelicum clementia coetum
Omnipatris, proprium qui mox post tempora natum
mittere virgineum miserans disponit in alvum,
ut sine principio Natus de Patre superno
carnem virgineo sub tempore sumeret alvo
omnes atque suo salvaret sanguine sacro.
Ne post haec generis humani callidus hostis
gauderet mundum laqueis retinere malignis,
sed Patris et Nati numen quoque Pneumatis almi
aequali forma pollens sub nomine trino
finetenus stabilem regnaret iure per orbem.

Angelus astrigerum postquam transcendit Olympum,
vix patiens Ioachim tantae praeconia causae
et tactus iaculo terroris denique magno,
stratus adusque solum doni virtute superni
pertimidus iacuit, necnon sine mente quievit

I advise you to bring to the Lord, along with a sacred drink offering, the food which you were intending to put on the table for me." Joachim quickly took a year-old lamb from his flocks, hoping that Ruben's past insults were at an end, and he sacrificed the lamb to the Lord, placing it over a fire as the law prescribed, happily rejoicing in his heart. The angel, after these offerings had been properly made as he had ordered, headed for the stars, borne aloft by the smoke of the altar.

Already then, little by little, the grace of the indulgent Father was beginning to shine on the world with clear rays, and the discord of former times was coming to a permanent end. Then for the first time the citizens of heaven promised that they would, one day, accept into their community the inhabitants of earth, whom they had previously spurned because of the faults of their father, Adam. And the indulgence of the Father of all beings was not concealed from the angelic host, the Father who was mercifully disposed, in the near future, to send his own Son into the Virgin's womb, so that the Son born with no beginning from the Father above might take on flesh in temporality from the Virgin's womb and by his sacred blood save everyone. Thus, the deceitful enemy of the human race would no longer be able to rejoice in holding the world in his wicked snares, but the divinity of the Father and the Son and the Holy Spirit, shining equal in nature under a triune name, might justly reign throughout the stable world until the end of time.

After the angel ascended to starry Olympus, Joachim, who could scarcely bear the tidings of so great a matter, and who was struck by a great bolt of terror, finally lay spread out on the ground terrified at the power of this heavenly

ipsius <a> sexta, ni fallor, forte diei
dum sol usque suum conclusit vespere cursum.
Interea pueri venerunt cum grege lassi,
cumque suum dominum terra videre locatum,
comminus astantes coeperunt discere tristes
causam terroris turbata mente recentis.
Ipsum percerte sed vix potuere levare.
Quis cum caelestis narrasset nuntia civis,
suaserunt illi iussis parere supernis
et rapido patriam cursu repedare relictam.
Qui gregibus lectis silvis discessit ab illis,
ac gaudens pueros secum deduxerat ipsos.
Et cum transisset spatium triginta dierum,
angelus oranti sanctae comparuit Annae
et cum pacificis deprompsit talia verbis:
"Exsurgens animo vultu quoque perge sereno
ad portam subito, quae dicitur 'aurea' vulgo;
illic forte tuum summa cum pace reversum
legalem dominum mox comperies fore vivum."
Quae citius dicto iussum complevit amandum;
impatiensque morae perrexit ad ostia portae
praestolata suum gavisa mente patronum.
Scilicet attonitis quem cum conspexit ocellis,
caro florigerum percurrerat obvia campum
ipsius et collo sese suspendit amando,
Altithrono grates reddendo denique tales:
"Laus tibi, cunctorum largitor summe bonorum,
qui mihi non merito concedis gaudia tanta!
Ecce virum proprium praesentem sentio salvum.
Tempore quae longo iam permansi viduata
quaeque fui sterilis, concepi gaudia prolis."

gift, and remained in a trance, if I am not mistaken, from about the sixth hour of that same day until the sun completed its course that evening.

Meanwhile, his weary servants arrived with the flock, and when they saw their master sprawled on the ground, stood next to him, sadly, and began with troubled hearts to inquire into the cause of this new terror. But, in fact, they were scarcely able to relieve him. When he had recounted to them the pronouncements of the heavenly citizen, they persuaded him to obey the commands from above and return by a quick route to the fatherland he had left behind. He collected his flocks and left those woods, and he happily led his servants home with him. And after an interval of thirty days had passed, an angel appeared to holy Anna as she was praying and announced these things with calming words: "Rise up with your heart and mind at ease, go immediately to the gate which is commonly called the golden gate; there, perchance, you will soon find that your lawful lord is returned alive in perfect peace." She, swifter than you could say it, carried out that agreeable order; and impatient of delay, she headed for the entrance of the gate, awaiting her protector with a happy heart.

Indeed, when she caught sight of him with her astonished eyes, she ran through the flowery field to meet her dear husband, and she hung upon his beloved neck, at last giving thanks to God enthroned on high as follows: "Praise be to you, supreme dispenser of all good things, who bestow on me such unmerited joys! Look, I perceive that my husband is here and is safe, while I who remained a long time widowed and sterile have conceived the joys of offspring."

Talibus auditis congaudens concinit omnis
plebs Hebraea Deo laudes cum pectore laeto.
Post haec noveno percerte mense peracto
venit summa dies, in qua praenobilis Anna
progenuit natam cunctis saeclis venerandam.
Postque dies octo primi venere vocati
pontifices, tantae solito qui more puellae
nomen et aptarent ipsam quoque sanctificarent.
Quis Ioachim preculas fudit presentibus istas:
"Rex caeli, stellis solus qui nomina ponis,
istius tenerae nomen dignare puellae
caelitus indiciis per te monstrare coruscis."
Dixerat, et subito sonuit vox fortis ab alto
mandans egregiam "Mariam" vocitare puellam,
"stella maris" lingua quod consonat ergo Latina.
Hoc nomen merito sortitur sancta puella,
est quia praeclarum sidus, quod fulget in aevum
Regis <in> aeterni claro diademate Christi.
Post haec annorum meta vergente duorum,
fortunata suam dum sumpsit ab ubere natam,
ablactando piam genetrix de more Mariam,
ocius in templo sistit cum munere digno
ipsam, quae templum Domini fuit immo futurum,
quo sociata sacris virguncula parva puellis
semper divinis illic perstaret in odis,
quem merito cives celestes laude frequentant.
Post haec, in templi subsistens limine sacri,
ascensum graduum subito ter quinque supinum,
immemor aetatis, iam plena Deo, puerilis,

Rejoicing when they heard these things, the entire Hebrew nation sang praises to God with a happy heart.

Afterward, when the ninth month had passed, most assuredly the day arrived at last on which noble Anna bore a daughter who shall be venerated for all time. And eight days later, the high priests were summoned and came according to the usual custom to assign a name appropriate to such a girl, and to purify the mother. In their presence, Joachim poured out these prayers: "King of heaven, you who alone give names to the stars, consent, I pray you, to indicate by clear signs from above a name for this tender girl."

He said this, and suddenly a mighty voice sounded from on high, ordering them to call the remarkable child "Mary," which is equivalent, then, to "star of the sea" in the Latin tongue. The saintly girl was rightfully allotted this name, because she is a brilliant star, which shines forever in the lustrous crown of Christ, the eternal King.

After this, when it was getting on toward the close of two years, as the fortunate mother was removing her daughter from her breast, weaning kind Mary according to custom, she presented the girl without delay in the temple with a suitable gift, the same girl who, in fact, was destined to become the temple of the Lord. Anna presented her so that the young maiden, in the company of holy girls, would always remain there, steadfast in singing divine odes to the Lord, whom the heavenly citizens rightly celebrate with praise.

After this, Mary, as she set foot upon the threshold of the sacred temple, all of a sudden ran fearlessly up the rising flight of thrice five steps, forgetful of her childish age, already then filled with God, and she did not turn her face

audacter currit, vultum nec retro reflexit,
quaerat ut astantes infantum more parentes.
His super accensi mirantur denique cuncti
astantes populi templi pariterque ministri.
Pontifices ipsi factum laudant quoque primi,
dicentes tanto quod tunc infantula facto
per se quid fieri praesignaret cito magni
et vere magni cunctis meritoque stupendi.
Quod credi maius, vel quod posset fore maius,
quam quod virgineo portavit ventre puella
magnum Factorem mundi propriumque parentem?
Nec mirum, sursum coepit si figere gressum,
infans lacteolis fuerat dum parvula membris.
Quam, Pater alme, tuo ditasti Flamine sacro,
dum fuerat sanctae genetricis condita ventre.
Praescius hanc solam certe consistere dignam
ad proprii partum Nati per saecula voti.
Qui post corporeae tectus velamine formae
ascensum graduum cunctis patefecit in aevum,
per quos ad patriam tendunt remeare relictam.
Cui Christus nomen; cui laus sit caelitus. Amen.
Scilicet et genetrix tali fetu bene felix
conlaudens Regem cecinit sic Anna perennem:
"Omnipotens rector, solus pietatis amator,
clementer proprio fecisti mira popello;
aspiciens humilem miserando meam quoque mentem
iam desperatae donasti gaudia natae.
Audeo percerte post haec tibi munera ferre,
nec vereor prohibere meum post haec inimicum
quominus stem sacris templi sociata ministris.

back, the way that children do, to look for her parents standing nearby.

Finally, in their excitement at these things, all the people who were standing nearby were amazed, as were the ministers of the temple. Even the chief priests themselves praised her deed, saying that by such an action, the little infant was even then showing an early sign that some great thing was soon to be done through her, truly a great thing that must rightly be a wonder to all.

What greater thing can be believed, or what thing can ever be greater, than that a girl carried in her virgin womb the great Creator of the world and her own parent? And it is no wonder if she started planting her steps upward while she was a little infant with limbs white as milk. You enriched her, gracious Father, with your Holy Spirit, while she was hidden in the womb of her saintly mother. You surely knew in advance that she stood alone in being worthy to give birth to your own Son, the hope of the ages. He, after he was covered in the veil of a bodily form, laid open to all people a stairway to eternity, by which they aim to return to the fatherland they had left behind. His name is Christ; heavenly praise be to him. Amen.

And indeed, her mother Anna, well pleased with such a child and joining in the praise of the eternal King, sang in this way: "All-powerful ruler, sole lover of mercy, in your indulgence you have done wondrous things for your people; and looking mercifully also on my humble desire, you have granted me the joys of a daughter after I had already given up hope. From now on I most assuredly have the courage to bring gifts to you, and from now on I have no fear that my enemy will prohibit me from standing in the company of the

Hinc te celestes conlaudant sedulo cives,
condignum carmen modulando perenniter. Amen."
His ita finitis orantis scilicet orsis
germine felices talis rediere parentes
indolis in templo parva remanente Maria.

Omnes humanae nequeunt comprendere linguae,
nec potis est stabilis, quamvis verbum sonet, orbis
istius infantis praeclaram dicere famam.
Sed nec mirandae vitam moresque puellae
quis laudare modis potis est per saecula dignis,
haec quia continuo cunis subtracta puella
maturis omni lucebat moribus orbi.
Nec quicquam membris gessit puerile tenellis;
ast in praeceptis fuerat iustissima legis
necnon carminibus semper studiosa Davidis.
Haec prudens, humilis, fervens dulcedine mentis,
omnibus atque placens, tota virtute refulgens.
Hanc hominis maledicentem non audiit auris,
offensam sed nec quisquam cognoverat umquam.
Semper erat mitis necnon gratissima cunctis,
et, quae nempe suo profluxit ab ore loquela,
nectare gratiolae fuerat condita supernae.
Et cum quis verbis illi benedixit amicis,
mox grates Domino curavit reddere summo,
nec sic divinis linguam retineret ab odis.
Exemplumque suis in se praenobile cunctis
preponit sociis iam cunctigenae bonitatis.
Ipsius faciem niveo candore nitentem
tradunt ardentis radios praecellere solis
necnon humanum penitus devincere visum.
Quid referam digitos operum satis arte probatos?

holy ministers of the temple. That is why the heavenly citizens eagerly join in praising you, eternally singing a worthy song. Amen." When she had completed this prayer, the parents returned home, happy to have a child of such noble character, and little Mary remained in the temple.

No human tongue can comprehend, nor can the steadfast world, speak as it may, describe the outstanding reputation of this infant. And no one can praise this wondrous girl's life and manners in ways that are fitting for all time, because from the moment she was taken from the cradle, this girl brightened the whole world with her mature behavior. And she did not do anything childish with her tender limbs; on the contrary, she was as correct as possible regarding the precepts of the law and always earnest about the psalms of David. She was prudent, humble, fired by sweetness of heart, and pleasing to everyone, resplendent in every virtue. No human's ear heard her speaking ill, and no one ever knew her to be angered. She was always gentle and most agreeable to everyone, and indeed the speech which flowed from her mouth had been seasoned with the nectar of sweet grace from above. And when someone greeted her with friendly words, she was careful straightaway to respond with thanks to the Lord most high, and so she never held her tongue back from singing divine odes. She also provided to all her companions a very noble example in herself of every kind of goodness. They say that her face, shining snowy white, surpassed the rays of the blazing sun and completely overpowered human sight. Why should I mention those fingers, well proven in the skill of weaving? Indeed, though just a little

Namque manu docta perfecit parva puella
. . .
Nempe sibi normam statuens ipsissima duram
omnibus in templo vivebat strictius ergo
virginibus reliquis illic pariter sociatis.
Nam tantum preculis studuit persistere sacris,
necnon divinis semper constanter in odis,
ex quo discussae noctis periere tenebrae,
Aurora spargente plagam lucem per eoam
altius usque polum Phoebo ascendente serenum
tertia iam solito devenerat hora diei.
Tunc usu digitos operis laxaverat albos
docte purpureis instando denique filis.
Sed mox ut nona Phoebus descendit in hora,
se precibus solito reddit famosa puella.
Ac studio mentis bene perduravit in illis,
usque per angelicum sumpsit sacra virgo ministrum
omni namque die missam sibi caelitus escam.
Et quam pontifices dederant de more potentes,
hanc studio mentis citius concessit egenis.
Denique caelestes lapsi de sidere cives
hanc crebro verbis consolabantur amicis,
spernere terrestrem quo mox didicisset amorem
et castam Regi mentem servare perenni.
Quisquis languidolis infirmus denique membris
hanc saltem tetigit, raptim salvus remeavit.
Cuius cum stabilem volitaret fama per orbem,
Abiathar reliquos exorat saepe sacerdos
pontifices templi, pretii non munere pauci,
vellent praeclaram quo disponsare Mariam
ipsius egregio legali foedere nato.

girl, with her expert hand she accomplished. . . . In fact, establishing for herself, on her own, a severe way of life, she lived then in the temple more strictly than all the rest of the virgins joined together there. Indeed, she only aspired to continue with her holy prayers, and was always steadfastly singing divine odes, from the time when the scattered shadows of night were disappearing, as Dawn was sprinkling her light through the eastern zone, until the third hour of the day had arrived in its regular way, as Phoebus ascended higher into the clear sky. At that time, she exhausted her milk-white fingers to perform their work, and then was skillfully intent on the purple threads. But at the ninth hour, as soon as Phoebus descended, the celebrated girl was accustomed to return to her prayers. And the holy virgin rightly continued at her prayers with an eager heart, until she took from her angelic minister the food sent to her from above, in fact, every day. And the food which the high priests gave her according to their custom, this, with an eager heart, she very speedily gave to the needy. Then the heavenly citizens, gliding down from the stars, would often comfort her with friendly words, so that she soon learned to reject earthly love and to keep her heart chaste for the eternal King. Finally, whoever was sick with weakened limbs and touched her, even lightly, instantly returned to health.

As her fame was spreading throughout the steadfast world, the priest Abiathar repeatedly asked the other pontiffs of the temple, with a bribe of no small value, to agree to the betrothal by lawful contract of the illustrious Mary to

Quod fieri vero prohibet virguncula casta,
incluta regalis spernens consortia stirpis,
se quoque finetenus testatur nobile corpus
eius coniugio percerte subdere nullo.
Talia pontifices cui mox dixere potentes:
"Nonne Deus colitur digneque potens veneratur
in plebis Iudae legali posteritate?
Nec decet innuptam talem remanere puellam."
Quis constans animo respondit talia virgo:
"Nam Deus in templo gaudet requiescere mundo
mentibus et sobriis, nec delectatur in illis,
crimine quos magno maculat lasciva libido.
Scimus Abel duplam merito sumpsisse coronam,
qui primus mundo iustus fuerat protoplasto:
unam martirii fratris de caede peracti,
atque magis nitidam pro virginitate secundam.
Credimus Heliam caelum petiisse secretum
corpore cum vero, mansit quia virgo potenter,
nec corpus maculis umquam violavit amaris.
Haec didici certe legis ratione docente
et discens animo mandavi sedula fixo
meque puellarem vovi retinere pudorem."
Postquam bis septem totos compleverat annos,
non hoc esse sui moris, dicunt Pharisaei,
aetatis tantae quod vellet virgo manere
post haec in templo Domini sub honore sacrato.
<Hinc> decreverunt populum concurrere cunctum,
ut pariter tantam temptarent volvere causam.
Et cum sub tectis templi consisteret omnis,
Abiathar, quem iam memini, sub lege sacerdos,

his own fine son. This, in truth, the chaste young virgin prohibited from happening, rejecting a distinguished marriage to a royal line, and furthermore she asserted that so long as she lived she most certainly would subject her noble body to no marriage. In turn, the high priests spoke words such as these to her: "Is it not by the lawful offspring of the people of Judah that our powerful God is worshiped and rightly venerated? It is not proper that such a girl as you should remain unmarried."

The virgin, steadfast in her heart, responded to them as follows: "Surely God is happy to rest in a pure temple and in sober minds, and he is not pleased with those whom wanton lust stains with a great sin. We know that Abel deservedly received a double crown, he who was the first just man when the world was newly created: he received one for the martyrdom accomplished when his brother slew him, and the second, which was more illustrious, for his virginity. We believe that Elijah traveled to a heavenly retreat in the actual flesh because he effectively remained a virgin, and he never violated his flesh with the bitter stains of sin. I learned these things with certainty from the instructive reasoning of the law, and learning them, I have diligently fixed them firmly in my mind, and I have vowed that I will keep my maidenly chastity." After she had finished twice seven years in their entirety, the Pharisees said it was not their custom that a girl of such an age should choose to remain any longer in the Lord's temple in sacred service. So, they decreed that the whole populace gather so that they could attempt to reflect upon the situation together. And when everyone was standing together under the roof of the temple, Abiathar, whom I have already mentioned, a priest under the law, ascended

ascensum graduum conscendit namque supinum
praesul, et astanti dicebat talia plebi:
"Ex quo constructum fuerat praenobile templum
istud per magni regis studium Salomonis,
ut scitis vere, manserunt semper in illo
forma conspicuae vultus, aetate tenellae,
natae nobilium famoso germine regum,
atque sacerdotum, vatum, pariterque priorum;
quae celebres omni merito mansere popello.
Certe perfecta sed mox aetate recepta
coniugibus tantae condignis sunt sociatae,
multo magisque deo placuerunt semper ab illo.
More sed insolito sperat se virgo Maria
posse placere viris Domini pro nomine spretis.
Nunc quia non constat votum se reddere tantum,
restat, ut Altithronum precibus digne rogitemus
ut nos forte suis faciat cognoscere iussis,
hanc cui legali fas sit cum foedere iungi."
Tali consilio consensu plebis adepto,
sortem pontifices miserunt primitus omnes
inter namque tribus Israelis duodenas;
quae mox egregiam Iudae signat fore dignam.
Qua designata prae cunctis scilicet una
praecepere viros eiusdem germinis omnes,
quos sine coniugibus fecit consistere casus,
collectos ergo concurrere sole secundo
et manibus virgas dextris conferre novellas.
His igitur cunctis toto conamine lectis,
advenit dignus senior Ioseph sociatus
illis incurvam portans sub iudice virgam.
At vero summus virgas tollendo sacerdos

the stairs leading upward, for in fact he was the one presiding, and he spoke as follows to the people standing there:

"From the time when this very noble temple was constructed through the efforts of our great king Solomon, as you truly know, our daughters have always dwelt in it, girls tender in age and conspicuously beautiful in appearance, the renowned offspring of noble kings, and also, likewise, of former priests and prophets; and they dwelt there, deservedly celebrated by all the people. But, surely, as soon as they had reached the age of maturity, such girls were united with suitable husbands, and they were always far more pleasing to God as a result. But, in an unconventional manner, the virgin Mary hopes she can find favor by rejecting men in the name of the Lord. Now since it is not right that she make such a vow, it only remains for us, in a fitting manner, to ask the One enthroned on high through our prayers to make known to us, perchance, by his commands, the man to whom it is right for her to be joined in a lawful marriage."

When that plan was accepted by consent of the people, first all the priests cast lots, that is to say, all the priests among the twelve tribes of Israel; this soon singled out the outstanding tribe of Judah as deserving. When this tribe had been designated before all others, that is to say, alone, they ordered all the men of that tribe, whom chance caused to be living unmarried, to assemble then together on the second day and to bring with them newly sprouted branches in their right hands.

And so, when by a great effort these men had been gathered together, the worthy old man Joseph came accompanying them, carrying to the ordeal a crooked branch. And truly the high priest, joyfully taking everyone's branches, and

gaudens cunctorum, Domino faciens holocaustum,
quid fieri iubeat, fusis precibus rogitabat.
Cui mox indiciis divinis ista iubentur,
tempore digesto sibi quae fuerant facienda.
Praemonitus virgas qui misit protinus ipsas
in templi sanctum famosi iure secretum,
demandans, quidni, collectim luce sequenti
Iudae regales iterum venisse nepotes
unumquemque suam rursum quoque sumere virgam.
Nam sibi pro signo dictum fuerat manifesto,
virgo quod haec credi deberet nobilis illi
de cuius virga volitaret rite columba,
quae petiisse polum temptaret protinus altum.
Dum ter mille suas retinerent denique captas
virgas personae, praedicto tempore certe,
nec signum populo praedictum redderet ulla,
obtulit incensum praesul venerabile rursum
seque dedit precibus devoto pectore fusis.
Cui mox caelesti dicetur voce precanti,
"Virgula namque brevis Ioseph iusti senioris,
quae iacet in templo nec sollicitatur ab ullo,
implebit merito signum memorabile sola."
His ita finitis, sonuit vox pontificalis
mandans in mediam Ioseph procedere turbam.
Hic erat abiectus forma nullaque decorus,
nec sibi complacuit sociis interfore tantis,
sed mage postremo gaudet remanere locello.
Qui mox ut vocem sensit se forte vocantem,
processit pavidus virgam conprendere iussus.
Ex qua continuo splendens egressa columba
haud tarde caelum fertur petiisse secretum.

making a burned offering to the Lord, asked in effusive prayers what the Lord ordered to be done. To the priest then these things were ordered by divine signs, and they had to be done by him at a specified time. As instructed, he immediately sent these branches, as law required, into the hidden sanctuary of that famous temple, demanding, of course, that the noble descendants of Judah collectively return on the following day, and that each one of them retrieve again his own branch. For it had been told to him by a clear sign, that this noble virgin ought to be entrusted to the man from whose branch a dove would duly fly, and the dove would attempt to travel straight to high heaven.

While three thousand individuals held the branches they had now reclaimed at the specified time, and indeed no branch rendered the sign that had been foretold to the people, the priest for a second time offered the venerable incense and with a devout heart committed himself to pouring forth prayers. Soon by a heavenly voice it was proclaimed to him as he was praying, "Indeed, none but the little branch of the just old man Joseph, which is lying in the temple and was not claimed by anyone, will deservedly fulfill the remarkable sign."

When these proclamations were finished, the priest's voice called out ordering Joseph to advance to the middle of the crowd. Joseph was humble and distinguished by no elegance, and he did not like to mingle in such company, but enjoyed, rather, remaining in the most unassuming place. As soon as he understood that the voice, as fated, was calling upon him, he advanced in fear to retrieve his branch as instructed. Immediately a splendid dove, emerging from it, is reported to have sought, without delay, a heavenly retreat.

His ita transactis, laudes plebs concrepat omnis
grates Altithrono reddentes pectore laeto,
cui placuit signo iustum monstrare novello.
Ipse sed aetatis non immemor ulterioris
protestans proceres se<se> genuisse nepotes,
magno percerte fertur rogitare pudore
pontifices, Mariam quo non vellent sibi pulchram,
ipsius proprio sed sponsam tradere nato.
Quod cum forte negant, se signatum quoque narrant,
nec cuiquam credi sanctam debere puellam
quam sibi, quem Dominus solum fecit fore dignum,
exorans alias coepit rogitare puellas
mitti cum Maria causa solaminis ergo.
Quae veluti connutritae sociaeque coaevae
illam colloquii scirent solamine dulci
absque mora consolari, ne virgo pudori
coniuge pro vetulo fieret subiecta tenella.
Quod mox pontifices fieri iussere potentes.
Nam senior frustra sudaverat ista rogando,
non sibi, sed Christo fuerat quia virgo dicata.
Postquam pontifices preculis cessere precantis,
Ioseph servandam suscepit namque puellam
et pariter missas (ni fallor, quinque) puellas.
Quarum sic ergo creduntur nomina dicta:
Sephiphora, Zabel, Susanna, Rebecca, Abigea.
Quis opus ad templi pertingens namque sacrati
traditur ornatum studiose perficiendum,
coccus cum bysso, linum cum vellere Serum.

After that happened, all the people shouted their praise, giving thanks with a joyous heart to the One enthroned on high, who had been pleased to identify the just man by this novel sign. But he himself, not unmindful of his very great age and protesting that he had already begotten noble descendants, is reported to have implored the priests, with great humility certainly, that they not choose to give the beautiful Mary to him as a spouse, but to give her instead to one of his own sons. When, as it happened, they rejected this, and said, likewise, that it was he who was designated, and that the holy girl should not be entrusted to anyone other than to him, whom alone the Lord had indicated as worthy, then he began to ask imploringly that additional girls be sent along with Mary as a source of solace. These girls, since they had been raised alongside her and were companions of the same age, would know right away how to console her with the sweet solace of conversation, so that the tender little virgin would not be exposed to embarrassment on account of her aged spouse. This the high priests then ordered to be done. In making these requests, to be sure, the old man had exerted himself in vain, because the virgin had been consecrated to Christ, not to him.

After the priests yielded to the gentle prayers of the suppliant, Joseph indeed received the girl into his protection, and likewise the other girls who were sent with her (five of them, if I am not mistaken). These, then, are the names by which they are believed to have been called: Sephiphora, Zabel, Susanna, Rebecca, and Abigea. Indeed, so that they could attentively carry out work pertaining to the decoration of the sacred temple, to these girls was given red dye along with linen, flax with Chinese fleece. But the shining

Purpura sed sanctae fulgens operanda Mariae
creditur ad velum Domini templi pretiosum.
His super accensae praesentes quippe puellae
opprobrii causa dixerunt taliter ergo:
"Num te reginam constat post haec fore nostram,
iam texenda tibi quia purpura creditur uni,
non parvo cum sis iunior tu tempore nobis?"
Quae tunc, ut semper, bene sustinuit patienter
talia nec verbo iam contradixerat ullo.
Astans sed citius custos semper sibi fidus
angelus astrigera dilapsus dixit ab aula,
"Non te, virgo, rogo, perturbent talia verba,
istae percerte quia vatum more locutae
iam nunc presaga dicebant voce futura.
Tu quia sola potenter eris regina perennis
necnon stelligeri dominatrix incluta caeli."
Post haec secreta residebat in aede quieta
purpureos digitis filos operans benedictis.
Angelus et summus Gabriel conspectibus eius
astitit, astrigera caelorum lapsus ab aula,
virgineumque decus verbis affatur amicis,
iuxta cunctorum narrans oracula vatum,
ipsius e casto nasci dignarier alvo
Altithroni prolem mundo satis antiquiorem,
virgineique modum partus narrat memorandum.
Ergo non nostris potis est exponier orsis
nobile colloquium longo sermone peractum
Virginis aeternae, Christi matris benedictae,
partus et tanti sacra narrantis paranymphi.
Sed nec dactylicis opus est nos psallere chordis

purple was entrusted to the saintly Mary to be worked into a precious curtain of the Lord's temple.

Angered indeed by this, the girls then face-to-face spoke insultingly as follows: "Is it decided that you will be our queen in the future, since to you alone now the purple is entrusted for weaving, although you are younger than we are in age, and not by a little?" Mary then, as always, bore such comments very patiently and did not at that time reply to them with a single word.

But standing very swiftly beside her, her ever-faithful guardian angel, having descended from the starry palace, said, "Virgin, I beg you, do not let such words disturb you, for these girls have surely spoken as prophets, and just now they were telling the future with prophetic utterances. For you alone will be a queen in power forever and also the celebrated mistress of starry heaven."

Afterward she sat in her home in quiet seclusion working the purple threads with her blessed fingers. And the archangel Gabriel stood before her eyes, having descended from the starry palace of the heavens, and he addressed her virginal honor with friendly words, telling her that in keeping with the predictions of all the prophets, the child of the One enthroned on high consented to be born from her chaste womb, a child far more ancient than the world, and he told her of the remarkable manner of the virgin birth.

It is, of course, not possible for that noble conversation to be explained in my words, that conversation carried out in a long discussion between the eternal Virgin, the blessed mother of Christ, and the groomsman who told her the sacred details of such a birth. And there is no need for me to sing in dactylic measures of the great grief of Joseph and the

magnum maerorem Ioseph durumque dolorem
frustra cordetenus quo iam fuerat cruciatus,
talem dum gravidam sensisset forte puellam,
qualiter et tristis solatur tempore noctis
virginis intactae iussus curam retinere
virginis et nati nobis de sidere missi.
Haec evangelici demonstrant cuncta libelli
nostras et fragiles excedunt denique vires.
His nos transmissis, constant quia cognita cunctis,
sermonem vobis tantum faciemus ab illis,
rarius in templo quae creduntur fore dicta.

Certe cum stabilem volitans urgueret in orbem
undique subiectos describi iussio lectos
Caesaris Augusti censumque sibi profiteri,
Ioseph ad patriam Bethlem perrexerat urbem
cum desponsata sibimet pregnante Maria.
Et cum famosis essent prope moenibus urbis,
aspexit, non corporeis, sed mentis ocellis,
comminus alma duos virguncula stare popellos,
unum ridentem necnon alium lacrimantem.
Quod Ioseph vetulo narrans audivit ab illo,
"Contine subiecto tantum te rite iumento
et noli, posco, narrare superflua verba."

Dixerat et iuvenem coram prospexit erilem,
qui sibi mysterium declaravit populorum
talia sacrata dicens pro virgine verba:
"Cur dicis Mariam non verbula vera locutam,
indignatus eam secretum cernere solam?
Nam flentem populum merito vidit Iudaeorum,
qui mox a Domino discedet corde maligno;

harsh pain by which he was tortured now deep in his heart and needlessly, when he sensed, by chance, that such a maiden was pregnant, and how he was consoled in his sadness during the night and was ordered to continue to care for the unblemished virgin, and for the virgin's child sent for our sake from the stars. The gospel books explain all these things, and they surpass in the end my feeble strength. I, passing over them because it is certain they are known to everyone, will make mention to you only of those things that are understood to be more rarely spoken of in church.

Assuredly, when Augustus Caesar's order was spreading through the steadfast world, driving his subjects, gathered from all sides, to be registered and to declare their property to him, Joseph traveled to his native city, Bethlehem, with Mary his betrothed, who was pregnant. And when they were close to the famous walls of the city, the blessed young virgin saw, not with her bodily eyes, but with the eyes of her heart, two crowds of people standing close by, one laughing and the other crying. Telling this to the old man Joseph, she heard from him, "Just keep yourself properly on that humble beast of burden and do not, I beg you, tell unnecessary tales."

No sooner had he said that than he saw before him a young man of the Lord, who explained to him the mystery of those crowds of people, speaking in the sacred virgin's defense words like these: "Why do you say that Mary has not spoken fitting words, being angry that she alone perceives this secret? For she sees the people of Judaea crying, and rightly so; they will soon part from the Lord with a malign heart; but she saw the Gentiles, in contrast, overflowing

contra gentilem sed laetitia fluitantem,
ad fidei magnum quia perveniet sacramentum."
  His dictis, Mariam blande conversus ad almam
tempus adesse sibi Christum narrat pariendi.
Quae de subiecto descendit iussa iumento
intrans speluncam sub terra rite locatam.
Quae male praesentis penitus fuit inscia lucis,
et quam continuae semper tenuere tenebrae.
Sed mox ut lucem genetrix paritura perennem
hanc adiit, radiis coepit fulgere coruscis.
Nec post haec ibi caelestis lux defuit omni
tempore, quo genetrix illic mansit bene felix.
  Noctis tranquillae medio libramine certe
illic haec eadem genuit virguncula prolem
gaudens divinam cunctis saeclis venerandam.
Cui nomen Iesus, cui sit laus, gloria, virtus.
Solvere qui veterum veniens oracula vatum
se pro salvando venturum praescia mundo,
pacem caelicolis fecit cum civibus orbis.
Quem genitum sacro castae de virginis alvo,
protinus angelicus circumstat denique coetus,
laudans submissis Factorem vocibus orbis,
orans et puerum nobis de sidere missum.
Sed mater subito cunctis veneranda Maria
collocat angusto praesepi membra tenella
Christi, panniculis Regem volvendo perennem.
  Et pius interea Ioseph digressus ab illa
mox obstetrices secum duxit mulieres,
quae Zelemi, Salome fuerant de nomine dictae.
Sola sed ingreditur Zelemi, Salomeque veretur
tangere speluncam pedibus splendore repletam.

with happiness, because they will soon come to the great sacrament of the faith."

When he had said these things, he turned soothingly toward dear Mary, and told her that her time was at hand for giving birth to Christ. She climbed down, as instructed, from the humble beast of burden, duly entering a cave located underground. It was entirely ignorant of light, which was not present there, and constant darkness always gripped it. But, as soon as the mother who was about to give birth to eternal light entered it, the cave began to shine with bright rays. And from then on, heavenly light did not cease in that place for the entire period during which that happiest of mothers resided there.

At the central midpoint of that tranquil night, assuredly, this same young virgin joyously bore in that place the divine child who shall be venerated by all ages. His name is Jesus; may glory, honor, and power be his. He, coming to fulfill the predictions of the ancient prophets, which foretold that he was coming to save the world, made peace between the citizens of heaven and those of earth. Him, born from the sacred womb of a chaste virgin, immediately then the angelic host surrounded, praising him in restrained voices as the Creator of the world, and praying to the child sent for our sake from the stars. But his mother Mary, venerated by all, immediately placed Christ's tender little limbs in a narrow manger, wrapping the eternal King in swaddling clothes.

And pious Joseph, who in the meantime had departed from her, before long brought back with him women who were midwives, who were called Zelemi and Salome by name. Zelemi, however, alone went in to Mary, and Salome was afraid for her feet to touch a cave filled with shining

Mox quoque virgineum Zelemi tractans piae partum,
exclamans signi dixit bene credula tanti,
"Quid sibi non nuptae partus vult iste novellus?
Editus ecce puer regali germine nuper
coniugis expertem bene declarat fore matrem.
Atque parens virgo natum lactat pie sola
uberibus castis de caelo iure repletis.
Non dolor est matri, nec est maculatio proli;
ordine divino fieri sed talia credo."
  Hanc Salome vocem spernens non ficta loquentem
dixerat auditis sese non credere verbis,
ni probet ipsa sacram palma tangendo Mariam.
Hinc ingressa suam coepit protendere dextram,
audacter castam temptans palpare Mariam;
sed talis poenam confert audacia dignam.
Dextraque continuo temptatrix debilitata
ingenti certe cruciatur iure dolore.
Tunc Salome clamans animo subtristis amaro
defectum dextrae subitum deflevit ademptae.
Moreque Iudaico proprium meritum recitando,
necnon iusticia sat confidens simulata,
talia Celsithrono fertur dare verba dolendo:
  "Testis cunctorum consolatorque laborum,
tu scis, praeceptis fueram quod sedula legis,
quodque tui causa semper fueram bene larga
pauperibus cunctis lectis de finibus orbis.
Qui maerens venit, de me quoque laetior ivit.
Et nunc pro meritis patior damnum grave tantis."
  Cui mox apparens iuvenis praelucidus infit:

light. And before long Zelemi, handling the virgin-born offspring of the pious woman and fully believing in that great sign, said, exclaiming, "What does it mean, this novel delivery of a woman who is not married? Look, this boy just now born of royal lineage makes clear that his mother has no knowledge of a spouse. And the virgin who bore him on her own piously nurses her son, since her chaste breasts have rightly been filled from heaven. The mother has no pain, nor is there a stain on the child; and what's more, I believe such things happen by God's order."

Salome, rejecting this declaration, although Zelemi was not speaking falsehoods, said that she would not believe the words she had heard, unless she could confirm them by touching holy Mary with her own hand. Therefore, entering the cave, she began to extend her right hand, rashly attempting to examine chaste Mary; but such rashness brought the appropriate punishment. The hand that made the attempt was immediately impaired and was afflicted with a pain that was severe indeed, and justly so. Then Salome, calling out in distress from a bitter heart, wept over the sudden loss of her dead right hand. And reciting her own merits according to Jewish custom, and quite confident in a pretense of justice, she is reported to have spoken, in pain, words like these to the One enthroned in heaven:

"Witness and consoler of all our labors, you know that I have been earnest about the commandments of the law, and that for your sake I have always been very generous to all the poor people gathered from the ends of the earth. Whoever came in sorrow, also departed from me more happily. And now for such great merits I suffer a heavy loss."

Then a very radiant young man appeared to her and

"Panniculos pueri solummodo tange tenelli,
accedens istas ad regales cito cunas,
ipseque maiori te restituet sanitati."
Haec ubi iussa sibi sequitur solamina dantis,
tangendo minimum pannorum denique filum,
sensit se subito salvam fore corpore toto,
et grates Domino reddebat voce canora,
qui sibi dignatur talem conferre salutem.

Ordine digesto postquam fuit ergo repleta
visio pastorum, signum sibimet quoque dictum
de parvo puero praesepibus inveniendo;
ipsius pueri quoque circumcisio Christi
nominis atque sui fulgens aptatio magni.
Reges astrologi solis de cardine lecti
advenere, Magi stellarum lege periti
quaerentes urbem famosam denique Salem.
Necnon Herodem constanti pectore regem
sollicitant regis de nativitate recentis,
se vidisse novam fantes nuperrime stellam,
quae regem natum demonstrarct Iudeorum.

His rex turbatus secreta mente profanus
accitis citius scribis audivit ab illis
certe Bethleis nasci quod Christus in oris
iuxta cunctorum deberet carmina vatum.
Scilicet atque Magis iussit cum fraude remissis,
ut puerum quaerant natum sibimet quoque monstrent,
quem cupit occidi simulans se velle precari.
Qui monstrante viam stella pergunt cito rectam,
intrant et pueri regalia tecta tenelli,
haud vario certe digestim picta colore,
sideris obsequio tanti sed rite polita.

began to speak: "Touch but the swaddling clothes of the tender little boy, going swiftly to that royal crib, and he himself will restore you to better health." When she followed the commands of the young man offering her solace, by touching then the slightest thread of the swaddling clothes, she sensed that she was suddenly healthy throughout her body, and she gave thanks in a melodious voice to the Lord, who saw fit to confer such health on her.

Then, in due order, after the vision of the shepherds was fulfilled and a sign was declared to them about finding a small child in a manger, the circumcision also of the Christ child took place and the splendid assignment of his great name. Kings came, astrologers gathered from the threshold of the sun, Magi learned in the law of the stars, seeking at last the famed city Jerusalem. And with their resolute hearts they made King Herod uneasy about the birth of a newly created king, saying they had very recently seen a new star, which indicated a king of the Jews had been born.

Disturbed in his innermost heart by these words, the impious king heard from his hastily summoned scribes that Christ, according to the predictions of all the prophets, surely ought to be born within the boundaries of Bethlehem. And, in fact, he deceitfully ordered the Magi when they were sent on their way, to seek out for him the child who was born and point out where he was, on the pretext that he wished to pray to the one he was eager to kill. They quickly set off, the star showing them the proper road, and they entered the tender little boy's royal dwelling, which was not decorated, to be sure, in a harmonious range of colors, but fittingly adorned by the attendance of such a star.

Proni vestigiis figentes oscula prolis,
orantes preculis humili quoque voce profusis,
trino caelestem venerantur munere Regem
hunc hominemque Deum designantes moriturum.
Qui mox in somnis moniti sub tempore noctis
ad patriam laeti redeunt per devia ducti.
His ita digestis, Herodes pessimus hostis
Augusti iussu Romam deducitur ergo,
quo vel purgaret, lex ut Romana doceret,
criminis inposita de magni se cito culpa,
vel capitis poenam iuste pateretur amaram:
namque reus maiestatis dicetur erilis.
Et merito talem patitur iam suspicionem,
qui cupit insidiis vulpino corde paratis
prolem caelestis divinam perdere Regis.
Hoc nam divino nutu factum fore credo,
quod tunc percerte Romam mandatur adire,
quo sibi subtracto legis mandamina cuncta
plenius in nato complerentur cito Christo.
Namque quater denis cursu duccnte peractis
virginei partus digestim rite diebus,
hic Factor membris caelorum namque tenellis
sistitur in proprio parvo cum munere templo.
Ulnis exceptus tremulis iusti Simeonis,
et mundi Dominus condignis est benedictus
odis ex ipso iusto Simeone vetusto,
necnon famosa praesagis vocibus Anna.
His quoque completis iuxta mandamina legis,
ad patriam Bethlem redierunt protinus urbem.
Nam post haec, binis mansurnis paene repletis,

Bowing down to plant kisses on the child's feet, praying also in profuse supplications in a humble voice, the Magi honored him with three gifts, symbolically marking him as the heavenly King, as God, and as mortal man. Having been warned in their sleep, the Magi then returned to their fatherland rejoicing, guided along back roads by night.

After these things had occurred, Herod, that most wicked of enemies, was then conducted to Rome by order of Augustus, either to exculpate himself, as Roman law prescribed, speedily from the guilt ascribed to him of a great crime, or to suffer justly the bitter penalty of capital punishment: for he was charged with high treason. And he now justifiably suffered such suspicion, because with the tricks he had prepared in his fox's heart he desired to destroy the divine offspring of the heavenly King. For I believe it happened by divine will that he was just then ordered to go to Rome, so that once he was out of the way, all the mandates of the law could be accomplished swiftly and more fully in the Christ child.

And indeed, when four times ten days had been completed, rightly following their course in order after the virgin birth, this Creator of the heavens with his tender limbs was placed, indeed, in his own temple with a small offering. He was taken up in the trembling arms of the just man Simeon, and he was blessed as the Lord of the world in worthy odes by that same just old man Simeon, and also in prophetic words by the renowned Anna. After these things too had been completed according to the mandates of the law, they returned straightaway to their fatherland, the city of Bethlehem.

Indeed afterward, when nearly two years were passed, the

hostis ab exilio veniens perversus amaro,
quod dixere Magi, volvebat mente dolenti,
se nati stellam Regis vidisse decoram.
Haec recolens, proceres regni rogitabat eriles,
an redeundo Magi venissent mente fideli,
vel quid de nato demandarent sibi Christo.
Qui mox responsis pariter dicunt bene firmis
se nescire, Magi fuerint si forte reversi,
nec quid de nato sese perdiscere Rege.

His super accensus, rex Herodes furibundus
mittens infantes occidi protinus omnes,
qui tunc Bethleis fuerant, praecepit, in oris,
se semper vivum sperans extinguere Christum
posse. Sed in somnis monitus, Ioseph venerandus
pergit in Aegyptum, vasti per devia secum
deducens eremi Iesum cum matre tenellum,
nocti terrestris Christo dominante timoris.
Talia sed solito fecit pietate superna,
Aegypti tenebras propria quo luce vetustas
mox illustraret per se penitusque fugaret.

Contigit ergo die quadam requiescere velle
iuxta speluncam sancta cum prole Mariam.
Quae sat lassa solo fuerat cum forte locata,
scilicet in gremio Iesum molli refovendo,
multi terribiles procedunt namque dracones
ex hac spelunca pro qua fuit ipsa locata.
Quos Ioseph pueri cernentes, obstupefacti
coeperunt certe magno clamare timore.
At puer e gremio matris surrexit amando
Iesus, sacratis stabat mitis quoque plantis

perverse enemy Herod returned from his bitter exile, and he turned over in his anguished mind what the Magi had said, that they had seen the beautiful star of the newborn King. Recollecting this, he asked the noble princes of the realm whether the Magi, with dutiful hearts, had visited them on their return, or whether they could report anything to him about the Christ child. They then replied uniformly with very firm responses that they did not know whether the Magi happened to have returned, and that they had not learned anything about the King who was born.

Incensed by these responses, King Herod in his rage issued an order for all the infants who were at that time within the boundaries of Bethlehem to be killed at once, hoping he could extinguish the ever-living Christ. But the venerable Joseph, warned in his sleep, journeyed into Egypt, taking the tender little Jesus and his mother along with him through the back ways of the vast desert, with Christ prevailing over the terrestrial fear of night. But he did these things in his usual way with heavenly piety, so that by his own light and of his own accord he might soon illuminate the long-standing darkness of Egypt and totally chase it away.

It happened then on a certain day that Mary wished to rest with her holy child near a cave. She was very tired, and when she had, perchance, placed herself on the ground, that is, when she was cuddling Jesus in her soft lap, many serpents, terrible indeed, proceeded from the cave before which she was seated. Seeing them, the dumbfounded servants of Joseph assuredly began to cry out in great fear. But the boy Jesus rose up from the beloved lap of his mother, and he stood meekly on his holy feet opposite the serpents

contra frendentes turbata mente dracones.
Qui subito proni ceciderunt mansuefacti,
orantes tacitis Factorem nutibus orbis;
ipseque digrediens eremi per devia vasti
illos praecessit sequier sese quoque iussit.
Quo Ioseph viso genetrix Christique sacrata
exanimes fragilis pro consuetudine carnis
facti, sat pavitant puerum laedique timebant.
Ipse sed, inspector mentis testis quoque cordis,
haec responsa dedit timidis conversus et inquit,
"Quare lactantes tantum tractabitis artus
in me, virtutem capitis nec mente perennem?
Quamvis humanis sim parvus homuncio membris,
vir tamen omnipotens summo sum numine pollens.
Condecet atque feras silvae mansuescere cunctas
me coram, rabie dimissa rite priore."
Post haec, magnanimes cum pardis namque leones,
necnon cunctigenae venerunt undique lectae,
ut sensere ferae prolem Factoris adesse,
orantes puerum submissa voce tenellum,
circa praeclaram gaudentes atque Mariam.
Quam super insolito pavitantem denique signo,
laetius intuitus fertur sic dicere Christus:
"Non te, Virgo, rogo, pollens, genetrix mea cara,
permoveat signi novitas carnaliter almi.
Obsequii sola veniunt istae quia causa,
non quod te vellent vel saltem laedere possent."
His quoque discessit dictis angustia cordis.
At vero belvae praecedebant bene laetae,
demonstrando viam per deserti loca rectam.

who were raging with agitated minds. They suddenly fell flat on the ground, tamed, praying to the Creator of the world with silent nods; and Jesus, continuing through the back roads of the vast desert, went ahead of them and ordered, as well, that they follow.

Joseph and the holy mother of Christ, when they had seen this, becoming pale in the normal way of feeble flesh, were very frightened and feared that the boy would be injured. But he, who looks into our mind and is the witness of our heart, having turned to his fearful parents, gave the following responses and said, "Why will you only treat me as breastfeeding flesh, and not grasp in your mind my eternal power? Although I am a small child with human limbs, I am, nevertheless, an all-powerful man, flourishing with the highest divinity. And it is appropriate that all the wild animals of the woods become tame in my presence, driving out their earlier fierceness, as is proper."

Now, after these things, greathearted lions came, along with panthers, and all kinds of creatures gathered from everywhere, as soon as these wild beasts sensed that the child of the Creator was present, and they prayed in a gentle voice to the tender little boy and frolicked about the illustrious Mary. Then, seeing her frightened by this unusual miracle, Christ is reported to have spoken very happily thus: "O mighty Virgin, my dear mother, I ask that the novelty of this propitious miracle not disturb you materially. For these creatures come solely for the sake of obedience, not because they want to harm you; nor could they anyhow." And so the anguish of her heart left her because of these words. And in truth the beasts very happily marched before them, showing them the right path through the desert regions. And not

Sed nec nocturnis discesserat ulla sub horis,
et Ioseph pecori sociatae mente fideli,
oblita rabie naturalique furore,
pacificae modici gustabant pascua faeni.
Inter quas ergo fuerat concordia tanta,
ut quondam timidi iunxere lupis latus agni,
et bovibus mites bene commansere leones.
Sed non immerito, caelorum pax quia vera,
quo regit immensum, firmavit foedere, caelum,
illarum mentes mutato more fideles.
Post haec, pausavit radiis lassata caloris
aestivi cara palmae Maria sub umbra,
et sursum versis claris aspexit ocellis
fructibus hanc palmam maturis esse refertam.
His visis, lingua formavit talia verba:
"Istius palmae nimium delector onustae,
si potis est fieri, de fructu denique vesci."
Cui senior vetulus legis moderamine iustus
haud blande dictis Ioseph mox obviat istis:
"Hoc miror certe nimium te dicere velle,
cum videas ramos magno de germine ductos
astris contiguos caelum pulsare profundum.
Ast ego praecogito summa tantummodo cura,
si saltem valeam puram comprendere lympham,
utribus in nostris quia nec est guttula fontis."
Haec heros igitur venerandus sic loquebatur,
ceu desperaret quod praesens omnia posset
Christus, corporeis tectus fuerat quia membris.
At puer, in gremio carae genitricis amando
accumbens, palmam gaudens se vertit ad ipsam,
functus et imperio praeclare quippe paterno

a single one left them even during the nocturnal hours, and having joined the flock of Joseph with loyal hearts, forgetful of their savagery and natural fierceness, they peacefully enjoyed the forage of a little hay. Among them then there was such concord that the once-timid lambs accompanied the wolves side by side, and the lions lived very calmly among the cattle. And not without cause, because the true peace of heaven, by the same covenant with which it rules the immense heaven, strengthened their hearts to be faithful, altering their nature.

After this, worn out by the rays of the summer's heat, Mary paused under the precious shade of a palm tree, and with her bright eyes turned upward she saw that this palm tree was filled with ripe fruit. Seeing this, she formed words like these with her tongue: "I would very much like, if it be possible, to eat of the fruit of this bountiful palm tree."

Joseph, the aging old man, just in conduct of the law, then confronted her in an unkind manner with these words: "I am certainly quite amazed that you say you desire this, since you can see that the branches extending to the stars from this great sprout strike the highest heaven. But I, with the greatest concern, am thinking ahead to whether I might at least be able to get hold of clean water, because there is not the slightest drop of liquid in our flasks." The venerable hero said these things, then, in that way, as if he despaired that Christ, though present, could do everything, since he was clad in bodily limbs. But the boy, reclining in the beloved lap of his dear mother, joyously turned himself toward that same palm tree, and carrying out, brilliantly indeed, his

ipsi continuo dicebat fronte serena,
"Arbor, flecte tuos summo de vertice ramos,
ut, quantum libeat, de te mater mea carpat."
Dixerat, atque suis arbor fortissima iussis
ante pedes Mariae parens inflectitur almae.
Fructu cumque suo penitus fuerat spoliata,
incurvata stetit nec surgens alta petivit,
opperit imperium Christi sed rite probatum.
Ipseque "Te subito," dixit, "nunc erige, palma,
ut sis lignorum post haec collega meorum,
quae paradisiacis constant plantata locellis.
Et radice tua deduc extemplo secreto
undas fonticuli fluitantes gurgite dulci!"
Quae citius dicto complentur denique cuncta.
At prolis comites, fontem lustrando recentem,
reddebant grates laetato pectore dulces,
atque sitim lymphis tristem dempsere novellis.
Cumque profecturi deserti per loca vasti
essent, ad palmam Iesus sic dixerat ipsam:
"De te quippe meo precepto, palmula, mando,
angelus ut caelo veniens dilapsus ab alto
tollat rite tuo ramum de vertice summo,
necnon hunc ipsum plantet mox in paradisum.
Et tibi gloriolam super hoc iam confero tantam,
ut post haec summi dicaris palma triumphi.
Et quisquis bello famose vicerit ullo,
de te vincenti dicetur protinus illi,
'Ad palmam magni venisti namque triumphi.'"
Haec ubi dicta dedit, dilapsus sidere venit
angelus, et tollens ramum divexit in altum.
Quo viso, cuncti praesentes obstupefacti

Father's command, at once said in a calm demeanor to the tree, "Tree, bend your branches from the very top, so that my mother may pluck from you as much as she pleases." So he spoke, and that mightiest of trees, obeying Christ's commands, bent itself down before the feet of dear Mary. When it had been thoroughly stripped of its fruit, it stood there bent over and did not seek to rise back up to the heights, but properly awaited the confirmed command of Christ. And he said, "Now straighten yourself up right away, palm tree, so that from now on you may be an associate of my trees, which stand planted in heavenly little places. And draw out secretly from your roots straightaway the waves of a spring, flowing with fresh water!" All these things then were accomplished sooner than they were spoken. And the companions of the child, surveying the new spring, offered sweet thanks with happy hearts, and they put an end to their dire thirst with these newly found waters. And when they were about to set out through the tracts of the vast desert, Jesus spoke to this same palm tree as follows: "Beloved palm tree, I mandate by my directive that an angel come gliding down from high heaven and take from you a branch, as is fitting, from your highest crown, and then plant this same branch in paradise. And for this service, I will now confer on you such glory that henceforth you will be called the palm of the greatest triumph. And whoever conquers gloriously in any battle, on account of you they will say to that conqueror, 'You have attained the palm of a great triumph indeed.'"

When he had delivered these words, an angel came gliding down from the stars, and taking the branch, carried it away on high. At the sight of this, all present were stupefied

in terram proni consternuntur tremefacti.
Quos Iesus subito solatur talia fando:
"Non opus est certe vobis formidinis ullae
hunc quia transferri ramum per sidera iussi,
ut mox deliciae magno plantetur in horto
et, velut hic in deserto mea iussa sequenda
implevit, magno nosmet studio satiando,
sic illic sanctis constet dulcedo perennis."
Talibus ac tantis signis iam sedulo visis,
Ioseph, virtutem prolis tractando perennem,
utitur his verbis submisso murmure fusis:
"Ecce calor nimius nostros male decoquit artus;
nunc, tibi si placeat, cuius regnum iuge constat,
praecipe per pelagi calles nos pergere vasti,
urbibus appositis quo certa quies data nobis
nos citius spatium faciat percurrere tantum."
Cui dixit Iesus divino numine clarus,
"Namque viam subito longam per me breviabo,
et quod ter denis potuit vix ante diebus
metiri, faciam diei spatio repedari."
His dictis, Sotinen viderunt ocius, urbem
Aegypti magnam famosis moenibus altam.
Hanc introgressi petierunt limina templi,
in quo stulta deos consuevit ponere falsos
gens pagana suos perverso more colendos.
Mox sed ut intravit sancta cum prole Maria,
omnia falsorum pariter simulacra deorum
in terram subito ciciderunt denique prona,
iam cognoscentes Regem venisse perennem
atque Deum verum magna virtute deorum.
Tunc est impletum, fuerat quod carmine dictum

and fell flat on the ground, trembling. Jesus at once consoled them, speaking thus: "Assuredly there is no need for you to have any fear because I ordered this branch to be transferred to the stars, so that presently it would be planted in the great garden of delights. And just as here in the desert it fulfilled my commands, obeying them and satisfying us with great zeal, so in the same way there it would be an eternal sweetness for the saints."

After carefully observing such great miracles, Joseph, coming to grips with the eternal power of his child, employed these words, pouring them forth in a humble whisper: "See how this excessive heat wickedly roasts our limbs; now, if it is pleasing to you, whose realm endures forever, order that we travel through the roads along the vast sea, so that the secure rest given us in the cities bordering it may allow us more quickly to pass over such a great distance." To him Jesus, glorious in his divine power, said, "In fact, I will shorten the long road immediately by my own power, and that distance which previously could scarcely be traveled through in thrice ten days, I will cause to be traversed in the space of one day."

After he said these things, they straightaway beheld Sotinen, the great lofty city of Egypt with its famous walls. When they had entered it, they sought the precinct of the temple, in which the foolish pagan race made a habit of setting up their false gods to be worshiped in a wicked manner. But as soon as holy Mary entered with her child, suddenly all the statues of false gods simultaneously fell on the ground prostrate, finally now recognizing that the eternal King and the true God of gods had come with great power.

Then was fulfilled what most assuredly had been foretold

olim percerte modulantis tale prophetae:
"Ecce super levem Dominus veniet cito nubem,
pro cuius sancta facie decet omnia nempe
Aegypti subito conquassari simulacra."
Haec Afrodisio postquam fuerant recitata,
urbis namque duci praedictae valde potenti,
illic cum sociis festinat pergere multis.
Quod cum pontifices templi sensere profani,
sperabant illum variis mox perdere poenis
hos, qui damna diis fecerunt talia stultis.
Ipse sed in terra cernens simulacra decora
obtutu prono passim volutare minuta,
lumine caelestis raptim succensus amoris.
Et fidei sacrae mutato denique corde
substitit atque suis gaudens dicebat amicis,
"Ecce patenter adest Dominus super omnia pollens.
Quem fortasse dii tacito cum murmure nostri
iure Deum verum contestantur fore solum.
Restat ut ipsorum prostrati more deorum
devota Regem veneremur mente perennem,
quae fecit regi memorantes iam Pharaoni,
qui sua plus iusto sprevit mandamina sacra,
ne nosmet foveam mortis detrudat in atram."
Dixerat atque solo prostratus corpore toto
volvitur ante pedes sanctae rogitando Mariae
gratiolam pueri constanter voce fideli,
quem mater gremio gaudens portavit amico.
O laudanda tuae virtutis gloria, Christe,
O miranda sacrae semper mutatio dextrae,
qui nutu tacito potis es disponere cuncta!
Quis volet ergo tuae pietatis munera magnae,

long ago in the song of a prophet, who chanted thus: "Behold, the Lord will soon come upon a swift cloud, and before his holy face it is surely fitting that all the statues of Egypt immediately be shattered."

After this story had been told to Aphrodisius, who was a very powerful leader of the aforesaid city, he hastened with many of his companions to go to that place. When the pagan priests of the temple perceived this, they hoped he would straightaway destroy with a variety of punishments these people, who had caused such injuries to their foolish gods. But Aphrodisius, seeing the beautiful statues tumbled in pieces here and there with their faces downward, was suddenly inflamed by the light of celestial love. And with his heart at last converted to the sacred faith, he stopped and joyfully said to his friends, "Behold, the Lord is clearly present, powerful over everything. Perhaps our gods with their silent whisper are rightly testifying that he alone is the true God. All that remains is for us, prostrate like these gods themselves, to venerate the eternal King with a devout heart, and to keep in mind what he has already done to our king, the Pharaoh, who unjustly rejected his sacred commands, lest he thrust us down into the black pit of death."

He spoke and then with his whole body prostrate on the ground, whirled before the feet of holy Mary, asking steadfastly in a faithful voice for a little grace from the child, whom the cheerful mother held in her loving lap.

Oh, the praiseworthy glory of your power, Christ, oh, the ever-miraculous change of your sacred right hand, you can ordain all things with a silent nod! Who then could hope to admire fittingly, or to tell with the praise they deserve, the

unice nate Dei summo similis Genitori,
mirari digne merita vel dicere laude,
qui nostri causa fecisti tanta stupenda?
Tu sine principio natus de Patre superno
per praecepta Patris complesti viscera matris
ex hac corpoream sumens sub tempore formam.
Quique vales proprio mundum concludere palmo,
panniculis stringi non raris haud respuisti.
Et qui stellato resides solio super aethra,
parvo praesepi contractus procubuisti.
Et qui multigenis imponis nomina stellis,
ac pluviae guttas, pelagi quoque solus arenas
rite potes numero per te comprendere certo,
ut fragiles pueri, patienter conticuisti,
tempore virgineas quo suxisti pie mammas.
Insuper Herodem nulla formidine regem,
sed sola certe fugisti pro pietate,
quo carnis veram demonstrares pie formam.
Et mox absque mora fecisti saxea corda
nam paganorum mollescere non domitorum
et sentire tuum solidum per tempora regnum,
quo te divinis moniti scirent fore signis
ipsum, qui solo fecisti secula Verbo,
et quem cunctorum cecinerunt carmina vatum.
Hinc Genitore tuo maneat per saecula cuncta
gloria de cunctis et laus aeterna creatis,
qui tibi dilecto nescivit parcere nato.
Et tibi, Christe, decus perpes, victoria, virtus,
sanguine qui mundum fuso redimis periturum,
Flamine cum Sacro saecli per tempora cuncta,
gratia caelestis per quem conceditur omnis!

benefits of your great kindness, sole son of God in the image of your supreme Father, who for our sake accomplished such amazing things? You, born of the Father above, without a beginning, at the behest of your Father filled your mother's womb, taking from her a corporeal form in temporality. And you who are able to enclose the world in the palm of your hand did not refuse to be wrapped in common swaddling clothes. And you who sit on a starry throne above the ether have lain confined in a small manger. And you who impose names on the various stars, and who alone through your own power can properly comprehend in a fixed number the drops of rain as well as the sands of the sea, you were patiently silent at that time when you piously sucked at the Virgin's breasts, as tender infants do. Furthermore, you fled from King Herod, not out of any fear, but assuredly out of piety alone, so that you could piously manifest the true form of flesh. And next without delay you made the stony hearts of the unconquered pagans grow soft indeed and recognize that your dominion is stable through all time, so that warned by divine miracles they might know that you yourself exist, you who by your Word alone made the world, and whom the songs of all the prophets have sung. And so may glory remain through all ages, and eternal praise from all his creations, for your Father, who did not hesitate to sacrifice you, his beloved son. And for you, Christ, may there remain endless honor, victory, and power, you who by pouring out your blood redeem the dying world, together with the Holy Spirit through all ages of the world, through whom all heavenly grace is granted!

Qualia retribuam Factori munera nunc iam
pro cunctis digne, mihimet quae reddidit ipse?
Qui pius indignam solita pietate famellam
me, licet exiles, fecit persolvere grates.
His super, angelicae caelorum, posco, catervae
collaudare Deum non cessent sedulo verum.

What kind of gifts may I now repay to my Creator that are worthy of all he has already given to me? He, in his accustomed mercy, mercifully allowed me, an unworthy little servant, to pay him my thanks, meager though they are. Therefore, I ask the angelic choirs of heaven that they not stop diligently praising in unison the true God.

De ascensione Domini

Hanc narrationem Iohannes episcopus
a Graeco in Latinum transtulit

Postquam corporeo Christus velamine tectus
temporis implevit spatium sacri venerandum,
quod cum terrigenis mansit dignanter homullis,
qui solus maculis potuit sine vivere cunctis,
ut per se mundo demonstraret redimendo
gaudia perpetuae quondam male perdita vitae;
postque triumphalem sanctamque piam quoque mortem,
quam nostri causa patienter pertulit ergo,
dum victor magno fregit luctamine tela
humani generis saevissima fortiter hostis,
sanguinis et pretium proprii gratis dedit amplum,
pro nobis animam deponens in cruce caram;
necnon gloriola surgentis rite peracta
atque quater denis diei spatiis replicatis,
in quis discipulis apparens sedulo caris,
esse sua nostram monstrat cum morte peremptam,
nec mortis vinclis se posse tenerier artis,
qui solus culpae fuerat sine sordibus Adae,
postremo caris isdem monstratur amicis,
montis oliviferi praecelso vertice quidni
astans astrigeram mox ascensurus ad aulam,
affaturque suos cum tali voce ministros:

On the Ascension of the Lord

Bishop John Translated This Account from Greek into Latin

After Christ, covered in a veil of flesh, completed that venerable interval of sacred time during which he graciously remained with mere earthly men, Christ who alone was capable of living entirely without sins, so that on his own he might point out to a world in need of redemption the joys of perpetual life that had been distressingly lost long ago; and after his triumphant and holy and also pious death, which indeed he bore patiently for our sake, when as the victor in a great struggle he forcefully shattered the fiercest weapons of the enemy of the human race and freely paid the ample price of his own blood, surrendering on the cross for our sake his precious life; and, moreover, after the precious glory of his resurrection was duly accomplished and an interval of four times ten days had unfolded, days in which he faithfully appeared to his beloved disciples and showed that by his own death ours was destroyed and that he could not be held by the tight chains of death, he who alone was free from the stain of Adam's guilt—then finally he revealed himself to those same beloved friends, standing, no doubt, on the lofty peak of the olive-bearing mountain as he was about to ascend to the starry palace, and he addressed his ministers in a

"Ut Pater in mundum me promisit sibi carum,
sic ego mitto meos dilectos vosmet amicos.
At vos, in gentes citius cunctas abeuntes,
illas perpetuae vitae mandata docete,
credentes sacra purgantes ocius unda
in Patris et Nati pariter quoque Flaminis almi
nomine, quo veteris deponant crimina sordis.
Et virtute mea varios depellite morbos,
necnon imperio praedones cogite vestro
saevos obsessum linquant ut pectoris antrum,
illis praedulcem servantes mentis amorem,
laedere vos odiis qui temptant semper amaris.
Ex hoc percerte possunt praenoscere cunctae
gentes discipulos vos esse satis mihi caros:
si colitis vestros puris animis inimicos.
    Fine tenus memores persistite scilicet omnes
quae vestri causa passus fuerim sine culpa.
Nonne meam faciem cherubin non cernere talem
possunt in regno, qualis nitet ergo, paterno?
Iudaei spurcis hanc sed petiere salivis,
maxillisque meis alapas tribuere malignas,
atque manus clavis ligno fixere cruentis,
de limo pulchrum quis plasmavi protoplastum,
cum quibus et caelos extendi denique celsos
(nam si respicio terram, pavitat tremefacta,
nec mis terroris potis est vim ferre potentis);
et praecedentes acriter caput atque moventes,
me male Iudaei deridebant scelerosi.
Haec cum damnandis paterer pacienter ab illis,
ipsos vindicta volui non perdere iusta.
Sed crucis in ligno mortem gratis patiendo,

speech like this: "As my Father sent me forth into this world that is so dear to him, so I send you, my beloved friends. But you, going forth very swiftly among all nations, are to teach them the commandments of eternal life, quickly cleansing the believers in sacred water in the name of the Father and of the Son and also of the Holy Spirit, so that they may lay aside the defects of ancient sin. And through my power drive out various diseases, and by your authority compel the savage plunderers to leave the cavern of the breast they have occupied, preserving that sweet love of your heart for those who attempt to injure you with their ever-bitter hatred. This is how all nations can most clearly understand in advance that you are my well-loved disciples: if you cherish your enemies with pure hearts.

Until the end you should all, in fact, remain mindful of what I have suffered for your sake, though I am without fault. Is it not true that the cherubim in my Father's kingdom cannot look at a face like mine because of how it shines? Yet the Jews attacked my face with their foul spit, and they showered spiteful blows on my cheeks, and they fastened my hands to the wooden cross with blood-soaked nails, the hands with which I fashioned that beautiful first-made man from mud, and with which I ultimately extended the lofty heavens (indeed, if I look down at the earth, it trembles terrified, and it cannot bear the force of my awful power); yet passing by me and severely wagging their heads, the wicked Jews derided me cruelly. While I was patiently enduring these things from those contemptible men, I was still unwilling to destroy them through justifiable vengeance. On the contrary, freely suffering death on the wood

oravi Patrem clementius omnipotentem
illis continuo dimittere crimina tanta,
suadens exemplo tali quae sunt facienda,
ut mea caelestis fieret doctrina fidelis,
et ne quis fictis auderet dicere verbis,
'Ecce, quod ipse pati respuit, nos ferre suasit,
et quod non fecit, faciendos nos fore dixit.'
Sponte prior mortis subii discrimina tristis
ceu pastor verus, cordis bonitate fidelis,
pro propriis animam ponens ovibus pie caram.
Necnon complevi multum pietate fideli
omnia quae vates de me dixere priores.
At nunc ascendo, cinctus virtute paterna,
ad Patrem victor summum super aethra locatum.
Sed non turbari cordis rogitabo fidelis
vestri secretum, quia non vos forte relinquam
ceu desolatos in mundo namque pupillos.
Sacri gratiolam vobis sed Flaminis almam
emittam citius, quae vos verum docet intus.
Insuper ipse dies vobiscum scilicet omnes
fine tenus maneo mundi per tempora cuncta."
   Haec ubi dicta dedit, conversus denique dixit
ad matrem propriam mansueta voce Mariam,
"Nec contristeris, rogito, Virguncula casta,
cum me praecelsos videas ascendere caelos,
te quia praeclaram mundi non linquo lucernam;
atque meum sanctum migrans non desero templum,
nec incorruptam vitae dimitto coronam,
inveni solam prae cunctis te quia castam
condignamque meum corpus generasse sacratum.
Certe de mundo cum te discedere mando,

of the cross, I mercifully prayed that my all-powerful Father grant them immediate remission from their great crimes, recommending by such an example what must be done to make my heavenly doctrine believable, and to ensure that no one would dare say with deceptive words, 'Look, he encouraged us to endure what he himself refused to suffer, and he said we ought to do what he did not do.' Of my own accord, going first, I endured the hazards of dire death like a true shepherd, from the goodness of a faithful heart, devotedly forfeiting my precious life for the sake of my own sheep. Furthermore, I fulfilled in very faithful generosity everything which the earlier prophets said concerning me. But now, girt with my Father's power, I ascend as a conqueror to my Father most high, who dwells beyond the ether. But I will continue to ask that the secret recesses of your faithful hearts not be troubled, because I will not unexpectedly leave you, in effect, like orphans abandoned in the world. Instead, I will swiftly send forth to you the Holy Spirit's loving grace, which will teach you inner truth. In addition, I myself will remain with you every day, that is to say, up to the end, through all the ages of the world."

When he had delivered these words, turning at last to his own mother Mary, he said in a tender voice, "Do not be sad, I beg you, precious chaste Virgin, when you see me ascending to heaven on high, because I am not leaving you behind, O brightly shining light of the world. And, while departing, I am not deserting you, my holy temple, and I am not dismissing you, the uncorrupted crown of life, for I have found you alone chaste before all others and worthy to have engendered my sacred body. Assuredly, when I order you to leave

ad te caelicolas non solum mitto catervas,
ipse sed adveniens animam sumam benedictam
multum sole quidem rutilanti splendidiorem.
Necnon angelicis deductam suaviter hymnis
ocius astrigeram ponam veneranter in aulam.
At nunc Iohannem tecum remanere fidelem
impero, qui gemmis fulget bene virginitatis,
ut tua vita magis praefulgeat incluta, castis
saepius obsequiis circumdata virginitatis."
    Ilicet angelicus dicentem talia coetus
ipsum dulcisonis laudans circumdedit hymnis,
et mons contegitur subito cum nube sereno.
Conveniunt illic veterum cunei quoque vatum.
Inter quos medius David rex, psallere doctus,
cantans in citharis hortatur talibus orsis
Natum caelestis solium petiisse Parentis:
"Exaltare super caelos, fortis Deus, altos,
atque super totam mundi tua gloria terram."
Scilicet angelicis suadens ait ista catervis:
"Exaltate Deum modulato carmine nostrum,
orantes in monte suo crebra prece sancto,
iste Deus Dominus noster constat quia sanctus."
    Et Christus Iesus vultu ridente reversus
discipulis iterum verbis dicebat amicis:
"Pax vobis, fratres, semper mihi rite fideles
velle meum qui fecistis necnon faciatis;
ecce meam stabilem vobis do denique pacem
ac vobis ipsam pacem dimitto perennem."
Haec ait, et citius, propria virtute levatus,
ascendit diri victor super aethera leti,

this world, I will not only send troops of angels to you, but coming myself, I will take up your blessed soul, which is much more splendid than the flaming sun. And without delay I will reverently place it, pleasantly attended by angelic hymns, in the starry palace. But now I command my faithful John to stay with you, John, who shines honorably among the jewels of virginity, so that your own illustrious life will shine forth even more outstandingly, being more frequently surrounded by the chaste observance of virginity."

Straightaway an angelic host surrounded him as he was saying these things, praising him with sweet-sounding hymns, and the mountain was suddenly covered with a bright cloud. Throngs of ancient prophets gathered there also. In their midst King David, skilled at playing, singing to his lyre, encouraged the Son to seek the throne of his celestial Father, beginning with words like these: "Be exalted above the high heavens, O mighty God, and may your glory be exalted above all the lands of the earth." He was clearly persuading the angelic hosts, when he said these things: "Exalt our God with your harmonious song, supplicating him on his holy mountain with frequent prayers, because it is established that he is our holy Lord and God."

And Jesus Christ, turning toward his disciples with a smiling face, again spoke in friendly words: "Peace to you, brothers, who are always properly faithful to me, you have carried out my wishes and should continue to do so; behold, I give to you at last my firmly established peace, and I grant this same peace to you forevermore." He said these things and very quickly ascended, raised up by his own power, beyond the heavens, a conqueror of dreadful death,

obsequio nubis circumsaeptus rutilantis.
Quem sursum fixis cum respexisset ocellis
plebs doctrix fidei claustris caeli patefactis
pergentem sursum, cunctis famulantibus astris,
mox duo nempe viri, stellato cardine lapsi,
astiterant illis induti vestibus albis.
Qui satis angelicis dixerunt talia verbis:
"Dicite, posco, viri, cur suspicitis, Galilaei,
vultibus attonitis stantes oculisque supinis?
Hic certe Iesus, vobis mirantibus unus
assumptus caelos qui transcendit super altos,
hac veniet iudex forma, qua pergit ad aethra."
Tunc David, Christum cernens super aethra levatum,
commovit citharam divina laude repletam,
haec et laetitia <psallebat> congrue magna:
"Ascendit Deus in iubilo magnus super astra,
necnon in tubae Dominus clangore sacratae."
Post haec intonuit solio vox Patris ab alto,
dicens ad proprium divino famine Natum,
"Tu meus es carus percerte Filius unus;
semper iure mihi qui multum complacuisti;
tu sine principio Verbum Patris quoque verum,
et mea de caelo solus sapientia vera.
At nunc in dextra victor requiesce paterna
gaudens, usque tuos ponam cunctos inimicos
sanctorum per saecla pedum tibi rite scabellum."
Postquam naturam iam de busto redivivam
humanam solio Christus Patris intulit alto,
omnes angelicae submissa voce catervae
laudabant ipsum qui regnaturus in aevum.

accompanied by a flaming cloud. When the band of teaching disciples, with their eyes fixed upward, were watching him ascend to the opened confines of heaven, attended by all the stars, then assuredly two men, having descended from the starry threshold, stood before them dressed in white clothes. They spoke in most angelic words as follows: "Tell me, I ask you, O men of Galilee, why do you look up, standing there with astonished faces and upturned eyes? Certainly, this Jesus, who alone has been taken up before your wondering eyes and surpassed the high heavens, this Jesus will come as a judge in the same form as he now goes to heaven."

Then David, seeing Christ raised up beyond the heavens, struck his lyre, which was overflowing in divine praise, and in great joy he appropriately sang these things: "Our great God has ascended in exultation above the stars, and our Lord has ascended in the blare of a sacred trumpet."

After this, the voice of the Father thundered from his lofty throne, saying to his own Son in divine speech, "You are most assuredly my one dear Son; rightly have you always been most pleasing to me; you are also the true Word of the Father without beginning, and you alone are my true wisdom from heaven. But now rest as a conqueror at the right hand of your Father, rejoicing, until I justly place all your enemies for all time beneath you as a footstool for your holy feet."

After Christ had delivered his human nature, revivified from the grave, to the high throne of his Father, all the angelic crowds in a humble voice praised him who will reign

Mortem devicit moriens mundumque redemit,
ut regnare suos faceret per saecula servos.

Haec quiqumque legat, miserandi pectore dicat,
“Rex pie, Hrotsvithe parcens miserere miselle
et fac divinis persistere caelitus odis
hanc; quae laudando cecinit tua facta stupenda.”

forever. By dying, he conquered death and redeemed the world, so that he could make his servants reign for all ages.

Whoever may read this should say with a merciful heart, “Merciful King, pity poor little Hrotsvit, sparing her, and allow her to continue by heavenly authority with her divine odes; she, praising you, has sung of your marvelous deeds.”

Passio sancti Gongolfi martyris

O pie lucisator, mundi rerumque parator,
qui caelum pingis sideribus variis
solus et astrigera regnans dominaris in aula,
numine cuncta tenens imperioque regens.
Tu qui per proprium fecisti saecula Natum
et rerum trinam ex nihilo machinam.
Quique protoplasto, de terra rite creato,
oris divini nectare nempe tui,
sensus vitalem sufflasti, forte, liquorem,
ut fixum digiti esset opus proprii.
Tu dignare tuae perfundere corda famellae
Hrotsvithae rore tis pie gratiolae,
carmine quo compto valeam pia pangere facta
sancti Gongolfi, martyris egregii,
et laudare tuum semper nomen benedictum.
Qui post bella tuis grata dabis famulis
praemia perpetuae, tenui pro vulnere, vitae,
mandans in regno vivere lucifluo.

Tempore quo regni gessit Pippinus eoi
Francorum sceptra regia pro populo
iureque magnifico rexit Burgundia regna,
subiectos frenis rite domando suis,
famosus iuvenis nutritur partibus illis
armis praevalidus, corpore conspicuus,

The Passion of Saint Gongolf the Martyr

O merciful sower of light, creator of the world and of the things of the world, you paint the heaven with diverse stars and alone are the master ruling in the astral palace, controlling everything by your will and ruling it by your command. You, through your own Son, made the world, and out of nothing you created the threefold structure of things. And you breathed the vital fluid of consciousness, as it happened, into the first-made man, who was duly created from the earth, with the nectar, assuredly, of your divine mouth, so that he would be a stable work of your own finger. May you deem it proper to shower the heart of your dear servant Hrotsvit with the dew of your kindly grace, so that I have the strength to record in an elegant poem the pious deeds of Saint Gongolf the illustrious martyr, and always to praise your blessed name. In exchange for a slight wound, you will give to your servants after their battles the welcome rewards of eternal life, summoning them to live in the kingdom that streams with light.

At the time when Pepin held the royal scepter of the eastern realm of the Franks for the benefit of the people, and he ruled the Burgundian realms with magnificent justice, duly guiding the subjects under his reins, a celebrated young man was brought up in those parts, very strong in arms and

nomine Gongolfus, morum probitate venustus.
   Omnibus hic carus extitit et placidus.
Illum nempe ferunt ortum de germine regum
   regalemque suis moribus egregiis.
Ipsius e matris gremio spes pendet in Illo
   qui Verbo cuncta condidit ex nihilo.
Germinis et tanti sese non credit honori,
   sed transit meritis almitiem generis.
Incluta nam genetrix tali foetu pie felix
   in mundi lucem fudit ut hanc sobolem,
ocius abluitur vetulis baptismate culpis
   quas protoplastes obtinuere patres.
Chrismatis unguento scripto sibi fonteque signo
   ascitur natis Ecclesiae nitidis.
Pascitur et plene fidei mox dogmate trinae,
   dum vagit cuna corpore lacteolo.
Lac quotiens suxit, totiens fidei sacra sumpsit
   suspensus matris uberibus geminis.
Talibus incubuit, lactis dum gurgite vixit.
   Hinc pulsus gravido ferbuit ingenio,
caniciemque senum membris meditando tenellis
   non raro sacris nempe vacat studiis.
Quem mox imberbem tota probitate vigentem
   gratia Pippini principis almifici
regali non immerito sisti iubet aula;
   ardenter talem corde colens iuvenem.
Sed pietas illum quamvis iustissima regis
   ditaret tantae munere gloriolae,
regius ut primis esset proconsul ab annis,
   turgenti fastu non tamen erigitur.

distinguished in physique, Gongolf by name, charming in the goodness of his manners. He was pleasing and dear to everyone. Indeed, they say he was born from a line of kings and was regal in his exceptional character. From the time he was in his mother's lap his hope hung on that One who with his Word created everything from nothing. And Gongolf did not place his trust in the glory of his great lineage, but by his merits he surpassed the beauty of his noble birth.

Indeed, when his renowned mother, piously rejoicing in such a progeny, brought forth this child into the light of the world, he was by baptism quickly cleansed of the ancient blemishes that our first-made parents had incurred. And when the sign of the cross had been written with the ointment of chrism on his brow, he was enrolled among the splendid sons of the Church. And presently he was fully fed on the dogma of faith of the Holy Trinity, while he was crying in a cradle, a tiny, milk-white body. Whenever he sucked milk, he took in the sacraments of the faith, suspended at the twin breasts of his mother. He devoted himself to such things, while he lived on that stream of milk. When he was driven from that source, he was aflame with abounding intelligence, practicing the white-haired maturity of old men while still of tender young limbs; for indeed it was not seldom that he spent his time on sacred studies.

Then, while Gongolf was still a beardless youth flourishing in all goodness, the favor of the beneficent prince Pepin ordered him to take a place in the royal palace, and not undeservedly; Pepin ardently cherished in his heart such a young man. But even though the most just piety of the king enriched him with a gift of such great glory that he was a royal proconsul from his early years, nevertheless, he was

Pectore sed tales humili fastidit honores
 suspirans aulae munera sidereae.
Nam patrii census fuerat sibi maxime partus,
 dividit et tanto pauperibus studio,
ceu Christum miseros inter sentiret egenos
 arridere suo munere fronte pio.
Saepe Iob atque viri normam tractando beati
 ipse manus manco, pes fuit et podagro;
se necnon orbo cautum praebebat ocellum,
 exemplum cunctis nobile dans populis.
Nec minus humanis sudavit denique causis
 aequalem primis se faciens dominis.
Nam, male si nostras aures simulata vetustas
 non rebus fictis luserat et dubiis,
hic, quem nostra manus cepit iam pingere, sanctus
 est assuetus iter quadrupedum sequier.
Sedulo venando, lassat quoque membra decora
 succumbens cari imperio domini.
Ipsius et telum numquam scit cedere victum,
 cum sint ferrati oppositi cunei,
aufert <praeclarum> semper sed ab hoste triumphum
 tutus divino caelitus auxilio.
Certe non nostrae possunt dictando camenae
 composito modulis texere dactylicis,
quantis dilectum signis variaverat istum
 Rex regum summa pro bonitate sua.
Sed tamen, inculto quamvis sermone, latrabo
 unum de claris pluribus et variis.
Ut res facta probat, turmas ducendo preibat
 capturus populum Marte satis tumidum.
Extitit et solito victor mox denique bello

not aroused by swollen pride. With a humble heart, he spurned such honors, desiring rather the rewards of the sidereal palace. In fact, the property of his father fell mostly to him, and he divided it among the poor with great zeal as though he sensed that Christ, in the midst of those pitiable and needy people, had a smile on his face because of Gongolf's pious work. Moreover, often reflecting upon the standard of the blessed man Job, he was a hand for the one-handed, and a foot for the lame; and additionally, he offered himself as a wary eye to the blind, providing a noble example to all the people. And in fact he labored no less over human affairs, making himself the equal of the foremost lords.

Indeed, if ancient tradition, falsely feigning, has not deceived my ears with fictitious and dubious reports, this holy man, whom my hand has already begun to portray, made a habit of following the trail of four-legged beasts. Hunting intently, he wearied his beautiful limbs, bowing to the authority of his cherished lord. And his weapon never learned to give up, defeated, when ironclad troops were arrayed against him, but always he carried off a splendid trophy from his enemy, protected by divine aid from heaven.

Certainly, my muses, versifying, are not able to weave into this work in dactylic meters the numerous signs by which the King of kings, in accord with his own supreme goodness, distinguished this beloved man. But nonetheless, even if in language unrefined, I will bellow out just one of his many notable and diverse wonders. As events prove, he went forth leading his troops, intending to capture a nation very arrogant in war. Straightaway then he was, as usual, the

eius non laeso sanguine purpureo,
gentibus adversis proprio quoque iure subactis
censum signavit; pace data rediit.
Contigit et ducente via se pergere iuxta
cuiusdam saepta pauperis opposita;
quis latuit pictum vernanti flore locellum
tectum multiplicis germinis atque comis.
Necnon fonticulus vitreo candore serenus
profluxit rivo rura rigans stridulo.
Hic ubi praeclaros senior deduxit ocellos
perlustrans liquidam fonticuli scatebram,
frigoreae captus lymphae paulisper amore
substitit et placitis tardat iter morulis.
Et mittens puerum venisse rogabat ad illum
domnum florigeri ipsius ergo loci.
Qui praecepta ducis complens extemplo iubentis,
quo fuerat iussus, egreditur citius.
Hunc dux ipse quidem dum respexit venientem,
aggreditur blandis protinus alloquiis
atque rogans humilis tota dulcedine mentis
formavit lingua talia verba sua:
"Dulcis amice, meis precibus sis, postulo, largus
et vendas purum hunc mihi fonticulum.
Qui clarus vitreis et suave sonantibus undis
prolambens arva irrigat ista tua.
Et mox argenti tibi pro mercede probati
largiter infundo pondera non modica."
Ast ubi tinnitum dando promissio laeta
aures personae intrat in exiguae,
laeta nitet facies, totae volitant quoque venae,
cordis secreto quae latuere loco.

victor in the war, and his royal blood was unshed. On the hostile races who were now brought under his authority he also imposed tribute. When he had made peace, he went back home. And as the road led him onward, he happened to pass near some poor man's fields that appeared in front of him; among them there lay hidden a small place painted with spring flowers, covered with leaves from many a sprout. Moreover, a clear little spring as bright as glass flowed through it, irrigating the countryside with its babbling stream. When the lordly man had set his splendid eyes upon it, surveying the limpid source of the little spring, he was seized with a passion for those cool waters, and he stopped briefly and postponed his journey amid these pleasant delays. And then, sending his servant, he asked the owner of this flowering place to come to him. Immediately the owner, following the mandates of the duke's summons, came quickly to where he had been summoned. Indeed, when the duke saw the man coming toward him, he approached him with pleasant words, and, asking with all the sweetness of his humble heart, he formed words like these with his tongue: "Sweet friend, I entreat you, be generous to my petitions and sell me this pure little spring. It is clear and with its glassy, soft-sounding waves, lapping at these fields of yours, it supplies them with water. And straightaway as payment to you I will pour out lavishly no small measure of verified silver."

And when this happy promise, with a ringing sound, entered the ears of the humble fellow, his happy face glowed, and all the veins lying hidden in a secret place in his heart

Tunc miser in talem coepit prorumpere vocem
  ultra, quam credas, spem dubiam sitiens:
"O nostrate decus, nulli pietate secundus,
  quem colit eous mente fide populus,
quid tibi, quid digni potis est mea lingula fari?
  Nonne tuis manibus est sita nostra salus?
Et quicquid mihi per verbum sancis faciendum,
  quamvis difficile sit satis atque grave,
attamen est aequum tibi me parere, beate,
  ut dulum summo exiguum domino.
Si placet hinc vetulum me transmigrare colonum,
  non contraluctor, sed tua iussa sequor."
Haec ait et pressis frenat sua verbula labris,
  nec post verbosa quid loquitur ligula.
Et contra vir regalis pie talia fantis
  suscepit dicta pro bonitate sua
et citius dicto solvit promissa misello
  illi centenos attribuens solidos.
Haec ubi perfecit, raptim redeundo migravit
  nitens ad patriam pergere posthabitam.
Tunc, qui non gnari fuerant signi venerandi,
  olim facturus quod fuit Altithronus,
blasphemare ducem tacitis cepere susurris
  et pietatis opus spernere ceu facinus.
Credite non latuisse dolum pietatis homullum,
  sed mox nudari clancula dicta sibi.
Qui dedit arguto vocem tunc nempe palato
  his verbisque suos alloquitur socios:
"Cur libet, O socii, vosmet reprehendere, cari,
  plus iusto verbis me satis illicitis,

fluttered as well. Then the poor man began to burst forth in speech like this, thirsting more than you could believe after a dubious hope: "O glory of our people, second to none in piety, whom the eastern people worship with faithful hearts, what, what can my little tongue say that is worthy of you? Is our salvation not placed in your hands? And whatever through your word you decree that I should do, although it be difficult and very burdensome, nevertheless it is right that I obey you, O blessed man, as a poor slave obeys the greatest master. If it pleases you that I, an aging farmer, move along to another place, I will not put up a fight against you, but will follow your orders." He said these things and restrained his words with his lips shut tight, and after this did not say a thing with his talkative little tongue.

And in response, the nobleman generously accepted the declarations of this speaker, such as they were, as befitted his own good nature, and no sooner said than done, he fulfilled his promises to that poor little fellow, paying him a hundred coins. When he had done these things, he moved on, making his return hurriedly, striving to get to the fatherland he had left behind. Then, those men, who were ignorant of the venerable miracle which the One enthroned on high was one day going to perform, began to slander the duke in quiet whispers and to despise his pious deed as though it were a crime.

Believe me, their deceit did not escape this esteemed man of piety, but soon their hidden words were laid bare to him. He then, you may be sure, gave voice to his sharp tongue and addressed his companions in these words: "O dear companions, why does it please you to criticize me unjustly, with words that are utterly improper, saying that out

causa stultitiae dicentes me tribuisse
nummos ignoto extraneoque viro?
Me vacuum tanti meritoque dolere lucelli
et bene mercati utpote fonticuli,
dextra ceu propria, census est quae pie larga,
aurum pro donis si dederim minimis.
Non decet hoc nostris vobis reserarier orsis,
quid velit addicti causa sibi pretii.
Mentes sed motas praestat componere vestras,
et rogo parcatis talibus alloquiis,
e vobisque virum caute nunc credite gnarum
emissis ventis aeribusque vagis,
ut iam semotum citius repetendo locellum
lustret, si vena fonticuli liquida
more suo flores inter bene multicolores
perstrepat undisono murmure per lubrica.
Tunc patet, ille lucris sese si iactat ab illis
rusticus ambobus, me vacuo penitus."
Haec postquam memorat, cursim quidam remeabat,
tantae dimenso atque viae spatio
oppido predictum lassus pervenit ad arvum,
quo fuerat domino vendita lympha pio.
Non tamen extemplo pedibus, quamvis curiosus,
attigit atrioli limina florigeri.
Applicat inpexis iuxta sed se paliuris
necnon hirsutis vepribus et tribulis,
quis fuit incultum solito rus undique tectum.
Nec spineta pede horruit appetere,
iungere praescriptis ardens sua lumina septis,
ut lustraret aquae amniculum vitreae.

of stupidity I have paid money to a man who is unknown and a stranger? And that I deservedly grieve that I have lost such a tidy little sum as well as the little spring so expensively purchased, as though with my own right hand, which is piously generous with money, I had given gold in exchange for lesser gifts. It is not proper for the rationale of this expenditure to be revealed to you through my words. But it is better to calm your unsettled minds, and I ask you to stop such talk, and now carefully entrust a knowledgeable man from your number to the unleashed winds and the wandering breezes, so that he may return swiftly to that now-distant place and investigate whether the clear vein of the little spring is babbling loudly in its normal way among the many-colored flowers, murmuring with its sounding waves along its slippery paths. Then it will be clear whether that peasant is congratulating himself on having the advantages from both these things, the money and the spring, while I am totally destitute."

After he related these things, one of them went running back, and when he had completed the distance of that long road, utterly exhausted, he came to the field in question, where the stream sold to his pious master had been. Yet even though he investigated carefully, he did not immediately touch the threshold of that flowery little plot with his feet. Instead, he entwined himself in the tangled brambles nearby and in the bristly briars and thorns, with which the uncultivated countryside was usually covered on all sides. And he was not afraid to assail the thickets with his foot, burning to get his eyes on the aforementioned hedges, so that he could examine the little river of glassy water. But

Sed tamen attonitis frustra prospexit ocellis,
fons quia desinerat prorsus et hinc aberat.
Tunc se iuncturas volvebat mente per artas
clare non posse cernere saepiculae.
Ac tractim rigida necnon cervice superba
incedens gressum vertit in atriolum
sperans, sub foliis quod forte lateret amoenis
florum multimodis undola tecta comis.
Cumque locum peteret fundumque sitire probaret
qui quondam validis luxuriavit aquis,
usque solum stratus vacua spe non bene lusus,
coepit harenosa lingere nempe loca
temptans, exiguam posset si lambere guttam.
Sed nec praesiccam tinxerat hinc ligulam.
Tandem Gongolfi sensit pia facta sacelli
se dolet et meritis credere nolle piis.
Hinc postquam rediit socios iterumque revisit,
aspexit nubem aere conspicuam
iuxta dulce caput Christi volitare famelli
instar candidoli denique pallioli.
Hanc capiens oculis, coepit depromere verbis
fontis defectum, quem didicit, subitum.
Suaserat et sociis dubium deponere cordis
et meritis sancti iam credulos fieri.
Talia colloquiis dum verba loquuntur amicis,
applicuere sui in propriis domini,
moenia florigero fuerant ubi structa locello
circum diffusis arboribus variis.
Hic Christi carus gressum direxit amicus,
mente libens atrio currere purpureo,

nevertheless, he looked in vain with his astonished eyes, because the spring had completely ceased to flow and had disappeared from there. Then he supposed that he could not see clearly enough through the tight structure of the little hedge. And moving along little by little with his proud neck still unbent he turned his step toward the little plot, hoping that by chance the little brook might be hiding under the pleasant foliage of the flowers, covered by all sorts of leaves. And when he got to the place and ascertained that the ground which had once been rich in robust waters was now dry, he spread himself on the ground, badly deceived with vain hope, and he in fact began to lick the sandy places, trying to see if he could lap up the smallest drop. But he did not thereby dampen his parched little tongue. Finally, he understood the pious deeds of saintly Gongolf, and he grieved that he had been unwilling to believe in his pious good works.

After he returned from this place and saw his companions again, he saw a cloud fluttering visibly in the air around the sweet head of the servant of Christ, like a white cloak, so to speak. Catching sight of it, he began to explain in words what he had discovered, the sudden disappearance of the spring. And he persuaded his companions to remove the doubt from their hearts and to become believers now in the merits of the saintly man. While they were speaking these words in friendly conversation, they got to the property of their master where walls had been constructed in a flowery spot with various trees scattered about. To this place the dear friend of Christ guided his step, glad at heart to run

et baculum tractis, gessit quem denique, nervis
in terram fixit moxque domum petiit.
Illic innumeri certabant rite ministri
instantes variis fortiter officiis;
ipsi qui mensas dapibus ponunt oneratas
poscentes tandem solvere sero famem.
Sed prius invalidam iussit procedere turbam
quam suevit mensa pascere saepe sua;
ac propriis ipsa manibus plene saturata
se tandem mensa applicat apposita.
Accumbunt pariter Franci per moenia fusi
gustantes bachica munera laetitia.
Interea somnum sidus suadebat eoum,
nox vicina nigras et minitat tenebras,
atque quies epulas subito sequebatur amica
serpens per membra ebrietate data:
dux pius insomnem coepit transducere noctem
intenta Dominum voce precando suum.
Postquam nox scissis discessit victa tenebris,
<et> lux orta plagam cinxerat aetheriam,
venerunt pueri tironum sorte potiti
portantes cari calciolas domini.
Et pulsant aulam, noctis pro tempore clausam,
orantes aditum iam fieri patulum.
Sed dux paulisper siluit somnum quoque finxit.
Post velut e somno evigilans gravido
solvere custodi vectes iubet interiores
pandere triclinium militibusque suum.
His introductis lympham manibus petit albis;
sed nutu Domini defuit altithroni.

over this rosy courtyard, and then tensing his muscles he stuck the rod he was carrying into the ground and went home. There, countless servants duly exerted themselves, valiantly intent on their various duties; and they set tables loaded with food, asking that he finally relieve his hunger late in the evening. But first he ordered a crowd to step forward, the infirm whom he often used to feed at his table; and when they had their fill from his hands, he finally placed himself at the table set before him. The Franks reclined side by side spread out through the halls, enjoying the offerings with Bacchic cheer.

Meanwhile, the eastern star was urging slumber, and the approaching night was threatening black darkness, and without warning a welcome rest succeeded the feast, slithering through limbs surrendered to drunkenness. The pious duke began to spend a sleepless night, praying to his Lord in an earnest voice.

After the night departed vanquished, with darkness sundered, and light had arisen and encircled the ethereal regions, the servants arrived who chanced to be serving as squires, carrying the slippers of their beloved master. And they beat at the chamber door, which was locked for the night, asking that open access be granted them. But the duke was silent for a time and pretended to be asleep. Later, as though waking from a deep sleep, he ordered the guard to remove the interior bars and to open his chamber to the soldiers. When they had been allowed entry, he asked for water for his white hands; but by the will of the Lord enthroned

Tunc vir securus Christi pietate beatus
unum de pueris ocius egregiis,
ut sibi deferret virgam, misit, memoratam,
quam sero proprium fixit in atriolum.
Qui cursu rapido saliendo per herbida rura
circumfert lubricos atque vagos oculos
inquirens baculum terrae †tempore† sepultum.
Et nactum tractis arripuit digitis
extraxitque solo parva remanente caverna,
post haec conspicuum ut fieret titulum.
Certe quo facto cecidit nubecula parva,
quae volitans aura ante fuit vacua.
Evomit et tumidas ipso disrupta locello
undas praescripti denique fonticuli,
mansuras scatebrae venas quoque fixit aquosae,
virgula praefixa quo fuit exigua.
At puer obstupuit vocemque per aera spargit
suadens militibus affore iam citius
illis atque novi narravit gaudia signi,
quae Rex militiae annuit angelicae.
Dum subito cuncti tanto signo tremefacti
tollunt mirantes ad superos facies
expansisque suis omnes ad sidera palmis
laudum carminula concinuere Deo.
Ecce palatinus pelvem manibus tulit unus,
implevit lympha quem cito conspicua,
laeto Gongolfum vultu quoque pergit ad almum,
ut sibimet signum diceret insolitum.
Et coram tanto subsistens fronte serena
consule de rostro haec dedit egregio:

on high, there was none. Then the blessed man, confident in the goodness of Christ, straightaway sent one of those outstanding servants to bring him that rod mentioned earlier, which he had fixed in his own little plot the previous evening.

The boy, leaping through the grassy fields at a swift pace, cast his lively and wandering eyes around, seeking for some time the rod buried in the ground. And when he found it, stretching out his fingers, he snatched it and drew it from the soil, leaving behind a small hole to be a clear marker afterward. To be sure, when this was done, that little cloud, which had previously been fluttering in the empty breezes, fell to the earth. And bursting open at that very spot, it then spewed out the swollen waves of the aforementioned little spring, and it also fixed permanent arteries for this watery source, in the place where the little rod had previously been fixed. But the boy was stupefied, and he spread the word through the breezes, urging the soldiers now to come very quickly, and he told them the joys of this new miracle, which the King of the angelic army had approved. While they were all trembling at this miracle, suddenly they raised their wondering faces to the angels above, and with their hands reaching toward the stars they all joined in singing canticles of praise to God. Look, one of the palace guards brought a bowl in his hands, which he quickly filled with the clear water, and he went with a happy face to blessed Gongolf, so he could tell him about this unusual miracle. And standing with a serene expression before the great consul, he delivered these words from his honorable mouth:

“Laetus,” ait, “merito sumas rarissima dona,
quae tibi non terra contulit exigua;
sed Rex ipse poli summo de vertice caeli
per nubis mirum miserat officium.
Hinc nos laetitiam constat nunc carpere magnam,
sortitus tantam es quia gloriolam.”
Ilicet econtra fatur dux ore sereno
reddens responsa talia voce pia:
“Non decet haec meritis,” inquit, “sat credere nostris,
umquam tantilli nil quia commerui.
Restat multiplices Christo sed pangere grates,
qui praesens famulis semper adest propriis.”
Dixerat et solito tinxit se fonte novello,
lotus et altithrono haec cecinit Domino:
“O semper pietas, nostrae spes unica vitae,
O vis divinae maxima gratiolae!
Odis quis potis est dignis opus omnipotentis
artificis mundi aequiperare Dei,
qui nova praeteritis reddit non dissona signis
omnia per Genitum saecla regens proprium?
Haec sunt virtutis propriae miracula, Christe,
qui quondam populo utpote Iudaico
petram iussisti latices effundere dulces
et fel triste laci dulce satis fieri.
Inde potestatis non immemor, agne Tonantis,
qua rerum trinam iure regis machinam,
hoc nunc et nostris voluisti credere terris
indicium magnae nobile gloriolae,
quo discant teretem degentes saepe per orbem
te semper solum esse fuisse Deum.

"Rejoicing," he said, "you should accept these rarest of gifts, well deserved, which the meager earth did not confer upon you; but rather the King of heaven himself from the highest peak of the sky sent them through the miraculous service of a cloud. It is certain that we will now reap great happiness from this, because you have been allotted such a precious honor."

Instantly the duke spoke in reply with a serene face, rendering the following responses in a kindly speech: "It is not entirely appropriate," he said, "to credit these things to my merits, because I have earned not the smallest shred of it ever. There is nothing else to do but sing abundant thanks to Christ, who always appears in person to his servants." He said this, and in his usual way he dipped himself in the novel fountain, and having bathed he sang these verses to the Lord enthroned on high:

"O everlasting mercy, sole hope of our life, O greatest force of the divine precious grace! Who is equal to the task of singing in worthy songs the work of God, the all-powerful creator of the world, who grants new miracles not discordant with those of the past, ruling all the ages through his own Son? These are miracles of your own power, Christ, inasmuch as you once for the Jewish people ordered a rock to pour out sweet waters, and you ordered the bitter bile of the lake to become very sweet. And so, not forgetting, O lamb of the Thunderer, the power with which you justly rule the threefold structure of things, now you have chosen to bestow also on our lands this noble proof of your great glory, so that the people living throughout the circle of the earth may learn again and again that you are and always have been the

Hoc quoque nunc, Iesu, donum concede precatu:
abluat ut morbos iste liquor varios,
quo te dulcisonis conlaudet vocibus omnis,
qui se salvatum sentiat et validum."
Haec ait, et vocem sequitur salus alma loquentem,
fitque salubris aqua: laus pia sit Domino!
Post haec per vasti volitans cito climata mundi,
proditrix signi Fama satis placiti
non solum patrios hortatur nempe colonos,
quis fungi dono contigit aurivago,
sed quoque languidolos de longinquo peregrinos
undique collectos accelerare citos
et nullo pretio medicinae sumere dona
gustando tantum fonticuli modicum.
Crebrius incultam videas procumbere turbam
volventem membra litore languidola,
ut possis variis obsessos credere morbis
affore Iudaici languidolos populi,
qui quondam quinis in porticibus Salomonis
fusi piscinae obice Bethsaidae.
Certabant medico lympham turbante superno,
primule quis morbos ablueret varios
(lege quidem tali miro sub sorte potiti,
ut mox illapsus exueret dedecus)
pluribus in lucem suspensis aegre sequentem.
Qui pro spe vitae efflagitant avide,
ut raptim medicus supero de cardine lapsus
turbaret modicam vel pede piscinulam.
Haud alias isti cupiere salutis avari
tangere vel guttam fonticuli minimam.

only God. Grant also now this gift, Jesus, on account of our prayer: that this liquid wash away various diseases, so that everyone may praise you in unison with sweet-sounding voices, everyone who perceives that he has been cured and is healthy." He spoke these words, and restorative healing followed the speaking of this appeal, and the water became health-giving: pious praise be to the Lord!

Afterward, flying swiftly through the regions of the vast world, Rumor, the revealer of this very pleasant miracle, encouraged not only the inhabitants of that land, to whom the enjoyment of this gift of the wandering breeze most assuredly fell, but also the sadly ailing pilgrims from distant lands who quickly assembled from all directions, to rush to receive the gifts of this medicine at no cost by tasting only a modest sip of the little fountain. Very frequently you could see this disheveled mob bent over, rolling their sickly limbs on the edge of the fount, so that you might think it was those sickly members of the Jewish race, afflicted with all sorts of diseases, who were there, those who in former times were sprawled on the five porches of Solomon's temple at the edge of the pool of Bethsaida. When an angelic healer stirred the water, they fought over who would be first to wash away his various infirmities (for by wondrous fate they were subject to a law such that whoever next slipped into the water after the angel would shed his infirmity), while many others were put off against their will until the next day. They avidly implored, so far as they had hope of life, that the healer, gliding down quickly from the threshold of heaven, would stir up the little pool at least with his foot. In just the same way, these people, eager for health, wanted to touch even the smallest drop from Gongolf's little fountain.

Et gustu primo, veteri sanitate recepta,
pulsabant odis sidera dulcisonis,
grates pro tanto reddentes munere Christo,
qui sancti meritis grata dedit miseris.
Laudibus aeque virum tollunt super aethera dignum,
tanta sui causa quod tenuere bona.
Si vacet aequales meritis protendere laudes
et mores tanti egregios duculi,
ante dies noctis peplo veletur Olympo,
quam metam nostra optineat ratio.
Haec sed linquentes doctis tractanda poetis
pingamus coepta nos fragili calamo.
Certe Francorum populus dum risit eous
illustris meritis et bonitate ducis,
blanditur magnis procerum precibus seniorum
hic Christi carus, gentis et omne decus,
quo sibi condignam vellet sociare puellam
federe legali coniugii soliti,
ne finem caperet subducta posteritate
inclita regalis prosapies generis.
His tandem monitus Gongolfus dux venerandus
sat tactus blandis atque patrum monitis
igni conspicuam proprio iungebat amicam
regalem genere et nitidam facie.
Hanc iussit liquidam semper deducere vitam,
compositam castis moribus et studiis.
Ei mihi, sed coluber cupidus, versutus, amarus,
ingenium nuptae illicit indocile.
Scilicet infelix Gongolfi clericus audax
ardebat propriam plus licito dominam.

And at the first taste, when they had gotten back their former health, they made the heavens reverberate with sweet-sounding odes, giving thanks for so great a gift to Christ, who on account of the merits of this saintly man gave favors to these miserable people. Equally in their praises they extolled this worthy man beyond the skies, since it was because of him that they enjoyed such great benefits.

If I had the time to articulate praises equal to his merits and to articulate the outstanding character of a duke so beloved, the day would be veiled in the cloak of night from Olympus before my plan reached its goal. But relinquishing those things that ought to be handled by learned poets, let me embroider with my delicate pen what I've begun. Certainly, while the tribe of Franks in the east was smiling on the merits and goodness of this illustrious duke, he was enticed by the great prayers of the noble elders, he the beloved of Christ and the entire glory of his race, to choose to join himself to a worthy girl in the legal bond of customary marriage, so that the distinguished line of his royal race, in the absence of descendants, not come to an end.

Ultimately, then, the venerable duke Gongolf, advised and very touched by the amiable advice of his seniors, joined to himself with proper passion a striking companion, regal by birth and beautiful in appearance. He ordered her always to lead a pure life consisting of chaste character and pursuits. But, ah me, the serpent, who was covetous, cunning, and bitter, seduced the foolish mind of the bride. That is to say, Gongolf's cleric, a miserable and rash man, burned illicitly for his master's wife. Oh the pain! She, poor wretch,

Pro dolor! Haec male victa dolo serpentis amaro
infelix citius aestuat in facinus.
Inherens servo cordisque calore secreto
legalem dominum respuit ob famulum.
Crimina tunc hostis scalpsit nudare feralis,
quae caluit proprio structa fuisse dolo.
Inpatiensque morae vacuas iaculabat in auras
divulgando suam denique laetitiam.
Dum fuerat vulgo res diffamata dolenda
Francorum gentis omnibus indigenis,
pulsu linguarum tenues conflatur ad aures
sancti Gongolfi consulis almifici.
Ut capit <auditu> latebras illapsa per artas
verbula non minimae nuntia maestitiae,
ingemuit tam triste nefas dignissimus heros,
angoris magno tangitur et iaculo.
Intus in angusto volvit quoque pectoris antro
res sibi diversas triste dolendo duas:
primule vindictam poenali lege parandam
pro sceleris tanti crimine terribili,
post vero veniam solitae pietatis amandam.
Et dolet ad tempus hinc nimium dubius.
Certe sed meritam solvit tandem pie poenam;
diffamare scelus nec placet ulterius.
Sollicitus tantum miserae crimen prohibere,
ne post haec temere viveret in scelere.
Cumque piam curis mentem laxaret in illis,
contigit atriolo currere se proprio
contra fonticuli sibimet prius ostia missi
nubis per mirum caelitus officium.

wickedly overpowered by the bitter deceit of the serpent, was very quickly burning to commit the crime. Clinging to the servant and with a secret warmth in her heart, she rejected her legal lord for the sake of his manservant. Then the beastly enemy was itching to expose these crimes, which he knew had been instigated by his own deceit. And impatient of delay, he proclaimed their crimes to the open air, publicizing, at last, his happiness.

While this grievous affair was being spoken of publicly among all the inhabitants of the Frankish nation, by the wagging of tongues it drifted into the tender ears of Saint Gongolf, the beneficent consul. When his hearing caught these whispers, slipping through the narrow recesses of his ears and bringing news not a little distressing, that most worthy hero lamented the transgression so dire and was wounded by a great shaft of anguish. Furthermore, deep inside in the narrow cavity of his chest, in his bitter grief he considered for himself two different options: first, that revenge should be taken through legal punishment for a terrible crime of such wickedness, but second, that the indulgence of his usual kindness should be embraced. And he grieved for some time afterward, being in great uncertainty. But in the end, he generously absolved her of the punishment she certainly deserved, and it did not please him to publicize the crime any further. He was concerned only to stop the sinning of the miserable woman, so that afterward she would not live thoughtlessly in sin.

And when he had wearied his generous heart over these cares, he happened to wander in his little courtyard right up against the mouth of the little spring that had earlier been sent to him from heaven through the miraculous good

Hic, ubi Gongolfus subsisteret ipse beatus,
coniunx lasciva affuerat subito.
Quam mox pacificis affatur denique verbis
talia dictando ore satis gravido:
"Parte tua famam didici persaepe sinistram,
quod corrupta toro sis male si proprio.
Differo sed vulgo tractare tui miserando,
donec forte sciam te-ne fuisse ream.
Nec mando multam subito concurrere turbam
accitam flendo undique concilio,
ut volvat gnarus subtili sorte senatus
causam terribilis et meritum sceleris.
Sed suadebo manum dextram te tinguere tantum
praesentis lympha fonticuli gelida;
et si non subito damni quid contigit ergo,
ultra iudicio non opus est alio."
Quae tunc plus iusto confidens corde superbo
confortante suam demone duritiam
fundo nudatam committit denique palmam
nil sperans damni posse sibi fieri.
Inter frigoreas ardens sed comperit undas,
quid posset nostri dextera celsa Dei.
Scilicet in madidis audax ardebat harenis,
uritur et flammis acriter aequoreis
et, quae pacificis fastidit cedere verbis,
cogitur aeternae cedere iustitiae.
O semper nostri facilis mutatio Christi,
O virtus iusti iudicis aequa Dei!
Nam, quae iactando tinxit se, triste dolendo
exuitur tincti pellicula brachii.
Nec mora, cum palmam retulit, quod forte negavit,
portavit crudum criminis indicium.

offices of a cloud. Here, when blessed Gongolf himself had come to a halt, suddenly his wanton wife appeared. He addressed her at once with words that proved conciliatory, saying the following with an expression most serious: "I have over and over encountered a sinister rumor concerning you, that you have been wickedly corrupted in a bed that is not your own. But I hesitated to handle the matter publicly out of pity for you, until I had a chance to know whether you are guilty. And I did not order a great crowd suddenly to gather, summoned from all sides to a lamentable assembly, so that a well-informed senate in a subtle decision might consider the case of your terrible crime and the appropriate punishment for it. But I will urge you only to wet your right hand in the cold water of this little spring here. And if nothing harmful suddenly happens as a result, there will be no need for any further judgment." She then, more confident than was warranted, with an arrogant heart, for the devil strengthened her obstinacy, did indeed entrust her naked hand to the depths, expecting that no harm could come to her. But burning amid the chilly waves, she discovered what the exalted right hand of our God can do. That is to say, the brazen woman burned amid the wet sands, and she blazed fiercely in the watery flames, and she who sneered at yielding to conciliatory words was forced to yield to eternal justice.

Oh the ever-simple recompense of our Christ! Oh the impartial power of God, the just judge! Indeed, she who boastfully immersed her hand burned off the skin of her immersed arm in dire pain. Straightaway when she pulled out her hand, it carried the raw proof of the crime which she

His ita digestis pavitat mens conscia fraudis,
ultra nec victae spes fuerat veniae,
tantum certa mori corruptelamque piari
letali poena ocius apposita.
Sed tristis meritam mentis mitigaverat iram
princeps Gongolfus, arbiter egregius,
mandans ut propria damnandus clericus ergo
expulsus subito pergeret e patria,
quo sua fine tenus mala defleret scelerosus
seclusus patria et datus exilio.
Et donat miseram veniae miseratus honore,
ultra sed proprio non locat in thalamo.
Post haec Gongolfi fama crescente beati,
laudatrix vitae quae fuit almificae,
vafer deceptor hominum captorque reorum,
evolvens bilem invidiae veterem
fraudibus omnigenis antiquae calliditatis,
temptavit famam evacuare bonam,
ne gens exemplo tali tantoque suasa
ante superba sua colla daret Domino.
Tempore tunc longo sudavit fraude maligna
laedere famosum, nec valuit, duculum,
in soles quia multo magis vis crevit amoris
illius magni cordibus in populi.
Postremo fraudis miserum circumdedit armis,
quem sceleris causa reppulit e patria.
Sanguinis huncque siti iussit fervere superbi,
nec scivit proprio parcere iam domino.
Tali suffusus subito cum felle misellus
in mortem iusti aestuat atque pii;

had casually denied. When things turned out this way, she trembled, her mind conscious of deceit, and the convict had no further hope of pardon, sure only of death and of atoning for her corruption by a lethal punishment swiftly imposed. But the princely Gongolf, an outstanding judge, softened the justified anger in his sad heart, ordering that the damnable cleric, expelled then from his own fatherland, depart immediately, so that the wicked man might weep for his evil deeds to the end of his days, secluded from his fatherland and consigned to exile. And pitying the pitiful woman, he granted her the honor of forgiveness, but he did not any longer lodge her in his own bedroom.

Afterward, when the reputation of the blessed Gongolf was increasing (reputation was the eulogist of his beneficent life), the cunning deceiver of men and catcher of the guilty, rolling out the ancient bile of his envy, attempted with all the stratagems of his ancient craftiness to do away with Gongolf's good reputation, so that, persuaded by so great an example, a once-arrogant nation would not bow its neck to the Lord. For a long time then he labored in his malicious trickery to injure the reputable and cherished duke, but he could not manage it, because day by day the power of love increased much more in the hearts of that great people.

Finally, with the weapons of his deceit, Satan besieged the wretched cleric, whom he had driven from his fatherland because of his crime. And he forced him to burn with thirst for noble blood, and now the cleric did not know how to spare his master. Suddenly suffused with such malice, the wretched little man was hot for the death of the just and

ac parili repetens ganeam feritate malignam,
illi nudavit omnia, quae studuit.
Ocius haec eius pravis (heu) subdita votis
optavit citius iam fieri facinus.
Tendit et insidias iusto clam nempe nefandas
inmemor antiquae (ah) penitus veniae,
qua se de poena solvit iam rite paranda
nec patitur vitam morte perire ream.
His ingrata, magis socio consensit iniquo
servilique lupa uritur igniculo.
Cumque polum tegeret tenebris nox conscia fraudis,
sensit damnanda tempus inesse lupa,
quo male Gongolfum possunt exstinguere sanctum,
haec et perverso nuntiat armigero.
Qui, resecans coxam stricto mucrone sacratam
sancti Gongolfi, martyris eximii,
deseruit patriam fugiens cum coniuge caram
raptus amore suae indomitae dominae.
Sed non legalis finem ceu nescit amoris,
sic vindicta suam nescit habere moram.
Viscera sed subito profudit caelitus acta,
pridem laetitia quae fuerant tumida.
Sicque miser celsa prostratus vindice dextra
vita mercatam perdiderat ganeam.
Nam martyr sanctus furtivo vulnere laesus
dum mortis gustum ebiberet rapidum,
necnon supremis moriens spiraret in horis,
astabat coetus comminus angelicus,
voce ciens stabilem corpus deponere testem
contextum venis fictile languidolis,
necnon angelicis blanditum suaviter hymnis,
mox caeli calles carpere sidereas.

pious Gongolf, and seeking again that malignant harlot with equal savagery, he revealed to her everything he had planned. She, speedily subdued, alas! by his depraved wishes, wanted the evil deed to happen more quickly now. And she set wicked snares for the just man, secretly, to be sure, forgetting entirely (ah me!) his former forgiveness, by which he freed her from the penalty that should already have been duly imposed, and did not allow her guilty life to end in death. Ungrateful for these kindnesses, the whore instead yielded to her evil accomplice and burned with a slavish spark. And when night, a partner of their crime, covered the sky with darkness, the damnable whore sensed that the time was at hand when they could wickedly extinguish the saintly Gongolf, and she announced this to her wicked champion. He, having drawn his sword, cut through the sacred thigh of saintly Gongolf, the excellent martyr, and abandoned his beloved fatherland in flight with Gongolf's wife, ravished by the love of his fierce mistress. But just as that man did not know the bounds of legal love, so vindication did not know how to tolerate delay. Instead, the cleric immediately shed his genitalia, which were carried off by heaven's authority, those parts so recently swollen in pleasure. And so, the wretched man was struck down from on high by God's chastising hand and lost that harlot he had bought with his own life.

Now, while the saintly martyr, injured by the stealthy wound, was drinking in the rapid draft of death and, dying, was in his final hours of drawing breath, an angelic host stood near at hand, and with one voice encouraged that steadfast martyr to put aside his earthen body, which was constructed of feeble veins, and then, sweetly charmed by angelic hymns, to seize the starry paths of heaven. The

Ocius expirans animam martyr bene lotam
agni lucenti sanguine purpurei
tollitur ex aura vehiturque per astra serena,
in caeli porta sistitur et Domino.
Hic sibi de Christi fertur mox laurea rara
et manibus bravii palmula perpetui;
lucentique stola cuneis coniungitur albis
per vulnus leti, quos tenet aula poli.
Funeris interea magni fit pompa parata,
ornant exsequiae corpus et exanime.
Plangebant cuncti casum tantique patroni,
ipsius famuli maxime sed miseri.
Eligiturque locus tumulo locuples venerando,
quem tradunt veteres Tul vocitare patres.
Illic Gongolfi condebant membra beati
sacros spargentes cum lacrimis cineres.
Post haec non raro visitabant ossa sacrata
quaerentes certum denique praesidium.
Sternuntur sacro procerum quoque corpora busto
pro vitae causis instabilis variis.
Ast, qui sceptra gerit, prostratus marmora lambit
et libat tumulo oscula marmoreo
munere spe dictis rogitans, quo martyris almis
pro meritis Christus sit sibi propitius.
Quid referam turbam templi pro limine iactam,
quidve loquar vota illius innumera?
Haec certe nullus potis est comprendere sensus,
nec possunt ullae dicere litterulae.
At contra vero testis prosperrimus ipsis
largitur talis munera dulcedinis,

martyr, very swiftly breathing out his soul, which was well washed in the resplendent blood of the purple lamb, was raised up beyond the tranquil air and carried through the stars and placed at the gate of heaven before the Lord. Here, then, the rarified laurel was brought to him from the hands of Christ, the palm of eternal reward; and through the wound of death he was joined in shining raiment to the white-robed troops whom the palace of heaven contains.

Meanwhile the pomp of a great funeral was prepared, and funeral rites honor his lifeless body. All men mourned the fall of so great a patron, but his servants were especially sad. A precious spot was chosen for his venerable tomb, a place which the ancient fathers report was called Toul. There they buried the limbs of the blessed Gongolf, sprinkling his sacred ashes with tears. Afterward they frequently visited his holy bones, seeking aid that was, in fact, certain. The bodies of noblemen also bowed down at his sacred tomb because of the various misfortunes of our unstable life. Indeed, the king, holding the scepter, on his knees kissed the marble, placing kisses on the marble tomb, asking by his service, his hope, his words, that Christ be favorable to him because of the cherished qualities of the martyr.

Why should I report on the crowd who threw themselves down before the entrance of the temple, or why speak of their countless vows? Certainly, none of our senses is able to comprehend these things, nor can any mere letters describe them. But, for his part, in truth, Gongolf, that most propitious martyr, lavishes on those people gifts of such sweet-

omnis ut absque mora sentit fore prospera cuncta,
efflagitant testem pro quibus egregium.
Hic certe laeto caecus visu reparato
haurit mox oculis lumina clara suis,
atque diu clausae reserantur vocibus aures,
et gressus plantis redditur invalidis.
Hic quoque de variis morbus depellitur aegris
mundatis membris denique languidolis.
Orsis non valeo digne praeclara monere
munera, quae populus hic metit egregius.
Nec solum cari refoventur amore patroni,
quis cives tanti contigit esse viri;
sed pariter terris habitantes forte remotis
sentiscunt promptum martyris auxilium.
Hinc se felicem iactat Tul terra per orbem,
quae molli gremio confovet ossa sacra.
Denique summatim coepi quia tangere sancti
Gongolfi facta martyris egregia,
restat, uti tenui repetam sermone misellam
illius indignam coniugio ganeam,
quodque dedit signum merito damnanda baratro
invita propriis conveniens meritis.
Certe victoris cum iam laetissima testis
pulsaret celsi sidera fama poli
totos et stabilis fines percurreret orbis
divulgans tantae gaudia gloriolae,
gaudens devotus quidam currebat homullus
e busto signis composito variis,
obvius atque lupae factus supra memoratae
substitit attonitis aspiciens oculis.

ness that each one straightaway perceives that all the things for which they are petitioning that excellent martyr will turn out well. Here certainly the blind man, with his sight happily restored, is soon drinking in with his eyes the clear light, and ears long closed are opened to voices, and the ability to walk is returned to lame feet. Here also disease is driven out of people with various sicknesses, and their weakened limbs are finally purified. I am not strong enough to inform you worthily in words about the magnificent gifts which this excellent people reaped. Not only are those who happen to be fellow citizens of such a man nurtured by the love of their dear patron, but equally those living, it may be, in remote lands begin to feel the ready aid of the martyr. So the land of Toul boasts of its good fortune throughout the world, for it caresses those sacred bones in its tender embrace.

Finally, in summation, because I have begun to touch upon the outstanding deeds of Saint Gongolf the martyr, all that remains for me is, in a few words, to return to that wretched harlot who was unworthy to be his wife, and to the proof which she unwillingly provided, she who deserved to be condemned to hell, a proof in conformity with what she deserved. When, assuredly, the most gratifying renown of this victorious martyr had already struck the stars of high heaven and his fame was coursing through all the lands of the steadfast earth, making known the joys of so great a glory, a certain devout man departed joyfully from that grave, which was adorned by many miracles. And being brought face to face with the aforementioned whore, he stopped, looking at her with astonished eyes. And he

Hanc quoque pro meritis dictis affatur amaris
conformans ligula talia verba sua:
"O nimis infelix flammis credenda meretrix;
iamne piget fraudis, paenitet aut sceleris,
in sanctum Domini non iusta mente patrati,
solo lascivi consilio socii?
Nam miserando tui pando medicamina sani
optima consilii mox capienda tibi;
suadens ut sacrum quaeras maerenda sepulchrum
abstergas fusis et maculas lacrimis,
illic exanimis sancte quia condita testis
prefulgent signis fragmina non minimis.
Et, licet indignam, spero te posse misellam,
si defles culpam, consequier veniam."
Pestiferis sed mens vitiis male dedita totis
ad vitae rectam rennuit ire viam;
solaque nunc laetae complectens lubrica vitae
non curat patriae gaudia perpetuae.
Sic haec infelix commissi criminis auctrix
fastidit verbis credere pacificis,
se quia credebat causis totam perituris
nec spem mansuris gestit habere bonis.
Scilicet auditis verbis non falsa loquentis
intorquens oculos subdola sanguineos
exagitat caput indomitum impatienter in illum
et latrat rostro talia pestifero:
"Cur loqueris frustra simulans miracula tanta
sedulo Gongolfi pro meritis fieri?
Haec, quae dicuntur, certe non vera probantur;
non desint signa illius ut tumulo,

addressed her with bitter words as she deserved, his tongue fashioning words like these: "O you whore, wretched beyond measure, you ought to be consigned to the flames; are you ashamed now of your deceit, or are you sorry for this crime, perpetrated with an unjust mind against the Lord's holy man, at the instigation of your wanton partner alone? Indeed, out of pity for you I will explain the best remedies of healthy advice, which you ought to immediately adopt; I encourage you to seek in sorrow the sacred sepulcher and wash away your stains with effusive tears, because the relics of the deceased martyr, buried there in a holy manner, shimmer with the greatest miracles. And even though you do not deserve it, you wretch, I hope that if you weep for your guilt, you can attain forgiveness."

Her mind, however, was maliciously devoted to all pestilential vices, and she refused to travel the proper road of life, and alone now, embracing the slippery slope of a merry life, she cared nothing for the joys of the eternal fatherland. So, the wicked authoress who perpetrated this crime refused to trust in the man's conciliatory words, because she entrusted herself totally to perishable things and had no desire to place her hope in goods everlasting.

For when she had heard the words of this man, who was not speaking falsehoods, she deceitfully rolled her bloodshot eyes and shook her wild head impatiently at him and barked the following from her pestilential mouth: "Why do you talk nonsense, pretending that such miracles are repeatedly happening because of the merits of Gongolf? These things that are being reported certainly cannot be proven true; in a word, portents are no more present at his tomb

haud alias quam mira mei miracula dorsi
proferat extrema denique particula!"
Dixerat, et verbum sequitur mirabile signum
illi particulae conveniens propriae:
ergo dedit sonitum turpi modulamine factum,
profari nostram quale pudet ligulam.
Et post haec verbum quotiens formaverat ullum,
reddidit incultum hunc totiens sonitum.
Ut, quae legalem respuit retinere pudorem,
sit risus causa omnibus immodica;
fine tenusque suae portet per tempora vitae
indicium proprii scilicet opprobrii.

than the lower extremity of my backside produces wondrous miracles!"

So she spoke, and a miraculous portent followed her word, appropriate to that particular part of her body: for it produced then a blast, made in an ugly tone, such as it would shame my modest tongue to pronounce. And after this, whenever she formed any word, she produced this same uncouth blast. The result was that this woman who had refused to maintain her lawful chastity was a joke to everyone for an immodest reason; and up to the very end, through the whole span of her life, she carried the proof, certainly, of her own disgrace.

Passio sancti Pelagii

PRECIOSISSIMI MARTYRIS QUI NOSTRIS TEMPORIBUS IN CORDUBA MARTYRIO EST CORONATUS

Inclite Pelagi, martyr fortissime Christi
et bone regnantis miles per saecula Regis,
respice Hrotsvitham miti pietate misellam;
me, tibi subiectam devota mente famellam,
quae te mente colo; carmen quoque pectore prono,
et fac exigui supero de rore rigari
pectoris obscurum iam mis clementius antrum,
quo possim laudum condigne mira tuarum
famosumque tuum calamo signare triumphum
et quam nobiliter mundum cum morte cruentum
vicisti, nitidam mercatus sanguine palmam.

Partibus occiduis fulsit clarum decus orbis
urbs augusta nova Martis feritate superba,
quam satis Hispanii cultam tenuere coloni,
Corduba famoso locuples de nomine dicta,
inclita deliciis, rebus quoque splendida cunctis,
maxime septenis sophiae repleta fluentis
necnon perpetuis semper praeclara triumphis.
Olim quae Christo fuerat bene subdita iusto,
fudit et albatos Domino baptismate natos.
Bellica sed subito virtus bene condita iura

The Passion of Saint Pelagius

A Most Precious Martyr Who in Our Times Was Crowned in Martyrdom in Córdoba

Renowned Pelagius, bravest martyr of Christ and good soldier of the King who reigns through the ages, look with gentle kindness at poor little Hrotsvit; look at me, your little servant, submitting to you with a devout heart, I who cherish you in my heart; look also at my poem with a favorable mind, and grant that the dark caverns of my meager mind be moistened more graciously now with dew from heaven, so that I can signal with my pen in a worthy way the wonders of your praises, and your famous triumph, and how you nobly conquered the world, which was bloodied with death, having purchased with your blood the shining palm of victory.

In the western regions of the world shone a noble beauty, a majestic city, haughty from the recent savagery of war, a most cultured place, which Spanish settlers held, wealthy and called by the famous name of Córdoba, renowned for its charms, splendid also in all things, especially filled with the sevenfold sources of flowing wisdom and ever glorious in endless triumphs. It had once been properly subject to Christ's justice, and it bore for the Lord in baptism its white-robed children. But a bellicose power suddenly

mutavit sacrae fidei spargendo nefandi
dogmatis errorem populum laesitque fidelem.
   Perfida nam Saracenorum gens indomitorum
urbis Marte petit duros huiusce colonos,
eripuit regni sortem sibi vi quoque clari,
exstinxitque bonum regem baptismate lotum.
Qui pridem merito gessit regalia sceptra
et cives iustis domuit quot tempora frenis.
Hostili ferro certe quo iam superato,
ac reliquo victo tanta de cede popello,
ductor barbaricae gentis, structor quoque pugnae,
vir sat perversus vita rituque profanus,
vindicat imperii sortem sibi denique tanti.
Collocat et socios populato rure nefandos
implens maerentem non paucis hostibus urbem.
Polluit et veterem purae fidei genetricem
barbarico ritu (quod nam miserabile dictu),
paganos iustis intermiscendo colonis,
quo sibi suaderent patrios dissolvere mores
deque profanato secum sordere sacello.
   Agmen sed tenerum Christo pastore regendum
iussum perversi respuit mox triste tyranni,
dicens malle mori, legem quoque morte tueri,
vivere quam stulte sacris famulando novellis.
Quo rex comperto non absque sui fore damno
sensit, si cunctis pariter praedivitis urbis,
quam crebro validae cepit luctamine pugnae,
civibus excidium mortis conferret amarum.

changed the well-established laws of its holy faith by spreading the error of a wicked dogma, and it wounded those faithful people.

Indeed, the perfidious tribe of wild Saracens attacked in war the hardy settlers of this same city, and forcefully wrested away for its own benefit the destiny of this noble realm, and killed the good king, who had been cleansed in baptism. He had deservedly held the royal scepter in earlier times and had tamed the citizens with the reins of justice for many a year. In fact, when this king had been conquered by the enemy's sword, and the rest of the people were vanquished in such a great slaughter, the commander of that barbaric tribe, the architect also of the battle, a man most perverse in his life and a pagan in religion, claimed for himself the destiny of that empire so great. And he placed his wicked associates in the devastated country, filling the grieving city with no small number of enemies. And he polluted that ancient mother of the pure faith with his barbaric religion (a thing which surely is wretched to relate), comingling pagans with the righteous settlers, so that the pagans would persuade the Christians to destroy their native customs and defile themselves, joining the pagans, in the pagan temple.

But the tender flock which was to be governed by Christ the shepherd soon rejected the dire command of a perverse tyrant, saying they preferred to die, and to preserve their law by their deaths, rather than to live thoughtlessly enslaved to newfangled forms of sacred ritual. When he learned this, the tyrant understood that he would not escape unscathed if he were to confer the bitter destruction of death simultaneously on all the citizens of this opulent city, which he had captured after the continued struggle of a

Ob quod, decretum prius immutando statutum,
sanxit mox legem vulgato dogmate talem:
ut quisquis Regi mallet servire perenni
et patrum mores olim servare fideles,
hoc faceret licito nulla post vindice poena.
Hac solum caute servata conditione:
ne quis praefatae civis praesumeret urbis
ultra blasphemare diis auro fabricatis,
quos princeps coleret, sceptrum quicumque teneret,
seu caput exacto citius subiungere ferro
et sententiolam leti perferre supremam.
His ita digestis, simulata pace quievit
obruta mille malis totiens urbs nempe fidelis.
Sed si quos ignis Christi succensit amoris,
martyriique sitis suasit corrumpere dictis
marmora quae princeps, comptus diademate supplex
corpore prostrato, veneratur ture Sabeo,
hos capitis subito damnavit denique poena.
Sed superos animae petierunt sanguine lotae.
Casibus his plures volvebat Corduba soles
subdita per longum paganis regibus aevum,
donec sub nostris quidam de germine regis
temporibus regnum suscepit sorte parentum.
Deterior patribus, luxu carnis maculatus,
Abdrahemen dictus, regni splendore superbus.
Qui nam Christicolis faciebat more parentis,
librans arbitrium fidei supra memoratum
nec satis iniustum solvit pietate decretum

mighty battle. For this reason, changing the decree that he had earlier established, he then sanctioned, by publishing an edict, a law to this effect: that whoever preferred to serve the eternal King and to preserve the faithful customs of their fathers from long ago, could do so legally with no punishment afterward in retribution. Only this condition must carefully be preserved: that no citizen of the aforementioned city should undertake any longer to blaspheme the gods made of gold, whom the king, or whoever held the scepter, worshiped, or he must undertake to submit his head straightaway under a drawn sword and to endure the supreme sentence of death.

When these things had been worked out in this way, under a pretense of peace, the city remained calm; though uprooted so many times by thousands of evils, it was still firm of faith. But if the fire of Christ's love inflamed any of those citizens, and the thirst for martyrdom persuaded them to violate with words those marble statues that the king, as a suppliant adorned with a crown and with his body prostrate, was venerating with Sabaean incense, these citizens, then, he immediately condemned to capital punishment. But their souls, cleansed by blood, went to heaven.

Amid these misfortunes many years rolled by in Córdoba, subjected, as she was, for a long time to pagan kings, until in our times one of the king's offspring, in his turn, took over the kingdom of his parents. He was worse than his fathers, stained by carnal lust, and was called Abd al-Rahman, a man proud of the splendor of his realm. He certainly acted in the manner of his father toward the Christians, keeping in place the decision about the Christian faith mentioned above, and he did not show mercy and revoke

auctor quod sceleris, populator perfidus urbis,
sanxit dum regem superaret Marte fidelem.
Sed volvens animo, servans quoque corde profundo,
saepius innocuo madefecit sanguine rura,
corpora iustorum consumens sancta virorum.
Qui Christo laudes ardebant pangere dulces
ipsius et stultos verbis reprehendere divos.
Insuper et tanto fastu se iactat in aula,
sacrilegus meritas cumulans sibi denique poenas,
ut regem regum semet fore crederet ipsum,
eius et imperio gentes omnes dare colla,
ullum nec tanta populum feritate refertum,
qui temptare suas auderet Marte catervas.

Dum tumuit fastu licito iactantius isto,
audiit inde locis gentem degere remotis,
Gallicia regione sitam, belloque superbam,
Christi cultricem, simulacrorumque rebellem.
Quae sua continuo temptaret spernere iura,
velle negans dominis olim fore subdita pravis.
Quo rex comperto fervebat daemonis ira,
corde gerens veterem serpentis denique bilem
volvebatque diu flammato dedecus astu,
quid faceret tantis, animo tractans, inimicis.
Tandem nempe dolo cunctis iam forte retecto
affatur proceres praedivitis urbis heriles
talia pestifero latrando verbula rostro:
"Non latet imperio reges succumbere nostro,
vivere nostrarum necnon moderamine legum
omnes, oceanus gentes quas circuit altus.
Sed, quae Gallicios retinet fiducia captos,

that very unjust decree which the author of the crime, the perfidious destroyer of the city, had sanctioned while he was conquering the Christian king in war. Instead, turning it over in his mind and safeguarding it deep in his heart, he again and again soaked the fields with innocent blood, devouring the saintly bodies of just men. These men burned to sing sweet praises to Christ and to rebuke by their words the senseless divinities of the king. Furthermore, this sacrilegious man vaunted himself in his palace with such pride, heaping up deserved punishments for himself in the end, that he believed he was the very king of kings, and that all nations submitted their necks to his authority, and that there was no people filled with such great ferocity that they dared to test his troops in war.

While swollen with this pride more haughtily than was proper, he heard of a nation inhabiting regions far removed from there, settled in the region of Galicia, and haughty in war, worshippers of Christ, and opponents of his idols. They continually attempted to reject his laws, saying that they never wanted to be subjected to depraved lords. When this became known to him, the king seethed with the wrath of a demon, bearing in his heart the ancient bile of the serpent, and in the end, he pondered this disrespect for a long time with flaming malice, turning over in his mind what he would do to such enemies. Finally, in fact, when his scheme was, perchance, now known to everyone, he addressed the noble heirs of that wealthy city, barking out words like these from his pestilential mouth: “It is no secret that kings submit to our authority, and that all nations encircled by the deep ocean live under the regulation of our laws. But I do not understand what audacity holds the Galicians hostage, so that

nescio, gratiolae respuant ut foedera nostrae
et tandem veteris sint ingrati pietatis.
Restat, ut armatis repetamus quippe lacertis
Gallicios hostes, agitando forte rebelles,
donec ex nostris strati per saecula telis
inviti nostris summittant colla catenis."
Haec postquam iactat causamque doli memorabat,
iussit collectis vulgus concurrere turmis,
armorum variis instructum denique signis,
pergeret ut gentem secum delere fidelem.
Ostentatque suum gemmato casside vultum
ferrea lascivis imponens tegmina membris.
Tali cumque locum peteret pompa memoratum
et gentem primo temptaret denique bello,
extemplo tantum sortitur namque triumphum,
ut iam bis senos una cum principe captos
illaqueat comites artis stringitque catenis.
His procerum damnis magna feritate paratis
cessit victa suis fidissima gens inimicis,
subditur atque iugo perversi regis iniquo.
Tunc restaurato rursus quoque foedere primo
loris procedunt vincti comites duodeni
cum concaptivo victi rectore popelli.
Qui citius vinclis dissolvuntur resolutis
exempti propriae pretio gazae numeroso;
sed ducis est pretium iussu regis duplicatum,
ultra quam propriis posset persolvere gazis.
Cumque sui causa regi deferret avaro
quicquid habere domi sibimet suevit pretiosi,
casu condicti parvum quid defuit auri.

they despise the treaties of our graciousness and, in a word, are ungrateful for our long-standing kindness. The only solution is to attack the Galician enemy again, our shoulders equipped with arms, pursuing the rebels, it may be, until, laid low for all time by our weapons, they unwillingly submit their necks to our chains."

After he had made these boasts and described the reason for his scheme, he ordered the people to meet in assembled squadrons, arrayed under the various insignia of the troops, so they could at last proceed with him to wipe out that faithful nation. And he presented his face in a jeweled helmet, putting iron coverings on his lewd limbs. When he attacked the aforementioned place with a great procession and was, then, testing that nation in a first skirmish, he immediately achieved so great a triumph, indeed, that he soon ensnared twelve counts, captured along with their leader, and shackled them in tight chains.

When these noblemen had been lost amid great savagery, that nation most faithful was conquered, yielded to its enemies, and was subjugated to the evil yoke of a perverse king. Then also, after the earlier treaty had again been restored, the twelve counts appeared, bound in leather cords along with their fellow captive, the leader of the conquered people. The counts very quickly had their chains removed, and they were released, redeemed by an extensive outlay of their personal treasures; but the ransom of the leader was doubled by order of the king, beyond what he was able to pay from his own treasury. And when, on his own behalf, he had delivered to the greedy king everything of value he normally kept for himself at home, it turned out that some small portion of the gold demanded was lacking. Perceiving this and

Quod rex sentiscens, fraudem quoque mente revolvens,
dixit nolle ducem populo dimittere dulcem,
ni prius indictum plene solvat sibi censum.
Non sitiens tantum pretii, quod defuit, aurum,
quantum rectorem populi gestit dare morti.
Cui fuerat natus praeclari germinis unus,
omni praenitida compostus corpore forma,
nomine Pelagius, formae splendore decorus,
consilio prudens, tota bonitate refulgens.
Qui vix transactis iam tunc puerilibus annis
attigit aetatis primos flores iuvenilis.
Cumque sat immitem patri sciret fore regem,
tali maerentem blanditur voce parentem:
"O mi care pater, mea suscipe verba libenter,
et, quae commoneo, sensu bene percipe prompto.
Calleo namque tuam senio decrescere vitam,
viribus et propriis nervos penitus vacuatos,
nec te posse quidem levis quid ferre laboris.
Ast ego sed validis dominabor quippe lacertis
ad tempusque potens dominis succumbere duris.
Quapropter moneo precibus blandisque rogabo
ut regi natum me deponas tibi carum,
donec sufficias pretium persolvere totum,
ne tua canities vinclis intercidat artis."
At senior contra dicebat voce severa:
"Desine tanta loqui, dulcissime, desine, fili!
Ne maerore meos ducas in tartara canos.
Nempe salute tua pendet tantum mea vita,
et sine te spatium valeo, pie, vivere nullum.
Tu decus omne meum, tu gloria magna parentum,
es quoque subiecti nobis spes sola popelli.

pondering treachery in his mind, the king said he was unwilling to return the sweet leader to his people, unless he had first paid to the king the specified sum in full. He was not thirsting for the value of the missing gold as much as he was eager to put the commander of that people to death.

This leader had one son of noble stock, his every limb adorned in radiant beauty, Pelagius by name, handsome in the splendor of his form, wise in his counsel, resplendent in all goodness. He already then, having scarcely gotten beyond his childhood years, had reached the first flower of a young man's age. And when he learned that the king would be utterly cruel to his father, he soothed his grieving parent with the following speech:

"O my dear father, accept my words willingly, and what I advise, comprehend it well with a ready understanding. For I am well aware that your life is declining into old age and your muscles have completely lost their proper strength, and that you cannot even endure any light sort of labor. But I, on the other hand, am master of strong shoulders indeed, and I am able for a time to submit to harsh masters. For this reason, I advise, and I will beg with soothing prayers, that you deliver me, your dear son, as security to the king, until you have the means to pay the entire ransom, so that your white-haired old age does not end in tight chains."

But the old man spoke against this in a harsh voice: "Stop saying such things, my dearest son, stop! Don't lead my gray hairs in sorrow to the underworld. In fact, my life hangs on your safety alone, and without you, kind one, I can live no time at all. You are my every honor, you are the great glory of your parents, you are also the sole hope of the people who

Quapropter patriam praestat me linquere caram
necnon Hispaniam vinctum penetrare superbam,
quam te grandaevae vinclis spem tradere vitae."
  Non tulit, ergo, patrem Pelagius ista loquentem,
sed mulcet dictis mentem cari genitoris,
et cogit blandis, quod suasit, velle loquelis.
Consensit precibus tandem genitor venerandus
tradidit et natum, semet redimendo, misellum.
Tunc rex Pelagium iussit perducere secum
et laetus rediit patriam victorque revisit.
  Nullus pro meritis credat factum fore regis
hoc, quod tam pulchra vincebat denique pompa.
Sed mage iudicio secreti Iudicis aequo,
ut populus tanto correptus rite flagello
fleret totius proprii commissa reatus,
vel quo Pelagius Christi pro lege necandus
forte locum peteret, quo se morti dare posset
necnon sanguineum pro Christo fundere rivum,
impendens animam Domino bene morte piatam.
  Postquam rex urbem tetigit saevus locupletem
portans praeclarum iusta de gente triumphum,
ilicet egregium Christi praecepit amicum
carceris in tenebras vinctum submergere nigras
deliciisque cibo nutritum pascere parvo.
  Corduba namque locum servat sub fornice taetrum,
oblitum lucis consignatumque tenebris;
maxima qui miseris fertur fore causa doloris.
Illic Pelagius praepollens pacis alumnus

are my subjects. For this reason, it is better that I leave my beloved fatherland and enter haughty Spain as a bound prisoner than that I surrender you, the hope of my aged life, to chains."

Pelagius did not tolerate his father saying such things any further, but he softened his beloved father's heart with words, and he compelled him with soothing language to want what he was urging. His venerable parent finally consented to his prayers, and handed over his poor little son, redeeming himself. Then the caliph ordered Pelagius to accompany him, and he happily returned to his fatherland and revisited it as a conqueror.

No one should think it came to pass on account of the king's merits that he was a victor then with a beautiful parade. But rather, one should think that it came about by the equitable judgment of the Judge of what is hidden, so that this people, duly chastised by such flagellation, would weep for the commission of all their sins, or so that Pelagius, destined to die for the law of Christ, might by chance reach that point where he could deliver himself to death and pour out a river of blood for Christ, properly laying down his soul, expiated by death, for the Lord.

After the savage king reached the wealthy city, holding a glorious triumph over that righteous nation, he immediately commanded that this noble friend of Christ be bound and plunged into the dark shadows of a prison, bound up, and that the child raised on delicacies be fed little food.

Now, Córdoba maintains a dreadful place under a vaulted roof, which had forgotten light and had been consigned to darkness; it was said to be the greatest cause of pain for the miserable inmates. There Pelagius, the shining child of

clauditur imperio regis cogente nefando.
Illic ergo viri venerunt sedulo primi
mulcendo mentem iuvenis causa pietatis.
. . .
necnon praedulcis gustassent ipsius oris
verbula rhetoricae circumlita melle loquelae,
optabant speciem vinclis absolvere talem;
haec et suaserunt regi iam sceptra tenenti.
  Ipsum felicis certe summum caput urbis
corruptum viciis cognoscebant sodomitis,
formosos facie iuvenes ardenter amare,
hos et amicitiae propriae coniungere velle.
Huius namque rei memores animo miseranti,
causa Pelagii, suaserunt talia regi:
  "Non decet ergo tuum, princeps fortissime, sceptrum,
duriter ut puerum mandes punire decorum
obsidis et teneros insontis stringere nervos.
Eius praenitidam velles si cernere formam
et tam mellitam saltem gustare loquelam,
quam cuperes iuvenem tibimet coniungere talem
gradu militiae necnon assumere primae,
corpore candidulo tibi quo serviret in aula!"
  His rex mollitus dictis, hac voce coactus,
iussit Pelagium nodis evellere duris,
omneque <cum> lavacro corpus detergere puro,
lotaque purpureo circumdare tegmine membra,
collum gemmatis necnon ornare metallis,
quo bene constructa posset fore miles in aula.
Caesaris imperio tunc haec urgente superbo,
extemplo nigris martyr producitur antris,
sistitur atque, toga regali comptus, in aula.

peace, was closed up by compulsion of the king's wicked order. There, then, the leading citizens came, eagerly soothing the heart of the young man out of kindness. . . . and when they had tasted from his sweet lips words smeared with the honey of rhetorical speech, they wanted to release such a beautiful specimen from chains; and they tried to persuade the king, who at that time held the scepter.

They knew for certain that the foremost leader of this prosperous city was corrupted by the vices of Sodom, that he ardently loved young men with pretty faces and wanted to join them to himself in affection. Indeed, mindful of this fact and with merciful intention, for Pelagius's sake, they urged the king as follows:

"It is unbecoming of your scepter, O bravest of kings, that you harshly command a pretty boy to be punished and the tender muscles of an innocent hostage to be shackled. If you were to choose to examine his lovely figure and at least sample his speech so sweet, how you would want to join such a young man to yourself and to raise him up in the first rank of the military, so that with his shining white body he might serve you in the palace!"

The king, softened by these words and impelled by this speech, ordered that they remove those harsh bonds from Pelagius, and wash his whole body in a cleansing bath, and wrap his clean limbs in a purple cloak, and decorate his neck with bejeweled metals, so that he could be a soldier in the finely furnished palace. Then, in accord with the haughty command of Caesar, straightaway the martyr was led out of the dark dungeon, and he was presented in the palace, handsome in his royal toga.

Cumque palatinis medius foret ille locatus,
vincebat socios vultus splendore togatos.
In quem conversis omnes mirantur ocellis
tum faciem iuvenis, tum dulcia verbula fantis.
Aspectu primo quoque rex suspensus in illo
ardebat formam regalis stirpis amandam.
Tandem Pelagium nimium mandavit amandum
in solio regni secum iam forte locari,
ignis ut ipsius fieret sibi sedulo iunctus.
Fronteque summisso libaverat oscula caro
affectus causa complectens utpote colla.

Non patitur talem Christi nam miles amorem
regis pagani luxu carnis maculati,
aurem regali ludens sed contulit ori
magno ridiculo divertens ora negata
fatus et egregio dicebat talia rostro:
"Non decet ergo virum Christi baptismate lotum
sobria barbarico complexu subdere colla,
sed nec Christicolam sacrato chrismate tinctum
daemonis oscillum spurci captare famelli.
Ergo corde viros licito complectere stultos,
qui tecum fatuos placantur caespite divos,
sintque tibi socii, servi qui sunt simulacri."

Sed rex econtra nulla commotior ira
molliter ephebum dicens mulcebat amandum:
"O lascive puer, iactas te posse licenter
spernere tam mitem nostri iuris pietatem
audacterque diis totiens illudere nostris.
Nec movet aetatis praesens damnum iuvenilis
et quod maerentes orbabis forte parentes?

And when placed in the midst of the courtiers, he surpassed his toga-clad companions in the splendor of his looks. When they turned their eyes on him, all were amazed, both at the face of the young man and at his charming little speeches when he was talking. At first sight, the king too was fixed on him, and he burned for the lovely figure of the royal child. Then he even ordered that the much-loved Pelagius be placed on the throne of the realm, right beside himself, as it were, so that the object of his passion might be joined constantly to him. And bending down his face, he would have taken a kiss from his darling, embracing his neck, as one would expect, out of affection.

Assuredly, the soldier of Christ did not tolerate that kind of love from a pagan king stained by carnal lust, but he moved his ear in mockery to the king's mouth, as a great joke diverting his own mouth in denial, and speaking from his noble lips, he said the following: "It is not proper, now, for a man cleansed in Christ's baptism to subject his sober neck to a barbaric embrace, and it is not proper for a Christian anointed with the sacred chrism to seek out the kiss of a petty servant of the filthy demon. Therefore, properly embrace in your heart those stupid men who join you in placating those fatuous divinities on a grass-covered altar, and let those men be your companions, who are enslaved to idols."

But the king, in reply, more aroused, but not in anger, gently soothed the lovable young man, saying: "O impudent boy, you boast that you can freely reject the kindness of my authority, which is so gentle, and that you can boldly mock our gods so many times. Doesn't the imminent loss of your young life disturb you? Doesn't it disturb you that you will, perhaps, leave your grieving parents childless? Our religion

Nostri blasphemos urget cultus cruciandos
subdere mox morti ferro iugulosque forari,
ni cedant et blasphemam respuant rationem.
Hortatu moneo quapropter quippe paterno,
talibus ut verbis parcas saevae rationis,
et mecum stabilem comportes mentis amorem,
nec temptes nostrum post haec offendere iussum,
magno sed studio serves mea dicta sequenda.
Te quia corde colo, necnon venerarier opto
tanto prae cunctis aulae splendore ministris,
alter ut in regno sis, me praestante, superbo."

Haec ait et dextra compressit martyris ora,
astrictim laeva complectens colla sacrata,
quo sic oscillum saltem configeret unum.
Callida sed testis confudit ludicra regis
osque petit subito pugno regale vibrato.
Intulit et tantum pronis obtutibus ictum,
sanguis ut absque mora stillans de vulnere facto
barbam foedavit necnon vestes madefecit.

Tunc rex non modicam tristis conversus in iram
iussit Pelagium, caelestis Regis alumnum,
trans muros proici iactum funda machinali,
crebro bellantes saxis quae perfodit hostes,
nobilis ut testis fluvii collisus harenis
urbem qui vasta propius circumfluit unda,
membratim creperet raptim fractusque periret.
Talia iactanti parebant forte ministri
mox et inauditam struxerunt denique poenam
funda Pelagium iacientes martyrizandum
urbis famosae trans maxima moenia longe.
Sed licet ingentes obstantes undique rupes

insists that blasphemers undergo torture, then that their throats be pierced with a sword till death, unless they yield and reject their blasphemous nature. For this reason, in fact, I advise you with fatherly counsel to refrain from these words of a savage nature, and to share with me an enduring love of the heart, and not to attempt after this to challenge my decree, but to observe with great care my words, which must be obeyed. I advise these things because I cherish you in my heart, and I hope to honor you in preference to all the ministers of the palace with such splendor, that you may be second in my proud kingdom, with me alone over you."

He said these things and held the martyr's face in check with his right hand, tightly embracing his holy neck with his left hand, so that in this way he might force at least one kiss on him. But Christ's martyr confounded the clever tricks of the king and instantly attacked his royal face with a resounding punch. And he conferred such a blow on that eager face, that immediately blood, dripping from the wound he had made, fouled the king's beard and soaked his clothes.

Then the king turned harsh in unrestrained wrath, and he ordered that Pelagius, the child of the celestial King, be hurled over the walls, shot from the mechanical catapult that breaks through warring enemies with a shower of rocks, so that the noble martyr of Christ, smashed on the sands of the river that flows nearby around the city with its vast waters, would be broken to bits quickly and die mangled. The ministers, as fate would have it, obeyed the king spouting such things to the breezes, and immediately, then, they arranged the unheard-of punishment, heaving Pelagius with the catapult to martyrdom far away over the mighty walls of the famous city. But even though the huge rocks projecting

artarent testis corpus praedulce cadentis,
attamen illaesus Christi permansit amicus.
Certe regales citius pervenit ad aures
martyris allisi corpus non posse secari,
infigi scopulis ripae quod iussit acutis.
Hic magis offensus, penitus fuerat quia victus,
mox caput exacto iussit succidere ferro
et sententiolam sic exercere supremam.
Denique lictores regalia iussa trementes
mox Christi testem gladio secuere fidelem,
funus et extinctum lymphis credunt retinendum.
Nam miles Regis, prostrata morte, perennis
victor stelligeri volitat per sidera caeli,
caelitus angelicis deductus suaviter hymnis.
Iudicis et veri, caeli super astra locati,
e dextra nitidam suscepit congrue palmam
pro nece martyrii laudando fine peracti.
Sed nec ferventis bravio fraudatur amoris,
quo semet vinclis pro vita denique patris
impendit, patriam linquens gentemque subactam.
Tandem nulla piis potis est depromere verbis
lingula laureolam caelesti luce coruscam,
qua bene servata fulget pro virginitate,
adiunctus turmis caelesti sede receptis
Agno cantamen modulando perenniter. Amen.
Postquam lictores regis decreta sequentes
funeris exuvias extincti sat generosas
lympharum gremio credunt in saxaque figunt,
ut sacri tumulo cineres essent sine digno,

on every side hemmed in the sweet body of the martyr as he fell, nevertheless that friend of Christ remained uninjured.

To be sure, it very quickly came to the royal ears that the body of the battered martyr, which he had ordered to be impaled on the sharp rocks of the shore, could not be pierced. The king, even more offended because he had been utterly vanquished, directly ordered that they draw a sword, cut off his head, and carry out in that way the ultimate sentence. Then the executioners, trembling at the royal orders, immediately cut down Christ's faithful martyr with a sword, and they entrusted his lifeless corpse to the waters for keeping.

Certainly this soldier of the eternal King, having laid death low, soared as a conqueror through the heavenly bodies of the starry sky, pleasantly escorted heavenward amid angelic hymns. And from the right hand of the true Judge stationed beyond the stars of heaven, he appropriately received the shining palm of victory for a martyr's death accomplished with a praiseworthy ending. But he was not cheated of the prize of ardent love for which he had, in the end, offered himself in chains for the life of his father, leaving behind his fatherland and his conquered nation. Really, no mere tongue can describe in devout words the laurel crown, sparkling with heavenly light, with which he shines brightly in exchange for having preserved his virginity, joined to the throng received at the heavenly throne, singing chants to the Lamb forever. Amen.

After the executioners, following the king's decrees, entrusted the noble remains of his lifeless corpse to the bosom of the waves and fixed them on the rocks, so that those holy remains would be without a worthy tomb, Christ, who does

Christus, qui proprios patitur non perdere sanctos
praeclari modicum capitis vel forte capillum,
non tulit in lympha testem remanere fidelem,
illi sed dignum provisit rite locellum,
qui sancti tumulo servaret membra sacrata.
  Nam piscatores lymphas remis resecantes,
fluctivagosque greges variis laqueis capientes,
litoris extrema viderunt corpus in ora
inter grandisonas agitari martyris undas.
Eminus hoc cautis cernentes nempe pupillis
illic vela dabant citius corpusque levabant.
Nec iam personae noscunt formam venerandae,
illita purpureo fuerant quia sanguine membra,
et caput egregium iacuit procul amne revulsum.
Sed tamen hoc sapiunt prompto quoque pectore credunt:
quod hic, quisquis erat, Christi pro lege cadebat,
illic hi soli quia damnantur capitali
poenae qui, sacra tincti baptismatis unda,
non metuunt crebro regis reprehendere sacra.
  Cumque, caput nanciscentes colloque locantes,
Pelagii faciem cognoverunt rutilantem,
rumpunt in tales miseranti pectore voces:
"Heu, iacet exanimis propriae spes unica gentis,
atque decus patriae tumuli sine sordet honore!
Nonne satis multis scimus nos vendere seclis
semper sanctorum corpuscula passa virorum,
quos capitis caedes monstraverat esse fideles?
Et quis laudabilis dubitet corpus fore testis,
quod truncum misere capitis iacet absque decore?"

not suffer his saints to lose, even by chance, the tiniest hair of their glorious heads, did not allow his faithful martyr to remain in the water, but rightly provided him a humble resting place, suitable for preserving the holy limbs of the saint in a tomb.

Indeed, fishermen cutting through the waves with their oars, and capturing in various nets the schools that wander the streams, saw the martyr's body on the extreme edge of the shore, being tossed amid the heavy-sounding waves. Noticing it in fact from afar with careful eyes, they set sail for that place and very quickly picked up the body. And they did not at this time recognize the features of that venerable individual, because his limbs were smeared with crimson blood, and his noble head lay far off, carried away by the river. But nonetheless they knew and believed with ready hearts that this person, whoever he was, had died for Christ's law, because in that place only those people were condemned to capital punishment who, after being dipped in the sacred water of baptism, were not afraid to criticize repeatedly the king's religion.

And when, after stumbling upon the head and placing it on the neck, they recognized the glowing face of Pelagius, they burst out in these words with pity in their hearts: "Alas, the sole hope of his nation lies dead, and the glory of his fatherland is slighted without the honor of a tomb! Are we not well aware that we have always sold for many shekels the martyred bodies of holy men, whose decapitation demonstrated that they were men of faith? And who could doubt that this is the body of a laudable martyr, because the trunk lies there pitifully, lacking the dignity of a head?"

Haec ubi dicta dabant, navi pia membra locabant,
et citius versis remigabant denique velis
famosae cunctis ad portam gentibus urbis.
Hic quoque subducta iam processere carina
et clam coenobium Christo petiere sacratum
intra non modicos urbis venerabile muros,
portantes pretio vendendum denique magno
extinctum testis funus venerabile terris.
Quod gaudens hymnis suscepit turba fidelis
suavibus, exsequias celebrans de more sacratas;
largiter et pretium nautis tribuit superauctum,
ardescens sancti mercari corpus amandi.
Quo nam mercato pretii non munere pauco,
eligitur tellus membris locuples retinendis.
In qua suprema busto pompa reparato,
glaebae sub cumulo conduntur fragmina sacra.
Quae mox stelligerae Regnator maximus aulae
in tumulo signis iussit fulgere coruscis,
in caelis anima satis ut regnante beata
aequa gloriola regnarent mortua membra.
Denique collectus cernens ex urbe popellus
non pauco variis obsessos tempore morbis,
mundatis illic foedis putredine membris,
salvari gratis, nulla mercede salutis,
nam rudem meriti sanctum titubat fore tanti,
illius ut causa fierent miracula tanta.
Tandem, coenobii princeps rectorque popelli
optima consilii tractans medicamina sani
sensit Celsithronum devota mente precandum,
quo iam dignanter solita pietate patenter
detegeret dubio causae secreta remoto.

After speaking these words, they placed his pious limbs in their boat, and with sails turned round they rowed back, then, most swiftly to the entrance of that city renowned among all nations. Here now, once their vessel was docked, they set forth and secretly sought out the venerable monastery dedicated to Christ within the high walls of the city, carrying what was then to be sold at a great price, the lifeless corpse of the martyr, venerable throughout the world. The faithful assembly received it, rejoicing with pleasant hymns, celebrating the sacred funeral rites according to custom, and they generously offered the sailors a greatly augmented price, being eager to purchase the body of the beloved saint. After they had purchased this prize at what was certainly no small price, a valuable piece of land was chosen for holding his limbs. In that spot, when the burial had been prepared with the finest ceremony, his holy remains were buried under a mound of sod. Then the greatest Ruler of the starry palace ordered these remains to shine in the tomb with brilliant miracles, so that while his soul was reigning so happily in heaven, his mortal limbs might reign in equal glory.

At length the people of the city gathered together, having observed that those afflicted for a long time with various diseases were freely healed at his tomb, their foul limbs cleansed from decay with no charge for the healing; indeed, they were uncertain whether this new saint was of such merit that such miracles occurred because of him. Finally, the leader of the monastery and guide of the people, meditating on the best remedies of sane counsel, understood that they should pray with devout hearts to the One enthroned on high, so that now in his accustomed mercy he might openly uncover the secrets of this case, and remove all

Quod mox personae sexus optant utriusque
parcius atque tribus satiatae sponte diebus
dulcibus instabant hymnis precibus quoque sacris.
His certe votis devota mente peractis
mitem mollitum Regem sensere polorum
esse suis preculis studioso murmure fusis
necnon iudicio dubiae pronum fore causae.
Et cito fornacem cogunt fervere minacem
ignibus appositis toto conamine structis.
Cumque focus gremio fureret fornacis in amplo,
mox caput abscisum Christi sumpsere famelli
talia blandiloquis palpantes verbula linguis:
"Rex pie, sidereae Dominator nobilis aulae,
omnia iudicio qui scis discernere iusto,
istius meritum sancti fac igne probari.
Et, si sit tantae fultus bonitatis honore,
eius ut ex meritis fierent haec dona salutis,
frontis pelliculam facito non tangere flammam,
verticis illaesos omnes quoque redde capillos.
Sin vero meriti constet fortasse minoris,
manda pro signo saltem laedi cute summa
iuxta naturam fragilis carnis perituram."
Talia dicentes clarum caput igne probandum
credunt flammivomis alte surgentibus undis.
Et tandem plenae spatium post unius horae
hoc ipsum rapidis extollunt denique flammis,
lustrantes oculis damnum ferretne caloris.
Quod iam splendidius puro radiaverat auro
expers ardoris penitus tantique caloris.

doubt. Immediately individuals of both sexes wanted this, and eating very sparingly by their own choice for three days, they dedicated themselves to sweet hymns and sacred prayers. When they had performed their vows with devoted hearts, they understood that the kind King of the heavens was mollified by their precious pleas, poured out attentively in whispered prayers, and that he was ready for a decision in this uncertain case. And swiftly they made a frightening furnace hot, setting the flames and heaping them up in concerted effort.

And when the hearth was raging in the ample interior of that furnace, then they took the severed head of Christ's dear servant, repeating tender words like these with persuasive tongues: "Merciful King, noble Lord-Master of the starry palace, you who know how to decide everything in righteous judgment, give a proof by fire of the worthiness of this saint. And, if he is fortified by the dignity of such great goodness, that these gifts of healing happen because of his merits, keep the flame from touching the tender skin of his face, and return every hair of his head unharmed as well. But if, in truth, he is perhaps of lesser merit, command that at least the surface of his skin be injured, as a sign, in keeping with the perishable nature of fragile flesh." Saying such things, they entrusted that lovely head to be tested by the fire with its flame-spewing waves surging to the heights. And finally, after the space of one full hour, they at last took it out of the fierce flames, scanning it with their eyes to see if it bore any damage from the heat. It now shone more splendidly than pure gold and was totally free of harm from the burning and the great heat.

Hinc sursum versis laudavit turba fidelis
vultibus altithronum modulanti carmine Christum,
qui totiens tantis fecit splendescere signis
fragmina constantis pro sese mortua testis.
Haec et mausoleo digne condens venerando
digno percerte supplex veneratur honore,
fine tenus meriti vulgo bene credula noti
caelitus atque dati semper gavisa patroni.

Then with their faces turned upward, the faithful crowd in a melodious song praised Christ enthroned on high, who so many times with miracles like these made the relics of a loyal martyr who died for his sake shine brightly. And properly burying these relics in a venerable mausoleum, the suppliant crowd most assuredly venerates them with proper honor, fully trusting, one and all, in his renowned merit until the end of time, and rejoicing forever that they were given such a patron by heaven.

Lapsus et conversio Theophili vicedomni

Postquam lux fidei, crescens per climata mundi,
Siciliam tenebris errorum solvit ab atris,
vir satis illustris nutritur partibus illis,
nobilitate potens, meriti splendore refulgens.
Hicce Theophilus fuerat de nomine dictus,
puri sacrata tinctus baptismatis unda.
Quem devota patrum divinis cura suorum
obsequiis igitur primis signavit ab annis,
atque sui dulcem pie sollicitando nepotem
cuidam pontifici credidit nimium sapienti,
quo nutriret eum studio florente docendum,
ipsius ingenuum mentisque rigaret agellum
de sophiae rivis septeno fonte manantis.

Cumque pio satis exhausti puero foret ipsi,
digno confestim provectus honore gradatim
perveniebat ad officium sibimet satis aptum,
quod lingua vulgi scimus "vicedom" vocitari.
Hac igitur tanti pompa splendoris adepta
pontifici se subiectum cleroque modestum
praebuit atque pium populo cunctisque benignum;
commisso<que> gregi studio praeerat vigilanti.

The Fall and Conversion of the Vicar Theophilus

After the light of faith, increasing through the regions of the world, had freed Sicily from the dark shadows of its errors, a very illustrious man was raised up in those parts, strong in nobility, glittering in the splendor of his worthiness. This man was called by the name Theophilus when he was dipped in the sacred water of pure baptism. The devoted love of his parents singled him out for the religious life, therefore, from his earliest years. And in kindly solicitude for their sweet descendant, they entrusted him to a certain priest who was extremely wise, so that he would raise him up to be educated with flourishing zeal, and so that he would water the noble field of his mind with the rivers of wisdom flowing from the sevenfold fountain of the liberal arts.

And when this same pious boy had drunk sufficiently from that fountain, quickly advancing step by step in well-deserved honor, he obtained an office quite suited to him, which we have learned is called in the vernacular tongue the "vicariate." When he had acquired, then, the pomp of such splendor, he behaved humbly toward his bishop and modestly toward the clergy, and also kindly toward the people and benignly to everyone; and he watched over the flock entrusted to him with vigilant energy. But especially to the

Maxime sed Christi minimis miserisque pupillis,
ac castis viduis necnon cunctis peregrinis
vestes et victum dextra tribuit bene larga,
hospitiumque vagis numquam claudebat egenis.
Hinc igitur concors omnis devotio plebis
affectu tenero cordis pendebat in illo:
ipsum ceu dulcem venerantur amando parentem.
    Interea vir summorum praesul meritorum
caelitus acceptum direxit ad aethera flatum.
Quo nam defuncto gremio terraeque locato,
consensus plebis clamat concorditer omnis,
respondens cleri votis eadem cupientis,
hunc fore praecipuis aptum meritis vicedomnum
ut culmen sedis captaret pontificalis
summi pontificis curamque teneret ovilis.
Hoc quoque persuadere suo metropolitano
pontifici scriptis festinabant cito missis.
Cuius iudicio statui pastor sapienti
debuit Ecclesiae tali condignus honore.
    Qui bonitate viri comperta namque benigni
se completurum promisit velle precantum.
Et venisse virum iussit maturius ipsum,
affectu populi tanto quem sensit amari.
Ille sed exsecrans talem constanter honorem
praesulis imperio parere negat veniendo,
donec invitus trahitur. Turbis glomeratur
et, cum pontificis praesentaretur ocellis,
stratus adusque solum voces spargebat in altum,
infectum vitiis sese dicens fore multis
non aptum sancto Christi populo dominari.

least of Christ's people, and to the unfortunate orphans, and to chaste widows, and to all strangers, he distributed food and clothing with a very generous hand, and he never closed the door of hospitality on the needy and homeless. For this reason, then, the unanimous devotion of the entire people, with the tender affection of their hearts, resided in him: they lovingly venerated him as a sweet parent.

Meanwhile the bishop, a man of the highest merits, had sent his spirit into the ethereal regions, and it was welcomed in heaven. Now, when he had died and been placed in the bosom of the earth, the consensus of all the people cried out in unison, responding to the wishes of the clergy, which desired the same thing, that this vicar was suited because of his special merits to secure the eminence of the episcopal throne, and to take on the care of the flock of the highest pontiff. They also hastened to persuade their metropolitan bishop of this, sending him letters right away. It is by his wise judgment that a shepherd ought to be appointed for the Church, one worthy of such an honor.

When he learned of the goodness of the man, who was indeed of a benign nature, he promised that he would fulfill the desire of the supplicants. And he ordered this same man to come to him very speedily, a man whom he understood was loved with great affection by the people. But Theophilus, steadfastly rejecting such an honor, refused to obey the order of the bishop and go to him, until at length he was dragged unwillingly. He was hemmed in by the crowds, and when he was presented before the eyes of the bishop, he spread himself on the ground and scattered his cries to high heaven, saying that he was tainted by many vices and not suited to be in charge of Christ's holy people.

His igitur querulis iterata voce profusis,
antistes summus cessit postremo coactus,
huncque, decus talis qui fastidivit honoris,
iniunctae vacuum curae concessit abire,
constituens alium rectoris nomine dignum.
Qui nam paucorum post intervalla dierum,
quorundam blandis clam seductus suadelis,
subiectis alium cito praeposuit vicedomnum,
atque Theophilum summis meritis venerandum
movit ab officio, multos quo fungitur annos.
Istec sed fragilis tolerans patienter honoris
damnum, trititiam pellit de pectore cunctam.
Gaudebatque satis sese iam posse vacare
tanto liberius studio Christi famulatus,
quanto curarum securus erat variarum.

Cuius mox mentem detestatur patientem
totius humani generis saevissimus hostis.
Et, qua primates decepit fraude parentes,
hac huiusce viri pulsat penetralia iusti,
adducens eius fragili saepissime menti
blanda potestatis delectamenta prioris
despectusque gravem facti nuperrime sortem.
Nec laqueos harum retraxerat insidiarum,
donec captivum Christi duxit sibi servum.
Nec mora, vir fortis, vita meritisque celebris,
mentis virtutem demens abiecerat omnem
nec temptamentis studuit restare nefandis;
sed victus cessit mentisque dolore tabescit.
Quique prius plebi sprevit princeps dominari,
affectat iuris pompas nunc inferioris.
Tandem seductus caecato corde misellus

Therefore, when Theophilus had repeatedly poured forth these complaints, the supreme priest was finally forced to yield, and allowed this man, who had rejected the distinction of such an honor, to go away without this duty being imposed on him, and instead he installed another man who was worthy of the name of rector. But now this other man, after an interval of a few days, having been covertly misled by the alluring arguments of certain individuals, hastily appointed a different vicar over his subjects, and he removed Theophilus, venerable on account of his supreme merits, from the position that he had held for many years. Theophilus, however, patiently accepted the loss of that fragile honor and drove all sadness from his heart. And he rejoiced greatly that he was now able to free himself up for the pursuit of his service to Christ more unreservedly, inasmuch as he was relieved of his various pastoral duties.

Then that most savage enemy of the whole human race cursed Theophilus's patient heart. And with the same fraud he had used to deceive our first parents, he attacked the inner thoughts of this just man, as often as possible recalling to his susceptible mind the tempting pleasures of his former power, and the heavy misfortune of the slight so recently done to him. And he did not withdraw the snares of this ambush until he had led the servant of Christ away as his prisoner. Straightaway the brave man, celebrated for his life and his merits, foolishly discarded every virtue of his heart and did not try to resist wicked temptations; instead, he gave up, overwhelmed, and withered from the pain in his heart. And this man who had earlier refused to govern his people as a leader desired now the pomp of a lesser office. Finally seduced, with his heart blinded, the poor little man hastily

quendam perversum petiit festinus Hebreum,
qui magica plures decepit fraude fideles.
Prolambensque suas prostrato corpore plantas
ipsius auxilium flagitat lacrimando nefandum.
Qui, super errantis lapsus gaudendo malignus,
nocte procul dubio iussit venisse futura,
promittens promptam despectus esse medelam,
si parendo suis vellet tantum suadelis
sub dicione sui post haec habitare magistri.
His hic infelix monitis captus male blandis
daemonis obsequio saevi gestit religari,
quo sic umbratilis munus meruisset honoris.
Quem non signatum signo sanctae crucis almo,
sed mage daemonicis confidentem suadelis
ocius ille magus secum duxit maledictus
trans urbem sub nocturnis secreto tenebris.
Intulit inque locum multo phantasmate plenum,
in quo tartarei steterant in veste coloni
alba, candelas plures manibus retinentes.
Inter quos medius princeps residebat iniquus,
qui rex est mortis proles quoque perditionis,
suadens damnandis astuta fraude ministris
impigre cunctis praetendere calliditatis
assuetae laqueos omnes captare paratos.
At magus errantem damnumque sui cupientem
mox ad concilium perducebat scelerosum,
prostratusque sui plantis extemplo magistri,
monstravit verbo causam, qua venerat illo.
Cui daemon saevus contra sic denique fatus:
"Dic," ait, "auxilii possim quid ferre fideli
ablutoque viro Christi baptismatis unda?

sought a certain nefarious Jew, who deceived many of the faithful with his deceitful magic. And he threw himself to the ground, kissing the man's feet, and begged in tears for his wicked aid. The Jew, malignly rejoicing over the fall of this sinner, ordered him to come without fail the next night, promising a ready cure for the slight Theophilus had received, if only he would choose, yielding to the sorcerer's encouragements, to live in the future under the power of the sorcerer's master.

Poor Theophilus, captured by this evilly alluring advice, was eager to be bound to the service of the savage demon, so that he would earn thereby the reward of a shadowy honor. That cursed sorcerer swiftly led Theophilus, marked no longer by the nurturing sign of the holy cross but trusting instead in demonic persuasions, through the city in secret, under the shadows of night. And he brought him to a place filled with many apparitions, where the inhabitants of Tartarus were clothed in white, holding many candles in their hands. In their midst presided the evil prince, who is the king of death and the progeny of perdition, encouraging his damnable assistants with clever deceit to lay energetically for everyone the snares of their customary cunning, snares prepared to capture all.

But the sorcerer conducted that sinner, who was eager for his own destruction, to this criminal gathering then and, prostrating himself at the feet of his master, immediately revealed in a speech why he had come to him. Then the savage demon addressed him in this way: "Tell me," he said, "what kind of help can I bring to a man who is faithful and has been cleansed in the water of Christ's baptism? If

Si meus esse cupit scriptis Christumque negabit
illiusque puellarem pariter genetricem,
per cuius partum patior nimium grave damnum,
illum continuo virtute mea relevabo.
Atque decus talis praestabo patenter honoris,
praesul ut ipse suis non contradicere iussis
apponat, cernens omnes illi famulantes,
qui nunc despectum spernunt, venerarier ipsum."
His nam blanditiis anguinae calliditatis
iste miser verbo non contradixerat ullo,
sed fieri gestit, quae perversus draco suasit.
Proditor atque <sui> totum se perditioni
sponte dedit proprii chartam scribens detrimenti,
in qua spirituum testatur velle nigrorum
esse sub aeternis socius per saecula poenis.
Hoc ubi perfecit, passim phantasma recessit,
ipseque cum pravo gaudendo redibat amico.
Facta namque die praesul praecepit adesse
cleri primates plebis pariterque priores.
Atque Theophilum, cunctis astantibus illis,
adductum verbis nimium blanditur amicis
ipsius subdens hilari vultu dicioni
. . .
Deflevitque piis sese peccasse lamentis,
abiecisse virum praesumebat quia sanctum.
Ast hic, e subitis tanti laetatus honoris
donis, plus aequo tollit se mente superba
iactanter subiectorum cuneos populorum
ipsius obsequiis cogens succumbere duris.
Et spreto penitus patriae caelestis honore

he wants to be mine and will deny Christ in writing, and will deny Christ's maidenly mother as well, through whose childbearing I have suffered a loss most grave, I will raise him up immediately with my power. And I will openly bestow on him a distinction of such honor, that the bishop himself will not intervene to contradict his commands when he sees that all men, who now reject Theophilus as an object of contempt, are serving him."

Now, against these inducements of viperish cunning that wretched man did not speak a single word, but was eager to bring about that which the evil serpent had urged. And he was his own betrayer and gave himself up totally to destruction of his own accord, signing the document of his own ruin, in which he swore his desire to be the companion of the black spirits in eternal punishment for all ages. When he had done this, the apparition vanished pell-mell, and Theophilus went home joyfully along with his depraved friend.

Now, in the morning the bishop ordered the highest-ranking members of the clergy and also the leaders of the people to attend him. And Theophilus, who was introduced when they were all present, he flattered with friendly words, subjecting himself with a happy face to his authority . . . And he deplored with pious laments that he had sinned, for presuming to oust that saintly man. But Theophilus, delighted by the sudden conferral of such honor, raised himself up unjustly in his prideful heart, haughtily forcing the crowds of his subjects to succumb to harsh service. And having completely rejected the glory of his heavenly fatherland, he

terrestris tantum pompae versatur amore.
Cumque diu vacuis inhiaret namque lucellis,
atque monente mago numquam cessaret iniquo
saevo multiplices Satanae persolvere grates
(ex cuius largis credidit solummodo donis
accessisse quidem tantam sibi prosperitatem),
tandem caelestis pietas immensa Parentis,
qui numquam cupit interitum mortemque reorum,
sed mage conversis laetam concedere vitam,
condoluit facti meritum periisse benigni,
quo quondam stabili fulsit celeberrimus orbi
istec sollicitans omnes clementer egentes.
Moreque divino pietas eadem veneranda
concutit errantem digna formidine mentem.

Nec mora compunctus summo maerore misellus
praeponit pavitans oculis saepissime cordis,
quanta negando Deum meruit tormenta per aevum,
et quibus in poenis iungi debebat Averni.
Haec quoque tractando secum maerore supremo
talia continuis fertur dixisse lamentis:
"Heu mihimet misero cunctis probris vitiato!
Ve mihi damnando proprii pro crimine voti,
qui Patris summi Prolem per scripta negavi
divinaeque simul dulcem Prolis genetricem!
Eheu, quam saevis tradar per saecula poenis!
Et quam continuis claudar sine <fine> tenebris!
Qui miser elegi subdi Satanae dicioni
atque tenebricolis Erebi sub limine iungi,
mundanae pompae vano seductus amore!

occupied himself only with the love of earthly display. And when he had for some time, in fact, panted after these vacuous and meager gains, and when, on the advice of the evil sorcerer, he had ceaselessly paid manifold thanks to cruel Satan (from whose generous gifts alone he believed that such prosperity, in fact, had come to himself), finally the immense mercy of the heavenly Father, who never desires the death and destruction of the guilty, but wants, instead, to grant a blessed life to those who have converted, grieved that the merit of Theophilus's good work had perished, the merit for which this same man had once shone forth as the most celebrated person in the fixed universe, caring mercifully for all those in need. And in a godly manner, this same venerable mercy shook the sinning heart of Theophilus with justified fear.

Immediately the poor little man, stung with the greatest remorse, trembling repeatedly, placed before the eyes of his heart the great torments which he had earned for eternity by denying God, and the punishments of Avernus to which he was due to be subjected. And pondering these things inwardly with supreme remorse, he is reported to have said the following, with endless laments: "Alas, poor me, defiled by every disgrace! Woe to me, destined for damnation for a crime of my own choosing, I who denied in writing the Son of the highest Father, and likewise the sweet mother of the divine Son! Alas, how savage the punishments to which I will be consigned for all time! And how perpetual the darkness in which I will be imprisoned without end! I, poor wretch, who chose to be subject to the power of Satan and to be yoked to the inhabitants of darkness under the threshold of Erebus, seduced by vain love of worldly pomp! What

Quid dicturus ero nimium peccator in illo
tempore iudicii sanctis ipsis metuendi,
quando factorum mercedem quisque suorum
accipiet dignam, satis aequa lance libratam,
pro diversorum qualitate quidem meritorum?
Vel quis forte mei tunc apponet misereri,
cum vix pro meritis iustus salvatur opimis?
Nam Christi Genetrix, caelique potens dominatrix
Flaminis atque sacri templum sine sorde coruscum,
haec eadem virgo partus post gaudia casta,
quae retro conversis fuerat mitissima cunctis
atque sui dulcem numquam tardat pietatem,
sola mihi veniae potis est medicamina ferre,
si pro me proprium dignatur poscere Natum.
Sed, si pollutis illam rogitare labellis
coepero, bacchanti nuper quam corde negavi,
me vereor flammis caelo consumier actis,
ferre meum facinus quia non patitur grave mundus.
Attamen instantis causa cogente doloris
eiusdem celerem supplex quaero pietatem,
quo clemens animam precibus solvat perituram."
Haec secum querulis nimium dicebat amaris
et saecli curis citius de corde repulsis.
Impiger ad templum properat sub honore dicatum
Virginis intactae Matrisque Dei venerandae
octiens et spatium transegit quinque dierum
illic, contrito deflens sua corde piacula.
Denegat atque sibi lacrimis satiatus amaris
omnia cultorum delectamenta ciborum
scilicet et requiem somni saepissime dulcem
pervigil in sacris summo conamine votis.

am I, an egregious sinner, going to say at the time of that judgment that must be feared by the saints themselves, when everyone will receive the payment he deserves for his deeds, meted out on a scale that is entirely fair, according, indeed, to the nature of his varying merits? Or who, perchance, will then intervene to pity me, when even a just man can scarcely be saved by his bountiful works? Assuredly the Mother of Christ, the powerful mistress of heaven, the shining, unblemished temple of the Holy Spirit, that same one who was a chaste virgin after the joys of childbirth, she who has proved most gentle to all who have turned back to Christ and has never held back her sweet kindness, she alone is able to bring the remedies of forgiveness to me, if she sees fit to ask her Son on my behalf. But, if I start to pray with my polluted lips to that woman whom I recently denied with a raving heart, I am afraid I will be devoured by heaven-sent flames, because the world cannot stand to endure my grievous crime. Nonetheless, being compelled by unrelenting pain, I will seek her ready kindness as a suppliant, so that by her prayers, merciful as she is, she may free my soul which is about to perish." He said these things to himself with extremely bitter self-reproaches and with all his concerns for the world driven swiftly from his heart. He energetically raced to the temple consecrated in honor of the unblemished Virgin and venerable Mother of God, and he spent an interval of five times eight days there, weeping over his sins with a contrite heart. And fed only on bitter tears, he denied himself all the pleasures of fine food, and, in fact, as often as possible he denied himself the sweet rest of sleep, staying awake in sacred prayers by the greatest effort.

Tali percerte corpus frangendo labore,
purgavit lacrimis animae maculas vitiatae.
His bene perfectis nimium cum lassus in horis
nocturnis molli dederat sua membra quieti,
astitit in somnis illi castissima Regis
aeterni genetrix, eadem mundi dominatrix,
scilicet auxilium, spes solamenque paratum
eius praesidium devota mente precantum.
Talibus et verbis terrebat corda paventis:
"O vir, cur nostri vigilas ad limina templi
vel cur posse mei celerem temet pietatem
praesumis sperare, meum qui denique Natum
me matremque sui perverso corde negasti?
Dic, rogo, quis oculis possim mis cernere Prolis
divinae vultum, caelesti luce coruscum,
quove modo solio praesens astare tremendo
eius praesumo tibimet veniam rogitando?
Ast omnes culpas in me fortasse patratas
affectu mentis tibi mox indulgeo gratis,
omne genus nimium quia diligo Christicolarum.
Illos praecipue tenero sed mentis amore
diligo, consolor, propriis amplector et ulnis,
quos exorantes crebris hymnisque vacantes
invigilare meo cerno saepissime templo.
Materni sed vis fortis me cogit amoris
hinc magis erga te nimio fervescere zelo,
quod praesumpsisti tradendus perditioni
blasphemando mei sanctum contemnere Natum.
Qui Deus aeternus de Patre Deo generatus
retro principii primordia cana sereni

Wrecking his body, to be sure, by such an endeavor, he purged the stains of his corrupted soul with his tears.

After he had fully performed these actions, when he was thoroughly exhausted and had surrendered his limbs to pleasant sleep in the nighttime hours, there stood before him in his dreams that most chaste mother of the eternal King, she who is also the mistress of the world, she, in fact, who is the aid, the hope, and the ready solace of those who pray for her assistance with devout intention. And she terrified the heart of that trembling man with the following words:

"Sir, why do you perform vigils at the threshold of my temple, or why do you presume that you can hope for my swift mercy, you who have, in short, denied my Son and me, his mother, in your corrupted heart? Tell me, I beg you, with what eyes can I look upon the face of my divine Son, shining in heavenly light, or in what way will I presume to stand in attendance at his terrifying throne seeking pardon for you? But for all the crimes you may have perpetrated against me, out of the affection of my heart I will freely forgive you straightaway, because I cherish greatly the entire race of Christians. But I cherish especially with a tender love of my heart, and I comfort and embrace in my arms, those whom I see praying, spending their time in frequent hymns, keeping vigils over and over in my temple. Yet the strong force of maternal love compels me in this case, instead, to rage with utmost fervor against you, because you have presumed, handing yourself over to destruction, to despise my saintly Son by blaspheming him. He, the eternal God, born from God the Father before the hoary origins of the serene

ex me dignatus sumpsit sub tempore corpus,
quod dedit humanae morti nationis amore."
Talia dicenti castae Christi Genetrici
vir maerens animo contra sic fatur amaro:
"O mea domna, scio nimiumque tabesco sciendo,
plus iusto quia deliqui spe captus inani.
Commisi cunctis facinus vitiis quoque peius
despiciendo Deum de te sine sorde profusum.
Hinc non sum dignus veniae conquirere munus;
sed tamen exemplum nobis tribuere salutis
sperandae multi, vario qui crimine lapsi
post lapsum scelerum veniam meruere suorum.
Nonne Ninivitae mitem Christi pietatem
sese condignis cruciantes namque lamentis
invenere trium post intervalla dierum?
Nonne David, propheta dei, princeps quoque regni
Iudaici, plebem Domini qui rexit erilem,
illicito nuptae subito praeventus amore,
non timet insidiis circumveniendo dolosis
insontem vita fraudare virum sine causa,
complexus carae licito quo posset habere?
Sed postquam vatis perterritus advenientis
admonitu culpas didicit deflere gemellas.
Delevit lacrimis tantae maculas cito sordis,
suscepit rursum prophetiae quoque donum.
Quid referam Petrum Christo testante beatum?
Qui, postquam ius solvendi pariterque ligandi
necnon stelligerae claves acceperat aulae
pro fidei rectae satis expressa ratione,
detestando deum sese cognoscere Christum
rennuit ancillae vocem metuendo nefandae.

creation, deigned to receive from me a temporal body, which he surrendered in death out of his love for the human race."

To the chaste Mother of Christ who spoke these words, the mournful man replied in the bitterness of his heart as follows: "O my mistress, I know, and the knowledge gnaws at me, that I have done wrong, being captivated unjustly by an empty hope. I have also committed a crime worse than all other vices by despising the God brought forth from you without stain. For this reason, I am unworthy to ask for the favor of your forgiveness; but nevertheless, many people have provided us an example of hoped-for salvation, people fallen into various sins, who earned forgiveness of their sins after falling. Did not the Ninevites, torturing themselves with appropriate laments, in fact discover the gentle mercy of Christ after an interval of three days? Was it not David, prophet of God and leader of the Jewish kingdom, who ruled the noble people of the Lord—was it not David, being suddenly overwhelmed by an unlawful love for a married woman, who was not afraid to cheat an innocent man out of his life with no justification, by entrapping that man in deceitful snares, so that he himself could enjoy the embraces of the beloved woman lawfully? But afterward, terrified by the warning of the prophet who came to him, he learned to repent of both his sins. He swiftly erased with his tears the stains of such sordidness, and he also received again the gift of prophecy. Why should I mention Peter, who by Christ's own testimony is blessed? He, after he had received the power of releasing and of binding as well as the keys to the starry palace for the very explicit reason of his true faith, denied that he knew Christ, renouncing God because he feared the voice of a wicked maid? Not once, or two

Nec semel aut binis vicibus sed denique ternis
ceu numquam visum carum negat ergo magistrum.
Sed, quia condigne lapsum deflevit ab ore
peccatum, veniae meruit medicamen opimae
scilicet atque gregi iussus praeesse fideli
princeps, Ecclesiae pastor fit iure sacrate.
Talibus ac tantis, aliis multisque figuris
admonitus similem me sperabam pietatem
a Christo citius per te conquirere posse."

Cui vultu blando dicebat sancta Maria
tristem mellifluae refovens dulcedine linguae,
"Si te commissum turbat facinusque nefandum,
condecet, ut cordis consensu confitearis
hoc, quod mendaci demens sermone negasti,
ipsum, quem peperi, Patris Natum fore summi,
qui iudex orbem veniet renovare per ignem.
Et post haec tandem pro te praesumo rogare."
Ille quidem rursus lacrimans infit vicedomnus:
"O dilecta Dei, <genetrix> sanctissima Christi,
quae miti refoves cunctos pietate fideles,
quo pacto, quo iure quidem contingere tandem
Altithroni nomen sanctum venerabile magnum
infelix ego pollutis praesumo labellis,
qui Christum, baptisma, crucem, Christi quoque matrem
te castam scriptis blasphemavi male pictis
cunctaque caelestis pia sacramenta salutis?"

His miserens querulis inventrix virginitatis
aiebat blandis iterum clementius orsis:
"Quamvis sis gravibus vitiis nimium maculatus,
attamen, ut monui, Dominum non sperne fateri,

times, but finally three times, as if he had never seen him, he denied, then, his beloved teacher. But, because he worthily repented the sin that had slipped from his mouth, he earned the remedy of bountiful forgiveness, and, indeed, he was ordered to be the leader over the faithful flock, and rightly became the shepherd of the holy Church. Incited by such examples, and by such great ones, and by many others, I was hoping I might speedily seek similar mercy from Christ through you."

To him holy Mary said with a soothing expression, reviving the sad man by the sweetness of her tongue, from which honey flowed, "If your transgression and wicked crime disturbs you, it is appropriate for you to confess in accordance with your heart this thing that you insanely denied in lying words, that the very person whom I bore was the Son of the Father on high, who will come as the judge to renew the world through fire. And after that I will presume at last to entreat on your behalf." The vicar, indeed, weeping once more, began as follows: "O beloved of God, holiest mother of Christ, who revive all the faithful with your gentle kindness, in what way, with what right, indeed, do I presume now to defile the great, holy, venerable name of the One enthroned on high—I, a poor wretch with polluted lips, I, who have blasphemed Christ, baptism, the cross, and also you, the chaste mother of Christ, and all the pious sacraments of heavenly salvation, with written declarations wickedly signed?"

She who was the founder of virginity, pitying these complaints, spoke again more mercifully, with soothing words: "Although you are deeply stained with serious faults, still, as I advised, don't refuse to confess the Lord, because he was

est quia factus homo nostri solummodo causa,
ut spem conversis veniae praeberet habendae."
Tunc istec demum, monitis parendo iubentis
cum lacrimis, tales spargebat ad aethera voces:
"Nunc supplex veneror, laudo, complector, adoro
ex Patre caelesti Christum sine tempore natum,
temporibus nostris missum de sede parentis,
ut de te casta necnon de Flamine sancto
indueret fragilis nostrae velamina carnis.
Huncque Deum verum necnon hominem fore plenum
non dubito, nostri causa qui pertulit ergo
opprobriis tangi, colaphis, alapis quoque caedi,
sacraque pulsari crebris sua terga flagellis,
atque sputis rutili speciem vultus maculari.
Cumque coronatus spinis et felle potatus,
quae sacra praedixit scriptura, per omne replevit.
Postremo sacris expansis in cruce palmis
ceu pastor verus bonitatis honore decorus
pro nobis animam moriens ponebat amandam
adque sepulchralem dignans suscepit honorem.
Hinc inferna petens Erebi quoque claustra resolvens
mortem destruxit mortis patremque ligavit
tartareoque suos traxit de carcere iustos.
Ac sic non parva victor comitante caterva
ad superos rediit proprium corpusque resumpsit,
quod fuit in busto clausum sub marmore magno.
Tertia quem vivum vidit lux omne per aevum,
discipulique sui crebro videre beati
ipsum nunc convescentem, nunc ergo loquentem
illis de regno dulci sermone futuro.
Post haec attonitis oculis cernentibus ipsis

made man solely for our sake, in order to offer to the converted the hope of attaining pardon."

Then at last Theophilus, tearfully obeying the admonitions of her command, cast words such as these into the upper air: "Now as a suppliant I revere, I praise, I embrace, I adore Christ, born from the heavenly Father outside time, who was sent in our times from his parent's throne, so that from you, uncorrupted, and from the Holy Spirit he might take on the covering of our fragile flesh. I do not doubt that this One is true God and also fully man, who for our sake, then, endured being touched by insults and jabs, also being cut down by blows, and his holy back being beaten over and over by whips, and the beauty of his radiant face being defiled by spit. And when he had been crowned with thorns and been given vinegar to drink, he fulfilled in every detail what sacred scripture had foretold. Finally, with his sacred palms stretched out on the cross, like a true shepherd, adorned by the honor of his goodness, dying for us, he gave up his beloved soul and deigned to receive the honor of burial. Then, seeking out also the infernal regions and opening the enclosures of Erebus, he destroyed death and bound the father of death, and dragged his own righteous people from the prison of Tartarus. And so, as a conqueror, accompanied by no small throng, he returned to the upper regions and took up again his own body, which had been closed up in a tomb beneath a great marble block. The third day saw him alive, now for all time, and his blessed disciples saw him repeatedly, sometimes dining with them, then again sometimes talking to them in sweet speech about the kingdom that was to come. After that, while they looked on with

ipsam, quam sumpsit, carnem super astra libravit,
in qua iudicium veniet celebrare futurum,
proque suis meritis reddet bona vel mala cunctis.
Haec ita credentem, cordisque fide retinentem,
atque tui deposcentem solitam pietatem
commenda me, Virgo, tuo, sanctissima, Nato
impetraque tuo veniam famulo sceleroso."

Haec ubi continuis deflevit verba querelis,
sancta Dei Genetrix eademque potens dominatrix
caelorum, verbis respondens inquit amicis,
"Propter mysterium sacri baptismatis almum,
345 quod suscepisti credentis more popelli,
336 et propter dulcem carae mis prolis amorem,
cuius te pretio sacri scio sanguinis amplo
emptum, pro mundo qui fusus erat perituro,
procedens sacris advolvor sedula plantis
eius, quem genui, cunctorum iudicis aequi.
Nec parcam preculis studio certante profusis
donec ipsius mitem cogo pietatem,
ut, tibi parcendo, dimittat tanta piacla."
344 His dictis subito discessit Virgo sacrata,
346 linquens promissi misero solamina sani.

Certe post triduum rursus veniebat ad illum
in visu veniae munus reserans reparatae;
et vultu laeto deprompsit talia verba:
"En tis, vir Domini, tristis compunctio cordis
est accepta Deo Patri Prolique perenni,
atque tuae lacrimae scelerum veniam meruere.
Sed nec tartareis poenis umquam capieris,
si post haec perstare cupis sine fraude fidelis."

astonished eyes, he raised above the stars the flesh he had 325
taken on, that flesh in which he will come to celebrate the
judgment that is to come, and in which he will render good
and evil to all according to their merits. Commend me, be-
lieving these things are so, and retaining them with the faith
of my heart, and appealing for your customary kindness,
O most holy Virgin, commend me to your Son, and obtain 330
forgiveness for your sinful servant."

When he had wept out these words in continual lamenta-
tion, the holy Mother of God, that same powerful mistress
of the heavens, responding in friendly words, said, "Because 335
of the gracious mystery of holy baptism, which you received 345
after the manner of the faithful people, and because of my 336
sweet love for my dear child, at the ample price of whose
sacred blood I know you have been redeemed, that blood
which was poured out for the world that was going to per-
ish, I will go and eagerly prostrate myself at the holy feet of 340
him whom I bore, of that fair judge of all. And I will not
spare profuse prayers in my zealous effort until I compel
his gentle mercy, forgiving you, to dismiss your great sins."
When she had said these things, the holy Virgin suddenly 344
departed, leaving the poor man the solace of her health- 346
giving promise.

After three days, assuredly she came again in a vision to
that man, disclosing the gift of forgiveness that had been
restored to him; and with a joyful expression she uttered
words to this effect: "Man of the Lord, look, the remorse of 350
your sad heart has proven acceptable to God the Father and
to his eternal Son, and your tears have earned you forgive-
ness for your sins. And furthermore, you will never be taken
away for hellish punishments if, from now on, you strive to

Ipse quidem contra mox dicebat prece blanda:
"Certe servabo sacrae fidei documenta,
nec post haec ultra male transgredior neglegendo
quicquam de vestris, mea domna piissima, iussis,
te quia post Dominum solam conferre medelam
spero, quo poenis pabulum non tradar amaris.
Sed non est mirum per te me iam fore salvum,
per quam de veteris letali crimine matris
omnem dante Deo mundum patet esse solutum.
Et quis te poscens spe non dubiaque requirens
desertus fuerat vel confusus remeabat?
Hinc ego criminibus sat supremis vitiatus
suppliciter fontem devota mente perennem,
alma Dei Genetrix, exoro tuae pietatis,
ut facias chartae litteras extemplo nefandae,
quis me subiunxi vastatoris dicioni,
eius de manibus miserum me sumere rursum.
Hinc animam formido meam quia forte misellam
tempore iudicii multo discrimine laedi,
si nunc praedoni non est abstracta feroci."
His dictis oculis iterum vigilabat apertis;
et se prosternens precibus crebro quoque deflens,
ieiunando trium cursus agit ergo dierum.
Post haec e somno cum surrexit mane summo,
invenit positam supra sua pectora chartam.
Qua visa membris mox contremuit resolutis
et grates Christo cordis reddebat ab imo
atque puellari pariter Christi Genetrici.
Post haec namque die sacra feliciter orta,
quae trahit a Domino nomen venerabile summo,

remain honestly faithful." He, in fact, responded straightaway with a pleasing prayer: "Certainly I will preserve the teachings of the sacred faith, and I will not in the future wickedly transgress any further, neglecting any of your commands, my kindest mistress, because I trust that, after the Lord, you alone will provide a remedy, so that I not be handed over as fodder for bitter punishments. But it is no wonder that I have already been saved through you, through whom it is clear that the entire world was freed, by God's gift, from the fatal crime of that mother of long ago. And who, asking you and seeking you with undoubting hope, has ever been abandoned, who ever went away perplexed? And so, I, deeply stained by the highest crimes, humbly pray with a devout heart, dear Mother of God, for the eternal font of your mercy, I pray that you see to it that I, poor wretch, retrieve at once the text of that wicked charter by which I subjugated myself to the power of the destroyer, that I retrieve it again from his hands. Because I am afraid my poor soul, in great danger at the time of judgment, may perchance be injured, if this charter is not now stripped from the fierce plunderer."

When he had said these things, he again performed vigils with his eyes wide open, and prostrating himself and repeatedly weeping in prayer, he spent a span of three days fasting. After that, when he arose very early in the morning from sleep, he found the document placed on his chest. Then when he saw it, he straightaway trembled, and his limbs gave way, and he rendered thanks to Christ from the bottom of his heart, and likewise to the maidenly Mother of Christ.

After that, in fact when that holy day was happily beginning which takes its venerable name from the Lord most

intrat in ecclesiam populis ex more repletam.
In qua tunc inter sacrae sollemnia missae
astantes evangelicis praesul docet orsis;
et coram cunctis sacram prostratus ad aram,
eiusdem quoque pontificis dans oscula plantis,
voce palam clara narravit ab ordine cuncta
quae vel mortiferis egit victus suadelis
vel quae perpetua meruit poscente Puella.
Haec ubi composita plene retulit ratione,
antistes facti tactus terrore stupendi
intonat his verbis mirantis voce profusis:
"Cuncti gaudentes huc iam properate fideles.
Et pia facta Dei laudantes mente fideli,
credite iam Dominum propria pietate benignum
in leto delectari numquam scelerosi,
sed plus conversis vitam dare velle futuram.
Eia, dilecti fratres, intendite cuncti,
quam pie peccantes Dominus tolerat bonus omnes,
quos scit converti post tristia facta piacli.
Quis non miretur, quis non supplex veneretur
laudandam mitem dulcem Christi pietatem,
illum quaerentes semper qua sublevat omnes?
Qui iam criminibus miserans parcebat et huius
ipsius illustris precibus sanctaeque parentis.
Per quam naturae periit maledictio nostrae
et per quam mundo venit benedictio cuncto.
Hinc memor esto, Dei Genetrix sanctissima, nostri.
Qui te mente, fide, voto laudamus et ore,
quo pius ipse gregem pastor servare fidelem
dignetur veteris depulsa fraude draconis.

high, he entered the church, which was filled with people as usual. In this church then, during the solemnities of the holy Mass, the bishop was instructing the bystanders in the words of the gospels; and in front of everyone, Theophilus, prostrating himself at the holy altar and also kissing the feet of this same bishop, publicly narrated everything in a clear voice right from the beginning, both what he had done when overcome by fatal persuasions, and what he had earned by the intercession of the perpetual Virgin. When he had fully reported these things in an orderly fashion, the presider, touched by the dread of this amazing affair, intoned in wondering tones, pouring out these words:

"Hurry to this place now, rejoicing, all you faithful people. And praising the merciful deeds of God with a faithful heart, believe now that the Lord, gracious in the mercy that is his, never takes pleasure in the death of a wicked man, but rather wishes to bestow the life to come on those who repent. Come on, beloved brothers, pay attention, all of you, to how mercifully the good Lord tolerates all those sinners he knows to be repentant after their dire acts of sin. Who would not be amazed, who would not humbly venerate the praiseworthy, gentle, sweet mercy of Christ, through which he always raises up all who seek him? He now mercifully has refrained from punishing the sins of this man too, because of the prayers of his own celebrated and holy mother. Through her the curse of our nature has perished, and through her a blessing has been bestowed upon the whole world. Wherefore be mindful of us, holiest Mother of God. We praise you with our heart, our faith, our vow, and our voice, so that the merciful shepherd himself may see fit to save his faithful flock, after he has repelled the fraud of the

At nos exiles nulla virtute potentes
te semper, Regis Mater non tacta perennis,
ac de te genitum Regem Dominumque polorum
efferimus crebris conclamantes simul odis;
peccato noster moriens periit quia frater,
sed, postquam periit, per te, sacra Virgo, revixit."
His dictis chartam comburebat maledictam
et mox misterium missae peragit studiose.
Hoc ubi complevit, miro splendore refulsit
instar surgentis Phoebi facies vicedomni,
quo mentis splendor lucens animae quoque candor
eius per faciem monstraretur rutilantem.
Hinc astans populus, nimia formidine tactus,
Altithrono grates coepit resonare tonantes,
cui placuit monstrare viri meritum venerandi.
Ipse quidem sacrum repetens extemplo locellum,
in quo caelestis donum meruit pietatis,
frangitur adversa fragilis valitudine carnis,
per spatiumque trium morbo crescente dierum.
Exemptus corruptibilis de carcere carnis
spiritus aethereàm plaudens ascendit ad aulam
auxilio sanctae fultus domnaeque Mariae.
Scilicet extinctum corpus nisu populorum
ipso rite loco tumulatur honore supremo,
in quo nactus erat veniam, quam flendo rogabat.
Talis erat desperati necnon scelerosi
finis, qui proprium didicit deflere reatum
et se condignis studuit punire lamentis.
Hinc laus et virtus Christo per saecula cuncta,
humani veterem generis qui straverat hostem

ancient serpent. But we who are feeble, possessed of no strength, O untouched Mother of the eternal King, will always exalt you and him who was born from you, the King and Lord of the heavens, while we are singing together in repeated odes; we will exalt you because our brother Theophilus perished, dying on account of sin, but, after he perished, he lived again through you, holy Virgin."

When he had spoken these things, he burned the cursed charter and then eagerly completed the mystery of the Mass. When he had finished this, the face of the vicar shone with a miraculous splendor like the rising of Phoebus, so that the radiant splendor of his heart and the brightness of his soul were made manifest through his brilliant face. Thereupon, the people standing around, touched by great fear, began to sound their thundering thanks to the One enthroned on high, whom it pleased to demonstrate the worth of this venerable man. Theophilus, indeed, going immediately to that holy chapel where he had earned the gift of celestial mercy, was seized with ill health in his frail body, his sickness increasing over the course of three days. His spirit ascended rejoicing to the ethereal palace, freed from the prison of corruptible flesh and supported by the aid of our lady, holy Mary. Needless to say, his dead body, by an effort of the people, was properly buried with the greatest honor on the very spot where he obtained the forgiveness he had sought by his weeping.

Such was the end of that desperate and sinful man, who learned to weep for his own faults and strove to punish himself with appropriate lamentations. So let there be praise and glory to Christ for all ages, he who laid low the ancient

plasma suae dextrae rapiens serpentis ab ore,
ipsius et dulci constet laus alma parenti,
quae pie solamen misero iam contulit. Amen.

<Appendix: Benedictio ad mensam>

Unicus Altithroni genitus retro tempora mundi,
qui miserans hominis descendit ab arce Parentis
et carnis veram sumpsit de Virgine formam,
virginis ut gustum primae deleret amarum,
consecret appositae nobis pie fercula mensae
has faciendo dapes gustantibus esse salubres.
Quod sumus et quod gustamus vel quicquid agamus,
dextera Factoris benedicat cuncta regentis.

enemy of the human race, snatching the creation of his own right hand from the serpent's mouth, and let there be gracious praise for his sweet mother, who in her kindness at that time brought consolation to this poor man. Amen.

Appendix: Blessing at Mealtime

May the only child, born of the One enthroned on high before the ages of the world began, who pitying mankind descended from the citadel of his Father and took the true form of flesh from the Virgin, so that he could destroy the bitter taste of the first virgin, may he graciously consecrate the dishes of the table set before us, making this feast healthful for those tasting it. Whatever we are, and whatever we taste, or whatever we may do, may the right hand of the Creator who rules everything bless it.

<Conversio cuiusdam iuvenis desperati per sanctum Basilium episcopum>

<Prologus 2. Ad Gerbergam abbatissam>

En tibi versiculos, Gerberg, fero, domna, novellos
iungens praescriptis carmina carminulis,
qualiter et veniam meruit scelerosus amandam
congaudens modulis succino dactylicis.
Spernere quos noli, nimium cum sint vitiosi,
sed lauda miti pectore facta Dei!

<Prefatio>

Qui velit exemplum veniae comprendere certum
necnon larga Dei peitatis munera magni,
pectore versiculos submisso perlegat istos
nec fragilem vilis sexum spernat mulieris,
quae fragili modulos calamo cantaverat istos.
Sed mage caelestem Christi laudet pietatem,
qui non vult digna peccantes perdere poena,
sed plus perpetuae conversos reddere vitae:
gaudens gaudebit, quod verum stare probabit,
quisquis praesentem perscrutatur rationem.

Tempore Basilius quo vir virtutibus almus
rexerat Ecclesiam iusto moderamine sanctam,

The Conversion of a Certain Desperate Young Man by Saint Basil the Bishop

Prologue 2. To Abbess Gerberga

Look! I bring you new little verses, Mistress Gerberga, appending these poems to the little poems I wrote before, and I sing joyously in dactylic meter of how a wicked man earned the forgiveness he desired. Do not despise these little verses, full of errors though they be, but praise God's works with a gentle heart!

Preface

Whoever may choose to learn about an unambiguous example of forgiveness and about the generous gifts of our magnificent God's mercy, should read these little verses with a humble heart and should not despise the frail sex of the simple woman who composed these songs with her frail pen. But rather, that person should praise the heavenly mercy of Christ, who does not want to destroy sinners with deserved punishment, but rather wants to return them, restored, to eternal life: whoever examines the present account will joyfully rejoice that it proves to be true.

At the time when Basil, a man revered for his virtues, ruled the holy Church with just moderation, having acquired the

sedem rectoris sortitus Cesariensis,
vir satis illustris degebat partibus illis,
nomine Proterius, cunctae plebi venerandus,
nobilitate potens, opibus rerum quoque pollens.
Unica feminei sexus proles fuit illi
(nec alius substantiolae mansit sibi magnae
heres), quam certe tenero dilexit amore.
Affectuque pio necnon pietate paterna
optans plus animam natae numquam morituram
ornari gemmis perfectae virginitatis,
quam corpus pompa mundi mortale caduca,
curavit sacris ipsam sociare puellis,
quae, consignatae Christo velamine sacro,
coenobii claustris pariter servantur in artis.
  Auctor sed scelerum, qui decepit protoplastum,
detestando viri votum laudabile iusti
ipsius proprium fecit fervescere servum
in supradictae dementer amore puellae.
Qui nimis infelix spiculis perfossus amoris,
quo magis ardescit, tanto plus corde tabescit,
indignum se coniugio meminit quia tanto,
nec audet nudare novum cordis cruciatum.
Tandem namque magum quaerens invenerat unum,
secretum cui tristitiae monstravit amarae
promittens illi non parvi dona lucelli,
si teneram prolis mentem proprii senioris
eius servili iam conglutinasset amori.
Cui mox perversus fraudis dicebat amicus,
"Nam fateor tantae non me valitudinis esse,
ut servo propriae iungam consortia domnae.
Sed, si rite meo satagis parere magistro,

episcopal see of Caesarea, a most distinguished man was living in those parts, Proterius by name, respected by all the people, mighty in nobility, and notable also for the wealth of his estate. He had one child, of the feminine sex (and there remained no other heir to his vast little piece of property), whom he certainly cherished with a tender love. And with kindly affection and paternal kindness, wanting the undying soul of his daughter to be adorned by the jewels of perfect virginity more than he wanted her mortal body to be adorned by the perishable pomp of the world, he took care that she join in association with the holy maidens, who, having been marked out for Christ by their sacred veil, were protected together within the narrow cloisters of a monastery.

But that author of crimes, who deceived the first-made man, detesting the praiseworthy vow of this just man Proterius, made one of the man's own slaves burn crazily with love for the aforementioned girl. This most unfortunate slave was pierced by the pricks of love; the more he blazed, the more he withered in his heart, because he was aware that he was unworthy of such a marriage, and he did not dare to expose this strange torturing of his heart. In the end, then, seeking out a sorcerer, he found one and indicated the secret of his bitter sadness to him, promising the sorcerer gifts of no small value, if he could bind fast the tender heart of his noble lord's daughter to a servant's love. To him the corrupted friend of deceitfulness then said, "I certainly confess that I do not have sufficient strength to join a slave in marriage to his own mistress. But, if you duly make an effort to

qui princeps aeternarum constat tenebrarum,
ipse potest certe complere tuum cito velle,
si post haec Christi nomen non vis venerari."
Cui male caecatus bacchanti corde misellus
se consensurum monitis promiserat istis.
Tunc magus ista suo mandat scribendo magistro:
"Princeps inferni, regnator magne profundi,
condecet ergo tuos semper temptare ministros,
si possint aliquos fontis baptismate lotos
assignare tibi subtractos de grege Christi,
ut, quae te sequitur, semper pars multiplicetur.
Hinc tibi namque virum misi gaudens satis istum,
eius propositum quo mox complendo secretum
ipsum discipulum facias tibi rite futurum."
Hanc ita perscriptam misero dederat quoque chartam
. . .
supra gentilis tumulum sub tempore noctis
. . .
Quod mox praeceptum <miser> amplectens male suasum
gaudens tendebat, quo se magus ire iubebat,
auxilium veteris supplex orando draconis,
interitum praebere suis qui temptat amicis.
Nec mora, tartarei cursim venere ministri
errantemque satis laeti duxere maligni
mox ad concilium crudele tenebricolarum.
Illic inventor sceleris cunctae quoque fraudis,
damnandus damnandarum princeps legionum,
consedit medius, corvino milite saeptus,
tendens incautis laqueos clam calliditatis.
Necnon insidias evolvens ante repertas
inquirit, scelerum faceret quid quisque suorum.

obey my master, who is the prince of eternal darkness, he can certainly fulfill your wish swiftly, if you are willing not to venerate the name of Christ in the future."

The poor slave, painfully blinded in his raving heart, promised he would consent to this advice. Then the sorcerer, writing to his master, communicates the following: "Prince of hell, great ruler of the abyss, it is right, then, that your ministers constantly explore whether they can enroll in your cause any of those who were washed in the font of baptism, having snatched them from the flock of Christ, so that the ranks of your followers may always be increased. For this reason, assuredly, I am delighted to send you this man, so that swiftly fulfilling his secret proposal, you may rightfully make him your future disciple." This document so inscribed, he had also given to the poor slave . . . over the tomb of a pagan at nighttime . . . Then the poor slave, embracing the order wickedly enjoined upon him, happily went where the sorcerer commanded him to go, praying as a suppliant for the aid of the ancient serpent, who attempts to bring death to his friends. Without delay the hellish ministers came running, and very happy in their wickedness, they soon led the sinner away to the savage assembly of the denizens of darkness. There the inventor of crime and of all deceit, the damnable prince of the damnable legions, sat among them, surrounded by his raven-black army, secretly setting his traps of trickery for the unwary. And revealing the traps he had previously devised, he asked what crimes each of his associates had committed.

Scilicet ut litteras perscrutatur sibi missas,
utitur his verbis, frendens velut ira leonis,
perterrendo virum saeva ratione misellum:
"Numquam Christicolae permansistis mihi fidi,
sed mox ut vestrum complevi velle iucundum,
protinus ad vestrum fugistis denique Christum,
me detestando penitus post munera tanta,
credentes talis certe Christum pietatis,
ut veniam nulli vellet tardare petenti,
reddere conversum mihimet nec post scelus ullum.
Quapropter domini natae complexibus uti
si cupias licito, Christum prius ore negato
Christicolisque datum Christi baptisma sacratum,
scilicet et mecum te velle fatere per aevum
poenis inferni permansuris cruciari;
hincque tuis manibus scriptam mihi porrige chartam:
ostendamque citus, quantum possit mea virtus."

His mox infelix servus monitis male captus
scribebat proprium ridenti pectore damnum,
interitusque sui causam taetro dedit hosti.
Qui mox damnando nimium gaudens super illo
laeto tartareos emisit corde ministros,
virginis ut miserae mentem facerent in amore
incesto proprii citius fervescere servi.

Ut mens blandiciis fragilis pulsatur amoris,
exclamat subito magna de stirpe creata,
optans praestari sibimet consortia servi,
atque patri proprio profudit talia verba:
"Iam miserere tuae, genitor dulcissime, natae
et citius meme iuveni, quem diligo, trade,
ne moriar tristis languens per taedia cordis."

Indeed, as he was scrutinizing the letter sent to him, he employed these words, growling like an angry lion, terrifying that poor little man in a savage manner: "You Christians never remain faithful to me, but as soon as I have granted the wish you desire, you instantly flee again to your Christ, cursing me utterly after receiving great rewards, believing with certainty that Christ is so merciful that he will not delay giving forgiveness to anyone seeking it, nor surrender to me any convert after his crime. For this reason, if lawfully
enjoying the embraces of your lord-master's daughter is 67
what you desire, first verbally deny Christ and the sacred 91
baptism of Christ that is given to Christians, and, of course, profess that you wish to be tortured along with me through eternity in the lasting punishments of hell, and then give me a document signed by your own hands, and I will quickly show you how much my power can accomplish."

Straightaway the unfortunate slave, badly taken in by this advice, signed off on his own destruction with a smiling heart, and he gave the vile enemy the means of destroying him. The enemy then, very happy about this man who was destined to be damned, with a glad heart sent forth his hellish ministers, so that they could swiftly make the heart of the pitiful maiden start burning with unchaste love for her own slave.

When her fragile heart was struck by the enticements of love, suddenly the girl born of noble stock cried out, desiring that marriage to a slave be arranged for her, and she poured out the following words to her father: "Now pity your daughter, O sweetest father, and hand me over very quickly to the boy whom I love, lest I perish, withering from the distress of a forlorn heart."

His pater auditis lacrimis dicebat amaris,
"Heu, heu, quid pateris vetuli spes unica patris?
Dic, rogo, quis verbis te decepit male blandis,
vel quis blandiciis circumvenit simulatis?
Nonne tibi patriam reddi cupiendo supernam
sponso caelesti Christo te denique vovi,
hunc casta solum coleres quo mente per aevum,
illius et laudes cum caelicolis resonares
addita virgineis mortis post vincula turmis?
Et tu lascivi fervescis amore famelli!
At nunc submissa, soboles mea, voce rogabo,
finem stultitiae pergas ut reddere tantae,
ne genus omne tuum male confundas generosum.
Si tamen in coepto temptas durare maligno,
turpiter absque mora peries, dulcissima proles."
Quae nam consilium penitus spernendo paternum,
vultu mordaci proprio dixit genitori,
"Si complere meum tardabis denique votum,
comperies caram citius prolem morituram."
Tunc senior, non sponte, minis devictus amaris
tradiderat sobolis servo consortia dulcis,
condonans substantiolam pariter pretiosam
ipsis. Hinc animo natae dicebat amaro,
"Infelix non felicis tu nata parentis,
dedecus atque dolor matris temet parientis,
totius et nostri generis confusio turpis,
congaude iam nunc servo miserae tibi caro,
et post aeternis poenis maerens capieris."
Tali coniugio Satanae cum fraude peracto,
condoluit Christus mundi salvator amandus
quos pius effusa salvavit sanguinis unda,

When her father heard these things, he said with bitter tears, "Ah me, ah me, what is happening to you, O one and only hope of your aged father? Tell me, I beg you, who has deceived you with his wickedly enticing words, indeed, who has beguiled you with counterfeit enticements? Wasn't it from my desire that the fatherland on high be granted to you, that I accordingly dedicated you to Christ, the celestial bridegroom, so that you might worship him alone with a chaste heart forever, and sing his praises along with the angels when you have been added to the virgin choirs after the chains of death? And you start burning with love for a lecherous little slave! But now I beg you, my child, in a humble voice, to stir yourself and put an end to this great stupidity, so that you not wickedly embarrass your entire noble family. But if you attempt to persist in this wicked enterprise, you will perish shamefully without delay, my sweetest child."

But she, utterly rejecting this paternal advice, said to her father with a caustic look on her face, "If you are slow, in the end, in fulfilling my wish, you will very quickly find that your dear child is dying." Then the elderly man, contrary to his wishes, defeated by these bitter threats, arranged the marriage of his sweet child to a slave, granting likewise a precious share of his property to them. So, in bitter spirits, he said to his daughter, "You unlucky daughter of no lucky parent, you disgrace and pain of the mother who bore you, you vile embarrassment of our entire family, enjoy now while you can that slave so dear to you, poor wretch, and afterward, grieving, you will be taken to eternal punishments."

When the marriage had been concluded with such treachery of Satan, Christ, the beloved savior of the world, was pained that those whom he had mercifully saved with the

hostis sub diri vinclis captos retineri.
Et placet auxilium lapsis praestare benignum.
Scilicet erranti mox narratur mulieri,
quod non catholicus fuerit coniunx miser eius,
nec limen templi vellet pede tangere sancti,
se quia serpentis iuri tradebat avari
sacra negans rectae fidei nomen quoque Christi.
Quae se deceptam cognoscens esse misellam
auribus intentis ut sensit verba loquentis,
in terram cecidit membris tremefacta solutis,
eruit et proprios summo de vertice pilos
necnon verberibus pulsavit sedulo pectus
cum lacrimis tales spargens super aethera voces:
"Quisquis praedulces non vult audire parentes,
numquam salvatur, quod hac ratione probatur.
Heu, heu, splendorem diei cur nata recepi?
Vel cur continuo non sum concessa sepulchro,
infelix foveam caderem ne mortis in atram?"
Haec dum tristitia dicebat continuata,
coniunx illius subito venit scelerosus
et de se falsas iuravit res fore dictas.
Quae mox constanti respondit voce neganti:
"Si reus ingentis culpae iam denique non sis,
laetus ad ecclesiam mecum cras pergito sanctam
illic et sanctae celebra sollemnia missae!"
Qua mox devictus iusta ratione misellus
causam commissi narravit namque piacli.
Illaque mollitiem iam deponens muliebrem
et sumens vires prudenti corde viriles,
mox ad Basilium currebat namque beatum,
necnon vestigiis coram prostrata sacratis

poured-out stream of his blood were held captive under the chains of the dire enemy. And it pleased him to offer gracious assistance to the fallen. Namely, it was soon reported to the sinful woman that her wretched husband was not a true believer, and he did not wish to touch the threshold of the sacred temple, because he had placed himself under the authority of the greedy serpent, denying the sacraments of the proper faith and also the name of Christ.

Realizing that she had been wretchedly deceived when she heard with attentive ears the speaker's words, she fell to the ground trembling with lifeless limbs, and tore out the hair from the top of her head, and earnestly pounded her chest with blows, tearfully scattering to the heavens cries such as these: "Whoever does not wish to listen to his sweet parents will never be saved, which is proven in this case. Ah me, ah me, why have I been born and received the light of day? Or why was I not consigned straightaway to the grave, so that I, unlucky one, would not fall into the black snare of death?"

While she was saying these things in endless sadness, her sinful husband suddenly came and swore that these things were said falsely about him. She immediately responded in a firm voice to him as he was making this denial: "If you are not, then, guilty at the present time of a great crime, go happily tomorrow with me to the sacred church and there take part in the solemnities of holy Mass!" Immediately overcome by this just plan, the poor slave told her the reason why he had, in fact, committed this sin. And she, now putting aside her womanly softness and acquiring manly strength in her wise heart, assuredly rushed straightaway to blessed Basil, and prostrate before his sacred feet employed

utitur his verbis turbato pectore fusis:
“Sancte Dei, clemens nobis succurre misellis
et trahe de taetris saevi nos faucibus hostis,
qui nostras fragiles iactat se perdere mentes!”
Cumque modum culpae denudavit sibi tantae,
vertitur ad servum praesul Domini scelerosum
ac coepit verbis illum rogitare benignis,
post scelus ad Christum vellet si vertere sensum.
Qui se salvari desperans dixerat illi,
“Si posset fieri, voluissem mente libenti.
Sed restat menti sceleris res facta volenti,
me quia per litteras hosti dederam male scriptas,
et nomen Christi caecato corde negavi.”
Ad quem vir Domini, “Curam tibi fingere noli,
ceu tibi sit veniae penitus spes dempta petendae.
Unicus ergo Patris, iudex mitissimus orbis,
ad se conversum qui numquam respuit ullum,
si defles culpam, gaudet praestare medelam.
Hinc iam mortiferum peccati linque profundum,
necnon ad certum pietatis confuge portum;
ad se tendentes qui salvos suscipit omnes.”
His igitur miserum monitis correxit homullum
necnon sponte suo nigro conclusit in antro,
illic ut sordes licito defleret enormes.
Post tres ergo dies iterum veniebat ad illum,
inquirens talem si posset ferre laborem.
Qui lassus nimium verbis responderat istis:
“Poenas spirituum patior vix namque nigrorum,
me quia continuis attrectant namque flagellis

these words, poured out from her troubled heart: "Holy man of God, mercifully aid us, poor wretches, and drag us from the vile jaws of the savage enemy, who boasts that he is destroying our fragile hearts!" And when she had exposed to him the extent of that great fault, the Lord's bishop turned to the criminal slave and began to ask him in kindly words whether he wished to turn his heart toward Christ after this crime. The slave, despairing that he could be saved, said to him, "If that could happen, I would have wished it with a willing heart. But the act of crime I committed stands firm against my wishful heart, for I have given myself to the enemy through a wickedly signed letter, and I have denied the name of Christ with a blinded heart."

To him the man of the Lord said, "Don't invent for yourself a reason for concern, as though the hope of seeking forgiveness had been entirely taken from you. Indeed, the only-begotten of the Father, the most lenient judge of the world, who never rejected anyone who converted to him, is happy to provide a remedy, if you repent of your fault. So now leave behind the lethal ocean of your sin, and flee to the certain haven of his mercy, which safely receives all who seek it." He reproved, therefore, the wretched little man by these admonitions, and he deliberately enclosed him in his own dark chamber, so that there he could lawfully weep over his enormous defilement.

After three days, then, Basil came again to him, asking if he was able to tolerate such hardship. The slave, quite exhausted, responded in these words: "Indeed, I can scarcely endure the punishments of the black spirits because they wear me down, in fact, with endless beatings, and they

atque petunt iaculis lapidum saepissime duris.
Insuper opprobriis opponunt semper amaris,
quod non invitus pridem sed gratis adirem
illos, ipsorum sine vi me dans dicioni."
Tunc animae medicus languescentis bene doctus
lassatum refici iussit statimque recessit.
Post tempus parvum veniebat denique rursum
quaerens, obscuro quid tunc pateretur in antro.
Qui dixit, "Certe melius valeo, pater alme,
longius horribiles tantum quia sentio voces."
Hinc praesul laetus secreto pectore factus
egreditur iuxta morem faciendo priorem.
Tandem post spatium veniens quadraginta dierum,
in quis peccatum lapsus deflevit amarum,
invenit laetum, quem credebat fore maestum.
Et cum laetitiam miraretur sibi caram,
peccator lacrimis iam mundatus bene largis
et certus veniae sancto dicebat amandae,
"Spero quidem per te me salvari, pater alme,
in somnis quia te vidi luctamen inire
pro me cum saevo necnon serpente maligno,
quem tu vicisti subito virtute superna."
Auribus intentis ut sensit verba loquentis
antistes, laudem Christi cecinit pietati
extraxitque loco captivi membra nigello,
et locat in propria noctis sub tempore cella,
quae fuit ecclesiae lateri coniuncta sacratae.
Illic et plebem iussit coire fidelem,
ut pariter preculis pernoctarent studiosis,
quo bonus errantem per consuetam pietatem

attack me incessantly with hard missiles of stone. Furthermore, they accuse me endlessly in bitter reproaches of having, in former times, not unwillingly but freely, approached them, giving myself into their power unforced."

Then that very learned healer of the ailing soul ordered that the exhausted man be fed, and he immediately departed. Then, after a short time, Basil came again, asking what the slave was suffering at that time in the dark chamber. He replied, "Assuredly, dear father, I am much stronger, because I hear the horrible voices only in the distance." Then the bishop, delighted deep in his heart, departed, acting according to his usual manner. Finally coming again after the space of forty days, during which the fallen man had wept over his bitter sin, he found the man happy whom he had expected would be sad. And while Basil was marveling at this happiness, attained at such a cost, the sinner, already well cleansed by bountiful tears and certain of loving forgiveness, said to the holy man, "I am confident indeed, dear father, that I am being saved through you, because in my dreams I saw you enter the battle with the savage and evil serpent on my behalf, and you conquered him quickly with heavenly strength."

When with attentive ears the bishop understood the speaker's words, he sang the praises of Christ's mercy and extracted the limbs of the captive from that dismal place, and when night was upon them, he placed him in a proper cell, which was joined to the side of the sacred church. There he ordered the faithful people to come together, so that they also might pass the night in earnest prayers, in order that the good shepherd through his accustomed mercy

pastor ovem turmis proprii iunxisset ovilis.
Ortus cumque nigras noctis sol expulit umbras,
dextra praedicti comprensa praesul homulli
intrat in ecclesiam secum quoque duxerat ipsum.
Ut limen sacris tetigit venerabile plantis,
affuit insidiis latitans clam daemon amaris
attraxitque virum magna vi denique rursum
illius arrepta secreta fraude sinistra.
Ad quem Basilius forti mandamine functus:
"Inprobe fur, Regis facturam redde perennis
et furto raptam victus cito desere praedam!"
Cui mox communis cunctorum dixerat hostis
perversis vacuas implens latratibus auras,
"Cur satagis proprium mihimet vi tollere servum?
Qui sua sponte meis submisit colla catenis.
Chartam percerte, mihimet quam reddidit ipse,
tempore iudicii Christo monstrabo futuri."
Cui sanctus rursum reddebat tale responsum:
"Ipsius Christi praecepto, iudicis aequi,
reddere litterulas spero te protinus ipsas."
His igitur dictis, oravit turba fidelis
Altithronum, preculis devoto pectore fusis,
fidum pastorem quo confortaret in hostem.
Nec mora, de summo cecidit scriptura dolosa
ante pedes sancti necnon pastoris amandi.
Tunc plebs corde pio gaudens cum praesule digno
sparsit adusque polum voces cum carmine laudum,
conlaudens Christum solita pietate benignum,

might unite this wandering sheep with the throngs in his own sheepfold. And when the sun had risen and dispelled the black shadows of night, the bishop, seizing the right hand of the aforementioned little man, entered into the church and led that man along with him.

When he touched the venerable threshold with his sacred feet, the demon was there, lurking unseen with his bitter snares, and he pulled the man again to himself, then, with great force, after grabbing his left hand in secret treachery. Basil delivered a strong command to this demon: "Wicked thief, return the creation of the eternal King, and abandon at once in defeat the booty you thievishly plundered!" To him then the common enemy of all, filling the empty breezes with perverse howling, said, "Why do you struggle to take my own slave from me by force? He submitted his neck to my chains of his own free will. That document, most certainly, which he himself gave to me, I will show to Christ at the time of the judgment that is coming."

To him the holy man again gave a response as follows: "By order of this same Christ, the impartial judge, I am confident you will at once surrender those very same letters." At these words, therefore, the faithful crowd asked the One enthroned on high, pouring out prayers from their devout breasts, to strengthen the faithful shepherd against the enemy. Without delay, that grievous document fell from on high at the feet of the holy and beloved shepherd.

Then the people, rejoicing in their pious hearts, along with the worthy bishop spread their voices to the heavens in a song of praise, in unison praising Christ, bountiful in his accustomed mercy, who had dragged back the captive out of

qui captum veteris retraxit ab ore leonis.
Nos quoque plaudentes spargamus ad aethera voces
laudantes Dominum ridenti pectore Christum,
qui nobis clemens talem veniae tribuit spem.
Ipsi namque decus soli, victoria, virtus,
laudum cantamen maneatque perenniter. Amen.

the mouth of the ancient lion. Let us too spread our applauding voices to the skies, praising with a smiling heart our Lord Christ, who has mercifully provided such hope of forgiveness to us. To this same One alone, indeed, may there remain honor, victory, power, and the chanting of praise forever. Amen.

Passio sancti Dionysii egregii martyris

Dum factor summae, mediae rationis et imae
in cruce supplicium mortis pateretur amarum,
orbem nocturnae circumduxere tenebrae;
et sol deposito radii splendore sereni
exsequias Domini celebrat famulamine tristi.
Quo mox astrologus viso Dionysius almus,
qui tunc Memphitidis artem discebat in oris,
quae docet astrorum motus solis quoque cursum,
obstupuit; libris coepitque requirere lectis,
si tunc eclipsis posset consistere solis.
Ast ubi non solitas sensit magus esse tenebras,
descripsisse diem dignum ducebat et annum
non dubitans designari quid forte stupendi,
quod post mysterium declarasset tenebrarum.
Coniectatque deum signis testantibus almis
hactenus ignotum mundo mox esse probandum.
Ast ubi de rivis prefatae debrius artis
Athenas petiit, sedem patriamque revisit.
Inter stultorum simulacra profana deorum
culte constructam poni praeceperat aram
hanc ipsam titulis decernens congrue pictis

The Passion of Saint Denis, an Outstanding Martyr

While the creator of what is highest, lowest, and in between was suffering the bitter penalty of death on the cross, nocturnal shadows encompassed the world; and the sun, after shedding the splendor of its serene shining, celebrated the funeral rites of the Lord in mournful service. Then, when he saw this, the revered astrologer Denis, who was at that time on the shores of Memphis, studying the discipline which teaches the motions of the stars and the course of the sun, was amazed; and he began to investigate in the books he had gathered whether an eclipse of the sun could be taking place at that time. But when this wise man understood that these were not ordinary shadows, he thought it worthwhile to write down the day and the year, having no doubt that something amazing was, perchance, being signaled, which afterward would explain the mystery of the shadows. And he conjectured that through the testimony of these propitious signs a god till then unknown would soon be revealed to the world. Moreover, when he was intoxicated by the rivers of that discipline mentioned above, that is, astronomy, he went to Athens and revisited his ancestral home. Among the profane statues of their senseless gods he ordered that an elegantly constructed altar be set up, stipulating that this same altar ought to be appropriately consecrated with a

ignoti sub honore dei debere sacrari.
Quam doctor Paulus cum conspexisset opimus,
quis sit hic ignotus, verbis rogitabat amicis.
Urbis cui primus Dionysius ipse beatus
exposuit causam, pro qua construxerat aram.
Et sic alternis certantibus ergo loquelis,
qui fuit incredulus, fidei cessit bene victus.
   Post haec egressus caeco dat lumina Paulus
quem properare quidem citius praecepit in urbem.
Hunc functum cernens praedictus lumine princeps,
et credens signo divino numine facto,
festinat subito Damari cum coniuge cara
pergere, quo Paulum cognoverat esse beatum,
ipsius multa iuris comitante caterva.
Qui pariter <cuncti> sacro baptismate tincti
prorsus delicti mundantur sorde veterni.
Et, qui dux plebis fuerat simulacra colentis,
praesul catholico praeponitur ergo popello.
   Hic praesul factus, mira bonitate decorus,
sedulus officium bene complevit sibi iunctum
absentes scriptis, praesentes denique dictis
ad verae cultum fidei ducendo sequendum.
Nam quondam pergens semen Verbi quoque spargens,
hospes iam vergente die fertur petiisse
sanctum presbyterum Cretensem nomine Carpum.
Qui male tristitia conturbabatur amara
necnon plus licito succensa ferbuit ira,
quidam gentilis quia perversis suadelis
fecit Christicolam fidei sacra spernere quendam.
Hunc ut presbyterum praesul sensit fore maestum,

written inscription in honor of the unknown god. When the glorious teacher Paul saw it, he asked in amicable words who this unknown god was. The blessed Denis himself, the leader of the city, explained to him the reason why he had constructed this altar. And so, while they were competing in arguments back and forth, this man who had been a nonbeliever yielded to the faith, positively overwhelmed.

Leaving afterward, Paul gave sight to a blind man and indeed ordered him to go very quickly to the city. The aforementioned leader of the city, Denis, observing that this man had obtained sight, and believing this miracle happened by divine will, hastened immediately to travel with his beloved wife Damaris to where he knew the blessed Paul was, and he was accompanied by a large group of those under his jurisdiction. Together they were all immersed in holy baptism, and they were utterly cleansed of the filth of the ancient sin. And the man who had been the leader of a people worshipping statues, was then appointed bishop over a Christian population.

This man, distinguished in his wondrous goodness, having become bishop, energetically and ably fulfilled the office entrusted to him, leading those who were absent by his writings and those present by his words, accordingly, to follow the worship of the true faith. Indeed, once while traveling and spreading the seed of the Word, when the day was already sinking toward the horizon, he is said as a guest to have sought out a holy priest, a Cretan named Carpus. This man was badly disturbed by a bitter rancor, and he burned with a wrath unjustly inflamed, because a particular pagan, using perverse arguments, had made a certain Christian reject the sacraments of the faith. When the bishop sensed

causam tristitiae verbis quaerebat amicis;
et tristem monitis blande mulcendo benignis
suaserat ut nimiam cordis deponeret iram
et pro damnandis exoraret scelerosis,
qui cito conversi Christoque reconciliati,
eius perciperent mitis munus pietatis.
Admonuitque crebro nulli debere negari
spem veniae, proprium vellet si flere reatum.
Sed qui tristitiae studuit spreta pietate,
econtra frendens cordisque furore tabescens
apposuit miseris duris maledicere verbis,
protestans illos neutra dignos fore vita,
qui vixisse Deo praesumpsissent sine vero.
Hac tam tristificia tandem ratione peracta
mente satis tristi componit membra quieti.
Nec mora, monstratur caelis illi patefactis
visio, quae fluctus animi compescuit eius.
Scilicet Altithronum miro splendore coruscum
viderat angelicis septum residere ministris,
de caeloque rogum raptim descendere magnum,
ceu foret emissus scelerum vindex aliquorum.
Hinc terras oculis rursum lustrando reflexis,
horrendum baratrum conspexit hiare deorsum,
anguibus impletum variis poenisque refertum.
Supra quod miseri plantis lapsantibus illi
haerebant ergo flentes in litore summo.
Egressi quoque serpentes illos cruciantes
cogebant secum baratrum penetrare profundum.
Quo viso Carpus maiore furore repletus
deflet, quod miseri non essent praecipitati,

that this priest was dejected, he asked in friendly words the cause of his despondency; and gently calming the sad man with kind admonitions, he urged him to put aside the inordinate anger of his heart and to pray for the doomed sinners, so that, swiftly converted and reconciled to Christ, they might receive the gift of his gentle mercy. And he repeatedly admonished the priest that the hope of forgiveness should be denied to no one, if that person were willing to weep for his sins. But the priest persisted in his rancor, rejecting kindness, and, on the contrary, gnashing his teeth and consumed by the rage in his heart, he put curses on the wretched sinners in harsh words, protesting that they who had presumed to live apart from the true God deserved neither the present life nor the future one. When this utterly depressing business was finally finished, he put his limbs to rest with a very sad heart. Without delay, the heavens opened up and a vision was revealed to him, which calmed the waves of his soul. Namely, he saw seated there the One enthroned on high, shining with wondrous splendor, surrounded by his angelic ministers; and he saw a great pyre descend violently from heaven, as though it had been sent out as an avenger of sins of some sort. From there, scanning the earth again with his eyes turned back downward, he saw a horrendous abyss gaping open below him, filled with snakes and brimming with all manner of punishments. At the top of this abyss the wretched men, their feet already slipping, were consequently holding on tightly, wailing on its highest edge. And snakes which were emerging from it compelled those tortured men to enter that vast abyss along with them. When he saw this, Carpus, filled with a greater madness, bemoaned that these wretches were not cast headlong into it, and again

voceque confusa rursum repetens maledicta,
ut divina reos, orat, mox ultio perdat.
Dixerat et Iesum solita pietate benignum
de summo caeli solio promptum misereri
. . .
infit non mitem Carpi causando dolorem:
"Percute, si possis, contra me, Carpe, rebellis,
qui cupis interitum sitienter adesse reorum.
En ego sum, caeli rector mortisque peremptor,
humana rursus pro gente pati pie promptus,
si non salvari possunt aliter scelerosi,
qui post commissum discunt deflere reatum.
Nec leve duco meae dextrae iam plasma perire,
quod pulchrum feci, quod corruptum reparavi.
Elige nunc dulcem vel sectando pietatem
in caelo mecum semper regnare per aevum,
vel per saevitiam dirae mentis male duram
supplicio baratri tradi sine fine profundi."
His nimium iustus monitis vir mansuefactus
exemplum cunctis imitandae fit pietatis.

Post haec summorum fama clarus meritorum
praesul disposuit Romam petiisse superbam,
optans cum Petro Paulo pariterque magistro
nomine pro Christi se mox impendere morti.
Palmam martyrii sed sumpserunt prius illi,
quam portas Romae veniens intraverat ipse;
discipulusque Petri Clemens venerabilis orbi
sedis apostolicae culmen rexit satis apte.
Qui nam pontificem pie suscepit venientem
illum condigne summoque colebat amore.
Denique post spatium decursi temporis amplum,

repeating his curses with a troubled voice, he prayed that divine vengeance immediately destroy the guilty. He said also that Jesus, gracious in his accustomed mercy, ready from the high throne of heaven to show mercy . . . Jesus began as follows, objecting to the harsh indignation of Carpus: "Strike against me, if you can, Carpus, you rebel, you who so thirstily desire the destruction of the guilty. Look, I am I, the ruler of the heaven and the destroyer of death, ready again to suffer mercifully for the human race, if those sinners who have learned to weep after committing a crime cannot be saved in any other way. And I do not think it unimportant if something fashioned by my hand perishes, something I made beautiful, something I restored when it was corrupted. Choose now either to rule ever at my side in heaven, administering sweet mercy through the ages, or to be handed over, on account of the wickedly harsh savagery of your dreadful heart, to the endless punishment of the profound abyss." The very just man, softened by these admonitions, became an example of piety for all to imitate.

Afterward the bishop, illustrious from the fame of his supreme merits, decided to travel to mighty Rome, choosing along with Peter and equally with his teacher Paul, to offer straightaway to die in the name of Christ. But they had received the palm of martyrdom before he himself had arrived and entered the gates of Rome; and Clement, venerable before the world, a disciple of Peter's, was ruling the summit of the apostolic see very suitably. He certainly received the arriving bishop in a kindly manner and celebrated him worthily with the greatest love. Finally, after a considerable

quo servi Domini commanserunt venerandi,
cum iam caelestis pietas mitissima Regis
aeternae radio lucis voluisset opimo
errorum tenebras veterum discindere nigras
quis tunc occiduae partes fuerant male cinctae,
papa prior monitus divino Flamine sanctus
pontifici verbis digno suadebat amicis
semina divini per gentes spargere Verbi.
"En," ait, "O miles Christi, frater Dionysi,
magna seges Domini crescit per climata mundi
praebens innumeras maturae messis aristas;
instantes messi sed constant oppido pauci.
Hinc tu, sacrorum bibulus qui fonte librorum
constas divini sciolus quam maxime cultus,
exemplo Pauli securus perge magistri
imperio populos Christi subiungere multos.
Et tibi credo potestatem dicionis eandem
quam Christum Petro scimus credidisse magistro,
et quam suscepi successor iure magistri
conversos pie solvendi sontesquc ligandi.
Accipe nunc Gallos tibi me tradente docendos,
doctrinaeque tui signetur Gallia sorti,
quo vir apostolicus digna celebreris alumna.
Nec vereare quidem gentes intrare rebelles,
quae restant vero frendentes more ferino;
sed tibi mercedis tantum confide perennis
in Patris astrigera summi servarier aula,
quantum pro Christo tuleris patiendo doloris."
   His papae blandis praesul monitus suadelis,
occiduae fines partis festinus adivit,
moenibus atque Paris gressum mox intulit urbis,

time had passed in which these venerable servants of the Lord remained together (for the gentle mercy of the celestial King had now long since wished, by a glorious ray of eternal light, to sunder the black shadows of ancient errors that then wickedly encircled the western lands), the saintly pope, warned in advance by the divine Spirit, urged the worthy bishop in friendly words to spread the seeds of the divine Word among the gentiles. "Look," he said, "O soldier of Christ, Brother Denis, the great crop of the Lord is increasing throughout the regions of the world, providing the boundless grain of a ripe harvest; but there are exceedingly few employed in the harvest. Therefore, you who drink from the font of sacred books and are especially knowledgeable about divine worship, go forth fearlessly, following the example of the teacher Paul, to add many people to the empire of Christ. And to you I entrust the same power of authority which we know Christ entrusted to the teacher Peter, and which I duly received as the teacher's successor, the power of loosing the piously converted and of binding the sinners. Consent now to teach the Gauls, since I am delivering them to you, and let Gaul be assigned by lot to your instruction, so that you may be celebrated there as an apostolic man by that worthy pupil. And do not be afraid to go among disobedient nations, who resist the truth, growling like wild animals; but be confident that an eternal reward is being stored up for you in the starry palace of the supreme Father, a reward that is as great as the pain you will endure suffering for Christ."

The bishop, advised by the flattering encouragements of the pope, went quickly to the borders of the western world, and he soon set foot within the walls of the city of Paris, in

in qua crebro loci pro fertilitate decori
Gallorum proceres concurrunt saepius omnes.
Hic ubi divini coepit sacra semina Verbi
spargere, signorum mox exercere per illum
Christus virtutes dignabatur pie plures,
quo tanto plebis mollescere corda rebellis
ad veniam possent, quanto crebro signa viderent.

Ast ubi credentis numerus populi magis auctus
inspirante dies Christo crevisset in omnes,
infremuit super hoc veteris fraus saeva draconis,
dedignans animas sese iam perdere tantas
quas prius errorum laqueis capiebat amaris.
Hinc pater ipse doli sceleris doctorque maligni
provocat iniustum regem mox Domitianum
Christicolis edicta necis dictare ferocis.
Qui decreta per omne suum mittens mala regnum
Christi cultores morti damnaverat omnes.
Cuius praecepto Sisinnius ergo nefando
praeses consensum praebens extemplo malignum
pontificem praesentari vinctum iubet illi,
quem fore Gallorum cognovit rite magistrum.
Ac primum flagris mactatum denique duris
necnon suppliciis affectum crebro cruentis
carceris in tenebras iussit concludier atras,
ipsius condiscipulos pariter quoque binos,
quos numquam caro sors cogit abesse magistro.

Sed nec carcereis praesul praeclarus in antris
destitit obsequium Domino persolvere dignum,
sed docuit plebem studiose convenientem
ac celebrat sacrae solito sollemnia missae.
Ast ubi caelestem debebat frangere panem,
lux nova tristifico subito fulgebat in antro.

which, on a regular basis, because of the abundance of that beautiful place, all the noble Gauls frequently meet. Here, when he had begun to spread the sacred seeds of the divine Word, straightaway Christ in his mercy saw fit to perform through him many manifestations of miracles, so that the more often they saw these miracles, the more the hearts of that disobedient folk would soften toward forgiveness.

But when the growing number of people who became believers had daily increased through Christ's inspiration, the savage treachery of the ancient serpent was thereby enraged, disdainful that he should lose so many souls which, until then, he had held in the bitter snares of sins. Therefore the father of deceit himself and the master of wicked crime soon provoked the unjust ruler Domitian to issue edicts of ferocious slaughter against the Christians. He sent these evil decrees through his entire realm and condemned all the worshipers of Christ to death. To his nefarious mandate, then, the governor Sisinnius immediately gave his wicked consent and ordered that the bishop be brought before him shackled, rightly recognizing in him the teacher of the Gauls. But first he ordered that the bishop be punished with harsh beatings and then that, weakened by repeated grisly tortures, he be confined in the dark shadows of a prison, and along with him two of his disciples as well, whom fate compelled never to be away from their beloved teacher.

The illustrious bishop, however, did not stop rendering proper service to the Lord in these cavernous prisons, but he energetically taught the people assembled there, and he celebrated the solemnities of the holy Mass in the customary way. But when he ought to have been breaking the heavenly bread, a new light suddenly shone in the dreary cave.

In qua sidereae regnator splendidus aulae,
scilicet angelica pariter comitante caterva
apparens carum consolabatur alumnum;
sanctaque dans illi mulcebat famine tali:
"Accipe, care meus, mis iam venerabile corpus,
cuius mysterium tibi mox complebo secretum;
namque tui merces mecum manet optima perpes.
Hisque salus summa Patris praestatur in aula,
consentire tuis qui dant operam pie iussis.
Certa constanter servaque fidem patienter,
quo crescant celebris tibi iam praeconia laudis.
Et, quodcumque sacris a me precibus rogitabis,
impetrare mei poteris dono pietatis."
Tali laetatus fortis solamine testis
nulla timet tormenta pati pro nomine Christi.
Post haec abstracti testes de carcere terni
praecepto mox praefecti cogente superbi,
an vellent duris, rogitantur, cedere poenis.
Qui bene concordes, clara quoque voce fatentes
Patrem cum Nato necnon cum Flamine sacro
esse Deum verum solumque perenniter unum,
testantur mox malle mori pro nomine Christi
membratim quoque suppliciis scindi redivivis,
quam sua colla diis umquam submittere falsis.
Hac magis offensus praeses ratione profanus
ceu leo non modica rugiens praeceperat ira
athletis Christi cervices mox resecari
et gladiis cunctos perimi baptismate lotos.
Cedibus innumeris, ut iussit, namque peractis
praesul cum sociis iunctus trahitur venerandus
ad loca martyrii damno capitum peragendi.

In this light the splendid ruler of the starry palace, accompanied of course by a crowd of angels too, appeared and consoled his dear pupil; and giving him the sacraments he soothed him with the following speech: "Receive now, my dear man, my venerable body, whose hidden mystery I will soon fulfill for you; indeed, your greatest reward remains with me in perpetuity. And in the highest palace of my Father salvation will be bestowed upon those who piously strive to follow your commands. Fight steadfastly and preserve the faith patiently, so that the proclamations of your celebrated glory may henceforth increase for you. And whatever you may ask of me in sacred prayers, you will be able to obtain by the gift of my mercy." The brave martyr was gladdened by such consolation, and he was not afraid to suffer any tortures in the name of Christ. Soon afterward the three martyrs were taken from the prison by the compulsory order of the haughty governor, and they were asked whether they wanted to submit to these harsh punishments. They were totally in agreement with one another, and professed in a ringing voice that the Father along with the Son and with the Holy Spirit was the true God, one and only forever, and then they swore that they preferred to die in Christ's name, even torn limb by limb in repeated tortures, than ever to bow their necks to false gods. The profane governor, offended all the more by their reasoning, roared like a lion in no small fury and ordered the necks of the athletes of Christ be cut through directly and that all who had been bathed in baptism be destroyed by swords. When countless slaughters had, in fact, been carried out as he ordered, the venerable bishop, joined by his companions, was dragged to the place of his martyrdom, which was to be carried out

Qui nam gaudentes Domino laudesque canentes
pergebant prompti semet mox dedere morti.
Praesul tunc oculis sursum manibusque levatis
Altithrono tales fundebat congrue grates:
“Mi Dee, mi factor, mi clementissime rector,
qui me vitali praestans aura pie vesci,
scilicet ingenii donasti luce profundi,
quo tis secretum scrutarer mysteriorum.
Te solum laudo, te corde tenus benedico,
et tibi devotas cunctis grates ago membris
pro cunctis donis mihi collatae pietatis.
Teque precor, maiestatis Rex magne perennis,
ut dare perpetuam mihimet dignere coronam
atque meis sociis pro te iam nunc morituris.
Tuque tuum populum serva pietate paterna,
quem pascens fidei tibimet sermone nutrivi.”
His ita poscentis precibus iam rite peractis,
una discipuli sancto cum praesule bini,
poplitibus positis cervicibus atque reflexis,
ictus lictoris susceperunt ferientis.
Quorum permansit celebris confessio talis,
ut, dum praecisis siluerunt corpora collis,
palpantes linguae laudes Domino cecinere.
Truncatum quoque pontificis corpus morientis
erigitur subito nitidum splendore sereno.
Atque caput brachiis portans proprium bene firmis
descendit recto gressu de monte profundo,
in quo martyrium consummavit pretiosum.
Transiliensque viae citius duo milia durae
venit adusque locum servando corpore dignum.

by decapitation. And in fact, rejoicing and singing praises to the Lord, they went promptly to surrender themselves straightaway to death. The bishop then, with his eyes and hands raised upward, appropriately poured out to the One enthroned on high thanks of this sort: "My God, my maker, my most merciful ruler, who kindly provided that I might feed on the breath of life, you have assuredly granted with the light of your profound intellect that I might behold the secret of your mysteries. I praise you alone, I bless you from the bottom of my heart, and I give you devout thanks with all my limbs for all the gifts of mercy that have been conferred upon me. And I pray to you, great King of eternal majesty, that you see fit to give a perpetual crown to me and to my companions who are now already preparing to die for you. And you in your paternal mercy should protect your people, whom I have nourished for you, feeding them by the preaching of faith."

When these prayers of the petitioner had now been duly completed, the two disciples together with the saintly bishop, positioned on their knees and with their necks bent over, received the blows of the executioner's stroke. Their glorious confession endured to such an extent that, while their bodies fell silent after their necks were cut, their quivering tongues still sang praises to the Lord. Furthermore, the truncated body of the dying bishop suddenly stood up, shining with serene splendor. And carrying his own head in his very able arms, he descended with a steady stride from the high mountain on which he had consummated this precious martyrdom. And swiftly traversing two miles of hard road he came to a place worthy to preserve his body. As he

Quem descendentem cursuque cito gradientem
coetus angelici comitantur luce sereni
"Alleluia" Deo resonantes voce sonora.
His signis factis convenit turba fidelis
martyris atque loco venerabile corpus in ipso,
quem sibi signavit, cum post gressus requievit,
impositum tumulo veneratur honore supremo
exsequias tanti luctu celebrando patroni.
Illic pro meritis eius testis venerandis
Christus virtutes fecit clarescere signis.
Nam visus caecis, <usus> linguae quoque mutis,
auditus surdis, solidus gressusque podagris
teste precante sacro donatur crebrius illo.
Et variis aegri morbis qui debilitati
adveniunt, laeti membris redeunt renovatis.
Hic quoque non raro maestis solamina grata,
et munus veniae scelerosis fertur ab arce
his qui sacra precum profundunt vota suarum
martyris ad tumulum proprium deflendo reatum.
Cuius continuo nos intercessio sancta
commendet Christo, scelerum veniamque precando
obtineat nostris ipsum pie parcere culpis,
et partem nobis vitae praestare perennis,
quo mereamur eum laeti laudare per aevum.
Qui post dura suis semper certamina sanctis
martyribus duplicis bravium praestabit honoris,
ut, dum congaudent animae super aethera sanctae,
non minus in tumulo laetentur mortua membra
signorum titulis crebro glorificata coruscis.
Ipsi summa salus, perpes victoria, virtus,
laus, honor, imperium, semper decus omne per aevum!

was descending and moving in a swift course, angelic hosts, serene with brilliance, accompanied him, singing "Alleluia" to God in a melodious voice.

When these miracles were finished, a faithful crowd gathered and venerated with the greatest honor the venerable body of the martyr, which had been placed in a tomb at the very place he had designated for himself when he rested after his walk; they venerated him, celebrating in mourning the funeral rites of such a great patron. In that place, because of the venerable merits of this martyr, Christ made his powers shine through miracles. For sight was given on many occasions to the blind, as well as the use of the tongue to the mute, hearing to the deaf, and a firm step to the lame, when that holy martyr prayed for it. And the sick who came there, debilitated by various diseases, returned happily with their limbs restored. Here also pleasing consolations were granted not infrequently to the grieving, and the gift of forgiveness was conferred from heaven on those sinners who poured out the sacred vows of their prayers at the tomb of the martyr, weeping for their sin.

May his saintly intercession continually recommend us to Christ and, by praying for the forgiveness of sins, may it obtain his merciful pardon for our faults, and offer us a share of eternal life, whereby we might earn the right to praise him happily forever. After their hard struggles, he will always offer to his saintly martyrs the prize of double honor, so that, while their saintly souls rejoice beyond the skies, their mortal limbs will be no less happy in the tomb, repeatedly glorified by the shining distinctions of miracles. To him may there be supreme salvation, perpetual victory, strength, praise, honor, authority, glory always and forever!

Passio sanctae Agnetis virginis et martyris

Virgo, quae vanas mundi pompas ruituri
et luxus fragilis cupiens contemnere carnis,
promeruit Regis vocitari sponsa perennis.
si velit angelicae pro virginitatis honore
ipsius astrigera sponsi caelestis in aula,
addita caelicolis, nitida fulgere corona,
atque sequens Agnum carmen cantare sonorum,
conservet purae sincero cordis amore
signum laudabilis, quod portat, virginitatis.
Quae<que> caput Christo signat velamine sacro,
haereat affectu tenero constanter in illo,
ac cunctis aliis ipsum praeponat amicis.
Qui rutilans nimium forma speciosus amoena
natos cunctarum merito vincit mulierum.
Cuius amore quidem ferventes congrue pridem
perplures sacrae constanti corde puellae
elegere mori saevis poenisque necari,
quam decus insignis corrumpere virginitatis.
Inter quas Agnes, mundo celeberrima virgo,
iure sui sponsi condigna laude decori
Christi dissimilem cunctis recitando decorem
virginibus sacris eius commendat amoris
pignus. Qui genitus sacra de Virgine solus
sponsus castarum necnon decus est animarum.

The Passion of Saint Agnes the Virgin and Martyr

The virgin who wants to reject the empty pomp of this world destined to perish and the licentiousness of the feeble flesh has earned the right to be called a spouse of the eternal King. If she should wish, for the honor of angelic virginity, to shine in the starry palace of this same celestial spouse, joined to those living in heaven, with a radiant crown, and to sing a resonant song following the Lamb, let her preserve in the sincere love of a pure heart the mark of the laudable virginity which she carries. And let the virgin who marks her head for Christ with the sacred veil attach herself with tender affection constantly to him, and let her prefer him to all her other friends. He, so radiantly handsome in his pleasing beauty, rightly surpasses the sons of all women. Indeed, properly fired by his love, long ago many sacred girls with an unwavering heart chose to die and to be put to death by savage tortures, rather than corrupt the honor of their distinguished virginity. Among these girls, Agnes, the most celebrated virgin in the world, with praise that was worthy of her beautiful spouse, rightly declaring Christ's beauty unlike all others, recommends to all sacred virgins the pledge of his love. He alone, born of the sacred Virgin, is the spouse and the glory of chaste souls.

Haec Agnes ergo, meritis clarissima virgo,
carmine non culto pangit quam nostra Camena,
urbis famosae praenobilis incola Romae,
prodiit almorum clara de stirpe parentum,
inclita nobilitas quos vexit et alma potestas.
Ortus atque sui respondens nobilitati
pulchra fuit facie, fideique decora nitore,
praecipuis nimium meritis mundoque celebris.
Quae nam tincta sacri pura baptismatis unda
et de delicti maculis mundata veterni
se totam Christo devovit mente benigna
nitens servata bene virginitate beata
spernere carnales affectus fortiter omnes
caelibis et vitae durum luctamen inire,
quo victrix hostis corruptelam suadentis
iungi caelicolis meruisset in aethere sanctis.

Ast ubi lustra duo celeri cursu revoluta
insuper et ternos aetatis transigit annos,
Simphronii comitis, praefecti scilicet urbis,
filius insignis iuvenilis stemmate floris,
illius formae decus ut vidit speciosae,
affectu nimio cordis suspensus in illa,
hanc sibi prae cunctis unam delegit amandam
se fortunatum credens et honoribus aptum,
si tam praepulchrae meruisset habere puellae
dulcia per propriae tempus consortia vitae.
Hinc illam multis adiit comitatus amicis.
Desponsare volens sponsam Christi venerandam,
pluraque de patris comportans munera gazis
stultus speravit, quod perpetrare nequivit,
virginis ut stabilem donis corrumpere mentem

This Agnes, then, a virgin most illustrious for her merits, whom my Muse celebrates in an unpolished poem, a very noble inhabitant of the renowned city of Rome, came from the distinguished stock of nourishing parents, whom outstanding nobility and nourishing power guided. And in keeping with the nobility of her origins, she was beautiful in appearance, attractive in the radiance of her faith, and very celebrated in the world for her exceptional merits. For after she was bathed in the pure water of sacred baptism and cleansed of the stains of the ancient guilt, she devoted herself entirely to Christ with a kindly heart, preserving intact her blessed virginity, staunchly striving to reject all carnal desires and to embark upon the arduous struggle of a celibate life, so that she, as a conqueror of the enemy who incites us to corruption, might deserve to be joined to the heaven-dwelling saints in the sky.

But when she had passed through twice five years, rolling along in their swift course, and three more years of her life on top of that, the son of Count Simphronius, that is, the son of the prefect of the city, a boy of flowering youth and distinguished by his noble birth, immediately upon seeing the beauty of her lovely figure, fixating on her with excessive affection of the heart, chose her for himself to be loved before all others, believing himself fortunate and suited to the honors, if he earned the right to have the sweet partnership of so very beautiful a girl throughout the span of his life. For this reason, he approached her, in the company of many of his friends. Wishing to espouse this venerable spouse of Christ, and carrying with him many gifts from among the treasures of his father, he foolishly hoped for a thing he could not accomplish, that he would be able to corrupt the

illius et turpi coniungere posset amori.
Sed Christi virgo, spernens ceu stercora dona,
pondus et oblati dedignans protinus auri,
splendorem quoque gemmarum rutilum variarum,
his verbis iuvenem causari fertur amentem:
"O fili mortis merito damnande perennis,
O fomes sceleris, contemptor et Omnipotentis,
discedens a me citius fugiendo recede.
Nec credas te posse meum pervertere purum
cor, quod amatoris praevenit nobilioris
dulcis amor. Pulchrum cuius fidei fero signum
in facie summa necnon in corpore toto,
quo me signavit strictimque sibi religavit,
ne mea mens alium iam praesumpsisset amicum
quaerere, sed solum complecti disceret illum,
qui virtute potens omnique decore refulgens
caelestes et mortales supereminet omnes.
Hunc sine matre Pater cani retro tempora mundi
in deitate parem nec maiestate minorem
omnipotens genuit; per quem sibi saecula fecit.
Et sine patre quidem mater pariebat eundem
Factorem proprium lactans sub tempore natum.
Cuius praepulchram mirantur denique formam
solaris splendor lunae renitens quoque candor,
laudantes radiis Dominum fulgentibus orbis.
Cuius et imperio famulantia sidera cuncta
illis iniunctum complent per tempora cursum.
Cui conclamantes condignis laudibus omnes
coetus angelici non desistunt famulari.
Mira cui bonitas est et praecelsa potestas,
gloria sublimis, perpes concordia pacis,

firm mind of the maiden with gifts and join her to his foul love. But the virgin of Christ, rejecting his gifts as excrement, and disdaining straightaway the measure of gold he offered, and also the shining glitter of various gems, is said to have assailed the crazy boy in these words: "O child deservedly condemned to eternal death, O inflamer of sin, and despiser of the Almighty, get away from me, departing very swiftly in flight. And do not imagine you can pervert my pure heart, because the sweet love of a nobler lover has claimed it first. I bear the lovely seal of his faith on my forehead and on my whole body, the seal by which he has marked me and bound me strictly to him, so that my heart not presume to seek another lover, but learn to embrace only him, who, powerful in strength and radiant in every beauty, surpasses all heavenly and mortal beings. His almighty Father bore him without a mother, before the eras of this aged world began, equal in deity and no less in majesty; through him he made the world for himself. And, indeed, without a father, a mother gave birth to this same one, nursing her own Creator, born into the temporal world. At his most lovely form, then, the splendor of the sun and also the shining whiteness of the moon marvel, praising the Lord of the earth with their bright rays. And obeying his command, all the stars complete the course assigned them through the seasons. Singing together with worthy praises, all the angelic hosts serve him without pause. He has wondrous goodness and excellent power, sublime glory, the perpetual con-

laudabilis pietas, nimiumque benigna voluntas.
Talis namque meus, quem diligo, constat amicus;
quem fateor solum prae cunctis esse colendum.
Ille quidem talis me desponsavit amoris
pignore ceu sponsam clara dotando corona,
atque meum gemmis collum cinxit pretiosis,
auribus et resplendentes suspendit inaures,
praebens ornatus varii claros mihi cultus.
Ipsius certe dulcedo fluxit ab ore,
quae me lactavit dulci pastuque cibavit
ceu nectar mellis suavis vel copia lactis.
Insuper et thalamum mihimet construxit in aevum
lucentem gemmis variis aurique metallis.
Organa melodiis in quo resonando canoris
carmen dulce mihi cantant per tempora saecli,
et pariter sponsi laudes modulantia cari,
illius affectum semper suadent mihi castum.
Affectu quem secreto <cum> cordis amabo,
nulla puellaris patior detrimenta pudoris.
Ast ubi forte sui merear complexibus uti
eius et in thalamum sponsarum more coruscum
duci, permaneo virgo sine sorde pudica.
Cui debebo fidem soli servare perennem.
Ipsi me toto cordis conamine credo."
His miser auditis, spiculis perfossus amoris,
ingemuit, crebro ducens suspiria longa,
hoc quia non meruit, caeco quod corde petivit.
Et super hoc maerens nimioque dolore tabescens,
decidit in lectum (stultissimus ille virorum!),
et simulans male languorem, celavit amorem,
qui sibi causa gravis fuerat non parva doloris.

cord of peace, laudable mercy, and an exceedingly gracious will. Such assuredly is my lover, the one I cherish; I avow that he alone ought to be worshipped before all others. He, indeed, has taken me as a spouse with a pledge of such love as though he were dowering his spouse with a shining crown, and he encircled my neck with precious gems, and he hung brilliant earrings on my ears, offering me the shining ornaments of various refinements. Certainly a sweetness flowed from his mouth, which nursed me and fed me with sweet food as though it were the nectar of honey or an abundance of milk. Furthermore, he constructed for me a bridal chamber for all time, shining with all kinds of gems and golden metals. Instruments inside this chamber, resounding in harmonious tunes, chant a sweet song for me through the ages of time, and singing likewise the praises of my dear spouse, they constantly encourage in me a chaste affection for him. When I love him with the secret affection of my heart, I suffer no loss of my girlish modesty. But when I, perchance, will have earned the right to enjoy his embraces and to be led into the gleaming bridal chamber as brides are led, I will remain a modest virgin without stain. For him alone I will be obliged to preserve my eternal faith. To him I entrust myself with every effort of my heart."

When he heard these words, the poor fellow, pierced by the shafts of love, groaned, repeatedly drawing long sighs, because he had not obtained what he had sought with his blind heart. And grieving over this and withering away with great pain, he sank into his bed (that most foolish of men!), and faking a serious illness, he concealed the love which was no small cause of his heavy pain. In a short time, it became

Nec mora, fit notum fama prodente sinistra
natum praefecti nimio languore ligari.
Conveniunt subito medici velut agmine facto;
apponunt variis aptas morbis medicinas,
harum sed iuveni nil proficiebat amenti.
Tandem senserunt quod mox patri retulerunt,
non hoc languoris signum, sed fortis amoris,
quod contristatus pateretur filius eius.
Quo pater audito, causa morbique reperta,
ut leo frendescens rapidam conversus in iram,
incepit percontari rabie furienti,
quis foret ille potestatis sic imperialis,
in quo spe vana virgo confisa superba
crederet esse sibi iunctum, contemnere natum
eius, qui plebi merito celeberrimus omni
esset condigne summo provectus honore.
Haec ubi disseruit nimioque furore latravit,
comperit hanc ipsam sacro baptismate lotam
Agnen, Christicolam primis fore semper ab annis,
et conservandae pro virginitatis amore
esse suum sponsum consueto dicere Christum.
Quo nam comperto laetatur corde maligno,
sperans <se> teneram merito debere puellam
saevis ad cultum poenis urgere deorum,
et sic posse suum tandem complere furorem,
quo pro contemptu nati furiebat aegroti.
Hinc illam citius sisti conspectibus eius
iussit. Et astantem nulloque metu trepidantem
primo suadelis nimium mulcebat amicis.
Tunc etiam probris dure cogebat amaris,
ut se sponte sui nati copularet amori

known through the betrayal of malicious rumor that the son of the prefect was bound fast with a great illness. The doctors convened instantly, as though ready for battle; they applied medicines appropriate for various diseases, but none of these medicines benefitted that crazy lad. Finally they recognized what they soon reported to his father: that it was not a symptom of illness, this thing which his distraught son was suffering, but of overpowering love. When the father had heard this, and when the cause of the disease was revealed, like a growling lion roused swiftly to anger, he began to ask in a furious frenzy, who that man of such imperial power was, for whose sake the proud virgin, trusting with vain hope, believed that it was her duty to refuse the son of a man who was deservedly the most renowned among all people and had rightfully been raised up to the highest honor. When he had said this and howled in excessive rage, he learned that this same Agnes had been bathed in holy baptism, that from her first years she had always been a Christian, and that from her desire to preserve her virginity she routinely said that Christ was her spouse. When he had learned this, he was gladdened in his wicked heart, expecting that he was rightly entitled to pressure the tender girl, with savage tortures, into worship of the gods, and in that way he would at last be able to put an end to his own rage, with which he was raging on account of her rejection of his ailing son. Then he ordered that she immediately be made to stand before him. And as she was standing there, not trembling with any fear, at first he tried to soothe her with the friendliest encouragements. Then also with bitter insults he sternly pressured her to join herself in love to his son, of her own accord, and to worship the images of the

et simulachra deum coleret Christumque negaret.
Sed virgo Christi nec suppliciis superari,
nec blandimentis potuit devincier ullis,
quin servaret amatori sine fraude priori,
quod pepigit, pactum signo fidei stabilitum.
Cui praeses pravam rursum renovans suadelam
dixit, "Si vere cupias intacta manere
virgo, deae magnae citius subiungere Vestae
eius sacricolis et consociare puellis,
quo condigna fias illi semper famulari."
Haec inquit praeses; contra sed sic ait Agnes:
"Si mihi iure tuum placuit contemnere natum,
qui ratione vigens, cunctis quoque sensibus utens
corporeis anima regitur numquam moritura
(quamvis sit merito baratro claudendus in imo
multis errorum pro commissis variorum,
ni, sanum sapiens et quandoquidem resipiscens,
se tingui faciat pura baptismatis unda),
quis te posse minis vel quis tandem suadelis
ad simulacrorum reris me cogere cultum?
Artificum cura quae conformata metallo
membrorum falsam portant solummodo formam,
mobilis officium complent nec corporis ullum,
neque suum quid viventis monstrant animalis.
Et quod ab his insensatis monstrisque profanis
solamen vitae mihimet sperare gerendae
possum? Quae vita sensuque carentia cuncto
nec sibi proficiunt mihi nec succurrere possunt"
Haec ubi dicta dedit, praeses Simphronius inquit,
"Florentem primis te nam cognosco sub annis,
ingenio parvam necnon aetate tenellam.

gods, and to deny Christ. But Christ's virgin was not to be overcome by any punishments, nor prevented by any enticements, from preserving for her earlier lover, without deception, the pledge confirmed by the seal of faith which she had made. Renewing his perverse encouragements, the governor said to her, "If you truly desire to remain an intact virgin, subjugate yourself immediately to the great goddess Vesta and join the girls who are her priestesses, so that you become worthy of serving her forever."

So spoke the governor; but Agnes answered in this way: "If it justifiably pleased me to reject your son, who is alive and endowed with vigorous reason, who has the use of all his bodily senses, and is governed by a soul which will never die (although he should deservedly be confined to the bottom of hell because of his frequent commission of various sins, unless, being in his right mind and one day returning to his senses, he has himself dipped in the pure water of baptism), by what threats or by what forms of persuasion, then, do you suppose you could possibly force me to worship statues? Fashioned out of metal by the skill of craftsmen, they bear only the false form of bodies, and they do not fulfill any of the functions of a moving body, nor do they display as their own any trait of a living being. And what solace in leading my life can I hope for from these unfeeling and unholy monstrosities? Lacking life and every sensation, they can do nothing for themselves, and they cannot help me."

When she had delivered these words, Governor Simphronius said, "I recognize, indeed, that you are in the flower of your first years, limited in intelligence and tender in age.

Hinc infantili parcendo simplicitati
prudenter te supporto, lasciva puella,
quo parcendo tuum citius te flectere collum
sub sacris Vestae plantis faciam venerandae
tureque nostrorum numen placare deorum.
Sed si tam mitem spernendo mei pietatem
contraluctaris, mea ne praecepta sequaris,
ultra non parco, sed vim iustam faciendo
mando sub obscenae latebris te claudier aedis,
in qua criminibus turpes gaudent mulieres.
Et faciam pollutarum sociam meretricum,
quo tu, quae clara polles de stirpe creata,
dedecus omne tuis sis et confusio turpis."
At sacra virgo minis minime trepidans super istis,
audacter mox praefecto dedit ista responsa:
"Si tu namque Deum scires hunc, quem colo, verum
illiusque potestatem sine fine vigentem,
qua semper proprios pie confortando ministros
antiqui fraudes hostis confringeret omnes,
talia verba tuo nolles profundere rostro,
nec mihi terrores totiens praeponere tristes.
Hinc ego, quae sectando fidem Christi meliorem,
illum cognosco necnon cognoscor ab illo:
ipsius dextra me defendente superna
spero delicti numquam maculis violari,
carnis spurcitias fragilis sed vincere cunctas."
His dictis saeva praeses commotior ira
caelestis sponsam Regis iussit venerandam
vestibus exutam, toto quoque corpore nudam,
concurrente trahi conventiculo populari
inque lupanaris nigrum concludier antrum,

For this reason, taking pity on your youthful simplicity, I will, in my prudence, transport you, impudent girl, to a place where, through my leniency, I will swiftly make you bend your neck at the sacred feet of the venerable Vesta and appease the divinity of our gods with incense. But if you resist, rejecting my kindness, which is so mild, and you do not follow my commands, I will spare you no longer, but exercising just authority, I will hand you over to be confined in the inner rooms of a bawdy house, where vile women revel in their sins. And I will make you the partner of debauched prostitutes, so that you, a distinguished young woman born from illustrious stock, become a total dishonor to your people and a vile disgrace."

But the holy virgin, not frightened in the least by these threats, then boldly gave the following responses to the prefect: "In fact, if you knew this God, the true One whom I worship, and his power flourishing without end, the power by which, constantly and mercifully strengthening his servants, he demolishes all the deceits of the ancient enemy, you would not want to spout such words from your mouth, nor to confront me with distressing terrors again and again. It is for this reason that I, following the better faith of Christ, know him and am known by him: I expect that, with his heavenly right hand to defend me, I will never be violated by the stains of sin, but will overcome all the filthiness of the fragile flesh."

The governor, more stirred to savage wrath by these words, ordered that the venerable spouse of the celestial King be stripped of her clothes, and with her whole body naked, be dragged, a common mob accompanying her, and be confined in the dark recesses of a brothel, where

in quo lascivi iuvenes rationis egeni
colloquio scelerosarum gaudent mulierum.
Sed Christus propriae praebens solamina sponsae
illam conviciis tangi non sustinet ullis.
Ast ubi distracto nudatur tegmine toto,
continuo bene densati crevere capilli.
Qui ductu longo lapsi de vertice summo
descendendo pedum plantas tetigere tenellas,
corpus et omne comis tegitur ceu tegmine vestis.
Utque lupanaris calcavit limina tristis,
extemplo suavis sensit dulcamen odoris
atque locum turpem miro splendore micantem
aspexit, tenebris qui sordebat prius atris.
Et cum sordidulum compulsa subintrat in antrum,
angelus Altithroni blande stetit obvius illi.
Custos indubius fuerat qui corporis eius,
obtulit et vestem niveo splendore micantem
eius mensurae conformatam satis apte.
Hac induta quidem direxit ad aethera vocem
assidue grates Christo resonando suaves,
cuius opem tanti sensit sub fasce pericli,
cuius et auxilio fuerat protecta paterno,
ne posset veteris corrumpi fraudibus hostis.
    Interea iuvenes, caecato corde furentes,
undique collectis cursim venere catervis,
certantes studio perversae mentis iniquo,
quis prior intraret, vel quis perdiscere posset
an virgo, suffulta sui munimine Christi,
haec, quae carnales semper contempsit amores,
iam nunc in coepto posset persistere voto.
Nec mora, cognoscunt nec contradicere possunt,

lusty young men devoid of reason enjoy converse with sinful women. But Christ, offering comforts to his own spouse, did not allow her to be touched by any abuse. Rather, when she was denuded, with all her clothing removed, immediately the hair on her head grew very thick. Falling in a long cascade, descending from the top of her head, it touched the tender soles of her feet, and her entire body was covered by her hair, as if by a covering of clothing. And when she set foot on the threshold of that dire brothel, straightaway she sensed the sweetness of a mild fragrance and saw that vile place shining with a wondrous splendor, which previously was sordid with gloomy darkness. And when under compulsion she entered that sordid cave, an angel of the One enthroned on high stood soothingly before her. Undoubtedly, he was the guardian of her body, and he brought her a shining garment of snow-white splendor, very properly tailored to her size. When she had put it on, indeed, she directed her voice to the heavens, ardently sounding sweet thanks to Christ, of whose aid she was conscious under the burden of this great danger, and by whose fatherly assistance she had been protected, so that she could not be corrupted by the wiles of the ancient enemy.

Meanwhile, the young men, raving in their blinded hearts, from all sides came swiftly in congested crowds, competing in the wicked ardor of their perverted minds, about who would enter first, or who would first discover whether this virgin, reinforced by the protection of her Christ, this virgin who had always rejected carnal love, could now any longer persist in the vow she had taken. In no time they learned and could not deny that no one will ever be

quod numquam longum quis confundetur in aevum,
qui credens Domino firma spe pendet in illo.
Nam quicumque sua compulsus mente superba,
ingreditur turpis latebras temerarius aedis,
ut radios lucis vidit mire rutilantis
angelicae praefulgentem vestisque nitorem,
correptus signi nimio terrore stupendi,
prostratus sacrae plantis extemplo puellae,
postulat errorum laxari vincla suorum.
Testaturque Deum verum fore iure colendum,
eius cultores qui consolabitur omnes.
Sicque locus scelerum domus efficitur precularum.
Tandem praefecti natus venit male sanus,
cuius sustinuit causa vim virgo beata.
Qui mox ingressus ridenti corde misellus
nec dixit laudem Domino nec reddit honorem,
gratia tristifico cuius radiabat in antro.
Sed detestabilem laetus tendebat in aedem,
amplexu dulci sperans se virginis uti
iam licito sacrae, cuius languebat amore.
Sed Christi pietas necnon praecelsa potestas
fortiter obsistens illi perversa volenti
a corruptela propriam protexit alumnam,
in reprobam miserum mortem tradebat et illum.
Nam mox ut rapido cursu properaverat illo,
quo supplex laudes Domino resonaverat Agnes,
infelix membris inprovisa resolutis
morte ruit pronus Christi virtute peremptus.

Quo pater audito miser advenit lacrimando,
stipatus multa populorum namque caterva.
Et sese miserum clamans spargebat in altum

ruined for eternity who, believing in the Lord, depends on him with unwavering hope. For whosoever, driven by his own proud heart, rashly entered the inner rooms of that disgraceful house, as soon as he saw the rays of light wondrously sparkling and the brilliant shine of her angelic garment, was seized with great terror at this stupendous miracle, and having immediately prostrated himself at the feet of the holy girl, asked that the chains of his sins be loosened. And he attested that the true God should justly be worshipped, the God who consoles all his adherents. And so that place of sinning was turned into a house of prayers. Last of all came the son of the prefect, in ill health, on whose account the blessed virgin had endured this violence. The little wretch immediately entered with a smiling heart, and he neither gave praise to the Lord nor rendered honor to him whose grace was radiating in that dreary cell. Instead, he happily headed into that detestable building, hoping that he might now lawfully enjoy the sweet embrace of the sacred virgin, for the love of whom he was wasting away. But the mercy of Christ and his extraordinary power, stoutly resisting that man who wanted to wrong her, protected his disciple from corruption, and handed over that miserable man to a vile death. For as soon as he had rushed, running swiftly, to where the suppliant Agnes was singing praises to the Lord, the unlucky fellow's limbs crumpled, and he fell on his face in an unforeseen death, destroyed by the power of Christ.

When his poor father heard this, he came in tears, surrounded by a truly great crowd of people. And proclaiming that he was wretched, he sent his cries to high heaven,

voces his sanctam verbis causando puellam:
"O mulier male crudelis, cui non muliebris
cordis inest feritas nimiumque cruenta voluntas
corpore sub tenero frendescens more ferino,
dic, quae causa meum cogit te perdere natum,
qui decus omne suis et spes fuerat genitoris,
quondam felicis talis de germine prolis,
sed nunc orbati misere pro funere nati?
Hinc patet ergo tuam mentem nimium vitiosam
de rivulis magicae fraudis bibulam satis esse,
florentem primis quia forte necare sub annis
subtractum dulci iuvenem vita voluisti."
At sacra conviciis virgo non frangitur istis
praefecto nec responsum reddebat acerbum,
dulcia sed resono profundens verba palato
dixit facunde bene composita ratione:
"Non ego causa necis iuveni fueram pereunti,
sed magis ipse sibi fuit incensor moriendi,
glorificare Deum stultus quia spreverat illum,
gloria tristifico cuius praefulget in antro.
Sed nunc, ut plane toto clarescat in orbe
eius maiestas necnon praecelsa potestas,
ipsius suavem supplex oro pietatem,
ut corpus rigidum iubeat recalescere rursum,
atque novum membris hominem reparet redivivis."
Dixit et astantes egredi praeceperat omnes.
Et prostrata solo fundensque preces lacrimando
praestari petit a Domino veniam sceleroso.
Cui mox oranti misero vitamque precanti
angelus astiterat procumbentemque levabat
praebens colloquiis illi solamen amicis.

accusing the saintly girl with these words: "O wickedly cruel woman, whose breast harbors an unwomanly ferocity and a determination that is too cruel, raging like a beast in a tender body, tell me what cause drove you to destroy my child, who had been every glory to his people and the hope of his father, a father once happy in the production of such an offspring but now miserably deprived by the death of the child? From this, then, it is clear that your heart is deeply corrupt and utterly drunk on the streams of your deceitful witchcraft, for you have casually chosen to destroy a young man, removing from sweet life one who was flowering in his prime years."

But the sacred virgin was not broken by these insults, nor did she return a bitter response to the prefect, but pouring out sweet words from her sonorous palate, she spoke eloquently and in reasonable terms: "I was not the cause of death of this young man who has died, but rather he was the instigator of his own death, because he foolishly refused to glorify that God whose glory shone brightly in the dreary cell. But now, so that his majesty and extraordinary power be plainly revealed throughout the world, as a suppliant I ask of his tender mercy that he order this young man's rigid body to grow warm again, and that he restore the man anew with reanimated limbs." She said this and ordered all those standing around to depart. And prostrate on the ground weeping, pouring out prayers, she asked that pardon be offered by the Lord to that sinner. Straightaway an angel stood by her as she was praying for the wretched boy and asking for his life, and the angel raised up the praying woman, offering her solace in friendly conversation. And with a word,

In verboque Dei iussit virtute potenti
extinctum subito flatu vixisse resumpto.
Qui citius dicto iussus surrexit ab humo
viribus et cunctis plene membris restitutis.
Ac laudum dulces spargens super aethera voces
grates continuo solvebat mente iucunda
Christo, victori mortis vitaeque datori.
Inde quidem prima prorsus forma renovata
processit vivus, qui morte fuit religatus.
Atque suo tristi se praesentando parenti
fit res gaudendi, fuerat cui causa dolendi.
Hinc crebro caelum pulsans clamore profundum
utitur et verbis suadens studiosius istis:
"Credite, Romani cives, rogo, credite cuncti
esse Deum Christum verumque perenniter unum
cum Patre celsithrono necnon cum Flamine sacro
semper regnantem sceptrum caelique tenentem.
Sub dicione sua qui complectens universa
cuncta gubernaclis regit immensae bonitatis.
Hic est orandus solusque colendus amandus.
Qui prius errantem necnon perversa volentem
morte repentina citius me praeveniendo
finem stultitiae dignabatur dare tantae.
Et post erranti promptus solito misereri
virginis Agnetis precibus sacrae studiosis
mollitus rursum vitae reddit renovatum."
At pater, ut natum prodire sui redivivum
perfectum specie vidit plenumque decore,
interitum lacrimis cuius deflevit amaris,
mox super insolita signi novitate stupendi
admirando pavet, laeto sed pectore gaudet.

by the powerful virtue of God he ordered the dead man to live, with his breathing suddenly resumed. Quicker than you could say it, he rose up from the ground as he had been ordered, with his strength and all his limbs fully restored. And sending the sweet sounds of praise above the heavens, he immediately paid thanks with a joyous heart to Christ, conqueror of death and giver of life. Then indeed, with his original form altogether renewed, he who had been bound fast by death, went forth alive. And presenting himself to his grieving father, he became a source of rejoicing to the man to whom he had been a cause of sorrow. For this reason, he made the high heavens resound with repeated shouts and used these words, in eager encouragement: "Believe all you Roman citizens, I beg you, believe that Christ is the true God forever, one with the Father enthroned on high and with the Holy Spirit, ruling always and holding the scepter of heaven. He, in his dominion, embraces all things and rules everything by the guidance of his immense goodness. He should be prayed to and alone should be worshipped, should be loved. When I was a sinner planning perverted things, he prevented me by sudden death, and he saw fit to put an end to my great foolishness. And afterward, ready in his accustomed manner to be merciful to a sinner, and softened by the fervent prayers of the holy virgin Agnes, he brought me back again, restored to life." But his father, when he saw his son come forth reborn, perfect in appearance and full of honor, the son whose death he had wept over with bitter tears, he straightaway trembled in wonder at the rare novelty of this astounding miracle, but he

Tunc amplectendo collum pietate paterna
mitia praedulci libaverat oscula proli.
Atque Deum verum clamans dixit fore Christum,
cuius tam celerem cognoscebat pietatem,
cuius et imperio mors succumbebat amara
reddens viventem, quem sorbebat morientem.
Scilicet astantes animis mirantibus omnes
tollunt in caelum laeti praeconia laudum
laudantes sanctum Domini nomen benedicti.
Hoc vix pontifices crudeli corde ferentes
commovere quidem non parvam seditionem,
Agnem sacrilegam dicentes et scelerosam
occidi poenis citius debere cruentis,
illius causa quia contemptum simulacra
cunctaque sacrorum paterentur iura suorum.
Hinc praeses, maestus turbato pectore factus,
condoluit sacrae subtristi mente puellae.
Ignorat tamen omnino dubius, super illa
quid sibi sectandum, vel quid restaret agendum.
Perdere non placuit, sed nec defendere quivit.
Tandem discessit maerens aliumque reliquit,
iudicis officio functum feritate lupina,
qui fuit Aspasius dictus rituque profanus.
Qui citus Agnetem proici praecepit in ignem
pontificum votis male concordando malignis.
Sed corpus castum nulla de sorde piandum,
ardor carnalis quod non succendit amoris,
ignis non laesit praesens, nec tangere quivit.
Denique divisae divino numine flammae
virgineis tribuere locum precibus spatiosum,
ac prorumpentes aestu nimioque furentes

rejoiced with a happy heart. Then embracing his neck with paternal affection, he gave soft kisses to his sweet child. And calling out, he declared that Christ was the true God, whose swift mercy he had experienced, and to whose power bitter death had succumbed, returning alive the boy whom it had swallowed up dying. Needless to say, all the bystanders, their hearts struck by wonder, happily raised to heaven hymns of praise, praising the holy name of the blessed Lord.

The pagan priests, scarcely tolerating this in their cruel hearts, stirred up an insurrection by no means small, saying that the sacrilegious and sinful Agnes ought to be swiftly put to death with bloody punishments, because on her account all the statues and entitlements of their sacred rites were exposed to contempt. Therefore the governor, now grown despondent in his troubled heart, grieved in sorrowful thought for the holy girl. And yet, completely bewildered, he did not know what course he should follow concerning her, or what remained for him to do. It was not his wish to destroy her, but he had no power to protect her.

Finally he withdrew sorrowfully and left another, a man of wolflike savagery, to perform the office of judge; he was called Aspasius and was a pagan by religion. He swiftly ordered Agnes to be tossed on a fire, in wicked accord with the malicious desires of the priests. But the fire's presence did not injure her chaste body, which needed no expiation for any sort of defilement, since the ardor of carnal love had not inflamed it, and the fire was not able to touch her. Finally, by divine will the flames were divided and provided a wide space for the virgin's prayers; then bursting out raging with

perdunt carnifices urendo primitus omnes.
Hinc circumstantem lambentes undique plebem
incredulam plures raptim stravere phalanges.
Sola sed immunis stabat pia virgo caloris,
inter flammarum crines ludens crepitantes.
Oravitque Deum versis ad sidera palmis,
hoc utens in fronte precis modulamine laudis:
"Omniparens Verbi genitor mundique creator,
qui cum dilecto regnans retro tempora Nato
amborumque coaeterno cum Flamine sacro,
digne laudaris, coleris, veneraris, amaris.
Te solum laudo, te laudando benedico,
et tibi devote grates persolvo perennes,
eiusdem quia fulta tui munimine Nati
numquam succubui serpentis fraude vetusti.
Corpore sed casto puro cordisque secreto,
carnis spurcitias pertransivi bene cunctas
poenas sacrilegi pariter superando tyranni.
Hinc gaudens in te nimium super hac pietate
ad te nunc animis festino venire iucundis
optans iura pati mortis citiusque resolvi,
quo merear vere contemplari sine fine
te, quem quaesivi, quem solum semper amavi.
Tu clemens animam pro te de corpore pulsam
intra claustra tui dignanter suscipe regni,
quo tu iure tuo pollens sub nomine trino,
Rex unus machinae rerum per saecula trinae
istaec cuncta regis sceptro summae Deitatis."
Scilicet orantis precibus iam rite peractis,
ignibus extinctis moritur subito rogus omnis;

great heat, they first destroyed all the executioners, burning them up. From there the flames, licking on all sides at the faithless people standing around, violently cut down many legions of them. Alone, however, the pious virgin remained standing, immune to the heat, reveling in the midst of the crackling tendrils of flame. And she appealed to God with her hands turned to the stars, employing this song of praise at the opening of her prayer: "Parent of all, progenitor of the Word, and creator of the world, who, ruling before all the ages along with your beloved Son and along with the Holy Spirit, who is coeternal with both of you, are rightly praised, worshiped, venerated, loved—you alone do I praise, and in praising bless, and I devotedly pay you endless thanks, because supported by the aid of that same Son of yours, I have never succumbed through the deceit of the old serpent. But with my body chaste and the secret chamber of my heart pure, I have successfully traversed all the foulness of the flesh, overcoming too the tortures of a sacrilegious tyrant. So, rejoicing greatly in you on account of this mercy, I am hurrying to come to you now in joyous spirits, choosing to suffer the laws of death and to be swiftly freed, so that I might truly earn the right to contemplate you endlessly, you whom alone I have always sought, and always loved. Mercifully receive this soul driven from its body for your sake, receive it worthily within the cloisters of your kingdom, where you, powerful in your own right under a triune name, rule as the one King of the threefold structure of things through all these ages, with the scepter of the highest Deity." And indeed, when the prayers of this suppliant were now duly completed, the flames were extinguished and the whole

et cinis ipse suis confrigescendo favillis
sic expers omnis factus fuit immo caloris,
ut nec scintillam sibi post servaverit ullam.
Hoc igitur signo iam clarescente stupendo,
quanto se virtus Christi plus detegit orbi,
tanto maioris rabiem spirando furoris
iniustus iudex animo cruciatur amaro.
Nec patitur sacram post haec superesse puellam,
per quam sunt crebro miracula tanta patrata.
Ense sed immisso, tenerum guttur penetrando,
martyris egregiae iugulum perfodit avare.
Et vice conversa, quod non speravit, agendo
illi profecit, cui gratis obesse cupivit,
transmittens caelo, quam subtraxit male mundo.
Ast ubi pro Christo letali vulnere laesa
extremum Domino flatum reddit moriendo,
atque fide salva gaudens obdormit in illo,
ocius angelici coetus de sidere lapsi
astantes animam, niveo candore coruscam
necnon caelestis perfusam luce nitoris,
blande suscipiunt laetique per aera tollunt,
congrue divinae laudis resonantibus hymnis.
Indeque transvectam celeres super aetheris ignes
ducunt astrigeram sponsi caelestis in aulam.
A quo continuo clarum rutilante corona
donatur purae pro virginitatis honore.
Nec minus ergo, sui signo donanda triumphi,
martyrii palmam sumpsit sine fine gerendam,
quo martyr felix, duplici certamine victrix
(corporis et mentis carni semper renitentis),

pyre suddenly died down; and the very ash growing cold in its embers became instead devoid of all heat to such an extent that afterward it did not preserve for itself even a tiny spark of it.

The more, then, that Christ's power was revealed to the world as this wondrous miracle shone forth, the more the unjust judge Aspasius, spewing a rage of even greater fury, was tortured in his bitter mind. Nor could he endure for the holy girl to survive after this, the girl through whom such great miracles were continually being performed. But with a sword inserted, penetrating her tender throat, he greedily pierced the neck of the illustrious martyr. And in turn, by doing this he accomplished a thing he had not anticipated for her, whom he had intended gratuitously to harm, sending to heaven this girl whom he had wickedly taken from the world. But when she was struck for Christ's sake by this lethal wound, and had rendered up her final breath, dying for the Lord, and when, with her faith unblemished, she joyfully rested in him, hosts of angels slipped swiftly down from the stars, they stood by her soul, which was shining in snowy whiteness and perfused with the light of heavenly radiance, and they gently received it, and joyfully carried it through the air, while hymns of divine praise were harmoniously resounding. And from there, they led it, transported above the swift fires of the ether, into the starry palace of its celestial spouse. By him she was immediately presented with a clearly shining crown for the honor of her pure virginity. And then also, being worthy of gifts as a sign of her triumph, she received the palm of martyrdom to bear forever, so that as a fortunate martyr, conqueror in a double contest (that of the body and of the mind ever resisting the flesh),

utens aeterni bravio decoris duplicato
inter virgineas fulgeret clara catervas,
lilia ceu pulchre roseo permixta rubore
inter delicias florum rutilat variorum.
 Interea quoque summorum sacra cura parentum
excultam magna, funus venerabile, pompa
in gremio terrae toto contexit honore.
Nec saltim bustum sacratae virginis ipsum,
quod pro servandis fuerat venerabile membris,
sollicitudo parentalis contempsit amoris,
sed sub nocturnis servat vigilantius horis.
At, dum pervigiles consueto more parentes
excubias proli celebrabant mente fideli,
caelitus his ipsis monstratur visio talis:
denique virgineas subito descendere turmas
viderunt, lapsas celeri de cardine caeli,
ornatas pulchre pleno comptasque decore.
Inter quas Agnen simili splendore nitentem
conspexere suam pro Christo martyrizatam;
a dextris cuius nive candidior stetit agnus.
Quos merito fidei scivit dignos venerari,
blande colloquiis illos affatur amicis
dicens: "Gaudete mecum gratulando per aevum,
sum quia luciflua Regis caelestis in aula
virginibus sacris sociata perenniter istis.
Et nunc in caelis illi coniungor amoris
amplexu dulci, quem semper mente fideli
in terris colui cupiens sine fine tueri."
His igitur dictis subito discessit ab illis.
Qui nimium laeti tanto solamine facti

experiencing the twofold reward of eternal glory, she might shine bright among the crowds of virgins, in the same way that a lily, beautifully mixed with rosy red, is resplendent among the delights of various flowers.

Meanwhile too the holy love of her noble parents buried her with great pomp, a corpse to be revered, in the bosom of the earth with all honor. Nor indeed was the place of burial of the sacred virgin, venerable because it preserved her limbs, neglected by the solicitude of paternal love, but was watched over even more vigilantly in the nighttime hours. And, while the watchful parents, as is customary, were standing vigil for their child with faithful hearts, a heavenly vision of this kind was shown to these same parents: in short, they saw crowds of virgins descending suddenly, having slipped down from the swiftly turning axis of heaven, beautifully adorned and arranged in full glory. Among them they caught sight of Agnes, shining in similar splendor, their own daughter who was martyred for Christ; on her right stood a lamb whiter than snow. She spoke gently to them in friendly conversation, knowing they deserved to be respected by virtue of their faith, saying: “Rejoice with me, giving thanks forever, because I am in the light-filled palace of the heavenly King, in the company of these holy virgins for all time. And now I am joined in heaven in love’s sweet embrace to the One whom I always worshipped on earth with a faithful heart, desiring to look on him endlessly.” When she had said these things, she suddenly departed from them. They were overjoyed by such solace and dried

siccabant lacrimas super eius morte refusas,
et laudes Domino psallebant voce canora,
qui post dura suis tribuit certamina sanctis
testibus aeternae clementer praemia vitae.

Amen.

EXPLICIT LIBER PRIMUS.

the tears they had poured out over her death, and they chanted praises in a sweet-sounding voice to the Lord, who mercifully provides to his saintly martyrs after their hard struggles the rewards of eternal life.

Amen.

HERE ENDS THE FIRST BOOK.

BOOK TWO

LIBER SECUNDUS

INCIPIT SECUNDUS DRAMATICA SERIE CONTEXTUS

Huius omnem materiam sicut et prioris opusculi sumpsi ab antiquis libris sub certis auctorum nominibus conscriptis, excepta superius scripta passione sancti Pelagii, cuius seriem martyrii quidam eiusdem in qua passus est indigena civitatis mihi exposuit; qui ipsum pulcherrimum virorum se
2 vidisse et exitum rei attestatus est veraciter agnovisse. Unde si quid in utroque falsitatis dictando comprehendi, non ex meo fefelli sed fallentes incaute imitata fui.

BOOK 2

HERE BEGINS THE SECOND BOOK, WOVEN IN A DRAMATIC SEQUENCE

All the material of this little work, just as of the earlier one, I have taken from ancient books written under the names of known authorities, with the exception of the passion of Saint Pelagius included above. The narrative of his martyrdom a certain native of the same city in which Pelagius himself was martyred expounded to me; he swore that he had seen that most handsome of men and that he knew the truth
about the outcome of the matter. So, if I have included any 2
sort of falsehood in writing either of these books, the error did not originate with me, but rather I have mistakenly followed writers who were themselves in error.

<Praefatio>

Plures inveniuntur Catholici, cuius nos penitus expurgare
nequimus facti, qui pro cultioris facundia sermonis, genti-
lium vanitatem librorum utilitati praeferunt sacrarum scrip-
2 turarum. Sunt etiam alii sacris inhaerentes paginis, qui licet
alia gentilium spernant, Terentii tamen figmenta frequen-
tius lectitant; et dum dulcedine sermonis delectantur, ne-
3 fandarum notitia rerum maculantur. Unde ego Clamor Vali-
dus Gandeshemensis, non recusavi illum imitari dictando,
dum alii colunt legendo, quo eodem dictationis genere, quo
turpia lascivarum incesta feminarum recitabantur, laudabi-
lis sacrarum castimonia virginum iuxta mei facultatem inge-
4 nioli celebraretur. Hoc tamen facit non raro verecundari,
gravique rubore perfundi, quod, huiusmodi specie dictatio-
nis cogente, detestabilem illicite amantium dementiam et
male dulcia colloquia eorum, quae nec nostro auditui per-
mittuntur accommodari, dictando mente tractavi; et stili
5 officio designavi. Sed <si> haec erubescendo neglegerem,
nec proposito satisfacerem, nec innocentium laudem adeo
plene iuxta meum posse exponerem. Quia quanto blanditiae

Preface

Many true Christians are found who prefer the vanity of pa-
gan books to the utility of the sacred scriptures on account
of the elegance of their more refined speech, and I cannot
entirely clear myself of this charge. There are also others, 2
adherents of sacred writings, who even though they reject
the other fictions of the pagans, nevertheless very fre-
quently read and reread those of Terence and, while they are
delighted by the sweetness of his speech, are stained by
becoming acquainted with unmentionably wicked things.
Therefore, I, the Strong Voice of Gandersheim, have not re- 3
fused to imitate him in my writing, since others embrace
him in their reading, so that in that same form of writing in
which the vile sexual transgressions of wanton women were
recounted, the laudable chastity of holy virgins might be
celebrated, as far as my limited ability permits. Nonetheless, 4
this not rarely makes me blush, and covers me in a deep red,
because, by the constraints of this genre of writing, I have
dealt in my mind, while composing, with the detestable
madness of unlawful lovers and with their wickedly sweet
conversations, things it is not permissible for us even to
hear; and I have written these things down using my pen.
But if I were to omit these things just because they make me 5
blush, I would neither fulfill my intention, nor would I pro-
pound to the best of my ability the praise of the innocent.
For, however much more prone the sweet words of mad

amentium ad illiciendum promptiores, tanto et superni Adiutoris gloria sublimior, et triumphantium victoria probatur gloriosior, praesertim cum feminea fragilitas vinceret,
6 et virilis robur confusioni subiaceret. Non enim dubito mihi ab aliquibus obici, quod huius vilitas dictationis multo inferior, multo contractior, penitusque dissimilis eius quem proponebam imitari, sit sententiis. Concedo. Ipsis tamen denuntio, me in hoc iure reprehendi non posse, quasi his vellem abusive assimilari, qui mei inertiam, longe praecesse-
7 runt in scientia sublimiori. Nec enim tantae sum iactantiae, ut vel extremis me praesumam conferre auctorum alumnis. Sed hoc solum nitor: ut licet nullatenus valeam apte, supplici tamen mentis devotione acceptum in Datorem retorqueam ingenium.

8 Ideoque non sum adeo amatrix mei, ut, pro vitanda reprehensione, Christi, qui in sanctis operatur, virtutem, quo-
9 cumque ipse dabit posse, cessem praedicare. Si enim alicui placet mea devotio, gaudebo. Si autem, vel pro mei abiectione, vel pro vitiosi sermonis rusticitate, nulli placet, memet ipsam tamen iuvat quod feci, quia dum proprii vilitatem laboris in aliis meae inscientiae opusculis heroico ligatam strophio, in hoc dramatica vinctam serie colo, perniciosas gentilium delicias abstinendo devito.

lovers are to entice us, so much the more sublime will be the glory of our celestial Helper, and so much the more glorious the victory of those who triumph, especially when feminine fragility conquers, and manly strength is subjected to shame.
Now, I do not doubt that some will reproach me, alleging 6
that the paltriness of my writing makes it far inferior, far more restricted, and entirely dissimilar in wording to that of the person whom I proposed to imitate. I grant that. Nevertheless, I protest against them that I cannot be justly reprimanded in this matter, as though I wanted, inappropriately, to be compared to those who, in their more elevated wis-
dom, far surpass my lack of skill. Nor indeed am I so arro- 7
gant that I would presume to compare myself even to the least learned pupils of these authorities. Instead, this is all I am trying to achieve: that, even though I am not strong enough in any way to do so sufficiently, nevertheless, I may, in the humble devotion of my heart, turn back onto the Giver the intelligence I have received.

And, therefore, I am not so much a lover of myself that, 8
in order to avoid criticism, I would cease, in whatever way he will grant me the ability, to preach the virtue of Christ,
who works through his saints. If indeed my devotion pleases 9
anyone, I will be happy. If, however, either on account of my inferior condition, or on account of the rusticity of my corrupt speech, it pleases no one, what I created will still gratify me, because while I adorned the inferiority of my labor in those other little products of my ignorance by tethering it to heroic meter, in this one I have done so by shackling it to a dramatic narrative, yet in both cases I have abstemiously avoided the pernicious charms of the pagans.

Epistola eiusdem ad quosdam sapientes huius libri fautores

Plene sciis et bene moratis, nec alieno profectui invidentibus, sed, ut decet vere sapientes, congratulantibus, Hrotsvit, nesciola nullaque probitate idonea, praesens valere, et perpes gaudere.

2 Vestrae igitur laudandae humilitatis magnitudinem satis
admirari nequeo, magnificaeque circa mei vilitatem be-
nignitatis atque dilectionis plenitudinem, condignarum re-
3 compensatione gratiarum remetiri non sufficio. Quia cum
philosophicis apprime studiis enutriti, et scientia longe ex-
cellentius sitis perfecti, mei opusculum vilis mulierculae,
vestra admiratione dignum duxistis. Et largitorem in me
operantis gratiae fraterno affectu gratulantes laudastis, arbi-
trantes mihi inesse aliquantulam scientiam artium quarum
subtilitas longe praeterit mei muliebre ingenium.

4 Denique rusticitatem meae dictatiunculae hactenus vix audebam paucis ac solummodo familiaribus meis ostendere. Unde paene opera cessavit dictandi ultra aliquid huiusmodi, quia sicut pauci fuere qui me prodente perspicerent, ita non

A Letter of the Same Woman to Certain Learned Patrons of This Book

To all those who are well educated and live properly, and who do not envy another's advancement, but instead, as is fitting for those who are truly wise, applaud it, Hrotsvit, a little know-nothing, quite unqualified in worth, sends her wishes for present health and perpetual joy.

I am unable, then, sufficiently to admire the magnitude 2
of your laudable humility, and I am inadequate to repay with a reimbursement of worthy thanks the fullness of your magnificent kindness and affection so far as it concerns my inferiority. Because, although you have been superbly nurtured 3
in philosophical studies, and although you have been far more excellently perfected in knowledge, you have considered this little work written by me, a lowly little woman, worthy of your admiration. And through your congratulations you have praised with brotherly affection the bestower of the grace that operates in me, thinking that there is present in me some little knowledge of those arts, whose subtlety far exceeds my womanly intelligence.

Moreover, I have scarcely dared until now to expose the 4
rusticity of my meager writing even to a few, and only to my friends. So it is that the effort of writing anything further of this sort almost came to a halt, because just as there were few who were paying attention while I was producing it, so

multi qui vel quid corrigendum inesset enuclearent, vel ad
5 audendum aliquid huic simile provocarent. At nunc quia
trium testimonium constat esse verum, vestris corroborata
sententiis fiducialius praesumo et componendis operam
dare, si quando Deus annuerit posse, et quorumcumque sa-
6 pientium examen subire. Inter haec diversis affectibus gau-
dio videlicet et metu in diversum trahor. Deum namque
cuius solummodo gratia sum id quod sum in me laudari
corde tenus gaudeo. Sed maior quam sim videri timeo, quia
utrumque nefas esse non ambigo, et gratuitum Dei donum
7 negare, et non acceptum accepisse simulare. Unde non de-
nego praestante gratia Creatoris per dynamin me artes scire,
quia sum animal capax disciplinae, sed per energian fateor
8 omnino nescire. Perspicax quoque ingenium divinitus mihi
collatum esse agnosco, sed magistrorum cessante diligentia
incultum, et propriae pigritia inertiae torpet neglectum.

9 Quapropter ne in me donum Dei annullaretur ob neglegentiam mei, si qua forte fila vel etiam floccos de panniculis a veste Philosophiae abruptis evellere quivi, praefato opusculo inserere curavi, quo vilitas meae inscientiae intermixtione nobilioris materiae illustraretur, et largitor ingenii, tanto amplius in me iure laudaretur, quanto muliebris sensus tardior esse creditur.

also there were not many who would either explain what in
my work ought to be corrected, or who would encourage me
to dare to attempt anything of a similar nature. But now, 5
because the testimony of three people constitutes truth,
strengthened by your opinions, I more confidently presume
both to devote my effort to compositions, if ever God will
grant me the ability, and to submit them to the judgment of
whoever is wise. Meanwhile, I am pulled in different ways 6
by different emotions, namely by joy and by fear. Assuredly
I am joyful from the bottom of my heart that God, by whose
grace alone I am what I am, is praised through me. On the
other hand, I am afraid to seem greater than I am, for I do
not doubt that both these things are crimes: to deny a gift of
God freely given, and to pretend to have received some-
thing that one has not received. So I do not deny that by the 7
gift of grace through the power of the Creator I know the
arts, because I am a creature capable of instruction; but I
confess that through my own energy I am entirely ignorant.
I also acknowledge that a perspicacious intelligence was di- 8
vinely conferred upon me, but it has been uncultivated since
the attentiveness of my teachers came to an end; and it lies
numb, neglected by the laziness of my own inertia.

For this reason, so that the gift of God not be nullified in 9
me because of my negligence, if I was able, by chance, to tear away any thread, or even patches of cloth ripped from the robe of Philosophy, I have been careful to insert them into the aforementioned little composition, so that the inferiority of my lack of knowledge would be brightened by the intermingling of a nobler material, and the bestower of my intelligence would be, justly, all the more praised through me, since womanly understanding is believed to be very dull.

10 Haec mea in dictando intentio, haec sola mei sudoris est
causa; neque simulando, me nescita scire iacto, sed quantum
11 ad me, "tantum scio quod nescio." Quia enim attactu vestri
favoris atque petitionis harundineo more inclinata, libellum
quem tali intentione disposui, sed usque huc pro sui vilitate
occultare, quam in palam proferre malui, vobis perscrutan-
dum tradidi. Decet ut non minoris diligentia sollicitudinis
eum emendando investigetis quam proprii seriem laboris.
12 Et sic tandem ad normam rectitudinis reformatum mihi
remittite, quo vestri magisterio praemonstrante, in quibus
maxime peccassem possim agnoscere.

This was my intention in writing, this was the sole reason 10
for my effort; and I do not deceptively boast that I know
things that are unknown to me, but so far as it concerns me,
"this only I know, that I know nothing." Indeed because, 11
touched by your favor and your request, bending like a reed,
I have surrendered this little book to your scrutiny, a little
book which I put in order for that very purpose, but which
until now I preferred to hide because of its inferiority, rather
than to bring it out into the open. It is proper that you in-
vestigate it, emending it with a diligence of no lesser atten-
tiveness than you would apply to a narrative that is your own
labor. And then at last send it back to me, reformed accord- 12
ing to the rules of proper grammar, so that by the guidance
of your teaching, I may learn in what ways I have particu-
larly erred.

<Conversio Gallicani I>

Conversio Gallicani principis militiae, qui iturus ad bellum contra Scithas sacratissimam virginem Constantiam, Constantini imperatoris filiam desponsavit. Sed in conflictu proelii nimium coartatus, per Iohannem et Paulum primicerios Constantiae conversus ad baptisma convolavit, caelibemque vitam elegit. Postea autem iubente Iuliano apostata in exilium missus martyrio est coronatus. Sed et Iohannes et Paulus eodem iubente, clam occisi, et in domo occulte sunt sepulti. Nec mora, percussoris filius, a daemonio arreptus, patris commissum, et martyrum confitendo meritum, iuxta eorum sepulchra salvatus una cum patre est baptizatus.

Constantinus imperator
Gallicanus
Constantia
Artemia
Attica
Iohannes
Paulus
Principes

I

Constantinus. Taedet me, Gallicane, morarum quia gentem quam scis Scitharum, Romanae solam resistere paci,

The Conversion of Gallicanus I

The conversion of Gallicanus, commander of the army, who, as he was about to go to war against the Scythians, got engaged to Constance, the emperor Constantine's daughter, a very saintly girl. But at a crucial moment in the battle, in dire straits, he was converted by John and Paul, the chief advisors of Constance, hurriedly had himself baptized, and chose the celibate life. Afterward, though, by order of Julian the Apostate, he was sent into exile and crowned with martyrdom. But both John and Paul, by Julian's order, were clandestinely killed, and they were secretly buried in the palace. Straightaway the son of their assassin was possessed by a demon; he acknowledged his father's crime and the merits of the martyrs; he was saved and baptized together with his father next to the tombs of the martyrs.

Constantine the Emperor	Attica
Gallicanus	John
Constance	Paul
Artemia	Princes

I

Constantine. I am tired of the delays, Gallicanus, because the Scythian nation, as you know, stands alone in refusing to make peace with Rome, and they have the temerity to

nostrisque temere praeceptis reluctari. Bello protrahis lacessere, cum pro tui strenuitate, id tibimet exercitii, ad defensionem non ignores patriae servari.

2 GALLICANUS. Tuis enim, O auguste Constantine, obnixe manibus pedibusque semper insistens obsequiis, tui augustalis excellentiae votis, effectu conabar respondere operis, nec umquam me subtraxi faciendis.

3 CONSTANTINUS. Si opus est monitu, nam memoriae fixum teneo. Unde monui, hortando potius quam arguendo, morem ut geras.

GALLICANUS. Id ipsum etiam nunc studebo.

CONSTANTINUS. Gaudeo!

GALLICANUS. Nec amore vitae abduci potero, quin peragam, quae iubes.

CONSTANTINUS. Placet, tuique in me benevolentiam laudo.

4 GALLICANUS. Sed summa implendae intentio servitutis, summam expetit recompensationem mercedis.

CONSTANTINUS. Nec iniuria.

GALLICANUS. Difficultas enim cuiuscumque laboris tolerabilius fertur, si haud incerta accipiendae spe mercedis relevatur.

CONSTANTINUS. Patet.

GALLICANUS. Unde ineundi praemium periculi, mihi quaeso proponas in praesenti, quo impigre dimicans sudore non frangar certaminis animatus spe retributionis.

oppose our orders. Still you hesitate to make war on them, even though you know it was because of your aggressiveness that this military exercise in defense of the fatherland was put under your command.

GALLICANUS. O venerable Constantine, I have always been resolute, striving with hands and feet, to serve you; I have tried to respond to the wishes of Your Venerable Excellence by carrying out my job, and I have never shied away from what had to be done. 2

CONSTANTINE. There is no need for a reminder, indeed it is fixed in my mind. It was for this reason that I brought it up, to encourage you to act in your accustomed manner, rather than to rebuke you. 3

GALLICANUS. I will get busy right now doing precisely that.

CONSTANTINE. I am delighted!

GALLICANUS. Not for the love of life could I be deterred from accomplishing what you order.

CONSTANTINE. That pleases me, and I applaud your good will toward me.

GALLICANUS. But the best intentions in performing a service require the best compensation as a reward. 4

CONSTANTINE. And not unjustly.

GALLICANUS. Surely the difficulty of any labor is more easily borne if it is lightened by the secure expectation of receiving a reward.

CONSTANTINE. Clearly.

GALLICANUS. So, I ask that you declare at once what reward you would propose for my undertaking this danger. Then, fighting vigorously, inspired by the hope of this reward, I will not break down from the toil of the contest.

5 Constantinus. Quod dignissimum omnique videbatur senatui gratissimum, numquam tibi negabam aut negabo praemium, scilicet nostrae adeptionem familiaritatis, praecipuaeque inter palatinos dignitatis.

Gallicanus. Fateor, sed id nunc haud molior.

Constantinus. Si aliud expetas, oportet proferas.

Gallicanus. Immo aliud.

Constantinus. Quid?

6 Gallicanus. Si praesumo dicere.

Constantinus. Et bene.

Gallicanus. Irasceris.

Constantinus. Nullo modo.

Gallicanus. Certe.

Constantinus. Non.

Gallicanus. Moveberis indignatione.

Constantinus. Ne id vereare.

7 Gallicanus. Dicam; iussisti. Constantiam tui natam, amo—

Constantinus. Et merito; decet ut erilem filiam honorabiliter ames, et amabiliter honores.

Gallicanus. Interrumpis dicenda.

Constantinus. Non interrumpo.

Gallicanus. Ipsamque, si tui annuerit pietas, desponsare gestio.

8 Constantinus. Non leve appetit praemium, sed summum, vobisque, O principes, ante insolitum.

Constantine. I have never withheld from you the reward 5
which seemed most worthy and most pleasing to the entire senate, nor will I deny it, namely admission to my inner circle of friends and special honors among the palace officials.

Gallicanus. I acknowledge as much, but that is not what I am now after.

Constantine. If there is something else you want, it is appropriate for you to state it.

Gallicanus. In fact, there is something.

Constantine. What?

Gallicanus. I do not presume to say. 6

Constantine. It will be alright.

Gallicanus. You will be angry.

Constantine. Not at all.

Gallicanus. I am sure you will.

Constantine. Not so.

Gallicanus. You will be stirred to indignation.

Constantine. Do not be afraid.

Gallicanus. I will speak; you have commanded it. I love 7
your daughter Constance—

Constantine. And properly so; it is right that you honorably love and lovingly honor my noble daughter.

Gallicanus. You are interrupting what I have to say.

Constantine. I won't interrupt.

Gallicanus. And, if your generosity will permit it, I am eager to marry her.

Constantine. He does not seek a trivial reward, but the 8
highest one, my lords, and one previously unheard of among you.

GALLICANUS. Eheu, dedignatur! Praescivi. Instate quaeso mecum precibus.

PRINCIPES. Decet tuam, Imperator egregie, dignitatem, ut, pro sui reverentia, hoc illi non abnuas.

CONSTANTINUS. Si abnuo quantum ad me, sed subtili primum inquisitione reor investigandum, an filia praebeat assensum.

PRINCIPES. Consequens est.

CONSTANTINUS. Ibo, ipsamque si velis, Gallicane, pro hac re appellabo.

GALLICANUS. Ac libens.

2

CONSTANTIA. Dominus imperator adit nos solito tristior; quid velit vehementer admiror.

CONSTANTINUS. Huc ades, O filia Constantia. Paucis te volo.

CONSTANTIA. Adsum, domine mi. Iube quid velis.

CONSTANTINUS. Anxietate cordis fatigor, gravique tristitia afficior.

CONSTANTIA. Ut te venientem adspexi, tristitiam deprehendi, et licet causam ignorarem, conturbata pertimui.

CONSTANTINUS. Tui causa contristor.

CONSTANTIA. Mei?

CONSTANTINUS. Tui.

CONSTANTIA. Expaveo! Quid est, domine mi?

CONSTANTINUS. Piget dicere, ne contristeris.

CONSTANTIA. Multo magis contristor, si non dixeris.

GALLICANUS. Oh no, he refuses! I saw it coming. Stand by me, please, with your entreaties.

PRINCES. It is in keeping with your dignity, O illustrious Emperor, out of respect for him, not to deny him this.

CONSTANTINE. I do not deny him, so far as it is up to me; but I think there must first be a careful inquiry to determine whether my daughter gives her consent.

PRINCES. That is reasonable.

CONSTANTINE. I will go, and if you wish, Gallicanus, I will address her on this matter.

GALLICANUS. I do wish it.

2

CONSTANCE. My lord the emperor is headed my way, sadder than usual; I very much wonder what it means.

CONSTANTINE. Come to me, Constance, my daughter. I would like a few words with you.

CONSTANCE. Here I am, my lord. Ask what you wish.

CONSTANTINE. I am worn out from anxious concern, afflicted with a heavy sorrow.

CONSTANCE. When I saw you approaching, I noticed your sorrow, and though I did not know the reason for it, I was terribly disturbed.

CONSTANTINE. I am distressed for your sake.

CONSTANCE. For my sake?

CONSTANTINE. For your sake.

CONSTANCE. I am shocked! What is it, my lord?

CONSTANTINE. I am ashamed to say, because it might upset you.

CONSTANCE. I will be much more upset if you do not say.

2 Constantinus. Gallicanus dux, cui frequens successus triumphorum primum inter principes dignitatis acquisivit gradum, cuiusque ope saepissime indigemus ad defensionem patriae . . .

Constantia. Quid ille?

Constantinus. Desiderat te sponsam habitum ire.

Constantia. Me?

Constantinus. Te.

3 Constantia. Malim mori.

Constantinus. Praescivi.

Constantia. Nec mirum, quia tuo consensu, tuo permissu, servandam Deo virginitatem devovi!

Constantinus. Memini.

Constantia. Nullis enim suppliciis umquam potero compelli, quin inviolatum custodiam sacramentum propositi.

4 Constantinus. Convenit. Sed hinc coartor nimium, quia si quod debet fieri, paterno more te in proposito permansum ire consensero, haud leve damnum patiar in publica re. Si autem—quod absit!—renitor, aeternis cruciandus poenis subiacebo.

Constantia. Si enim divinum desperarem adesse auxilium mihi quam maxime, mihi potissimum esset dolendum.

Constantinus. Verum.

Constantia. Nunc autem nullus relinquitur locus maestitiae praesumenti de Domini pietate.

Constantinus. Quam bene dicis, mea Constantia.

5 Constantia. Si meum digneris captare consilium, praemonstrabo qualiter utrumque evadere possis damnum.

Constantinus. O utinam!

Constantine. General Gallicanus, whose frequent mili- 2
tary triumphs have gained him the highest rank among the nobles, and whose aid in defending the country I have so often needed . . .

Constance. What about him?

Constantine. He wants you to become his wife.

Constance. Me?

Constantine. You.

Constance. I would rather die. 3

Constantine. I foresaw that.

Constance. No wonder, since by your consent, by your permission, I vowed to remain a virgin for God!

Constantine. I am aware.

Constance. By no punishments can I ever be forced not to keep inviolate the sacred vow of my commitment.

Constantine. That is as it should be. But that is why I'm 4
so distressed, because if the proper thing is done, namely, that I approve, as a father should, of your keeping your commitment, I will suffer no small damage as a ruler. If however—God forbid!—I oppose you, I will suffer the torments of eternal punishment.

Constance. Indeed, if I had any doubt that divine aid is abundantly at my disposal, I would be terribly grieved.

Constantine. Truly.

Constance. Now, however, there is no place for sadness, for I take the Lord's mercy for granted.

Constantine. How rightly you speak, my Constance.

Constance. If you think it proper to take my advice, I will 5
show you how you can avoid both of these evils.

Constantine. If only!

Constantia. Simula prudenter peracta expeditione, ipsius votis te satisfacturum esse. Et ut meum concordari credat velle, suade, quo suas interim filias, Atticam ac Artemiam, velut pro solidandi pignore amoris mecum mansum ire, meosque primicerios, Iohannem et Paulum, secum faciat iter arreptum ire.

Constantinus. Et quid, si victor revertetur, mihi erit agendum?

Constantia. Reor Omnipatrem prius esse invocandum, quo ab huiusmodi intentione Gallicani revocet animum.

6 Constantinus. O filia, filia, quantum dulcedine tuae allocutionis amaritudinem dulcorasti maesti patris, adeo, ut pro hac re nulla post haec movear sollicitudine.

Constantia. Non est necesse.

Constantinus. Eam et Gallicanum laeta promissione circumveniam.

Constantia. Vade in pace, mi domine.

3

Gallicanus. Curiositate frangar, O principes, antequam quid mis senior augustus tam diu cum herili filia agat experiar.

Principes. Suadet illi, velle quae desideras.

Gallicanus. O utinam praevaleret suasio!

Principes. Forsitan praevalebit.

2 Gallicanus. Silete! Quiescite! Augustus revertitur, non ut abiit obscuro, sed vultu admodum sereno.

Principes. Bona fortuna!

CONSTANCE. Prudently pretend that when the campaign is completed you will satisfy his wishes. And in order that he believe that my wish is in accord with his, persuade him to make his daughters Attica and Artemia remain with me for the duration, as a pledge for strengthening our love, and to make my chamberlains, John and Paul, undertake the expedition with him.

CONSTANTINE. And what will I do if he returns victorious?

CONSTANCE. I think the Father of everything must be called on in advance, so that he may turn Gallicanus's mind away from any intention to marry.

CONSTANTINE. O daughter, daughter, with your sweet 6
words you have so thoroughly sweetened the bitterness of your father's sorrow that from now on I will not worry about this.

CONSTANCE. There is no need to worry.

CONSTANTINE. I should go and try to circumvent my difficulties with Gallicanus through this encouraging promise.

CONSTANCE. Go in peace, my lord.

3

GALLICANUS. I will die of curiosity, princes, before I learn what my venerable lord is doing for so long with his noble daughter.

PRINCES. He is persuading her to want what you desire.

GALLICANUS. If only his persuasion might succeed!

PRINCES. Perhaps it will succeed.

GALLICANUS. Silence! Be quiet! The emperor is returning, 2
not with a gloomy expression as when he left, but with a somewhat cheerful expression.

PRINCES. Good luck!

GALLICANUS. Si enim, ut dicitur, speculum mentis est facies, serenitas faciei mansuetudinem forte designat eius animi.

PRINCIPES. Ita!

4

CONSTANTINUS. Gallicane.

GALLICANUS. Quid dixit?

PRINCIPES. Procede, procede, vocat te.

GALLICANUS. Dii propitii favete!

2 CONSTANTINUS. Perge securus, Gallicane, ad bellum. Reversus enim accipies quod desideras praemium.

GALLICANUS. Illudisne me?

CONSTANTINUS. Si illudo.

GALLICANUS. Me felicem, si unum scirem.

CONSTANTINUS. Quid unum?

GALLICANUS. Eius responsum.

CONSTANTINUS. Filiae?

GALLICANUS. Ipsius.

3 CONSTANTINUS. Iniusta satis ratio in hac re verecundae virginis responsum quaerere. Consequentia autem rerum monstrabit eius assensum.

GALLICANUS. Si hunc scirem, responsum flocci facerem.

CONSTANTINUS. Licet experiare.

GALLICANUS. Exopto.

4 CONSTANTINUS. Sui primicerios Iohannem et Paulum tecum commoratum iri decrevit usque in diem nuptiarum.

GALLICANUS. Quam ob causam?

GALLICANUS. If, as they say, the face is indeed the mirror of the mind, then maybe the serenity of his face indicates that his mind is at ease.

PRINCES. Just so!

4

CONSTANTINE. Gallicanus.

GALLICANUS. What did he say?

PRINCES. Go, go, he's calling you.

GALLICANUS. May the gracious gods favor me!

CONSTANTINE. March off to war carefree, Gallicanus. 2
When you return, you will, in fact, get the reward you desire.

GALLICANUS. Are you joking with me?

CONSTANTINE. I am not joking.

GALLICANUS. How happy I would be, if I knew one thing for sure.

CONSTANTINE. What thing?

GALLICANUS. Her reply.

CONSTANTINE. My daughter's?

GALLICANUS. Hers.

CONSTANTINE. It is very unreasonable in such a matter to 3
ask for a modest maiden's reply. The outcome, however, will reveal her consent.

GALLICANUS. If I were certain of that, I wouldn't care about her reply.

CONSTANTINE. You may put it to the test.

GALLICANUS. I'm eager to try.

CONSTANTINE. She has decided that her chamberlains John 4
and Paul will stay with you until the day of the wedding.

GALLICANUS. Why?

CONSTANTINUS. Quo illorum ex confabulatione ipsius vitam, mores, consuetudinem, possis praenoscere.

GALLICANUS. Bonum consilium, mihique quam maxime placitum.

CONSTANTINUS. Scilicet tui filias secum versa vice desiderat interim mansum ire, quatenus illarum per sodalitatem tibi fiat morigera.

GALLICANUS. Euax, euax! Omnia meis respondent votis.

CONSTANTINUS. Fac ut adducantur citius.

GALLICANUS. Statis milites? Currite, abite, adducite filias ad obsequium sui dominae.

5

MILITES. Assunt illustres Gallicani natae, tuae familiaritati, era Constantia, pro sui pulchritudinis, sapientiae, et probitatis perspicuitate satis aptae.

2 CONSTANTIA. Placet. Introducantur honorifice. Amator
virginitatis et inspirator castitatis, Christe, qui me, preci-
bus martyris tuae Agnetis, a lepra pariter corporis et ab
errore eripiens gentilitatis invitasti ad virgineum tui ge-
nitricis thalamum, in quo tu manifestus es verus Deus.
Retro exordium, natus a Deo Patre. Idemque verus homo
3 ex matre natus in tempore. Te veram et coaeternam Patris
sapientiam, per quam facta sunt omnia, et cuius dispo-
sitione consistunt et moderantur universa, suppliciter
exoro, ut Gallicanum, qui tui in me amorem surripiendo

CONSTANTINE. So that by speaking with them you may learn in advance about her life, her character, her habits.

GALLICANUS. A good idea, and one that pleases me immensely.

CONSTANTINE. Naturally she wants your daughters, in ex- 5
change, to stay with her in the meantime, so that through a close relationship with them she may become more pleasing to you.

GALLICANUS. Hurrah, hurrah! Everything is just as I wish.

CONSTANTINE. Have them brought here as soon as possible.

GALLICANUS. Soldiers, why are you just standing there? Hurry, go, bring my daughters here to wait on their lady.

5

SOLDIERS. Here are the illustrious daughters of Gallicanus; they are most worthy of your friendship, Lady Constance, because of the brightness of their beauty, wisdom, and goodness.

CONSTANCE. That pleases me. Let them be introduced with 2
honor. O Christ, lover of virginity and inspirer of chastity, you, through the prayers of Agnes your martyr, snatching me equally from the leprosy of the body and the error of paganism, have invited me to the virginal marriage bed of your mother, in which you were made manifest as true God. Before the beginning of time, you were born from God the Father. In time, you were born as true man
from your mother. You, the true and coeternal wisdom of 3
the Father, through whom all things were made, and by whose disposition everything exists and is controlled, I ask as a suppliant, that you restrain Gallicanus, who is trying surreptitiously to extinguish the love for you that

conatur exstinguere, post te trahendo, ab iniusta intentione revocare. Suique filias digneris tibi assignare sponsas, et instilla cogitationibus earum tui amoris dulcedinem, quatenus exsecrantes carnale consortium, pervenire mereantur ad sacrarum societatem virginum.

ARTEMIA. Ave, Constantia, imperialis era.

4 CONSTANTIA. Salvete sorores, Attica et Artemia. State, state, ne procidatis. Sed libate mihi osculum amoris.

ARTEMIA. Tuum ad obsequium, domina, alacri mente venimus. Tuae dicioni summa devotione nos subicimus, tantum ut tua nobis abundet gratia.

5 CONSTANTIA. Unum Dominum habemus in caelis, cui debetur devotio nostrae servitutis. In cuius fide et dilectione condecet nos servata corporis integritate unanimiter perseverare, ut mereamur aulam caelestis patriae cum palma virginitatis introire.

6 ARTEMIA. In nullo reluctamur, sed tis in omnibus praeceptis parere nitimur, praecipue in agnitione veritatis, et servandae proposito virginitatis.

CONSTANTIA. Congrua satis responsio, vestraque ingenuitate condigna. Nec dubito quin divinae inspiratione gratiae ad credendum estis praeventae.

ARTEMIA. Qui posset fieri ut, servientes idolis, sanum saperemus sine illustratione supernae pietatis?

7 CONSTANTIA. Stabilitas vestrae fidei spem mihi excitat de credulitate Gallicani.

ARTEMIA. Admoneatur tantum, haud dubium quin credat.

CONSTANTIA. Advocentur Ioannes et Paulus.

is in me; restrain him from his unjust plan, by drawing him to you. And I ask that you see fit to designate his daughters as your spouses, and instill in their thoughts the sweetness of your love, so that despising carnal union, they earn admission to the society of holy virgins.

Artemia. Hail, Constance, imperial lady.

Constance. Greetings sisters, Attica and Artemia. Stand 4
up, stand up, don't bow down. Give me a kiss of love instead.

Artemia. We come with hearts ready to serve you, lady. We submit to your command with the greatest devotion so that your grace will abound in us.

Constance. We have one God in heaven to whom we owe 5
devotion and service. In his faith and love we ought to persevere in single-mindedness, preserving the purity of our bodies, so that we earn the right to enter the palace of the celestial kingdom with the victory palm of virginity.

Artemia. We have no hesitation and will try to obey your 6
every command, especially by recognizing the truth and by leading a life that preserves our virginity.

Constance. A very satisfactory response, and one worthy of your noble stature. I do not doubt that you had already come to your faith through the inspiration of divine grace.

Artemia. How could it be possible that we, who were servants of idols, could understand sanely except by the illumination of heavenly mercy?

Constance. Your steadfast faith gives me hope that Galli- 7
canus will become a believer.

Artemia. Let him only be guided, and there is no doubt that he will believe.

Constance. Summon John and Paul.

6

IOHANNES. Praesto sumus, era, quid vocasti?

CONSTANTIA. Ite citi ad Gallicanum et inhaerentes eius lateri, suadete illi paulatim mysterium nostrae fidei, si forsan illum Deus dignetur per vos lucrari.

PAULUS. Deus det proventum, nos adhibemus frequentationes hortamentorum.

7

GALLICANUS. Opportune advenitis, Iohannes et Paule. Suspensis diu animis vestrum praestolabar adventum.

IOHANNES. Ut vocem iubentis dominae hausimus, tibi ad obsequendum convolavimus.

GALLICANUS. Multo magis vestro quam aliorum delector obsequio.

PAULUS. Nec inmerito, nam vulgo dicitur, quod dilecti socius et ipse sit dilectus.

GALLICANUS. Verum.

IOHANNES. Dilectio mittentis herae reconciliatur nos familiaritati tuae.

2 GALLICANUS. Non nego. Convenite, congregamini tribuni et centuriones, omnesque mei iuris milites. Adsunt Iohannes et Paulus, quorum detinebar absentia ne pergerem.

TRIBUNI. Praecede; collectim comitantur.

GALLICANUS. Capitolium et templa primum nobis intranda, numinaque deorum placanda sunt ritu sacrificiorum, quo prosperentur exitum pugnae.

6

John. We are here, lady. Why have you called?

Constance. Go quickly to Gallicanus and, clinging to his side, convince him little by little of the mystery of our faith. Perhaps God will see fit to convert him through you.

Paul. May God grant us success! We will provide repeated encouragements.

7

Gallicanus. You've come just in time, John and Paul. I have long been holding my breath, awaiting your arrival.

John. As soon as we heard our lady's request, we rushed to serve you.

Gallicanus. Your service pleases me far more than any others'.

Paul. And rightly so, for it is commonly said that the friend of someone dear is also himself dear.

Gallicanus. That is true.

John. Our love for the lady who sent us should commend us to your affection.

Gallicanus. I will not deny it. Come, tribunes and centu- 2
rions and every soldier under my command, gather together. John and Paul are here; I was prevented by their absence from setting out.

Tribunes. Lead the way; we'll follow all together.

Gallicanus. First, we must go to the Capitoline Hill and to the temples, and we must placate the will of the gods with ritual sacrifices, so that they favor the outcome of the battle.

TRIBUNI. Necesse.

IOHANNES. Subtrahamus nos interim.

PAULUS. Decet.

8

IOHANNES. En dux egreditur. Ascendamus equos, offeramus nos obviam.

PAULUS. Ac cito.

GALLICANUS. Unde venitis? Ubi fuistis?

IOHANNES. Stravimus, sarcinulas praemisimus, quo expediti tuum iter possimus comitari.

GALLICANUS. Placet.

9

GALLICANUS. O tribuni, pro Iuppiter aspicio innumerabilis exercitus legiones, variis armorum instrumentis horribiles!

TRIBUNI. Hercle hostes!

GALLICANUS. Resistamus fortiter, et congrediamur viriliter!

TRIBUNI. Si est utilis nostri congressio cum tantis.

GALLICANUS. Et quid mavultis?

TRIBUNI. Submittere colla.

GALLICANUS. Nolit hoc Apollo.

TRIBUNI. Edepol faciendum! En undique secus circumdamur, vulneramur, perimimur.

GALLICANUS. Eh heu! Quid erit cum tribuni me spernunt, se tradunt?

2 IOHANNES. Fac votum Deo caeli, te Christianum fieri, et vinces.

Tribunes. A necessary measure.

John. We should remove ourselves while this is happening.

Paul. That is proper.

8

John. Look, the general is approaching. We should mount our horses and go to meet him.

Paul. Yes. And quickly.

Gallicanus. Where are you coming from? Where have you been?

John. We saddled the horses and sent our packs ahead, so we could join your march unimpeded.

Gallicanus. I approve.

9

Gallicanus. O tribunes, I see, by Jove, the legions of an enormous army, bristling with an array of weapons!

Tribunes. By Hercules, it's the enemy!

Gallicanus. We must stand firm and fight bravely!

Tribunes. There is no use our fighting against so many.

Gallicanus. And what would you prefer?

Tribunes. To surrender.

Gallicanus. Apollo will not allow it!

Tribunes. By Pollux, it must be done! We are surrounded on every side; we are being wounded; we are being slaughtered.

Gallicanus. Oh woe! What will happen when the tribunes abandon me and surrender themselves?

John. Make a vow to the God of heaven that you will be- 2
come a Christian; then you will defeat them.

GALLICANUS. Voveo, et opere implebo.

HOSTES. Heus rex Bradan, sperandae fortuna victoriae alludit nos. En dextrae languescunt, vires fatiscunt, sed et inconstantia pectoris cogit nos discedere ab armis.

BRADAN. Quid dicam ignoro. Ipsa quam toleratis me urget passio. Restat ut nos duci tradamus.

HOSTES. Alias non evademus.

3 BRADAN. Dux Gallicane, noli in nostri perniciem saevire. Sed parce et utere ut libet nostra servitute.

GALLICANUS. Ne trepidetis, ne formidetis, sed datis obsidibus facite vos tributarios imperatoris, et vivite beate sub Romana pace.

HOSTES. Tuo arbitrio pendet, quot qualesque accipere quantumque pondus solvendi census nobis velis imponere.

GALLICANUS. Solvite procinctum mei milites! Nemo laedatur, nemo perimatur. Amplectamur foederatos, quos publicos insectabamur inimicos.

4 IOHANNES. Quanto magis valet intenta precatio, quam humana praesumptio!

GALLICANUS. Verum.

PAULUS. Quam efficax his aderit superna miseratio, quos Deo commendat humilis devotio!

GALLICANUS. Perspicuum.

IOHANNES. Sed quod vovetur in perturbatione, solvendum est in tranquillitate.

GALLICANUS. I do make that vow, and I will fulfill it by my action.

ENEMY SOLIDER. Oh, King Bradan, fate has cheated us of the victory we had hoped for. Look, our hands are weary, our strength is sapped; furthermore, our wavering courage compels us to give up the fight.

BRADAN. I don't know what to say. The pain you are suffering, afflicts me too. Our only choice is to surrender to the general.

ENEMY SOLDIERS. There is no other escape.

BRADAN. General Gallicanus, don't be savage and kill us. In- 3
stead, spare us and benefit from our enslavement, however you please.

GALLICANUS. Do not tremble, do not be afraid; just surrender hostages and pay tribute to the emperor, then live contentedly under Roman peace.

ENEMY SOLDIERS. It is up to you how many and what sort of hostages you want to receive, and what burden you wish to impose on us by way of taxes.

GALLICANUS. Lower your weapons, soldiers! No one should be injured, no one killed. Let us embrace as our allies those we were pursuing as public enemies.

JOHN. Earnest prayer is so much stronger than human pre- 4
sumption!

GALLICANUS. That is true.

PAUL. What a powerful presence heavenly compassion will be to those men, whose humble devotion commends them to God!

GALLICANUS. That is clear.

JOHN. But what was sworn in times of trouble must be carried out in the times of peace.

GALLICANUS. Assentio. Unde quantocius baptizari gestio, ac reliquum vitae in Dei obsequio vacare.

PAULUS. Iustum.

10

GALLICANUS. Ecce, in introitu nostro proruunt Romani urbicolae, insignia laudum ferentes ex more.

IOHANNES. Consequens est.

GALLICANUS. Sed nec nostrae nec deorum fortitudini titulus debetur triumphi.

PAULUS. Nullo modo, sed vero Deo.

GALLICANUS. Unde templa arbitror transeunda.

IOHANNES. Recte arbitraris.

GALLICANUS. Et limina apostolorum, supplici confessione esse intranda.

PAULUS. O te tali opinione felicem! Nunc testaris te verum Christicolam.

11

CONSTANTINUS. Admiror, O milites, cur Gallicanus tam diu se subtrahat nostris conspectibus.

MILITES. Ut urbem intravit, gressum ad domum sancti Petri concite tetendit, terra tenusque prostratus, pro recepta victoria grates impendit Altithrono.

CONSTANTINUS. Gallicanus?

MILITES. Ipse.

CONSTANTINUS. Incredibile.

MILITES. En accedit. Ipsum potes sciscitari.

GALLICANUS. I agree, so I want to be baptized as soon as possible and spend the rest of my life in service to God.

PAUL. That is just.

10

GALLICANUS. Look, the Roman citizens are rushing out to celebrate our arrival, bearing the banners of victory according to custom.

JOHN. It is to be expected.

GALLICANUS. But the credit for this triumph is not owed to our fortitude, nor to that of the gods.

PAUL. No, but to the one true God.

GALLICANUS. And therefore, I think we ought to avoid the temples.

JOHN. You judge rightly.

GALLICANUS. And the shrines of the apostles ought to be visited with prayer and a profession of faith.

PAUL. How fortunate you are in that thought! Now you provide proof that you are a true Christian.

11

CONSTANTINE. I wonder, soldiers, why Gallicanus has kept himself out of my sight for so long.

SOLDIERS. When he entered the city, he went straight to the church of Saint Peter, and bowed down to the ground, he gave thanks to the One enthroned on high for the victory won.

CONSTANTINE. Gallicanus did that?

SOLDIERS. Gallicanus himself.

CONSTANTINE. That is incredible.

SOLDIERS. Look, here he comes. You can ask him.

12

CONSTANTINUS. Diu te, Gallicane, sustinui, ut modum exitumque experirer proelii.

GALLICANUS. Dicam digestim.

CONSTANTINUS. Hoc interim parvi pendo, quo edisseras quod magis exopto.

GALLICANUS. Quid est?

CONSTANTINUS. Cur iturus deorum templa, et revertens intrares apostolorum tecta?

GALLICANUS. Rogas?

CONSTANTINUS. Curiose.

GALLICANUS. Expono.

CONSTANTINUS. Exopto.

2 GALLICANUS. Fateor, sacratissime imperator, iturus ut obiecisti sacella intravi, meque daemoniis et diis supplex commisi.

CONSTANTINUS. Hoc Romanis antiquitus fuit in more.

GALLICANUS. Mala consuetudo.

CONSTANTINUS. Pessima.

3 GALLICANUS. Quo peracto tribuni cum suis legionibus advenere, meque euntem undiquesecus saepsere.

CONSTANTINUS. Pomposo admodum apparatu egrediebaris.

GALLICANUS. Promovimus, hostes impegimus, comisimus, victi sumus.

CONSTANTINUS. Romani victi?

GALLICANUS. Penitus.

12

CONSTANTINE. I have been waiting a long time for you, Gallicanus, so I could hear the course and outcome of the battle.

GALLICANUS. I will give an orderly account.

CONSTANTINE. I care little about that at the moment; you may tell me instead something I am more eager to hear.

GALLICANUS. What is it?

CONSTANTINE. Why did you enter the temples of the gods when you were preparing to leave, and the churches of the apostles when you returned?

GALLICANUS. Is there need to ask?

CONSTANTINE. I am curious.

GALLICANUS. I will explain.

CONSTANTINE. I am eager to hear.

GALLICANUS. I confess, most sacred emperor, that, setting 2
out as you have charged, I entered the sanctuaries and entrusted myself as a suppliant to demons and idols.

CONSTANTINE. This has been the practice among the Romans since ancient times.

GALLICANUS. It is an evil custom.

CONSTANTINE. The worst.

GALLICANUS. When that was finished, the tribunes and the 3
legions came, and they surrounded me on every side as I marched out.

CONSTANTINE. You departed with quite a parade.

GALLICANUS. We advanced, we engaged the enemy, we battled, we were conquered.

CONSTANTINE. The Romans were conquered?

GALLICANUS. Totally.

CONSTANTINUS. O res dira, omnibusque saeclis inaudita!

4 GALLICANUS. Ego quidem nefanda sacrificia iteravi, nec aderant qui adiuvarent dii. Sed invalescente congressione plurimi ex nostris interiere.

CONSTANTINUS. Confundor audiendo.

GALLICANUS. Tandem tribuni me spreverunt, se tradiderunt.

CONSTANTINUS. Hostibus?

GALLICANUS. Ipsis.

5 CONSTANTINUS. Ah, quid fecisti?

GALLICANUS. Quid possem facere, nisi fugam captare?

CONSTANTINUS. Non!

GALLICANUS. Etiam!

CONSTANTINUS. Quantis tunc angustiis urgebatur constantia tui pectoris!

GALLICANUS. Maximis.

CONSTANTINUS. Et quomodo evasisti?

6 GALLICANUS. Mis familiares socii Iohannes et Paulus suaserunt mihi, votum fecisse Creatori.

CONSTANTINUS. Salubre.

GALLICANUS. Experiebar. Ut os ad vovendum aperui, caeleste iuvamen sensi.

CONSTANTINUS. Quo pacto?

7 GALLICANUS. Apparuit mihi iuvenis procerae magnitudinis, crucem ferens in umeris et praecepit, ut stricto mucrone illum sequerer.

CONSTANTINUS. Quisquis ille erat, caelitus missus fuerat.

GALLICANUS. Comprobavi. Nec mora astiterunt mihi a dextra laevaque milites armati, quorum vultum minime agnovi, promittentes auxilium sui.

CONSTANTINUS. Caelestis militia!

CONSTANTINE. Oh what a dire thing, unheard of in previous ages!

GALLICANUS. I repeated, indeed, the wicked sacrifices, and 4
there were no gods there to help us. But as the battle surged, a great many of our soldiers died.

CONSTANTINE. I am distressed hearing this.

GALLICANUS. Finally, the tribunes deserted me and surrendered themselves.

CONSTANTINE. To the enemy?

GALLICANUS. To the enemy.

CONSTANTINE. Ah me! What did you do? 5

GALLICANUS. What could I do other than to take flight?

CONSTANTINE. No!

GALLICANUS. Yes!

CONSTANTINE. What pains must then have afflicted your steadfast heart!

GALLICANUS. The greatest pains.

CONSTANTINE. And how did you escape?

GALLICANUS. My dear companions John and Paul per- 6
suaded me to make a vow to the Creator.

CONSTANTINE. Sound advice.

GALLICANUS. I tried it. As soon as I opened my mouth to make the vow, I felt heavenly aid.

CONSTANTINE. In what way?

GALLICANUS. There appeared before me a young man of 7
towering height, carrying a cross on his shoulders; and he ordered me to follow him with my sword drawn.

CONSTANTINE. Whoever he was, he was sent from heaven.

GALLICANUS. As I discovered. Straightaway, armed soldiers surrounded me on the right and on the left. I did not recognize their faces, but they promised me their assistance.

CONSTANTINE. A heavenly host!

8 Gallicanus. Non ambigo. At ubi sequens praecedentem securus inter medias hostium ingrederer acies, perveni ad regem eorum, nomine Bradan. Qui mox incredibili metu correptus, pedibusque meis provolutus, se cum suis subdidit, professus censum principi Romani orbis fine tenus solvendum.

Constantinus. Grates prosperitatis auctori, qui in se sperantes non patitur confundi.

Gallicanus. Experimento didici.

9 Constantinus. Vellem experiri, quid deinde profugi actitarent tribuni.

Gallicanus. Maturabant reconciliari.

Constantinus. Recepistin' gratis?

Gallicanus. Ego illos gratis, qui me periclis, qui se inimicis? Haud ita!

Constantinus. Et qui?

Gallicanus. Proposui promerendae gratiae pretium.

Constantinus. Quale?

Gallicanus. Videlicet sectam Christicolarum. Quam qui elegerit, gratiam susciperet priorem honoremque ampliorem; qui vero spreverit, gratia simul privaretur et militia.

Constantinus. Recta propositio tuaque auctoritate condigna.

10 Gallicanus. Ego quidem baptismate imbutus totum me Deo subiugavi, in tantum ut tuae, quam prae omnibus dilexi, abrenuntiarem filiae, quo abstinens coniugii placerem Virginis Proli.

GALLICANUS. I have no doubt. And then following the 8
leader, I marched safely through the enemy's ranks and
came to their king, whose name is Bradan. He was immediately seized by an incredible fear and, throwing himself at my feet, surrendered himself and his army, promising to pay taxes to the ruler of the Roman world till the end of time.

CONSTANTINE. Thanks be to the author of our success, who does not allow those who trust in him to be confounded.

GALLICANUS. I have learned this from experience.

CONSTANTINE. I should like to know what the tribunes 9
who deserted did next.

GALLICANUS. They were in a hurry to be reconciled.

CONSTANTINE. Did you take them back freely?

GALLICANUS. Did I freely take back men who had surrendered me to danger and themselves to the enemy? Certainly not!

CONSTANTINE. What then?

GALLICANUS. I set a price for earning forgiveness.

CONSTANTINE. And what kind of price?

GALLICANUS. Why, Christianity. Whoever chose to adopt it would be restored to their former favor and even higher honors; but whoever rejected it would be removed at once from my favor and from the army.

CONSTANTINE. That is a proper proposal and one that is worthy of your dignity.

GALLICANUS. I myself, fresh from baptism, have surren- 10
dered myself entirely to God, so much so that I would break my engagement to your daughter, whom I love more than all other women, in order to find favor with the Virgin's Son by abstaining from marriage.

Constantinus. Accede propius, ut irruam in tuos amplexus. Nunc quidem, nunc cogor tibi detegere, quod ad tempus studebam velare.

Gallicanus. Quid?

Constantinus. Id videlicet quod mea tuaeque natae eidem quam elegisti student religioni.

Gallicanus. Gaudeo!

Constantinus. Tantoque servandae virginitatis flagrant amore, ut nec minis, nec blandimentis revocari possunt ab intentione.

Gallicanus. Perseverent exopto.

11 Constantinus. Introeamus in palatium, ubi ipsae commorantur.

Gallicanus. Praecede; sequar.

Constantinus. Ecce occurrunt, cum augusta Helena, mei genetrice gloriosa! Omnibusque lacrimae fluunt prae gaudio.

13

Gallicanus. Vivite feliciter, O sanctae virgines, perseverantes in Dei timore! Decusque virginitatis inviolatum servate, quo dignae inveniamini amplexibus Regis aeterni.

Constantia. Eo liberius servabimus, quo te non contraluctari sentimus.

2 Gallicanus. Non contraluctor. Non renitor. Non prohibeo. Sed vestris in hoc votis libens concedo, in tantum ut nec te, O mea Constantia, quam haud segniter emi vitae pretio, aliud quam coepisti velle cogo.

Constantine. Come closer so I can rush into your arms. Now, indeed, now I am compelled to reveal to you what, for a time, I was eager to conceal.

Gallicanus. And what is that?

Constantine. The fact, namely, that my daughter and your daughters practice the very same religion that you have chosen.

Gallicanus. I am delighted!

Constantine. They are inflamed with such a desire to preserve their virginity that neither by threats nor bribes can they be dissuaded from their resolution.

Gallicanus. I hope they persevere.

Constantine. Let's go into the palace, where they are 11
waiting.

Gallicanus. Lead the way; I will follow.

Constantine. Look, they are coming to meet us, accompanied by the empress Helena, my glorious mother! Everyone is crying for joy.

13

Gallicanus. Holy virgins, live happily, remaining constant in the fear of God! And preserve the unblemished honor of your virginity, so that you may be found worthy of the embraces of the eternal King.

Constance. We will preserve it all the more openly, since we understand that you are not opposed.

Gallicanus. I am not opposed. I do not resist. I do not 2
prohibit you. Rather, I am happy to yield to your wishes in this matter, so much so that I will not force you, my dear Constance, whose hand I was quick to acquire even at the cost of my life, to choose any other course than the one on which you have embarked.

CONSTANTIA. Haec mutatio dextrae excelsi.

GALLICANUS. Si in melius mutatus non essem, tuae promissioni assensum non praeberem.

3 CONSTANTIA. Amicus pudicitiae virginalis et fautor totius bonae voluntatis, qui te ab iniusta intentione revocavit meamque virginitatem sibi signavit, dignetur nos pro corporali discidio quandoque associatum ire in aeterno gaudio.

GALLICANUS. Fiat! Fiat!

14

CONSTANTINUS. Cum vinculum Christi amoris in unius nos societate coniungat religionis, decet ut, quasi gener augustorum, honorifice nobiscum habites intra palatium.

GALLICANUS. Nulla magis est vitanda temptatio quam oculorum concupiscentia!

CONSTANTINUS. Refragari nequeo.

GALLICANUS. Unde non expedit me frequentius virginem intueri, quam prae parentibus, prae vita, prae anima a me scis amari.

CONSTANTINUS. Ut libet.

2 GALLICANUS. Ecce, habes quadruplicatum exercitum Christo favente et me laborante. Patere ut nunc militem imperatori, cuius iuvamine vici, et cui debeo quicquid feliciter vixi.

CONSTANTINUS. Ipsum decet laus et iubilatio. Ipsi debet famulari omnis eius plasmatio.

Constance. The hand of God on high produced this transformation.

Gallicanus. If I had not been changed for the better, I would not grant my approval of your promise to take vows.

Constance. May the lover of maidenly chastity and the 3
patron of all good will, who dissuaded you from your unworthy plan and designated my virginity for himself, judge us worthy on account of our separation in this life to be one day joined together in eternal joy!

Gallicanus. May it be so! May it be so!

14

Constantine. Since the bond of Christ's love joins us in the fellowship of a single religion, it is right that you live with us in honor, as son-in-law of the emperor and empress, in the palace.

Gallicanus. No temptation ought to be more strenuously avoided than lust of the eyes!

Constantine. I cannot argue with that.

Gallicanus. So, it is not a good idea for me frequently to see this maiden, whom, as you know, I love more than my parents, than my life, than my soul.

Constantine. As you wish.

Gallicanus. Look, you now have, by Christ's aid and by 2
my efforts, an army four times as large as before. Let me now fight for the imperial Lord through whose assistance I was victorious, and to whom I owe every happiness I have enjoyed in life.

Constantine. He deserves praise and jubilation. All his creation ought to serve him.

GALLICANUS. Sed illi potissimum, quis in necessitate largius praestat auxilium.

CONSTANTINUS. Ut asseris.

3 GALLICANUS. Partem possessionis quae ad filias pertinet excipio, partemque ad susceptionem peregrinorum mihi reservo. De reliquo, proprios servos libertate donatos ditari, pauperumque necessitates volo sustentari.

CONSTANTINUS. Prudenter possessa disponis, nec expers fies aeternae retributionis.

4 GALLICANUS. Me ipsum etiam sancto viro Hilariano in urbe Ostensi individuum sodalem ardeo associatum iri, quo ibidem reliquum vitae in Dei laude pauperumque vacem susceptione.

CONSTANTINUS. Simplex esse cui semper est posse sinat tui esse prosperis successionibus iuxta sui velle vigere, et perducat te ad gaudia aeternitatis, qui regnat et gloriatur in unitate Trinitatis.

GALLICANUS. Amen.

GALLICANUS. But especially those to whom he more abundantly offered aid when they were in need.

CONSTANTINE. As you say.

GALICANUS. I reserve one share of my property which goes to my daughters, and one share for myself to provide assistance to pilgrims. From the remainder, I want my slaves, who are now granted their freedom, to be endowed, and the needs of the poor to be relieved. 3

CONSTANTINE. You dispose of your property wisely, and you will not be without an eternal reward.

GALLICANUS. Furthermore, I am eager to join up with the holy man Hilarianus in the city of Ostia, as his inseparable companion, so that I might spend there the remainder of my life praising God and assisting the poor. 4

CONSTANTINE. May that singular Being who is ever powerful grant that you prosper with good success according to his will, and may he who reigns and is glorified in the unity of the Trinity lead you to the joys of eternity!

GALLICANUS. Amen.

<Conversio Gallicani 2>

Iulianus imperator Milites
Consules

1

Iulianus. Incommodum satis nostro probatur esse imperio, quod Christiani libero utuntur arbitrio, et iactant se leges debere sequi, quas accipiebant temporibus Constantini.

Consules. Turpe si pateris.

Iulianus. Non patiar.

Consules. Decet.

2 Iulianus. O milites, accingimini, et nudate Christicolas possessionibus propriis obiciendo sententiam Christi dicentis, "*Qui non renuntiaverit omnibus quae possidet, non potest meus esse discipulus.*"

Milites. In nobis non erit mora.

2

Consules. En milites revertuntur.

Iulianus. Secundusne vester reditus?

Milites. Secundus!

Iulianus. Et cur tam citus?

The Conversion of Gallicanus 2

Julian the Emperor   Soldiers
Consuls

I

Julian. It has proven to be a great nuisance to our empire that the Christians exercise their free will and boast that they ought to follow the laws they secured in the time of Constantine.

Consuls. What a disgrace if you tolerate that!

Julian. I will not tolerate it.

Consuls. That is proper.

Julian. Soldiers, arm yourselves and strip the Christians of 2
their property, taunting them with the dictum of Christ,
who said, "*Whoever does not renounce all that he has, cannot
be my disciple.*"

Soldiers. We will not delay.

2

Consuls. Look, the soldiers are returning.

Julian. Is your return propitious?

Soldiers. Propitious indeed!

Julian. And so why are you back so soon?

MILITES. Dicemus: Castella, quae Gallicanus sibi retinuit, decrevimus intrasse, tuaeque servituti usurpasse, sed si quis ex nostris pedem admovit, leprosum seu inergumi-num se esse cognovit.

IULIANUS. Revertimini, ipsumque compellite vel patriam deserere, vel idolis sacrificare!

3

GALLICANUS. Ne fatigemini, O milites, inutilia suadendo, quia in aestimatione aeternae vitae flocci facio, quicquid habetur sub sole. Unde patriam desero, et exsul pro Christo Alexandriam peto, optans ibidem coronari martyrio.

4

MILITES. Gallicanus, ut iussisti, patria expulsus Alexandriam petiit. Ibique a Rautiano comite tentus, gladio est peremptus.

IULIANUS. O bene factum!

MILITES. Sed Iohannes et Paulus te fastidiunt.

IULIANUS. Quid agunt?

MILITES. Libere vagant; thesauros Constantiae erogant.

IULIANUS. Advocentur!

5

MILITES. Adsunt.

SOLDIERS. We'll explain: We decided to enter the castle which Gallicanus retained for himself and to commandeer it for your purposes, but whenever one of us set foot in it, he immediately discovered he had become a leper or was possessed.

JULIAN. Go back at once, and force him either to leave the country, or to sacrifice to the gods!

3

GALLICANUS. Don't wear yourselves out, soldiers, trying uselessly to persuade me, because in expectation of eternal life, I don't care about anything under the sun. So, I'll leave this land and for the sake of Christ go as an exile to Alexandria, hoping there to be crowned in martyrdom.

4

SOLDIERS. As you ordered, Gallicanus was expelled from the country, and he went to Alexandria. There he was taken into custody by the magistrate Rautianus, and died by the sword.

JULIAN. Oh, well done!

SOLDIERS. But John and Paul still scorn you.

JULIAN. What are they doing?

SOLDIERS. They are wandering around freely; they are distributing the wealth of Constance.

JULIAN. Have them summoned!

5

SOLDIERS. Here they are.

IULIANUS. Non nescio vos, Iohannes et Paule, a cunabulis augustorum mancipatos fuisse obsequio.

IOHANNES. Fuimus.

IULIANUS. Unde decet ut meo inhaerentes lateri serviatis in palatio, in quo nutriti estis a puero.

PAULUS. Haud serviemus.

IULIANUS. Mihin' non servietis?

IOHANNES. Diximus.

2 IULIANUS. Num non videor augustus?

PAULUS. Sed dissimilis prioribus.

IULIANUS. In quo?

IOHANNES. Religione et merito.

IULIANUS. Vellem plenius audire.

PAULUS. Et volumus dicere. Gloriosissimi et famosissimi imperatores, Constantinus, Constans, et Constantius, quorum famulabamur imperio, fuere viri Christianissimi, et gloriabantur se servos esse Christi.

3 IULIANUS. Memini. Sed non opto eos in hoc sequi.

PAULUS. Deteriora imitaris. Qui ecclesias frequentabant, et, excusso diademate, prostrati Iesum Christum adorabant.

IULIANUS. Ad haec me non cogitis.

IOHANNES. Ideo illis es dissimilis.

PAULUS. Nam quia adorabant Creatorem, augustalis apicem dignitatis ornabant, et beatificabant insignibus suae probitatis et sanctitatis, prosperisque ad vota successionibus pollebant.

IULIANUS. Certe et ego.

JULIAN. I am not unaware that you, John and Paul, were assigned to imperial service from the time you were born.

JOHN. So we were.

JULIAN. So it is proper that, staying by my side, you serve in the palace, where you were raised since childhood.

PAUL. We will not serve you.

JULIAN. You will not serve me?

JOHN. That's what we said.

JULIAN. What then, am I not the emperor? 2

PAUL. But you are not like your predecessors.

JULIAN. In what way?

JOHN. In religion and in merit.

JULIAN. I'd like to hear a fuller explanation.

PAUL. And we'd like to tell you: The most honorable and famous emperors, Constantine, Constans, and Constantius, under whose authority we served, were the most Christian of men, and they were proud to be servants of Christ.

JULIAN. I recall that. But I don't choose to follow them in 3
this respect.

PAUL. The examples you follow are worse. They were often in church and, casting aside their crowns, bowed down and worshiped Jesus Christ.

JULIAN. You could not force me to do those things.

JOHN. That's how you are unlike them.

PAUL. Precisely because they worshipped the Creator, they were the epitome of imperial dignity, and they blessed it by the marks of their probity and sanctity, and they excelled in successfully achieving their goals.

JULIAN. And certainly I do as well!

Iohannes. Non simili modo, quia eos divina comitabatur gratia.

4 Iulianus. Frivola! Ego quondam stultus talia exercui, et clericatum in Ecclesia obtinui.

Ionhannes. Placetne tibi, O Paule, clericus?

Paulus. Diaboli capellanus.

Iulianus. At ubi nihil utilitatis inesse deprehendi, ad culturam deorum me inflexi, quorum pietas me provexit ad fastigium regni.

Iohannes. Abrupisti nostri orationem, ne audires iustorum laudem.

Iulianus. Quid ad me?

5 Paulus. Nihil. Sed subiungendum est quod ad te. Postquam enim mundus eis non erat dignus habendis, suscepti sunt inter angelos, tibique infelix res publica relinquebatur regenda.

Iulianus. Cur "infelix" iuxta id temporis?

Iohannes. Ex qualitate rectoris.

Paulus. Reliquisti omnem religionem, et imitatus es idolatriae superstitionem. Pro hac iniquitate et a tuis conspectibus et a tuorum societate nos subtraximus.

6 Iulianus. Licet satis multis iniuriis a vobis dehonestatus sim, adhuc tamen parcens audaciae, cupio vos inter primos in palatio extollere.

Iohannes. Ne fatiga te, quia nec minis nec blandimentis cogimur cedere.

JOHN. Not in the same way, because divine grace was their companion.

JULIAN. Nonsense! I was once foolish enough to perform 4
those rites, and I became a priest in your Church.

JOHN. How do you like this priest, Paul?

PAUL. He is the devil's chaplain.

JULIAN. But when I had determined that there was nothing beneficial in those practices, I turned myself to the worship of the Roman gods, whose goodwill has elevated me to the peak of power.

JOHN. You interrupted our speech to avoid hearing us praise the just men who were your predecessors.

JULIAN. How does that concern me?

PAUL. Not at all. But I must add something that does con- 5
cern you. For after the world was no longer worthy to hold them, they were taken up among the angels, and then this unfortunate state was left for you to rule.

JULIAN. Why do you call it "unfortunate" after that point in time?

JOHN. Because of the caliber of its ruler.

PAUL. You have abandoned all religion and have aped the superstition of idolatry. Because of that depravity, we have removed ourselves from your sight as well as from your society.

JULIAN. Even though I have been disrespected by you with 6
a great many insults, I will, nonetheless, still pardon your audacity; I want to raise you to the highest ranks in the palace.

JOHN. Do not trouble yourself, because neither by flattery nor by threats can we be compelled to yield.

7 IULIANUS. Decem dierum dabo indutias, quo tandem resipiscentes ultro maturetis reconciliari gratiae nostrae dignitatis. Sin autem, quod faciendum est faciam, ne ultra vobis ludibrium fiam.

PAULUS. Quod facturus eris, hodie perfice, quia nec ad tui salutationem, nec ad palatium, nec ad culturam deorum nos poteris revocare.

IULIANUS. Abite! Discedite! Quae monui perpetrate!

IOHANNES. Acceptas non flocci faciamus indutias, sed facultates caelo praemittamus, nosque ieiuniis et obsecrationibus Deo interim commendemus.

PAULUS. Consequens est.

6

IULIANUS. Vade, Terrentiane! Sumptis tecum militibus et compelle Iohannem et Paulum deo Iovi sacrificare. Si autem obstinato restiterint pectore, perimantur. Non palam, sed nimium occulte; quia palatini fuere.

7

TERRENTIANUS. Imperator Iulianus, cui servio, misit vobis, Iohannes et Paule, pro sui clementia aureum simulachrum Iovis, cui tura gratis imponere debetis. Quod si nolueritis, capitalem sententiam subibitis.

IOHANNES. Si Iulianus sit tuus dominus, habeto pacem cum illo et utere eius gratia. Nobis non est alius, nisi Dominus

Julian. I will grant you ten days of indulgence, so that, finally returning to your senses, you may be ready and willing to get back in my good graces. But if not, I will do what must be done, so that I not be an object of ridicule to you any longer. 7

Paul. Whatever you are going to do, you might as well do it today, because you cannot induce us to offer you fealty, nor to come to the palace, nor to worship your gods.

Julian. Get out of here! Leave! Do as I told you!

John. We couldn't care less about the indulgence we've received, but we should turn our thoughts to heaven and recommend ourselves to God in the meantime through fasting and praying.

Paul. That is the logical course.

6

Julian. Go, Terrentianus! Take with you some soldiers, and make John and Paul sacrifice to the god Jupiter. But if their hearts remain obstinate, and they resist, have them destroyed. Not publicly, but very secretly; after all, they were court officials.

7

Terrentianus. The emperor Julian, in whose service I am acting, has sent you, John and Paul, as a display of kindness, a golden effigy of Jupiter. You must burn incense to it of your own free will. If you don't, you will be sentenced to death.

John. If Julian is your lord, keep your peace with him and enjoy his favor. We have no Lord other than Jesus Christ.

Iesus Christus. Pro cuius amore desideramus mori, quo mereamur aeternis gaudiis perfrui.

2 TERRENTIANUS. Quid tardatis, milites? Stringite ferrum, et interficite imperatoris deorumque rebelles. Interfectos clam in domo sepelite, nullumque sanguinis vestigium relinquite.

MILITES. Et quid dicemus rogati?

TERRENTIANUS. Simulate, quasi exilio sint destinati.

IOANNES. PAULUS. Te, Christe, cum Patre et sancto Spiritu regnantem, unum Deum sub hoc periculo invocamus. Te moriendo laudamus. Tu suscipe animas pro te de lutea habitatione eliminatas.

8

TERRENTIANUS. Eh heu, O Christicolae, quid patitur unicus filius meus?

CHRISTICOLAE. Stridet dentibus, sputa iacit, torquet insana lumina, nam plenus est daemonio.

TERRENTIANUS. Vae patri! Ubi agitatur?

CHRISTICOLAE. Ante sepulcra martyrum Iohannis et Pauli; humi provolvitur, seque ipsorum precibus torqueri fatetur.

2 TERRENTIANUS. Mea culpa, meum facinus! Nam meo hortatu, meo iussu, ipse infelix, impias manus in sanctos martyres misit.

CHRISTICOLAE. Si te hortante deliquit, te compatiente poenas luit.

For love of him we choose to die, so that we earn the pleasure of eternal joy.

Terrentianus. Why are you stalling, soldiers? Draw your 2
swords and kill these men who rebel against our emperor and our gods. Bury their corpses secretly indoors, and leave no trace of blood.

Soldiers. And if we are asked about them, what are we going to say?

Terrentianus. Pretend that they were sent into exile.

John and Paul. You Christ, who reign with the Father and the Holy Spirit as one God, we invoke in this peril. Dying, we praise you. Receive our souls, cleansed for your sake of their earthly abode.

8

Terrentianus. Alas, Christians, what is it my one and only son is suffering?

Christians. He is gnashing his teeth, foaming at the mouth, rolling his eyes insanely, for he is possessed by a demon.

Terrentianus. Pity his poor father! Where does my son suffer?

Christians. In front of the tombs of the martyrs, John and Paul; he is rolling on the ground and claims that he is tormented by their prayers.

Terrentianus. It is my fault, my crime! For it was by 2
my encouragement, by my order that the poor boy laid wicked hands on the holy martyrs.

Christians. If he sinned at your behest, you suffer along with him while he is punished.

Terrentianus. Ego quidem miser parui iussis impiissimi imperatoris Iuliani.

Christicolae. Ideo namque ipse divina perculsus est ultione.

Terrentianus. Scio. Eoque magis expaveo, quo nullum hostem Dei servorum impunitum evasisse meminero.

Christicolae. Recte.

Terrentianus. Quid si curram, et paenitens sceleris sacris provolvar tumulis?

Christicolae. Veniam mereberis, si tamen baptismate mundaberis.

9

Terrentianus. Gloriosi testes Christi, Iohannes et Paule, imitamini exemplum magistri eadem iubentis, et orate pro persecutorum delictis. Este compatientes orbati patris angustiis, et misereamini furientis nati miseriis, quo ambo tincti fonte baptismatis perseveremus in fide sanctae Trinitatis.

2 Christicolae. Parce, Terrentiane, lacrimis, et parce anxietati cordis. En filius tuus resipiscit, et per martyrum suffragia sanum recepit.

Terrentianus. Gratias Regi aeternitatis, qui suis militibus tantum praestitit honoris, ut non solum animae gaudent in caelis, sed etiam mortua in tumulis ossa variis fulgent miraculorum titulis, in testimonium sui sanctitatis, praestante Domino nostro Iesu Christo qui vivit <et regnat Deus in unitate Spiritus sancti per omnia saecula saeculorum. Amen.>

Terrentianus. Poor me, I was only obeying the orders of Julian, the wickedest of emperors.

Christians. For that reason, no doubt, your son was struck down by divine retribution.

Terrentianus. I know. And I am all the more afraid because I know that no enemy of your God's servants has escaped unharmed.

Christians. And rightly so.

Terrentianus. What if I run to prostrate myself at their holy tombs, repenting of my crime?

Christians. You will earn forgiveness, but only if you are also cleansed in baptism.

9

Terrentianus. John and Paul, glorious martyrs of Christ, imitate both the example and the bidding of your master, and pray for the sins of your persecutors. Have compassion upon the pain of a father who has lost a child, and pity the miseries of a son who is raving, so that both of us, dipped in the baptismal font, may continue believing in the Holy Trinity.

Christians. Terrentianus, spare your tears, and spare the 2
anxiety of your heart. Look, your son is recovering his senses, and through the aid of the martyrs he has regained his health.

Terrentianus. Thanks be to the eternal King, who gives such honor to his soldiers that not only do their souls rejoice in heaven, but even the dead bones in their tombs shine forth through all manner of miraculous signs, in witness to their sanctity, by order of our Lord Jesus Christ, who lives and reigns as God in the unity of the Holy Spirit for ever and ever. Amen.

<Passio sanctarum virginum Agapis, Chioniae, et Hirenae>

Passio sanctarum virginum Agapis, Chioniae, et Hirenae, quas sub nocturno silentio Dulcitius praeses clam adiit, cupiens earum amplexibus saturari. Sed mox ut intravit, mente captus; ollas et sartagines, pro virginibus amplectendo, osculabatur donec facies et vestes horribili nigredine inficiebantur. Deinde Sisinnio comiti ius super puniendas virgines cessit, qui, etiam miris modis illusus, tandem Agapem et Chioniam concremari, et Hirenam iussit perfodi.

Diocletianus	Hirena
Agapes	Dulcitius
Chionia	Milites

I

Diocletianus. Parentelae claritas ingenuitatis vestrumque serenitas pulchritudinis exigit vos nuptiali lege primis in palatio copulari. Quod nostri iussio annuerit fieri, si Christum negare nostrisque diis sacrificia velitis ferre.

The Passion of the Holy Virgins Agape, Chionia, and Hirena

The passion of the holy virgins Agape, Chionia, and Hirena, whom the governor Dulcitius visited in the still of the night, yearning to satisfy his hunger for their embraces. But as soon as he entered, he lost his mind; he kissed the pots and pans, hugging them instead of the maidens, until his face and clothes were infected with a horrible blackness. Then he ceded the authority to punish the girls to Count Sisinnius, who, also mocked in wondrous ways, at last ordered Agape and Chionia to be incinerated, and Hirena to be pierced by an arrow.

Diocletian	Hirena
Agape	Dulcitius
Chionia	Soldiers

I

Diocletian. The brilliance of your noble parentage and the fairness of your beauty demand that you be coupled in legal marriage to men of the first rank in the palace. My order will assure that this is done, if you are willing to deny Christ and bring sacrifices to our gods.

2 AGAPES. Esto securus curarum, nec te gravet nostrum praeparatio nuptiarum, quia nec ad negationem confitendi nominis, nec ad corruptionem integritatis, ullis rebus compelli poterimus.

3 DIOCLETIANUS. Quid sibi vult ista, quae vos agitat, fatuitas?

AGAPES. Quod signum fatuitatis nobis inesse deprehendis?

DIOCLETIANUS. Evidens magnumque.

AGAPES. In quo?

DIOCLETIANUS. In hoc praecipue, quod relicta vetustae observantia religionis, inutilem Christianae novitatem sequimini superstitionis.

AGAPES. Temere calumniaris statum Dei omnipotentis. Periculum.

DIOCLETIANUS. Cuius?

AGAPES. Tui, reique publicae quam gubernas.

DIOCLETIANUS. Ista insanit; amoveatur!

4 CHIONIA. Mea germana non insanit, sed tui stultitiam iuste reprehendit.

DIOCLETIANUS. Ista inclementius bacchatur; unde nostris conspectibus aeque subtrahatur, et tertia discutiatur.

5 HIRENA. Tertiam rebellem tibique penitus probabis renitentem.

DIOCLETIANUS. Hirena, cum sis minor aetate, fito maior dignitate.

HIRENA. Ostende, quaeso. Quo pacto?

DIOCLETIANUS. Flecte cervicem diis, et esto sororibus exemplum correctionis et causa liberationis.

Agape. Do not be concerned, and do not let the prepara- 2
tion of marriages for us weigh heavily upon you, because we cannot be compelled by any means either to renounce our profession of Christ's name or to corrupt our integrity.

Diocletian. What is the meaning of this idiocy agitating 3
you?

Agape. What sign of idiocy do you detect in us?

Diocletian. One that is evident and great.

Agape. In what way?

Diocletian. In this way in particular, that having abandoned the observance of the old religion, you are following the useless novelty of Christian superstition.

Agape. You are rashly insulting the standing of God the Almighty. That's dangerous.

Diocletian. To whom?

Agape. To you, and to the state you are governing.

Diocletian. This woman is insane; take her away!

Chionia. My sister is not insane, but justly criticizes your 4
stupidity.

Diocletian. This woman is even more severely deranged; so, she too should be removed from my sight, and the third one should be examined.

Hirena. You will find the third one a rebel who totally re- 5
jects you.

Diocletian. Hirena, although you are a minor in age, make yourself an elder in dignity.

Hirena. Show me, please. How?

Diocletian. Bow your neck to the gods, and be for your sisters an example of reform and the reason for their being freed.

6 HIRENA. Conquiniscant idolis, qui velint incurrere iram Celsitonantis. Ego quidem caput, regali unguento delibutum, non dehonestabo pedibus simulacrum submittendo.

DIOCLETIANUS. Cultura deorum non adducit inhonestatem, sed praecipuum honorem.

7 HIRENA. Et quae inhonestas turpior, quae turpitudo maior, quam ut servus veneretur ut dominus?

DIOCLETIANUS. Non suadeo tibi venerari servos, sed dominos principumque deos.

HIRENA. Nonne is est cuiusvis servus, qui ab artifice pretio comparatur ut empticius?

8 DIOCLETIANUS. Huius praesumptio verbositatis tollenda est suppliciis.

HIRENA. Hoc optamus, hoc amplectimur: ut pro Christi amore suppliciis laceremur.

DIOCLETIANUS. Istae contumaces nostrisque decretis contraluctantes catenis irretiantur, et ad examen Dulcitii praesidis sub carcerali squalore serventur.

2

DULCITIUS. Producite, milites, producite quas tenetis in carcere.

MILITES. Ecce quas vocasti.

DULCITIUS. Papae! Quam pulchrae, quam venustae, quam egregiae puellulae!

MILITES. Perfectae decore.

DULCITIUS. Captus sum illarum specie.

MILITES. Credibile.

HIRENA. Let those people cower before idols who want to incur the wrath of the Thunderer on high. I, at least, will not dishonor my head, which was daubed with royal chrism, by submitting at the feet of statues. 6

DIOCLETIAN. Worship of the gods does not bring dishonor, but an exceptional honor.

HIRENA. And what dishonor is filthier, what filthiness is greater, than that a slave be venerated as a lord? 7

DIOCLETIAN. I am not encouraging you to venerate slaves, but the lords and gods of princes.

HIRENA. Is this not someone's slave, this thing which is bought as merchandise from a craftsman for a price?

DIOCLETIAN. The arrogance of this babbling must be stopped by torture. 8

HIRENA. That is what we desire, that is what we embrace: to be wracked by torture for the love of Christ.

DIOCLETIAN. These obstinate women, fighting against my decrees, should be entangled in chains, and they should be kept in the prison's squalor for examination by the governor Dulcitius.

2

DULCITIUS. Bring them forth, soldiers, bring forth those women you are holding in the prison.

SOLDIERS. Here are the women you requested.

DULCITIUS. Oh my! How beautiful, how charming, how exquisite these little girls are!

SOLDIERS. Flawless in their loveliness.

DULCITIUS. I am captivated by their appearance.

SOLDIERS. Quite understandable.

2 DULCITIUS. Exaestuo illas ad mei amorem trahere!

MILITES. Diffidimus te praevalere.

DULCITIUS. Quare?

MILITES. Quia stabiles fide.

DULCITIUS. Quid si suadeam blandimentis?

MILITES. Contemnunt.

DULCITIUS. Quid si terream suppliciis?

MILITES. Parvi pendunt.

DULCITIUS. Et quid fiet?

MILITES. Praecogita.

3 DULCITIUS. Ponite illas in custodiam, in interiorem officinae aedem, in cuius proaulio ministrorum servantur vasa.

MILITES. Ut quid eo loci?

DULCITIUS. Quo a me saepiuscule possint visitari.

MILITES. Ut iubes.

3

DULCITIUS. Quid agant captivae sub hoc noctis tempore?

MILITES. Vacant hymnis.

DULCITIUS. Accedamus propius.

MILITES. Tinnulae sonitum vocis a longe audiemus.

2 DULCITIUS. Observate pro foribus cum lucernis. Ego autem intrabo, et vel optatis amplexibus me saturabo.

MILITES. Intra. Praestolabimur.

Dulcitius. I am burning to entice them to make love to 2
me!

Soldiers. We doubt you will succeed.

Dulcitius. Why?

Soldiers. Because they are firm in their faith.

Dulcitius. What if I tempt them with flatteries?

Soldiers. They will reject them.

Dulcitius. What if I terrify them with punishments?

Soldiers. They will think nothing of it.

Dulcitius. Then what shall be done?

Soldiers. Give it some thought.

Dulcitius. Put them under guard, in the inner room of my 3
office, the one in whose vestibule the servants' pots and pans are stored.

Soldiers. Why there?

Dulcitius. So that they can be visited by me all the more frequently.

Soldiers. As you order.

3

Dulcitius. What are the prisoners doing at this time of night?

Soldiers. They spend their time singing hymns.

Dulcitius. Let's go closer.

Soldiers. We will listen to the sound of their ringing voices from a distance.

Dulcitius. Keep watch with the lanterns outside the 2
doors. I, however, am going to enter, and perhaps I will get my fill of their charming embraces.

Soldiers. Enter. We'll be waiting for you.

4

Agapes. Quid strepit pro foribus?

Hirena. Infelix Dulcitius. Ingreditur.

Chionia. Deus nos tueatur!

Agapes. Amen.

2 Chionia. Quid sibi vult collisio ollarum, caccaborum, et sartaginum?

Hirena. Lustrabo. Accedite quaeso, per rimulas perspicite.

Agapes. Quid est?

Hirena. Ecce, iste stultus, mente alienatus, aestimat se nostris uti amplexibus.

Agapes. Quid facit?

3 Hirena. Nunc ollas molli fovet gremio, nunc sartagines et caccabos amplectitur, mitia libans oscula.

Chionia. Ridiculum.

Hirena. Nam facies, manus, ac vestimenta, adeo sordidata, adeo coinquinata, ut nigredo quae inhaesit similitudinem Aethiopis exprimat.

Agapes. Decet ut talis appareat corpore, qualis a diabolo possidetur in mente.

4 Hirena. En parat egredi. Intendamus, quid illo egrediente agant milites pro foribus exspectantes?

5

Milites. Quis hic egreditur? Daemoniacus, vel magis ipse diabolus? Fugiamus.

4

Agape. What's making that noise in front of the doors?

Hirena. That wretch Dulcitius. He's coming in.

Chionia. God save us!

Hirena. Amen.

Chionia. What's the meaning of this clanging of pots and 2
pans and skillets?

Hirena. I'll have a look. Come here, if you please, peer through the cracks.

Agape. What is it?

Hirena. Look, that fool has lost his mind and thinks he's enjoying our embraces.

Agape. What's he doing?

Hirena. Now he's fondling the pots in his tender lap, now 3
he's hugging the pans and the skillets, offering gentle kisses.

Chionia. It's ridiculous.

Hirena. In fact, his face, hands, and clothes are so dirty, so filthy, that the blackness clinging to them makes him look like an Ethiopian.

Agape. It is appropriate he appear that way in his body, since he is possessed by the devil that way in his mind.

Hirena. Look, he's preparing to leave. Let's watch what the 4
soldiers waiting at the door do when he leaves.

5

Soldiers. Who is this emerging? A demoniac, or rather, the devil himself? Let's run.

DULCITIUS. Milites, quo fugitis? State, exspectate, ducite me cum lucernis ad cubile.

MILITES. Vox senioris nostri, sed imago diaboli. Non subsistamus, sed fugam maturemus. Phantasma vult nos pessumdare.

DULCITIUS. Ad palatium ibo, et quam abiectionem patiar, principibus vulgabo.

6

DULCITIUS. Hostiarii introducite me in palatium, quia ad imperatorem habeo secretum.

HOSTIARII. Quid hoc vile ac detestabile monstrum, scissis et nigellis panniculis obsitum? Pugnis tundamus; de gradu praecipitemus; nec ultra huc detur liber accessus.

2 DULCITIUS. Vae, vae, quid contigit? Nonne splendidissimis vestibus indutus? Totoque corpore videor nitidus? Et quicumque me aspicit, velut horribile monstrum fastidit. Ad coniugem revertar, quo ab illa quid erga me actum sit experiar. En solutis crinibus egreditur, omnisque domus lacrimis prosequitur.

7

CONIUX. Heu, heu, mi senior Dulciti, quid pateris? Non es sanae mentis, factus es in derisum Christicolis.

DULCITIUS. Nunc tandem sentio me illusum illarum maleficiis.

DULCITIUS. Soldiers, why do you flee? Stop, wait, lead me with the lanterns to my room.

SOLDIERS. It is the voice of our lord, but the semblance of the devil. Let's not stand here, but make a speedy flight. This phantom wants to harm us.

DULCITIUS. I will go to the palace, and I will make known to the princes what a humiliation I am suffering.

6

DULCITIUS. Guards, lead me into the palace, for I have confidential business with the emperor.

DOORMEN. What is this vile and detestable monster, covered in torn and blackened rags? We should pummel him with blows; we should throw him off the stairs; he should not be given free access beyond this point.

DULCITIUS. Fie, fie, what is happening? Am I not dressed in 2
the most splendid clothes? And doesn't my entire body
seem elegant? And yet, whoever looks at me despises me
as though I'm a horrible monster. I will return to my wife,
to learn from her what has happened to me. Look, she
is coming out with her hair disheveled, and the whole
household follows in tears.

7

WIFE. Alas, alas, my lord Dulcitius, what are you suffering? 7
You are not in your right mind; you have become a laugh-
ingstock to the Christians.

DULCITIUS. Now finally I understand that I have been ridiculed by the witchcraft of those women.

CONIUX. Hoc me vehementer confudit, hoc praecipue contristavit: quod quid patiebaris ignorasti.

DULCITIUS. Mando ut lascivae praesententur puellae, et abstractis vestibus publice denudentur, quo versa vice quid nostra possint ludibria experiantur.

8

MILITES. Frustra sudamus; in vanum laboramus. Ecce vestimenta virgineis corporibus inhaerent velut coria. Sed et ipse qui nos ad exspoliandum urgebat praeses stertit sedendo, nec ullatenus excitari potest a somno. Ad imperatorem adeamus, ipsique rerum quae geruntur propalemus.

9

DIOCLETIANUS. Dolet nimium quod praesidem Dulcitium audio adeo illusum, adeo exprobratum, adeo calumniatum. Sed ne viles mulierculae iactent se impune nostris diis, deorumque cultoribus illudere, Sisinnium comitem dirigam ad ultionem exercendam.

10

SISINNIUS. O milites, ubi sunt lascivae, quae torqueri debent, puellae?

MILITES. Affliguntur in carcere.

SISINNIUS. Hirenam reservate, et reliquas producite.

MILITES. Cur unam excipis?

WIFE. This disturbs me profoundly; this distresses me above all: that you did not know what you were suffering.

DULCITIUS. I command that those wanton girls be brought before me, and that they be exposed in public, stripped of their clothes, so that they in turn can learn the power of my mockery.

8

SOLDIERS. We toil in vain; we labor to no purpose. Look, the clothes cling like skin to their virgin bodies. But also, the governor who urged us to strip them is sitting there snoring and cannot be aroused from sleep in any way. Let's go to the emperor and reveal to him what is happening.

9

DIOCLETIAN. It pains me very much that I hear Governor Dulcitius is so ridiculed, so disparaged, so insulted. But to prevent those vile little women from boasting with impunity that they have ridiculed our gods and the worshippers of our gods, I will send Count Sisinnius to exact punishment.

10

SISINNIUS. Soldiers, where are those wanton girls who are to be tortured?

SOLDIERS. They are suffering in prison.

SISINNIUS. Hold back Hirena, and bring out the others.

SOLDIERS. Why are you excluding one of them?

SISINNIUS. Parcens infantiae. Forte facilius convertetur, si sororum praesentia non terrebitur.

MILITES. Ita.

II

MILITES. Praesto sunt, quas iussisti.

SISINNIUS. Praebete assensum, Agapes et Chionia, meis consiliis.

AGAPES. Si praebebimus.

SISINNIUS. Ferte libamina diis.

AGAPES. Vero et aeterno Patri, eiusque coaeterno Filio, sanctoque amborum Paraclyto, sacrificium laudis sine intermissione libamus.

SISINNIUS. Hoc vobis non suadeo, sed poenis prohibeo.

AGAPES. Non prohibebis, nec umquam sacrificabimus daemoniis.

2 SISINNIUS. Deponite duritiam cordis, et sacrificate. Sin autem, faciam vos interfectum iri, iuxta praeceptum imperatoris Diocletiani.

CHIONIA. Decet ut in nostri necem obtemperes iussis tui imperatoris, cuius nos decreta contemnere noscis. Si autem parcendo moram feceris, aequum est ut tu interficiaris.

3 SISINNIUS. Non tardetis, milites, non tardetis. Capite blasphemas has, et in ignem proicite vivas.

MILITES. Instemus construendis rogis, et tradamus illas bacchantibus flammis, quo finem demus conviciis.

SISINNIUS. Out of consideration for her youth. Perhaps she will be converted more easily, if she is not terrified by the presence of her sisters.

SOLDIERS. Just so.

II

SOLDIERS. Here they are, the ones you ordered.

SISINNIUS. Give your assent, Agape and Chionia, to my advice.

AGAPE. We will not give it.

SISINNIUS. Make sacrifices to the gods.

AGAPE. To the true and eternal Father, and to his coeternal Son, and to the holy Paraclete of both, we continually offer a sacrifice of praise.

SISINNIUS. That is not what I am urging you to do; on the contrary, I will prevent it with punishments.

AGAPE. You will not prevent it, nor will we ever sacrifice to demons.

SISINNIUS. Give up this hardness of heart, and sacrifice. 2
But if you don't, I will have you killed, according to the order of the emperor Diocletian.

CHIONIA. It is appropriate that in killing us you obey the orders of your emperor, whose decrees you know we despise. If, however, you delay out of pity, it is only right that you yourself be killed.

SISINNIUS. Do not delay, soldiers, do not delay. Seize these 3
blasphemers, and toss them alive into the fire.

SOLDIERS. Let's get busy constructing the pyres, and let's hand them over to the raging flames, so we can put an end to their insults.

4 Agapes. Non tibi, Domine, non tibi haec potentia insolita, ut ignis vim virtutis suae obliviscatur, tibi obtemperando. Sed taedet nos morarum; ideo rogamus solvi retinacula animarum, quo extinctis corporibus tecum plaudant in aethere nostri spiritus.

5 Milites. O novum, O stupendum miraculum! Ecce, animae egressae sunt corpora, et nulla laesionis repperiuntur vestigia. Sed nec capilli, nec vestimenta ab igne sunt ambusta, quo minus corpora.

Sisinnius. Proferte Hirenam.

12

Milites. Eccam.

Sisinnius. Pertimesce, Hirena, necem sororum, et cave perire exemplo illarum.

Hirena. Opto exemplum earum moriendo sequi, quo merear cum eis aeternaliter laetari.

Sisinnius. Cede, cede meae suasioni.

Hirena. Haud cedam facinus suadenti.

2 Sisinnius. Si non cesseris, non citum tibi praestabo exitum, sed differam, et nova in dies supplicia multiplicabo.

Hirena. Quanto acrius torqueor, tanto gloriosius exaltabor.

Sisinnius. Supplicia non metuis? Admovebo quod horrescis.

Hirena. Quicquid irrogabis adversi, evadam iuvamine Christi.

AGAPE. Not for you, Lord, not for you is the power unprec- 4
edented to make fire forget the violence of its strength in obedience to you. But we are weary of the delays, so we ask that you release the bonds of our souls, so that when our bodies have perished, our spirits may rejoice with you in heaven.

SOLDIERS. Oh, what a new, oh, what a stupendous miracle! 5
Look, their souls have left their bodies, and no traces of a wound are to be found. And neither their hair nor their clothes were burned by the fire, much less their bodies.

SISINNIUS. Bring out Hirena.

12

SOLDIERS. Here she is.

SISINNIUS. Learn to tremble, Hirena, at the death of your sisters, and avoid destruction by their example.

HIRENA. I want to follow their example in dying, so that I earn the right to rejoice with them for eternity.

SISINNIUS. Give in, give in to my encouragement.

HIRENA. I will not give in to anyone encouraging wrongdoing.

SISINNIUS. If you do not give in, I will not provide you with 2
a quick death but will stretch it out, and I will multiply new tortures for you daily.

HIRENA. The more bitterly I am tortured, the more gloriously I will be exalted.

SISINNIUS. Are you not afraid of tortures? I will apply some that will horrify you.

HIRENA. With the aid of Christ I will escape from whatever adversity you inflict.

3 SISINNIUS. Faciam te ad lupanar duci, corpusque tuum turpiter coinquinari.

HIRENA. Melius est ut corpus quibuscumque iniuriis maculetur, quam anima idolis polluatur.

SISINNIUS. Si socia eris meretricum, non poteris polluta ultra intra contubernium computari virginum.

HIRENA. Voluptas parit poenam, necessitas autem coronam. Nec dicitur reatus, nisi quod consentit animus.

4 SISINNIUS. Frustra parcebam, frustra miserebar huius infantiae.

MILITES. Praescivimus nullatenus ad deorum culturam potest flecti, nec terrore umquam potest frangi.

SISINNIUS. Non ultra parcam.

MILITES. Rectum.

5 SISINNIUS. Capite illam sine miseratione, et trahentes cum crudelitate, ducite ad lupanar sine honore.

HIRENA. Non perducent.

SISINNIUS. Quis prohibere poterit?

HIRENA. Qui mundum sui providentia regit.

SISINNIUS. Probabo.

HIRENA. Ac citius libito.

SISINNIUS. Ne terreamini milites fallacibus huius blasphemae praesagiis.

MILITES. Non terremur, sed tuis praeceptis parere nitimur.

SISINNIUS. I will see to it that you are taken to a brothel 3
and that your body is vilely debauched.

HIRENA. It is better that the body be stained by injuries of any kind whatsoever, than that the soul be polluted by idols.

SISINNIUS. If you are the partner of prostitutes, you will no longer be able, after you've been defiled, to be counted among the cohort of virgins.

HIRENA. Pleasure breeds punishment, but what we are forced to do brings us a crown. And it is not called guilt, unless the mind consents to it.

SISINNIUS. In vain did I spare her, in vain did I pity her 4
youth.

SOLDIERS. We already knew that she could not be forced in any way to worship the gods, nor be broken by any fear.

SISINNIUS. I will spare her no longer.

SOLDIERS. Right.

SISINNIUS. Seize her without mercy, and dragging her cru- 5
elly, lead her in disgrace to a brothel.

HIRENA. They will not accomplish that.

SISINNIUS. Who will prevent it?

HIRENA. He who rules the world by his providence.

SISINNIUS. I will put it to the test.

HIRENA. As quickly as you please.

SISINNIUS. Don't be afraid, soldiers, of the deceitful prophesies of this blasphemer.

SOLDIERS. We are not afraid, but are eager to obey your commands.

13

SISINNIUS. Qui sunt hi qui nos invadunt? Quam similes sunt militibus quibus Hirenam tradidimus. Ipsi sunt. Cur tam cito revertimini? Quo tenditis tam anheli?

MILITES. Te ipsum quaerimus.

SISINNIUS. Ubi est quam traxistis?

MILITES. In supercilio montis.

SISINNIUS. Cuius?

MILITES. Proximi.

2 SISINNIUS. O insensati et hebetes, totiusque rationis incapaces.

MILITES. Cur causaris? Cur voce et vultu nobis minaris?

SISINNIUS. Dii vos perdant.

MILITES. Quid in te commisimus? Quam tibi iniuriam fecimus? Quae tua iussa transgressi sumus?

SISINNIUS. Nonne praecepi, ut rebellem deorum ad turpitudinis locum traheretis?

3 MILITES. Praecepisti, nosque tuis praeceptis operam dedimus implendis, sed supervenere duo ignoti iuvenes asserentes se ad hoc ex te missos, ut Hirenam ad cacumen montis perducerent.

SISINNIUS. Ignorabam.

MILITES. Agnoscimus.

SISINNIUS. Quales fuerunt?

MILITES. Amictu splendidi, vultu admodum reverendi.

4 SISINNIUS. Num sequebamini illos?

MILITES. Sequebamur.

SISINNIUS. Quid fecerunt?

13

SISINNIUS. Who are these men who approach us? How similar they are to those soldiers to whom we entrusted Hirena. They are the same. Why have you returned so swiftly? Where are you going so out of breath?

SOLDIERS. We are looking for you.

SISINNIUS. Where is the girl you were dragging away?

SOLDIERS. On top of the mountain.

SISINNIUS. Which one?

SOLDIERS. The closest one.

SISINNIUS. Oh, you are senseless and dull-witted, incapable 2
of all intelligent thought.

SOLDIERS. Why do you accuse us? Why do you threaten us with your voice and expression?

SISINNIUS. May the gods destroy you!

SOLDIERS. What have we done to you? How have we hurt you? What orders of yours have we transgressed?

SISINNIUS. Did I not order you to drag that opponent of the gods to a place of degradation?

SOLDIERS. You did order it, and we made an effort to carry 3
out your orders, but two unknown young men intervened, saying they had been sent by you for this purpose, to lead Hirena to the top of the mountain.

SISINNIUS. I was ignorant of this.

SOLDIERS. We realize that now.

SISINNIUS. What did they look like?

SOLDIERS. They were splendidly dressed, very respectable in appearance.

SISINNIUS. Did you follow them? 4

SOLDIERS. Yes, we followed them.

SISINNIUS. What did they do?

MILITES. A dextra laevaque Hirenae se locaverunt, et nos huc direxerunt, quo te exitus rei non lateret.

SISINNIUS. Restat ut ascenso equo pergam, et qui fuerint, qui nos tam libere illuserunt, perquiram.

MILITES. Properemus pariter.

14

SISINNIUS. Hem, ignoro quid agam. Pessumdatus sum maleficiis Christicolarum. En montem circueo, et semitam aliquotiens repperiens, nec ascensum comprehendere, nec reditum queo repetere.

2 MILITES. Miris modis omnes illudimur, nimiaque lassitudine fatigamur. Et si insanum caput diutius vivere sustines, te ipsum et nos perdes.

SISINNIUS. Quisquis es meorum, strenue extende arcum, iace sagittam, perfode hanc maleficam.

MILITES. Decet.

3 HIRENA. Infelix erubesce, Sisinni, erubesce, teque turpiter victum ingemisce, quia tenellae infantiam virgunculae absque armorum apparatu nequivisti superare.

SISINNIUS. Quicquid dedecoris accedit, levius tolero, quia te morituram haud dubito.

HIRENA. Hinc mihi quam maxime gaudendum, tibi vero dolendum, quia pro tui severitate malignitatis in Tartara damnaberis. Ego autem martyrii palmam virginitatisque receptura coronam intrabo aethereum aeterni Regis thalamum. Cui est honor et gloria in saecula.

SOLDIERS. They placed themselves on the right and left of Hirena, and sent us here, so that the outcome of this affair would not be hidden from you.

SISINNIUS. All I can do now is get on a horse and go find out who these young men were who so freely mocked me.

SOLDIERS. We'll go too.

14

SISINNIUS. Phew, I have no idea what I'm doing. I've been outdone by the witchcraft of the Christians. Look how I circle the mountain, and whenever I find the path, I can't figure out how to ascend, nor how to get back again.

SOLDIERS. We are all being mocked in wondrous ways, and 2
we are worn out by great fatigue. And if you allow her crazy head to survive any longer, you will destroy yourself as well as us.

SISINNIUS. Whichever of my soldiers is present, draw your bow boldly, send an arrow, pierce that witch.

SOLDIERS. Just so.

HIRENA. Blush, wretched Sisinnius, blush, and lament that 3
you were disgracefully defeated, because you could not prevail over the youth of a tender little virgin without the use of weapons.

SISINNIUS. Whatever dishonor comes, I will bear it more lightly, because I have no doubt that you are going to die.

HIRENA. This is the cause of the greatest rejoicing for me, but of the greatest grief for you, because you will be condemned to Tartarus for the severity of your evil will. I, however, will receive the palm of martyrdom and the crown of virginity, and I will enter the heavenly chamber of the eternal King. His is the honor and glory forever.

<Resuscitatio Drusianae et Calimachi>

Resuscitatio Drusianae et Calimachi, qui eam non solum vivam sed etiam prae tristitia atque execratione illiciti amoris in Domino mortuam plus iusto amavit. Unde morsu serpentis male periit. Sed precibus sancti Iohannis apostoli, una cum Drusiana resuscitatus, in Christo est renatus.

CALIMACHUS	ANDRONICUS
AMICI	SANCTUS IOHANNES
DRUSIANA	FORTUNATUS

I

CALIMACHUS. Paucis vos, amici, volo.

AMICI. Utere quantum libet nostro colloquio.

CALIMACHUS. Si aegre non accipitis, malo vos interim sequestrari aliorum a collegio.

AMICI. Quod tibi videtur commodum, nobis est sequendum.

CALIMACHUS. Accedamus in secretiora loca, ne quis superveniens interrumpat dicenda.

AMICI. Ut libet.

The Raising from the Dead of Drusiana and Callimachus

The raising from the dead of Drusiana and of Callimachus, who loved her more than was right, not only while she was living, but also, because of his grief and the abomination of his illicit love, after she had died in the Lord. So, he perished dreadfully from a snakebite. But through the prayers of Saint John the Apostle, raised up along with Drusiana from the dead, he was reborn in Christ.

Callimachus	Andronicus
His Friends	Saint John
Drusiana	Fortunatus

1

Callimachus. I'd like a few words with you, my friends.

Friends. Converse with us as much as you please.

Callimachus. If you don't take it amiss, I would rather you be separated from the company of others while we talk.

Friends. Whatever seems good to you, we will accommodate.

Callimachus. Let's go to a more isolated place, so that no one coming upon us can interrupt what we need to discuss.

Friends. As you please.

2

CALIMACHUS. Anxie diuque gravem sustinui dolorem, quem vestro consilio relevari posse spero.

AMICI. Aequum est, ut communicata invicem compassione patiamur, quicquid unicuique nostrum utriusque eventu fortunae ingeratur.

CALIMACHUS. O utinam voluissetis meam passionem compatiendo mecum partiri!

AMICI. Enuclea quid patiaris, et si res exigit compatiemur; sin autem, animum tuum a nequam intentione revocare nitimur.

2 CALIMACHUS. Amo.

AMICI. Quid?

CALIMACHUS. Rem pulchram, rem venustam.

AMICI. Nec in solo, nec in omni, ideo atomum quod amas per hoc nequit intellegi.

CALIMACHUS. Mulierem.

AMICI. Cum "mulierem" dixeris, omnes comprehendis.

CALIMACHUS. Non omnes aequaliter, sed unam specialiter.

AMICI. Quod de subiecto dicitur, non nisi de subiecto aliquo cognoscitur. Unde si velis nos enarithmum agnoscere, dic primam ousiam.

3 CALIMACHUS. Drusianam.

AMICI. Andronici huius principis coniugem?

CALIMACHUS. Ipsam.

2

CALLIMACHUS. I have anxiously and for a long time suffered a heavy affliction, which I hope through your advice can be lightened.

FRIENDS. It is only fair that, in shared suffering, we suffer together whatever good or bad fortune is inflicted on any one of us.

CALLIMACHUS. Oh, if only you would choose to share my suffering, suffering along with me!

FRIENDS. Explain what you are suffering, and if the situation requires it, we will share your suffering; but if not, we will try to distract your mind from any harmful preoccupation.

CALLIMACHUS. I am in love. 2

FRIENDS. In love with what?

CALLIMACHUS. Something beautiful, something charming.

FRIENDS. This description does not apply to only one thing, nor to everything; therefore, from what you have said, it is not possible for the single, indivisible thing which you love to be understood.

CALLIMACHUS. Woman.

FRIENDS. When you say "woman," you include all of them.

CALLIMACHUS. Not all equally, but one specifically.

FRIENDS. What is said about a subject cannot be understood unless it is about some particular subject. So, if you want us to understand one particular thing among a multitude, name for us its prime essence.

CALLIMACHUS. Drusiana. 3

FRIENDS. The nobleman Andronicus's wife?

CALLIMACHUS. The same.

Amici. Erras, socie; est lota baptismate.

Calimachus. Inde non curo, si ipsam ad mei amorem attrahere potero.

Amici. Non poteris.

Camilachus. Cur diffiditis?

Amici. Quia rem difficilem petis.

Calimachus. Num ego primus huiusmodi rem peto? Et non multorum ad audendum provocatus sum exemplo?

4 Amici. Intende, frater: ea ipsa quam ardes, sancti Iohannis apostoli doctrinam secuta, totam se devovit Deo, in tantum ut nec ad torum Andronici, Christianissimi viri, iam dudum potuit revocari; quo minus tuae consentiet vanitati.

Calimachus. Quaesivi a vobis consolationem, sed incutitis mihi desperationem.

Amici. Qui simulat, fallit; et qui profert adulationem, vendit veritatem.

5 Calimachus. Quia mihi vestri auxilium subtrahitis, ipsam adibo, eiusque animo mei amorem blandimentis persuadebo.

Amici. Haud persuadebis.

Calimachus. Quippe vetar Fatis!

Amici. Experiemur.

3

Calimachus. Sermo meus ad te, Drusiana, praecordialis amor.

FRIENDS. You're making a mistake, colleague; she has been cleansed in baptism.

CALLIMACHUS. I don't care about that, so long as I can entice her to love me.

FRIENDS. You can't.

CALLIMACHUS. Why have you no confidence?

FRIENDS. Because it is a difficult thing you are seeking.

CALLIMACHUS. Am I the first person to seek this sort of thing? And am I not emboldened to risk it by the example of many others?

FRIENDS. Pay attention, brother: this particular woman you 4
burn for follows the teaching of Saint John the Apostle and has dedicated herself entirely to God, so much so that she has not for a long time now been induced to return to the bed of Andronicus, a most Christian husband; it is far less likely she will consent to your foolishness.

CALLIMACHUS. I sought consolation from you, but you inflict hopelessness on me.

FRIENDS. Whoever dissimulates, deceives; and whoever offers flattery, sells out the truth.

CALLIMACHUS. Since you deny me your assistance, I will go 5
to her, and with sweet talk I will persuade her heart to love me.

FRIENDS. You will not persuade her.

CALLIMACHUS. No doubt I will be denied by the Fates!

FRIENDS. We shall see.

3

CALLIMACHUS. I'd like a word with you, Drusiana, dear love of my heart.

DRUSIANA. Quid mecum velis, Calimache, sermonibus agere, vehementer admiror.

CALIMACHUS. Miraris?

DRUSIANA. Satis.

CALIMACHUS. Primum de amore.

DRUSIANA. Quid de amore?

CALIMACHUS. Id scilicet, quod te prae omnibus diligo.

2 DRUSIANA. Quod ius consanguinitatis, quaeve legalis conditio institutionis, compellit te ad mei amorem?

CALIMACHUS. Tui pulchritudo.

DRUSIANA. Mea pulchritudo?

CALIMACHUS. Immo.

DRUSIANA. Quid ad te?

CALIMACHUS. Pro dolor hactenus parum; sed spero quod attineat postmodum.

3 DRUSIANA. Discede, discede, leno nefande. Confundor enim diutius tecum verba miscere; quem sentio plenum diabolica deceptione.

CALIMACHUS. Mea Drusiana, ne repellas te amantem tuoque amore corde tenus inhaerentem, sed impende amori vicem.

DRUSIANA. Lenocinia tua parvi pendo, tuique lasciviam fastidio, sed te ipsum penitus sperno.

4 CALIMACHUS. Adhuc non repperi occasionem irascendi, quia, quid mea in te agat dilectio, forte erubescis fateri.

DRUSIANA. Nihil aliud nisi indignationem.

CALIMACHUS. Credo te hanc sententiam mutatum ire.

DRUSIANA. Non mutabo, percerte.

CALIMACHUS. Forte.

DRUSIANA. I greatly wonder, Callimachus, what you wish to discuss with me.

CALLIMACHUS. You wonder?

DRUSIANA. Very much.

CALLIMACHUS. First, about love.

DRUSIANA. What about love?

CALLIMACHUS. This—namely, that I love you before all others.

DRUSIANA. What right of kinship, or what lawfully estab- 2
lished marriage incites you to love me?

CALLIMACHUS. Your beauty.

DRUSIANA. My beauty?

CALLIMACHUS. Indeed.

DRUSIANA. What has that to do with you?

CALLIMACHUS. Alas, till now very little; but I hope that it will concern me in the future.

DRUSIANA. Go away, go away, you wicked lech. Indeed, I am 3
ashamed to speak with you any longer; I believe you are full of diabolical deception.

CALLIMACHUS. My Drusiana, don't reject one who loves you and clings to you with a love deep in his heart, but pay back his love in turn.

DRUSIANA. I care little for your lechery, and your lust nauseates me, but you yourself I totally despise.

CALLIMACHUS. So far, I find no reason to be angry, because 4
it may well be that you are embarrassed to admit what my love is stirring up inside you.

DRUSIANA. Nothing but indignation.

CALLIMACHUS. I believe you will change your mind.

DRUSIANA. I most certainly will not change it.

CALLIMACHUS. Perhaps.

Drusiana. O insensate et amens! Cur falleris? Cur te vacua spe illudis? Quo pacto, qua dementia reris me tuae cedere nugacitati? Quae per multum temporis, a legalis toro viri me abstinui?

Calimachus. Pro deum atque hominum fidem, si non cesseris, non quiescam, non desistam, donec te captiosis circumveniam insidiis.

4

Drusiana. Eh heu, Domine Iesu Christe! Quid prodest castitatis professionem subiisse, cum is amens mea deceptus est specie? Intende, Domine, mei timorem. Intende quem patior dolorem. Quid mihi, quid agendum sit, ignoro. Si prodidero, civilis per me fiet discordia. Si celavero, insidiis diabolicis sine te refragari nequeo. Iube me in te, Christe, ocius mori, ne fiam in ruinam delicato iuveni.

Andronicus. Vae mihi infortunato! En, improvise mortua est Drusiana. Curro sanctumque Iohannem advoco.

5

Iohannes. Cur nimium contristaris, Andronice, cur fluunt lacrimae?

Andronicus. Heu, heu, domine, taedeo vitae propriae!

Iohannes. Quid pateris?

Andronicus. Drusiana, tui assecla.

Iohannes. Quid illa? Estne homine exuta?

Andronicus. Hem, est.

DRUSIANA. Oh, you senseless and crazy man! Why do you deceive yourself? Why do you delude yourself with vain hope? In what way, by what madness, do you imagine I will yield to your nonsense, I who have abstained for so long from the bed of my lawful husband?

CALLIMACHUS. By the faith of gods and men, if you do not yield, I shall not rest, I shall not cease, until I beguile you by deceitful tricks.

4

DRUSIANA. Ah, alas, Lord Jesus Christ! What use is it to have taken a vow of chastity, when this crazy man is ensnared by my beauty? Look at my fear, Lord. Look at the pain I am suffering. I do not know what I . . . what I should do! If I expose him, there will be a public uproar because of me. If I conceal what happened, I cannot resist his devilish snares without you. Order me, Christ, swiftly to die in you, so that I not become the cause of ruin to that spoiled young man.

ANDRONICUS. Woe to me, poor wretch! Look here, Drusiana has died unexpectedly. I will run and call Saint John.

5

JOHN. Why are you so distressed, Andronicus, why the flood of tears?

ANDRONICUS. Alas, alas, my lord, I am weary of this life!

JOHN. What is the matter?

ANDRONICUS. It's Drusiana, your disciple.

JOHN. What about her? Has she shed this human coil?

ANDRONICUS. Unfortunately, it is so.

2 IOHANNES. Multum disconvenit, ut pro his fundantur lacrimae, quorum animas credimus laetari in requie.

ANDRONICUS. Non dubitem licet, quin, ut asseris, anima aeternaliter laetetur corpusque quandoque incorruptum resuscitetur, hoc tamen me vehementer exurit, quod ipsa me praesente mortem, ut adveniret, optando invitavit.

IOHANNES. Agnovistin' causam?

ANDRONICUS. Agnovi tibique enucleam, si quando ex tristitia hac convalescam.

3 IOHANNES. Accedamus, exsequiasque diligenter celebremus.

ANDRONICUS. Marmoreum in proximo sepulchrum habetur, in quod funus ponatur, servandique cura sepulchri Fortunato nostro relinquatur procuratori.

IOHANNES. Decet ut tumuletur honorifice. Deus laetificet animam in requie.

6

CALIMACHUS. Quid fiet, Fortunate, quia nec morte Drusianae revocari possum ab amore.

FORTUNATUS. Miserabile!

CALIMACHUS. Pereo, nisi me adiuvet tua industria.

FORTUNATUS. In quo possum adiuvare?

CALIMACHUS. In eo: ut vel mortuam me facias videre.

JOHN. It is very unseemly to shed tears for those whose 2
souls we believe are rejoicing in rest.

ANDRONICUS. Even though I do not doubt what you say, that her soul will rejoice forever and that one day her body will be resurrected unblemished, still it pains me terribly that in my very presence she willingly invited death to come.

JOHN. Do you know the reason?

ANDRONICUS. I do know, and I will reveal it to you, if I ever get over this sadness.

JOHN. Let's go and carefully perform the funeral rites. 3

ANDRONICUS. There is a marble sepulcher not far away; her corpse should be placed in it, and responsibility for guarding the sepulcher should be left to my steward Fortunatus.

JOHN. It is appropriate that she be buried honorably. May God gladden her soul in rest.

6

CALLIMACHUS. What will happen, Fortunatus, since I cannot be induced even by Drusiana's death to give up my love.

FORTUNATUS. How pitiful!

CALLIMACHUS. I will die unless your industry comes to my aid.

FORTUNATUS. In what way may I be of assistance?

CALLIMACHUS. In this way: arrange for me to see her, even though she is dead.

FORTUNATUS. Corpus adhuc integrum manet, ut reor, quia non languore exesum, sed levi, ut experiebare, febre est solutum.

CALIMACHUS. O me felicem, si numquam experirer!

2 FORTUNATUS. Si placabis muneribus, dedam illud tuis usibus.

CALIMACHUS. Quae in praesenti ad manus habeo, interim accipe, nec diffidas te multo maiora accepturum fore.

FORTUNATUS. Eamus cito.

CALIMACHUS. In me non erit mora.

7

FORTUNATUS. Ecce corpus, nec facies cadaverosa, nec membra sunt tabida. Abutere ut libet.

CALIMACHUS. O Drusiana, Drusiana, quo affectu cordis te colui, qua sinceritate dilectionis te viscera tenus amplexatus fui; et tu semper abiecisti, meis votis contradixisti. Nunc in mea situm est potestate, quantislibet iniuriis te velim lacessere.

2 FORTUNATUS. Atat! Horribilis serpens invadit nos!

CALIMACHUS. Ei mihi, Fortunate! Cur me decepisti? Cur detestabile scelus persuasisti? En tu morieris serpentis vulnere, et ego commorior prae timore.

8

IOHANNES. Accedamus, Andronice, ad tumulum Drusianae, quo animam Christo commendemus prece.

Fortunatus. Her corpse is still intact, I imagine, since it was not eaten away by disease, but released by a mild fever, as you know.

Callimachus. Oh, lucky me, if I had never known that!

Fortunatus. If you will favor me with a gratuity, I will de- 2
liver the corpse to you, to use as you please.

Callimachus. For the time being, take what I have to hand, and do not doubt that you will get far greater rewards in the future.

Fortunatus. Let's go quickly.

Callimachus. There will be no delay on my part.

7

Fortunatus. Look at her body: her face is not that of a cadaver, and her limbs are not decayed. Abuse her as you please.

Callimachus. O Drusiana, Drusiana, with what heartfelt desire I have worshiped you, with what sincere love deep in my innermost parts I have embraced you; and you always rejected me, you denied my wishes. Now I have the power to assault you with as many outrages as I choose.

Fortunatus. Oh, oh! A dreadful snake is attacking us! 2

Callimachus. Ah me, Fortunatus! Why did you deceive me? Why did you convince me to perform this detestable crime? See now, you will die from the serpent's bite, and I will die of fear along with you.

8

John. Andronicus, we should go to Drusiana's tomb, so we can commend her soul to Christ through prayer.

ANDRONICUS. Hoc decet tui sanctitatem, ut non obliviscaris in te confidentem.

2 IOHANNES. Ecce, invisibilis Deus nobis apparet visibilis, in pulcherrimi similitudine iuvenis.

ANDRONICUS. Expaveo!

IOHANNES. Domine Iesu, cur iuxta id loci dignatus es servis tuis manifestari?

DOMINUS. Propter Drusianae eiusque, qui iuxta sepulchrum illius iacet, resuscitationem apparui, quia nomen meum in his debet gloriari.

3 ANDRONICUS. Quam subito receptus est caelo!

IOHANNES. Ideo causam penitus non intellego.

ANDRONICUS. Maturemus gressum. Forte re experieris in perventione, quod asseris te minus intellegere.

9

IOHANNES. In nomine Christi, quid est hoc quod video miraculi? Ecce aperto sepulcro corpus Drusianae foras est eiectum, iuxta quod iacent duo cadavera, amplexu serpentis circumflexa.

2 ANDRONICUS. Coniecto, quid significet. Is, ipse Calimachus, Drusianam dum viveret illicite amavit; quod illa aegre ferens, in febrem prae tristitia incidit, et mortem ut adveniret invitavit.

IOHANNES. Hoc amore castitatis coegit.

3 ANDRONICUS. Post cuius occasum, hic amens, infelicis languorem amoris et negati taedium conglomerans sceleris, tabescebat animo, eoque magis aestuabat desiderio.

IOHANNES. Miserabile.

ANDRONICUS. It is in keeping with your holiness that you do not forget one who put her faith in you.

JOHN. Look—God, who is invisible, appears visible to us, in 2
the form of a most beautiful young man.

ANDRONICUS. I'm terrified!

JOHN. Lord Jesus, why have you seen fit to reveal yourself to your servants in this place?

LORD. I have appeared for the sake of resurrecting Drusiana, and also this man who lies near her sepulcher, because my name should be glorified in them.

ANDRONICUS. How quickly he was taken back to heaven! 3

JOHN. That's why I do not understand this situation at all.

ANDRONICUS. Let's hurry up. Perhaps when we get there, you will work out what you say you do not understand.

9

JOHN. In the name of Christ, what is this miracle I see? Look here, the sepulcher has been opened, the body of Drusiana has been cast out, and next to her lie two cadavers, wrapped in the coils of a snake.

ANDRONICUS. I can guess what this means. He, Callima- 2
chus here, loved Drusiana improperly while she was alive; she took it badly, and fell into a fever from despair, and invited death to come.

JOHN. She was compelled to do this by her love of chastity.

ANDRONICUS. After her death, this crazy young man, com- 3
pounding the sickness of his unfulfilled love and the annoyance of having been denied his crime, wasted away in spirit, and so burned more in desire.

JOHN. How wretched.

4 Andronicus. Non ambigo, quin hunc improbum servum mercede conduceret, quo illi patrandi occasionem facinoris praeberet.

Iohannes. O nefas incomparabile!

Andronicus. Ideo ambo, ut video, morte sunt consumpti, ne effectum administrarent sceleri.

Iohannes. Nec iniuria.

5 Andronicus. In hoc tamen illud est vel maxime admirandum, cur huius qui pravum voluit resuscitatio, magis quam eius qui consensit, divina sit voce praenuntiata, nisi quia forte hic carnali deceptus delectatione, deliquit ignorantia, iste autem sola malitia.

6 Iohannes. Quanta supernus Arbiter districtione cunctorum facta examinat, quamque aequa lance singulorum merita pensat—id non obvium nec cuiquam explicabile fore potest, quia divini subtilitas iudicii longe praeterit humani sagacitatem ingenii.

Andronicus. Ideo admirando deficimus, quia rerum quae geruntur causas, docte internoscere nequimus.

Iohannes. Eventus post facta docet persaepe rerum discrimina.

7 Andronicus. Verum age iam, beate Iohannes, quod acturus es. Fac ut resuscitetur Calimachus, quo solvatur huiusmodi ambiguitatis nodus.

Iohannes. Reor prius invocato Christi nomine anguem proturbandum; post vero Calimachum suscitandum.

ANDRONICUS. I have no doubt he bribed this worthless slave to offer him the opportunity of perpetrating an outrage. 4

JOHN. Oh, wickedness beyond compare!

ANDRONICUS. And so, these two men were devoured by death, as I see it, so that they could not bring their crime to fruition.

JOHN. And not unjustly.

ANDRONICUS. What I especially wonder at in all this is why 5
the resurrection of this man who wanted to do a depraved thing was foretold in the divine message, rather than the resurrection of that man, who was his accomplice; unless maybe because this one, deceived by carnal desire, erred through ignorance, but that one solely from malice.

JOHN. With what severity the heavenly Judge examines 6
everyone's deeds, and how he weighs the merits of individuals in an impartial scale—that cannot be obvious nor explicable to anyone, because the subtlety of divine judgment far surpasses the comprehension of human intelligence.

ANDRONICUS. And so, in our amazement, we come up short, because we are unable to distinguish knowledgeably the causes of the things that happen.

JOHN. The outcome of things, after the fact, very often teaches us the distinctions.

ANDRONICUS. But do now, blessed John, what you are plan- 7
ning to do. Resurrect Callimachus, so that the knot of this ambiguity may be unraveled.

JOHN. I suppose the snake should be run off first, by invoking Christ's name; afterward, truly, Callimachus should be resurrected.

ANDRONICUS. Recte reris ne ultra laedatur morsu serpentis.

8 IOHANNES. Discede ab hoc, crudelis bestia, quia serviturus est Christo.

ANDRONICUS. Licet irrationale animal sit, haud surda tamen aure quod iussisti obaudivit.

IOHANNES. Non mea, sed Christi virtute paruit.

ANDRONICUS. Ideo citius dicto evanuit.

9 IOHANNES. Deus incircumscriptus et incomprehensibilis, simplex et inaestimabilis, qui solus es id quod es, qui diversa duo socians ex hoc et hoc hominem fingis, eademque dissocians unum quod constabat resolvis: iube ut, reducto halitu, disiunctaque compagine rursus conliminata, Calimachus resurgat plenus ut fuit homo, quo ab omnibus magnificeris, qui solus miranda operaris.

10 ANDRONICUS. Amen. Ecce vitales auras carpit, sed prae stupore adhuc quiescit.

IOHANNES. Calimache, surge in Christi nomine, et utcumque se res habeat confitere, sed et quantislibet obnoxius sis vitiis proferas, ne nos vel in modico lateat veritas.

11 CALIMACHUS. Negare nequeo, quin patrandi causa facinoris accesserim, quia infelici languore tabescebam, nec illiciti aestum amoris compescere poteram.

IOHANNES. Quae dementia, quae insania te decepit, ut castis praesumeres fragmentis alicuius iniuriam conferre dehonestatis?

ANDRONICUS. You suppose correctly, so he isn't bitten again by the snake.

JOHN. Get away from this man, cruel beast, for he is going 8
to be a servant of Christ.

ANDRONICUS. Even though it is an irrational animal, still it did not turn a deaf ear to what you ordered.

JOHN. It did not obey because of my power, but because of Christ's.

ANDRONICUS. And so, quicker than words, it vanished.

JOHN. O God, uncircumscribed and incomprehensible, 9
simple and inestimable, you who alone are what you are, you who, combining two different things, create man from disparate components and, separating these same things, dissolve the unity that once was: order that Callimachus rise again in his complete human form, with his breath returned and the disunion of his body and soul repaired; do this so that you will be glorified by all, you who alone work wonders.

ANDRONICUS. Amen. Look, he is drawing the breath of life, 10
but he is still paralyzed by stupor.

JOHN. Callimachus, rise in the name of Christ, and confess what happened, but also declare whatever sins you have committed, so the truth not be hidden from us, even in a small detail.

CALLIMACHUS. I cannot deny that I came here to perpe- 11
trate a crime, because I was withering away from a miserable sickness, and I could not keep in check the heat of my illicit love.

JOHN. What madness, what insanity deceived you, that you presumed to inflict the injury of degradation on someone's chaste remains?

CALIMACHUS. Propria stultitia, huiusque Fortunati fraudolenta deceptio.

12 IOHANNES. Num triplici infortunio adeo infelix effectus es, ut nefas quod voluisti perficere posses?

CALIMACHUS. Nullatenus. Licet non defuisset velle, possibilitas tamen omnino defuit posse.

IOHANNES. Quo pacto impediebaris?

CALIMACHUS. Ut primum distracto tegmine conviciis temptavi lacessere corpus exanime, iste Fortunatus, qui fomes mali et incensor exstitit, serpentinis perfusus venenis periit.

ANDRONICUS. O factum bene!

13 CALIMACHUS. Mihi autem apparuit iuvenis aspectu terribilis. Qui detectum corpus honorifice texit. Ex cuius flammea facie candentes in bustum scintillae transiliebant, quarum una resiliens mihi in faciem ferebatur. Simulque vox facta est dicens, "Calimache morere ut vivas." His dictis, exspiravi.

IOHANNES. Opus caelestis gratiae, quae non delectatur in impiorum perditione.

14 CALIMACHUS. Audisti miseriam meae perditionis. Noli elongare medelam tuae miserationis.

IOHANNES. Non elongabo.

CALIMACHUS. Nam nimium confundor, corde tenus contristor, anxio, gemo, doleo, super gravi impietate mea.

IOHANNES. Nec inmerito! Quippe grave delictum, haud leve paenitudinis exspectat remedium.

Callimachus. My own stupidity, and the fraudulent deception of this man Fortunatus.

John. Did you become, through a triple misfortune, so un- 12
lucky as to perform the wickedness you desired?

Callimachus. Not at all. Even though the will was there, nonetheless, the power to carry it out was entirely lacking.

John. How were you impeded?

Callimachus. As soon as her shroud was removed and I tried to assault her lifeless body with outrages, this man Fortunatus, who was the fomenter of evil and its igniter, died, soaked in the serpent's venom.

Andronicus. Oh, well done!

Callimachus. But a young man of dreadful countenance 13
appeared to me. He respectfully covered the denuded body. From his flaming face, gleaming sparks leaped forth onto the tomb, one of which, bouncing back, was carried into my face. And at the same time there was a voice saying, "Callimachus, die so that you may live." After he said that, I expired.

John. This is the work of heavenly grace, which takes no pleasure in the damnation of the wicked.

Callimachus. You have heard the misery of my damna- 14
tion. Do not withhold the remedy of your compassion.

John. I will not withhold it.

Callimachus. For I am very ashamed, I am distressed deep down in my heart, I am anxious, I am moaning, I am in pain over my grave impiety.

John. And not undeservedly! A heavy crime, to be sure, can hardly expect a light remedy of repentance.

15 CALIMACHUS. O utinam reserarentur secreta meorum viscerum latibula, quo interni amaritudinem quam patior doloris perspiceres, et dolenti condolores.

IOHANNES. Congaudeo huiusmodi dolori, quia sentio te salubriter contristari.

CALIMACHUS. Taedet me prioris vitae, taedet delectationis iniquae.

IOHANNES. Nec iniuria.

16 CALIMACHUS. Paenitet me quod deliqui.

IOHANNES. Et merito.

CALIMACHUS. Displicet omne quod feci, in tantum ut nullus amor, nulla voluptas sit vivendi, nisi renatus in Christo merear in melius transmutari.

IOHANNES. Non dubito, quin superna in te appareat gratia.

17 CALIMACHUS. Ideo ne moreris, ne pigriteris lapsum erigere, maerentem consolationibus attollere, quo tuo monitu, tuo magisterio, a gentili in Christianum, a nugace in castum transmutatus virum, tuoque ducatu semitam arripiens veritatis, vivam iuxta divinae praeconium promissionis.

18 IOHANNES. Benedicta sit unica progenies divinitatis, idemque particeps nostrae fragilitatis, qui et, fili Calimache, parcendo occidit, et occidendo vivificavit, quo suum plasma mortis specie ab interitu liberaret animae.

ANDRONICUS. Res insolita, omnique admiratione digna.

CALLIMACHUS. Oh, I wish the secret hiding places inside 15
me were unlocked, so that you could see the bitterness of inner pain I suffer, and you would have pity upon the sufferer.

JOHN. I am glad for that kind of pain, because I feel you are distressed for your own good.

CALLIMACHUS. I am weary of my earlier life; I am weary of that wicked pleasure.

JOHN. That is only just.

CALLIMACHUS. It pains me that I have sinned. 16

JOHN. And rightly so.

CALLIMACHUS. I am displeased by all I did, so much so that I have no love, no desire for living, unless, reborn in Christ, I earn the right to be changed for the better.

JOHN. I have no doubt that heavenly grace is beginning to operate in you.

CALLIMACHUS. Then do not delay, do not be slow to raise 17
up a man who has fallen, to sustain with consolation one who is grieving, so that through your admonitions, through your teaching, I may be transformed from a gentile to a Christian, from a fool to a chaste man, and through your leadership, taking the path of truth, I may live according to the preaching of the divine promise.

JOHN. Blessed be the only child of the divinity, the same one 18
who shares our frailty, who also, Callimachus my son, killed you by sparing you, and by killing you, gave you life, so that, by the appearance of death, he could free his creation from the ruin of its soul.

ANDRONICUS. This is a strange business, deserving nothing but wonder.

19 IOHANNES. O Christe, mundi redemptio, et peccatorum propitiatio, qualibus laudum praeconiis te talem celebrem ignoro. Expaveo tui benignam clementiam et clementem patientiam. Qui peccantes nunc paterno more tolerando blandiris; nunc iusta severitate castigando ad paenitentiam cogis.

20 ANDRONICUS. Laus eius divinae pietati. Quis auderet credere, quisve praesumeret sperare, ut hunc, quem criminosis intentum vitiis Mors invenit, et inventum abstulit, tui miseratio ad vitam excitare, ad veniam dignaretur reparare? Sit nomen tuum sanctum benedictum in saecula, qui solus facis stupenda mirabilia.

21 ANDRONICUS. Eia, sancte Iohannes, et me consolari ne tardes. Nam coniugalis amor Drusianae meam haud patitur mentem consistere, nisi et ipsam quantocius videam resurrectum ire.

IOHANNES. Drusiana, resuscitet te Dominus Iesus Christus.

DRUSIANA. Laus et honor tibi, Christe, qui me fecisti reviviscere.

CALIMACHUS. Sospitatis auctori grates, qui te, mea Drusiana, resurgere dedit in laetitia, quae gravi cum tristitia die fungebaris extrema.

22 DRUSIANA. Decet tui sanctitatem, venerande pater Iohannes, ut resuscitato Calimacho qui me illicite amavit, et hunc resuscites, qui mei proditor funeris extitit.

CALIMACHUS. Ne dignum ducas, Christi apostole, hunc proditorem, hunc malefactorem a vinculis mortis absolvere, qui me decepit, me seduxit, meque ad audendum horribile facinus provocavit.

JOHN. O Christ, redemption of the world, and propitiation of sinners, I do not know by what hymns of praise I may celebrate your qualities. I tremble at your kind gentleness, and your gentle patience. Sometimes you talk softly to sinners, tolerating them like a father; at other times, castigating them with just severity, you compel them to repentance. 19

ANDRONICUS. Praise be to his divine mercy. Who would dare to believe, or who would presume to hope, that your mercy would see fit to stir this man to life, to restore this man to forgiveness, this man whom Death found intent upon sinful vices, and carried off when he came upon him? May your holy name be blessed forever, you who alone perform amazing miracles. 20

ANDRONICUS. Ahem, Saint John, don't be slow to console me as well. For my spousal affection for Drusiana will not let my mind rest, unless I see that she too is going to be resurrected as quickly as possible. 21

JOHN. Drusiana, may the Lord Jesus Christ resurrect you.

DRUSIANA. Praise and honor to you, Christ, you have made me come back to life.

CALLIMACHUS. Thanks be to the author of your health, who granted that you rise again in joy, my Drusiana, you who spent your last day in great distress.

DRUSIANA. It suits your sanctity, venerable father John, since you brought Callimachus back to life, a man who loved me in an unlawful manner, that you also bring this man back to life, who was the betrayer of my corpse. 22

CALLIMACHUS. You should not think it proper, apostle of Christ, to absolve from the chains of death this betrayer, this evildoer, who deceived me, led me astray, and provoked me to venture upon this horrible crime.

IOHANNES. Non debes illi invidere gratiam divinae clementiae.

CALIMACHUS. Non est enim dignus resurrectione, qui auctor exstitit perditionis alienae.

23 IOHANNES. Lex nostrae religionis docet, ut homo homini dimittat, si ipse a Deo dimitti ambiat.

ANDRONICUS. Iustum.

IOHANNES. Quando etiam Dei unigenitus idemque virginis primogenitus, qui solus innocens, solus inmaculatus, solus sine veterni sorde fuit delicti, in mundum venit, omnes sub gravi onere peccati depressos invenit.

ANDRONICUS. Verum.

24 IOHANNES. Sed licet nullum iustum, nullum misericordia inveniret dignum, neminem tamen sprevit. Neminem suae gratia pietatis privavit, sed se ipsum omnibus tradidit, suique dilectam animam pro omnibus posuit.

ANDRONICUS. Si innocens non occideretur, nemo iuste liberaretur.

IOHANNES. Ideo in hominum non delectatur perditione, quos suo emptos meminit pretioso sanguine.

ANDRONICUS. Gratias illi.

25 IOHANNES. Unde aliis Dei gratiam non debemus invidere, quam ex nullis praecedentibus meritis in nobis gaudemus abundare.

CALIMACHUS. Terruisti me monitu.

IOHANNES. Ne autem tuis videar reniti votis, non suscitetur per me, sed per Drusianam, quia ad hoc implendum a Deo accepit gratiam.

JOHN. You should not begrudge him the grace of divine clemency.

CALLIMACHUS. Surely a man does not deserve resurrection, who was the author of another's damnation.

JOHN. The law of our religion teaches that a man should for- 23
give another man, if he himself desires to be forgiven by God.

ANDRONICUS. That is just.

JOHN. Moreover, when the only-begotten son of God, the same one who was firstborn of the Virgin, he who alone is without fault, alone unblemished, alone was without stain of the ancient sin—when he came into the world, he found everyone oppressed by the heavy burden of sin.

ANDRONICUS. Truly.

JOHN. But even though he found no one just, no one deserv- 24
ing of mercy, still he rejected nobody. He deprived nobody of the grace of his kindness, but gave himself up for all men, and forfeited his precious soul for the sake of all.

ANDRONICUS. If an innocent man had not been killed, no man would justly be freed.

JOHN. So, he is not pleased by the damnation of men; he is mindful that they were redeemed by his precious blood.

ANDRONICUS. Thanks be to him.

JOHN. For this reason, we should not begrudge others the 25
grace of God, which we are glad abounds in us, though our prior works did nothing to deserve it.

CALLIMACHUS. You have terrified me by your warning.

JOHN. But so that I not seem to oppose your wishes, he should not be brought back to life by me, but by Drusiana, because she has received from God the grace to accomplish this.

26 DRUSIANA. Divina substantia, quae vere et singulariter es sine materia forma, quae hominem ad tui imaginem plasmasti, et plasmato spiraculum vitae inspirasti: iube materiale corpus Fortunati reducto calore in viventem animam iterum reformari, quo trina nostri resuscitacio tibi in laudem vertatur, Trinitas veneranda.

IOHANNES. Amen.

27 DRUSIANA. Expergiscere, Fortunate, et iussu Christi retinacula mortis dirumpe.

FORTUNATUS. Quis me apprehensa manu erexit? Quis vocem, ut resurgerem, dedit?

IOHANNES. Drusiana.

FORTUNATUS. Num me suscitavit Drusiana?

IOHANNES. Ipsa.

FORTUNATUS. Nonne ante aliquot dies improvisa morte fuerat consumpta?

IOHANNES. At nunc vivit in Christo.

FORTUNATUS. Et cur manet Calimachus gravi vultu modestus, nec perfurit solito more in amore Drusianae?

IOHANNES. Quia a nequam intentione transmutatus, vere est Christi discipulus.

FORTUNATUS. Non!

IOHANNES. Etiam!

28 FORTUNATUS. Si, ut asseris, Drusiana me suscitavit, et Calimachus Christo credit, vitam repudio, mortemque sponte eligo, quia malo non esse, quam in his tantam abundanter virtutum gratiam sentiscere.

DRUSIANA. Divine being, you are truly and singularly form without matter, you have fashioned man in your own image, and into what you fashioned, you breathed the breath of life. Command that the material body of Fortunatus, its warmth restored, be reformed again into a living soul, so that our three resurrections may be turned into praise of you, O venerable Trinity. 26

JOHN. Amen.

DRUSIANA. Wake up, Fortunatus, and by the command of Christ, break the bonds of death. 27

FORTUNATUS. Who took my hand and raised me up? Who gave the command that I rise again?

JOHN. Drusiana.

FORTUNATUS. Did Drusiana raise me from the dead?

JOHN. She herself.

FORTUNATUS. Did she not perish in an untimely death a few days ago?

JOHN. But now she is alive in Christ.

FORTUNATUS. And why does Callimachus remain calm, with a serious expression, and not rage as usual on account of his love for Drusiana?

JOHN. Because he has been diverted from his wicked purpose and is truly a disciple of Christ.

FORTUNATUS. No!

JOHN. Yes!

FORTUNATUS. If, as you claim, Drusiana resuscitated me and Callimachus believes in Christ, I refuse to live, and I freely choose death, because I would rather not exist, than see such a dispensation of virtues abounding in them. 28

29 IOHANNES. O admiranda invidia diaboli, O malitia serpentis antiqui! Qui et protoplastis mortem propinavit, et super iustorum gloria semper gemit. Iste infelicissimus Fortunatus, diabolicae amaritudinis felle plenissimus, comparatur malae arbori amaros fructus facienti. Unde excisus a collegio iustorum, et abiectus a consortio deum timentium, mittatur in aeterni ignem supplicii, cruciandus sine alicuius intermixtione refrigerii.

30 ANDRONICUS. Ecce turgescentibus serpentinis morsibus ad occasum rursus vergitur, et citius dicto morietur.

IOHANNES. Moriatur, sitque incola gehennae. Qui propter alieni invidiam profectus recusavit vivere.

ANDRONICUS. Terribile!

31 IOHANNES. Nihil terribilius invido, nihil scelestius superbo.

ANDRONICUS. Uterque miserabilis.

IOHANNES. Una eademque persona utroque semper laborat vitio, quia neutrum sine altero.

ANDRONICUS. Expone enucleatius.

IOHANNES. Nam qui superbit invidet, et qui invidet superbit, quia mens invida dum alienam laudem nec patitur audire, et in sui comparatione perfectiores ambit vilescere, dedignatur subici dignioribus, et superbe conatur praeferri comparibus.

ANDRONICUS. Patet.

JOHN. Oh, the amazing envy of the devil, oh, the malice of 29
the ancient serpent! He administered the drink of death to the first-made humans and has always bemoaned the glory of the righteous. This most wretched fellow Fortunatus, abundantly filled with the gall of diabolic bitterness, is like an evil tree, producing bitter fruit. Therefore, he should be cut off from the community of the righteous, and expelled from the society of those who fear God, and sent into the fire of eternal punishment, to be tortured without the admixture of any relief.

ANDRONICUS. Look, the serpent's bites are swelling up, he 30
is sinking again into death, and he is dying quicker than words.

JOHN. Let him die, and let him live in hell. Because of his envy of another's improvement, he refused to live.

ANDRONICUS. How awful!

JOHN. There is nothing more awful than an envious man, 31
nothing more wicked than a proud man.

ANDRONICUS. Both are wretched.

JOHN. One and the same person always labors under both of these vices, because neither exists without the other.

ANDRONICUS. Please explain more clearly.

JOHN. In fact, whoever is proud has envy, and whoever envies is proud, because the envious mind, while it cannot endure hearing another praised, and while it aims to belittle those who in comparison to itself are more accomplished, does not consent to being subjugated to those who are worthier, and proudly tries to be preferred to its equals.

ANDRONICUS. That's clear.

32 IOHANNES. Unde iste miserrimus vulnerabatur mente, quia se his inferiorem aestimari non sustinuit, in quis ampliorem Dei gratiam lucere non nescivit.

ANDRONICUS. Nunc tandem intellego, quod inter surgentes minime est computatus, quia ocius erat moriturus.

IOHANNES. Dignus est enim utraque morte, quia et commendatum funus afficiebat iniuria, et resurgentes iniusto insectabatur odio.

ANDRONICUS. Infelix est mortuus.

33 IOHANNES. Recedamus, suumque diabolo filium relinquamus. Nos autem diem istum, et pro miranda Calimachi mutatione, et pro utriusque resuscitatione, cum laetitia agamus, gratias ferentes Deo, aequo iudici, secretorumque discretissimo cognitori, qui solus omnia subtiliter examinans, omnia recte disponens, unumquemque iuxta quod dignum praenoscit, praemiis suppliciisve aptabit. Ipsi soli honor, virtus, fortitudo, et victoria, laus et iubilatio, per infinita saeculorum saecula. Amen.

JOHN. So, this most wretched man was wounded at heart 32
because he could not stand to be esteemed less than these others, in whom he was not unaware that a more ample grace of God shines.

ANDRONICUS. Now finally I understand why he was not numbered among those who would be brought back to life, because he was going to die again so swiftly.

JOHN. He deserved, in fact, both his deaths, because he inflicted injury on a corpse entrusted to him, and he attacked the risen with unjust hatred.

ANDRONICUS. A wretched death.

JOHN. Let's go, and let's leave to the devil his own son. We, 33
however, should spend this day in joy, both for the wondrous conversion of Callimachus, and for the resurrection of these two, offering thanks to God, the just judge, the most discerning knower of secrets, who alone examines all things subtly, arranges all things correctly, has knowledge beforehand of every person after his deserts, and will assign rewards or punishments fittingly. To him alone be honor, virtue, fortitude, and victory, praise and jubilation, through the infinite age of ages. Amen.

<Lapsus et conversio Mariae, neptis Abrahae>

Lapsus et conversio Mariae, neptis Abrahae eremicolae, quae, ubi viginti annos solitariam vitam egit, corrupta virginitate, saeculum repetiit, et contubernio meretricum admisceri non metuit. Sed post biennium, praefati Abrahae monitis, illam sub amatoris specie quaerentis, reducta, larga effusione lacrimarum continuaque exercitatione ieiuniorum, vigiliarum, atque orationum, per vicenos annos emundavit maculas criminum.

ABRAHAM MARIA
EFFREM

I

ABRAHAM. Tune, frater et coeremita Effrem, commodum ducis meae adhuc confabulationi vacare, an, quoadusque divinas expleas laudes, me vis praestolari?

EFFREM. Nostrorum confabulatio Eius debet esse laudatio, qui se congregatis in suo nomine medium spopondit interesse.

The Fall and Conversion of Mary, Niece of Abraham

The fall and conversion of Mary, niece of Abraham the hermit, who, after living a solitary life for twenty years, returned to the world because her virginity had been corrupted, and she was not afraid to mingle in the company of prostitutes. But after two years, through the counsels of the aforementioned Abraham, who sought her out in the disguise of a lover, she was led back; with a great outpouring of tears and a ceaseless performance of fasts, vigils, and prayers, she cleansed away the stains of her sins for the next twenty years.

Abraham Mary
Effrem

1

Abraham. Do you, Effrem, brother and fellow hermit, think it convenient to spend time at present conversing with me, or do you want me to wait until you finish your divine praises?

Effrem. A conversation between us ought to be a form of praise of the One who promised that he would be there in the midst of those gathered in his name.

ABRAHAM. Nihil aliud locuturus accessi, nisi quod divinae voluntati non nescio concordari.

2 EFFREM. Quare nec ad momentum quidem me subtraho, sed tuo affectui totum dedo.

ABRAHAM. Quiddam agendum mihi exaestuat mente, in quo tuum velle meis votis exopto respondere.

EFFREM. Si unum cor, unaque nobis anima iubetur esse, idem velle idemque cogimur nolle.

3 ABRAHAM. Est mihi neptis tenella, utriusque parentis solamine destituta. In quam pro compassione orbitatis nimio affectu ducor. Cuiusque causa, continua sollicitudine fatigor.

EFFREM. Et quid tibi, triumphator saeculi, cum curis mundi?

ABRAHAM. Id scilicet curo, ne immensa eius serenitas pulchritudinis alicuius obfuscetur sorde coinquinationis.

EFFREM. Huiusmodi cura si est vituperanda.

ABRAHAM. Spero.

EFFREM. Cuius est aetatis?

4 ABRAHAM. Si unius rotatus mansurni apponeretur, duas Olympiades vitali aura vesceretur.

EFFREM. Immatura pupilla.

ABRAHAM. Ideo non deest mihi cura.

EFFREM. Ubi deget?

ABRAHAM. In meis mansiunculis. Nam rogatu propinquorum nutriendam eam suscepi, sed eius gazas pauperibus erogare decrevi.

ABRAHAM. I have come intending to speak of nothing other than that which I know is in concord with the divine will.

EFFREM. Then not even for a second will I keep myself from 2
you, but surrender myself totally to your will.

ABRAHAM. Something I must do is troubling my mind; I hope that your desires correspond to my wishes regarding this thing.

EFFREM. If we are ordered to be of one heart and one soul, we are compelled to have the same desires and the same aversions.

ABRAHAM. I have a niece of very tender age, deprived of the 3
comfort of both her parents. I am drawn to her with great affection out of compassion for her orphaned state. And for her sake, I wear myself out with constant worry.

EFFREM. And what have you to do with secular concerns, you who have triumphed over worldly things?

ABRAHAM. I am worried in particular about this, that the great clarity of her beauty not be darkened by the stain of some contamination.

EFFREM. There is no criticizing a concern of that nature.

ABRAHAM. I hope that is so.

EFFREM. Of what age is she?

ABRAHAM. If the revolution of one year were added, she 4
would already be enjoying the breath of life for two Olympiads.

EFFREM. An immature little ward.

ABRAHAM. That is why I am not lacking in concern.

EFFREM. Where does she live?

ABRAHAM. In my humble dwellings. For I took her in to raise her at the request of my relatives, but I decided to distribute her wealth to the poor.

Effrem. Despectio temporalium condecet animum caelo intentum.

5 Abraham. Exaestuo mente, gestiens illam Christo desponsari, eiusque tirocinio mancipatum iri.

Effrem. Laudabile.

Abraham. Cogor nomine.

Effrem. Quid vocatur?

Abraham. Maria.

Effrem. Maria?

Abraham. Ita.

Effrem. Tanti excellentiam nominis decet stemma virginitatis.

6 Abraham. Non diffido quin, si nostris suaviter hortamentis provocetur, ad cedendum facilis experiatur.

Effrem. Accedamus, eiusque cogitationi caelebis securitatem vitae instillemus.

2

Abraham. O adoptiva filia, O pars animae Maria, cede meis paternis monitionibus meique comparis Effrem saluberrimis institutionibus, et nitere ut auctricem virginitatis, quam aequivoco aequiparas nomine, imiteris et castitate.

2 Effrem. Multum disconvenit, filia, ut quae, cum Dei genitrice Maria, per mysterium nominis praemines in axe inter sidera numquam casura, inferior meritis terrae volutes in fimis.

Effrem. Contempt for temporal things is appropriate for a mind intent on heaven.

Abraham. My mind is burning, eager that she be promised 5
in marriage to Christ and handed over for apprenticeship in his service.

Effrem. That is laudable.

Abraham. I am compelled to do it by her name.

Effrem. What is she called?

Abraham. Mary.

Effrem. Mary?

Abraham. Yes.

Effrem. The crown of virginity suits the excellence of such a name.

Abraham. I do not doubt that if she is sweetly enticed by 6
our encouragements, she will prove amenable to yielding.

Effrem. Let us go, and let us instill in her mind the security of a celibate life.

2

Abraham. O foster daughter, O half of my soul, Mary, yield to my paternal advice and to the very salutary instructions of my colleague Effrem, and strive to imitate also in chastity the founder of virginity, with whom you share the same name.

Effrem. It would be very unsuitable, daughter, that you 2
who, together with Mary the mother of God, are preeminent through the mystery of your name among the never-setting stars in heaven, should wallow in the muck of the earth, falling short of your potential.

MARIA. Mysterium nominis ignoro, unde quid circuitione verborum significes haud intellego.

3 EFFREM. Maria interpretatur "maris stella," circa quam videlicet fertur mundus et rotatur polus.

MARIA. Cur "maris stella" dicitur?

EFFREM. Quia numquam occidit, sed navigantibus recti semitam itineris dirigit.

4 MARIA. Et qui posset fieri, ut ego, tantilla ex lutea materia confecta, eo attingerem meritis, quo mysterium rutilat nominis?

EFFREM. Illibata corporis integritate, puraque mentis sanctitate.

MARIA. Grandis est honoris, hominem aequari astrorum radiis.

5 EFFREM. Nam si incorrupta et virgo permanebis, angelis Dei fies aequalis. Quibus tandem stipata, gravi corporis onere abiecto, pertransies aera, supergradieris aethera, instabilemque planetarum et cursum perlustrans solis, ducta per semitas zodiacum percurres circulum, nec subsistendo temperabis gressum, donec iungaris amplexibus Filii Virginis in lucifluo thalamo sui genetricis.

6 MARIA. Qui haec parvi pendit, asinum vivit. Unde praesentia despicio, memet ipsam denego, quo merear ascribi gaudiis tantae felicitatis.

EFFREM. Ecce nanciscimur in pectore infantili senilis maturitatem ingenii.

MARY. I don't know the mystery of my name, so I do not understand what you mean by this roundabout use of words.

EFFREM. Mary means "the star of the sea," that is, the star around which the cosmos turns and the sky is rotated. 3

MARY. Why is that star called "the star of the sea"?

EFFREM. Because it never sets, but directs sailors on the path of the proper course.

MARY. And how can it be that I, such a little thing, fashioned from mud, could by my own merits get to that place from which the mystery of my name sparkles? 4

EFFREM. By the unimpaired integrity of your body, and the pure holiness of your mind.

MARY. It is a mark of great honor that a human be compared to the rays of the stars.

EFFREM. Indeed, if you remain uncorrupted and virgin, you will become equal to the angels of God. Surrounded by them, in the end, when you have cast off the heavy burden of the body, you will pass through the air, you will walk above the heavens, and passing through the unsteady course of the planets and sun, led along the paths, you will run through the circle of the zodiac signs, and you will not interrupt your progress by stopping until you are joined in the embraces of the Son of the Virgin, in the light-filled chamber of his own mother. 5

MARY. Anyone who devalues such things lives like an ass. For this reason, I despise the things of the world, I deny my own self, so that I may earn the right to be included in the joys of such happiness. 6

EFFREM. Behold, we encounter in this infant breast the maturity of an elder's intelligence.

ABRAHAM. Gratia Dei est, id quod est.

EFFREM. Negari nequit.

7 ABRAHAM. Sed licet Dei gratia sit illustrata, imbecillem tamen aetatem suo uti non prodest arbitrio.

EFFREM. Verum.

ABRAHAM. Ideo faciam illi exiguam absque introitu cellulam meis mansiunculis contiguam, per cuius fenestram Psalterium ceterasque divinae legis paginas illam crebrius visitando instruam.

EFFREM. Convenit.

8 MARIA. Tuo, pater Effrem, interventui me committo.

EFFREM. Caelestis sponsus, cuius affectu in tenella aetate inhaesisti, tueatur te, filia, ab omni fraude diabolica.

3

ABRAHAM. Frater Effrem, si quid mihi utriusque casu fortunae ingeritur, te primum adeo, te solum consulo. Unde ne sis adversus querimoniae quam prosequor, sed fer opem dolori quem patior.

2 EFFREM. Abraham, Abraham, quid pateris? Cur plus licito contristaris? Numquam fuit fas eremicolae conturbari saecularium more.

ABRAHAM. Incomparabilis luctus mihi contigit, intolerabilis dolor me afficit.

EFFREM. Ne fatiga me longa verborum circuitione, sed quid patiaris expone.

Abraham. It is by the grace of God, that it is so.

Effrem. That cannot be denied.

Abraham. But even if she is illuminated by the grace of 7
God, still it is not good for one at that fragile age to use her own judgment.

Effrem. True.

Abraham. Therefore, I will make her a small cell without an entranceway next to my humble dwellings, through the window of which I will instruct her in the Psalter and the other pages of divine law, visiting her very frequently.

Effrem. That is suitable.

Mary. I entrust myself to your supervision, Father Effrem. 8

Effrem. May the celestial spouse, to whose affection you have attached yourself at a very tender age, protect you, daughter, from every diabolic deceit.

3

Abraham. Brother Effrem, if anything happens to me, whether of good or bad fortune, you are the first one I turn to, the only one I consult. For this reason, do not be hostile to this complaint I describe, but bring aid for the pain which I suffer.

Effrem. Abraham, Abraham, what are you suffering? Why 2
are you unjustly distressed? It has never been right for a hermit to be anxious like a layman.

Abraham. An incomparable grief has touched me; an intolerable pain afflicts me.

Effrem. Do not wear me out with this long roundabout use of words, but explain what you are suffering.

3 ABRAHAM. Maria, mis optima filia, quam per bis bina lustra summa diligentia nutrivi, summa solertia instruxi . . .

EFFREM. Quid illa?

ABRAHAM. Ei mihi, periit!

EFFREM. Qualiter?

ABRAHAM. Miserabiliter! Deinde evasit latenter.

4 EFFREM. Quibus insidiis circumvenit eam fraus antiqui serpentis?

ABRAHAM. Per illicitum cuiusdam simulatoris affectum, qui monachico adveniens habitu simulata eam visitatione frequentabat, donec indocile iuvenilis ingenium pectoris ad sui amorem inflexit, adeo ut per fenestram ad patrandum facinus exsiliret.

EFFREM. A! Contremisco auditu.

5 ABRAHAM. At ubi ipsa infelix se corruptam sensit, pectus pulsavit, faciem manu laceravit, vestes scidit, capillos eruit, voces in altum eiulando dedit.

EFFREM. Nec iniuria. Huiusmodi namque ruina, toto lacrimarum fonte est lugenda.

ABRAHAM. Lamentabatur namque se quod fuerat non esse.

EFFREM. Vae illi miserae!

ABRAHAM. Lugebat se nostris contraria monitis egisse.

EFFREM. Ac valde.

ABRAHAM. Deflevit se vigiliarum, orationum, ieiuniique sudores evacuasse.

Abraham. Mary, my dearest daughter, whom for twice two 3
lustra I raised with the greatest diligence, whom I instructed with the greatest care . . .

Effrem. What about her?

Abraham. Woe to me, she is ruined!

Effrem. How?

Abraham. Miserably! And then she ran off secretly.

Effrem. By what snares did the deceit of the ancient ser- 4
pent entrap her?

Abraham. Through the illicit affection of some charlatan, who, arriving in monk's clothing, visited her regularly under the pretense of inspection, until he had twisted the untutored nature of her young heart into loving him, to the point that she jumped out the window to perform the evil deed.

Effrem. Ah! I tremble to hear it.

Abraham. But when that poor girl realized that she was 5
corrupted, she pounded her breast, tore her face with her hand, ripped her clothes, pulled out her hair, and with a howl she sent her cries to the sky.

Effrem. Not unjustly. For ruin of this kind must be mourned with an entire fountain of tears.

Abraham. She lamented indeed that she was no longer what she had been.

Effrem. Woe to that poor girl!

Abraham. She mourned that she had acted contrary to our admonitions.

Effrem. And very much so.

Abraham. She wept that she had made all her sweating over vigils, prayers, and fasts meaningless.

EFFREM. Si in tali compunctione perseveraret, salva fieret.

6 ABRAHAM. Haud perseveravit, sed peiora prioribus apposuit.

EFFREM. Viscera tenus conturbor, totisque membris resolvor.

ABRAHAM. Postquam enim hisce lamentis se punivit, nimietate victa doloris, praeceps ferebatur in foveam desperationis.

EFFREM. Eh heu, quam gravis perditio!

ABRAHAM. Et quia veniam desperavit posse promereri, saeculum repetere vanitatique elegit deservire.

7 EFFREM. Hem, par victoria spiritalibus in sorte eremitarum nequitiis antea fuit insolita.

ABRAHAM. Sed nunc daemonum sumus praeda.

EFFREM. Mirum qui fieri posset, ut te ignorante evaderet.

8 ABRAHAM. Interim fueram consternatus mente ex ostensae visionis terrore, qua si mens non fuisset laeva, mihi praefigurabatur eius ruina.

EFFREM. Vellem modum visionis audire.

ABRAHAM. Putabam me ante fores cellulae stetisse, et ecce draco mirae magnitudinis nimiique fetoris rapido impetu adveniens candidulam secus me columbam reperiens cepit, devoravit, subitoque non comparuit.

EFFREM. Evidens visio.

Effrem. If she would persevere in such remorse, she would be saved.

Abraham. She has not persevered, but added even worse 6
deeds to the earlier ones.

Effrem. I'm shaken to the core; all my limbs have gone limp.

Abraham. After she had punished herself with these laments, overcome by an excess of grief, she was carried headfirst into a pit of despair.

Effrem. Oh my, how heavy the loss!

Abraham. And because she despaired that she could deserve forgiveness, she chose to go back into the world and to be a slave to its vanity.

Effrem. Alas, rarely has there been before now a compara- 7
ble victory for spiritual evil among those living as hermits.

Abraham. But now we are the prey of the demons.

Effrem. It is a wonder how it could be possible for her to run away without your knowing it.

Abraham. At the time my thoughts were overwhelmed by 8
fear because of a vision revealed to me, in which, had my mind not been distracted, her ruin was foretold to me.

Effrem. I should like to hear the tenor of this vision.

Abraham. I imagined I was standing before the doors of my little cell, and—hark!—a dragon of wondrous size and of incredible stench swooped in with a swift attack, and found a little white dove beside me; the dragon grabbed it, devoured it, and suddenly disappeared.

Effrem. This vision is clear.

9 Abraham. At ego, ubi expergiscens mente quae videbam tractavi, verebar aliquam Ecclesiae imminere persecutionem, quae fideles quosdam attraheret in errorem.

Effrem. Verendum erat.

Abraham. Unde prostratus in orationem Praecognitorem futurorum supplicavi, ut mihi detegeret solutionem somnii.

Effrem. Recte egisti.

10 Abraham. Tertia demum nocte cum lassa sopori membra dedissem, putabam eundem draconem mei vestigiis disruptum volutasse, ipsamque columbam absque laesione emicuisse.

Effrem. Laetificor auditu. Nec ambigo, quin tua quandoque ad te revertatur Maria.

11 Abraham. Postquam evigilans huius solamine visionis temperabam tristitiam prioris, mentem recepi, ut reminiscerer alumnae. Illud quoque si sine tristitia memini: quod ipsam in duorum intervallo dierum divinae innitentem laudi solito non sensi.

Effrem. Sero meministi.

12 Abraham. Fateor. Accessi, manu fenestram pulsavi, filiam saepius nominando vocavi.

Effrem. A, frustra vocasti!

Abraham. Hoc adhuc non sensi, sed cur neglegenter in divinis ageret rogavi. Sed nec levis tinnitum responsi recepi.

13 Effrem. Et quid tunc fecisti?

Abraham. But when I awoke and went over in my mind the things I had seen, I feared that some persecution of the Church was imminent, which would draw some of the faithful into error. 9

Effrem. That was cause for fear.

Abraham. And so, prostrate in prayer, I begged the One with foreknowledge of the future that he reveal to me the meaning of this dream.

Effrem. You acted properly.

Abraham. Then on the third night, when I had surrendered my weary limbs to sleep, I imagined this same dragon writhing, crushed by my feet, and the dove springing forth without a scar. 10

Effrem. I'm glad to hear it. And I have no doubt that someday your Mary will return to you.

Abraham. After waking up, because of the comfort of this vision, I moderated my distress at the earlier one, and I regained my senses so that I thought again of my foster child. And I also recollected, not without distress, that in the intervening two days I had not heard her occupied with divine worship in her customary way. 11

Effrem. You were slow to recollect that.

Abraham. I confess it. I went to her, I knocked at the window with my hand, I called to my daughter by name, over and over. 12

Effrem. Ah, you called in vain!

Abraham. I had not yet realized this, but I asked why she was performing her divine prayers so negligently. But I got not the faintest tinkle of a response.

Effrem. And what did you do then? 13

ABRAHAM. Ubi abesse quam quaerebam deprehendi, viscera discutiebantur timore, membra contremuerunt pavore.

EFFREM. Nec mirum. Certe et ego id ipsum nunc patior audiendo.

14 ABRAHAM. Deinde flebilibus sonis auras pollui, rogitans quis lupus meam agnam raperet, quis latro meam filiam captivaret.

EFFREM. Iure conquestus fuisti eius perditionem quam nutristi.

15 ABRAHAM. Tandem accesserunt qui, veritatem scientes, res sese ita ut tibi nunc exposui habere ipsamque vanitati dixerunt deservire.

EFFREM. Ubi moratur?

ABRAHAM. Ignoratur.

16 EFFREM. Quid fiet?

ABRAHAM. Est mihi fidelis amicus qui civitates villasque peragrans non quiescet, donec quae illam terra susceperit agnoscet.

EFFREM. Quid si experietur?

ABRAHAM. Habitum mutabo ipsamque sub amatoris specie adibo, si forte meo monitu post grave naufragium revertatur ad pristinae quietis portum.

17 EFFREM. Et iam quid fiet si carnium esus vinique haustus apponetur?

ABRAHAM. Haud abrogabo, ne agnoscar.

EFFREM. Recta prorsus laudabilique discretione uteris, si artioris frenas observantiae aliquantisper laxabis, quo errantem Christo lucreris.

ABRAHAM. When I understood that the one I was seeking was not there, my innards were rattled with fear, my limbs trembled in horror.

EFFREM. No wonder. I too, to be sure, hearing this, am now experiencing the very same thing.

ABRAHAM. Next, I defiled the breezes with tearful sounds, 14
asking what wolf carried off my lamb, what thief held my daughter captive.

EFFREM. You have justly lamented the loss of the one you raised.

ABRAHAM. Finally, some people came forward who knew 15
the truth of the matter, and they said that things were just as I have now explained them to you, and that she was a slave to the world's vanity.

EFFREM. Where is she living?

ABRAHAM. It's a mystery.

EFFREM. What will be done? 16

ABRAHAM. I have a faithful friend who will not rest, criss-crossing towns and villages, until he learns what land has taken her in.

EFFREM. What then, if she is discovered?

ABRAHAM. I will change my clothing, and I will approach her in the guise of a lover, to see if, by chance, through my counsel, she may return after this grave shipwreck to the harbor of her former tranquility.

EFFREM. And now what will happen if a supper of meats and 17
a drink of wine is served to you?

ABRAHAM. I will not refuse it, so that I will not be recognized.

EFFREM. You are using proper and laudable sense indeed, if you relax for a time the restraints of our stricter observance in order to win back a sinner to Christ.

Abraham. Eo magis ad audendum incitor, quo te mihi in hoc concordari re experior.

18 Effrem. Qui clancula cordium cognoscit, qua intentione unaquaeque res geratur intellegit. Nec in discretissimo eius examine reus praevaricationis habetur, qui, a strictioris rigore conversationis ad tempus descendendo, imbecillioribus assimilari non respuit, quo efficatius animam revocet quae erravit.

19 Abraham. Tuum est interim me precibus adiuvare ne impediar diabolica fraude.

Effrem. Ipsum summum bonum, sine quo nihil fit boni, faciat tuum velle in bono consummari.

4

Abraham. Num ille est meus amicus, quem ante hoc biennium pro inquisitu direxi Mariae? Ipse est.

Amicus. Ave, venerande pater.

Abraham. Ave, affabilis amice. Diu te sustinui, sed nunc advenire desperavi.

2 Amicus. Ideo moram feci, quia te ambigua re sollicitari non praesumpsi. At ubi veritatem investigavi, reditum maturavi.

Abraham. Vidistin' Mariam?

Amicus. Vidi.

Abraham. Ubi?

Abraham. I am even more inspired to undertake this adventure, since I find in fact that you concur with me in this matter.

Effrem. The One who knows the secret places of our 18
hearts also knows with what intention every single thing is done. And in his most discerning judgment, a man will not be considered guilty of falsehood who, departing for a time from the rigor of our stricter way of life, does not refuse to intermingle with those who are weaker, in order more effectively to call back a soul that has gone astray.

Abraham. It is your job, in the meantime, to aid me with 19
your prayers, so that I might not be impeded by the devil's treachery.

Effrem. May God, the highest good, without whom nothing good happens, make sure that your wish is accomplished for the good.

4

Abraham. Isn't that my friend, whom I sent two years ago in search of Mary? It is he.

Abraham's Friend. Hello, venerable father.

Abraham. Hello, gentle friend. I waited a long time for you, but I had by now lost hope that you would come.

Abraham's Friend. I have been delayed because I did not 2
presume to worry you with an unsubstantiated report. But when I had tracked down the truth, I hastened my return.

Abraham. Have you seen Mary?

Abraham's Friend. I have seen her.

Abraham. Where?

AMICUS. In proxima civitate.

ABRAHAM. Cum quibus moratur, quibusque assimilari nititur?

AMICUS. Piget dicere.

ABRAHAM. Quare?

AMICUS. Quia dictu miserabile.

ABRAHAM. Dic, obsecro.

3 AMICUS. In domo cuiusdam lenonis habitationem elegit, qui tenello amore illam colit. Nec frustra: nam omni die non modica illi pecunia ab eius amatoribus adducitur.

ABRAHAM. A Mariae amatoribus?

AMICUS. Ab ipsis.

ABRAHAM. Qui sunt eius amatores?

AMICUS. Perplures.

4 ABRAHAM. Ei mihi! O bone Iesu, quid hoc monstri est, quod hanc, quam tibi sponsam nutrivi, alienos amatores audio sequi.

AMICUS. Hoc meretricibus antiquitus fuit in more, ut alieno delectarentur in amore.

5 ABRAHAM. Affer mihi sonipedem delicatum et militarem habitum, quo, deposito tegmine religionis, ipsam adeam sub specie amatoris.

AMICUS. Ecce omnia.

ABRAHAM. Affer, obsecro, et pilleum, quo coronam vellem capitis.

AMICUS. Hoc maxime opus est ne agnoscaris.

ABRAHAM. Quid si unum solidum quem habeo mecum afferam, quo stabulario pro mercede tribuam?

AMICUS. Aliter ad colloquium Mariae non potes pervenire.

Abraham's Friend. In a nearby city.

Abraham. With whom is she living, whose habits is she adopting?

Abraham's Friend. I hate to say it.

Abraham. Why?

Abraham's Friend. Because it is a wretched thing to say.

Abraham. Tell me, please.

Abraham's Friend. She chooses to live in the home of a 3
certain pimp, who worships her with tender love. And not without reason, for every day no small amount of money accrues to him from her lovers.

Abraham. From Mary's lovers?

Abraham's Friend. From them.

Abraham. Who are her lovers?

Abraham's Friend. There are many of them.

Abraham. Ah me! O benevolent Jesus, what a monstrous 4
thing it is to hear that this woman, whom I raised to be your spouse, pursues other lovers.

Abraham's Friend. It has long since been the custom of prostitutes to take pleasure in the love of strangers.

Abraham. Bring me a fine horse and a soldier's clothing, so 5
that without my religious garb I may go to her in the guise of a lover.

Abraham's Friend. Here is everything you requested.

Abraham. Please bring me a hat too, to hide the top of my head.

Abraham's Friend. That is especially necessary, so that you won't be recognized.

Abraham. What do you think, should I bring with me the one gold coin I have, to pay the tavern keeper for her fee?

Abraham's Friend. You will not be able to have a conversation with Mary otherwise.

5

ABRAHAM. Salve, bone stabularie.

STABULARIUS. Quis loquitur? Hospes, salve!

ABRAHAM. Estne apud te locus viatori ad pernoctandum aptus?

STABULARIUS. Est plane. Nostra hospitiola nulli sunt neganda.

ABRAHAM. Laudabile.

STABULARIUS. Intra, ut tibi praeparetur cena.

2 ABRAHAM. Magnas grates tibi pro hilari susceptione debeo, sed adhuc maiora a te expeto.

STABULARIUS. Quae voles, ut concessurum efflagita.

ABRAHAM. Accipe vile munus quod defero, et fac ut praepulchra, quam tecum observari experiebar, puella nostro intersit convivio.

STABULARIUS. Cur illam desideras videre?

3 ABRAHAM. Quia nimium delector in eius agnitione, cuius pulchritudinem a quam pluribus laudari audiebam saepissime.

STABULARIUS. Quisquis laudator eius formae exstitit, nihil fefellit, nam praenitet venustate vultus prae ceteris mulieribus.

ABRAHAM. Ideo ardeo in amore eius.

STABULARIUS. Miror te in decrepita senectute iuvenculae mulieris amorem spirare.

ABRAHAM. Percerte nullius alius rei causa accessi, nisi eam videndi.

5

Abraham. Hello, good taverner.

Tavern Keeper. Who is speaking? Greetings, customer!

Abraham. Is there a place in your establishment suitable for a traveler to spend the night?

Tavern Keeper. By all means, there is. Our humble lodgings are denied to no one.

Abraham. That's commendable.

Tavern Keeper. Enter, so that a meal may be prepared for you.

Abraham. I owe you great thanks for this cheery reception, 2
but I have still greater things to ask of you.

Tavern Keeper. State what you want, so it may be granted.

Abraham. Take this humble gift which I bring you, and have that gorgeous girl, whom I've discovered is in your keeping, join me in conversation.

Tavern Keeper. Why do you want to see her?

Abraham. Because I will have great pleasure in the acquain- 3
tance of a woman whose beauty I have so very often heard praised by so many men.

Tavern Keeper. Whoever this celebrator of her beauty was, he was not mistaken, for the charm of her face is radiant beyond that of all other women.

Abraham. For that reason, I burn with love for her.

Tavern Keeper. I am surprised that in your frail old age you aspire to the love of a woman who is a very young girl.

Abraham. Most assuredly I came for no other reason than to see her.

6

Stabularius. Procede, procede, Maria, tuique pulchritudinem nostro neophytae ostende.

Maria. Ecce venio.

Abraham (*secum dicit*). Quae fiducia, quae constantia mentis mihi post haec, cum hanc quam nutrivi in eremi latibulis meretricio cultu ornatam conspicio? Sed non est tempus ut praefiguretur in facie, quod tenetur in corde. Erumpentes lacrimas viriliter stringo, et simulata vultus hilaritate internae amaritudinem maestitudinis contego.

2 Stabularius. Fortunata Maria, laetare, quia non solum ut hactenus tui coaevi, sed etiam senio iam confecti te adeunt, te ad amandum confluunt.

Maria. Quicumque me diligunt, aequalem amoris vicem a me recipiunt.

Abraham. Accede, Maria, et da mihi osculum.

Maria. Non solum dulcia oscula libabo, sed etiam crebris senile collum amplexibus mulcebo.

Abraham. Hoc volo.

3 Maria. Quid sentio? Quid stupendae novitatis gustando haurio? Ecce odor istius flagrantiae praetendit flagrantiam mihi quondam usitatae abstinentiae.

Abraham. Nunc, nunc est simulandum; nunc lascivientis more pueri iocis instandum, ne et ego agnoscar prae gravitate, et ipsa se reddat latibulis prae pudore.

6

TAVERN KEEPER. Come out, come out, Mary, and display your beauty to our new convert.

MARY. Here I am, I'm coming.

ABRAHAM *(SAYS TO HIMSELF)*. What confidence, what steadiness of mind can I have now, after seeing this woman whom I raised in the shelter of my hermitage tricked out in the dress of a prostitute? But now is not the time to reveal by my expression what is held in my heart. I will repress in a manly way the tears bursting out of me, and I will cover up the bitterness of my inner sorrow by feigning happiness in my expression.

TAVERN KEEPER. O fortunate Mary, rejoice, because now 2
not only, as in the past, your contemporaries, but also those already consumed by old age are coming to you; they are pouring in to make love to you.

MARY. Whoever loves me will get an equal repayment of love from me.

TAVERN KEEPER. Come here, Mary, and give me a kiss.

MARY. I will not only offer sweet kisses, but I'll also soothe your aged neck with frequent embraces.

ABRAHAM. That's what I want.

MARY. What am I feeling? What kind of wondrous novelty 3
do I taste and breathe? See here, the smell of this fragrance puts me in mind of the fragrance of chastity that was once so familiar to me.

ABRAHAM *(TO HIMSELF)*. Now, even now, I must put on an act; now I must devote myself to flirting, like a lustful boy, so I won't be recognized by my serious demeanor, and she won't retreat to her private rooms out of shame.

MARIA. Vae mihi infelici! Unde cecidi, et in quam perditionis foveam corrui!

4 ABRAHAM. Hic non est aptus querelae locus, ubi convivarum confluit conventus.

STABULARIUS. Domna Maria, cur suspiria trahis? Cur mades lacrimis? Nonne per biennium hic conversabaris, et numquam ex te gemitus prorupit, numquam tristior sermo prodiit?

5 MARIA. O utinam fuissem ante biennium morte absumpta, ne ad tanta devenirem flagitia!

ABRAHAM. Non ut tua tecum peccata plangerem adveni, sed ut tuo iungerer amori.

MARIA. Levi compunctione permovebar, ideo talia fabar. Sed epulemur, et laetemur, quia ut monuisti, hic non est tempus peccata plangendi.

6 ABRAHAM. Affatim refecti, affatim sumus inebriati tua largitate administrante, O bone stabularie. Da licentiam a cena surgendi, quo lassum corpus in stratu componam, dulcique quiete recreem.

STABULARIUS. Ut libet.

MARIA. Surge, domine mi, surge, tecum pariter tendam ad cubile.

ABRAHAM. Placet. Nullatenus cogi possem, ut te non comitante exirem.

7

MARIA. Ecce triclinium ad inhabitandum nobis aptum; ecce lectus haud vilibus stramentis compositus. Sede ut tibi detraham calciamenta, ne tu ipse fatigeris discalciando.

MARY. Oh, poor me! From what a height I have fallen, and into what a pit of damnation I have collapsed!

ABRAHAM. This is not a suitable place for lament, where an 4
assembly of banqueters is pouring in.

TAVERN KEEPER. Lady Mary, why do you sigh? Why are you soaked in tears? You have lived here for two years, and such a groan has never burst forth from you, a sadder word has never issued from you; is it not so?

MARY. Oh, if only I had been taken by death two years ago, 5
so that I would not have come to such degradation!

ABRAHAM. I did not come to cry over your sins with you, but to be united with you in love.

MARY. I was overwhelmed by a trivial regret, that's why I said those things. But let's eat, let's be merry, because as you reminded me, here there is no time for crying over sins.

ABRAHAM. We are filled to the brim, drunk to overflowing 6
from your generous service, O good barkeep. Give me leave to rise from the table, so I can put my weary body in bed, and restore myself with sweet sleep.

TAVERN KEEPER. As you wish.

MARY. Rise, my lord, rise; I'll accompany you to the bedroom.

ABRAHAM. That pleases me. I could not have been forced by any means to leave without you.

7

MARY. Look here, a suitable chamber for us to occupy; look, a bed covered in no mean linens. Sit, so I may strip off your sandals, to save you the trouble of removing them.

Abraham. Muni prius seris ostium, ne quis introeundi inveniat aditum.

Maria. Super hoc ne solliciteris, faciam ut nulli ad nos tribuatur accessus facilis.

2 Abraham. Tempus, ablato capitis velamine, quis sim, aperire. O adoptiva filia, O meae pars animae Maria, agnoscisne me senem, qui te paterno more nutrivi, qui te caelestis Regis unigenito desponsavi?

Maria. Ei mihi, pater et magister meus Abraham est qui loquitur.

3 Abraham. Quid contigit tibi filia?

Maria. Gravis miseria.

Abraham. Quis te decepit, quis te seduxit?

Maria. Qui protoplastos prostravit.

Abraham. Ubi est angelica illa quam in terris egisti conversatio?

Maria. Prorsus perdita.

Abraham. Ubi est verecundia tua virginalis? Ubi continentia admirabilis?

Maria. Evacuata.

4 Abraham. Quam mercedem, nisi resipiscas, pro ieiuniorum, orationum, vigiliarum, sudore ultra potes sperare, cum velut lapsa ab altitudinem caeli dimersa es in profundum inferni?

Maria. Eh heu!

5 Abraham. Quare me despexisti, quare deseruisti, quare eventum tuae perditionis mihi non indicasti, quo ego cum dilecto meo Effrem, dignam pro te paenitentiam agerem?

ABRAHAM. First secure the door with bolts, so that no one may find a way to enter.

MARY. Don't worry about that, I will make sure that no one has easy access to us.

ABRAHAM. It is time to remove the covering of my head and 2
reveal who I am. O foster daughter, O Mary, you who are half of my soul, do you recognize me, the old man who raised you as a father, who betrothed you to the only-begotten of the heavenly King?

MARY. Ah me, it is my father and teacher Abraham who is speaking.

ABRAHAM. What happened to you, daughter? 3

MARY. Grave misery.

ABRAHAM. Who deceived you, who seduced you?

MARY. The one who laid low the first humans.

ABRAHAM. Where is that angelic way of life that you lived on earth?

MARY. Totally lost.

ABRAHAM. Where is your virgin modesty? Where your admirable chastity?

MARY. Gone.

ABRAHAM. Unless you come to your senses, what reward for 4
the toil of your fasts, prayers, and vigils can you hope for any longer, since you are as fallen from the heights of heaven as you are sunk in the depths of hell?

MARY. Ah, woe!

ABRAHAM. Why did you disregard me, why did you abandon 5
me, why did you not make known to me the misfortune of your fall, so that with my beloved Effrem I could have done proper penance for you?

MARIA. Postquam lapsa in peccatis corrui, tuae sanctitati polluta proximare non praesumpsi.

6 ABRAHAM. Quis umquam a peccato exstitit immunis, nisi solus Filius Virginis?

MARIA. Nullus.

ABRAHAM. Humanum est peccare; diabolicum est in peccatis durare. Nec iure reprehenditur, qui subito cadit, sed qui citius surgere neglegit.

MARIA. Ei mihi infelici!

7 ABRAHAM. Cur decidis, cur in terra iaces immobilis? Erigere et quae dicam percipe.

MARIA. Pavore concussa corrui, quia vim paternae monitionis ferre nequivi.

ABRAHAM. Attende mei in te dilectionem, et depone timorem.

MARIA. Nequeo.

8 ABRAHAM. Nonne tui causa desiderabilem eremi habitationem reliqui, omnemque regularis observantiam conversationis propter te evacuavi, in tantum ut ego, vetus eremicola, factus sum lascivientium conviva? Et, qui diu silentio studebam, iocularia verba ne agnoscerer proferebam? Cur dimisso vultu terram inspicis? Cur respondendo mecum verba miscere dedignaris?

9 MARIA. Proprii conscientia reatus confundor, ideo nec oculos ad caelum levare, nec sermonem tecum praesumo conserere.

ABRAHAM. Noli diffidere, filia, noli desperare, sed emerge de abysso desperationis, et fige in Deo spem mentis.

MARY. After I had fallen and collapsed into sin, I did not presume to come near your saintly person, polluted as I was.

ABRAHAM. Who was ever able to live free from sin, except 6
only the Son of the Virgin?

MARY. No one.

ABRAHAM. It is human to sin; it is diabolical to go on living in sin. It is not right to reprimand one who has unexpectedly fallen, but one who refuses to rise up again quickly.

MARY. Oh, poor me!

ABRAHAM. Why do you fall down, why do you lie immobile 7
on the ground? Stand up and listen to what I am saying.

MARY. I collapsed struck by fear, because I could not bear the force of paternal reproach.

ABRAHAM. Consider my love for you, and put aside your fear.

MARY. I cannot do it.

ABRAHAM. Did I not leave the pleasant confines of my her- 8
mitage, did I not abandon all observance of my way of life under monastic rules for your sake, so much so that I, an aged hermit, became the drinking partner of lustful young men? And so much so that I, who for so long sought silence, uttered frivolous words in order not to be recognized? Why do you look at the ground with your face turned away? Why do you refuse to reply to me?

MARY. I am ashamed by recognition of my own guilt, so I 9
don't presume to raise my eyes to heaven, nor to join with you in conversation.

ABRAHAM. Do not lack confidence, daughter, do not despair, but rise out of this abyss of despair and place in God the hope of your heart.

Maria. Enormitas peccatorum prostravit me in desperationis profundum.

10 Abraham. Peccata quidem tua sunt gravia, fateor; sed superna pietas maior est omni creatura. Unde tricas rumpe, datumque paenitendi spatiolum pigritando noli neglegere, quatenus superabundet divina gratia, ubi superabundavit facinorum abominatio.

Maria. Si ulla promerendae spes veniae inesset, studium paenitendi minime deesset.

11 Abraham. Miserere mei, quam pro te subii, lassitudinis; et depone perniciosam desperationem, quam omnibus commissis non nescimus esse graviorem. Qui enim peccantibus Deum misereri velle desperat, irremediabiliter peccat, quia sicut scintilla silicis pelagus nequit inflammare, ita nostrorum acerbitas peccaminum divinae dulcedinem benignitatis non valet immutare.

12 Maria. Non enim supernae magnificentiam pietatis nego, sed proprii enormitatem sceleris considerando, ad dignae satisfactionem paenitentiae vereor non sufficere.

Abraham. In me sit iniquitas tua, tantummodo revertere ad locum unde existi, et ini secundo conversationem quam deseruisti.

13 Maria. In nullo umquam tui renitor votis, sed quae iubes obtemperanter amplector.

Abraham. Nunc fateor te vere meam quam nutrivi filiam. Nunc censeo te prae omnibus fore diligendam.

Mary. The enormity of my sins has cast me down into the depths of despair.

Abraham. Your sins are indeed grievous, I admit it; but the 10
kindness of heaven is greater than all creation. So put an end to this nonsense, and don't neglect out of laziness what little time is allotted for penance; for when the abomination of our sins has overflowed, God's grace does likewise.

Mary. If there were any hope of earning forgiveness, there would be no lack of enthusiasm for penance.

Abraham. Have pity upon my fatigue, a fatigue to which I 11
subjected myself for your sake; and put aside this destructive despair, which we know is a graver evil than any sins. For whoever despairs of God's desire to be merciful to sinners sins irredeemably, because just as a spark of flint cannot light a sea on fire, so the bitterness of our sins is not strong enough to alter the sweetness of divine beneficence.

Mary. I assuredly do not deny the greatness of heavenly 12
mercy, but considering the enormity of my own wickedness, I fear I am inadequate to the achievement of suitable penance.

Abraham. Let your iniquity be upon me, only return to the place you left, and for a second time enter upon the way of life that you abandoned.

Mary. In no way will I ever struggle against your wishes, 13
but will obediently embrace what you order.

Abraham. Now I admit that you are truly the daughter I raised. Now I believe that you must be loved more than everyone else.

14 Maria. Aliquantulum auri vestiumque possideo. Quid tua de his auctoritas decreverit exspecto.

Abraham. Quae adquisisti peccando, cum ipsis peccatis sunt abicienda.

Maria. Rebar pauperibus eroganda seu sacris esse altaribus offerenda.

Abraham. Non satis acceptabile munus Deo esse comprobatur, quod criminibus adquiritur.

Maria. Nulla super his ultra sollicitudine fatigar.

15 Abraham. Matuta nitescit; lucescit; abeamus.

Maria. Tuum est, pater amande, ut ad instar boni pastoris praecedas repertam ovem. Et ego, paribus incedens vestigiis, subsequor praecedentem.

Abraham. Haud ita! Sed ego pedibus incedam; te autem equo superponam, ne itineris asperitas secet teneras plantas.

16 Maria. O, quem te memorem? Quam tibi gratiarum impendam recompensationem? Qui me indignam miseratione, non terrore, cogis. Sed miti condescensione ad paenitentiam hortaris.

Abraham. Nihil aliud a te expeto, nisi ut reliquum vitae inhaerendo insistas Dei obsequio.

17 Maria. Spontanea mente inhaeream, pro viribus insistam. Et si facultas desit posse, numquam tamen deerit velle.

MARY. I have a little bit of gold and some clothing. I await 14
your authoritative pronouncement concerning them.

ABRAHAM. Whatever you acquired through sinning should be cast out with the sins.

MARY. I was considering whether they should be bestowed upon the poor, or offered at the sacred altars.

ABRAHAM. Whatever was acquired by wicked deeds is not fully sanctioned as an acceptable gift to God.

MARY. I will no longer be bothered by concern for these things.

ABRAHAM. Dawn is beginning to shine; it is becoming light; 15
we should go.

MARY. It is for you, beloved father, to take the lead in front of the sheep that was found, like a good shepherd. And I will follow your lead, proceeding at the same pace.

ABRAHAM. That cannot be! Rather, I will go on foot; you, however, I will place on a horse, so that the roughness of the journey not cut the tender soles of your feet.

MARY. Oh—what should I call you? What repayment of 16
thanks could I bestow on you? You urge me, unworthy as I am, through mercy, not terror. Rather, you encourage me by your kind indulgence to repent.

ABRAHAM. I want nothing else from you, except that you devote the rest of your life to the service of God, clinging to him.

MARY. I will cling to him with a willing heart, I will devote 17
myself to him with all my strength. And if the ability to achieve this is lacking, nevertheless, the desire will never be lacking.

ABRAHAM. Convenit ut, quo studio deserviebas vanitati, famuleris divinae voluntati.

MARIA. Fiat precor tuis meritis, ut in me perficiatur voluntas divinitatis.

ABRAHAM. Maturemus reditum.

MARIA. Maturemus, nam me taedet morarum.

8

ABRAHAM. Quanta celeritate asperi difficultatem itineris transcurrimus!

MARIA. Quod devote agitur, facile perficitur.

ABRAHAM. Ecce tua deserta cellula.

MARIA. Ei mihi! Ipsa mei sceleris est conscia, ideo ingredi formido.

2 ABRAHAM. Et merito. Fugiendus est quippe locus in quo hostem sequitur triumphus.

MARIA. Et ubi me decernis compunctioni vacare?

ABRAHAM. Ingredere in cellulam interiorem, ne vetustus serpens decipiendi ultra inveniat occasionem.

MARIA. Non contraluctor, sed quae iubes amplector.

3 ABRAHAM. Familiarem meum Effrem accedam, quo ipse, qui solus mecum tuae condoluit perditioni, congaudeat inventioni.

MARIA. Competit.

ABRAHAM. It is fitting that you subject yourself to God's will with the same zeal with which you were enslaved to vanity.

MARY. I pray it may turn out through your merits that God's will may be accomplished in me.

ABRAHAM. Let's hurry home.

MARY. Let's hurry, for I am tired of delays.

8

ABRAHAM. How quickly we have progressed through the difficulty of a hard journey!

MARY. Whatever is undertaken devoutly is easily accomplished.

ABRAHAM. Look, here is your empty little cell.

MARY. Ah me! The cell itself is aware of my wickedness, so I am afraid to enter it.

ABRAHAM. And rightly so. Indeed, a place where the enemy 2
met with success should be shunned.

MARY. And where have you decided I should spend my time in contrition?

ABRAHAM. Go into the little interior cell, so that the ancient serpent may find no opportunity for deceiving you further.

MARY. I will not resist, but will embrace what you command.

ABRAHAM. I will go to my friend Effrem, so that he, who 3
alone condoled with me for your loss, may rejoice for your recovery.

MARY. That is appropriate.

9

Effrem. Num mihi aliquid affers gaudii?

Abraham. Ac magni.

Effrem. Placet, nec dubito quin Mariam nanciscereris.

Abraham. Nanciscebar plane, et gaudens reduxi ad ovile.

Effrem. Divinae gratia visitationis factum credo.

Abraham. Procul dubio.

2 Effrem. Vellem scire qualiter iuxta id temporis vitam, moresque ordinaverit.

Abraham. Iuxta meum velle.

Effrem. Hoc illi expedit vel maxime.

Abraham. Quicquid ipsi agendum proposui, quamvis difficile, quamvis grave, haud abrogavit subire.

Effrem. Laudabile.

3 Abraham. Nam induta cilicio continuaque vigiliarum et ieiunii exercitatione macerata, artissimae legis observatione corpus tenerum animae cogit pati imperium.

Effrem. Aequum est, ut iniquae sordes delectationis eliminentur acerbitate castigationis.

Abraham. Quisquis eius lamenta intellegit, mente vulneratur. Quisquis compunctionem sentit, et ipse compungitur.

Effrem. Solet fieri.

9

Effrem. Have you brought me some cause for joy?

Abraham. For great joy.

Effrem. I am pleased. I have no doubt you have gotten Mary back.

Abraham. I got her back completely, and I have returned her to the fold, rejoicing.

Effrem. I believe this has happened thanks to divine assistance.

Abraham. Without question.

Effrem. I should like to know how she will now arrange her 2
life and her habits.

Abraham. According to my wishes.

Effrem. That will benefit her a great deal.

Abraham. Whatever I have proposed that she should do, however difficult, however serious, she did not refuse to undertake it.

Effrem. That is commendable.

Abraham. Indeed, dressed in a penitential robe and emaci- 3
ated by the continuous performance of vigils and of fasting, she is forcing her tender body, by observing the strictest regimen, to be subservient to her soul.

Effrem. It is only fair that the wicked stains of pleasure be eliminated by the ferocity of punishment.

Abraham. Whoever knows of her sorrows will be wounded in his heart. Whoever is aware of her contrition will himself be contrite.

Effrem. That often happens.

4 ABRAHAM. Elaborat pro viribus ut, quibus causa fuit perditionis, fiat exemplum conversionis.

EFFREM. Consequens est.

ABRAHAM. Nititur ut quanto exstitit foedior, tanto appareat nitidior.

5 EFFREM. Iucundor audiendo, praecordialique laetor gaudimonio.

ABRAHAM. Et merito. Nam phalanges angelicae gaudentes Dominum laudant super peccatoris conversione.

EFFREM. Nec mirum. Nullius namque iusti magis delectatur perseverantia, quam impii paenitentia.

6 ABRAHAM. Unde in illa tanto iustius laudatur, quanto ultra resipisci posse desperabatur.

EFFREM. Congratulantes laudemus, laudantes glorificemus unigenitum et venerabilem, dilectum et clementem Dei Filium, qui non vult perire quos sui sacro redemit sanguine.

ABRAHAM. Ipsi honor, gloria, laus, et iubilatio, per infinita secula. Amen.

ABRAHAM. She toils to the best of her ability to become an 4
example of conversion to those for whom she was the cause of ruin.

EFFREM. That is reasonable.

ABRAHAM. She struggles to appear as much cleaner now, as she was dirtier then.

EFFREM. I am happy to hear it, and I rejoice with heartfelt 5
joy.

ABRAHAM. And rightly so. For the angelic hosts, rejoicing, praise the Lord for the return of a sinner.

EFFREM. It is no wonder. The perseverance of any just person is, indeed, not more pleasing to him than the repentance of an unrighteous one.

ABRAHAM. And so, he is praised all the more justly in her 6
case, since it was beyond hope that she could return to her senses.

EFFREM. Giving thanks, let us praise; giving praise, let us glorify the only-begotten and venerable, the beloved and kind Son of God. He does not want those men to perish whom he redeemed with his own sacred blood.

ABRAHAM. To him may there be honor, glory, praise, and jubilation, for ever and ever. Amen.

<Conversio Thaidis>

Conversio Thaidis meretricis, quam Pafnutius eremita aeque ut Abraham sub specie adiens amatoris convertit. Et data paenitentia, per quinquennium in angusta cellula conclusit, donec, digna satisfactione Deo reconciliata, quinta decima peractae paenitentiae die obdormivit in Christo.

PAFNUTIUS THAIS
DISCIPULI

I

DISCIPULI. Cur obscurum, pater, vultum nec solito geris, Paphnuti, serenum?

PAFNUTIUS. Cuius cor contristatur, eius et vultus obscuratur.

DISCIPULI. Pro qua re contristaris?

PAFNUTIUS. Pro iniuria Factoris.

DISCIPULI. Quae haec iniuria?

PAFNUTIUS. Ipsa, quam a propria patitur creatura ad sui imaginem condita.

DISCIPULI. Terruisti nos dictu.

The Conversion of Thais

The conversion of Thais, a prostitute, whom the hermit Paphnutius converted, going to her in the disguise of a lover, just as Abraham did. And having assigned penance to her, he enclosed her for five years in a cramped little cell, until through proper recompense she was reconciled to God. On the fifteenth day after she had completed her penance, she rested in Christ.

Paphnutius	Thais
His Students	

I

Students. Why do you have a dark expression on your face, Father Paphnutius, and not your usual serene one?

Paphnutius. Whoever has a sad heart also has a dark face.

Students. Why are you sad?

Paphnutius. Because of an injustice to the Creator.

Students. What is this injustice?

Paphnutius. One that he suffers from his own creation, fashioned in his own image.

Students. You have terrified us by saying this.

2 PAFNUTIUS. Licet illa impassibilis maiestas affici non possit iniuriis, tamen ut usum nostrae fragilitatis metaphorice transferam in Deum: Quae maior iniuria dici potest quam quod eius imperio, cuius gubernaculis maior mundus obtemperanter subditur, solus minor contraluctetur?

3 DISCIPULI. Quis est "minor mundus"?

PAFNUTIUS. Homo.

DISCIPULI. Homo?

PAFNUTIUS. Porro.

DISCIPULI. Qui homo?

PAFNUTIUS. Omnis.

DISCIPULI. Qui potest fieri?

PAFNUTIUS. Ut placuit Creatori.

DISCIPULI. Non sapimus.

PAFNUTIUS. Non obvium est perpluribus.

DISCIPULI. Expone!

PAFNUTIUS. Intendite.

DISCIPULI. Ac prompta mente.

4 PAFNUTIUS. Sicut enim maior mundus ex quattuor contrariis elementis, sed ad nutum Creatoris secundum harmonicam moderationem concordantibus, perficitur, ita et homo non solum ab eisdem elementis sed etiam ex magis contrariis partibus coaptatur.

5 DISCIPULI. Et quid magis contrarium quam elementa?

PAFNUTIUS. Corpus et anima, quia licet illa sint contraria, tamen sunt corporalia. Anima autem nec mortalis ut corpus, nec corpus spiritalis ut anima.

DISCIPULI. Ita.

PAPHNUTIUS. Even though that invulnerable majesty can- 2
not be affected by injustices, nevertheless, to apply, metaphorically speaking, the experience of our own fragility to God: What greater injustice can be named than that the lesser world alone opposes the authority of God, to whose governance the greater world obediently submits?

STUDENTS. What is this "lesser world"? 3

PAPHNUTIUS. Man.

STUDENTS. Man?

PAPHNUTIUS. Certainly.

STUDENTS. Which man?

PAPHNUTIUS. Every man.

STUDENTS. How can that be?

PAPHNUTIUS. It pleased the Creator that it be so.

STUDENTS. We don't understand.

PAPHNUTIUS. It is not clear to many.

STUDENTS. Please explain!

PAPHNUTIUS. Pay attention.

STUDENTS. We will, and with attentive minds.

PAPHNUTIUS. Just as, in fact, the greater world is created 4
out of four elements, which are contrary, but which come together at the will of the Creator in a harmonious arrangement, so also man is fashioned not only from these same elements, but also from even more contrary parts.

STUDENTS. And what is more contrary than the elements? 5

PAPHNUTIUS. The body and the soul. Because even though the elements are contrary, still they are material. The soul, however, is not mortal like the body, nor is the body spiritual like the soul.

STUDENTS. Just so.

PAFNUTIUS. Si tamen dialecticos sequimur, nec illa contraria esse fatemur.

DISCIPULIS. Et quis potest negare?

PAFNUTIUS. Qui dialectice scit disputare, quia ousiae nihil est contrarium, sed receptatrix est contrariorum.

6 DISCIPULI. Quid sibi vult quod dixisti, "secundum harmonicam moderationem"?

PAFNUTIUS. Id scilicet, quod sicut pressi excellentesque soni harmonice coniuncti quiddam perficiunt musicum, ita dissona elementa convenienter concordantia unum perficiunt mundum.

DISCIPULI. Mirum quomodo dissona concordari, vel concordantia possint dissona dici.

PAFNUTIUS. Quia nihil ex similibus componi videtur, nec ex his quae nulla ratione proportionis iunguntur et a se omni substantia naturaque discreta sunt.

7 DISCIPULI. Quid est musica?

PAFNUTIUS. Disciplina una de philosophiae quadruvio.

DISCIPULI. Quid est hoc quod dicis "quadruvium"?

PAFNUTIUS. Arithmetica, geometrica, musica, astronomica.

DISCIPULI. Cur "quadruvium"?

PAFNUTIUS. Quia sicut a quadruvio semitae, ita ab uno philosophiae principio harum disciplinarum prodeunt progressiones rectae.

PAPHNUTIUS. If, however, we follow the dialecticians, we will declare that the elements are not contrary either.

STUDENTS. And who can make such a denial?

PAPHNUTIUS. One who knows how to argue like a dialectician, because nothing is contrary to its essence, but essence is the repository of contraries.

STUDENTS. What does it mean, what you just said, "in a har- 6
monious arrangement"?

PAPHNUTIUS. Namely this, that just as deep and high-pitched sounds, joined harmoniously, create some sort of music, so also the discordant elements, coming together concordantly, create one world.

STUDENTS. It is a miracle how discordant things can be concordant, or how concordant things can be called discordant.

PAPHNUTIUS. It is because nothing seems to be composed of similar things, nor from things that are not joined in some kind of proportion and that are totally different from one another in their substance and nature.

STUDENTS. What is music? 7

PAPHNUTIUS. One of the disciplines of the quadrivium of philosophy.

STUDENTS. What is this thing you call "the quadrivium"?

PAPHNUTIUS. Arithmetic, geometry, music, and astronomy.

STUDENTS. Why is it called "quadrivium"?

PAPHNUTIUS. Because just as paths extend outward from a four-way intersection, so do the right and proper advancements of these disciplines extend from one starting point in philosophy.

8 DISCIPULI. Veremur quiddam investigando rogitare de tribus, quia coeptae scrupulum disputationis capedine mentis vix penetrare quimus.

PAFNUTIUS. Difficile captu.

DISCIPULI. Dic nobis de ea, superficie tenus, cuius mentionem in praesenti fecimus.

PAFNUTIUS. Perparum dicere scio quia eremicolis est incognita.

9 DISCIPULI. Quid agit?

PAFNUTIUS. Musica?

DISCIPULI. Ipsa.

PAFNUTIUS. Disputat de sonis.

10 DISCIPULI. Utrum est una an plures?

PAFNUTIUS. Tres esse dicuntur, sed unaquaeque ratione proportionis alteri ita coniungitur, ut idem quod accidit uni, non deest alteri.

DISCIPULI. Et quae distantia inter tres?

PAFNUTIUS. Prima dicitur mundana sive caelestis, secunda humana, tertia quae instrumentis exercetur.

11 DISCIPULI. In quo constat caelestis?

PAFNUTIUS. In septem planetis et in caelesti sphaera.

DISCIPULI. Quo modo?

PAFNUTIUS. Eo videlicet, quo illa quae in instrumentis, quia tot spatia, pares productiones, eaedem symphoniae repperiuntur in his, quae et in chordis.

12 DISCIPULI. Quid sunt spatia?

STUDENTS. In trying to learn about one thing, we are afraid 8 to ask about three different things, because with the capacity of our mind we can scarcely penetrate the tiniest bit of the discussion you have begun.

PAPHNUTIUS. It is difficult to grasp.

STUDENTS. Tell us, at least superficially, about the thing we just now mentioned.

PAPHNUTIUS. I have very little to say, because it is a thing unknown to hermits.

STUDENTS. What is it about? 9

PAPHNUTIUS. Music?

STUDENTS. Yes, that.

PAPHNUTIUS. It concerns sounds.

STUDENTS. Is there one kind, or many? 10

PAPHNUTIUS. There are said to be three, but each one is joined to another by reason of its proportion, such that the same thing that can be said of the one, is not irrelevant to the other.

STUDENTS. And what distinction is there among the three?

PAPHNUTIUS. The first is called worldly or celestial, the second human, the third is what is performed with instruments.

STUDENTS. Of what does the celestial one consist? 11

PAPHNUTIUS. Of the seven planets and the celestial sphere.

STUDENTS. How so?

PAPHNUTIUS. In the same way, namely, as the one which is performed with instruments, because just as many intervals, an equal number of productions, and the same consonances are found in the planets as are found in the strings of instruments.

STUDENTS. What are intervals? 12

PAFNUTIUS. Dimensiones, quae numerantur inter planetas sive inter chordas.

DISCIPULI. Et quid productiones?

PAFNUTIUS. Idem quod toni.

DISCIPULI. Nec horum notitia nos tangit.

PAFNUTIUS. Tonus fit ex duobus sonis, et possidet rationem epogdoi numeri sive sesquioctavi.

13 DISCIPULI. Quanto velocius praeposita investigando satagimus transire, tanto difficiliora nobis non desinis apponere.

PAFNUTIUS. Hoc exigit huiusmodi disputatio.

DISCIPULI. Edissere summotenus aliquantulum de symphoniis, quo saltim sciamus significationem nominis.

PAFNUTIUS. Symphonia dicitur modulationis temperamentum.

DISCIPULI. Quare?

14 PAFNUTIUS. Quia nunc quattuor, nunc quinque, nunc octo sonis perficitur.

DISCIPULI. Quia tres esse cognoscimus, singularum vocabula dinoscere cupimus.

PAFNUTIUS. Prima dicitur "diatesseron," quasi "ex quattuor," et possidet proportionem "epitritam" sive "sesquitertiam." Secunda "diapente," quae constat "ex quinque" et est in ratione "hemiolei" sive "sesquialteri." Tertia "diapason"; haec fit in duplo perficiturque sonitibus octo.

15 DISCIPULI. Num sphaera et planetae proferunt sonum ut mereantur comparationem chordarum?

PAFNUTIUS. Ac maximum.

PAPHNUTIUS. Distances, which are calculated between planets, or between strings.

STUDENTS. And what are productions?

PAPHNUTIUS. The same things as tones.

STUDENTS. We have no understanding of tones either.

PAPHNUTIUS. A tone is made of two sounds, and it has the ratio of nine to eight, the sesquioctave.

STUDENTS. However much more swiftly we struggle to ad- 13
vance in our investigation of these propositions, so much the more difficult are the things you keep piling on us.

PAPHNUTIUS. A discussion of this kind requires it.

STUDENTS. Explain to us, just touching the surface, a little bit about consonances, so that we may at least understand the meaning of the word.

PAPHNUTIUS. Consonance is said to be the blending of a set of pitches.

STUDENTS. Why so?

PAPHNUTIUS. Because it is created sometimes by four 14
tones, sometimes by five, and sometimes by eight.

STUDENTS. Because we know there are three of these, we want to learn the names of each one.

PAPHNUTIUS. The first is called "diatesseron," that is to say, "from four," and it has the "epitrite" proportion of four to three, also called "sesquitertia." The second is "diapente" which means "from five," and it is in the "hemiolic" ratio of three to two, also called "sesquialter." The third is "diapason"; it occurs in a two to one ratio and is created by eight sounds.

STUDENTS. Do the sphere and the planets produce a sound 15
such that they deserve to be compared with strings?

PAPHNUTIUS. Yes, and it is the greatest sound.

DISCIPULIS. Cur non auditur?

PAFNUTIUS. Multifariam exponunt. Alii autumant non au-
diri posse propter assiduitatem, alii propter aeris spissitu-
16 dinem. Quidam autem ferunt, quod tanti enormitas soni-
tus artos aurium nequeat intrare meatus. Sunt etiam qui dicunt quod sphaera tam iucundum, tam dulcem efferat sonum, ut si audiretur omnes in commune homines, semet ipsis neglectis omnibusque postpositis studiis, ducentem sonum ab oriente sequerentur in occidentem.

DISCIPULI. Praestat ut non audiatur.

PAFNUTIUS. Hoc a Creatore praesciebatur.

17 DISCIPULI. Sit satis de ista; prosequere de humana.

PAFNUTIUS. Quid de illa?

DISCIPULI. In quo percipiatur.

PAFNUTIUS. Non solum, ut dixi, in compagine corporis et animae, necnon in emissione, nunc gravis nunc clarae, vocis, sed etiam in pulsibus venarum atque in quorundam mensura membrorum, sicut in articulis digitorum, in quibus easdem proportiones mensurando repperimus, quas in symphoniis praemisimus, quia musica dicitur convenientia non solum vocum, sed etiam aliarum dissimilium rerum.

18 DISCIPULI. Si praesciremus quod huiusmodi nodus quaestionis tam difficilis ad solvendum esset insciis, maluissemus "minorem mundum" nescire, quam tantum difficultatis subire.

Students. Why doesn't anyone hear it?

Paphnutius. The explanations are various. Some affirm that it cannot be heard because it is continual, others because of the thickness of the air. Certain men, however, 16
say the immensity of such a sound cannot enter the narrow channels of our ears. There are also those who maintain that the sphere brings forth a sound so pleasing, so sweet, that if it could be heard, all men, united, would follow the sound, forgetting about themselves and abandoning all their pursuits, as it led them from east to west.

Students. It's better no one hears it.

Paphnutius. The Creator knew that in advance.

Students. That should suffice regarding celestial music; 17
proceed with human music.

Paphnutius. What about it?

Students. How is it perceived?

Paphnutius. Not only, as I said, in the joining of the body and the soul, nor in the utterance—sometimes deep, sometimes high-pitched—of the voice, but also in the throbbing of the veins and in the measurements of certain parts of our bodies, such as in the joints of our fingers, in which we find, when we measure them, the same proportions we mentioned before in explaining the concordances, because music is said to be a coming together not only of voices, but also of other things that are dissimilar.

Students. If we had known beforehand that the knot of 18
this kind of questioning would be so difficult to unravel for the unlearned, we would have preferred not to know about the "lesser world," rather than to undergo such difficulty.

PAFNUTIUS. Nil officit quod elaborastis, cum ante ignorata experti estis.

DISCIPULI. Verum. Sed taedet nos philosophicae disputationis, quia nequimus sensu emetiri scrupulum tuae rationis.

19 PAFNUTIUS. Cur me illuditis, qui plane sum nescius, non philosophus?

DISCIPULIS. Et unde tibi haec quae nos fatigando protulisti?

PAFNUTIUS. Tenuem scientiae guttulam, quam de plenis sciorum pateris effluentem, non ad colligendum residens, sed casu praeteriens, repertam elambi, vobiscum communicare studui.

20 DISCIPULI. Gratulamur tuae benignitati, sed terremur sententia Apostoli dicentis, "Nam *stulta mundi elegit Deus, ut confunderet* sophistica."

PAFNUTIUS. Sive stultus sive sophista perversa operatur, confusionem a Deo meretur.

DISCIPULI. Ita.

PAFNUTIUS. Nec scientia scibilis Deum offendit, sed iniustitia scientis.

DISCIPULI. Verum.

21 PAFNUTIUS. Et in cuius laudem dignius iustiusque scientia artium retorquetur, quam in eius qui scibile fecit et scientiam dedit?

DISCIPULI. In nullius.

PAPHNUTIUS. It did no harm for you to work at it, since now you have learned things you previously didn't know.

STUDENTS. True. But we are tired of this philosophical disputation, because we can't wrap our minds around even the tiniest bit of your reasoning.

PAPHNUTIUS. Why do you make fun of me, since I am 19
plainly an ignorant man, not a philosopher?

STUDENTS. And what is the source of these things you have uttered, wearing us out?

PAPHNUTIUS. This slender little drop of knowledge, which I lapped up from the full platters of wise men when I found it spilling out as I was passing by fortuitously, not stopping to gather it in—this little drop I have attempted to share with you.

STUDENTS. We thank you for your kindness, but we fear the 20
pronouncement of the Apostle, who says, "For *God chose the foolish things of the world, in order to confound* sophistries."

PAPHNUTIUS. Whether it is a fool or a wise man doing perverse things, he deserves to be confounded by God.

STUDENTS. Just so.

PAPHNUTIUS. It is not the knowledge of what is knowable that offends God, but the injustice of the one who knows it.

STUDENTS. True.

PAPHNUTIUS. And in whose praise is knowledge of the arts 21
more properly and more justly directed, than in praise of him who made it knowable and who bestowed the knowledge?

STUDENTS. No one's.

Pafnutius. Quanto enim mirabiliori lege Deum *omnia in numero et mensura et pondere posuisse* quis agnoscit, tanto in eius amore ardescit.

Discipuli. Nec iniuria.

Pafnutius. Sed quid moror in istis, quae vobis minimum afferunt delectationis?

22 Discipuli. Enuclea nobis causam tui maeroris, ne diutius frangamur pondere curiositatis.

Pafnutius. Si quando experiemini, auditu non delectabimini.

Discipuli. Haud raro contristatur qui curiositatem sectatur. Sed tamen hanc nequimus superare, quia familiaris est fragilitati nostrae.

23 Pafnutius. Quaedam impudens femina moratur in hac patria.

Discipuli. Res civibus periculosa.

Pafnutius. Haec miranda praenitet pulchritudine, et horrenda sordet turpitudine.

Discipuli. Miserabile! Quid vocatur?

Pafnutius. Thais.

Discipuli. Illa meretrix?

Pafnutius. Ipsa.

24 Discipuli. Eius infamia nulli est incognita.

Pafnutius. Nec mirum, quia non dignatur cum paucis ad interitum tendere, sed prompta est omnes lenociniis suae formae illicere, secumque ad interitum trahere.

Discipuli. Lugubre!

PAPHNUTIUS. The more anyone recognizes that *God ordered all things in measure, and number, and weight,* by a very miraculous law, the more that person will burn with the love of God.

STUDENTS. That is just.

PAPHNUTIUS. But why do I dwell on these things that bring you no pleasure?

STUDENTS. Explain to us the cause of your sorrow, so we will 22
not be wracked any longer by the weight of curiosity.

PAPHNUTIUS. If you ever learn the answer, you will not be pleased by hearing it.

STUDENTS. The man who follows the dictates of his curiosity is not infrequently sad. But still we cannot overcome this impulse, because it is natural to our fragile human nature.

PAPHNUTIUS. There is a certain indecent woman living in 23
this country.

STUDENTS. A dangerous thing for the citizens.

PAPHNUTIUS. She sparkles from wondrous beauty, and is sordid from horrendous filth.

STUDENTS. How awful! What's her name?

PAPHNUTIUS. Thais.

STUDENTS. The prostitute?

PAPHNUTIUS. The same.

STUDENTS. Her ill repute has escaped no one. 24

PAPHNUTIUS. And no wonder, for it is not enough for her to go to ruin with just a few men, but she is ready to seduce all men with the enticements of her beauty, and drag them all to ruin along with her.

STUDENTS. How tragic!

25 Pafnutius. Nec solum nugaces vilitatem suae familiaris rei dissipant illam colendo, sed etiam praepotentes viri pretiosae varietatem suppellectilis pessumdant, non absque sui damno hanc ditando.

Discipuli. Horrescimus auditu.

Pafnutius. Greges amatorum ad illam confluunt.

Discipuli. Se ipsos perdunt.

26 Pafnutius. Qui amentes dum caeco corde quis illam adeat contendunt, convitia congerunt.

Discipuli. Unum vitium parit aliud.

Pafnutius. Deinde inito certamine nunc ora naresque pugnis frangendo, nunc armis vicissim eiciendo, decurrentis illuvie sanguinis madefaciunt limina lupanaris.

Discipuli. O nefas detestabile!

27 Pafnutius. Haec iniuria quam deflevi Factoris, haec est causa mei doloris.

Discipuli. Merito super hoc contristaris. Nec dubitamus quin tecum contristentur cives patriae caelestis.

28 Pafnutius. Quid si illam adeam sub specie amatoris, si forte revocari possit ab intentione nugacitatis?

Discipuli. Qui tuae cogitationi instillavit velle, ipse praestet efficaciam posse.

Pafnutius. Fulcite me interim precibus assiduis, ne superer insidiis vitiosi serpentis.

PAPHNUTIUS. It is not only silly young men who are wasting 25
what little family fortune they have in worshiping her, but even very powerful men are destroying all sorts of precious possessions, enriching her, at the cost of damage to themselves.

STUDENTS. We are horrified to hear this.

PAPHNUTIUS. Flocks of lovers stream to her.

STUDENTS. They are destroying themselves.

PAPHNUTIUS. These crazy men, while battling with blinded 26
hearts over who can be with her, heap insults on one another.

STUDENTS. One sin gives rise to another.

PAPHNUTIUS. Then, when the battle begins, sometimes they destroy one another's faces and noses with punches, sometimes they discharge missiles at one another; with the filth of their gushing blood, they soak the threshold of that brothel.

STUDENTS. Oh what a detestable crime!

PAPHNUTIUS. This injustice to the Creator which I was la- 27
menting, this is the cause of my pain.

STUDENTS. You are rightly sad about this. And we have no doubt that the citizens of the heavenly kingdom share your sadness.

PAPHNUTIUS. What if I go to her disguised as a lover, to see 28
if she might by chance be recalled from her frivolous intentions?

STUDENTS. The One who instilled this desire in your mind, he will ensure that it can be successful.

PAPHNUTIUS. Meanwhile, you must all support me with continuous prayers, so that I not be overcome by the snares of the vicious serpent.

DISCIPULI. Qui regem prostravit tenebricolarum, largiatur tibi contra hostem triumphum.

2

PAFNUTIUS. Ecce iuvenes in foro. Illos primum adibo, et ubi hanc quam quaero inveniam rogabo.

IUVENES. En ignotus quidam nos adit. Experiemur quid velit.

PAFNUTIUS. Heus, iuvenes, quid estis?

IUVENES. Urbicolae huius civitatis.

2 PAFNUTIUS. Avete!

IUVENES. Et tu salve, sive sis huius patriae indigena sive advena.

PAFNUTIUS. Advena nunc advenio.

IUVENES. Cur advenis? Quid quaeris?

3 PAFNUTIUS. Non est dicendum.

IUVENES. Quare?

PAFNUTIUS. Quia mihi secretum.

IUVENES. Melius ut proferas. Quia si non es nostras, difficile poteris aliquid inter nos negotium absque consilio peragere incolarum.

PAFNUTIUS. Quid si dixero, et dicendo aliquod mihi impedimentum excitavero?

IUVENES. Non a nobis.

4 PAFNUTIUS. Laetis promissionibus cedo, vestraeque fidei confidens secretum enucleo.

IUVENES. Nihil nostra de parte infidelitatis; nihil tibi obviabit contrarietatis.

Students. May the One who laid low the king of the denizens of darkness bestow on you a triumph over the enemy.

2

Paphnutius. See here, there are young men in the marketplace. I'll approach them first, and ask where I may find this woman I'm looking for.

The Young Men. Look, some stranger is approaching us. Let's find out what he wants.

Paphnutius. Say, fellows, who might you be?

The Young Men. We are citizens of this city.

Paphnutius. Greetings! 2

The Young Men. And welcome to you, whether you are a native of this land or a stranger.

Paphnutius. I come now as a stranger.

The Young Men. Why have you come? What are you looking for?

Paphnutius. I cannot talk about it. 3

The Young Men. Why?

Paphnutius. It is a private matter.

The Young Men. It would be better to state it. Because if you are not from our country, it will be difficult to do any business without the assistance of the locals.

Paphnutius. What if I tell you, and by telling I create an obstacle to my plan?

The Young Men. There will be no obstacle from us.

Paphnutius. I yield to these propitious promises, and 4
trusting in your good faith, I will reveal my secret.

The Young Men. There is no lack of faith on our part; no obstruction will bar you.

5 Pafnutius. Quorundam relatu comperi mulierem secus vos commorari, omnibus amabilem omnibus affabilem.

Iuvenes. Nosti eius nomen?

Pafnutius. Novi.

Iuvenes. Quid vocatur?

Pafnutius. Thais.

Iuvenes. Ipsa nostratium est ignis.

Pafnutius. Ferunt illam mulierum pulcherrimam, omnium esse delicatissimam.

Iuvenes. Qui retulere, nihil fefellere.

6 Pafnutius. Ipsius causa difficilis prolixitatem viae surripui. Ipsam ut viderem adveni.

Iuvenes. Nullum tibi obstat impedimentum eam videndi.

Pafnutius. Ubi moratur?

Iuvenes. Ecce mansio in proximo.

Pafnutius. Haec quam indice proditis?

Iuvenes. Ipsa.

Pafnutius. Illo pergam.

Iuvenes. Si placet, tecum pergemus.

Pafnutius. Malo ire solus.

Iuvenes. Ut libet.

3

Pafnutius. Tu istaec intro, Thais, quam quaero?

Thais. Quis hic qui loquitur ignotus?

Pafnutius. Amator tuus.

PAPHNUTIUS. I have learned from the report of certain 5
men, that a woman lives here among you, loving to all, friendly to all.

THE YOUNG MEN. Do you know her name?

PAPHNUTIUS. I do know it.

THE YOUNG MEN. What is she called?

PAPHNUTIUS. Thais.

THE YOUNG MEN. She is the fiery passion of all the men here.

PAPHNUTIUS. They say she is the most beautiful of women, the finest of all.

THE YOUNG MEN. Whoever said that was not lying.

PAPHNUTIUS. For her sake I secretly took a long journey on 6
a difficult road. I have come to see her.

THE YOUNG MEN. No barrier stands in the way of your seeing her.

PAPHNUTIUS. Where does she live?

THE YOUNG MEN. Right there, the house closest to us.

PAPHNUTIUS. This one you are pointing at?

THE YOUNG MEN. The very same.

PAPHNUTIUS. I'll go there.

THE YOUNG MEN. If you like, we will go with you.

PAPHNUTIUS. I would prefer to go alone.

THE YOUNG MEN. As you please.

3

PAPHNUTIUS. You there, inside, are you Thais, the woman I am searching for?

THAIS. Who is this unknown man speaking to me?

PAPHNUTIUS. One who loves you.

THAIS. Quicumque me amore colit, aequam vicem amoris a me recipit.

2 PAFNUTIUS. O Thais, Thais, quanta gravissimi itineris currebam spatia, quo mihi daretur copia tecum fandi tuique faciem contemplandi.

THAIS. Nec aspectum subtraho, nec colloquium denego.

3 PAFNUTIUS. Secretum nostrae confabulationis desiderat solitudinem loci secretioris.

THAIS. Ecce cubile bene stratum et delectabile ad inhabitandum.

PAFNUTIUS. Estne hic aliud penitius, in quo possimus colloqui secretius?

4 THAIS. Est etenim aliud <tam> occultum, tam secretum, ut eius penetral nulli praeter me nisi Deo sit cognitum.

PAFNUTIUS. Cui deo?

THAIS. Vero.

PAFNUTIUS. Credis illum aliquid scire?

THAIS. Non nescio illum nihil latere.

PAFNUTIUS. Utrumne reris illum facta pravorum neglegere, an sui aequitatem servare?

THAIS. Aestimo ipsius aequitatis lance singulorum merita pensari, et unicuique, prout gessit, sive supplicium sive praemium servari.

5 PAFNUTIUS. O Christe, quam miranda tuae circa nos benignitatis patientia! Qui te scientes vides peccare, et tamen tardas perdere.

THAIS. Whoever honors me with love, gets back an equal share of love from me.

PAPHNUTIUS. O Thais, Thais, I have traveled vast expanses 2
of a most difficult journey to have the opportunity to
speak to you, and to look upon your face.

THAIS. I will not deprive you of the sight, nor deny you conversation.

PAPHNUTIUS. The secret nature of our conversation re- 3
quires the privacy of a more secret spot.

THAIS. Here is a bedroom, well equipped, and a delightful place for us to make ourselves at home.

PAPHNUTIUS. Is there another room here more remote, in which we may speak more secretly?

THAIS. There is in fact another, so hidden, so secret, that its 4
inner chamber is known to no one besides me, except
God.

PAPHNUTIUS. What god?

THAIS. The true one.

PAPHNUTIUS. Do you believe he is somehow informed?

THAIS. I am not unaware that nothing escapes him.

PAPHNUTIUS. Do you suppose that he ignores the deeds of the wicked, or that he administers his justice?

THAIS. I reckon that the just deserts of individuals are balanced in the scale of his justice, and either punishment or reward awaits each person, according to how he has acted.

PAPHNUTIUS. O Christ, how wondrous is the patience of 5
your kindness toward us! You see that those who know
about you commit sins, and yet you take your time in de-
stroying them.

THAIS. Cur contremiscis mutato colore? Cur fluunt lacrimae?

PAFNUTIUS. Tui praesumptionem horresco. Tui perditionem defleo, quia haec nosti et tantas animas perdidisti.

THAIS. Vae, vae, mihi infelici!

6 PAFNUTIUS. Tanto iustius damnaberis, quanto praesumptiosius scienter offendisti maiestatem Divinitatis.

THAIS. Heu, heu, quid agis? Quid infelici minitaris?

PAFNUTIUS. Supplicium tibi imminet gehennae, si permanebis in scelere.

THAIS. Severitas tuae correptionis concussit penetral pavidi cordis.

7 PAFNUTIUS. O utinam esses viscera tenus concussa timore, ne ultra praesumeres periculosae delectationi assensum praebere.

THAIS. Et quis post haec locus pestiferae delectationi in meo corde potest relinqui, ubi solum intestini maeroris amaritudo consciique reatus nova dominatur formido?

PAFNUTIUS. Hoc opto, quo, resectis vitiorum spinis, emergere possit vinum compunctionis.

8 THAIS. O si crederes, O si sperares me, sordidulam, milies millenis sordium oblitam offuscationibus, ullatenus posse expiari, seu ullo compunctionis modo veniam promereri!

THAIS. Why are you trembling and changing color? Why are you drenched in tears?

PAPHNUTIUS. I am horrified by your audacity. I am crying over your damnation, because you know these things, and you have destroyed so many souls.

THAIS. Alas, alas, poor me!

PAPHNUTIUS. You will be all the more justly condemned, 6
because in your audacity you have knowingly offended the majesty of the Divinity.

THAIS. Woe, woe, why do you do this? Why do you threaten an ill-fated woman?

PAPHNUTIUS. The punishment of hell is hanging over you, if you persist in sin.

THAIS. The severity of your scolding has shaken the inmost chamber of my frightened heart.

PAPHNUTIUS. Oh, would that you were shaken to the core 7
with fear, so that you would no longer dare to consent to this dangerous pleasure.

THAIS. And, from now on, what place can possibly remain in my heart for this deadly pleasure, where only the bitterness of gut-wrenching grief and the new horror of a guilty conscience hold sway?

PAPHNUTIUS. This is what I was hoping for, so that when the thorns of your vices have been cut out, the wine of sorrow might emerge.

THAIS. Oh, if you could only believe, oh, if you could only 8
hope that I, sordid little me, smeared with the blackness of thousands of thousands of impurities, could in any way be cleansed, or that I, by any manner of remorse, might earn forgiveness!

PAFNUTIUS. Nullum enim <tam> grave peccatum, nullum tam immane est delictum, quod nequeat expiari paenitentiae lacrimis, si effectus sequetur operis.

THAIS. Ostende, quaeso, mi pater, quo effectu operis promereri queam munus reconciliationis.

9 PAFNUTIUS. Contemne saeculum, fuge lascivorum consortia amasionum.

THAIS. Et quid mihi tunc erit agendum?

PAFNUTIUS. In secretum locum secedendum, in quo te ipsam discutiendo possis lamentari enormitatem tui delicti.

THAIS. Si hoc speras proficere, non addo momentum morulae.

PAFNUTIUS. Non dubito quin prosit.

10 THAIS. Da mihi aliquantuli spatium tempusculi, ut proferam mammonam quam male collectam diu servavi.

PAFNUTIUS. Ne solliciteris pro ea; non desunt qui utentur inventa.

THAIS. Non ob id sollicitor, ut vel mihi servare vel amicis vellem dare. Sed nec egenis conor dispensare, quia non arbitror pretium piaculi aptum esse ad opus beneficii.

11 PAFNUTIUS. Recte arbitraris. Et quid de congestis actum ire meditaris?

THAIS. Igni tradere et in favillam redigere.

PAFNUTIUS. Quam ob rem?

PAPHNUTIUS. There is no sin so grievous, no transgression so monstrous, that it cannot be purged by the tears of penance, if the fulfillment of action follows.

THAIS. Show me, I beg you, my father, by what fulfillment of action I may earn the reward of reconciliation.

PAPHNUTIUS. Reject the world, flee the company of lustful 9
lovers.

THAIS. And then what must I do?

PAPHNUTIUS. You must retreat to a remote place where, examining your circumstances, you can mourn the enormity of your transgression.

THAIS. If you have hope that it will be beneficial, I will not delay for a second.

PAPHNUTIUS. I have no doubt that it will be profitable.

THAIS. Grant me the space of a short delay, so that I may 10
bring out the ill-gotten riches which I have long been
saving up.

PAPHNUTIUS. Do not worry yourself about them; there is no lack of people who will make use of them once they discover them.

THAIS. I am not worried because I want to save them for myself, or because I want to give them to friends. And I will not attempt to distribute them to the poor, because I do not think the profits of sin are suitable for doing good deeds.

PAPHNUTIUS. You think rightly. And what do you contem- 11
plate doing with these piles of things?

THAIS. Setting them on fire and reducing them to ash.

PAPHNUTIUS. For what reason?

THAIS. Ne retineantur in mundo quae male adquisivi, non absque mundi Factoris iniuria.

12 PAFNUTIUS. O quam mutata es ab illa quae prius eras, quando illicito amore flagrabas, avaritiae calore aestuabas!

THAIS. Fortasse mutabor in melius, si annuerit Deus.

PAFNUTIUS. Non est difficile immutabili eius substantiae res ut libet mutare.

THAIS. Ibo, et quae cogitavi opere complebo.

PAFNUTIUS. Vade in pace, citiusque ad me revertere.

4

THAIS. Convenite, properamini, nequam amatores mei.

AMATORES. Vox Thaidis nos vocantis. Adventum maturemus, ne illam tardando offendamus.

THAIS. Accelerate, accedite, ut queam vobiscum verba miscere.

2 AMATORES. O Thais, Thais, quid sibi vult rogus quem construis? Cur preciosarum varietatem divitiarum iuxta rogum congeris?

THAIS. Rogatis?

AMATORES. Admiramur satis.

THAIS. Exponam citius.

AMATORES. Hoc optamus.

3 THAIS. Aspicite.

AMATORES. Quiesce, quiesce, Thais! Quid agis? Num insanis?

THAIS. Non insanio sed sanum sapio.

Thais. So that the things I wickedly acquired, and not without injury to the Creator of the world, not be retained in the world.

Paphnutius. Oh, how you are changed from the woman 12
you were before, when you were blazing with improper
love, boiling from the heat of greed!

Thais. Perhaps I will be changed for the better, if God will give his approval.

Paphnutius. It is not difficult for one of his immutable substance to change things as he pleases.

Thais. I will go, and I will carry out in deed what I planned.

Paphnutius. Go in peace, and return very quickly to me.

4

Thais. Gather around, hurry up, my worthless lovers.

Her Lovers. The voice of Thais is calling us. Let's hurry to her, so that we will not offend her by delay.

Thais. Make haste, gather round, so I can exchange some words with you.

Her Lovers. O Thais, Thais, what is the meaning of this 2
bonfire you are building? Why have you piled up all sorts
of precious riches next to it?

Thais. Do you need to ask?

Her Lovers. We are quite amazed.

Thais. I will explain very soon.

Her Lovers. That is what we want.

Thais. Watch. 3

Her Lovers. Calm down, calm down, Thais! What are you doing? Are you insane?

Thais. I am not insane, but sanely wise.

Amatores. Ut quid haec perditio quadringentarum auri librarum, cum aliarum diversitate gazarum?

Thais. Omne quod iniuste a vobis extorsi, igne volo cremari, ne ullus fomes vobis relinquatur sperandi me ultra vestro amori cedendi.

4 Amatores. Subsiste paulisper! Subsiste et materiam tuae perturbationis detege!

Thais. Non subsisto, nec sermonem vobiscum confero.

Amatores. Cur dedignando nos fastidis? Num alicuius infidelitatis nos arguis? Nonne semper satisfecimus tuis votis? Et tu iniquo odio nos gratis insectaris.

Thais. Dimittite! Nolite vestem meam attrahendo scindere! Sit satis quod hucusque peccando vobis consensi. Finis instat peccandi, tempusque nostri discidii.

5 Amatores. Quo tendit?

Thais. Ubi nemo vestrum posthac me videbit.

Amatores. Papae, quid hoc monstri est, quod nostri delicias Thais, quae divitiis affluere semper laboravit, quae mentem a lascivia numquam retraxit, et se voluptati penitus dedit, tanta auri gemmarumque insignia absque retractatione perdidit, et nos sui amasiones dedignando sprevit subitoque non comparuit?

5

Thais. En, pater Pafnuti, venio ad sequendum tibi promptissima.

Her Lovers. Why the destruction of four hundred pounds of gold, with all manner of other treasures?

Thais. I want to burn up in this fire everything I unjustly extorted from you, so no spark of hope will remain in you of my yielding to your passion any longer.

Her Lovers. Stop a moment! Stop and explain the nature 4
of your distress!

Thais. I will not stop, nor will I discuss it with you.

Her Lovers. Why do you disdainfully reject us? Do you accuse us of some infidelity? Have we not always satisfied your demands? And now you gratuitously chase us away with unwarranted hatred.

Thais. Let go of me! Do not tear my clothes by tugging at me! Let it suffice that I went along with you until now in sinning. The end of my sinning is at hand, and it is time for us to be separated.

Her Lovers. Where is she going? 5

Thais. Where none of you will ever see me again.

Her Lovers. Heavens, what is this disaster, that our sweetheart Thais, who always worked to be flush with riches, who never took her mind off sex, and who devoted herself completely to pleasure, this same Thais has destroyed, without restraint, such ornaments of gold and jewels, and she has rejected us, her lovers, disdainfully, and suddenly disappeared?

5

Thais. See, Father Paphnutius, I have come, completely ready to follow you.

PAFNUTIUS. Quia moram in veniendo fecisti, coartabar nimis, verendo te iterum implicitam esse secularibus negotiis.

THAIS. Ne id vereare, quia multo aliud mihi versatur in mente, nam res familiares iuxta velle meum disposui, meisque amasionibus publice abrenuntiavi.

2 PAFNUTIUS. Quia his abrenuntiasti, superno amatori iam nunc poteris copulari.

THAIS. Tuum est mihi velut radio praescribere, quid me oporteat factum ire.

PAFNUTIUS. Sequere me.

THAIS. Sequar enim ambulatione; O utinam sequerer et actione!

6

PAFNUTIUS. Ecce coenobium in quo sacrarum virginum nobile commoratur collegium. Eo loci gestio te mansum ire agendae spatium paenitentiae.

THAIS. Non contraluctor.

PAFNUTIUS. Intrabo; et abbatissam, ductricem virginum, pro tui susceptione placabo.

THAIS. Quid iubes me interim agere?

PAFNUTIUS. Mecum pergere.

THAIS. Ut iubes.

2 PAFNUTIUS. Ecce abbatissa occurrit. Admiror quis illi nos adesse tam cito retulerit.

THAIS. Fama, quae nulla stringitur mora.

PAPHNUTIUS. Because you were delayed in coming, I was very anxious, fearing you were again involved in worldly affairs.

THAIS. You need not fear that, because something far different is occupying my mind, for I have disposed of my property according to my plan, and I have renounced my lovers publicly.

PAPHNUTIUS. Because you have renounced them, you may 2
now be coupled with your heavenly lover.

THAIS. It is for you to prescribe for me, as though with a pointer, what it is necessary for me to do.

PAPHNUTIUS. Follow me.

THAIS. Indeed, I will follow you with my feet; I hope I may follow you also in my actions!

6

PAPHNUTIUS. Here is the convent in which a noble community of consecrated virgins lives. I am eager that you should live in this place to do your time of penance.

THAIS. I will not resist.

PAPHNUTIUS. I will enter; and I will convince the abbess, the leader of the virgins, to take you in.

THAIS. What would you like me to do in the meantime?

PAPHNUTIUS. Come with me.

THAIS. As you order.

PAPHNUTIUS. Look, the abbess is coming to meet us. I won- 2
der who reported to her so swiftly that we are here.

THAIS. It was Rumor, who is constrained by no delays.

7

PAFNUTIUS. Opportune occurris illustris abbatissa; te ipsam quaero.

ABBATISSA. Gratanter advenis, venerande pater Pafnuti. Benedictus tui adventus, dilecte Dei.

PAFNUTIUS. Beatitudinem aeternae benedictionis infundat tibi gratia Omniparentis.

ABBATISSA. Unde hoc mihi ut sanctitas tua dignaretur invisere exiguitatem habitationis meae?

2 PAFNUTIUS. Opus est tuo iuvamine in aliqua sollicitanda necessitate.

ABBATISSA. Iube solummodo levi famine, quid me velis agere, et ego tui iussa complere tuisque votis studebo pro viribus satisfacere.

3 PAFNUTIUS. Attuli capellam semivivam, dentibus luporum nuper abstractam, quam tui miseratione foveri, tui sollicitudine gestio mederi, quoadusque abiecta haedinae pellis austeritate ovini velleris induatur mollitie.

ABBATISSA. Expone enucleatius.

4 PAFNUTIUS. Istaec quam vides meretricio more vitam instituit.

ABBATISSA. Miserabile!

PAFNUTIUS. Seseque totam lasciviae dedit.

ABBATISSA. Semet ipsam perdidit!

PAFNUTIUS. At nunc, me hortante Christoque cooperante, frivola quae sectabatur odiendo refugit, et castum sapit.

ABBATISSA. Mutationis auctori grates!

7

PAPHNUTIUS. Well met, illustrious abbess, the very person I was seeking.

ABBESS. You arrive as one most welcome, venerable Father Paphnutius. Your arrival is blessed, O beloved of God.

PAPHNUTIUS. May the grace of the Parent of us all pour the blessing of eternal benediction upon you.

ABBESS. To what do I owe it that your holiness thought it right to visit my insignificant residence?

PAPHNUTIUS. Your assistance is needed in a troubling diffi- 2
culty.

ABBESS. You have only to say in a fleeting word what you want me to do, and I will make an effort to carry out your orders and to satisfy your wishes with all my strength.

PAPHNUTIUS. I have brought to you a little goat, only half 3
alive, just now snatched from the jaws of wolves. I am eager that she be coddled in your mercy, that she be cured by your solicitude, until the time when she has thrown away the roughness of her goat's hide and can be dressed in the softness of a sheep's wool.

ABBESS. Please explain more clearly.

PAPHNUTIUS. This woman you see here arranged her life in 4
a whorish manner.

ABBESS. How wretched!

PAPHNUTIUS. And she devoted herself completely to sex.

ABBESS. She has ruined herself!

PAPHNUTIUS. But now, by my encouragement and with Christ's aid, she has rejected the worthless things she was pursuing, hating them, and has come to know chastity.

ABBESS. Thanks be to the author of this conversion!

5 Pafnutius. Quia enim aegritudo animarum, aeque ut corporum, contrariis curanda est medelis, consequens est ut haec, a solita saecularium inquietudine sequestrata, sola in angusta retrudatur cellula, quo liberius possit discutere sui crimina.

Abbatissa. Hoc potissimum prodest.

6 Pafnutius. Manda, ut quantotius cellula construatur.

Abbatissa. Parvo spatio perficiatur.

Pafnutius. Nullus introitus, nullus relinquatur aditus, sed solummodo exigua fenestra, per quam modicum possit victum accipere, quem statutis diebus et horis illi debebis parce praebitum ire.

7 Abbatissa. Vereor quod delicatae teneritudo mentis aegre patiatur difficultatem tanti laboris.

Pafnutius. Ne id vereare, nam grave delictum forte desiderat semper remedium.

Abbatissa. Verum.

8 Pafnutius. Taedet me magis morarum, quia timeo illam corrumpi visitatione hominum.

Abbatissa. Cur taedium pateris? Cur illam non includis? Ecce, cellula quam desiderasti est perfecta.

9 Pafnutius. Placet. Ingredere, Thais, habitaculum, tuis facinoribus deflendis satis congruum.

Thais. Quam breve, quam obscurum, et quam incommodum tenellae mulieri ad inhabitandum.

10 Pafnutius. Cur habitaculum exsecraris? Cur ingredi horrescis? Decet ut quae hactenus fuisti indomite vaga, nunc tandem in solitario refreneris loco.

Paphnutius. Since, in fact, the sickness of souls, just as the 5
sickness of bodies, must be cured by uncongenial remedies, it follows that she, sequestered from the normal disturbance of worldly affairs, must be thrust alone into a confined little cell, where she may freely examine her sins.

Abbess. This will benefit her very powerfully.

Paphnutius. Order a tiny cell to be built as soon as possi- 6
ble.

Abbess. It should be completed in a short time.

Paphnutius. No entranceway, no opening is to be permitted her, but only a tiny window, through which she may receive that little bit of food, which on established days and at fixed times you should sparingly provide to her.

Abbess. I am afraid that the tenderness of her pleasure- 7
loving mind may ill endure the difficulty of such a trial.

Paphnutius. Do not be afraid of that, for a serious transgression always needs a strong remedy.

Abbess. That is true.

Paphnutius. I am more concerned about delays, because I 8
fear she will be corrupted by the visits of men.

Abbess. Why suffer any concern? Why do you not shut her in? Look, the little cell which you wanted is finished.

Paphnutius. I am pleased. Go, Thais, into this little hovel, 9
which is quite well suited for lamenting your misdeeds.

Thais. How small, how dark, and how unpleasant for a very tender woman to inhabit.

Paphnutius. Why do you curse your little hovel? Why are 10
you afraid to enter? It is appropriate that you, who have been wandering untamed up to this point, should now finally be bridled in an isolated place.

THAIS. Mens assueta lasciviae haud raro impatiens est austerioris vitae.

PAFNUTIUS. Ideo debet habenis disciplinae stringi, quoadusque desinat contraluctari.

11 THAIS. Quod iubet tua paternitas, non recusat subitum ire mea vilitas. Sed quaedam inoportunitas inest huic habitationi, difficilis ad sufferendum meae fragilitati.

PAFNUTIUS. Quae haec inoportunitas?

THAIS. Erubesco dicere.

PAFNUTIUS. Ne erubescas, sed penitus detege.

12 THAIS. Quid inoportunius, quidve poterit esse incommodius, quam quod in uno eodemque loco, diversa corporis necessaria supplere debebo? Nec dubium, quin ocius fiat inhabitabilis, prae nimietate fetoris.

PAFNUTIUS. Formida perpetis crudelitatem gehennae, et desine transitoria pertimescere.

THAIS. Fragilitas mei cogit me terreri.

PAFNUTIUS. Convenit ut male blandientis dulcedinem delectationis luas molestia nimii fetoris.

13 THAIS. Non recuso, non nego. Me sordidam non iniuria foedo sordidoque habitatum ire in tugurio. Sed hoc dolet vehementius, quod nullus est relictus locus, in quo apte et caste possim tremendae nomen Maiestatis invocare.

PAFNUTIUS. Et unde tibi tanta fiducia, ut pollutis labiis praesumas proferre nomen impollutae Divinitatis?

THAIS. A mind accustomed to luxury is not infrequently intolerant of a more austere lifestyle.

PAPHNUTIUS. For that reason, such a mind should be constrained by the reins of discipline, until it stops resisting.

THAIS. Whatever your paternal solicitude orders, my vile- 11
ness will not refuse to submit to. But there is a particular inconvenience in this dwelling, which it will be difficult for my fragile nature to endure.

PAPHNUTIUS. What is this inconvenience?

THAIS. I am embarrassed to say.

PAPHNUTIUS. Do not be embarrassed, but reveal it completely.

THAIS. What could be more inconvenient, or what could be 12
more unpleasant, than that in one and the same place I be obligated to perform a variety of bodily necessities? There is no doubt that this place will quickly become uninhabitable from the overwhelming stench.

PAPHNUTIUS. Dread the cruelty of eternal hell, and stop being afraid of transitory things.

THAIS. My tender nature compels me to be terrified.

PAPHNUTIUS. It is appropriate that you wash away the sweetness of this wickedly soothing pleasure through the discomfort of excessive stench.

THAIS. I will not refuse, I will not say no. It is not unjust 13
that I, filthy as I am, should live in a filthy, dirty hut. But it pains me very greatly that there is no place left where I could appropriately and chastely invoke the name of the awesome Majesty.

PAPHNUTIUS. And from where do you get such confidence, that you would presume with your polluted lips to utter the name of the unpolluted Divinity?

14 THAIS. Et a quo veniam sperare cuiusve salvari possum miseratione, si Ipsum prohibeor invocare cui soli deliqui, et cui uni devotio orationum debet offerri?

PAFNUTIUS. Debes plane orare non verbis, sed lacrimis, non sonoritate tinnulae vocis, sed compuncti rugitu cordis.

THAIS. Et si vetar Deum verbis orare, quomodo possum veniam sperare?

PAFNUTIUS. Tanto celerius mereberis, quanto perfectius humiliaberis. Dic tantum: "Qui me plasmasti, miserere mei."

15 THAIS. Opus est eius miseratione, ne frangar in dubio certamine.

PAFNUTIUS. Certa viriliter, ut possis triumphum obtinere feliciter.

THAIS. Tuum est pro me orare, ut merear palmam victoriae.

PAFNUTIUS. Non opus est monitu.

THAIS. Spero.

16 PAFNUTIUS. Tempus est ut optatas solitudinis repetam latebras, et caros visitem discipulos. Tuae igitur sollicitudini, tuae pietati, venerabilis abbatissa, hanc captivam committo, ut et corpus delicatum mediocriter foveas necessariis, et animam sufficienter reficias saluberrimis monitis.

ABBATISSA. Ne solliciteris pro ea, quia eam materno affectu fovebo.

PAFNUTIUS. Vadam.

ABBATISSA. In pace.

Thais. And from whom can I hope for forgiveness, or by 14
whose mercy can I hope to be saved, if I am prohibited from invoking the name of the One against whom alone I have sinned, and to whom singularly the devotion of my prayers should be offered?

Paphnutius. You plainly ought to pray not with words, but with tears, not with the pleasant sound of your carillon voice, but with the groan of a remorseful heart.

Thais. And if I am not allowed to pray to God with words, how can I hope for forgiveness?

Paphnutius. You will earn forgiveness all the more quickly if you are humbled more completely. Say only: "You who made me, have mercy on me."

Thais. His mercy is required, so that I not be broken in this 15
uncertain struggle.

Paphnutius. Struggle like a man, so that you may happily triumph.

Thais. Your duty is to pray for me, so that I earn the palm of victory.

Paphnutius. There is no need to remind me.

Thais. I hope that is so.

Paphnutius. It is time for me to return to my longed-for 16
lair of solitude, and to visit my dear disciples. To your care, therefore, to your kindness, venerable abbess, I commit this captive, so that you may tend to her delicate body with the minimum required and also amply strengthen her soul with the most salubrious admonitions.

Abbess. No need to worry yourself about her, for I will tend to her with maternal affection.

Paphnutius. I will go.

Abbess. In peace.

8

DISCIPULI. Quis pulsat portam?

PAFNUTIUS. Ehe!

DISCIPULI. Vox Pafnutii patris nostri.

PAFNUTIUS. Amovete pessulum.

DISCIPULI. O pater, salve.

PAFNUTIUS. Avete.

DISCIPULI. Coartabamur nimium pro diutina absentia tui.

PAFNUTIUS. Iuvat quod abfui.

2 DISCIPULI. Quid actum est de Thaide?

PAFNUTIUS. Iuxta meum velle.

DISCIPULI. Ubi moratur?

PAFNUTIUS. In exigua cellula deflet sui commissa.

3 DISCIPULI. Laus sit summae Trinitati.

PAFNUTIUS. Et benedictum nomen eius tremendum, nunc et per aevum.

DISCIPULI. Amen.

9

PAFNUTIUS. Ecce tres mansurni paenitentiae Thaidis transiere, et ego ignoro, utrumne Deo acceptabilis sit eius compunctio. Surgam et vadam ad fratrem meum Antonium, quo mihi manifestetur per eius interventum.

8

Students. Who is knocking on the door?

Paphnutius. Hello there!

Students. It is the voice of our father Paphnutius.

Paphnutius. Undo the latch.

Students. O father, salutations.

Paphnutius. Greetings.

Students. We were very anxious because of your long absence.

Paphnutius. My absence was beneficial.

Students. What was done about Thais? 2

Paphnutius. It was according to my wishes.

Students. Where is she living?

Paphnutius. In a tiny little cell, she is crying over her sins.

Students. Praise be to the Trinity on high. 3

Paphnutius. And blessed be his awesome name, now and forever.

Students. Amen.

9

Paphnutius. Look now, three years of the penance of Thais have passed, and I do not know whether her remorse is acceptable to God. I will get up and go to my brother Anthony, so that all may be made clear to me through his intervention.

10

ANTONIUS. Quid insperatae iucunditatis accidit, quid novi gaudii mihi contigit? Num hic est frater et coeremicola meus Pafnutius? Ipse est.

PAFNUTIUS. Sum etenim.

ANTONIUS. Bene, frater, venisti. Bene me adveniendo laetificasti.

PAFNUTIUS. Haud minus tripudio tui visu, quam tu mei adventu.

2 ANTONIUS. Quae haec causa, tam acceptabilis, tam grata nobis, quae te huc duxit de tuis latibulis?

PAFNUTIUS. Enucleo.

ANTONIUS. Hoc desidero.

PAFNUTIUS. Ante hoc triennium morabatur secus nos quaedam meretrix nomine Thais, quae non solum sese perditioni dedit, sed etiam perplures secum ad interitum trahere consuevit.

ANTONIUS. Heu gemenda consuetudo!

3 PAFNUTIUS. Hanc sub specie amatoris adii, et lascivientem animum, nunc suavibus hortamentis blandiendo mulcebam, nunc acrioribus monitis minitando terrebam.

ANTONIUS. Hoc temperamentum eius lasciviae fuit necessarium.

PAFNUTIUS. Tandem cessit, et spreta reprehensibili consuetudine castitatem elegit, seseque in angustissima cellula concludi consensit.

4 ANTONIUS. Delector audiendo in tantum ut omnes praecordiorum venae intrinsecus exsiliant gaudendo.

10

Anthony. What an unexpected pleasure has occurred, what new source of joy has befallen me? Is this not my brother and fellow hermit Paphnutius? It is he.

Paphnutius. I am, in fact, he.

Anthony. It is good you have come, brother. You have made me very happy by coming.

Paphnutius. I rejoice no less at the sight of you than you do at my arrival.

Anthony. What is the reason, so agreeable, so pleasing to me, which led you here from your lair? 2

Paphnutius. I will explain.

Anthony. I am eager to hear.

Paphnutius. Three years ago there lived among us a certain prostitute named Thais, who not only delivered herself to damnation, but also used to drag many others with her to eternal death.

Anthony. Oh, what a lamentable way of life!

Paphnutius. I went to her disguised as a lover, and at times I soothed her lascivious mind, enticing it with soft encouragements, and at times I terrified her mind, threatening it with very bitter warnings. 3

Anthony. This restraining of her wantonness was necessary.

Paphnutius. Finally, she yielded, and abandoning her reprehensible way of life, she chose chastity, and agreed to be locked up in the tiniest possible cell.

Anthony. I am so delighted to hear this, that all the veins of my heart are fluttering for joy deep inside me. 4

PAFNUTIUS. Decet tui sanctitatem. Et ego quidem, licet supra modum gaudeo de conversione, si levi tamen conturbor sollicitudine, eo quod vereor eius teneritudinem aegre ferre diutinum laborem.

ANTONIUS. Ubi adest vera dilectio, non deest pia compassio.

PAFNUTIUS. Unde tuam dilectionem efflagito, ut tu tuique discipuli mecum in orationibus concordando velitis persistere, quoadusque caelitus demonstretur utrumne benignitas divinae miserationis adhuc <ad> indulgentiam mollita sit paenitentis lacrimis.

ANTONIUS. Consentimus tuae petitioni libenter.

PAFNUTIUS. Nec dubito vos a Deo exauditum iri clementer.

II

ANTONIUS. Ecce evangelica promissio in nobis est impleta.

PAFNUTIUS. Quae haec promissio?

ANTONIUS. Ea videlicet, quae consentientes in oratione promisit omnia impetrare posse.

PAFNUTIUS. Quid est?

ANTONIUS. Paulo meo discipulo ostensa est quaedam visio.

PAFNUTIUS. Voca illum.

ANTONIUS. Paule, accede, et quae vidisti Pafnutio expone.

PAPHNUTIUS. That suits your holiness. But I, on the other hand, though pleased beyond measure about her conversion, nevertheless am troubled by no small anxiety, for I fear her delicate nature cannot tolerate extended toil.

ANTHONY. Where there is true love, there is no lack of kindly compassion.

PAPHNUTIUS. For this reason I make an urgent demand on your love, that you and your disciples be willing to persevere in prayers, in concord with me, until it be shown by a heavenly sign, whether the kindness of divine mercy has yet been softened to indulgence by the tears of this penitent woman.

ANTHONY. We agree to your request willingly.

PAPHNUTIUS. I have no doubt that you will be listened to indulgently by God.

II

ANTHONY. Look, the promise of the gospel has been fulfilled in us.

PAPHNUTIUS. Which promise is that?

ANTHONY. The one, namely, which promises that those who unite in prayer can accomplish everything.

PAPHNUTIUS. What has happened?

ANTHONY. Some sort of vision has been revealed to my disciple Paul.

PAPHNUTIUS. Summon him.

ANTHONY. Paul, come here and explain to Paphnutius what you have seen.

2 PAULUS. Videbam in visione lectulum candidulis palliolis in caelo magnifice stratum. Cui quattuor splendidae virgines praeerant, et quasi custodiendo astabant. At ubi iucunditatem mirae claritatis aspiciebam intra me dicebam: "Haec gloria nemini magis congruit, quam patri et domino meo Antonio."

ANTONIUS. Tali me non dignor beatitudine.

PAULUS. Quo dicto, intonuit vox divina dicens: "Non, ut speras, Antonio, sed Thaidi meretrici servanda est haec gloria."

3 PAFNUTIUS. Laus dulcedini tuae miserationis, Christe, unice Dei, quod mei tristitiam tam pie dignatus es consolari.

ANTONIUS. Dignus est laudari.

PAFNUTIUS. Ibo et mei captivam visitabo.

ATONIUS. Tempus est, ut illi et spem veniae et solamen promittas beatitudinis aeternae.

12

PAFNUTIUS. Thais, mea adoptiva filia, aperi fenestram ut te videam.

THAIS. Quis loquitur?

PAFNUTIUS. Pafnutius, pater tuus.

THAIS. Unde mihi iucunditas tantae laetitiae, ut tu me peccatricem dignareris visitare?

PAFNUTIUS. Licet per hoc triennium absens essem corpore, haud modicum tamen sollicitatus sum pro tui salute.

THAIS. Non dubito.

PAUL. I saw in a vision a small bed in heaven, magnificently covered with shining white cloths. Four splendid virgins were in charge of it, and they stood next to it as if guarding it. But while I was admiring the pleasant quality of its wondrous brilliance, I kept saying to myself, "This glory suits no one more than my father and lord, Anthony." 2

ANTHONY. I do not deserve such a blessing.

PAUL. When I said that, a divine voice thundered, saying, "It is not, as you imagine, for Anthony, but for the prostitute Thais that this glory has been reserved."

PAPHNUTIUS. Praise be to the sweetness of your mercy, Christ, only-begotten of God, because you have so kindly seen fit to console my sadness. 3

ANTHONY. He deserves to be praised.

PAPHNUTIUS. I will go and visit my captive.

ANTHONY. It is time for you to promise her both the hope of forgiveness and the consolation of eternal happiness.

12

PAPHNUTIUS. Thais, my adopted daughter, open the window so I can see you.

THAIS. Who is speaking?

PAPHNUTIUS. Paphnutius, your father.

THAIS. To what do I owe the pleasure of such happiness, that you see fit to visit me, a sinner?

PAPHNUTIUS. Even though I have been absent in body for three years, nevertheless, I have been concerned in no small measure for your salvation.

THAIS. I do not doubt it.

2 PAFNUTIUS. Expone mihi historiam tuae conversationis modumque compunctionis.

THAIS. Hoc possum exponere, quod non nescio me nihil dignum Deo egisse.

PAFNUTIUS. Si Deus iniquitates observabit, nemo sustinebit.

3 THAIS. Si tamen quid fecerim vis scire, numerositatem meorum scelerum intra conscientiam quasi in fasciculum collegi, et pertractando mente semper inspexi, quo sicut naribus numquam molestia fetoris, ita formido gehennae non abesset visibus cordis.

PAFNUTIUS. Quia te compunctione punisti, ideo veniam meruisti.

THAIS. O utinam!

4 PAFNUTIUS. Da manum ut te educam.

THAIS. Noli pater venerande, noli me sordidulam his immunditiis abstrahere, sed sine in loco meis meritis condigno mansum ire.

PAFNUTIUS. Tempus est ut levigato timore incipias vitam sperare, quia tui paenitentia acceptabilis est Deo.

THAIS. Eius pietati laudem ferant omnes angeli, quia non sprevit humilitatem cordis contriti!

5 PAFNUTIUS. Esto stabilis in Dei timore et permane in eius dilectione. Post quindecim namque dies homine exues, et tandem felici cursu peracto, superna favente gratia transmigrabis ad astra.

PAPHNUTIUS. Tell me the story of your way of life, and the manner of your remorse. 2

THAIS. I can tell you this, that I am well aware that I have done nothing worthy of God.

PAPHNUTIUS. If God will mark our iniquities, who shall stand it?

THAIS. If, however, you wish to know what I have done, I have gathered together in my conscience the multitude of my crimes, as if in a booklet. And going over it in my mind, I have constantly examined it, so that, just as the nuisance of the stench is never absent from my nose, so the fear of hell is not out of sight of my heart. 3

PAPHNUTIUS. Because you have punished yourself with remorse, you have thereby earned forgiveness.

THAIS. If only it were so!

PAPHNUTIUS. Give me your hand so that I may lead you out. 4

THAIS. Do not, venerable father, do not remove me, filthy as I am, from this sordidness, but allow me to remain in a place that is in keeping with what I deserve.

PAPHNUTIUS. It is time that you begin, having lightened your fear, to hope for life, because your penance is acceptable to God.

THAIS. Let all the angels give praise for his mercy, because he did not reject the humility of a contrite heart!

PAPHNUTIUS. Be firm in your fear of God and persist in loving him. Fifteen days from now, you will strip off your human body, and then, having completed the course of your life successfully, through the favoring grace of heaven you will ascend to the stars. 5

THAIS. O utinam mererer poenas evadere, vel saltim clementius exuri mitiori igne. Non est enim hoc mei meriti, ut doner beatitudine interminabili.

PAFNUTIUS. Gratuitum Dei donum non pensat humanum meritum, quia, si meritis tribueretur, gratia non diceretur.

6 THAIS. Unde laudet illum caeli concentus, omnisque terrae surculus, necnon universae animalis species atque confusae aquarum gurgites, quia non solum peccantes patitur, sed etiam paenitentibus praemia gratis largitur.

PAFNUTIUS. Hoc illi antiquitus fuit in more, ut mallet misereri quam ferire.

13

THAIS. Noli abire pater venerabilis, sed adesto mihi pro solacio in hora meae dissolutionis.

PAFNUTIUS. Non abeo, non discedo, donec, anima super aethera plaudente, corpus tradam sepulturae.

2 THAIS. En incipio mori.

PAFNUTIUS. Nunc est tempus orandi.

THAIS. Qui plasmasti me, miserere mei, et fac felici reditu ad te reverti animam quam inspirasti.

Thais. Oh, would that I deserved to avoid punishment, or at least to be burned more mercifully by a gentler flame. That I be endowed with endless happiness is assuredly not in keeping with what I deserve.

Paphnutius. The freely given gift of God does not consider what a human deserves, because if it were given according to our merits, it could not be called grace.

Thais. For this reason the heavenly host should praise him, 6
and every sprouting plant on earth, and also every kind of animal, and the swirling whirlpools of the seas, because not only does he tolerate sinners, but he also freely distributes rewards to the penitent.

Paphnutius. It has been his practice since olden times, that he prefers to show sinners mercy, not to strike them down.

13

Thais. Do not leave, venerable father, but remain to console me in the hour of my dying.

Paphnutius. I will not leave, I will not go away, until I hand over your body to the grave, while your soul is rejoicing above in heaven.

Thais. Behold, I am beginning to die. 2

Paphnutius. Now is the time to pray.

Thais. You who made me, have mercy on me, and make my soul return to you in a happy journey, my soul into which you breathed life.

3 Pafnutius. Qui factus a nullo, vere es sine materia forma;
cuius simplex esse hominem, qui non est id quod est, ex
hoc et hoc fecit consistere. Da diversas partes huius
solvendae hominis prospere repetere principium sui ori-
ginis, quo et anima caelitus indita caelestibus gaudiis
intermisceatur, et corpus in molli gremio terrae suae
4 materiae pacifice foveatur. Quoadusque, pulverea favilla
coeunte et vivaci flatu redivivos artus iterum intrante,
haec eadem Thais resurgat perfecta ut fuit homo, inter
candidulas oves collocanda, et in gaudium aeternitatis in-
ducenda, tu qui solus <es> id quod es <et> in unitate Tri-
nitatis regnas et gloriaris per infinita saecula saeculorum.

PAPHNUTIUS. You who were created out of nothing, you are 3
truly form without matter; your simple being made man exist out of disparate elements, man who is not what he is. Allow the various parts of this dying woman to return successfully to the beginning of their origin, where her soul that came from heaven may mingle with heavenly joys, and her body may peacefully be caressed in the soft bosom of the earth, which is of the same matter as the
body. Allow this until the time when these dusty ashes 4
come together again, and the living breath enters again into her restored limbs, and the very same Thais may rise again, perfect as when she was alive, deserving a place among the unblemished sheep, and being inducted into the joys of eternity—you, who alone are what you are, and who reign in the unity of the Trinity, and are glorified through infinite ages of ages.

<Passio sanctarum virginum Fidei, Spei, et Caritatis>

Passio sanctarum virginum Fidei, Spei, et Caritatis, quas, earundem veneranda genetrice Sapientia praesente, et maternis admonitionibus ad tolerandas passiones hortante, Diocletianus imperator diversis suppliciis interfecit. Quarum etiam corpora, martyrio consummata, sancta mater Sapientia collegit; et aromatibus condita, quinto ab urbe Roma miliario honorifice sepelivit. Ipsa quoque quadragesima die, iuxta earum sepulchra, finita oratione sacra spiritum praemisit caelo.

Antiochus	Fides
Hadrianus	Spes
Sapientia	Caritas

I

Antiochus. Tuum igitur esse, O imperator Hadriane, prosperis ad vota successionibus pollere, tuique statum imperii feliciter absque perturbatione exoptans vigere, quicquid rem publicam confundere, quicquid tranquillum mentis reor vulnerare posse, quantocius divelli penitusque cupio labefactari.

The Passion of the Holy Virgins Faith, Hope, and Charity

The passion of the holy virgins Faith, Hope, and Charity, whom the emperor Diocletian killed through a variety of tortures in the presence of their venerable mother Wisdom, who was encouraging them with maternal admonitions to endure their martyrdoms. Their holy mother Wisdom also gathered up their bodies, brought to perfection through martyrdom, and after embalming them with spices, she buried them honorably at the fifth mile marker from the city of Rome. She herself also, forty days later, beside their tombs, sent her spirit on to heaven, after she had finished a sacred prayer.

Antiochus	Faith
Hadrian	Hope
Wisdom	Charity

I

Antiochus. Hoping that your very being, O Emperor Hadrian, will flourish in prosperous success according to your wishes, and that the condition of your empire will thrive in good fortune without disruption, it is my desire that whatever I deem capable of upsetting the government, whatever I deem capable of injuring the tranquility of your mind, be torn away most expeditiously and be destroyed completely.

HADRIANUS. Nec iniuria, nam nostri prosperitas tui est felicitas, cum summos dignitatis gradus in dies tibi augere non desistimus.

2 ANTIOCHUS. Congratulor tuae almitati. Unde, si quid experior emergere, quod tuo potentatui videtur contraluctari, non occulo sed impatiens morae profero.

HADRIANUS. Et merito, ne reus maiestatis esse arguaris, si non celanda celaveris.

ANTIOCHUS. Huiusmodi commisso reatus numquam fui obnoxius.

HADRIANUS. Memini, sed profer si quid scias novi.

3 ANTIOCHUS. Quaedam advena mulier hanc urbem Romam nuper intravit, comitata proprii fetus pusiolis tribus.

HADRIANUS. Cuius sexus sunt pusioli?

ANTIOCHUS. Omnes feminei.

HADRIANUS. Numquid tantillarum adventus mulierculaarum aliquid rei publicae adducere poterit detrimentum?

ANTIOCHUS. Permagnum.

HADRIANUS. Quod?

4 ANTIOCHUS. Pacis defectum.

HADRIANUS. Quo pacto?

ANTIOCHUS. Et quod maius potest rumpere civilis concordiam pacis, quam dissonantia observationis?

HADRIANUS. Nihil gravius, nihil deterius. Quod testatur orbis Romanus, qui undiquesecus Christianae caedis sorde est infectus.

HADRIAN. And rightly so, for my prosperity is your blessing, since I continue daily to raise you to the highest honors.

ANTIOCHUS. I am grateful for your kindness. That is why, if 2
I discover that anything is developing which seems to challenge your authority, I do not hide it, but I bring it forward, impatient of any delay.

HADRIAN. And for good reason, so that you are not charged with treason if you have concealed what should not be concealed.

ANTIOCHUS. I have never been guilty of committing that sort of crime.

HADRIAN. I know that, but if you have learned any news, produce it.

ANTIOCHUS. A certain foreign woman recently entered the 3
city of Rome, accompanied by three small children whom she herself bore.

HADRIAN. What sex are these little children?

ANTIOCHUS. They are all female.

HADRIAN. The arrival of such insignificant little women cannot bring any harm to the government, can it?

ANTIOCHUS. A very great harm.

HADRIAN. Which is?

ANTIOCHUS. A disturbance of the peace. 4

HADRIAN. How?

ANTIOCHUS. Indeed, what can possibly disrupt the concord of civil peace more than discord in religious observance?

HADRIAN. There is nothing more serious, nothing worse. The Roman world bears witness to this, for it has been infected on every side by the filth of Christian massacre.

5 Antiochus. Haec igitur femina cuius mentionem facio hortatur nostrates avitos ritus deserere, et Christianae religioni se dedere.

Hadrianus. Num praevalet hortamentum?

Antiochus. Nimium; nam nostrae coniuges fastidiendo nos contemnunt, adeo ut dedignantur nobiscum comedere, quanto minus dormire.

Hadrianus. Fateor periculum.

6 Antiochus. Decet tui personam praecavere.

Hadrianus. Consequens. Advocetur, et in nostri praesentia an velit cedere discutiatur.

Antiochus. Vin' me illam advocare?

Hadrianus. Volo percerte.

2

Antiochus. Quid vocaris, O mulier advena?

Sapientia. Sapientia.

Antiochus. Imperator Hadrianus iussit te in palatio praesentari suis conspectibus.

Sapientia. Palatium cum nobili filiarum comitatu intrare non trepido, et minacem imperatoris vultum comminus aspicere non formido.

2 Antiochus. Invisum genus Christicolarum semper promptum est principibus ad resistendum.

Sapientia. Princeps universitatis, qui nescit vinci, non patitur suos ab hoste superari.

Antiochus. Mitiga effluentiam verborum, et perge ad palatium.

ANTIOCHUS. Well then, this woman whom I mentioned is 5
encouraging our people to abandon their traditional rituals, and to devote themselves to the Christian religion.

HADRIAN. Her encouragement is not having any success, is it?

ANTIOCHUS. Too much; in fact, our wives are fed up and reject us, to the point that they refuse to eat with us, let alone sleep with us.

HADRIAN. I admit that is dangerous.

ANTIOCHUS. It suits your character to take precautions. 6

HADRIAN. That follows. Let her be summoned and questioned in my presence as to whether she wishes to yield.

ANTIOCHUS. Do you want me to summon her?

HADRIAN. I want that most assuredly.

2

ANTIOCHUS. What are you called, foreign woman?

WISDOM. Wisdom.

ANTIOCHUS. The emperor Hadrian has ordered you to present yourself in the palace before his eyes.

WISDOM. I am not afraid to enter the palace in the noble company of my daughters, and I have no fear of looking at the emperor's threatening face at close range.

ANTIOCHUS. The hateful Christian race is always ready to 2
resist our rulers.

WISDOM. The ruler of the universe, who cannot be conquered, does not allow his people to be overcome by the enemy.

ANTIOCHUS. Tone down that torrent of words and make your way to the palace.

Sapientia. Monstra viam praeeundo. Nos subsequimur accelerando.

3

Antiochus. Hic ipse est imperator quem in solio residentem conspicis. Praecogita quid loquaris.

Sapientia. Hoc prohibet Christi sententia, promittens nobis insuperabilis sapientiae dona.

2 Hadrianus. Huc ades, Antioche.

Antiochus. Praesto sum, domine.

Hadrianus. Numquid hae sunt mulierculae quas deferebas pro Christiana religione?

Antiochus. Sunt plane.

Hadrianus. Uniuscuiusque pulchritudinem obstupesco, sed et honestatem habitus satis admirari nequeo.

Antiochus. Desine, O mi senior, admirari, et coge illas deos venerari.

3 Hadrianus. Quid si illas primule aggrediar blanda allocutione, si forte velint cedere?

Antiochus. Melius est, nam fragilitas sexus feminei facilius potest blandimentis molliri.

Hadrianus. Illustris matrona, blande et quiete ad culturam deorum te invito, quo nostra perfrui possis amicitia.

4 Sapientia. Nec in cultura deorum tuis votis satisfacere, nec amicitiam tecum gestio inire.

Hadrianus. Adhuc mitigato furore, nulla in te moveor indignatione, sed pro tua tuique filiarum salute, paterno sollicitor amore.

WISDOM. Go ahead of us, showing the way. We will follow quickly.

3

ANTIOCHUS. This is the emperor himself, whom you see sitting on the throne. Think beforehand what you will say.

WISDOM. A pronouncement of Christ's forbids thinking in advance; it promises us gifts of invincible wisdom.

HADRIAN. Approach, Antiochus! 2

ANTIOCHUS. I am here, master.

HADRIAN. Are these the young women you have denounced for practicing Christianity?

ANTIOCHUS. They certainly are.

HADRIAN. I am stunned by the beauty of every one of them, and furthermore, I cannot sufficiently admire the respectability of their dress.

ANTIOCHUS. Stop admiring them, my lord, and make them worship our gods.

HADRIAN. Should I approach them first with flattering 3
words, in case they choose to give in?

ANTIOCHUS. That is better, for the frailty of the feminine sex can more easily be placated by flatteries.

HADRIAN. Noble matron, I tenderly and calmly invite you to worship the gods, so that you can enjoy my friendship.

WISDOM. I am eager neither to satisfy your wishes in regard 4
to the worship of the gods, nor to enter into friendship with you.

HADRIAN. My wrath is still in check; I am not roused against you by any anger, but I am, with paternal affection, distressed for your safety and for that of your daughters.

5 Sapientia. Nolite, meae filiae, serpentinis huius satanae lenociniis cor apponere, sed meatim fastidite.

Fides. Fastidimus, et animo contemnimus frivola.

Hadrianus. Quid murmurando loqueris?

Sapientia. Filias affabar paucis.

6 Hadrianus. Videris esse summis natalibus orta. Sed tamen patriam, genus, nomenque tuum ex te plenius cupio ediscere.

Sapientia. Licet sanguinis superbia nobis sit parvi pendenda, tamen clara ex stirpe me originem non nego trahere.

Hadrianus. Credibile.

Sapientia. Nam eminentiores Italiae principes fuere mei parentes, et vocor Sapientia.

Hadrianus. Claritas ingenuitatis rutilat in facie, et sapientia nominis fulget in ore.

7 Sapientia. Frustra blandiris. Non flectimur tuis suadelis.

Hadrianus. Dic cur advenires, vel quare nostrates adires.

Sapientia. Nullius alius rei nisi agnoscendae veritatis causa, quo fidem quam expugnatis plenius ediscerem, filiasque meas Christo consecrarem.

8 Hadrianus. Expone vocabula singularum.

Sapientia. Una vocatur Fides, altera Spes, tertia Caritas.

Hadrianus. Quot annos aetatis volverunt?

Sapientia. Placetne vobis, O filiae, ut hunc stultum arithmetica fatigem disputatione?

Wisdom. Do not open your hearts, my daughters, to this 5
Satan's serpentine seductions, but despise them as I do.

Faith. We despise them, and in our hearts, we scorn his frivolous words.

Hadrian. What are you saying in a whisper?

Wisdom. I was telling my daughters a few things.

Hadrian. You seem to be of the highest birth. But never- 6
theless, I want to learn more fully from you about your native land, your race, and your name.

Wisdom. Even though we ought to make little of the glory of our bloodline, still I do not deny that I trace my origin from distinguished ancestry.

Hadrian. I believe you.

Wisdom. Indeed, very prominent rulers of Italy were my parents, and I am called Wisdom.

Hadrian. The brilliance of your nobility shines on your face, and the wisdom of your name sparkles in your voice.

Wisdom. You flatter us in vain. We will not be bent by your 7
cajolery.

Hadrian. Tell me why you have come, or why you sought out our people.

Wisdom. For no other reason than for the sake of learning the truth, so that I might understand more fully the faith which you are attacking and consecrate my daughters to Christ.

Hadrian. Tell me the names of each of them. 8

Wisdom. One is called Faith, the second Hope, the third Charity.

Hadrian. How old are they?

Wisdom. Girls, would it please you if I torment this fool with a discourse on arithmetic?

FIDES. Placet, mater, nosque auditum praebemus libenter.

9 SAPIENTIA. O imperator, si aetatem inquiris parvularum, Caritas imminutum pariter parem mansurnorum complevit numerum. Spes, autem, aeque imminutum sed pariter imparem. Fides vero superfluum impariter parem.

10 HADRIANUS. Tali responsione fecisti me, quae interrogabam, minime agnoscere.

SAPIENTIA. Nec mirum, quia sub huius definitionis species, non unus cadit numerus sed plures.

11 HADRIANUS. Expone enucleatius, alioquin non capit meus animus.

SAPIENTIA. Caritas duas Olympiades iam volvit. Spes, duo lustra. Fides, tres Olympiades.

12 HADRIANUS. Et cur octonarius numerus, qui duabus constat Olympiadibus, et denarius, qui duobus lustris perficitur, "imminutus" dicitur? Vel quare duodenarius, qui tribus Olympiadibus impletur, "superfluus" esse asseritur?

13 SAPIENTIA. Omnis namque numerus "imminutus" dicitur, cuius partes coniunctae, minorem illo numero, cuius partes sunt summae, quantitatem reddunt, ut VIII. Est autem octonarii medietas, IV; pars quarta, II; pars octava, I;
14 quae in unum redactae, septem reddunt. Similiter, denarius habet dimidiam partem, V; quintam autem, II; deci-
15 mam vero, I; quae simul copulatae, VIII, colligunt. E contrario autem "superfluus" dicitur, cuius partes augendo

Faith. It would please us, mother, and we willingly volun-
teer to listen.

Wisdom. O emperor, if you ask the age of my little girls, 9
Charity has completed a deficient, evenly even number
of years. Hope, on the other hand, also a deficient num-
ber, but an evenly odd one. Faith, meanwhile, an abun-
dant, oddly even number of years.

Hadrian. By such a response, you have not made me un- 10
derstand what I asked.

Wisdom. No wonder, since not a single number, but many
numbers, fall under a definition of this type.

Hadrian. Explain more clearly, otherwise my mind will not 11
absorb it.

Wisdom. Charity has already completed two Olympiads.
Hope, two lustra. Faith, three Olympiads.

Hadrian. And why is the number 8, which makes up two 12
Olympiads, and the number 10, which is comprised of
two lustra, called "deficient?" And why is the number 12,
which amounts to three Olympiads, said to be "abun-
dant?"

Wisdom. In fact, every number is called "deficient" whose 13
parts, when added together, render a sum that is smaller
than that number whose parts were totaled, as for exam-
ple, the number 8. Now there is a half part of 8, which is
4; a fourth part, which is 2; and an eighth part, which is 1;
and when these parts are added together, they total 7.
Similarly, the number 10 has a half part, which is 5; a fifth 14
part, on the other hand, which is 2; and indeed, a tenth
part, which is 1; these parts joined together amount to 8.
In contrast, however, a number is called "abundant" 15
whose parts when added together are greater than that

crescunt, ut xii. Est enim duodenarii medietas, vi; pars tertia, iv; pars quarta, iii; pars sexta, ii; pars duodecima,
16 i. Hic cumulus redundat in sedecim. Ut autem principalem non praeteream, qui, inter inaequales intemperantias, medii temperamentum limitis sortitus est: ille numerus "perfectus" dicitur; qui suis aequus partibus nec auget nec minuit, ut, vi. Cuius partes, id est, iii, ii, i, eundem senarium restituunt. Simili quoque ratione, xxviii, ccccxcvi, viii milia cxxviii, perfecti dicuntur.

17 Hadrianus. Et quid reliqui?

Sapientia. Omnes superflui sive imminuti.

18 Hadrianus. Quis numerus pariter par?

Sapientia. Qui potest in duo aequalia dividi, eiusque pars in duo aequalia, partisque pars in duo aequalia, ac deinceps per ordinem, donec in insecabilem incurrat unitatem; ut viii et xvi, omnesque qui ab his in duplo fiunt.

19 Hadrianus. Et quis est pariter impar?

Sapientia. Qui in partes aequales recipit sectionem, eiusque partes mox indivisibiles permanebunt, ut x, et omnes qui ab imparibus in duplo fiunt. Hic namque numerus superiori est contrarius, quia in illo solus minor terminus divisione est solutus; in isto autem solus maior terminus divisioni est aptus; in illo quoque omnes eius partes nomine et quantitate sunt pariter pares; in isto, autem, si

number, as for example the number 12. There is, in fact, a half part of 12, which is 6; a third part, which is 4; a fourth part, which is 3; a sixth part, which is 2; and a twelfth part, which is 1. The aggregation of these totals 16. In order, 16
however, that I not pass over the most important number, that number which, among unequal extremities, is allotted the moderation of the middle course: that number is called the "perfect" number; it is equal to its parts, being neither greater than nor less than they, as for example, the number 6. Its parts—namely, 3, 2, and 1—add up to the number itself, 6. Also, by a similar reckoning, the numbers 28, 496, and 8,128 are called "perfect" numbers.

HADRIAN. And what about the rest? 17

WISDOM. They are all either abundant or deficient.

HADRIAN. What is an evenly even number? 18

WISDOM. It is a number that can be divided into two equal parts, and each part of that into two equal parts, and a part of this part can be divided into two equal parts, and so on continuously, until it comes to the indivisible unity; for example, 8 and 16, and all the numbers that result from the doubling of these.

HADRIAN. And what is evenly odd? 19

WISDOM. It is a number that can be split into equal parts, and these equal parts will immediately remain indivisible, like 10, and all the numbers that result from the doubling of odd numbers. This number, to be sure, is in contrast to the previous one, because in that one only the lower extremity is indivisible, in this one, however, only the greater extremity can be divided; in that one also all of its parts, the divisor and the quotient, are evenly even, in

denominatio fuerit par, quantitas impar, si quantitas par, denominatio impar.

20 Hadrianus. Nec "terminum" quem dixisti agnosco, nec "denominationem" seu "quantitatem" scio.

Sapientia. Quando quantilibet numeri digestim disponuntur, primus minor terminus et postremus maior dicitur, quando autem divisionem faciendo, quota pars sit numeri dicimus, "denominationem" facimus, cum autem quot in unaquaque parte sint enumeramus, "quantitatem" exponimus.

21 Hadrianus. Et quis est impariter par?

Sapientia. Qui non solum unam recipit sectionem sicut pariter impar, sed etiam et secundam, aliquoties autem et tertiam vel plures, sed tamen usque ad indivisibilem non perveniet unitatem.

22 Hadrianus. O quam scrupulosa et plectilis quaestio ex istarum aetate infantularum est orta!

Sapientia. In hoc laudanda est supereminens Factoris sapientia, et mira mundi Artificis scientia, qui non solum in principio, mundum creans ex nihilo, omnia in numero, et mensura, et pondere posuit, sed etiam in succedentium serie temporum et in aetatibus hominum miram dedit inveniri posse scientiam artium.

23 Hadrianus. Diu te sustinui ratiocinantem, quo te mihi efficerem obtemperantem.

this one, however, if the divisor were even, the quotient would be odd, if the quotient were even, the divisor would be odd.

HADRIAN. I do not understand this "extremity" which you mentioned; and I do not know what "divisor" or "quotient" mean. 20

WISDOM. When any numbers you choose are arranged in a series, the first in the series is the lower extremity, and the last is the greater extremity. Now when doing division, when we are talking about what portion of a number it is, that is the "divisor," but when we are enumerating how many there are in each part, we are describing the "quotient."

HADRIAN. And what is an oddly even number? 21

WISDOM. That is a number which is subject not only to one division like the evenly odd, but also to a second division, and sometimes, moreover, also to a third division, or more; but nevertheless, it will not arrive at the indivisible unity.

HADRIAN. Oh, what a meticulous and complicated discussion has arisen from the age of these infants! 22

WISDOM. In this we must praise the extraordinary wisdom of the Maker, and the wondrous knowledge of the Creator of the world, who not only in the beginning, creating the world out of nothingness, arranged everything according to number, and measure, and weight, but also in the course of the following times and in the ages of man he provided us the ability to discover for ourselves the wondrous knowledge of the arts.

HADRIAN. I have tolerated your calculating for a long time, in order to make you obedient to me. 23

Sapientia. In quo?

Hadrianus. In cultura deorum.

Sapientia. In hoc utique non consentio.

Hadrianus. Si reniteris, tormentis afficieris.

Sapientia. Corpus quidem suppliciis lacessere poteris, sed animum ad cedendum compellere non praevalebis.

Antiochus. Dies abiit; nox incumbit. Non est tempus altercandi, quia instat hora cenandi.

Hadrianus. In custodiam iuxta palatium ponantur, et triduanae indutiae illis ad tractandum praestentur.

24 Antiochus. Observate istas, o milites, omni sollicitudine. Nullam illis occasionem evadendi relinquite.

4

Sapientia. O dulces filiolae, O carae pusiolae, nolite super carceralis angustia custodiae contristari, nolite imminentium minis poenarum terreri.

Fides. Licet corpuscula pavescant ad tormenta, mens tamen gliscit ad praemia.

Sapientia. Vincite infantilis teneritudinem aetatulae maturi sensus fortitudine.

2 Spes. Tuum est nos precibus adiuvare, ut possimus vincere.

Sapientia. Hoc indesinenter exoro, hoc efflagito: ut perseveretis in fide, quam inter ipsa crepundia vestris sensibus non desistebam instillasse.

Wisdom. About what?

Hadrian. About the worship of the gods.

Wisdom. About that I will not comply in any way.

Hadrian. If you resist, you will be forced by tortures.

Wisdom. You may indeed assail my body with punishments, but you will not succeed in compelling my mind to yield.

Antiochus. The day has gone; the night is coming. There is no time for arguing, since the dinner hour is at hand.

Hadrian. Have them placed under guard near the palace, and let them have three days of respite for thinking things over.

Antiochus. Soldiers, guard these women with all dili- 24
gence. Give them no opportunity to escape.

4

Wisdom. O my sweet little daughters, O my dear little girls, do not be distressed by the strains of our incarceration. Do not be terrified by the threats of imminent punishments.

Hope. Even if our small bodies begin to tremble at the torments, our minds are still eager for rewards.

Wisdom. Overcome the fragility of your tender youth with the strength of mature understanding.

Hope. It is your place to assist us with prayers, so that we 2
can overcome.

Wisdom. I pray for this constantly; I ask this of you earnestly: that you persevere in the faith which I have not ceased to instill in your thoughts since you were in the cradle.

3 CARITAS. Quod sugentes ubera in cunabulis didicimus, nullatenus oblivisci quibimus.

SAPIENTIA. Ad hoc vos materno lacte affluenter alui, ad hoc delicate nutrivi: ut vos caelesti non terreno sponso traderem, quo vestri causa socrus aeterni Regis dici meruissem.

4 FIDES. Pro ipsius amore sponsi promptae sumus mori.

SAPIENTIA. Delector ex vestra ratione magis quam nectareae dulcedinis gustamine.

SPES. Praemitte nos ante tribunal iudicis, et experieris quantum eius amor nobis attulit temeritatis.

SAPIENTIA. Hoc exopto: ut vestra virginitate coroner, ut vestro martyrio glorificer.

SPES. Consertis palmulis incedamus, et vultum tyranni confundamus.

SAPIENTIA. Exspectate donec instet hora vocationis nostrae.

FIDES. Taedet nos morarum. Tamen est exspectandum.

5

HADRIANUS. Antioche, iube illas Italicas nobis repraesentari captivas.

ANTIOCHUS. Procede, Sapientia, teque cum filiabus imperatori repraesenta.

SAPIENTIA. Pergite mecum, filiae, constanter; et perseverate in fide unanimiter, ut possitis palmam percipere feliciter.

CHARITY. What we learned sucking at your breasts in the cradle, we cannot forget in any way. 3

WISDOM. That is why I fed you bountifully with a mother's milk, that is why I nourished you tenderly: that I might hand you over to a heavenly bridegroom, not an earthly one, so that because of you I might deserve to be called the mother-in-law of the eternal King.

FAITH. For the love of that same bridegroom, we are ready to die. 4

WISDOM. I am more delighted by your plan than by the taste of nectar's sweetness.

HOPE. Send us on ahead of you before the tribunal of the judge, and you will learn how much boldness our love of Christ has brought us.

WISDOM. This is what I want: to be crowned because of your virginity, to be glorified because of your martyrdom.

HOPE. Let's join our tender hands and go, and let's confound that tyrant to his face.

WISDOM. Wait until the hour of our calling is at hand.

FAITH. We are tired of delays. Nevertheless, we must wait.

5

HADRIAN. Antiochus, order those captive Italian women to be brought again before us.

ANTIOCHUS. Advance, Wisdom, and present yourself again, along with your daughters, to the emperor.

WISDOM. Come along with me, daughters, steadfastly; and persevere in the faith with a single mind, so that you may have the good fortune to receive the palm of victory.

SPES. Pergimus. Ipseque nobiscum comitetur, pro cuius amore ad mortem ducemur.

2 HADRIANUS. Triduanas vobis indutias praestabat nostri serenitas, unde, si quid tractaretis utilitatis, cedite iussionibus nostris.

SAPIENTIA. Summum igitur utile tractavimus, id scilicet ut non cedamus.

3 ANTIOCHUS. Cur dignaris cum hac contumace verba miscere, quae te insolenti fatigat praesumptione?

HADRIANUS. Debeone illam dimittere impunitam?

ANTIOCHUS. Nequaquam!

HADRIANUS. Et quid?

ANTIOCHUS. Hortare puellulas, et si renitantur, infantiae ne parcas. Sed fac ut illae necentur, quo rebellis mater funeribus natarum acrius torqueatur.

HADRIANUS. Faciam quae hortaris.

ANTIOCHUS. Ita demum praevalebis.

4 HADRIANUS. Fides, intuere venerabilem magnae Dianae imaginem, et fer sacrae deae libamina, quo possis uti eius gratia.

FIDES. O stultum imperatoris praeceptum, omni contemptu dignum!

HADRIANUS. Quid murmuras subsannando? Quem irrides fronte rugosa?

FIDES. Tui stultitiam irrideo; tui insipientiam subsanno.

HADRIANUS. Mei?

FIDES. Tui.

ANTIOCHUS. Imperatoris?

HOPE. We are coming. And may the Lord, for whose sake we will be led to death, also accompany us.

HADRIAN. My serenity granted you a three-day reprieve; so, 2
if you have drawn any useful lesson from it, yield to my orders.

WISDOM. We have, indeed, drawn the most useful lesson, namely that we should not yield.

ANTIOCHUS. Why do you think it worth your while to ex- 3
change words with this obstinate woman, who fatigues you with her insolent presumption?

HADRIAN. Should I send her away unpunished?

ANTIOCHUS. Certainly not!

HADRIAN. What then?

ANTIOCHUS. Pressure the little girls, and if they resist, have no mercy on their tender age. Rather, have them killed, so that the rebellious mother may be tortured more bitterly by the deaths of her daughters.

HADRIAN. I will do what you urge.

ANTIOCHUS. In that way you will finally succeed.

HADRIAN. Faith, look at this venerable image of the great 4
Diana, and make offerings to this sacred goddess, so that you can enjoy her favor.

FAITH. Oh, what a stupid command the emperor makes; it deserves total contempt!

HADRIAN. What are you whispering jeeringly? Whom are you mocking with that furrowed brow?

FAITH. I am mocking your stupidity; I am jeering at your idiocy.

HADRIAN. Mine?

FAITH. Yours.

ANTIOCHUS. The emperor's?

Fides. Ipsius.

Antiochus. O nefas!

5 Fides. Quid enim stultius, quid insipientius videri potest, quam quod hortatur nos contempto creatore universitatis venerationem inferre metallis?

Antiochus. Fides, insanis!

Fides. Antioche, mentiris.

Antiochus. Nonne haec summa insania et magna est dementia, ut rerum principem dixisti insipientem?

Fides. Dixi, et dico, dicamque quamdiu vixero.

Antiochus. Breve tempus vivere et cito debes consumi morte.

Fides. Hoc opto, ut moriar in Christo.

6 Hadrianus. Duodecim centuriones alternando scindant flagris eius membra.

Antiochus. Nec iniuria.

Hadrianus. O fortissimi centuriones, accedite, meique iniuriam vindicate.

Antiochus. Iustum.

Hadrianus. Perquire, Antioche, anne velit cedere.

7 Antiochus. Vin' adhuc, Fides, solita conviciorum obiectione imperatorem dehonestare?

Fides. Cur solito minus?

Antiochus. Quia prohiberis verberibus.

Fides. Verbera non compellunt me tacere, quia nullo afficior dolore.

Antiochus. O infelix pertinacia, O contumax audacia!

8 Hadrianus. Corpus fatiscit per supplicia, et mens tumet superbia.

FAITH. Yes, his.

ANTIOCHUS. Oh, the wickedness!

FAITH. What indeed can be stupider, what more idiotic, 5
than his encouraging us to reject the creator of the universe and to offer veneration to metallic objects?

ANTIOCHUS. Faith, you are insane!

FAITH. Antiochus, you are a liar.

ANTIOCHUS. Is it not the greatest insanity and the greatest dementia, that you called the ruler of the state an idiot?

FAITH. I called him that, I do call him that, and I will call him that so long as I live.

ANTIOCHUS. You deserve to live a short time and to be consumed swiftly by death.

FAITH. This is what I choose, to die for Christ.

HADRIAN. Let twelve centurions, taking turns, tear her 6
limbs with whips.

ANTIOCHUS. That is only just.

HADRIAN. O centurions, bravest of men, go to it, and avenge the injustice done to me.

ANTIOCHUS. That is fair.

HADRIAN. Ask her, Antiochus, whether she wants to give in.

ANTIOCHUS. Faith, do you still want to dishonor the em- 7
peror with your usual hurling of insults?

FAITH. Why any less than usual?

ANTIOCHUS. Because you will be deterred by beatings.

FAITH. Beatings cannot compel me to be silent, because I feel no pain.

ANTIOCHUS. Oh, miserable stubbornness, oh, obstinate audacity!

HADRIAN. Her body is growing weak from the punish- 8
ments, and yet her mind is swelling with pride.

FIDES. Erras, Adriane, si reris me fatigari suppliciis. Non ego quidem sed infirmi tortores deficiunt, et sudore ob lassitudinem fluunt.

9 HADRIANUS. Fac, Antioche, ut gemellae pectoris particulae abscidantur, quo saltem rubore coerceatur.

ANTIOCHUS. O utinam possit ullo coerceri modo!

HADRIANUS. Forsan coercebitur.

FIDES. Inviolatum pectus vulnerasti, sed me non laesisti. En pro fonte sanguinis unda prorumpit lactis.

10 HADRIANUS. In craticulam substratis ignibus assanda ponatur, quo vi vaporis enecetur.

ANTIOCHUS. Digna est ut miserabiliter pereat, quae tuae iussioni contraluctari non trepidat.

FIDES. Omne quod paras ad dolorem, mihi vertitur in quietem. Unde commode pauso in craticula, ceu in tranquilla navicula.

11 HADRIANUS. Sartago plena pice et cera ardentibus rogis superponatur, et in ferventem liquorem haec rebellis mittatur.

FIDES. Sponte insilio.

HADRIANUS. Consentio.

FIDES. Ubi sunt minae tuae? Ecce, illaesa inter ferventem liquorem ludens nato, et pro vi caumatis sentio matutini refrigerium roris.

12 HADRIANUS. Antioche, quid ad haec est agendum?

ANTIOCHUS. Ne evadat providendum.

Faith. You are mistaken, Hadrian, if you suppose I am weakened by these punishments. It is not I, in fact, but the feeble torturers who are growing weak, and they are drenched in sweat from exhaustion.

Hadrian. Antiochus, have the nipples of both her breasts 9
cut off, so she may be coerced, at the very least, by blushing.

Antiochus. I wish she could be coerced, in any fashion!

Hadrian. Maybe she will be coerced.

Faith. You have wounded my unviolated breast, but you have not injured me. Look, instead of a fountain of blood, a stream of milk is pouring out.

Hadrian. Let her be put on a grate with fire spread under 10
it, to roast, so that she is killed by the power of the heat.

Antiochus. A woman who is not afraid to oppose your commands deserves to die miserably.

Faith. Everything you do to hurt me becomes tranquility for me. So, I rest on this grate pleasantly, as though on a peaceful raft.

Hadrian. Let a cauldron full of pitch and wax be placed on 11
the burning pyres, and let this rebel be thrown into the boiling liquid.

Faith. I will jump in of my own accord.

Hadrian. Go ahead.

Faith. Where are your threats? Look, I'm swimming unharmed, playing in the boiling liquid, and I feel the refreshment of morning dew, instead of the violence of the heat.

Hadrian. Antiochus, what should be done about this? 12

Antiochus. We must see to it that she does not escape punishment.

HADRIANUS. Capite truncetur!

ANTIOCHUS. Alioquin non vincetur.

13 FIDES. Nunc est gaudendum, nunc in Domino exsultandum.

SAPIENTIA. Christe, triumphator diaboli invictissime, da tolerantiam Fidei meae filiae.

FIDES. O mater veneranda, dic vale ultimum tuae filiae. Liba osculum tuae primogenitae, nec afficiare ullo maerore cordis, quia tendo ad bravium aeternitatis.

SAPIENTIA. O filia, filia, non confundor, non contristor, sed valedico tibi exsultando. Et osculor os oculosque prae gaudio lacrimando, orans ut sub ictu percussoris inviolatum serves mysterium tui nominis.

14 FIDES. O uterinae sorores, libate mihi osculum pacis, et parate vos ad tolerantiam futuri certaminis.

SPES. Adiuva nos oratione assidua, ut mereamur sequi tua vestigia.

FIDES. Este obtemperantes monitis nostrae sanctae parentis, quae nos hortabatur praesentia fastidire, quo meruissemus aeterna percipere.

CARITAS. Maternis libenter obtemperamus monitis, quo perfrui mereamur aeternis bonis.

FIDES. Percussor, accede, et iniunctum tibi officium me necando imple.

15 SAPIENTIA. Abscissum morientis filiae caput amplectendo, impressisque labris crebrius deosculando, congratulor tibi, Christe, qui tantillulae victoriam praestitisti puellulae.

Hadrian. Off with her head!

Antiochus. She will not be conquered any other way.

Faith. Now is the time for rejoicing, now is the time to exult in the Lord. 13

Wisdom. Christ, most invincible conqueror of the devil, grant endurance to my daughter Faith.

Faith. O revered mother, say your last farewell to your daughter. Plant a kiss on your firstborn, and do not be afflicted by any grief in your heart, because I am going to my eternal reward.

Wisdom. O daughter, daughter, I am not distressed, I am not saddened, but I joyfully wish you farewell. And I kiss your mouth and eyes, crying for joy, praying that under the blow of the executioner you preserve the inviolate mystery of your name.

Faith. O sisters, born from the same womb, plant a kiss of 14
peace upon me, and prepare yourselves to endure the coming struggle.

Hope. Assist us with constant prayer, so that we earn the right to follow in your footsteps.

Faith. Obey the advice of our holy mother, who always encouraged us to reject the things of the present, so that we might earn the right to receive those things that are eternal.

Charity. We gladly obey our mother's advice, so that we may earn the right to enjoy eternal benefits.

Faith. Approach, executioner, and carry out the job entrusted to you, by killing me.

Wisdom. Embracing the severed head of my dying daugh- 15
ter, and kissing it repeatedly with my lips pressed to it, I give thanks to you, Christ, who have given victory to such a great little girl.

16 HADRIANUS. Spes, cede meis hortamentis paterno affectu tibi consulentis.

SPES. Quid hortaris? Quid consulis?

HADRIANUS. Ut caveas pertinaciam imitari sororis, ne similibus intereas poenis.

SPES. O utinam admeruissem illam imitari patiendo, quo illi assimilarer in praemio!

17 HADRIANUS. Depone callum pectoris, et conquinisce turificando magnae Dianae, et ego te propriae prolis vice excolo, atque extollo omni dilectione.

SPES. Paternitatem tuam repudio; tua beneficia minime desidero, quapropter vacua spe deciperis, si me tibi cedere reris.

HADRIANUS. Loquere parcius ne irascar.

18 SPES. Irascere. Nec sollicitor.

ANTIOCHUS. Miror, auguste, quod ab hac vili puellula tam diu calumniari pateris. Ego quidem disrumpor prae furore, quia illam audio tam temere in te latrare.

HADRIANUS. Hactenus infantiae parcebam. Ultra non parcam, sed meritam ultionem inferam.

ANTIOCHUS. O utinam!

19 HADRIANUS. O lictores, adite, et hanc rebellem usque ad interneciem crudis nervis caedite.

ANTIOCHUS. Decet ut severitatem sentiat tui furoris, quia lenitatem parvi pendit pietatis.

HADRIAN. Hope, yield to my exhortations, the exhortations of one counseling you with fatherly affection. 16

HOPE. What do you exhort? What do you counsel?

HADRIAN. That you avoid imitating the stubbornness of your sister, so that you not perish through similar punishments.

HOPE. Oh, may I prove worthy in imitating her suffering, so that I may resemble her in my reward!

HADRIAN. Put aside the hardness of your heart and bow down, burning incense to Diana, the great goddess, and I will care for you as my own child, and I will raise you up with all my love. 17

HOPE. I reject you as a father; I have no desire for your favors. So, you are deceived by an empty hope if you suppose I will yield to you.

HADRIAN. Speak more moderately, so I do not get angry.

HOPE. Get angry. I don't care. 18

ANTIOCHUS. I am amazed, imperial lord, that you tolerate being insulted by this vile little girl for so long. I, for one, am bursting with rage, because I hear her barking at you so arrogantly.

HADRIAN. I was, till now, sparing her because of her youth. I will spare her no further but will bring on the punishment she deserves.

ANTIOCHUS. I wish you would!

HADRIAN. Executioners, come here, and beat this rebel to death with rough leather straps. 19

ANTIOCHUS. It is right that she feel the severity of your rage because she thought so little of the leniency of your kindness.

Spes. Hanc pietatem exopto, hanc lenitatem desidero.

20 Antiochus. O Sapientia, quid murmurando loqueris, stans sublevatis oculis iuxta cadaver exstinctae prolis?

Sapientia. Invoco Omniparentem, quo eandem tolerantiae perseverantiam, quam praestitit Fidei, praestet et Spei.

21 Spes. O mater, mater, quam efficaces, quam exaudibiles experior esse tui preces. Ecce te orante anheli tortores levatis dextris librant ictum, et ego nullum doloris sentio tactum.

Hadrianus. Si flagra parvi pendis, acrioribus poenis coartaberis.

Spes. Infer, infer quicquid crudele, quicquid excogites letale. Quanto plus saevis, tanto magis victus confunderis.

22 Hadrianus. In aera suspendatur, et ungulis laceretur, quoadusque evulsis visceribus et nudatis ossibus deficiat, et membratim crepat.

Antiochus. Imperialis iussio, et congrua satis ultio!

Spes. Vulpina fraude loqueris, et versipelli astutia, Antioche, adularis.

Antiochus. Quiesce infelix! Verbositas tua nunc est finienda.

Spes. Non ut speras evenerit, sed tibi tuoque principi nunc etiam confusio aderit.

23 Hadrianus. Quid sentio novae dulcedinis? Quid odoror stupendae suavitatis?

HOPE. *This* is the kindness I want; *this* is the leniency I desire.

ANTIOCHUS. O Wisdom, what are you saying in your mur- 20
muring, standing there with your eyes raised upward next to the corpse of your dead child?

WISDOM. I am calling on the Father of us all, to grant to Hope the same steadfastness of endurance that he granted to Faith.

HOPE. O mother, mother, I feel how powerful your prayers 21
are, how worthy to be heard. Look, while you are praying, the panting executioners raise high their hands and mete out their blows, but no sensation of pain touches me.

HADRIAN. If you think little of these lashes, you will be tortured by harsher punishments.

HOPE. Bring it on, bring on whatever cruel, whatever deadly thing you can devise. The more you rage, the more embarrassed you will be when defeated.

HADRIAN. Have her strung up in the air, and let her be torn 22
with hooks, until she expires with her guts ripped out and her bones bared, and let her crack limb by limb.

ANTIOCHUS. A command worthy of an emperor, and a very suitable punishment!

HOPE. You speak with the deceit of a fox, Antiochus, and you grovel with shape-shifting craftiness.

ANTIOCHUS. Silence, you wretch! Your blabbering must now be stopped.

HOPE. It will not turn out as you hope, but even now there will be embarrassment for you and that ruler of yours.

HADRIAN. What is this strange sweetness I perceive? What 23
is this wondrous scent I smell?

SPES. Decidentia frusta mei lacerati corporis dant flagrantiam paradisiaci aromatis, quo nolens cogeris fateri, me non posse suppliciis laedi.

HADRIANUS. Antioche, quid enim mihi est agendum?

ANTIOCHUS. Novis cruciatibus incumbendum.

24 HADRIANUS. Aeneum vas plenum oleo et adipe, cera atque pice, ignibus superponatur, in quod ligata proiciatur.

ANTIOCHUS. Si in ius Vulcani tradetur, forsitan evadendi aditum non nanciscetur.

SPES. Haec virtus Christo non est insolita, ut ignem faciat mitescere mutata natura.

25 HADRIANUS. Quid audio, Antioche, velut sonitum inundantis aquae?

ANTIOCHUS. Heu, heu, domine!

HADRIANUS. Quid contigit nobis?

ANTIOCHUS. Ebulliens fervor confracto vase ministros combussit, et illa malefica illaesa comparuit.

HADRIANUS. Fateor, victi sumus.

ANTIOCHUS. Penitus.

26 HADRIANUS. Caput abscidatur!

ANTIOCHUS. Alias non absumetur.

SPES. O Caritas dilecta, O soror unica, ne formides tyranni minas. Ne trepides ad poenas. Nitere constanti fide imitari sorores, ad caeli palatium praecedentes.

CARITAS. Taedet me vitae praesentis. Taedet terrenae habitationis, quod saltem ad modicum temporis separor a vobis.

Hope. The sundered scraps of my lacerated body give off the fragrance of a heavenly aroma, so that even unwillingly you will be compelled to admit that I cannot be harmed by your punishments.

Hadrian. Antiochus, what on earth should I do?

Antiochus. We must resort to new forms of torture.

Hadrian. Have a bronze pot full of oil and fat, wax and 24
pitch, be placed over a fire, and let her be bound up and thrown into it.

Antiochus. If she is handed over to the justice of Vulcan, perhaps she will find no avenue for escape.

Hope. The power to make fire gentle, changing its nature, is not unknown to Christ.

Hadrian. What's this sound I hear, Antiochus, like flood- 25
ing water?

Antiochus. Alas, alas, my lord!

Hadrian. What is happening to us?

Antiochus. The boiling heat has broken the vessel and burned up our servants, and that witch has emerged unharmed.

Hadrian. I admit, we are defeated.

Antiochus. Totally.

Hadrian. Off with her head! 26

Antiochus. She will not be destroyed any other way.

Hope. O beloved Charity, my only sister, do not fear the threats of this tyrant. Do not tremble at the punishments. Try with steadfast faith to imitate your sisters, who are leading the way to the palace of heaven.

Charity. I am tired of my present life. I am tired of this earthly dwelling, because I will be separated at least briefly from you.

SPES. Depone taedium, et tende ad praemium. Non enim diu separabimur, sed ocius in caelo coniungemur.

CARITAS. Fiat, fiat.

27 SPES. Euge, mater illustris, gaude! Nec tangaris de mei passione materni affectus dolore. Sed praefer spem maerori cum me videas pro Christo mori.

SAPIENTIA. Nunc quidem gaudeo, sed tunc tandem perfecte exultans gaudebo, quando tui sororculam, pari conditione extinctam, caelo praemisero; et ego subsequar postrema.

SPES. Perennis Trinitas restituet tibi in aevum plenum absque diminutione filiarum numerum.

28 SAPIENTIA. Confortare, filia. Percussor invadit nos evaginato gladio.

SPES. Libens excipio gladium. Tu, Christe, suscipe spiritum pro tui confessione nominis eiectum de habitaculo corporis.

29 SAPIENTIA. O Caritas, suboles incluta, spes uteri mei unica, ne constristes matrem bonam tui certaminis consummationem exspectantem, sed sperne praesens utile, quo pervenias ad gaudium interminabile, quo tui germanae fulgent coronis illibatae virginitatis.

30 CARITAS. Fulci me, mater, precibus sacris, quatenus merear interesse illarum gaudiis.

SAPIENTIA. Exoro te, fine tenus in fide solidatum iri, nec dubito tibi perenne tripudium donatum iri.

HOPE. Put aside your weariness and reach for your reward. Indeed, we will not be separated for long, but we will be joined together soon in heaven.

CHARITY. Let it be so, let it be so.

HOPE. Very well, illustrious mother, rejoice! And do not let 27
the pain of motherly affection touch you because of my suffering. Rather, put hope ahead of grief when you see me dying for Christ.

WISDOM. I am indeed rejoicing now, but later I shall finally rejoice in perfect exultation, when I have sent your little sister before me to heaven, after she has died in a similar fashion; and I will follow, coming last.

HOPE. The everlasting Trinity will restore to you for eternity the full number of your daughters, without any decrease.

WISDOM. Be strong, daughter. The executioner is approach- 28
ing us with his sword drawn.

HOPE. I gladly receive the sword. You, Christ, receive my spirit, released from its enclosure in my body because I confessed your name.

WISDOM. O Charity, my glorious child, sole hope of my 29
womb, do not distress your mother, who is expecting a happy outcome of your struggle, but reject what is beneficial in the present, so that you may come to unending joy where your sisters are shining with the crowns of unviolated virginity.

CHARITY. Support me, mother, with your holy prayers, so 30
that I may earn the right to share in their joys.

WISDOM. I pray that you will be strong in faith to the end, and I have no doubt you will be granted eternal rejoicing.

31 HADRIANUS. Caritas, saturatus conviciis tui sororum nimiumque exacerbatus sum prolixa ratione earum. Unde diu tecum non contendo, sed vel obtemperantem mei votis ditabo omnibus bonis, vel contraluctantem afficiam malis.

CARITAS. Bonum corde tenus amplector, et malum omnino detestor.

32 HADRIANUS. Hoc tibi potissimum salubre, mihique est placabile. Ideoque leve quiddam tibi praepono meae pietatis gratia.

CARITAS. Quid?

HADRIANUS. Dic tantum, "Magna Diana," et ego ultra ad sacrificandum te non compello.

CARITAS. Percerte non dico.

HADRIANUS. Quare?

33 CARITAS. Quia mentiri nolo. Ego quidem et sorores meae, eisdem parentibus genitae, eisdem sacramentis imbutae, sumus una eademque fidei constantia roboratae. Quapropter scito nostrum velle, nostrum sentire, nostrum sapere, unum idemque esse, nec me in ullo umquam illis dissidere.

34 HADRIANUS. O iniuria, quod a tantilla etiam contemnor homullula!

CARITAS. Licet tenella sim aetate, tamen gnara sum te argumentose confundere.

HADRIANUS. Abstrahe illam, Antioche, et fac ut suspensa in eculeo, atrociter verberetur.

ANTIOCHUS. Vereor quod verbera non praevaleant.

HADRIAN. Charity, I have had my fill of the insults of your sisters, and I am extremely irritated by their protracted arguing. For that reason, I am not going to fight with you for long, but I will either enrich you with all sorts of goods, if you comply with my wishes, or I will assail you with evils if you resist. 31

CHARITY. I embrace what is good with all my heart, and I thoroughly detest what is evil.

HADRIAN. This is a very healthy attitude for you, and it is pleasing to me. And so, I propose to you something easy, by the grace of my kindness. 32

CHARITY. What?

HADRIAN. Just say, "Diana is great," and I will not compel you any further to perform sacrifices.

CHARITY. I will certainly not say that.

HADRIAN. Why?

CHARITY. Because I do not want to lie. I, indeed, and my sisters, born of the same parents, imbued in the same sacraments, we are all firm in one and the same constancy of faith. Understand, therefore, that our wish, our sentiment, our wisdom, is one and the same, and that I do not ever differ from them in any matter. 33

HADRIAN. Oh, how unjust, that I am even despised by such a tiny little person! 34

CHARITY. Even though I am of very tender age, nevertheless I know how to confound you by arguing.

HADRIAN. Take her away, Antiochus, and have her hung on the rack, and savagely beaten.

ANTIOCHUS. I'm afraid beatings will have no effect.

35 HADRIANUS. Si non praevaleant, iube tribus continuis diebus ac noctibus fornacem succendi, et illam inter bacchantes flammas proici.

CARITAS. O iudicem impotentem! Qui diffidit se absque armis ignium octennem infantem superare posse.

HADRIANUS. Abi, Antioche, et iniunctum officium perfice.

36 CARITAS. Saevitiae quidem tuae satisfaciendo parebit, sed me minime nocebit, quia nec verbera mei corpusculum lacerare, nec flammae comam vel vestes poterunt obfuscare.

HADRIANUS. Experietur.

CARITAS. Experiatur.

6

HADRIANUS. Antioche, quid pateris? Cur tristior solito regrederis?

ANTIOCHUS. Quando causam tristitiae experieris, haud minus constristaberis.

HADRIANUS. Dic, ne celes.

ANTIOCHUS. Illa lasciva, quam mihi cruciandam tradidisti puellula, me praesente flagellabatur. Sed ne tenuis quidem cutis summotenus disrumpebatur. Deinde proieci illam in fornacem igneum colorem prae nimio ardore exprimentem.

2 HADRIANUS. Cur dissimulas loqui? Expone exitum rei.

ANTIOCHUS. Flamma erupit, et quinque milia hominum combussit.

HADRIANUS. Et quid contigit illi?

ANTIOCHUS. Caritati?

HADRIAN. If they should have no effect, order a furnace to 35
be heated for three days and three nights without pause, and for her to be thrown in among the raging flames.

CHARITY. You impotent judge! You have no confidence that you can conquer an eight-year-old child without fire as a weapon.

HADRIAN. Go, Antiochus, and perform the job as ordered.

CHARITY. Indeed, he will obey, satisfying your savagery. But 36
he will not hurt me because beatings cannot tear my little body, nor can flames blacken my hair or clothes.

HADRIAN. He will put that to the test.

CHARITY. Let him do so.

6

HADRIAN. Antiochus, what is the matter? Why do you return abnormally sad?

ANTIOCHUS. When you find out the cause of my sadness, you will be just as upset.

HADRIAN. Tell me, do not hide it.

ANTIOCHUS. That wanton little girl you handed over to me for torturing was whipped in my presence. But not even the surface of her tender skin was broken. Then I hurled her into the furnace, which appeared fiery in color from the immense heat.

HADRIAN. Why do you refrain from speaking? Explain the 2
outcome of the affair.

ANTIOCHUS. The flame erupted, and it burned up five thousand men.

HADRIAN. And what happened to her?

ANTIOCHUS. To Charity?

HADRIANUS. Ipsi.

ANTIOCHUS. Ludens inter flammivomos vapores vagabat. Et illaesa laudes deo suo pangebat. Illi etiam qui diligenter inspexere ferebant tres candidulos viros cum illa deambulasse.

3 HADRIANUS. Erubesco illam ultra videre, quia nequeo illam laedere.

ANTIOCHUS. Restat ut perimatur gladio.

HADRIANUS. Hoc fiat absque mora.

7

ANTIOCHUS. Detege duram Caritas cervicem, et sustine percussoris ensem.

CARITAS. In hoc non renitor tui votis, sed libens pareo iussis.

SAPENTIA. Nunc, nunc, filia, gratulandum nunc in Christo est gaudendum. Nec est quae me mordeat cura, quia secura sum de tua victoria.

2 CARITAS. Imprime mihi, mater, osculum, et commenda iturum Christo spiritum.

SAPIENTIA. Qui te in meo utero vivificavit, ipse suscipiat animam quam caelitus inspiravit.

CARITAS. Tibi, Christe, gloria qui me ad te vocasti cum martyrii palma.

SAPIENTIA. Vale, proles dulcissima. Et cum Christo iungaris in caelo, memento matris. Iam patrona effecta te parientis.

HADRIAN. Yes, to her.

ANTIOCHUS. She wandered around playing among the spewing flames of heat. And, unharmed, she sang songs of praise to her god. Furthermore, those who looked closely reported that three men, shining white, walked around with her.

HADRIAN. I am ashamed to see her again, because I cannot 3
harm her.

ANTIOCHUS. The only thing left to do is to kill her with a sword.

HADRIAN. Let it be done without delay.

7

ANTIOCHUS. Uncover your stubborn neck, Charity, and suffer the executioner's sword.

CHARITY. I will not oppose your wishes in this regard, but freely obey your commands.

WISDOM. Now, now, daughter, we must give thanks to Christ, we must rejoice in Christ. And no concern is eating away at me, for I am certain of your victory.

CHARITY. Give me a kiss, mother, and send my soul on its 2
way to Christ.

WISDOM. May the One who gave you life in my womb welcome back the soul which he breathed into you from heaven.

CHARITY. Glory to you, Christ, who have called me to yourself, with the victory palm of martyrdom.

WISDOM. Goodbye, my sweetest child. And when you are joined with Christ in heaven, remember your mother. You have now become the protectress of the one who bore you.

8

Sapientia. Convenite illustres matronae et mearum cadavera filiarum mecum sepelite.

MAtronae. Corpuscula aromatibus condimus et exsequias honorifice celebramus.

Sapientia. Grandis benignitas et mira pietas, quam mihi impenditis meique mortuis.

Matronae. Quae tibi sunt commoda exsequimur mente devota.

Sapientia. Non dubito.

2 Matronae. Ubi vis eligere locum sepulturae?

Sapientia. Tertio miliario ab urbe, si vobis non displicet prolixitas.

Matronae. Non displicet, sed elata funera sequi placet.

9

Sapientia. Ecce locus.

Matronae. Hic nempe servandis reliquiis est aptus.

Sapientia. Flosculos uteri mei tibi, terra, servandos committo, quos tu materiali sinu foveto, donec in resurrectione maiori reviridescant gloria. Et tu, Christe, animas interim imple splendoribus, dans pacificam requiem ossibus.

Matronae. Amen.

2 Sapientia. Grates vestrae humanitati pro solamine quod contulistis meae orbitati.

8

Wisdom. Come together, illustrious matrons, and join me in burying the corpses of my daughters.

Matrons. We will embalm their little bodies with fragrant spices, and we will celebrate their funerals honorably.

Wisdom. It is a great kindness and a wondrous piety which you pay me and my deceased daughters.

Matrons. With a faithful heart we will do whatever pleases you.

Wisdom. I do not doubt it.

Matrons. Where do you want to choose as the place of 2
burial?

Wisdom. At the third milestone from Rome, if the distance does not displease you.

Matrons. It does not displease; rather it is a pleasure to follow the funeral procession.

9

Wisdom. Here is the place.

Matrons. This place is certainly appropriate for preserving their remains.

Wisdom. The little flowers of my womb, O earth, I entrust to you for safekeeping. Embrace them in your earthly bosom, until in the resurrection they bloom again in greater glory. And you, Christ, meanwhile fill their souls with splendors, and give peaceful rest to their bones.

Matrons. Amen.

Wisdom. I give thanks to your humanity for the comfort 2
which you have offered in my bereavement.

Matronae. Utrumne vis nos hic tecum morari?

Sapientia. Non.

Matronae. Cur non?

Sapientia. Ne ex meo commodo vobis ingeratur molestia. Sit satis, quod tres noctes mecum permansistis. Abite in pace, revertimini cum salute.

3 Matronae. Vis nobiscum abire?

Sapientia. Minime.

Matronae. Et quid meditaris agere?

Sapientia. Hic remanere, si forte veniat mea petitio, et impleatur quod desidero.

Matronae. Quid petis? Quid desideras?

Sapientia. Id solummodo, ut oratione completa moriar in Christo.

Matronae. Restat ut expectemus donec et te sepulturae tradamus.

4 Sapientia. Ut libet. Adonai, Emmanuel, quem retro tem-
pora divinitas edidit Omniparentis, et in tempore virgini-
tas genuit matris, qui ex duabus naturis unus Christus
mirifice consistis, nec diversitate naturarum unitatem
personae dividens, nec unitate personae diversitatem na-
5 turarum confundens, tibi iubilet iucunda serenitas ange-
lorum dulcisque harmonia siderum. Te quoque collaudet
totius scibilis rei scientia, omneque quod ex elemento-
6 rum formatur materia. Quia tu, qui solus cum Patre et
Spiritu sancto, es forma sine materia, ex Patris voluntate
et Spiritus sancti cooperatione non respuisti fieri homo,

MATRONS. Do you want us to remain here with you?

WISDOM. No.

MATRONS. Why not?

WISDOM. So that no trouble be brought upon you for my convenience. Let it suffice that you have remained with me for three nights. Go in peace, return home in good health.

MATRONS. Do you want to go with us? 3

WISDOM. No.

MATRONS. And what are you planning to do?

WISDOM. I plan to remain here to see if my prayer may be answered, and if what I desire may be fulfilled.

MATRONS. What is your prayer? What do you desire?

WISDOM. Only this: that when I am done praying, I may die in Christ.

MATRONS. All that remains is for us to wait until we may place you also in a tomb.

WISDOM. Whatever you wish. Adonai, Emmanuel, whom 4
the divine Father of all brought forth before time, and
whom the virginity of your mother bore in time, you who
from two natures miraculously comprise one Christ, nei-
ther dividing the unity of your person by the diversity of
your natures, nor confusing the diversity of your natures
by the unity of your person, for you let the joyous seren- 5
ity of the angels and the sweet harmony of the stars be
jubilant. Let also the knowledge of everything knowable,
and everything which is formed from the matter of the
elements, join in praising you. Because you, who alone 6
with the Father and the Holy Spirit are form without
matter, by the Father's will and with the cooperation of
the Holy Spirit did not refuse to become man, suffering

passibilis humanitate, salva divinitatis impassibilitate. Et ut nullus in te credentium periret, sed omnis fidelis aeternaliter viveret, mortem nostram non dedignatus
7 es gustare, tuaque resurrectione consumere. Te etiam, perfectum Deum hominemque verum, recolo promisisse omnibus qui pro tui nominis veneratione vel terrenae usum possessionis relinquerent, vel carnalium affectum propinquorum postponerent, centenae vicissitudinem mercedis recompensari, et aeternae bravium vitae debere donari. Huius spe animata promissi, feci quod iussisti,
8 sponte omittens suboles quas peperi. Unde tu pie promissa solvere ne moreris, sed fac me, quantocius absolutam corporeis vinculis, ex receptione filiarum laetificari. Quas pro te mactandas obtulisse non distuli, quo te illis Agnum virginibus sequentibus et novum canticum modulantibus ego iocunder audiendo, illarumque laetificer gloria, et quamvis non possim canticum virginitatis di-
9 cere, te tamen cum illis merear aeternaliter laudare. Qui non ipse qui Pater, sed idem es quod Pater, cum quo et Spiritu sancto unus Dominus universitatis, unusque Rex summae et mediae atque imae rationis, regnas et dominaris per interminabilia immortalis aevi saecula.

Matronae. Suscipe, Domine. Amen.

in your humanity, with the impassibility of your divinity
preserved. And so that no one who believes in you may
die, but so that all the faithful may live forever, you did
not disdain to taste our death, and to destroy it by your
resurrection. I remember also that you, as perfect God 7
and true man, have promised to all who give up the use of
earthly possessions for the veneration of your name, or
put aside the love of their blood relations, will be repaid
one hundred times in return, and will be granted the re-
ward of eternal life. Animated by the hope of this prom-
ise, I have done what you ordered, willingly giving up the
children whom I bore. So, do not hesitate to fulfill what 8
you mercifully promised, but allow me, freed as soon as
possible from my bodily chains, to rejoice in the recep-
tion of my daughters. I did not put off presenting them
to be sacrificed for your sake, so that I might rejoice hear-
ing those virgins following you, the Lamb, and singing a
new song, and so that I could revel in their glory, and,
though I myself cannot sing a song of virginity, so that I
might yet earn the right along with them to praise you
forever. You are not yourself the Father, but you are the 9
same as the Father, with whom and with the Holy Spirit,
as the one Lord of the universe, and as the one King of all
that is above, in the middle, and down below, you rule and
are Lord through the endless ages of immortal time with-
out end.

MATRONS. Receive her, Lord. Amen.

Dicat amen

D
I
C
A
T
*A*spice, nupta Deo, quae sit tibi gloria terris;
quae maneant caelis, aspice, nupta Deo.
*M*unera laeta capis, festiva fulgida taedis;
ecce venit sponsus, munera laeta capis.
*E*t nova dulcisono modularis carmina plectro,
sponsa, hymno exultans et nova dulcisono.
*N*ullus ab altithrono comitatu segregat Agni,
quam affectu tulerat nullus ab altithrono.

QUICUMQUE VIAM CUPIT IRE SALUTIS.

Let Him Say Amen

<D>
<I>
<C>
<A>
<T>
O bride of God, observe what glory you have on earth;
what glories remain for you in heaven, O bride of God, observe.
You are acquiring blessed gifts, shining festive with torches;
look, your bridegroom is arriving, you are acquiring blessed gifts.
And new songs on a sweet-sounding lyre you sing,
O spouse, rejoicing in a hymn and new songs on a sweet-sounding lyre.
From the high-throned companionship of the Lamb no one separates you;
no one ever deprived you of affection from the high-throned.

LET HIM SAY AMEN, WHOEVER WISHES TO TRAVEL THE ROAD OF SALVATION.

Iohannes, sive tituli in libro apocalypsis

1

Iohannes caelum virgo vidit patefactum
et nitido rerum Patrem solio residentem,
ordine bis duodenorum pulchro seniorum
stipatum, claris qui praefulsere coronis,
omnes induti vestes candoris opimi.
Vidit et in dextra Regis librum residentis,
secretum cuius potis est vir cernere nullus.
Angelus hic, dignum quaerens, non repperit ullum,
solvere qui clausi posset signacula libri.

2

Istec Iohannem consolatur lacrimantem,
Agnum solvendis aptum testando sigillis.

3

Ecce, patent Agno libri secreta perempto;
cui mox caelicolae laudem proni cecinere.

John, or Inscriptions for the Book of the Apocalypse

1

John: the virgin saw the sky opened up and the Father of everything sitting on a shining throne, surrounded by a beautiful row of twice twelve elders, who dazzled in their bright crowns, all dressed in garments of a splendid whiteness. And he saw in the right hand of the seated King a book, whose secret no man is able to discern. The angel here, seeking a worthy man, does not find anyone who can undo the seals of the closed book.

2

Here he consoles the weeping John by affirming that the Lamb is the appropriate one to undo the seals.

3

See here, the secrets of the book are revealed to the slain Lamb; to him then the heavenly host, bowing down, sang praise.

4

En, testes, clara clamantes voce sub ara,
accipiunt vestes nitido candore micantes.

5

Angelus a solis veniens ortu rutilantis
designat Regis servos in fronte perennis.

6

Post haec candidulas aspexit stare catervas,
Agnum laudantes palmas manibusque ferentes.

7

Ecce, silent media caeli cives velut hora.

8

Hic iuxta sacram cum turibulo stetit aram,
et tulit incensum, signans sacra vota piorum.

9

En, mulier pulchre fulget, circumdata sole,
bis senum nitida stellarum compta corona;
cuius vult natum serpens sorbere tenellum.

4

Look here, the martyrs, clamoring in a resounding voice below the altar, receive garments sparkling with a shining whiteness.

5

An angel coming from the rising of the glowing sun places a mark on the forehead of the servants of the eternal King.

6

Next, John observed the crowds standing there covered in white, praising the Lamb and carrying palm fronds in their hands.

7

See here, the citizens of heaven are silent for about half an hour.

8

Here the angel stood with a censer next to the sacred altar, and he bore incense, which signifies the sacred prayers of the pious.

9

Look here, a woman shines beautifully, surrounded by the sun, adorned with a shining crown of twice six stars; the serpent wants to swallow her tender little son. But the dragon

Sed draco proteritur, puer ad Dominumque levatur,
et draco de caelo cecidit proiectus in arva.

10

Hic Agnum stantem supra Syon aspice montem
et nova virgineum modulantem cantica coetum.

11

Haec fera congreditur sanctis, virtute draconis.
Quam prostravit equo Verax egressus in albo;
iste ligat veterem sub Tartara saeva draconem.

12

En, vitae libri mortisque tenentur aperti,
et surgent vivi, fuerant qui morte soluti,
quis sua pro meritis dantur mox praemia cunctis.

is trampled underfoot, and the boy is raised up to the Lord, and the dragon fell from heaven, hurled headlong to the ground.

10

See here the Lamb standing on Mount Sion, and a group of the chaste singing new songs.

11

This wild beast with the power of the dragon attacks the holy men. The one called True, carried on a white horse, defeated it; he bound the ancient dragon under savage Tartarus.

12

Look here, the books of life and death are held open, and those people will arise living who had been undone by death; to all of them proper rewards will soon be given, according to their merits.

BOOK THREE

LIBER TERTIUS

Praefatio ad gesta Ottonis

Gerbergae illustri abbatissae, cui, pro sui eminentia probitatis, haud minor obsequela venerationis quam pro insigni regalis stemmate generositatis, Hrotsvit Gandeshemensis, ultima ultimarum sub huiusmodi personae dominio militantium, quod famula herae.

2 O mea domina, quae rutilanti spiritalis varietate sapien-
tiae perlucetis, non pigescat vestri almitiem perlustrare
3 quod vestra confectum si ignoratis ex iussione. Id quidem
oneris mihi imposuistis, ut gesta Caesaris augusti, quae nec
auditu umquam affatim valui colligere, metrica percurrerem
4 ratione. In huius sudore progressionis, quantum meae insci-
5 tiae difficultatis obstiterit, ipsa coniicere potestis, quia haec
eadem nec prius scripta repperi, nec ab aliquo digestim sufficienterque dicta elicere quivi. Sed veluti si aliquis nescius ignoti per latitudinem saltus esset iturus, ubi omnis semita nivali densitate velaretur obducta; hicque nullo duce, sed solo praemonstrantium nutu inductus. Nunc per devia erraret, nunc recti tramitem callis improvise incurreret, donec tandem, emensa arboreae medietate spissitudinis, locum

BOOK 3

Preface to the Deeds of Otto

To the illustrious abbess Gerberga, to whom reverent obedience is owed no less for the eminence of her goodness than for the distinguished lineage of her regal nobility, I, Hrotsvit of Gandersheim, the lowest of the low among those enlisted under the authority of this illustrious person, offer what a servant ought to offer to her lady.

O my mistress, you who shine forth in the dazzling diver- 2
sity of your spiritual wisdom, may it not distress your grace
to examine that which you are not unaware was compiled
at your command. Indeed, you imposed on me the burden 3
of surveying in metrical form our august emperor's deeds,
which I have never been able adequately to gather from oral
sources. In the effort of advancing this agenda, you can 4
yourself imagine how great a difficulty confronted my igno-
rance, because I have not found a prior written account of 5
these things, nor have I been able to elicit from anyone a spoken account that was orderly and sufficient. But I have been just like some inexperienced man who was about to travel across the breadth of an unfamiliar woodland, where every path was veiled, covered by dense snow; and this man was led onward not by any guide, but solely by gestures from people pointing the way. Sometimes he would wander through backroads, sometimes he would unwittingly stumble upon the trail of the right path, until finally, having traversed the midpoint of this wooded thicket, he would find a

optatae comprehenderet quietis. Illicque gradum figens, ul-
terius progredi non praesumeret, usque dum vel alio super-
6 veniente induceretur, vel praecedentis vestigia subsequere-
tur. Haud aliter ego magnificarum prolixitatem rerum iussa
ingredi, regalium multiplicitatem gestorum, nutando et
vacillando aegerrime, transcurri. Hisque admodum lassata,
competenti in loco pausando, silesco, nec augustalis pro-
7 ceritatem excellentiae sine ducatu appono subire. Si enim
facundissimis disertissimorum sententiis, quas vel modo
scriptas, vel ocius de his rebus, non dubito, fore scribendas,
fuerim animata, fortasse nanciscerer unde mei rusticitas ve-
8 laretur aliquantisper. Nunc autem omne latus tanto magis
caret defensione, quanto minus ulla fulcitur auctoritate.
Unde etiam vereor me temeritatis argui, tendiculasque mul-
torum non devitare convicii, eo quod pomposis facetae
urbanitatis exponenda eloquentiis praesumpserim dehones-
9 tare, inculti vilitate sermonis. Si tamen sanae mentis exa-
men accesserit, quae res recte pensare non nescit, quanto
sexus fragilior scientiaque minor, tanto venia erit facilior;
praesertim cum si meae praesumptionis, sed vestrum causa
iussionis, huius stamen opusculi coeperim ordiri.

place of welcome rest. And planting his foot there, he would
not presume to go further, until either he was led by some-
one chancing upon him, or he could follow the tracks of 6
someone leading the way. In precisely this fashion, having
been ordered to enter upon a vast expanse of magnificent
things, I have worked my way through a multiplicity of royal
exploits, tottering and faltering with great difficulty. And
now quite worn out thereby, pausing in a suitable place, I
will grow silent, and I will not make an effort to approach
the nobility of his august excellence without guidance. But 7
if someday I should be inspired by the most eloquent state-
ments of the most articulate persons, statements which
have either already been written, or which, I do not doubt,
will very soon be written about these things, perhaps then
I may acquire the resources whereby my rusticity may be,
to some extent, veiled. Now, however, all of my flanks are 8
greatly in need of defending, since they are unsupported by
any authority. Hence, I also fear that I will be accused of au-
dacity, and that I will not be able to avoid the snares of many
men's reproaches, alleging that I have presumed to defile, by
the vileness of my uncultivated language, things that ought
to be expounded in the splendid eloquence of refined
urbanity. If, nevertheless, the judgment of a sane mind will 9
approach this matter, a mind which is not ignorant of how
to weigh the circumstances correctly, to the extent that my
gender is weaker and my knowledge inferior, so much the
more easily will forgiveness be granted; and this is especially
the case since it was not because of my presumption, but
because of your command, that I began to spin the thread of
this little work.

10 Cur tamen aliorum iudicia formido? Quae vestri solummodo censurae, si quid fefelli, obnoxia existo? Vel cur nequeam devitare convicia? Quae solummodo silentio studere debeo, ne, si seriem pro sui vilitate nulli ostendendam velim propalari, merito omnium succumbam reprehensioni. Vestro autem, vestrique familiarissimi, cui hanc rusticitatem sanxistis praesentatum iri, scilicet archipraesulis Wilhelmi, iudicio, quoquomodo factum sit, aestimandum relinquo.

Yet, why do I fear the judgments of others? I am liable to your censure alone, if I have failed in any respect. Or why should I not be able to avoid reproaches? I need only to practice silence to avoid the condemnation of everyone, which would be merited if I wished a text to be published that ought to be shown to no one because of its vileness. But to your judgment, and to the judgment of your very particular friend, to whom you have decreed that this rustic composition will be presented, namely Archbishop William, I leave this work, however it has turned out, to be evaluated.

<Prologus ad Ottonem I imperatorem>

Pollens imperii regnator Caesariani,
Oddo, qui Regis pietate favente perennis,
in sceptris augustalis praeclarus honoris,
Augustos omnes superas pietate priores,
quem plures gentes passim metuunt habitantes,
muneribus variis Romanus donat et orbis!
Exiguum munus ne spernas carminis huius,
iste sed oblatus laudum placeat tibi census.
Quem postrema gregis solvit tibi Gandeshemensis,
quem dulcis patrum collegit cura tuorum,
continuumque tibi debet studium famulandi.
Forsan gestorum plures scripsere tuorum,
et sunt scripturi post haec insignia multi.
Sed non exemplum quisquam mihi praebuit horum,
nec scribenda prius scripti docuere libelli.
Causa sed est operis tantum devotio mentis,
haec et ad audendum suadebat opus metuendum.
Nam sat formido, quod gesta tui modulando
incaute sim falsa sequens, non vera retexens:
sed non hoc suasit mala mis praesumptio mentis
nec summa veri contempta sponte fefelli.
Sed res, ut scripsi, sese sic prorsus habere,
ipsi dicebant, mihi qui scribenda ferebant.
Hinc, augustalis pietas non spernat honoris,
quod supplex humilis gessit devotio mentis.

Prologue to Emperor Otto I

O powerful ruler of the empire of the Caesars, Otto, who through the kindly favor of the eternal King, brilliant in the sovereignty of your imperial honor, surpass all previous emperors in piety, many people, living in diverse places, revere you, and the Roman world confers manifold gifts on you! Do not reject the meager gift of this poem; rather, this tribute of praises I offer ought to please you. The lowest member of the flock at Gandersheim pays you this tribute, the flock which the sweet care of your parents brought together, and which owes you its unending efforts to be of service. It may be that a great many men have written about the distinctions of your deeds, and many in the future are going to write of them. But no one provided me a transcript of these things, nor have books previously written taught me what ought to be written. The only reason for this work is the devotion of my heart, and this devotion persuaded me to hazard a work which I ought to have feared. For I am quite afraid that in versifying your deeds I may be incautiously following what is false, not recounting what is true: but no evil presumption of my mind persuaded me to do this, nor have I willingly erred, despising the full extent of the truth. Rather, the men who told me what to write have themselves asserted that the facts are precisely as I have written them. For this reason, the kindness of your imperial distinction should not reject what the suppliant devotion of a humble

Et, cum te libri laudantes congrue multi
post haec scribantur meritoque placere probentur:
ordine postremus non sit tamen iste libellus,
quem prius exemplo constat scriptum fore nullo.
Et, licet imperii teneas decus Octaviani,
non dedigneris vocitari nomine regis,
donec, perscripto vitae regalis honore,
ordine digesto necnon sermone decoro
dicatur sceptri decus imperiale secundi.

heart has brought you. And, although many books appropriately praising you may be written in the future, and may deservedly prove to be pleasing, nevertheless, this little book of mine should not be the last in your ranking, for it is certain that it was written earlier, without any model. And, even though you now hold the distinction of Octavian's imperial power, you should not disdain to be referred to by the name of king until such time as the imperial distinction of your second scepter may be told in orderly arrangement and in beautiful language, now that the glory of your time as king has been written.

<Prologus ad Ottonem II imperatorem>

Oddo, Romani praefulgens gemmula regni,
Oddonis flos augusti splendens venerandi,
cui Rex altithronus perpes quoque Filius eius
praestitit imperium pollens in vertice rerum:
vilem ne spernas vilis textum monialis.
Quem praesentari, si digneris reminisci,
ipse tui claris iussisti nuper ocellis.
Et cum perspicias maculis sordescere crebris,
ad celerem tanto veniam mox pronior esto
in monstrando tuis quantum plus pareo iussis.
Si tis praecepto non urgerer metuendo,
non foret ullomodo mihimet fiducia tanta,
ut tibi praesentis scrutandum rusticitatis
auderem satis exiguum praeferre libellum.
Qui praestante Deo patri subiunctus in aula
ipsius et monitis promptus parere paternis
par decus imperii retines concorditer ampli
comportans dextra sceptrum regale tenella.
Sed quia te memini sublimiter assimilari
nato famosi regis David Salomoni,
qui, genitore suo praesente iubenteque sancto,
optata regnum suscepit pace paternum,
ipsius exemplo te contentum fore spero.
Qui, cum regnando resideret in arce superba,
prudenter legum condens decreta sacrarum

Prologue to Emperor Otto II

Otto, most precious gem of the Roman realm, shining forth, splendid flower of the venerable emperor Otto, to whom the King enthroned on high, and also his eternal Son, provided a powerful empire at the head of the world: do not reject the lowly writing of a lowly nun. You yourself, if you deign to recall, recently ordered it to be laid before your brilliant eyes. And when you see it is marred by frequent faults, you should be, then, all the more ready to grant a swift pardon, the more obedient I am to your commands in showing it to you. If I were not urged on by fear of your order, I would in no way have such confidence as to dare to offer for your perusal this very meager little book in its present rusticity. You, by God's will, joined to your father in his palace, and ready to obey his paternal admonitions, harmoniously hold an equal glory of vast imperial power, carrying the royal scepter in your tender young hand. But since I recall that you have been sublimely compared to Solomon, the son of the renowned king David, who, while his saintly father was still present and giving orders, received his father's kingdom in welcome peace, I hope you will be content to follow Solomon's example. When he was sitting on the lofty citadel, ruling as king, prudently establishing the decrees of

ac penetrans animo rerum secreta profundo,
nunc libet et minimis mentem laxare rimandis.
Sed nec conflictum fastidit rite duarum
solvere iudicii celeri discrimine recti,
prolem restitui verae mandans genetrici.
Hinc, supplex te posco quidem, nostrum Salomonem,
ut, licet imperii tenearis sollicitandi
cura, digneris tamen et propriae monialis
ludendo seriem nunc lectitare recentem;
quo male compositis verbis mox decidat omnis
rusticitas oris de tractibus imperialis
nominis, et titulo signata tui venerando
despectus nimia meriti tueantur ab aura.

sacred laws, and penetrating the secrets of nature with his profound intelligence, sometimes he was pleased to ease his mind by examining even the most insignificant things. But rightly, he did not shrink from resolving the conflict of the two women by a swift decision of proper justice, ordering that the child be restored to his true mother. For this reason indeed, as a suppliant I ask you, our own Solomon, that although you are detained by your concern for an anxiety-provoking empire, nevertheless you should consider it proper now, in your leisure, also to read attentively this new narrative by your own nun, so that all the rusticity of speech caused by the badly composed words may soon fall away from these discourses on your imperial fame, and bearing the seal of approval of your venerable title, they may be safe from too strong a blast of well-deserved scorn.

<Gesta Ottonis>

Postquam Rex regum, qui solus regnat in aevum,
per se cunctorum transmutans tempora regum
iussit Francorum transferri nobile regnum
ad claram gentem Saxonum (nomen habentem
a "saxo" per duritiam mentis bene firmam),
filius Oddonis magni ducis et venerandi,
scilicet Henricus, suscepit regia primus
iusto pro populo moderamine sceptra gerenda.
Hic pollens quantae fuerat bonitatis honore,
et quanta populos rexit pietate subactos,
qualiter et reges meritis tunc temporis omnes
praeminet eximiis, excedit denique vilis
huius carminuli textum, nimium vitiosi.
Nam fuit immitis reprobis, blandus quoque iustis,
summo conservans studio legalia iura,
aequa satis meritis reddens quoque praemia cunctis.
Huic rex pacificus dederat de sidere Christus
eius civilem vitae per tempora pacem.
Omine felici, tenuit quoque culmina regni,
ni fallor, denos labentis temporis annos
necnon bis ternos, multum feliciter actos,
corregnante sua Mathilda coniuge clara.
Cui nunc in regno non compensabitur ulla,
quae posset meritis illam superare supremis.

The Deeds of Otto

After the King of Kings, who alone reigns forever, transforming of his own accord the tenures of all kings, ordered that the noble kingdom of the Franks be transferred to the glorious Saxon people (who take their name from the word "rock" because of the very firm hardness of their minds), then the son of Oddo, the great and venerable duke, namely Henry, was the first to take up the royal scepter, bearing it with moderation for the benefit of a righteous people.

He was powerful in the excellence of so much goodness, and ruled his subject peoples with so much kindness, and so far surpasses all the kings of that time in his outstanding merits that he transcends, in fact, the account of this paltry little poem, which is highly deficient. For he was firm with the wicked and tender with the just, preserving legal rights with the greatest energy, and also distributing quite equitable rewards to all, according to their merits. From heaven, Christ the peace-bringing king had granted to him civil peace throughout his lifetime. Under happy auspices, he held the highest authority in his kingdom, if I am not mistaken, while a period of ten years passed away, and six more as well, years very happily lived, with his illustrious wife Mathilda ruling alongside him. There is no woman now in the kingdom comparable to her, none able to surpass Mathilda in lofty merits.

Trina quibus Deitas dederat tres denique natos,
iam tunc felici disponendo pie genti,
ne post Henrici mortem regis venerandi,
imperium regni male surriperent scelerosi,
hi sed regalis nati de germine stirpis
rexissent regnum concordi pace paternum,
quamvis dissimiles his servarentur honores,
binis regnanti subiectis, scilicet, uni.

Inter quos primus fulsit ceu lucifer ortus
Oddo micans radiis nimium clarae bonitatis,
gratia quem Regis, solita pietate, perennis
rectorem plebi praevidit rite fideli.
Hic aetate prior fuerat, meritis quoque maior,
congruus et sceptris defuncto patre gerendis.
Non opus est verbis eius summam probitatis
dicere vel pueri meritum laudabile tanti.
Cui Christus talem iam nunc augessit honorem,
possidet ut Romam pollenti iure superbam,
quae semper stabilis summum fuerat caput orbis.
Edomat et gentes, Christo favente, feroces,
quae prius Ecclesiam laniabant saepe sacratam.
Post hunc, Henricus fuerat feliciter ortus,
impositoque patris famosus nomine regis.
Provida quem Domini pariter sapientia Christi
dignatur servare ducem populo bene fortem,
belliger ut fortis, belli doctissimus artis,
fortiter Ecclesiam praemuniret venerandam,
ceu murus iaculis obstans fortissimus hostis.
Post hunc, Ecclesiae pastor Brun nascitur almae.
Gratia pontificis quem duxit summa perennis
dignum catholici curam gestare popelli.

To Henry and Mathilda the triune Deity, already then making kindly arrangements for this fortunate people, had given, indeed, three sons, so that after the death of the venerable King Henry, wicked men might not wrongfully seize power in the kingdom, but, instead, these sons sprung of royal stock might rule their father's kingdom in peaceful concord, even though they were to have unequal honors, that is, two of them would be subordinate to the one who was ruling.

First among them, Otto shone forth like the morning star arisen, sparkling with the rays of a most illustrious goodness, Otto, whom the grace of the eternal King, in his accustomed mercy, duly provided as ruler for the faithful people. He was the first in age, also the greatest in merits, and suited to bearing the scepter when his father had died. There is no need to explain in words the sum of his goodness or the laudable merit of such a child. Christ has already now begun enhancing him with such dignity that he controls with powerful justice haughty Rome, which has always been the supreme head of the orderly world. And, with Christ's aid, Otto is taming fierce peoples, who often in the past tore apart the sacred Church. After him, Henry was happily born, and he was renowned because the name of his father, the king, was given to him. In like manner, the provident wisdom of Christ the Lord rightly saw fit to preserve him as a brave leader for his people, so that as a brave warrior, supremely trained in the arts of war, he might bravely protect the venerable Church, like the bravest bulwark opposing the enemy's weapons. After him, Bruno was born, a shepherd for the blessed Church. The supreme grace of Christ the eternal priest considered him worthy to take care

Hinc quoque divino nutu patris pia cura
ipsum servitio Christi fecit religari,
abstractum gremio carae nutricis amando,
ut regni pompis posset constare relictis
miles stelligera semper Regnantis in aula.
At Christus, Patris sapientia vera perennis,
tironem refovendo suum clementius istum,
ipsi dona dedit tantae praeclara sophiae,
quod non est illo penitus sapientior ullus
inter mortales fragilis mundi sapientes.

His igitur pueris regali more nutritis
ipsorum patri famoso denique regi
Henrico placuit (factis quod rite replevit),
ut, vitae calidas sospes dum carperet auras,
ipse suo primogenito regique futuro
Oddoni dignam iam disponsaret amicam,
quae propriae proli digne posset sociari.
Hanc non in proprio voluit conquirere regno,
trans mare legatos sed transmisit bene cautos
gentis ad Anglorum terram sat deliciosam,
demandans ut continuo, cum munere misso,
Aeduuardi regis natam peterent Eaditham.
Quae patre defuncto iam tunc residebat in aula,
fratre suo regni sceptrum gestante paterni,
quem peperit regi consors non inclita regni.
Istius egregiae genetrix clarissima domnae,
altera sed generis mulier satis inferioris.

Haec nam versiculis proles quam scriptito regis,
haec, inquam, fama cunctis fuerat bene nota:
nobilitate potens, primis meritis quoque pollens,
edita magnorum summo de germine regum.

of a Christian population. For this reason also, with divine approval, the kindly concern of his father had him bound to the service of Christ, removed from the beloved breast of his dear nurse, so that after he had left behind the pomp of his father's kingdom, he might be a soldier in the starry palace of the One who rules forever. But Christ, who is the true wisdom of the eternal Father, very mercifully nurturing this young recruit of his, gave him illustrious gifts of such understanding, that there is no one more thoroughly wise than he among the mortal sages of this frail world.

So, after these boys had been raised in royal fashion, it then pleased their renowned father King Henry (and he duly carried it out by his actions), that, while he himself was still alive, enjoying the warm breezes of life, he would already betroth to his firstborn son, the future king Otto, a worthy companion who could worthily be united to his own child. He did not want to look for her in his own realm, but sent suitably circumspect legates across the sea to the very agreeable land of the nation of the Angles, ordering that straightaway, with the gift he was sending, they ask for Edith, the daughter of King Edward. She was at that time, after her father's death, already living in the palace, since her brother held the scepter of their father's realm, her brother whom an ignoble consort had borne to the king of the realm. The mother of this excellent Lady Edith was most illustrious, but the other consort was a woman of quite inferior lineage.

Now, this descendant of the king about whom I write these little verses, she, I say, was well known to all by reputation: strong in nobility, mighty also in the finest merits, born from the highest line of great kings. Her serene face was of

Cuius praeclaro facies candore serena
regalis formae miro rutilabat honore.
Ipsaque perfectae radiis fulgens bonitatis
in patria talis meruit praeconia laudis,
ut fore iudicio plebis decernitur omnis
optima cunctarum, quae tunc fuerant, mulierum.
Nec mirum meritis si lucebat bene primis,
germen sanctorum quam producebat avorum.
Hanc tradunt ergo natam de stirpe beata
Oswaldi regis, laudem cuius canit orbis,
se quia subdiderat morti pro nomine Christi.
At regis nostri venientes denique missi
ad fratrem domnae iam tunc residentis in arce
illi nudabant quaecumque secreta ferebant.
Quae sibi percerte comperta satis placuere,
moxque suae dulci narrabat voce sorori
exhortans illam regi parere fideli,
illam qui propriae proli voluit sociari.
Cumque suae monitis menti instillaret amicis
Oddonis dulcem, pueri regalis, amorem,
colligit innumeras summo conamine gazas.
Ast ubi collecti visum fuerat satis ipsi,
praedictam sociis domnam comitantibus aptis
trans mare percerte summo direxit honore
condonans illi gazas nimium pretiosas.
Necnon germanam secum transmisit Adivam,
quae fuit aetatis meriti pariterque minoris,
quo sic maiorem prorsus conferret honorem
Oddoni, nato famosi regis amando,
egregiae binas stirpis mittendo puellas,

shining whiteness and glowed with the wondrous distinction of regal beauty. And resplendent with the rays of perfect goodness, she earned in her fatherland proclamations of such praise, that she was perceived in the judgment of all the people to be the best of all women then alive. And it is no surprise if she shone brightly with the finest merits, she whom a lineage of holy ancestors produced. For they say that she was born from the blessed line of King Oswald, whose praise the whole world sings, because he surrendered himself in death for the name of Christ.

But the legates of our king, coming then to the brother of the lady, who was already at that time living in the castle, exposed to him whatever secret messages they were bearing. What he learned certainly pleased him very much, and soon he spoke to his sister in a sweet voice, encouraging her to obey this trustworthy king, who wished to make her a companion for his own child. And while he was instilling in her heart by his friendly advice a sweet love for the royal child Otto, he gathered with great effort countless treasures. And when it seemed to him that enough had been gathered, he sent the aforementioned lady in the company of suitable companions across the sea, certainly with great honor, granting her those treasures so precious. Likewise, he sent her sister along with her, Adiva, who was inferior both in age and in merit, so that he could confer an altogether greater honor on Otto, the beloved son of the renowned king, by sending two girls of excellent lineage, so

ut sibi, quam vellet, sponsam licito sociaret.
Aspecto primo sed mox Eadit veneranda,
iure placens cunctis habitu summae bonitatis,
regali nato censetur congrue digna.
Haec illi dulcem peperit clarissima prolem
nomine Liudulfum tantis genitoribus aptum.
Quem populus merito dilexit amore tenello,
exoptans prolongari vitam satis ipsi.
    Istis sic habitis, instabat denique finis
Henrici regis. Cuius mortem gemit omnis
illius imperio populus iurique subactus.
Quo nam defuncto regnum susceperat Oddo,
eiusdem primogenitus regis venerandus;
et voto cuncti iam respondente popelli
unguitur in regem, Christo praestante, potentem.
Cui Rex gratiolae caeli munuscula tantae
contulit, ut digne cunctis celeberrimus ipse,
gestorum reges fama praecelleret omnes,
oceanus refluis quos nam circumfluit undis.
Insuper, e tantis ipsum sacra dextra Potentis
protegit insidiis occulta fraude paratis,
et tam magnificis ornat persaepe triumphis,
ut credas regem David regnare fidelem
iam nunc, antiquis fulgentem rite triumphis.
Nec solum gentes frenis moderat bonitatis,
quae prius imperio patris dederant sua colla,
sed multo plures certe sibi vindicat ipse
subdens gentiles Christi servis nationes,
quo pax Ecclesiae fieret stabilita sacratae.
Ad bellum certe quoties processerat ipse,
non fuerat populus quamvis virtute superbus,

that Otto might lawfully join to himself as a spouse whichever he chose. But then, at first sight, the venerable Edith, who was rightly pleasing to all on account of the supreme goodness of her nature, was appropriately judged worthy of the royal son. This most illustrious woman bore him a sweet child, Liudolf by name, a fitting child for such parents. The people rightly cherished him with a tender love, desiring that his life be extended for a very long time.

These things occurred as I have described, and then the end of King Henry was at hand. All the people subject to his power and justice mourned his death. But after he died, Otto, the venerable firstborn of that same king, took control of the kingdom; and at once in accordance with the desire of the entire population, he was anointed, by Christ's provision, as a mighty king. On him the King of heaven conferred precious gifts of such beloved grace that he was rightly the most celebrated of men in all respects, and he exceeded in the fame of his deeds all the kings whom the ocean with its flowing waves now flows around. Additionally, the sacred right hand of the Almighty protected him from great treacheries prepared with hidden deceit and adorned him so often with such magnificent triumphs that you would think that even now it is the faithful King David ruling, rightfully illustrious from his ancient triumphs. Not only did he control under the reins of his goodness those nations which had earlier subjected their necks to the authority of his father, but he certainly claimed for himself many more, making pagan tribes subject to the servants of Christ, so that there would be stable peace for the holy Church. Certainly, whenever he himself went to war, there was not a nation, however proud they might be of their strength,

laedere qui posset vel exsuperare valeret
ipsum celestis fultum solamine Regis.
Eius nec cessit telis exercitus ullis,
ni sua spernendo, forsan, regalia iussa,
illic pugnaret quo rex idem prohiberet.
At dux Henricus, frater regis venerandus,
princeps in regno fuerat tunc nempe quieto
post regem, plebi merito venerabilis omni.
Qui sibi condigne legali iunxit amore
Arnulfi natam, ducis egregii, generosam
nomine Iudittam, vultus splendore coruscam,
ac fulgore magis cunctae nitidam bonitatis.
His ita digestis, fuerat pax undique nostris
ad tempus modicum libitoque minus populorum,
bellorum certe saevo clangore tacente.
O quam tranquillum ridens deduceret aevum
fortunata satis nostrae res publica gentis,
quae nimis imperio regis regitur sapientis,
si non antiqui mala calliditas inimici
turbaret nostrum secreta fraude serenum!
Denique devictis aligenorum bene telis
exoritur nostris subito discordia fortis,
laeserat et plebem bellum civile fidelem
plus quam bellorum structura frequens variorum.
Huius causa mali fuerat non parva dolendi
denique conflictus quorundam non moderatus.
Ex quibus Henrico quaedam pars mente benigna
devovit regis fratri ius vernulitatis,
pars Evurhardo comiti studium famulandi.
At cum quisque sui peteret solamina domni,
hinc gravior dominis discordia nascitur ipsis.

which could wound him, or which was powerful enough to conquer that man who was supported by the aid of the heavenly King. His army did not yield to anyone's weapons, unless, perhaps, ignoring his royal orders, it was fighting in a place where the king himself had prohibited it to go.

But Duke Henry, the esteemed brother of the king, was at that time the first citizen in this peaceful kingdom—first after the king, that is—and he was deservedly respected by all the people. He worthily joined to himself in lawful love a noble daughter of the excellent duke Arnulf, Judith by name, brilliant in the splendor of her face, and even more shining from the brilliance of her complete goodness. These things were accomplished as I have described, then there was peace on all sides for our people for a short time, and for a shorter time than the people would have liked, while the savage clang of wars, assuredly, was silent.

Oh, what a peaceful age the happily flourishing government of our people would have experienced, ruled by command of a very wise king, if the wicked cunning of the ancient enemy had not disturbed our serenity with his hidden deceit! And then, after the weapons of foreigners were effectively vanquished, a powerful discord suddenly rose up in our ranks, and civil war wounded our faithful people more than the constant waging of various external wars had done. Now the cause of this grievous wickedness was not a small one; it was an unrestrained conflict between certain individuals. Among them one faction with kindly intention promised to Henry, the king's brother, their oath of vassalage, and one faction promised to Count Eberhard their eagerness to serve. But since each faction attempted to aid its own lord, thereby a more serious discord was generated

Tandem percerte conflictu progrediente,
praedictus praeses male collectas legiones
mox ad castellum Baduliki capiendum
ex improviso mittens sub nocte nigella,
duxit captivum fratrem regis generosum,
Henricum, vinclis palmas stringendo cruentis
eius candidolas, ornamentis magis aptas.
Atque suas gazas disperdens innumerosas,
ad sua mox prolem secum deduxit herilem,
utitur ut socio proprii domini quoque nato.
Quo rex comperto, maerens sub corde secreto,
deflevit tristis nimium miserabile factum.
Vix quoque germani damnum patiens grave cari,
nobile mox Abrahae factum sequitur patriarchae,
quod miserans egit dum Loth ex hoste redemit.
Militibusque suis summo conamine lectis,
necnon immodica tota de gente caterva,
pompa regali pergit solamina fratri
ferre sub ingenti cordis languore dolentis.
Nec mora, quem venit fratrem refovere redemit,
auctores tanti condemnavitque piacli,
suspendens quosdam ligno reprobis reparato,
quosdam de patria mandans discedere cara.
His bene dispositis regis iussu sapientis,
protulit antiqui rursum mala fraus inimici
inventum sceleris primo mage deterioris,
cunctis horrendum saeclis meritoque stupendum.
Denique, praedictus postquam rediens Evurhardus
praeses ab exilio patriam remeabat amandam,
hoc sibi gratiola regis praestante benigna.
Gislberhto comiti vinclis sociatus amoris

between the lords themselves. Finally, when the conflict was well and truly underway, the aforementioned leader Eberhard hastily sent his maliciously collected troops to take the castle of Belecke by surprise on a darkish night, and he led away as a captive the noble brother of King Otto (that is, Henry), binding with cruel chains his delicate white hands, which were more suited to jewelry. And plundering his countless treasures, he then led that noble scion away with him to his own lands, treating as an enemy the son of his own lord. When King Otto discovered this, grieving in his inmost heart, he wept sadly over this most pitiable deed. And scarcely enduring the grievous loss of his beloved brother, he soon followed the noble action of the patriarch Abraham, performed in pity when he redeemed Lot from the enemy. With his soldiers, chosen with the greatest care, and with no small crowd drawn from the whole nation, Otto set out in a royal procession to bring relief to his royal brother, under the great affliction of an aching heart. Without delay, he redeemed the brother he came to rescue, and he condemned the authors of that great crime, hanging some of them from a wooden scaffold prepared for the wicked, and ordering some to go into exile from their beloved fatherland.

When the wise king had duly settled these things by his orders, the wicked treachery of the ancient enemy brought forth anew a criminal scheme, this one far worse than the first one, a scheme which will terrify and amaze future ages. Indeed, after returning from exile, the aforementioned leader Eberhard came again to his beloved fatherland, the kindly grace of the king providing him this opportunity. He allied himself to Count Gilbert by bonds of

consilium dederat (quod non tibi, Christe, placebat),
ut caperent iustum regem, Domini benedictum,
et quod plus, iusto non iustam vim faciendo
illum mox proprio deprivarent male regno.
Hoc quoque consilium perversa mente repertum
Henrico regis fratri suasere fidelis,
mulcentes nimium verbis ipsum male blandis,
quo prius illatum nollet iam reddere damnum,
ipsorum votis sed plus parendo nefandis
susciperet regnum depulso fratre regendum.
Qui male blanditis tandem victus suadelis
(pro dolor!), ipsorum se promisit fore promptum
votis ac firmis hoc confirmaverat orsis.
Sed spero certe non se sic corde tenere,
illis consensum sed vi praebere coactum.
Qui male namque spei vacuae solamine capti
sperabant regem populos olim dominantem
ipsorum fragili citius subiungere iuri.
Sed Rex de caelis, iudex aequissimus orbis,
cunctorum solus qui cognoscit cogitatus,
vanaque mortalis potis est disperdere cordis,
commentum tanti sceleris virtute potentis
dextrae confregit, qua cuncta creata creavit.
Scilicet, insidias christo Domini reparatas
vertit in auctores tanti meritoque piacli.
Quique suo laqueos domino tendere malignos,
ex ipsis ipsi primum sunt illaqueati.

Non me plus licito tantae sophiae fore iacto,
ut sperem plene verbis edicere posse,
quanta gratiolae Christus virtute supernae
saepius hunc ipsum regem digne benedictum

love and offered him a plan (which was not pleasing to you, Christ), to seize the just king whom the Lord had blessed and, what is more, by doing unjust violence to the just king, quickly and maliciously to deprive him of his own realm. Once they had conceived this plan in their evil minds, they also urged it on Henry, the brother of the faithful king, enticing him very wickedly with flattering words not to seek to repay the harm they had previously done him, but in compliance to their evil wishes to take the kingdom and rule, once his brother was driven out. In the end, overcome by these wickedly enticing arguments (alas!), he promised he was amenable to their desires, and he confirmed this with strong words. But I certainly hope that he did not feel this way in his heart, but was compelled by force to give his acquiescence to them. They, to be sure, wickedly deceived by the comfort of vain hope, expected quickly to subjugate to their feeble authority the king who had long ruled the people. But the King of the heavens, the fairest judge of the world, who alone knows the thoughts of all men and is able to destroy the empty hopes of a mortal heart, shattered the fiction of this great crime by the power of that mighty right hand with which he created all creation. That is to say, he turned the plots that were prepared for the anointed man of the Lord against the inventors of that great crime, and rightly so. And those who set evil traps for their lord were entrapped first themselves by their own devices.

I do not improperly claim for myself such wisdom that I could hope to be able fully to explain in words the great power of heavenly grace by which Christ so often saw to it that this same king, deservedly blessed, safely escaped

fecit multiplices salvum percurrere fraudes
necnon insidias hostili parte paratas.
Sed nec hoc fragilis fas esse reor mulieris
inter coenobii positae secreta quieti,
ut bellum dictet, quod nec cognoscere debet.
246 Haec perfectorum sunt conservanda virorum
249 sudori, quis posse dedit sapientia mentis
250 omnia compositis sapienter dicere verbis.
248 Hoc dico solum (recte quod dicere possum):
247 principium qui cunctarum finis quoque rerum,
251 qui solus semper fecit miranda potenter,
quique David regem toties de fraude fidelem
eripiens Sauli, sceptrum regni dedit ipsi,
hunc pariter regem, David pietate sequentem,
protexit de millenis persaepe periclis.
Denique, cum solus praepauco milite saeptus,
esset ab adversis circumdatus undique turmis,
insuper atque fugam propriae partis male factam
pectore maerenti ferret nimiumque dolenti,
credere nec paucis sese praesumeret ipsis
illum qui reliquis non deseruere relapsis,
saepe ratus tantum se mox graviter moriturum.
Ocius auxilii fultus virtute superni
miratur turbae se iam superare cruentae
tantas absque suae fraudes discrimine vitae.
At si forte suos pugna crescente sinistra
audivit socios letali vulnere laesos,
praedicti regis lacrimans mox utitur orsis,
quae maerens dixit, tristi cum pectore sensit
ictibus angelici populum gladii periturum.
"En, qui peccavi," dixit, "facinusque peregi;

manifold intrigues and plots laid by a hostile party. And what is more, I do not consider it the right of a frail woman living in the seclusion of a peaceful monastery to make pronouncements about war, with which she should not even be acquainted. These things should be kept for the exertions of excellent men, to whom wisdom has given the strength of mind to say everything wisely in well-composed words. I say only that which I am properly competent to say: God, who was the beginning of all things and is the end of all things, who alone has always mightily performed wondrous things, and who so many times snatched the faithful King David from the treachery of Saul and gave David the scepter of the kingdom, he likewise repeatedly protected from thousands of dangers this king of ours, who followed King David in his piety. Indeed, alone and accompanied by a very small army, Otto was surrounded on all sides by hostile troops, and since, in addition, he bore in his grieving and very mournful heart the desertion wickedly carried out by part of his own forces, and he did not presume to entrust himself to those few who did not desert him when the others slipped away, he often thought only that he was soon going to die painfully. But very quickly, supported by the power of aid from above, he was amazed that he now prevailed over that cruel mob's great treacheries, with no danger to his own life. But as this woeful battle was escalating, if he chanced to hear that his companions were wounded by a lethal injury, he then tearfully used the words of the aforesaid King David, words which he had spoken in sorrow when he perceived with a sad heart that his people were perishing by the blows of an angel's sword. "Look, it is I who have sinned," he said,

hinc ego vindictae dignus sum denique tantae!
Hi quid fecerunt, damnum qui tale tulerunt?
Iam nunc, Christe, tuis parcens miserere redemptis,
ne premat insontes iusto plus vis inimica!"
Has igitur preculas miserans, divina potestas
parcebat regis, solita pietate, ministris.
Et dedit optatum miserans ex hoste triumphum,
iusto praedictos comites examine perdens.

Ipso, namque, die quo decepti vacua spe
speravere suis constringendum fore vinclis
regem, qui merito tenuit regalia sceptra,
ex improviso praeses proruperat Udo
adducendo quidem multam secum legionem;
ac subiit validum forti luctamine bellum.
Nec mora, percussus periit gladiis Evurhardus,
Gislberhtus saevis fugiens quoque mergitur undis.
At rex interea nescit tam fortia bella
averso quidni residens in litore Reni,
nec tunc auxilii scivit solamina tanti
iam miserante deo, subito casu, sibi missa.
Denique dum pugnae sensit discrimina tantae
haud gaudens inimicorum de morte suorum,
sed plus tantorum maerens de caede virorum
sumpsit non modicum, Davidis more, lamentum,
qui super occisum doluit regem pie Saulum.

Ast ubi victores laeti venere videntes
illius fusis vultum lacrimis madefactum,
haud aptum tanto luctum dixere triumpho,
sed reddi grates Regi debere perenni,
qui tunc impleri fecit pietate fideli,

"and carried out this crime; so, it is I who deserve, in the end, such vengeance! What have these men done, these men who have suffered such destruction? Already now, Christ, have mercy, sparing those whom you have redeemed, so that the enemy's violence does not unjustly afflict the innocent!" Therefore, taking pity on these humble prayers, divine power, in its accustomed mercifulness, spared the king's ministers. And taking pity, it granted the hoped-for triumph over the enemy, destroying the aforementioned counts by a just judgment.

In fact, on that very day on which these men, deceived by empty hope, expected to shackle in their chains the king who rightly held the royal scepter, Count Udo unexpectedly burst onto the scene, leading along with him, moreover, a large legion; and with a brave effort, he entered into the mighty battle. Straightaway Eberhard perished, struck by the sword, and Gilbert, fleeing, was drowned by the savage waves. But the king meanwhile was unaware of these fierce battles, for he was encamped on the opposite shore of the Rhine, and he did not know the relief of the great assistance which was at that time, by a sudden chance, sent to him by a merciful God. Then, when he learned of the losses of that great conflict, he was not so much happy about the death of his enemies, but rather sad because of the slaughter of such great men, and he raised no small lamentation, following the example of David, who mourned piously over the killing of King Saul.

But when the happy victors came and saw Otto's face soaked in flowing tears, they said that mourning was hardly suitable for such a triumph, but they ought to give thanks to the eternal King, who had then seen fit to fulfill with

quod patet in libro regis scriptum Salomonis,
dicentis iustum de tristitia liberandum,
necnon iniustum pro iusto mox fore dandum.
His mentem regis demulcendo suadelis,
ipsum tristitiam cogunt deponere tantam,
et bene victrici congaudentem legioni,
se post bella suis blandum praebere ministris.
Qui nam laetitiam vultu monstrans moderatam,
sed clam subtristem servans in corde dolorem
reddebat grates imo de pectore Christo,
non dederat propriis ipsum quia tunc inimicis
praedam, sed dextra protegit rite superna.
Ipsius titulum tanti clarumque triumphi
non sibi, sed Christi designavit pietati.

His ita digestis, modicum tempus requievit
civilis belli populus luctamine lassus.
Sed nec sic veteris finem sumpsit dolus hostis,
qui semper fragiles temptat pervertere mentes
post factum facinus suadens superaddere peius.
Fertur percerte quorundam pectora bile
tanto pestiferi tandem penetrare veneni,
ut mortem regi vellent inferre fideli
ipsius et fratrem populo praeponere regem.
Nec timuere diem Paschae sanctum maculare,
si posset fieri, fuso cum sanguine iusti.
Sed non consensit tanti commissa piacli
Agnus paschalis, qui pro nobis redimendis
se dedit electum Patri moriens holocaustum.
Sed mox consilium cunctis nudavit eorum,
et sic insontis salvatus erat bene sanguis.
Quique rei placiti sunt inventi scelerosi,

faithful mercy what is plainly written in the book of King Solomon, who says that the just man must be delivered out of sadness, and then the unjust must be offered up instead of him. Soothing the king's mind by these encouragements, they obliged him to put aside his great sadness and, rejoicing fully in his victorious legion, to present himself calmly to his ministers after the battles. Otto, indeed, showing a modest degree of cheerfulness in his expression, but secretly maintaining a sad pain deep in his heart, gave thanks to Christ from the bottom of his heart, because Christ had not then handed him over as booty to his enemies, but had protected him as he ought with his heavenly right hand. And Otto assigned the outstanding distinction of this great triumph not to himself, but to the mercy of Christ.

These things were accomplished as I have described, and then for a short time the people rested, worn out from the struggle of civil war. But the trickery of the ancient enemy did not therefore come to an end. He always tries to pervert frail minds, encouraging them, after they have committed one crime, to add to it an even worse one. It is said, most assuredly, that he penetrated the hearts of certain men with such a bile of pestilent poison, that in the end they wanted to bring death on their faithful king and to impose his brother on the people as king. And they were not afraid to pollute the holy day of Easter, if such a thing were possible, by shedding the blood of a just man. But the paschal Lamb did not consent to the commission of such a crime, the Lamb who gave himself up for our redemption, dying as the chosen offering to his Father. Instead, he immediately exposed their plan to everyone, and thus the blood of an innocent was properly saved. And those who were found guilty

pro modulo culpae poenis damnantur amaris.
Quidam iudicio, quidni, dantur capitali,
quidam de patria longe pelluntur amanda.
  Post haec Henricus, frater regis generosus,
Christi gratiola tactus sub corde secreto
secum tractavit summoque dolore revolvit,
contra iustitiam quicquid perfecerat umquam.
Hoc quoque deflevit nimiis persaepe lamentis,
quod male blanditis horum cessit suadelis,
ipsum qui verbis corruperunt simulatis.
Sed quamvis talem ferret sub corde dolorem,
praesentare tamen, spatii per tempora longi,
non se regali praesumebat faciei.
Absens sed cordis studio florente dolentis
optabat veniae dari munus sibi dulce.
Tandem, percerte forti devictus amore,
ilico poenalem proicit de corde timorem,
et sub nocturnis nimium secreto tenebris
adveniens, in regalem se contulit urbem,
in qua natalem Regis celebrare perennis
rex pius obsequiis coepit sollemniter aptis.
Depositisque suis ornamentis pretiosis,
simplicis et tenuis fruitur velamine vestis
inter sacratos noctis venerabilis hymnos
intrans nudatis templi sacra limina plantis.
Nec horret hiemis saevum frigus furientis,
sed prono sacram vultu prostratus ad aram
corpus frigoreae sociavit nobile terrae,
sic, sic, maerentis toto conamine cordis,
optans praestari veniae munus sibi dulce.
Quo rex comperto victus pietate benigna

of the wicked plan were condemned to bitter punishments according to the extent of their guilt. Some, of course, were handed over after trial for capital punishment; some were driven far off from the beloved fatherland.

After this, Henry, the noble brother of the king, touched deep in his heart by the sweet grace of Christ, examined himself and in the greatest pain turned over in his mind everything he had ever done unjustly. And he very often, with great lamentation, wept over the fact that he had yielded to the wickedly enticing arguments of those men, who had corrupted him with their fraudulent words. But even though he bore such great pain in his heart, still he did not presume, for an extended period of time, to present himself before the face of the king. But absent, with an increasing desire in his aching heart, he hoped that the sweet gift of pardon would be given to him. In the end, clearly overcome by strong love, he suddenly cast the fear of punishment from his heart, and very secretly arriving under cover of nocturnal darkness, he brought himself into the royal city, where the pious king had solemnly begun to celebrate the birth of the eternal King with appropriate services. And having taken off his precious ornaments, he wore only a covering of simple, light cloth, and with bare feet he entered the sacred precinct of the church amid the sacred hymns of that venerable night. And he did not tremble at the savage cold of the raging winter, but with his face cast downward, prostrate at the sacred altar, he joined his noble body to the chilling earth, hoping with every effort of his grieving heart that thus, even thus, the sweet gift of pardon would be offered to him. When King Otto learned of this, overcome by kindly

instantisque memor festi cunctis venerandi,
in quo caelicolae pacem mundo cecinere,
laeti Rege suo tenera de Virgine nato,
ut pie salvaret mundum merito periturum,
pro diei tantae pacem portantis honore
condoluit miserans fratri commissa fatenti.
Atque suam pie gratiolam concessit habendam
illi cum veniae dilecto munere plenae.
Necnon post aliquot spatii tempuscula parvi
ipsius iuri proceres subiunxerat omnes
famosae nimium gentis Baioariorum,
ipsum nempe ducem merito faciendo potentem.
Et post haec ultra fuerat discordia nulla
inter eos, animis fraterno foedere iunctis.
Avaresque per hunc saevi saepissime victi
post haec Ottonis regnum regis spatiosum
non laedunt telis consueto more cruentis,
tangere nec contingentes audent nationes
ex terrore ducis tanti nimium tremefacti.
Hic quia prudentis functus valitudine mentis,
his hominum monstris bellis obstans iteratis,
ad nos pergendi calles secluserat omnes.
Insuper, et primus, Christi munimine tutus,
audenter cum subiectae plebis legione
eiusdem populi patriam petiit scelerosi
impugnans gentem cunctis retro namque rebellem.
Scilicet et spoliis rerum captis variarum,
quas sibi communes collegerunt prius hostes
orbis perplures devastantes regiones,

generosity and bearing in mind the feast day, venerable to all, that was at hand, the feast day on which the angels prophesied peace for the world, rejoicing that their King was born from a tender Virgin in order to save through his mercy a world which was rightly going to perish, he, Otto, for the honor of such a peace-bringing day, mercifully felt compassion for his brother, who admitted his mistakes. And to him Otto generously granted acceptance into his favor, along with the precious gift of a full pardon. Additionally, after some short intervals of time had passed, he subjected to Henry's authority all the noblemen of the very renowned race of Bavarians, rightly making him, in fact, their mighty duke. And after this there was no further discord between them, once their hearts were joined in a brotherly covenant.

The savage Avars, who had been frequently conquered by Henry, did not subsequently harm the vast kingdom of King Otto in their usual way with bloody weapons, and the neighboring nations did not dare to touch his realm, they were so terrified by their fear of such a duke as Henry. Because he relied on the strength of a prudent mind, obstructing these monstrous men by a series of wars, he closed off all the routes for marching against us. Furthermore, he was the first one, safely under the protection of Christ and accompanied by a legion of subject peoples, to invade the fatherland of that wicked race of Avars, attacking a nation that was previously, in fact, hostile to everyone. And indeed after Henry had taken spoils of various kinds, which our common enemies had earlier collected for themselves when they were laying waste to many regions of the world, he also

uxores procerum soboles rapuit quoque dulces.
Et sic prostratis rediit gaudens inimicis.
Istis sic habitis, properata diecula tristis
venerat ingentem nostris augendo dolorem,
in qua praefulgens meritis regina supremis
Aedit praesentis vitae discessit ab oris,
ipsius imperio genti faciens famulanti
tristitiam necnon nimium cordis cruciatum
eius in abscessu. Magno quam denique luctu,
et non immerito, flevit plebecula cuncta.
Quam plus maternae fovit pietatis amore,
quam dominatricis iussis confringeret artis.
Cui licet a Christo requiem sine fine perennem,
necnon laetitiam iustis retro reparatam,
praestari citius iam non dubitaverit ullus
(qui meritum vitae scivit laudabile castae
ipsius ac mitem, gessit quam denique, mentem),
attamen, humanae pro consuetudine causae,
non mirum, populus planctum si sumpsit amarum,
dum sibi tam subito fuerat spes tanta retracta.
Et facies domnae nimium regalis amandae,
necnon subiecti praefulgens gloria regni
mandatur terrae gremio servanda sub amplo,
donec assurgat non corruptumque resumat,
quod nunc includit tumulus, praenobile corpus.
Haec igitur puerum supra paucis memoratum,
acriter orbatum dimittebat, Liudulfum,
feminei dulcem sexus unam quoque prolem,
nomine Liudgardam, summa bonitate coruscam,
moribus et facie similem matri venerandae.
In quas, percerte, soboles mox stirpis amandae

carried off the wives of their leading men and their sweet children. And so, he returned, rejoicing over our humbled enemies.

These things occurred as I have described, and then a sad day arrived, increasing the great pain among us, the day on which Queen Edith, who shone with the highest merits, departed from the shores of the present life, creating by her departure sadness and a great torment of the heart for those subject to her authority. All the common people, then, cried over her in great grief, and not undeservedly. She had cared for them with the love of maternal kindness more than she had crushed them with an empress's restrictive commands. Although no one now doubted that perpetual rest without end would swiftly be provided for her by Christ, and also the happiness that is prepared in advance for the just (no one, that is, who knew the laudable merit of her chaste life and, in sum, the gentle heart which she possessed), nonetheless, in light of the normal practice of the human condition, it is no wonder if the people took up bitter lamentation, when such great hope had been removed so suddenly from them. And the regal form of their much-loved lady, who was also the shining glory of her subject realm, was committed to the ample bosom of the earth for preservation, until such time as she would rise up and reassume that most noble and uncorrupted body, which her tomb now enclosed.

She, therefore, left behind the boy briefly mentioned above, Liudolf, bitterly orphaned; she also left behind one sweet child of the feminine sex, whose name was Liutgard, gleaming with the greatest goodness, and like her venerable mother in appearance and manners. Most assuredly, the entire populace was soon drawn with a great affection of heart

affectu cordis populus deducitur omnis
magno, pro meritis summis utriusque parentis.
Sed magis, ac iuste, dulci fervebat amore
erga regalem puerum dominum Liudulfum,
ipsum spe mentis tota complexus amantis.
Hicque sibi naturales imitans bene mores
extiterat cunctis blandus dulcedine mentis,
mansuetus, clemens, humilis, nimiumque fidelis.
Hinc quoque gratiolam, Christo praestante benigno,
tantam promeruit meritam—digneque recepit
gentibus in cunctis patris imperio religatis—
ut, quicumque suae saltim praepaucula famae
verbula conciperet latebris propensius auris,
ipsius in dulcem totus raperetur amorem
absentem venerans animis dominum studiosis.
Quem pater egregius, rex et senior venerandus,
dilectae matris mortem graviter patientem,
affectu patrio necnon pietate benigna,
digno percerte iam sublimavit honore,
subiecti faciens regni digne dominari.
Necnon Liudgardam simili causa venerandam,
unica feminei quae spes sexus fuit illi,
gratiola parili coluit, provexit, amavit.
Hanc quoque Conrado vinclis sociavit amoris,
egregio strenuoque duci, nimium quoque forti,
munere qui talis dignus constabat honoris.
Utque suo subdi nato faceret Liudulfo
multum devotae perfecto mentis amore
Francorum gentis dominos praenobilis almos
necnon primates Suevorum scilicet omnes,
ipsi legali praepulchram foedere iungi

to these children of beloved lineage, on account of the supreme merits of both of their parents. But the people burned more, and rightly so, with sweet love toward the princely boy, Master Liudolf, embracing him with every hope of their loving hearts. And he, fully adopting the manners that came naturally to him, pleased everyone by the sweetness of his heart; he was gentle, merciful, humble, and exceedingly faithful. For this reason, by Christ's kind provision, he also earned such deserved favor—and he rightly received it from all the peoples subject to his father's authority—that whoever listened with a willing ear to even a few words about his renown was completely seized with a sweet love for him, and venerated their absent master with eager hearts. His outstanding father, the king and venerable seigneur, with paternal affection and beneficent kindness elevated Liudolf to honors that were certainly deserved when the boy was grievously suffering from the death of his beloved mother, and he rightly made Liudolf the master of a subject realm. And Liutgard, who deserved to be honored for a similar reason, and who of the feminine sex was his sole hope, Otto cherished with an equal favor, he promoted her, he loved her. He also united her in the bonds of love to Conrad, an outstanding and steadfast duke, also a very brave one, who was recognized as worthy of a gift of such honor. And in order to make the revered lords of the noble race of Franks, and all the leaders of the Swabians as well, subject to his son Liudolf with the perfect love of very devoted hearts, Otto ordered that a very beautiful woman be joined

Idam iussit, Herimanni natam ducis almi,
qui fuit illustris princeps in partibus illis.
Haec quoque regalis fuerat consortia prolis
pro meritis propriae probitatis digna subire.
Ac vice reginae summo veneratur honore,
rege iubente quidem per consuetam pietatem.
Illam nec habitare locis voluit segregatis
rex idem nati digne succensus amore,
sed ceu reginam regnum transire per amplum,
quo sic dilectus sentiret filius eius
dulcia gratiolae semper munuscula magnae
ipsi cum sponsa regni sociatus in aula.
    Interea rex Italicus gravido Hlotharius
infectus morbo mundo discessit ab isto
Italiae regnum linquens merito retinendum
summae reginae, sibi quam sociavit amore.
Regis Rothulfi fuerat quae filia magni,
edita magnorum longo de stemmate regum.
Cui nomen clarum dictavit summa parentum
nobilitas, illam digne vocitans Aethelheitham.
Haec quoque regalis formae praeclara decore,
atque, suae causis personae sedula dignis,
factis regali respondit nobilitati.
Scilicet ingenio fuerat praelucida tanto,
ut posset regnum digne rexisse relictum,
si gens ipsa dolum mox non dictaret amarum.
Denique, defuncto quem praedixi Hluthario,
pars quaedam plebis fuerat, quae, retro rebellis
menteque perversa propriis dominis inimica,
restituit Beringarii regnum dicioni,
quod, patre defuncto, raptum violenter ab illo,

to Liudolf in legal marriage, Ida the daughter of the revered Duke Herman, an illustrious prince in the Swabian regions. She also deserved elevation to marriage with the king's son by merit of her own goodness. And she was venerated with the highest honor, in the place of the queen, the king having, in fact, ordered it in his customary generosity. And this same king did not want Ida to live in distant places, since he was honorably stirred by love for his son Liudolf, but rather Otto wanted her to travel through his vast realm as a queen, so that his beloved son might thereby understand the sweet gifts of Otto's great favor, always joined, along with his wife, to Otto in the royal court.

Meanwhile the Italian king Lothar, infected with a serious disease, departed this world, appropriately leaving the kingdom of Italy to be retained by the excellent queen, whom he had joined to himself in love. She was the daughter of the great King Rudolf, and had been born from a long line of great kings. The supreme nobility of her parents dictated that she bear an illustrious name, and they worthily called her Adelaide. She was also outstanding in the elegance of her royal beauty, and, being attentive to causes that were worthy of her person, she showed herself by her actions to be equal to her regal nobility. That is to say, she was very clearly of such native intelligence, that she could have worthily ruled the kingdom left to her, if that nation had not soon insisted upon bitter treachery. In the end, after this Lothar whom I mentioned had passed away, there was a faction of the populace which, having previously been rebellious, of evil intention, and hostile to their own lords, returned to Berengar's control the kingdom over which he had wept when his father died, since that kingdom was

olim per † manus regis deflevit Hugonis.
Optato certe qui sublimatus honore
detegit, invidiae quicquid sub pectore tristi
gessit, dum regni deflevit damna paterni.
Felleque plus iusto cordis succensus amaro,
fudit in insontem concretum quippe furorem
iniustam vim reginae faciens Aethelheithae,
quae regnans illi damnum non fecerat ullum.
Nec solum celsae solium sibi proripit aulae,
sed simul aerarii claustris eius reseratis,
omne quod invenit dextra tollebat avara,
aurum cum gemmis varii generis quoque gazis,
necnon regalis sertum praenobile frontis;
ornatus nec particulam dimiserat ullam.
Nec timuit propriis illam spoliare ministris
obsequiis quoque personis regalibus aptis
regalique potentatu (miserabile dictu!).
Postremo quoque pergendi pariterque manendi,
quo vellet, libertatem male denegat omnem,
solam cum sola committens namque puella
servandam cuidam comiti sua iussa sequenti.
Qui iussis captus regis non iusta iubentis
non metuit propriam culpae sine crimine domnam
clausam carcereis claustris servare cubilis,
circumdiffusis custodum denique turmis,
ut mos personas est servari scelerosas.
Sed, qui de vinclis Petrum tollebat Herodis,
hanc, quando voluit, miti pietate redemit.
Certe dum variis animo foret anxia curis,
nullaque spes sibimet certi solaminis esset,
praesul Adhelhardus, factum deflens miserandum,

violently snatched from him at that time by the hand of King Hugh. Berengar, to be sure, when elevated to the honor he had long desired, revealed all the treachery he had carried in his dire chest while he wept over the loss of his father's realm. And unjustly inflamed with a bitter rancor of the heart, he poured out against an innocent woman his compounded fury, doing in fact unjust violence to Queen Adelaide, who had done no harm to him while she was queen. He not only grabbed for himself the throne of the lofty palace, but, simultaneously, from the locked chambers of its treasury, he took with his greedy hand everything that he found, gold with jewels of various kinds, and treasures, and even the noble crown of the royal head; nor did he leave behind any piece of finery. And he was not afraid to despoil her of her personal attendants, and also of those individuals suited to royal service, and of her royal power (it is horrible even to mention it!). Finally, he likewise wickedly denied her all freedom to go or stay where she wished, consigning her, in fact, alone, with only a single servant girl, to be guarded by a certain count, who answered to the orders of Berengar. This count, himself a prisoner to the orders of a king who did not give just orders, was not afraid to keep his own lady, who was guiltless of any crime, closed up in a prisonlike enclosure of rooms, with, moreover, crowds of guards scattered all around, in the way that criminals are customarily kept. But he who removed Peter from the chains of Herod, with gentle mercy redeemed her, when it pleased him.

To be sure, while she was distressed in her mind by many concerns, and she had no hope of assured aid, Adelhard the bishop, deploring this miserable state of affairs and scarcely

vixque suae damnum carae patiens grave domnae,
illi transmisit missum mox, namque secretum.
Utque fugam caperet, monitis suasit studiosis,
ac peteret muris urbem structam bene firmis,
quae caput ipsius constabat pontificatus,
hic loca praesidii mandans tutissima certi
illi, condignum quoque praeberi famulatum.
His nam regales monitis pulsantibus aures,
inclita de mandatelis regina benignis
laetior exoptat vinclis absolvier artis.
Quid faceret tamen ignorat, quia nulla patebat
ianua, quae somno pressis custodibus alto
illam nocturnis pateretur abire sub horis.
Sed nec personam causa famulaminis ullam
subiectam sibi carcereis possedit in antris,
ipsius implendis esset quae sedula iussis,
ni supradictam solummodo namque puellam
necnon presbyterum vitae laudabilis unum.
His ubi continuis narraret cuncta lamentis,
quae maerens animo multum volvebat amaro,
voti communis placito, visum fuit illis
res melius verti, studio si forte latenti
sub terra foveam facerent fodiendo secretam,
per quam de vinclis possent evadere duris.
Haec ita percerte constant completa fuisse
ocius auxilio Christi praesente benigni.
Nam, caute fovea iuxta placitum reparata,
advenit libertati nox apta recenti,
in qua, dum somnus plebis perserperet artus,
tantum cum sociis regina piissima binis
custodum fraudes fugiens evaserat omnes.

able to endure the grievous injury to his dear lady, straightaway sent her a message, in secret, of course. And he persuaded her by energetic warnings to take flight and to seek the city, well fortified with strong walls, which constituted the seat of his bishopric, enjoining upon her that here the safest place of assured protection would be provided for her, and also an appropriate household staff. Indeed, with these warnings ringing in her royal ears, the renowned queen, happier as a result of these kindly injunctions, hoped to be freed from her tight chains. Still, she did not know what to do, because no door was open that allowed her to depart in the night hours when her guards were weighed down by deep sleep; and further, because she did not have in the dungeons of her prison a single person by way of a servant, subject to her, who would be diligent in carrying out her orders—no one, that is, excepting only the aforementioned maid and a single priest of praiseworthy life. When, in constant lamenting, she had told them everything that she was turning over and over in her bitter heart, grieving, it seemed to them, in accord with their shared desire, that things would turn out for the better, if, perchance, in a concealed effort they were to make, by digging, a secret underground tunnel through which they could escape their harsh chains. There is no doubt, accordingly, that these things were swiftly done through the ready aid of the merciful Christ. Indeed, when the tunnel had been carefully prepared to their satisfaction, a night arrived that was suitable for their renewed freedom, a night on which, while sleep was twining itself around the limbs of the people, that kindest of queens, fleeing with only her two companions, evaded all the treachery of her

Atque viae spatium noctis sub tempore tantum
pertransit, plantis quantum valet ergo tenellis.
Sed mox ut scissis cessit nox furva tenebris,
atque polus radiis coepit pallescere solis,
abscondens in secretis se cautius antris,
nunc vagat in silvis, latitat nunc denique sulcis
inter maturas Cereris crescentis aristas
donec nox, solitis rediens induta tenebris,
obtegit rursum nebulo terram tenebroso.
Tunc iterato viam studuit percurrere coeptam.
  Denique custodes, illam non invenientes,
narrabant factum comiti nimium tremefacti,
cura cui conservandae fuit indita domnae.
Qui, terrore gravis percussus corde timoris,
pergit cum sociis illam perquirere multis.
Et cum deficeret nec iam dinoscere posset
quo regina suum tulerit clarissima gressum,
detulit ad regem Beringarium timidus rem.
Hic quoque continuo nimiam conversus in iram,
circumquaque suos subito mittebat alumnos
praecipiens illos nullum transire locellum,
sed caute cunctas iam perlustrare latebras,
si forsan latebris regina lateret in ullis.
Ipseque cum fortis sequitur turba legionis,
ceu qui vult hostes bello superare feroces;
et rapido segetem cursu peragravit eandem,
in cuius sulcis latuit tunc domna recurvis,
haec quam querebat, Cereris contecta sub alis.
Sed, licet huc illucque locum percurreret ipsum,
in quo non parvo iacuit terrore gravata,
et quamvis circumpositos disiungere culmos

guards. And she traveled under night's protection as much of the distance of her journey as she was then able to go on her tender feet. But then as dark night receded, and the shadows were broken up, and the sky began to grow pale with the sun's rays, Adelaide, very cautiously concealing herself in secret recesses, sometimes roamed in the woods, sometimes hid in the furrows among the ripened sheaths of growing grain, until night, returning draped in its usual shadows, covered the land again in a shadowy cloud. Then she was eager again to continue the journey she had begun.

The guards, then, not finding her, explained in great fear to the count what had happened, that is, to the count to whose care the safekeeping of the lady had been entrusted. He, struck with a terror of grave fear in his heart, set out with many of his allies to look for her. And when he failed and could not yet learn where the most illustrious queen had turned her steps, he timidly reported the situation to King Berengar. The king was instantly stirred to great anger, and he too immediately sent his minions in every direction, ordering them not to overlook any little place, but carefully now to examine all the hideouts, in case the queen was perhaps hiding in any hideout. And he himself followed with a horde of a mighty legion, like one intending to conquer savage foes in war; and in rapid course he traveled through the same field, among whose alternating furrows the lady was then hiding, the one he was seeking, who was covered under the stalks of grain. But even though he ran here and there through the very place where, weighed down by no small fear, she lay hidden, and although he tried with all his energy

nisibus extenta cunctis temptaverit hasta,
non tamen invenit, Christi quam gratia texit.
Ast ubi confusus rediit nimium quoque lassus,
praesul Adelhardus mox advenit venerandus
induxitque suam gaudenti pectore domnam
intra, namque, suae muros urbis bene firmos.
Hicque sibi digne toto servivit honore,
donec maiorem Christo miserante decorem
regni suscepit, pridem quam maesta reliquit.
 Denique nostrates quidam tunc experientes
reginam domino desolatam fore caro
(cuius praedulcem gustaverunt pietatem
quando per Italiam coeperunt pergere Romam),
eius multiplicem recitati sunt pietatem
crebrius Ottoni, magno tunc denique regi,
Augusto sed Romani nunc denique regni,
nullam dicentes aliam consistere dignam
tecta sub ipsius thalami regalia duci
post obitum domnae flendum cunctis Eadithae.
Et rex, laetatus tantae dulcedine famae,
pectore volvebat tacito per tempora longa,
quo pacto sibi reginam coniungeret istam,
quae fuit insidiis regis circumdata tantis.
Venit et in mentem praedictum denique regem,
qui quondam patriis fuerat depulsus ab arvis
eius et auxilio citius miserante reductus,
ingratum fore nunc donis tantae pietatis.
Hinc quoque mox aditum sibimet providerat aptum
ipsius Italicum iuri subiungere regnum.
Hoc ubi colloquio sensit narrante paterno,
patris amor verus, spes et gentis, Liudulfus

to separate with an extended lance the stalks standing on all sides, nevertheless he did not find that woman, whom the grace of Christ protected. But when Berengar too went home confused and exhausted, then the venerable bishop Adelhard arrived, and he led his lady with a happy heart, yes, within the very strong walls of his city. And here he duly ministered to her with every honor, until by Christ's mercy she received the dignity of a kingdom greater than the one she had sadly just left behind.

Eventually then some of our countrymen, learning that the queen was bereft of her dear lord (the same queen whose sweet kindness they had themselves enjoyed when they journeyed through Italy to Rome), frequently recited her manifold kindnesses to Otto, at that time a great king, but now, finally, emperor of the Roman realm, telling him that no one but Adelaide was worthy to be led under the royal roof of his wedding chamber, after the death of Lady Edith, mourned by all. And the king, delighted by the sweetness of such a reputation, for a long time meditated with a silent heart how to join to himself this queen, who was surrounded by the snares of King Berengar, which were so great. And at length it occurred to him that King Berengar, who at one time had been driven from his native lands and had been swiftly restored by Otto's merciful aid, was being ungrateful for the grants of such kindness. Hence, also, Otto soon provided himself with a suitable opening for annexing the Italian kingdom to his own jurisdiction. When, from a fatherly conversation explaining it, Liudolf learned the situation, he, who was the true love of his father and the hope of his

non sua sollicitans, patris sed commoda tractans
praepaucis secum sociis secreto resumptis,
taliam petiit. Fortique manu penetravit
exortans patris imperio populum dare colla;
moxque redit clarum referens sine Marte triumphum.
Quo rex comperto populis narrantibus, Otto
corde super natum laeto plaudebat amandum,
ipsius causa qui nam discrimina tanta
audacter subiit, gentem turbando ferocem.
Utque labor talis non frustraretur amoris,
ipse quidem gentem festinus adivit eandem
plebis non parva propriae comitante caterva.
Regalis pompae vario comptusque decore
Alpibus accinctas altis intraverat oras.
His Beringarius compertis obstupefactus
non bellum movit, regi non obvius exit,
sed se salvandum castello protinus apto
intulit, in tutis posito firmisque locellis.
At rex famosus noster, virtute superbus,
audacter satis ignotas pertransiit oras,
Italici Papiam regni cepit quoque domnam.
Qua certe capta cuncti velut agmine facto
quaerentes regem proceres venere recentem,
certabantque suo iuri se subdere magno.
Quos nam more suo suscepit mente benigna
promittens ipsis eius munus pietatis,
si post haec illi servirent mente fideli.
Istis sic habitis, crebro tractamine cordis,
reginae satis egregiae memor est Aedelheithae
regalem certe cupiens, quandoque, videre

nation, not worrying about his own convenience, but considering his father's, set out for Italy, secretly taking a few of his companions with him. And with this brave force he penetrated Italy, exhorting the people to surrender their necks to his father's authority; and he soon returned, bringing back a glorious triumph without warfare. When King Otto became aware of this from people's accounts, with a happy heart he rejoiced over his beloved son, who for his father's sake had boldly undertaken dangers which were certainly great, by agitating a fierce nation. And so that such a labor of love not be in vain, Otto himself hastily went to this same nation, accompanied by no small crowd of his own people. And enhanced by the varied splendor of a royal procession, he entered those lands girded by the lofty Alps.

When he learned these things, Berengar was stunned, and neither started a war, nor went out to confront the king, but for his own safety took himself instantly to a suitable castle, located in a safe and fortified spot. But our renowned king, proud of his own strength, very boldly crossed through those unknown lands, and also seized Pavia, the dominant city of the Italian kingdom. Assuredly, once Pavia was taken, all the nobles, marching in step, came looking for their new king and competed with one another to place themselves under Otto's great authority. In his usual fashion, he received them with a gentle heart, promising them the gift of his kindness, if they would serve him in the future with a faithful heart.

These things occurred as I have described, and then Otto thought again, repeatedly turning the matter over in his heart, of the very illustrious Queen Adelaide, wanting no

ipsius faciem, cuius didicit bonitatem.
Unde quidem mandatelis secretius actis,
quae fuerant pacis necnon praedulcis amoris,
sub signo fidei firmae mandaverat illi,
hoc quoque suadelis exhortabatur amicis,
ut celeri Papiam cursu peteret, populosam
urbem, quam cum tristitia dimisit amara,
quo praestante sacra Regis pietate perennis
hic modo sublimem gaudens captaret honorem,
quo prius ingentem fuerat perpessa dolorem.
His mandatelis cessit regina benignis,
et quo iussa fuit pariter comitantibus ivit
permultis subiectorum cuneis populorum.
Ut rex hoc sensit, cuius mandamine venit,
ipsius Henricum fratrem praecepit amandum
huius in occursum regredi trans litora Padi,
ut sublimandam regni splendoribus heram
tanti compositus ducis ornaret famulatus.
Qui studio mentis praecepta sequens senioris
egreditur certe cum regali legione,
castraque reginae gaudens petiit venerandae,
in quis cum sociis residebat denique multis
illam condigne summo comitatus honore,
donec regali presentaret faciei.
Quae merito regi statim placuit satis ipsi
eligiturque sui consors dignissima regni.
Tunc rex se novitate rei cernens retineri,
tempore ne patrias instante rediret ad oras,
Liudulfum placuit carum praemittere natum,
ut gens Saxonum fortis volitaret ad illum,
et regnum sub patrono staret bene tanto.

doubt to see, at some point, the regal features of this woman, of whose good character he had been informed. For this reason, in fact, through very secretly delivered directives, which were of peace as well as of sweet love, under seal of his stable faith he directed her—and he also exhorted the same thing by amicable encouragements—to go by a quick route to Pavia, a populous city, which she had left in bitter distress, so that by provision of the sacred mercy of the eternal King she could now joyously receive high honor in this place, where earlier she had suffered great pain. The queen yielded to these kindly directives, and she went where she was ordered, with a vast cohort of her subject peoples accompanying her as well. When King Otto, by whose directive she was coming, learned this, he ordered his beloved brother Henry to go back across the shores of the Po to meet her, so that the orderly obeisance of so great a leader might celebrate the noble woman who was to be elevated to the splendors of the realm. Henry, following the instructions of his seigneur with a diligent mind, certainly went out with a royal legion, and he joyfully sought out the camp of the venerable queen, where she was then living with many associates, and he duly attended her with the highest honor, until he could present her to the king in person. She instantly proved very pleasing to the king himself, and rightly so, and she was chosen as a right worthy consort of his kingdom.

Then the king, recognizing that he would be detained by this new situation, and so, for the present time, could not return to his paternal lands, was pleased to send his dear son Liudolf ahead, so that the mighty race of Saxons would rush to his side, and the realm would stand steady under such a

Qui parens iussis devota mente parentis,
ad patriam rediit, curam regnique recepit,
omnia prudenter necnon nimium sapienter
complens in patria quae tunc fuerant facienda.
Interea dux Henricus, regis venerandus
frater, in Italia cordis conamine summo
obsequiis operam gessit regalibus aptam,
officium non germani solummodo cari,
sed mage ius servi studio complendo benigno.
Hinc non immerito regi placuit satis ipsi,
est quoque reginae fraterno iunctus amore;
affectuque pio fuerat dilectus ab illa.
Tunc rex Italicum peragraverat undique regnum
primates regni propriae subdens dicioni.
His quoque completis iuxta votumque locatis,
ne Beringarius regnum raperet sibi rursum,
Conradum cum non paucis ex agmine lectis
in Papia residere ducem iussit sapientem,
cui veneranda suae dederat consortia natae.
Ipseque continuo rediit cum coniuge clara
intendens patriae sedem festinus adire.
Quem gavisa quidem plebs suscepit venientem,
Altithrono grates spargens super aethera dulces,
qui miserando suae plebis solita pietate,
quem pius elegit, regem cum pace reduxit.
    Hac ita laetitia dignis rebus celebrata
advenit dux Conradus cum pace reversus
adducens Beringarium supra memoratum
ipsius ingenii captum sic arte profundi,
gratis ut Ottoni venit se subdere regi.

protector. Liudolf, obeying the orders of his parent with a devout heart, returned to his fatherland, and he undertook to care for the kingdom, accomplishing prudently and very wisely everything that needed, at that time, to be done in the fatherland. Meanwhile, Duke Henry, the venerable brother of the king, with the greatest effort of his heart, carried out in Italy the work appropriate to his royal offices, fulfilling with generous zeal not only the duty of a dear brother, but more the obligation of a kindly vassal. For this reason he not undeservedly pleased the king himself very much, and he was joined also with brotherly love to the queen; and he was beloved by her with a dutiful affection. Then the king traveled all over the Italian kingdom, subjecting the noblemen of the realm to his personal authority. After he had completed and arranged these things according to his wishes, so that Berengar could not again seize the kingdom for himself, Otto ordered Conrad, the wise duke to whom he had granted a respectable marriage with his daughter, to live in Pavia with a good many chosen soldiers from his army. And he himself immediately returned with his illustrious wife, intending to go straight to the heart of his fatherland. The joyous people, in fact, received him on his arrival, broadcasting their sweet thanks to the One enthroned above the heavens, who, taking pity on his people in his accustomed mercy, had brought back, along with peace, the king whom he had compassionately chosen.

Thus, the happy event was celebrated with worthy activities, and then Duke Conrad arrived, returning in peace, leading with him the aforementioned Berengar, whom he had captured by the skill of his profound ingenuity, so that Berengar came freely in order to subject himself to King

Tunc idem rex, qui semper fecit sapienter,
hunc regem certe digno suscepit honore,
restituens illi sublati culmina regni –
ista percerte tantum sub conditione,
ut post haec causis non contradiceret ullis
ipsius imperio, multis longe metuendo,
sed ceu subiectus iussis esset studiosus.
Hoc quoque sollicitis decrevit maxime dictis:
ut post haec populum regeret clementius ipsum,
quem prius imperio nimium corrupit amaro.
Qui, se complendis simulans promptum fore iussis,
ocius abscessit patriam laetusque petivit.
Ast ubi sublimem regni possederat arcem,
laesus suadelis quorundam namque sinistris,
mox infelici graviora quidem iuga genti
infert, vi magna pro despectu sibi facto;
se regnum pretio contestans emere magno
nec fore culpandum, si ius fregisset avorum,
sed magis Ottoni culpae meritum reputari,
ipsi primates plebis qui venderet omnes.
Haec res ad regem mox ut pervenit eundem,
in Beringarium iusta succenditur ira
corde super populi damnis maerens miserandi
in meliusque statum studuit convertere rerum.
Et faceret citius Christi munimine fultus,
si non fortunae restaret causa sinistrae.
Namque decore sui florente per omnia regni,
cum se gauderet cunctis fulgere secundis,
protulit antiqui renovata lues inimici
fraudis commentum cunctis per saecla dolendum

Otto. Then this same king, who always acted wisely, by all means received King Berengar with worthy honors, restoring to him the highest position in the realm that had been taken from him—but, to be sure, only under this condition, that in the future he would not for any reasons contradict Otto's imperial authority, respected by many far and wide, but like a subject he would be attentive to Otto's orders. This also Otto especially decreed with careful words: that in the future Berengar would govern more mildly his own people, whom he had previously harmed by his excessively cruel exercise of power. Berengar, pretending that he was ready to carry out these orders, very quickly departed and happily headed for his fatherland. But when he was in possession of the lofty citadel of his kingdom, assailed, to be sure, by the sinister arguments of certain men, he soon applied even heavier yokes to his unfortunate people, acting with great violence because of the disrespect done to him. He asserted that he had paid a great price for the kingdom and that he should not be blamed if he had broken the law of his ancestors, but rather responsibility for the crime should be ascribed to Otto, who had sold to him all the leaders of the people. As soon as this situation came to King Otto's attention, he was inflamed with justified anger against Berengar, grieving in his heart over the injuries to the pitiable people, and he was eager to change the state of things for the better. And supported by the aid of Christ, he would have acted very swiftly, if only ill fortune had not stood in his way. For in fact, while the honor of his realm was flourishing in every way, when he was rejoicing that he was shining with everything in his favor, the renewed scourge of the ancient enemy brought forth a plan of deceit, one to be lamented by all for

iam tunc pacificum temptans confundere regnum.
Hoc ut quantocius posset patrare malignus,
regni rectores primum turbaverat omnes
sperans interitum plebis mox esse futurum.

Denique famosi natus regis Liudulfus,
ut cognovit amicitiae signis satis aptis,
quanto perfectae fidei dilexit amore
Henricum regis fratrem regina fidelis,
quodque suae fidei studio se subdidit omni,
tangitur interni iaculis secreto doloris,
haud ira fervens, odii nec felle tabescens,
sed super amisso carae genitricis amore
ex aegri latebris ducens suspiria cordis.
Deceptusque malis permultorum suadelis,
pertimuit fragilis pro consuetudine mentis,
quod post non uti donis deberet honoris
condigni, sed forte locum subire secundum.
(Quod fieri Christus numquam permitteret aequus,
si staret regnum iusta sub pace quietum.)
Ast ubi subtristi vultu saepissime patri
monstratur maestus, solito nec more serenus,
752 sunt qui decepti serpentis fraude dolosi
. . .
1137 sed quo regalem patris hinc augeret honorem.
His rex compertis ex prosperitate fidelis
laetatus prolis, tota dulcedine mentis,
haec illi mandat scriptis extemplo remissis:
“In saeclum saecli maneat laus Omnipotenti,
qui dedit in tantis temet gaudere secundis!

all time, for the devil was attempting even then to overturn the peaceful kingdom. In order to be able to perpetrate this plan as swiftly as possible, the evil one first stirred up all the rulers of the kingdom, hoping that the destruction of the people would soon occur.

At length, Liudolf, the son of our renowned king, when 735
he noticed through very proper signs of friendship how great was that affection of perfect faith by which the queen loved Henry, the brother of the faithful king, and that she held herself by every effort to her pledge of faithfulness to
Otto, then Liudolf was secretly wounded by shafts of inner 740
pain, not boiling with anger, nor withering from the poison of hatred, but drawing sighs from the hidden depths of his aching heart over the lost love of his own dear mother. And
deceived by the evil arguments of a great many people, he 745
was terrified, as is usual for a tender mind, that in the future he might not enjoy the conferment of worthy honor, but perchance might have to tolerate second place. (Christ in his fairness would never permit this to happen, if the king-
dom were standing quietly under a just peace.) But when in 750
his grief he had so frequently presented himself to his father with a very sad expression, and was not calm in his normal
way, there were some who were deceived by the treachery of 752
the cunning serpent. . . .

. . . but in order to increase his father's royal honor thereby. 1137
When the king learned of these things, he was gladdened by the success of his faithful child, and with all sweetness of
intention he immediately sent the following to him in a 1140
written missive: "May praise endure for ever and ever to the Almighty, who allowed you to rejoice in such favorable

Grates atque tibi dentur, carissime fili,
quem constare quidem penitus cognosco fidelem,
haud obscura tuae fidei quia signa dedisti,
cum per te regnum cupiens augescere nostrum
signasti nobis proprii decus omne laboris.
Hinc ego gratanter, quae fecisti sapienter,
accipiens, vice conversa condigna rependo,
hoc ipsumque tibi regnum committo regendum,
imperio subdi nostro quod constituisti.
Praecipioque tibi iussis, dilecte, paternis,
ut, quem victrici populum dextra superasti,
absque mora tecum facias firmare tenendum
foedus, cum iuramento structum metuendo."
Haec dux Liudulfus decreta legens venerandus,
laetior ex mandatelis tantae pietatis,
iussus cum iuramento religat sibi firmo
ad patris obsequium populum digne moderandum.
His bene dispositis summo cum foedere pacis,
ardens absentis faciem meruisse parentis,
coniugis et carae dulci devictus amore
ac prolis geminae longe post terga relictae,
posthabitae fines patriae placuit repedare,
quo post exilii pondus nimium grave duri
posset quandoquidem patriae captare quietem.
Utque celer morulis haec impleret sine cunctis,
non iter optatum pondus tardaverit ullum,
collectim proprias iussit praemittere gazas.
Ipsius et faciem turbam praecedere totam,
quam belli causa secum deduxerat illo,
promittens ipsum vita comitante futurum
ad fines patriae spatii post tempora parvi.

successes! And let thanks be given, my dearest son, to you, for I know you have remained entirely faithful, because you have given clear signs of your faith, since in your desire to expand our kingdom through your own initiative you have assigned to us all the glory of your own labor. So, gratefully accepting what you have wisely achieved, I repay to you in return what you have earned, and I assign to you, to rule, this same kingdom which you have made subject to our empire. And I advise you, beloved son, with paternal injunctions, that without delay you make this people, whom you have conquered with your victorious hand, establish a binding treaty with you, confirmed by a dreadful oath." Reading these decrees, and made happier by directives of such kindness, the venerable Duke Liudolf, as ordered, bound to himself with a strong oath this people, who were to be worthily ruled in the service of his father.

After he had properly arranged these things with an excellent peace treaty, Liudolf longed to obtain an audience with his absent parent, and, overcome by sweet love for his dear wife and the twin children he had left behind, he was pleased to march back to the borders of the fatherland from which he had departed, so that after the very heavy burden of a hard exile, he could at last enjoy the tranquility of his fatherland. And in order swiftly to fulfill these plans without delays, he ordered all his personal treasures to be gathered up and sent ahead, and no burden hindered the longed-for journey. And he ordered the entire throng, which he had led there with him for the sake of war, to return ahead of himself, promising that, if he lived, he would be at the borders of the fatherland in a brief space of time. This also he specified

Hoc quoque melliflui verbis signaverat oris:
in quis castellis, in quis voluitque locellis
sumptus hospitii dignos sibimet reparari.
Hac moti fama nostrates desiderata
affectu cordis gaudebant interioris.
Omneque maeroris pondus cunctique doloris,
quod prius absentis causa tulerant senioris,
ex animo deponentes communiter omnes
causam laetitiae duxerunt esse supremae,
si post paucorum meruissent ergo dierum
cursus, promissi iuxta praeconia laeti
. . .
aeque ferens sceptrum capitis diademaque pulchrum,
atque sui cultus omnes regalis amictus,
ornatus sed maioris suscepit honoris
augusto summo pariter mox conbenedicta.
Hactenus Oddonis famosi denique regis
gesta, licet tenui Musa, cecini modulando.
Nunc scribenda quidem constant quae fecerat idem
augustus solium retinens in vertice rerum.
Tangere quae vereor, quia femineo prohibebor
sexu, nec vili debent sermone revolvi:
qualiter invicti duro luctamine belli
obtinuit constructa locis castella marinis,
quae Beringarius coniunx possedit et eius,
ac illum, iuramento cogente peracto
misit in exilium misera cum coniuge Willa;
qualiter et, recti compunctus acumine zeli,
summum pontificem, quaedam perversa patrantem
eius nec monitis dignantem cedere crebris,
Sedis Apostolicae fraudari fecit honore

by words from his honeyed mouth: in what castles, in what places he wanted appropriate expenditures for hospitality to be prepared for him. Stirred by this longed-for news, our people rejoiced with affection deep in their hearts. And the entire burden of all that pain and sorrow which they had previously endured on account of the absence of their seigneur, they all, in common, put out of their minds, and they considered it grounds for supreme happiness, if after the passing of a few days, in accordance with the reports of his happy promise, they should obtain. . . .

. . . bearing the scepter as well as the beautiful diadem on her head, and all the garments of her regal dress, but she received the adornments of a greater honor, soon being equally blessed along with the supreme emperor.

Up to this point, then, albeit with my slender Muse, I have sung in meter the deeds of the renowned King Otto. Now, indeed, there remain to be written those things which this same man accomplished while holding the throne at the head of the state as emperor. I am afraid even to touch on these things, because I am held back by my feminine gender, and the following matters should not be unfolded in common language: how in the hard struggle of victorious battle Otto took possession of castles constructed in coastal areas, castles which Berengar and his wife had owned, and, by compelling the performance of an oath, Otto sent him into exile along with his pitiable wife, Willa; and how, inspired by the sting of righteous zeal, he brought it about that the supreme pontiff, who was committing certain evil deeds and did not deign to yield to Otto's repeated warnings, was stripped of the honor of the Apostolic See, and Otto

constituens alium rectoris nomine dignum;
qualiter et, regno tranquilla pace quieto,
nostrates adiens, illic iterumque revertens,
necnon amborum retinens decus imperiorum
ipsius prolem post illum iam venientem,
scilicet Oddonem, nutricis ab ubere regem,
ad fasces augustalis provexit honoris
exemploque sui digne fecit benedici.
Haec igitur nostris nequeunt exponier orsis,
sed quaerunt seriem longe sibi nobiliorem.
Hinc ego tantarum prohibente gravedine rerum
ultra non tendo, finem sed provide pono,
post haec incepto ne succumbam male victa.
His ita finitis et summatim replicatis
est ingens Regis pietas oranda perennis,
quo pius augustos praestet deducere nostros
instantis vitae tempus feliciter omne;
et, fultos semper cunctis ad vota secundis,
Ecclesiae multos custodes servet in annos,
nobis solamen dantes clementius. Amen.

appointed another who was worthy of the name of leader; and how, with the kingdom calm in tranquil peace, Otto came to our country, and then returned again to Italy, and, maintaining the glory of both his dominions, he elevated his child, already following after him, namely, Otto II, a king from the time he was at his nurse's breast, to the insignia of imperial honor and worthily made sure that the child was blessed in the same way he himself had been. These things, in conclusion, cannot be expounded in my words, but require a far nobler narrative. Prevented by the gravity of such matters, therefore, I will go no further, but deliberately make here an end, so that I not fail in the endeavor, badly defeated.

So, since these things are finished and have been summarily related, I must beseech the great mercy of the eternal King, that he, in his mercy, see to it that our emperors live out the entire span of their present lives prosperously; and that he preserve the guardians of his Church for many years, always supported by everything favorable to their wishes, mercifully granting us comfort. Amen.

<Prooemium ad primordia coenobii Gandeshemensis>

Prooemium

Ecce meae supplex humilis devotio mentis
gliscit felicis primordia Gandeshemensis
pandere coenobii, quod cura non pigritanti
construxere duces Saxonum iure potentes,
Liudulfus magnus, clarus quoque filius eius
Oddo, qui coeptum perfecit opus memoratum.

Proem to the Origins of the Gandersheim Convent

Proem

Lo, the self-effacing devotion of my humble mind is eager to unfold the origins of the blessed convent Gandersheim, which the powerful dukes of the Saxons righteously constructed with no idle pains: the great Liudolf, and also his illustrious son Oddo, who completed the remarkable work that had been begun.

Primordia coenobii Gandeshemensis

Ordo nunc rerum deposcit debitus harum,
ut prius illustris constructio Gandeshemensis
apto coenobii recinatur carmine nostri.
Quod nam construxisse ducem reverenter eundem
constat Saxonum, quem praedixi, Liudulfum.
Hic, praenobilium natus de stirpe parentum,
ortus atque sui respondens nobilitati
moribus egregiis usuque suae probitatis,
inter Saxones crevit laudabilis omnes.
Namque fuit strenuus, forma nimiumque decorus,
prudens in verbis, in cunctis cautus agendis;
atque sui generis solus spes et decus omnis.
Hinc nam Francorum magni regis Hludowici
militiae primis ascriptus paene sub annis,
ex ipso digne summo sublatus honore,
gentis Saxonum mox suscepit comitatum.
Ac cito maioris donatus munere iuris
principibus fit par, ducibus sed nec fuit impar.
Quique suos omnes vicit pietate parentes,
non minus insignis pompa vincebat honoris.
Cui coniunx ergo fuerat praenobilis Oda
edita Francorum clara de stirpe potentum,
filia Billungi, cuiusdam principis almi,
atque bonae famae generosae scilicet Aedae.
Haec igitur crebro precibus consueverat Aeda

The Origins of the Gandersheim Convent

The due order of these things now demands first of all that the construction of our illustrious Gandersheim convent resound in a fitting song. It is established, to be sure, that it was this same duke of the Saxons whom I already mentioned, Liudolf, who reverently constructed it. He, born of the stock of very noble parents, and reflecting the nobility of his origin in his excellent manners and in the employment of his goodness, grew estimable among all the Saxons. For he was vigorous and very handsome in appearance, prudent in speaking, cautious in everything he had to do; and he was the sole hope of his race and all its glory. For this reason surely, having been enrolled in the army of Louis, the great king of the Franks, almost from his earliest years, and having been rightfully raised up by him to the highest honors, he soon obtained the position of count of the Saxon people. And being soon endowed with a gift of even greater authority, he became an equal to princes, and he was not unequal to the dukes. And this man who surpassed all his ancestors in piety, surpassed them no less in the splendor of his distinguished honor.

His wife, then, was the very noble Oda, born from the illustrious stock of the mighty Franks, the daughter of a certain beloved ruler named Billung, and of a noblewoman of good reputation, namely Aeda. This Aeda, indeed, in her prayers repeatedly made a habit of committing herself and

se totamque suam Domino committere vitam.
Saepius atque piis insistens sedula factis,
promeruit, bene promissis edocta supernis,
discere, baptista Christi referente beato,
quod sua progenies, saeclis quandoque futuris,
possessura foret iuris decus imperialis.
Ergo nocturnas quondam scindente tenebras
aurora lucis splendore suae rutilantis,
haec prostrata sacram solito iacuit secus aram,
sacratam sub Baptistae Iohannis honore,
oratu pulsando iugi penetralia caeli.
Cumque piam studiis mentem laxaret in illis,
vidit prona pedes hominis propius sibi stantis.
Ac, commota parum, volvebat pectore multum,
quis foret ille, suum qui conturbare secretum
praesumpsisset in hac hora precibus satis apta.
Fronteque de terra modicum conversa levato
aspexit iuvenem miro splendore micantem,
indutum vestis velamine flavicomantis,
ceu foret e pilis curvi contexta cameli.
Cuius candori nimio pulchrae faciei
barbula parva, nigris sociata colore capillis,
quoddam splendentis praestabat stemma nitoris.
Quem matrona videns nec mortalem fore credens
obstupuit mentis iuxta morem muliebris
procumbens subito magno terrore coacta.
Ille sed affatu blando trepidam refovendo
inquit, "Ne trepides nec perturbata pavescas;
sed cognosce gravis pulso terrore timoris,
quis sim: magna tibi portans solamina veni.
Nam sum Iohannes, liquidis qui tinguere lymphis

her whole life to the Lord. Being zealously engaged in pious deeds, time after time, and well instructed by heavenly promises, she was privileged to learn from the mouth of the blessed baptizer of Christ that her offspring, in some future age, would hold the honor of imperial authority.

For on a certain occasion, when dawn was breaking up the nocturnal shadows with the splendor of its glowing light, she lay prostrate in her usual manner beside a sacred altar consecrated in honor of John the Baptist, pummeling the inner chambers of heaven with her constant prayer. And while she was wearying her pious mind in these pursuits, she saw from her prone position the feet of a man standing very near to her. And so, a little disturbed, she pondered a great deal in her heart who this man could be, who had presumed to disturb her privacy at an hour which was appropriate for prayers. And turning herself, with her forehead raised a little off the ground, she saw a young man glittering with wondrous splendor, wearing a cloak of light-colored cloth, as if it were woven from the hairs of a humpbacked camel. To the whiteness of his very beautiful face, a short beard the same color as his black hair provided a kind of garland of splendid brightness. Seeing him and believing he was not mortal, the matron was struck dumb, in accordance with the nature of a woman's heart, and bowed down suddenly, compelled by great fear. But he, comforting the frightened woman with gentle speech, said, "You should not be afraid, nor should you tremble in distress; but drive out the terror of this grave fear and learn who I am: I have come to bring you great comforts. For I am John, who earned the distinction of

Christum promerui. Quia nos crebro coluisti,
nuntio virginibus sacris tua clara propago
instituet claustrum, pacem regnique triumphum,
dum sua religio studio steterit bene firmo.
Hinc tua progenies saeclis quandoque futuris
culmine pollentis tanto clarescet honoris,
ut terrenorum nullus tunc tempore regum
iure potentatus illi valeat similari."
Dixerat, et subito rediens penetraverat aëthra,
linquens matronae solamen dulce benignae.

Huius magnifici decoris promissio grandis
progeniem domnae claram specialiter Odae
signavit: de qua natus dux inclitus Oddo
sceptris Henricum regem genuit satis aptum.
Qui pater augusti fuit Oddonis venerandi,
eius qui, Regis fultus virtute perennis,
postquam Saxonum rexit, patris vice, regnum,
nutu divino benedictus, namque, secundo:
imperii sedem Romani dignus eadem
ac sceptrum iuris susceperat imperialis,
aequivocumque sui natum, pariter benedictum
disponente pia Regis bonitate perennis,
imperii sedem conscendere fecit eandem
atque pari similis splendore frui dicionis.
Haec igitur modici demonstrat pagina libri
plenius, e causis rerum quem scripsimus harum.
Nunc ad opus coeptum devote perficiendum
est convertendus stilus noster studiosus.

Ast ubi Liudulfo fuerat venerabilis Oda
foedere legali coniuncta, suo seniori,
inter nostrates celebris profecerat omnes

baptizing Christ in the clear waters. Because you have repeatedly honored me, I proclaim that an illustrious descendant of yours will establish a cloister for holy virgins, a source of peace and a triumph for his kingdom so long as his devotion remains on a firm footing. Thereafter, one of your descendants at some point in the coming centuries will shine from such a height of abundant honor, that none of the earthly kings at that time will be comparable to him in the authority of their power." After he said these things, he returned suddenly, ascending to the heavens, leaving sweet solace to the kindly matron.

The great promise of this magnificent honor expressly pointed to the illustrious progeny of Lady Oda: her son the renowned Duke Oddo begat King Henry, who was well suited to the scepter. Henry was the father of the august and venerable Otto, the one who, supported by the power of the eternal King, after he had ruled the kingdom of the Saxons as the successor of his father Henry, by divine assent was blessed for a second time: in fact, he obtained the throne of the Roman Empire, being worthy of the same, as well as the scepter of imperial authority. And he saw to it that the son who bore his name, who was equally blessed through the kindly disposing mercy of the eternal King, ascended to the same throne of imperial power and enjoyed an equal splendor of similar sovereignty. The pages, indeed, of a little book which I wrote about the circumstances of these things describe them more fully. Now, my eager pen must be directed devotedly to completing this work I have begun.

So, when the venerable Oda had been joined to Liudolf, her seigneur, in lawful marriage, she advanced among all our people, celebrated for her manners and deeds, walking the

moribus et factis callem gradiens bonitatis.
Exemploque suae vivens matris venerandae,
se totam Domino commendabat prece sacra,
corde tenens matris monitum claustri faciendi.
Hinc nam legalem non raro sui seniorem
exhortabatur blandis nimium suadelis
ut de gazarum construxisset propriarum
sumptu coenobium divinis laudibus aptum,
in quo sacrandae Domino velamine sacro
finetenus castae possent habitare puellae
atque vacare sui sancti famulamine sponsi.
His ergo monitis vir concedendo fidelis
coniugis electae precibus consenserat apte;
ac sic communi similis conamine voti
deservire Deo coeperunt protinus ambo.
  Quis fuit ecclesiae possessio denique parvae
trans ripas Gandae supra montana locatae,
unde locum celebrem vocitabant "Gandeshemensem."
Illic, obsequio Domini digne celebrando
dum locus investigari posset magis aptus,
communi multas vita iunxere puellas.
Atque sui natam decreverunt Hathumodam
his habitu similem fieri sociamque perennem.
Utque puellaris rectrix fore posset ovilis,
primitus hanc ipsam reverenter ad instituendam
tradebant abbatissae cuidam venerandae.
Quae praelatarum vice succedendo priorum
tunc Herifordensem sortita fuit sibi sedem.
Tali divinum meditati sunt famulatum
nisu Liudulfus coniunx insignis et eius.

path of goodness. And, living by the example of her own venerable mother, she commended herself completely to the Lord through sacred prayer, holding in her heart the prophecy her mother Aeda had received about building a cloister. For this reason, assuredly, she not rarely exhorted her lawful seigneur with most gentle encouragements to build with an outlay from his own treasuries a monastery suitable for divine worship, where chaste girls consecrated to the Lord under the sacred veil could live their lives to the end and spend their time in the service of their holy bridegroom. Her faithful husband, yielding to her advice, appropriately gave his consent to the entreaties of his chosen spouse; and so, in their common pursuit of the same desire, both of them immediately began to serve God.

They had possession, further, of a small church located in the mountains across the banks of the river Gande, from which this celebrated place got the name "Gandersheim." There, while properly performing service to the Lord until a more suitable place could be found, they brought together a number of girls for a communal life. And they decided that their own daughter Hathumoda should become like them in her way of life, and become their permanent companion. And in order that she could be the leader of a maidenly flock, first of all they reverently handed over this same daughter to a certain venerable abbess for instruction. This woman, succeeding in place of earlier religious leaders, was at that time appointed to the position of authority in Herford Abbey. By such exertions, Liudolf and his remarkable wife practiced their service to God.

Post haec, acceptis proprii scriptis senioris,
scilicet almifici regisque pii Hludowici,
eius permissu, cum non modico comitatu,
Romam pergebant. Sanctique Patris visitabant
sedem muneribus dignis precibusque benignis
ipsius auxilio deposcentes sua vota
iuxta velle Dei sese persolvere posse.
Isdem temporibus, possedit papa beatus
Sergius Ecclesiae primatum namque regendae.
Hic ubi perlegit cartas regis sibi missas,
sensit honore ducem summo dignum venientem;
et perquirendo causam, qua venerat illo,
affatu miti blandum se praebuit illi.
Quem ceu pontificem summum merito venerandum
exorans dux Liudulfus cum coniuge pronus
utitur his verbis tota dulcedine mixtis:
"Inclite papa, tuis ne sis durus peregrinis;
qui de longinquis terrarum venimus oris
muneribus nostri famulatus te venerari.
Nitimur ardentis toto conamine mentis
condere coenobium Domini sub honore sacrandum.
Unde quidem visum nobis est maxime iustum,
a te consilii solamen quaerere certi,
et studium nostri tibi rite precando fateri,
qui caput Ecclesiae toto dominaris in orbe;
quo, si forte tibi placeat devotio nostri,
auxilium praebente tua pietate paterna,
quod votis gerimus, factis bene perficiamus.
Ac tu, consilium cuius merito flagitamus,
susceptis donis clementi pectore nostris
scilicet et Regis compulsus amore perennis,

Afterward, having received documents from their own seigneur, namely, the beloved and pious King Louis, and with his permission, Liudolf and Oda set off for Rome with no small entourage. And they visited the seat of the Holy Father, asking with worthy gifts and kindly prayers for his assistance, so that they could fulfill their vows according to God's will. At that time, the blessed Pope Sergius, in fact, held the first place of authority in ruling the Church. When he finished reading the letter the king had sent him, he understood that a leader deserving of the greatest honor was coming; and inquiring into the reason why Liudolf had come there, with his gentle address he showed himself welcoming to him. Entreating him as the right venerable supreme pontiff, Duke Liudolf, bowing down along with his wife, employed these words, mingled with all sweetness: "Illustrious pope, do not be hard on your pilgrims; we have come from the borders of distant lands to venerate you with the offering of our service. We strive with every effort of our fervent hearts to build a sacred monastery in honor of the Lord. For this reason, indeed, it seemed to us especially right that we seek from you the comfort of assured advice, and that we profess our aim by praying uprightly to you, who as head of the Church rule throughout the world; we do these things so that, if by chance our devotion should please you, your paternal kindness might offer its assistance, and we might successfully accomplish in fact what we entertain in hope. But you, whose advice we rightly seek, accept our gifts with a merciful heart, and moved, moreover, by love of the

praesta sanctorum nobis sacra pignora, quorum
omnis coenobii constructio possit honori
apte signari sacris meritisque tueri.
Utque sit absque iugo regum per saecla potentum
nec terrenorum patiatur vim dominorum,
hoc rectoris apostolici solum dicioni
tradimus ad defendendum pariterque regendum."

Haec dux. Et summus Praesul sic Sergius orsus
inquit, "Te miti complector pectore, fili,
consortemque tuam pariter complector amandam.
Atque piis studiis gaudens congaudeo vestris
nec vobis credo fas esse negare petita.
Hic duo rectores fuerant aliquando potentes,
praesul Anastasius, sedis sanctissimus huius,
et coapostolicus sacer Innocentius eius.
Qui, post pastorem Petrum Paulumque magistrum,
Ecclesiae meritis celebres fulsere supremis.
Quorum tam magna servantur corpora cura
hactenus a cunctis huius rectoribus urbis,
ut nec particulam quisquam subtraxerat umquam,
pleno membrorum numero remanente sacrorum.
Sed quia iure piis concedere debeo votis,
amborum vobis donabo pignora gratis
corporibus sacris abscisa patenter ab ipsis,
si sacramento confirmatis mihi facto
haec in coenobii venerari iam memorati
finetenus templo vestri munimine facto,
nocte dieque sacris illic resonantibus hymnis
necnon accenso praeclaro lumine semper.
Hoc et apostolici iuris, sicut petiistis,
coenobium nostri designamus dicioni,

eternal King, furnish us with sacred relics of saints, in whose honor the construction of the entire monastery may suitably be dedicated, and through whose holy merits it may be watched over. And so that it may be free for all time from the yoke of powerful kings and not suffer the violence of earthly lords, we entrust it solely to the authority of the apostolic ruler to defend and guide."

These were the words of the duke. And the supreme pontiff Sergius spoke as follows, saying, "I embrace you with a tender heart, my son, and I embrace your beloved wife equally. And I joyously rejoice with you in your pious efforts, and I do not believe it is right to deny what you have asked for. There were once two powerful rectors here, the priest Anastasius, the holiest of this see, and his fellow apostle, holy Innocent. They, after the shepherd Peter and the teacher Paul, shone famously for their supreme services to the Church. Their bodies have been preserved to the present day with such great care by all the rulers of this city, that no one ever removed even a small piece, and the number of their holy limbs remains complete. But because I am rightly obligated to yield to your pious desires, I will freely donate to you relics of both of these men, cut from their sacred bodies in plain sight, if you confirm to me by making an oath that in the monastery just mentioned these relics will be venerated until the end of time, in a temple built through your generosity, with sacred hymns resounding there day and night, and with a brilliant light burning perpetually. And, as you have requested, we will designate this monastery as being under the sovereignty of our apostolic authority,

ut terrenorum sit securum dominorum."
His dux promissis laetatus corde verendis
mandatis se pontificis summi fore sacris
mox responsurum factis, inquit, studiosis,
. . .
qui foret ecclesia dignus mox aedificanda.
  Ut fert multorum sententia vera scientum,
proxima coenobio fuerat tunc silvula, cincta
collibus umbrosis, quibus et nos cincimur ipsis.
Necnon in silva fuerat sita parvula villa,
in qua Liudulfi soliti stabulare subulci
intra saepta viri cuiusdam, lassa quieti
corpora nocturnis sua composuere sub horis,
dum sibi commissos debebant pascere porcos.
Hic quondam, cum sanctorum venerabile festum
esset cunctorum mox post biduum celebrandum,
sub noctis claras tenebris ardere lucernas
in silva multas ipsi videre subulci.
His visis, cuncti mirabantur stupefacti
quid nova splendentis vellet sibi visio lucis,
miro nocturnas scindens splendore tenebras.
Hocque domus patri narraverunt tremefacti,
demonstrando locum, quem lux perfuderat, ipsum.
Qui, visu clare cupiens audita probare,
extra tecta domus, illis habitans sociatus,
insomnem coepit noctem servare sequentem;
non claudens oculos, somno suadente gravatos,
donec accensas rursus rutilare lucernas
aucto vincentes numero videre priores,
ipso quippe loco, sed prisca, qua prius, hora.
Ominis hoc signum felicis namque serenum,

so that it may be safe from earthly lords." The duke, gladdened in his heart by these awe-inspiring promises, said that he would straightaway respond to the sacred orders of the supreme pontiff with energetic actions . . . who would soon be worthy to build the church.

As the true opinion of many wise men reports, there was at that time next to the monastery a little forest, surrounded by shady hills, the same hills that now surround us. Furthermore, there was located in this forest a tiny little farmhouse, in which the swineherds of Liudolf used to find stable room among the pens of a certain man, and in which they quietly rested their weary limbs in the nighttime hours, while they were pasturing the pigs entrusted to them. Here once, when the venerable feast of All Saints was about to be celebrated in two days' time, these same swineherds saw in the dark of night a number of shining lanterns burning in the forest. When they saw this, they were all dumbfounded, wondering what this strange vision of shining light might mean, sundering the nocturnal darkness with wondrous splendor. And, trembling, they related this to the father of the house, showing him the very place the light had filled. He, wanting to verify clearly by sight the things he had heard, set out to spend the following sleepless night beyond the walls of the house, staying in the company of the swineherds; and he did not close his eyes, though they were heavy from sleep's urging, until they saw again the burning lanterns blazing, in increased numbers, surpassing the previous numbers, and, in fact, it was on the very same spot as before, but at an earlier hour. And truly this clear sign of an auspicious omen,

ut Phoebus radios spargebat ab aethere primos,
fit notum fama cunctis prodente iucunda.
Nec latuisse ducem dignum potuit Liudulfum,
aures sed, citius dicto, pulsaverat eius.
Ipseque sacrata festi mox nocte futuri
observans caute, si quicquam postea tale
caelitus ostensi monstraret visio signi,
cum multis silvam pernox conspexerat ipsam.
Nec mora, cum nebula terras nox texerat atra,
undique silvestris per girum denique vallis
in qua fundandum fuerat praenobile templum,
ordine disposito cernuntur lumina plura.
Quae simul arboreas umbras noctisque tenebras
clare pollentis scindebant luce nitoris.
Hinc simul astantes, Domino laudem referentes,
omnes esse locum firmabant sanctificandum
eius ad obsequium, qui luce repleverat illum.
227 At dux caelesti non ingratus pietati
229 consensuque suae dilectae coniugis Odae,
228 arboribus mox succisis spinisque resectis
omnino vallem mundari iussit eandem.
Silvestremque locum, faunis monstrisque repletum,
fecit mundatum divinis laudibus aptum.
Hinc, quos poscit opus, prius acquirens sibi sumptus
protinus ecclesiae construxit moenia pulchrae
. . .
quae splendor lucis designavit rutilantis.
Hac igitur causa fuerat iam coepta secundo
coenobii sub honore Dei constructio nostri.
Interea lapides structurae convenientes

when Phoebus was spreading his first rays from the upper air, became known to all as the happy word went forth. And it could not escape the worthy Duke Liudolf, but faster than words could say, it was drumming in his ears. And next Liudolf himself carefully kept watch on the holy night of the coming feast, to see whether the appearance of a manifest sign from heaven would reveal anything of a similar sort again; and he along with many others watched over that forest throughout the night. And before long, when night had covered the earth in a black cloud, at length, on all sides in a circle around that wooded valley in which that very noble temple was to be built, more lights were seen in an orderly arrangement. They pierced at the same time the shadows of the trees and the darkness of the night with the clear light of a powerful brightness. Therefore, those present, giving praise to the Lord, immediately all affirmed that this place should be consecrated to serve the one who had filled it with light. For his part, the duke was not ungrateful for this heavenly mercy, and in concord with his beloved wife Oda, he ordered that this same valley be cleared straightaway, with the trees cut down and the briars cut back. And he made that wooded place, which was full of fauns and monsters, a clearing suitable for divine worship. Then, first obtaining the funds that the project required, he immediately built the walls of a beautiful church . . . which the splendor of the shining light had designated. And for this reason, then, the construction of our monastery was now begun under the favorable patronage of God. At this time, stones appropriate

non potuere locis nancisci prorsus in illis;
unde moram templi patitur perfectio coepti.
Abbatissa sed a Domino sperans Hathumoda
impetrare fide credentes omnia posse,
frangebat sese nimio persaepe labore
nocte dieque Deo sacris studiis famulando.
Et, subiectarum multis illi sociatis,
caelitus auxilii petiit solamina ferri,
ne non perfectum remaneret opus bene coeptum.
Nec mora, caelestem, quam quaerebat, pietatem
sensit adesse sui votis promptam misereri.
Nam ieiunando sacris precibusque vacando
cum prostrata die quadam iacuit secus aram,
vocis mansuetae <monitis compellitur ire>
atque sequi volucrem, quem, iam progressa, sedentem
cerneret in saxi cuiusdam vertice magni.
Ipsaque, complectens animo praecepta parato,
egreditur dictis credens ex corde iubentis.
Ac caementariis secum sumptis bene gnaris
perrexit citius, quo duxit Spiritus almus,
donec ad coeptum pervenit nobile templum.
Illic candidulam vidit residere columbam
in designati praecelso vertice saxi.
Quae mox expansis volitans praecesserat alis,
temperat atque suum non sueto more volatum,
posset ut aereos directo tramite sulcos,
cum sociis gradiendo, sequi virguncula Christi.
Cumque columba locum volitans venisset ad illum,
quem nunc non sterilem magnis scimus fore petris,
descendens terram rostro percusserat illam,
sub cuius lapides latuerunt aggere plures.

for the structure could not readily be acquired in these parts, so the completion of the temple experienced a delay after it was begun. But Abbess Hathumoda, trusting that believers can obtain everything from the Lord by faith, continuously wore herself out in immense labor, serving God with her holy efforts night and day. And, with many of her subordinates accompanying her, she asked that the relief of assistance be delivered from heaven, so that the work not remain unfinished which had begun so well. Without delay, she became aware that the heavenly mercy she was seeking had arrived, ready to take pity on her wishes. For as she fasted and spent her time in sacred prayers, one day when she lay prostrate next to the altar she was inspired by the counsel of a gentle voice to go out and to follow a bird that she would see on the way, perched on top of a certain huge rock. And, embracing these instructions with a ready heart, she set out, trusting sincerely in the words of the voice that instructed her. And taking well-trained masons with her, she very quickly went where the Holy Spirit led her, until she came to the noble temple, already under construction. There she saw a precious white dove sitting on the lofty peak of the designated rock. The dove at once went on ahead, flying with spread wings, and moderated its flight in an unusual way, so that the cherished virgin of Christ, walking along with her companions, could follow in a straight path the furrow the dove cut through the air. And when the dove had come in its flight to a place which (we now know) is not lacking in large stones, it descended and struck with its beak the earth, under an embankment of which many

Quo certe viso Christi dignissima virgo
emundare locum socias praeceperat ipsum
et molem terrae circumfodiendo secare
tellurisque gravem fodiendo scindere molem.
Quo facto, praestante pia bonitate superna,
copia magnarum monstratur multa petrarum,
unde monasterii cum templo moenia coepti
omnia materiam possent traxisse petrinam.
Hinc, magis atque magis, toto conamine mentis,
factores templi, Domini sub honore sacrandi,
instabant operi mox nocte dieque recenti.

Sed dux Liudulfus, primus qui conditor eius
exitit et cura cuius processit origo
omnis structurae precibus poscentibus Odae,
(pro dolor!) ad summum non duxit opus studiosum.
Sed naturalis saeva tactus nece mortis,
cogitur ante suum Factori reddere flatum,
quam perfecta domus Domini foret inclita prorsus.
Commisitque suae carae moriendo relictae
atque suis natis, ducibus supra memoratis,
totius instantis pondus curamque laboris,
exorans votis, ut complerent, studiosis,
omnem coenobii structuram perficiendi.
Cuius in antiquo corpus venerabile templo
tunc gremio terrae commendatum fuit apte;
ossa sed, annorum post decursus aliquorum,
sunt hinc ecclesia translata locanda novella.
Forsan ad hoc illum mundo Deus abstulit isto,
dum vix aetatis febres tetigit mediocris:
illustris domnae post haec ut plenius Odae
mens intenta deo posset tractare superna

stones lay hidden. Assuredly, when that most worthy virgin of Christ saw this, she ordered her companions to clear out that very spot and to cut away the heavy mass of soil by digging. When this was done, by provision of the merciful goodness of heaven, a great abundance of huge rocks was revealed, from which all the walls of the monastery they had begun, along with its temple, were able to draw stone building material. And so, more and more, with every effort of their hearts, the builders of that temple, which was to be dedicated in honor of the Lord, devoted themselves then night and day to their new work.

But Duke Liudolf, who was the original builder of the monastery, and through whose concern the creation of the entire structure proceeded in response to the insistent prayers of Oda, did not bring to completion (alas!) this work for which he was so eager. But struck by the savage destruction of a natural death, he was forced to return his spirit to its Maker, before that renowned house of the Lord could be entirely finished. And dying, he committed to the dear wife he left behind and to their children, that is, those dukes mentioned above, the weight and management of the whole pressing work, entreating them, with urgent prayers, to complete all the construction of the monastery that remained to be done. His venerable body was then duly entrusted to the bosom of the earth in the older temple; but, after the passing of some years, his bones were transferred from there for placement in the new church. Perhaps God took him away from this world when he had barely reached the torments of middle age for this reason: so that after his death, the mind of the illustrious Lady Oda, more fully intent on God, could deal with heavenly matters,

expers carnalis totius prorsus amoris.
Nec tamen auxilii solamen denegat illi,
sed praestabat opem solita pietate recentem,
qua suffulta suas posset ditescere nonnas
omnibus his rebus, noster quibus indiget usus.
Ergo, sui natam, Liutgard de nomine dictam,
nutu clementis Regis praestante perennis,
elegit clarus Francorum rex Hludowicus
regni consortem sibimet sociamque perennem;
filius illius, cuius dono Liudulfus
suscepit primum propriae gentis dominatum.
Quae regina quidem nobis ad prosperitatem
facta suae dignum sanctae matri famulatum,
<consensu> regis, praebens, proprii senioris,
<maxima> coenobio permisit commoda nostro.
Interea Christi virgo felix Hathumoda,
cum gregis undenos curam bis gesserat annos,
ocius in Christo moriens transivit ad astra;
Gerbergae tenerum commisit ovile regendum.
Haec fuit illustri cuidam nimiumque potenti
desponsata viro Bernrad de nomine dicto,
sed sese Christo clam consecraverat ipsa,
caelesti fervens sponso, velamine sacro,
omnino sponsum spernens animo moriturum.
Nec tamen extemplo pro seditione cavenda
auro fulgentes potuit deponere vestes,
induitur solito sed vestitu pretioso.
Interea venit, quem sponsa Dei reprobavit,
uti colloquiis eius quaerens manifestis.
Audivit vero, votum quia fecerit ipsa
velle puellarem caste servare pudorem.

being altogether free of all carnal passion. Still, he did not deny her the consolation of his assistance, but rather with his customary mercy offered her a new source of wealth, fortified by which she was able to endow her nuns with all the things which our way of life requires. To wit, her daughter, who was called by the name of Liutgard, was chosen with the approval of the merciful eternal King by Louis, the illustrious king of the Franks, as his royal consort and his eternal partner; he was the son of that man by whose gift Liudolf had first received dominion over his people. Liutgard indeed, when she became queen, displayed toward our prosperity, with the consent of the king, her seigneur, a devotion worthy of her holy mother, and provided the greatest advantages to our monastery.

Meanwhile, the happy virgin of Christ, Hathumoda, when she had taken care of her flock for twice eleven years, passed swiftly to the stars, dying in Christ. She entrusted her tender lambs to Gerberga for ruling. This Gerberga had been betrothed to a certain illustrious and very powerful man, who was called by the name of Bernrad, but she had secretly consecrated herself to Christ with the holy veil, burning for her celestial spouse, and altogether spurning in her heart a mortal spouse. Nevertheless, in order to avoid a quarrel, she could not immediately put aside her shining gold clothes, but continued to dress herself, as usual, in precious clothing. In the meantime, Bernrad, whom the bride of God had rejected, came, looking to have a frank conversation with her. He had heard, in truth, that she had made a vow that she wished chastely to preserve her girlish modesty.

Quae cum tardaret cito nec procedere vellet,
quod prius audierat, verum fore valde timebat.
Impatiensque morae domnam precibus placat Odam,
donec ipsa suam iussit procedere natam,
ornatam pulchre cultu vestis pretiosae
necnon gemmatis sponsarum more metallis.
Ast ubi Bernradus vidit, quam desideravit,
his verbis caram causari fertur amicam:
"Non raro didici fama prodente sinistra,
quod tu nitaris nostrum disrumpere pactum
et fidei foedus servandum solvere prorsus.
At nunc ad bellum citius properare futurum
praecepto regis cogor, nostri senioris;
hinc, tempus quidni non est hoc discutiendi.
Si redeam certe sospes comitante salute
scito procul dubio, quod te mihimet sociabo,
atque tui votum penitus pessumdabo vanum."
Dixerat et dextra permotus mente levata
iurat per gladium, per candidulum quoque collum,
iuxta posse sui factis praedicta repleri.
Respondens ergo Gerberg ait ore modesto,
"Christo me totam committo meam quoque vitam,
utque fiat de me iuxta Domini rogo velle."
His ita colloquiis mutuo sermone peractis,
Bernrad mox abiit, casuque suo cito sensit
nil contra Dominum quemcumque valere superbum.
Et, quia plus iusto deliquit inania fando,
decidit in bello, victus virtute superna;
ac Christi virgo sponsi caelestis amori
se mox coniunxit, quem caste semper amavit.

When she delayed and was in no hurry to appear before him, he was very much afraid that what he had earlier heard was true. And impatient of delay, he sought to win the favor of Lady Oda by his entreaties, until she ordered her daughter to appear, beautifully adorned in an outfit of rich cloth and with precious metals covered in jewels, in the manner of a bride. But when Bernrad saw the one he loved, he is said to have pleaded with his beloved fiancée in these words: "I have heard more than once through the wagging of evil tongues that you are eager to break our engagement and to dissolve altogether an oath of fidelity that ought to be preserved. But now I am compelled by order of the king, our seigneur, to rush off in haste to the coming war; therefore, this is, no doubt, not the time for discussing this. Assuredly, if I return unharmed and in possession of my health, you should know beyond any doubt that I will join you to myself, and I will utterly do away with your pointless vow of chastity." He said this, and raising his right arm, confused in his mind, he swore by his sword, and also by her dear white neck, to accomplish in his actions what he had declared, so far as he was able. Then Gerberga spoke, responding in a mild voice, "I entrust myself and my life totally to Christ, and I ask that it be done with me according to the Lord's will." When this conversation was completed by this mutual exchange, Bernrad promptly departed, and he soon learned by his misfortune that anyone who is proud can do nothing against the Lord. And, because he had sinned unjustly by speaking empty words, he fell in battle, conquered by heavenly power; and the virgin of Christ soon joined herself to the love of her heavenly spouse, whom she had always chastely loved.

Cuius primatus sexto, ni fallor, in anno
Brun dux Ecclesiam promptus defendere sanctam
incursu de saevorum satis Ungariorum,
(pro dolor!) ex ipsis Domini pravis inimicis
occiditur binis cum praesulibus venerandis
omnibus atque viris propriae pariter legionis.
Quo mox occiso, iunior frater suus Odo,
dux factus populi dono regis Hludowici,
respondit factis sanctae voto genetricis.
Ac studio simili concordans nititur illi
cultibus ecclesiam dignis ornare novellam,
quae post haec anno fuerat sacranda secundo.
Moenia coenobii perfecit <et> omnia nostri
commoda mansuris illic per saecla puellis.

His bene perfectis, iuxta praecepta parentis
eligitur, domna poscente videlicet Oda,
ipsa dies templo condigne sanctificando,
in cuius noctis medio quam pluribus illo
tertio conspicuae quondam fulsere lucernae;
et quod cunctorum pariter venerabile festum
sanctorum vasti fuerat per climata mundi
principio mensis celebrandum rite Novembris.
Hac fama templi passim resonante sacrandi,
undique permultae mox confluxere catervae,
optantes diei praesentes esse celebri.
Scilicet, aurorae primo candore micante,
omnis nostrarum collectim turba sororum,
susceptis patronorum gratulando piorum
corporibus sacris pergit, resonantibus hymnis,
ad loca coenobii summo conamine structi.
Tunc tandem cunctis ad cultum rite paratis

In the sixth year of his rule, if I am not mistaken, Duke Bruno, who was quick to defend the holy Church against an incursion of very savage Hungarians, was killed (alas!) by those same depraved enemies of the Lord; he was killed along with two venerable bishops and all the men of his legion as well. As soon as Bruno was killed, his younger brother Oddo, having been made duke of the people by the gift of King Louis, answered his holy mother's wishes by his deeds. And with a zeal that matched hers he strove in harmony with her to adorn the new church in suitable elegance, and it was consecrated in the second year after this. He completed the walls of our monastery and all things necessary for the girls who were going to live there through the ages.

When these things had been fully completed, in accord with the instructions of his parent, that is, at the request of Lady Oda, the day was chosen for appropriately dedicating the temple, that same day on which, in the middle of the night, the bright lights had once shone for the third time on a great many people there; and this was the very day as well that the venerable feast of All Saints was duly celebrated throughout the regions of the vast world, the first day of the month of November. With the fame of that sacred temple resounding far and wide, huge crowds poured in from all sides, hoping to be present on that celebrated day. Indeed, at the first shining light of dawn, the whole assembly of our sisters as a group, giving thanks for the reception of the sacred relics of our kindly patrons, amid resounding hymns, proceeded to the site of the monastery, which had been built with the greatest effort. Then finally, when everything had been duly prepared for the observance of the feast day,

festi, Wicberhtus, praesul Domini benedictus,
dedicat hoc templum Domini sub honore decorum
omnibus ad laudem sanctis per saecla perennem,
quorum tunc festum digne fuerat celebrandum.
Hoc nam facta fuit clari sacratio templi
centum mansurnis octo vicibus revolutis
octonis denis uno pariter superaucto,
postquam Virgo puellaris sine sorde pudoris
saeclorum Regem peperit propriumque parentem.
Tunc coepere locis primum silvestribus illis
carmina divinae laudis clare resonare.
Exin et illius nostri collectio coetus
illic permansit Domino iugiter famulando.
Et, licet abbatissa gregem Gerberga recentem
caute servaret crebris monitisque doceret
conservare suae fuerant quae congrua vitae,
contra propositum nec quid patrare profanum,
domna tamen conversando venerabilis Oda
intra claustra monasterii, cura vigilanti,
scrutatur coniunctarum persaepe sororum
actus et studium, mores, vitae quoque cursum,
ne vel contempta maiorum lege sequenda
vivere lege sua reprobe praesumeret ulla,
vel locus illiciti foret ullius peragendi;
exemploque suo praemonstravit facienda.
Et, ceu prudentis dulcis dilectio matris
nunc terrore suas prohibet delinquere natas,
nunc etiam monitis bona velle suadet amicis,
sic haec sancta suas caras instruxit alumnas
nunc dominatricis mandando iure potentis,
nunc etiam matris mulcendo more suavis,

Wigbert, the blessed bishop of the Lord, dedicated this beautiful temple in honor of the Lord, for eternal glory through the ages, to all the saints whose feast day was worthily celebrated on that day. Indeed, the consecration of that famous temple was performed on the day when the eight hundred and eightieth year plus one rolled around in turn after the Virgin without blemish to her maidenly modesty bore the King of the ages who was also her own parent. Then in those forested places songs of divine praise began for the first time to resound loudly. And from that day onward, the assembly of this group of ours has remained there continuously serving the Lord. And, even though Abbess Gerberga was carefully protecting the members of her new flock and instructing them with frequent admonitions to observe those things which were appropriate to their way of life, and not to do anything profane, contrary to their proposed way of life, nevertheless, the venerable Lady Oda, living within the cloister of the monastery, with constant attention regularly scrutinized the actions and effort, the manners, and the way of life of the assembled sisters, so that no one would presume, in contempt for following the law of our ancestors, to live wickedly following her own law, and so that there would be no place for doing anything illicit; and she showed them what to do by her own example. And, just as the sweet love of a prudent mother sometimes by fear prevents her daughters from sinning, and sometimes by friendly counsels persuades them to choose what is good, so this saintly woman instructed her cherished students, sometimes by the righteous commanding of a powerful overseer, and sometimes in the soothing manner of a tender mother,

quo vita simili cunctae communiter uni
servirent Regi, iubilant cui sidera caeli.
Praeterea, quas maternae pietatis amore
nutrivit, vere magno veneratur honore,
has ipsas vocitando suas saepissime domnas.
Nam, quoties neptes eius proceresque nepotes,
quos praepollentis decus extollebat honoris,
eius ad implendum convenerunt famulatum,
certantes donis illam donare coruscis
regis ut illustrem socrum propriamque parentem,
illos mox verbis affari dicitur istis:
"Exhortans moneo vos, o mea pignora cara,
ut maturetis condignis primule vestris
muneribus nostras large ditescere domnas.
Hic servire piis debent quae sedulo nostris
patronis, quorum meritis precibus quoque sacris
successus nobis optatae prosperitatis
necnon regalis decus accedebat honoris."
Hac ratione suam stirpem persuaserat omnem
erga coenobii cultum pie sollicitari.
Et loca, quae generi dono regis Hludowici
possessura quidem proprium suscepit in usum,
permittente sua, pariter, pietate benigna,
ecclesiae tradi faciebat Gandeshemensi.
Nec rex ipse locum sublimavit minus illum
Liudgardis pie reginae bonitate precante,
sed tradens illo largitur praedia multa
in ius Gerbergae, nostrae rectricis amandae,
ipsius illustris reginae namque sororis.
Quae rex Arnulfus, successor scilicet huius,
posthac per scriptum regali iure statutum

so that by a similar way of life, they could all jointly serve the one King, in whom the stars in the sky rejoice. Furthermore, the women she raised with the love of maternal kindness, she truly respected with great honor, very frequently calling these same women her own mistresses. Indeed, as often as her granddaughters and noble grandsons, who were exalted by the distinction of very great honor, convened to fulfill their service to her, competing to endow her with splendid gifts, both as the illustrious mother-in-law of the king and as their own parent, she is reported to have addressed them straightaway in these words: "By way of encouragement I advise you, my dear children, to hasten to be first in lavishly endowing our mistresses with your worthy gifts. It is their duty here to serve attentively our pious patrons, by whose merits and holy prayers the success of welcome prosperity as well as the distinction of royal honor has come to us." By such reasons, she persuaded all her offspring out of piety to be solicitous regarding the support of the monastery. And the places which she had received by the gift of her son-in-law King Louis to hold, in fact, for her own use, by permission of his kind generosity, she, likewise, had transferred to the church of Gandersheim. And the king himself honored that place no less, through the goodness of Queen Liutgard's pious petitioning, but he granted to it many estates, transferring them to the authority of Gerberga, our beloved leader, and the sister, indeed, of the illustrious queen herself. King Arnulf, that is, Louis's successor, afterward confirmed these gifts by royal authority through a written statute,

firmat vinetis eius dono superauctis.
Ac sic coenobio succedunt prospere plura,
summorum meritis intercedentibus almis
pontificum, quorum constat sub honore dicatum.
Sed ne plus iusto fragiles extollere mentes
suaderet talis successus prosperitatis,
utque probaretur felix nostri dominatrix,
vere Iudicii salubris censura superni
perplures horum mundo subtraxerat isto,
quorum coenobium fuerat solamine fultum.
   Ergo rege pio iam defuncto Hludowico,
qui regum primus nostros tradebat in usus
regali prius obsequio loca debita multa,
necnon chirographis eius sub nomine scriptis
iura monasterii firmaverat omnia nostri,
eius post annos discessus denique paucos,
Liudgardis regina, sui dignissima regni
consors, tantorum quae nobis causa bonorum
extitit, e mundo discessit (pro dolor!) isto,
non sine nostrarum magno rerum detrimento.
Cui nam consimilis successit causa doloris,
abbatissa bonis Gerberg quia dedita curis,
quae, praedictorum suffulta iuvamine regum
necnon reginae germano foedere iunctae,
coenobium donis ornavit saepe coruscis
usibus et quaestum nostris superaddidit amplum,
postquam bis denos binos quoque praefuit annos
officio vice rectricis perfuncta prioris
deposito fragilis mortali pondere carnis
Factori flatum reddebat ab aethre receptum.
Orbatumque sui dimisit ovile sorori
Christinae procurandum sancteque tuendum.

adding as his own gift some vineyards. And, thus, many things went on prosperously for the monastery, thanks to the gracious intercessions of those popes to whose honor the monastery is dedicated. But in order that the success of such prosperity not persuade weak minds to exalt themselves more than is just, and so that our fortunate overseer might be tested, the truly salubrious censure of the heavenly Judge removed from this world a great many of those people by whose assistance the monastery had been supported.

And so, the pious King Louis was now dead, he who had been the first king to hand over for our uses many places previously subject to royal service and who had confirmed with handwritten documents in his own name all the rights of our monastery; then a few years after his departure, Queen Liutgard, that most worthy consort of his realm, who was the source of such great benefactions to us, departed from this world (alas!), not without great detriment to our affairs. And in fact, an equal source of pain ensued, because Abbess Gerberga, who was devoted to honorable concerns, and who, supported by the assistance of the aforementioned kings and of the queen joined to her by a sisterly bond, had often adorned our monastery with splendid gifts and added on top of that an ample income for our uses, this Gerberga, after she had been in charge for twice ten years plus two, functioning in her turn as the ruling prioress, put off the mortal burden of her frail flesh and returned to her Maker the spirit she had received from heaven. And she surrendered the orphaned congregation to her sister Christina to be cared for and to be watched over religiously.

Quae praefatarum mores sectando sororum,
atque sui vitam bene praemeditando gerendam,
illis fit similis magnae forma probitatis,
quis fuit aequalis provectu nobilitatis.
Mater et illius, stabilem corrumpere cuius
mentem nullarum potuit mutatio rerum,
quominus obsequio Domini fieret studiosa,
provocat exemplis illam, monitis quoque crebris,
ut, sese semper circumspiciens sapienter,
commissum caute sibimet servaret ovile,
necnon factorum iuxta meritum variorum
nunc pie subiectas monitis mulceret amicis,
nunc etiam verbis iuste terreret acerbis,
ne quem divini ritum cultus violari
torpens affectus cordis permitteret eius.
Ipsaque domna sui studio laudabilis Oda,
quae, claris splendens radiis mirae bonitatis,
sat dilecta Deo fuerat, celebris quoque mundo,
semper maternae solito pietatis amore,
eius adoptivis studuit conquirere natis
quicquid nonnarum deposcere sciverat usum.
Ottonisque ducis clari devotio grandis
concordando suae votis carae genetricis,
auxilio regum quibus exhibuit famulatum,
ipsum virgineum coetum Christi famularum
fovit clementer necnon provexit amanter.
Nec propriae vitae compelli quivit amore,
ut vel eas damno laedendo tangeret ullo
vel minus impleret, quae mater digna iuberet.
Ac sic concessae sibimet per tempora vitae
omni ferventis studuit conamine mentis

Christina, following the practices of her aforementioned sisters, and earnestly planning to live her life properly, became in the example of her great goodness just like her sisters, just as she was their equal in the prominence of her nobility. And her mother Oda, whose steady mind no change of any circumstances could corrupt in such a way that she would be less intent on her service to the Lord, encouraged Christina by examples, and also by frequent admonitions, that, always wisely looking around her, she carefully protect the flock entrusted to her, and also that, according to the merits of their various deeds, she should sometimes be gentle to her subordinates in a kindly way with friendly admonitions, and sometimes justly frighten them with stern words, so that no flagging dedication in her own heart would allow any ritual of divine worship to be violated. And Lady Oda herself, praiseworthy for her zeal, shining with the bright rays of a wondrous goodness, who had been very much loved by God and was also celebrated in the world, out of the customary love of her maternal kindness, was always eager to get for her adopted daughters whatever she knew the employment of nuns demanded. And the grand devotion of the brilliant Duke Oddo, in concord with the wishes of his dear mother, and with the aid of the kings to whom he rendered service, graciously provided for this virginal congregation of handmaids of Christ and lovingly forwarded their interests. And he could not be compelled even at the cost of his own life, either to lay a hand on them, wounding them by any injury, or to fall short in fulfilling what his worthy mother ordered. And so throughout the periods of life granted to him, he endeavored with every effort of his ardent spirit to pro-

coenobio patronorum praebere suorum
ipsius auxilii semper tutamina certi.
Nec vice terribilis metui petiit senioris,
sed bene mansueti genitoris ad instar amari.
Unde loco, non inmerito, permansit in illo
hactenus insignis laus illius pietatis.
Nos quoque permotae tantae dulcedine famae,
necdum maternis quae tunc prorupimus alvis,
sed fuimus vere longo post tempore natae,
haud minus illius constanter amore flagramus,
quam quae praesentem contemplabantur eundem
atque suae donis ditabantur pietatis.
Hic igitur talis praeclarae vir pietatis,
qui pius urbicolis tribuit bona talia nostris,
morte sui matrem nostri domnamque potentem
praeveniendo prior, vetiti pro crimine pomi,
quod protoplastes degustavere parentes,
exuitur membris limoso stamine textis
(pro dolor!) atque seris clausit sua lumina mortis,
coetu nostrarum circumvallante sororum
pernimio domni fletu lectum morituri.
Cuius ad exequias summo nisu celebrandas
undique nostrates confluxerunt lacrimantes
atque sui loetum cari senioris amarum
omnes immodicis pariter flevere lamentis.
Sed luctum procerum vulgi pariterque lamentum
vicit nonnarum miseranda querela suarum.
Quae, pro defectu mentis solito muliebris,
vivere spernentes citiusque mori cupientes
in lacrimando modum voluerunt ponere nullum.
Hinc patris eiusdem cari domnique benigni

vide to the monastery of his patrons the protections of his ever-assured assistance. And he did not seek to be feared in the manner of a dreaded seigneur, but to be well loved on the model of a gentle parent. And so, not undeservedly, praise for his remarkable kindness has endured in that place up to the present day. We, also, are deeply moved by the sweetness of such a reputation, we who at that time had not yet emerged from our mothers' wombs, but were, in truth, born a long time later, and we burn no less constantly with love for him, than those women who looked upon him in person and were enriched by the gifts of his kindness.

This man, then, of such outstanding kindness, who had kindly distributed such goods to the residents of our community, preceded his own mother, our powerful mistress, by going before her in death, the death caused by the crime of the forbidden fruit that our first parents tasted. And he stripped off his mortal limbs, woven from threads of clay, (alas!) and shut his eyes behind the bars of death, while a group of our sisters, with abundant tears, surrounded our dying lord's bed. To his funeral, which was celebrated with the greatest exertion, our countrymen poured in from all sides in tears, and all in equal measure wept with immoderate laments over the bitter death of their beloved seigneur. But the pitiable grief of his own nuns surpassed the sorrow of the nobles as well as the lamentation of the commoners. The nuns, from the normal weakness of a woman's heart, scorning life and desiring a very swift death, wanted to place no limit on their weeping. For this reason, they kept the body of this beloved father and beneficent lord unburied for

corpus per triduum conservabant inhumatum,
ceu sese lacrimis sperarent posse refusis
extincti flatum citius revocare reductum.
Tandem concilium sapiens satis advenientum
decernens vanae spei debere reniti,
ocius in tumulo non absque dolore parato
sed luctu nimio circumstantum madefacto,
membra ducis tanti digne servanda locari
fecit, in ecclesiae medio quam struxerat ipse.
Illic, nostrarum studio certante sororum,
continuis precibus, dilectus spiritus eius
semper Celsithroni commendatur pietati,
quo det ei requiem clemens sine fine perennem.
  Scilicet ante dies octo totidem quoque noctes,
quam ducis occasus miserabilis accidit huius,
ipsius nato, regi quandoque futuro,
nascitur Henrico famosus filius Oddo,
qui fuit electus Regis pietate perennis
primus Saxonum rex post patrem strenuorum
augustus Romanorum pariterque potentum.
  Mensibus hinc senis cursu volitante peractis,
dum decus hoc tanti clarum generis fuit ortum,
in quo laeta procul dubio promissa repleta
Christi baptistae creduntur primitus esse,
istius exiguae quae mox in vertice musae
Aedae namque suae memini fore dicta parenti,
Oda nimis felix, nostri spes et dominatrix,
cum decies denos septem quoque vixerat annos,
vitam fine bono consummans transit ad astra,
expectans spe felici tempus redeundi
flatus atque resurgendi de pulvere pleni

three days, as if they hoped by pouring out tears that they could promptly recall the withdrawn spirit of the deceased. Finally, a very learned conclave of the assembled people, deciding that they had to resist vain hope, saw to it that the limbs of this great duke were swiftly placed in a tomb, prepared not without pain but drenched by the great grief of the bystanders, to be worthily preserved in the middle of the church he had himself constructed. There, by the competing zeal of our sisters, amid continuous prayers, his beloved spirit was commended to the kindness of the One ever enthroned on high, to grant him, mercifully, eternal rest without end.

In fact, eight days and as many nights before the pitiable death of Duke Oddo had occurred, there was born to his child Henry, who was one day to become king, a famous son, another Otto, who by the mercy of the eternal King was chosen the first king of the hardy Saxons, after his father Henry, and likewise emperor of the mighty Romans.

When, rolling along in their course, six months had passed from the time when this shining glory of so great a family was born, in whom without doubt those happy promises of Christ's baptizer are thought to have been first fulfilled, promises which at the start of this little poem of mine I mentioned were spoken, in fact, to his ancestor Aeda, six months, I say, after he was born, the very blessed Oda, our overseer and hope, after she had lived for ten times ten years plus seven more, concluded her life with a virtuous ending and passed to the heavens, awaiting with blessed hope the time of her spirit's returning and of her full body's rising

corporis, in tumulo quod nunc sub tegmine duro
iuxta natarum requiescit busta suarum.
  Nec Christina, suis quae sola remansit alumnis,
iam tunc instantis grandis dulcedo doloris,
plus quam bis ternos post matrem vixerat annos.
Sed reddens animam Factore vocante beatam,
iungitur in lucis patria pacisque perennis
eius germanis, quarum pollebat honoris
heres et sanctae sectatrix inclita vitae.
Quas matri cunctas in caelo consociatas,
alme Pater, tecum praesta gaudere per aevum
illius et regni mercede perenniter uti,
quod retro cuncta tuis servasti saecula caris,
quo te cum Nato necnon cum Flamine sacro
solum rectorem caelestibus imperitantem
dulci laetitiae laudantes voce iucundae
<perstent divinis semper veneranter in odis.>

from the dust, her body which rests now in a tomb under a sturdy roof next to the graves of her own daughters.

And Christina, who alone remained for her charges, and already then was a great source of sweetness in their pressing pain, did not live more than twice three years after her mother. But returning her blessed soul when her Maker called her, she was joined in the fatherland of light and eternal peace to her sisters; she flourished as the heiress of their distinction, and as a renowned follower of the holy life. Grant, O caring Father, that all these women, joined to their mother in heaven, rejoice with you for eternity and enjoy forever the reward of that kingdom, which before all time you reserved for those dear to you, so that praising you, along with your Son and the Holy Spirit, as the sole ruler governing the heavens, in a sweet voice of blessed joy, they might ever reverently persist in their divine odes.

Appendix

Iussimus haec scribi vobismet prorsus amori.
Econtra preculis tandem succurrite nobis,
ut pariter patriam mereamur adire supernam,
quae specie nivea tenet hoc, quod lectio supra.

Appendix

We have ordered that these things be written for you entirely because of our love. In turn, then, come quickly to our aid with your prayers, so that equally we may deserve to attain the heavenly fatherland, which preserves in a snow-white beauty what the reading above describes.

Abbreviations

Berschin = Walter Berschin, ed., *Hrotsvit. Opera omnia* (Munich, 2001)

BHL = *Bibilotheca Hagiographica Latina antiquæ et mediæ ætatis,* edited by the Socii Bolandiani (Brussels, 1898–1901)

CCSL = Corpus Christianorum Series Latina

CSEL = Corpus Scriptorum Ecclesiasticorum Latinorum

DMLBS = *Dictionary of Medieval Latin from British Sources,* ed. R. E. Latham, 17 vols. (Oxford, 1975–2013)

Homeyer = Helene Homeyer, ed., *Hrotsvithae opera. Mit Einleitungen und Kommentar* (Munich, 1970)

Lewis and Short = Charlton T. Lewis and Charles Short, *A Latin Dictionary* (Oxford, 1975)

MGH = Monumenta Germaniae historica

PL = J. P. Migne, *Patrologiae cursus completus: Series Latina* (Brussels, 1841–1865)

Strecker = Karl Strecker, ed., *Hrotsvithae opera* (Leipzig, 1906)

von Winterfeld = Paul von Winterfeld, ed., *Hrotsvithae opera,* MGH Scriptores rerum Germanicarum in usum scholarum 34 (Berlin, 1902)

Note on the Texts

The Latin text follows Walter Berschin's Teubner edition, *Opera omnia* (Munich, 2001), except as noted in the Notes to the Texts. The titles and line numbering are Berschin's unless noted; but I have not included his divisions within the individual books (*Pars prior, Pars posterior,* and so on). Punctuation, capitalization, and orthography are accommodated to the English translation and follow the guidelines of the Dumbarton Oaks Medieval Library.

C = Cologne, Historisches Archiv, W* 101.

M = Munich, Bayerische Staatsbibiliothek, CLM 14485

M^2 = correction in M by early hand

$M^?$ = correction in M of unknown date

H1 = Hildesheim, Dombibliothek 534 *(The Origins of the Gandersheim Convent)*

H2 = Hannover, Niedersächsische Landesbibliothek, MS XXIII 167 *(The Origins of the Gandersheim Convent)*

Berschin = Walter Berschin, ed., *Opera omnia* (Munich, 2001)

Homeyer = Helene Homeyer, ed., *Hrotsvithae opera* (Munich, 1970)

Strecker = Karl Strecker, ed., *Hrotsvithae opera,* 2nd ed. (Leipzig, 1930)

von Winterfeld = Paul von Winterfeld, ed., *Hrotsvithae opera,* MGH Scriptores rerum Germanicarum in usum scholarum 34 (Berlin, 1902)

Note on the Texts

Notes to the Texts

Book 1

The Conversion of a Certain Desperate Young Man by Saint Basil the Bishop

36 supradictae: supra dicte *von Winterfeld, Strecker, Homeyer, Berschin*

Book 2

The Fall and Conversion of Mary, Niece of Abraham

5.1 loquitur? Hospes, salve *C*: loquitur hospes? *M, von Winterfeld, Strecker, Homeyer, Berschin*

The Passion of the Holy Virgins Faith, Hope, and Charity

3.21 pariter impar: pariter par *M, von Winterfeld, Strecker, Homeyer, Berschin*

Book 3

The Deeds of Otto

486 olim per † manus regis deflevit Hugonis: Olim per manus regis defleuit Hugonis *M*; Olim per regis manus defleuit Hugonis M^2; Olim per regis manus /// Hugonis M^2; Olim per manus regis devenit Hugonis *von Winterfeld*; Olim per manus regis. . . . Hugonis *Strecker*; olim per † manus regis devenit Hugonis *Berschin*

The Origins of the Gandersheim Convent

79 fecit *H2, von Winterfeld, Strecker, Homeyer*: facit *H1, Berschin*

Notes to the Translations

Book I

Preface

1 *This little book*: The first book of Hrotsvit's writings in the Munich manuscript (Bayerische Staatsbibiliothek, CLM 14485, hereafter, M) comprises eight major poems, in dactylic hexameters, on sacred subjects, all except the second being versified biographies of saints. Also included are short prose prefaces and prologues, as well as introductory poems, metrical codas, and verse prayers. Some of these appear to be integral parts of one or another of the larger poems, while others may be separate texts. It seems clear that Hrotsvit is responsible for the composition of these peripheral pieces, and perhaps also for the selection and arrangement of them within the book. This prose introduction, a general address to Hrotsvit's readers, precedes the first book.

3 *apocryphal*: Hrotsvit means something like "noncanonical sacred texts" and is referring in particular to the Gospel of Pseudo-Matthew, one of her primary sources for the *History of the Birth of Mary*.

6 *environs*: The Latin *area* can mean "area, zone" as well as "threshing floor"; Hrotsvit is playing on these two meanings, the latter extending the metaphor of harvesting, gleaning, and fruitful labor introduced by the verb "gathered."

Gandersheim: Gandersheim Abbey, in Lower Saxony, the religious community to which Hrotstvit belonged.

7 *Rikkardis*: Otherwise unknown.

Gerberga: This is the second abbess of that name at Gandersheim, hence often called Gerberga II; see the note below to the *History of the Birth of Mary* 1.

8 *talent of . . . intelligence*: Hrotsvit refers to the parable of the talents (Matthew 25:14–30) but plays on two meanings of *talenta:* "talent" in the English sense of skill, and the ancient coin called a "talent," as in the parable.

minimal: *Extremus* could mean "least" (emphasizing the humility topos) or "ultimate, lasting, final."

History of the Birth of Mary

title *Prologue 1. To Abbess Gerberga*: This dedicatory poem of six elegiac couplets follows the prose *Preface* after two blank lines in M; these were apparently left blank for a title that was never added (until the fifteenth century). After the poem are five blank lines, which take up the remainder of the page (fol. 2v). The elaborate title to the poem proper *(Historia nativitatis . . . Domini),* in broadly spaced capital letters, begins on the following complete page (fol. 3r). Although it appears from the layout in M that the dedicatory prologue constitutes a separate poem (a dedication of the book as a whole), it has traditionally been numbered as the first twelve lines of the first poem in the book. Hrotsvit dedicates her work to the abbess of her convent, Gerberga II.

1 *royal line*: Gerberga was the daughter of Duke Henry I of Bavaria (d. 956)—himself the son of Henry the Fowler, king of East Francia (919–936)—and she was the niece of Otto I, "the Great" (king 936–973, emperor 962–973). Her mother was Judith (d. after 985), daughter of Duke Arnulf of Bavaria (d. 937).

title *The History . . . of the Lord*: The first and the longest of Hrotsvit's hagiographical poems recounts the birth and childhood of Mary, the mother of Jesus, as well as the birth and infancy of Jesus. Hrotsvit's source was the Gospel of Pseudo-Matthew, ed. Jan Gijsel, *Libri de nativitate Mariae,* Corpus Christianorum

Series Apocryphorum 9 (Turnhout, 1997), English trans. Bart D. Ehrman and Zlatko Pleše, *The Apocryphal Gospels: Texts and Translations* (New York, 2011), an apocryphal work of the sixth or seventh century (on the date, see Gijsel, *Libri de nativitate Mariae,* 11–13). Following the verse prologue of twelve verses, the poem proper starts with an introductory prayer to Mary of thirty-two verses, also in elegiac couplets, asking Mary and Christ for inspiration; then follow 859 verses in dactylic hexameter, the last six of which are a coda giving thanks to God and asking the heavenly choirs to praise him.

Saint James: Some of the manuscripts of Pseudo-Matthew erroneously attribute the work to James, the brother of Jesus (see Gijsel, *Libri de nativitate Mariae,* 15), and Hrotsvit used a manuscript of this type. The rubric in M led to the mistaken claim, especially in early scholarship on Hrotsvit, that her source was the Protoevangelium of Saint James (also called the Gospel of James or the Infancy Gospel of James), rather than, or in addition to, the Gospel of Pseudo-Matthew. The Protoevangelium is an earlier account of much of the same material found in the Gospel of Pseudo-Matthew, and it was one of the main sources of Pseudo-Matthew.

31 *donkey*: Balaam's ass; see Numbers 22:28–30.

33 *angel's word*: Luke 1:26–38.

41–44 *lazy ingrates . . . virgin choirs*: Hrotsvit alludes to the parable of the wise and foolish virgins, Matthew 25:1–13.

43 *regal*: Hrotsvit's adjective *purpureus* (purple) refers both to "royal purple" and to the color of blood.

45 *five thousand years*: Each of the six ages of the world (see following note) was thought to last one thousand years (see 2 Peter 3:8); five of the ages were completed, and the sixth had begun with the birth of Jesus.

46 *sixth age*: According to Augustine (*De catechizandis rudibus* 22), the six ages of the world were (1) from Adam to Noah, (2) from Noah to Abraham, (3) from Abraham to David, (4) from David to the Babylonian captivity, (5) from the Babylonian captivity to the birth of Jesus, and (6) from the birth of Jesus onward.

48–49 *prophets . . . predicted*: Hrotsvit seems to mean passages like Jeremiah 23:5–6 and Isaiah 7:14, but she may particularly have Micah 5:2 in mind.

51 *old law*: That is, the law of the Hebrew Bible (the Christian Old Testament).

58 *true shepherd*: Jesus.

89 *Ruben*: Not known except from Pseudo-Matthew and sources derived from it.

90 *addressed him with bitter words*: Compare Virgil, *Aeneid* 10.591.

147 *cut through the air . . . on wings*: Virgil, *Georgics* 1.406.

150 The verse may be corrupt; *perorat* (prayed) has been corrected in M (the original reading is unclear), and there is no internal rhyme. Karl Strecker, ed., *Hrotsvithae opera* (Leipzig, 1906; 2nd ed., Lepizig, 1930), proposed *per omnem* (through the entire [day]) and a lacuna after this line.

law of the Psalms: I take *lex Psalmorum* to mean "the guiding principle of the book of Psalms" and assume Hrotsvit is referring to Psalms 1:1–2, "Happy is the man who has not walked in the counsel of the ungodly . . . but his will is in the law of the Lord, and on his law he shall meditate day and night." In other words, Anna, who is sad *(maesta),* follows the prescription for what will make her happy *(beata)* laid out in Psalms 1:1–2: to meditate day and night on God's law.

193 *If your regard for me . . . is assured*: Compare Virgil, *Aeneid* 4.125 and 7.548, "tua si mihi certa voluntas." Hrotsvit substitutes *gratia* (grace), a more Christian term, for Virgil's *voluntas* (regard, esteem).

247 *golden gate*: The eastern gate of the Temple Mount in Jerusalem.

265 *the day arrived at last*: Virgil, *Aeneid* 2.324.

276 *star of the sea*: The interpretation of the name *Mariam* as *stella maris* (star of the sea) is found in Jerome, *De nominibus Hebraicis,* ed. PL vol. 23, cols. 841–42; Bede, *Homeliarum evangelii libri II,* ed. D. Hurst, in *Opera homiletica; Opera rhythmica,* ed. D. Hurst and J. Fraipont, CCSL 122 (Turnhout, 1955), book 1, homily 3, lines 53–55; and elsewhere.

352 Strecker posits a line lost after this one, on the basis of the par-

allel passage in Pseudo-Matthew 6:1 (Gijsel, *Libri de nativitate Mariae,* 333): "Insistebat . . . in lanificio, et omnia quae mulieres antiquae non poterant facere, ista in tenera aetate posita explicabat" (She was intent on wool working, and everything the elderly women were not able to do, she at a tender age could accomplish). The passage in Pseudo-Matthew makes clear that the *opera* (works) mentioned in verse 351 are specifically works of spinning and weaving.

387 *is . . . venerated*: *Veneror* is normally a deponent verb in Classical Latin, but it is here used passively.

394 *Abel*: See Genesis 4:2–18; he is named by Christ (Matthew 23:35) as the first martyr.

398 *Elijah*: The reference is to 4 Kings (2 Kings) 2:11.

411 *under the law*: This refers to the period after Moses and before Christ.

461 *was proclaimed*: The use of a future tense *(dicetur)* as a historic present is unusual.

503 *Chinese fleece*: Literally, "fleece of the Seres"; the Seres were a people of eastern Asia, occupying portions of modern China, who exported silk to the West.

547 *betrothed*: Hrotsvit is following the account in Luke 2:6, "cum Maria desponsata sibi uxore praegnante" (with Mary his espoused wife, who was with child), but omitting the noun *uxore* (wife), and so calling more attention to her still-betrothed state. That their marriage is not consummated, but she is pregnant—a source of public shame to Joseph—is the subtle justification Hrotsvit offers for Joseph's harsh words in lines 553–54, words for which the angel scolds him.

599 *rightly*: *Iure* could be either "rightly" or "with juice, liquid." Gonsalva Wiegand takes it in the latter sense and interprets it as "milk" (*ius* is not attested elsewhere as "milk" or "breast milk"): "The Non-Dramatic Works of Hrotswitha: Text, Translation, and Commentary" (PhD diss., Saint Louis University, 1936), 47 and 72.

612–13 Hrotsvit is alluding to the parable of the Pharisee and the publican (Luke 18:9–14). The former's prayer is a self-righteous justification of his own merits, while the latter's is simply "O God, be merciful to me, a sinner." The self-justifying prayer of Salome is likened by Hrotsvit to that of the Pharisee.

644 *the boundaries of Bethlehem*: Compare Sedulius, *Carmen paschale* 2.73.

656 *symbolically marking*: For this sense of *designare,* see DMLBS, under 1 *designare* 4, "to indicate allegorically, symbolize." These lines are not represented in Pseudo-Matthew; Hrotsvit elaborates them based on patristic allegorical exegesis of the three gifts as denoting Christ's kingship, incarnation, and sacrificial death; see Helene Homeyer, ed., *Hrotsvithae opera* (Munich, 1970), 72, citing, for example, Bede, *In Matthaei evangelium expositio,* ed. PL vol. 92, col. 13C.

659–71 Hrotsvit's discourse on the journey of Herod to Rome to defend himself on a charge of treason (the purpose of which is to provide an explanation for why Herod waited two years before ordering the slaughter of the Innocents) is not found in Pseudo-Matthew as it is preserved to us, but Homeyer assumes it was in an expanded version known to Hrotsvit and notes that at least the detail that Herod initiated the massacre "a year later when he returned from Rome" is found in one version of Pseudo-Matthew. The account given by Hrotsvit is not preserved in other sources, but scattered details of it appear elsewhere. See Homeyer, *Hrotsvithae opera,* 72. It is possible that Hrotsvit has conflated various Herods (Herod the Great, Herod Agrippa, Herod Antipas), as suggested by Wiegand, "The Non-Dramatic Works of Hrotswitha," 72.

664 *was charged*: Future tense for historic present, as in verse 461.

666 *fox's heart*: At Luke 13:32, Jesus calls Herod Antipas "that fox," lending some support to the idea that Hrotsvit has conflated various Herods (see note to verses 659–71).

682 *years*: Latin *mansurnus* (month) in the sense of *annus* (year) is not recorded in any of the dictionaries in the *Database of Latin Dictionaries,* but Hrotsvit uses it several times in this sense; see Paul von Winterfeld, ed., *Hrotsvithae opera,* MGH Scriptores rerum Germanicarum in usum scholarum 34 (Berlin, 1902), 377.

701–2 *darkness*: The name Egypt was etymologized as *tenebrae* (darkness); see Jerome, *Liber interpretationis Hebraicorum nominum,* ed. P. de Lagarde, CCSL 72 (Turnhout, 1959), 66, 73, 77.

721 *looks into our mind and is the witness of our heart*: See Wisdom 1:6 and Proverbs 24:12.

745 *forgetful*: *Obliviscor* is normally a deponent verb in Classical Latin, but it is used here passively.

748–49 *that*: *Ut* is used here with indicative verbs *(iunxere, commansere)* to express result.

754 *Mary*: Exceptionally, the first syllable of *Mariam* scans long here, contrary to the norm and to Hrotsvit's practice elsewhere. Perhaps the passage is defective, a short syllable before *Mariam* having fallen out of the text. The following parallels in which the first syllable of *Maria* scans long—compiled by Walter Berschin and Tino Licht, for whose assistance I am most grateful—seem, however, to justify the preservation of the text as found in M: *Carmina Centulensia* 1.3, ed. Ernst Dümmler, MGH Poetae Latini aevi Carolini 2 (Berlin, 1884), 623; *Passio metrica sancti Arnulfi* 807, ed. Wilhelm Harster, *Novem vitae sanctorum metricae* (Leipzig, 1887), 115; and, in a metrical *titulus* in the manuscript known as the "Evangelistary of Henry III," Bremen, Universitätsbibliothek, b. 21, fol. 62v.

765 *thinking ahead*: The first *o* in *praecogito* is short here.

768 *said*: The *e* in *loquebatur* is short here.

775 *Tree, bend your branches*: See Fortunatus, *Carmina* 2.2.25.

819 *cities bordering it*: Hrotsvit writes only "cities placed near it" *(urbibus appositis),* but Pseudo-Matthew has "through maritime cities" *(per civitates maritimas),* clarifying Hrotsvit's meaning.

825 *Sotinen*: According to some versions of Pseudo-Matthew, this city was in the region of Hermopolis (Lower Egypt).

837–39 *Behold . . . shattered*: Isaiah 19:1.

856 *what he has already done to our king, the Pharaoh*: See Exodus 5–12.

864 *change of your . . . hand*: See Psalms 76(77):11–12.

873 *enclose the world in the palm of your hand*: See Isaiah 40:12.

877 *impose names on the various stars*: See Psalms 146(147):4.

891 *Father*: *Genitore* is equivalent to *genitori* (dative).

898–904 *What kind . . . true God*: This coda is treated by some scholars as a separate poem. No blank lines precede it in M, and there is no separate title. It is only set off from the preceding lines in the same way as the internal divisions of the poem (that is, with a slightly enlarged first letter, here *Q[ualia]*); such divisions are rendered in the present edition by indentation of the first line of each.

On the Ascension of the Lord

title Hrotsvit's *Ascension* deals with Christ's bodily ascension to heaven on the fortieth day after his resurrection. It tells of the gathering of his disciples and Mary on the Mount of Olives on his last day on earth, and it includes speeches by Christ, David, angels, and God. In her first poem, *History of the Birth of Mary,* Hrotsvit deals with Christ's human beginnings, and in this one, with the final moments of his human life.

Bishop John: Hrotsvit's principal source is a Greek sermon, printed as pseudo-Chrysostom, *Sermo in sanctam assumptionem servatoris nostri, Patrologia Graeca* 64:45–48, where it is accompanied by an eighteenth-century Latin translation by Walther Taylor. She states in the rubric that she knew the work in a Latin translation, which does not appear to have survived. The identity of the Bishop John *(Iohannes episcopus)* named by Hrotsvit as the translator is uncertain; perhaps she, or her source, has conflated the putative author (John Chrysostom) and the translator.

13 Hrotsvit's use of the pseudo-Chrysostom sermon begins with this verse, with the mention of the Resurrection ("gloriola surgentis rite peracta"), and continues through verse 140.

20 *olive-bearing mountain*: Mount Olivet, or the Mount of Olives, is the site of the Ascension according to Acts 1:12.

23 *this world that is so dear to him*: It is not entirely clear whether *sibi carum* (dear to him) modifies *mundum* (world) or *me* (me). In the latter case, read: "sent me, I who am so dear to him." But the verse may allude to John 3:16, "Sic enim Deus dilexit mundum ut filium suum unigenitum daret" (For God so loved the world, as to give his only begotten Son), which would favor *sibi carum* modifying *mundum.*

23–24 Compare John 20:21.

25–26 Compare Matthew 28:19–20.

30–32 Compare Matthew 10:8.

33–34 Compare Luke 6:27–28.

35–37 Compare John 13:35.

47 Compare Psalms 103(104):32.

48 *my*: *Mis* is equivalent to *mei.*

49 *passing by*: Compare Matthew 27:39.

54–55 Compare Luke 23:34.

62–63 Compare John 10:11.

66–67 Compare John 20:17.

68–70 Compare John 14:1, 14:18.

71–72 Compare John 14:26.

73–74 Compare Matthew 28:20.

75 *When he . . . words*: Virgil, *Aeneid* 2.790, and commonly elsewhere in Virgil and other poets.

101–2 Compare Psalms 56(57):6 and 56(57):12.

104–5 Compare Psalms 98(99):9.

109–12 Compare John 14:27.

113–26 Compare Acts 1:9–11. These lines are not represented in the pseudo-Chrysostom sermon, which was Hrotsvit's source.

130–31 Compare Psalms 46(47):6.

134 Compare Matthew 3:17.

136 Compare John 1:1.

138–40 Compare Psalms 109(110):1.

147–50 *Whoever may read . . . deeds*: Some scholars treat these lines as a separate poem. The four verses, a coda in which Hrotsvit addresses the reader, follow *Ascension* in M, but there is no title in the manuscript, and no blank lines separate them from *Ascension.* They were meant to be separated by a slightly larger initial letter *(H[aec]),* and there is a blank space in the manuscript to accommodate it, but the initial was never added.

The Passion of Saint Gongolf the Martyr

title According to the earliest *Life* of Saint Gongolf (BHL 3328), edited by G. Henschenius, *Acta sanctorum Maii* (Antwerp, 1680), vol. 2, pp. 644–48, as well as by W. Levison, MGH Scriptores rerum Merovingicarum 7 (Hannover, 1920), 155, which was Hrotsvit's primary source, he was an eighth-century Burgundian nobleman, with property near Varennes in eastern France (today, Varennes-sur-Amance, department of Haute-Marne, roughly halfway between Nancy and Dijon). A courtier under Pepin (Hrotsvit interprets this as Pepin the Short, who died in 768), Gongolf was a hunter and a soldier, and might more accurately be described as the victim of a very bad marriage than as a martyr in any familiar sense. Mortally wounded by his wife's lover, he died after seeing both of them punished. When miracles were observed at his tomb, he began to be venerated as a saint; his feast day is variously the eleventh or the thirteenth of May. Relics of Gongolf were held in Varennes, Trier, Toul, and Mainz. Alone of Hrotsvit's legends, *Gongolf* is written in elegiac couplets.

1–18 A metrical prayer precedes *Gongolf* proper in M. It has no title but is separated from the end of the *Ascension* by three blank lines, apparently intended for a title that was never added (until the fifteenth century). This title should have been for *Gongolf* as a whole, not just for this prayer. The prayer begins with a pen-work letter *O,* three lines tall, the size and degree of decoration indicating that the prayer is integral to *Gongolf,* for the initial letter beginning the poem proper at line 19 is less elaborate. There is a rubric following the prayer, on a single line, *Passio sancti Gongolfi martyris* (The Passion of Saint Gongolf the Martyr), and there is also, inexplicably, a blank line between verses 19 and 20.

1 *O merciful sower of light*: Compare Prudentius, *Cathemerinon* 3.1: *O . . . lucisator . . . pie.* This Prudentian poem is entitled *Hymnus ante cibum* (Hymn before a Meal), so Hrotsvit's decision to begin the poem that introduces *Gongolf* with a clear allusion to this hymn (the term *lucisator,* "sower of light," appears only here and in Prudentius's hymn) may be evidence that Hrotsvit's sacred poems were intended to be read in refectory. See also below the note to *Theophilus* 448–55, about the closing prayer for "Blessing at Mealtime."

6 *threefold structure*: That is, earth, water, and air.

10 *of your own finger*: The sense is "of your own hand," but Hrotsvit is alluding to God's writing the Ten Commandments with his finger, Exodus 31:18.

19–21 Hrotsvit places Gongolf in the period of Pepin the Short (714–768), who became Mayor of the Palace, and thereby *de facto* ruler of the Merovingian kingdom, in 741, and ruled over Francia jointly with his elder brother Carloman. After Carloman retired (747) and Childeric III, the last of the Merovingian monarchs, was deposed (751), Pepin became sole king of the Franks, ruling from 751 until 768. As such, he was ruler of "the eastern realm of the Franks" (lines 19–20), which had previously been his brother Carloman's, as well as of the "Burgundian realms" (line 21), originally part of his own division. Pepin was the father of Charlemagne.

53 *proconsul*: Hrotsvit loosely refers to Gongolf by a variety of Roman titles, including *dux, consul,* and *proconsul,* all of them meaning something like "leader," "civic official," "statesman."

61–62 Compare Job 29:15.

119–20 *our people . . . the eastern people*: The farmer is emphasizing that the local Burgundians ("our people") as well as the ("eastern") people of East Francia celebrated Gongolf. See note on lines 19–21.

152 *gold in exchange for lesser gifts*: The expression derives ultimately from Homer, *Iliad* 6.119–236, where Glaucus trades his gold armor for Diomedes's bronze armor, a classic example of a witless exchange. Hrotsvit may know the story from the pseudo-Acro scholia to Horace, *Sermones* 1.7.16–17, ed. Otto Keller, *Pseudacronis scholia in Horatium vetustiora* (Leipzig, 1904), vol. 2, p. 91.

219 *eastern star was urging slumber*: Hrotsvit must mean the evening star (the planet Venus); to be sure, Venus is both the morning star and the evening star, but is in the west in the evening. Compare Virgil, *Aeneid* 2.9.

221–22 *rest . . . slithering*: Compare Virgil, *Aeneid* 2.268–69.

222 *drunkenness*: *Ebrietate = ebrietati* (dative).

231 *Duke*: See note on *Gongolf* 53.

243 The verse does not scan properly (*tempore* should have a short *o*); see Homeyer, *Hrotsvithae opera,* 109, for various conjectures, none of them very satisfactory.

266 *consul*: See note on *Gongolf* 53.

289 *a rock to pour out sweet waters*: Compare Exodus 17:6.

290 *the bitter bile of the lake*: Compare Exodus 15:23–25.

292 *threefold structure*: See note on *Gongolf* 6.

313–24 The account of the pool of Bethsaida is from John 5:2–4.

315 *porches of Solomon's Temple*: Compare John 10:23.

335 *the cloak of night*: Compare Prudentius, *Cathemerinon* 5.28.

362 *knew*: *Caluit = calluit,* cf. von Winterfeld, *Hrotsvithae opera,* 544, *callere.*

368 *consul*: See note on *Gongolf* 53.

383 *wearied*: *Laxaret = lassaret.*

392 *not*: This use of *si* to mean *non,* derived from the Vulgate, often implies the ellipsis of a clause; see the discussion in Homeyer, *Hrotsvithae opera,* 18n37.

494 According to the earlier *Life* of Gongolf, he was originally interred in Varennes, and his remains were later transferred to Toul.

501 Pepin is said to have visited Gongolf's grave.

The Passion of Saint Pelagius

title *Pelagius* is the only one of Hrotsvit's legends that is not based, at least in part, on a preexisting prose work. It tells the story of Pelagius, a thirteen-year-old boy martyred in Córdoba in 925. According to Hrotsvit's account, Pelagius was a hostage at the court of Abd al-Rahman III (ca. 889–961) and was executed after he resisted the caliph's sexual advances and refused to respect the Muslim faith. Hrotsvit learned of Pelagius, she says (*Here Begins the Second Book, Woven in a Dramatic Sequence* 1), from the oral report of an eyewitness, perhaps someone connected to the diplomatic missions between Caliph Abd al-Rahman and Otto I in the 950s. The earliest prose account of Pelagius, by Raguel, edited by J. Papebroch, *Acta sanctorum Junii* (Antwerp, 1709), vol. 5, pp. 206–9, is roughly contemporary with Hrotsvit's poem, but it is unclear that either writer knew the other's work.

1–11 After the title given above, *Pelagius* opens with an introductory verse address to the saint, requesting his aid for the poet. The poem proper begins at verse 12, with an enlarged capital letter *(P[artibus]),* following a line left blank for a title or subtitle that was not added (until the fifteenth century).

7 *my meager mind*: *Mis* is here equivalent to *mei.*

12–16 *majestic city . . . Córdoba*: Compare Prudentius, *Peristephanon* 11.199, where the phrase *urbs augusta* (majestic city) is used of Rome. Compare also Virgil, *Aeneid* 1.12–14, describing Carthage.

13 *war*: Mars, the god of war, stands by metonymy for war (so also at verses 25, 79, 90).

17 *sevenfold sources*: Seven rivers, that is, the seven liberal arts.

21 *well-established laws*: Compare Prudentius, *Cathemerinon* 10.115 *(bene condita iura).*

24 *Saracens*: Hrotsvit uses the term loosely for all Arabs or Muslims.

29 *for many*: *Quot* is here equivalent to *tot.*

32 *commander*: That is, Abd al-Rahman I (731–788).

33 *pagan*: Hrotsvit refers to Muslims as pagans, since non-Christian, and she seems to assimilate them with the ancient pagans attacked by early Christian writers (in particular, attributing to them the worship of idols).

37 *mother of the pure faith*: *Purae fidei genetrix* refers to the city of Córdoba as the nourisher of the Christian faith before the Muslim conquest of the city, but Hrotsvit may have additionally in mind "Mother Church," or she may even imagine a specific church, for example, the Great Mosque of Córdoba, as having been converted from Christian to Muslim use (though in either of these cases *mater* would be the expected term, not *genetrix*). There was a medieval Arabic tradition that the Great Mosque was built on the site of a Church of Saint Vincent, though that claim is rejected by modern scholars; see Nuha N. N. Khoury, "The Meaning of the Great Mosque of Cordoba in the Tenth Century," *Muqarnas* 13 (1996): 80–98. It is, at any rate, unclear how Hrotsvit could have been aware of that tradition.

40 *the Christians*: *Sibi* is here equivalent to *eis.*

41 *defile themselves*: The force of *sordere* with *secum* is reflexive.

44 *their law*: That is, Christian teaching, or the New Testament.

45 *newfangled forms of sacred ritual*: It is also possible to take *sacer* in a negative sense (cursed, accursed); in that case, the sense would be "stupidly enslaved to accursed novelties."

74 *Abd al-Rahman*: Abd al-Rahman III (ca. 889–961), emir and caliph of Córdoba from 912 until 961.

85 *vaunted himself in his palace*: Compare Virgil, *Aeneid* 1.140: "se iactet in aula / Aeolus."

92 *inhabiting*: In *degere,* the second *e* is long, as commonly in Medieval Latin (see von Winterfeld, *Hrotsvithae opera,* 298).

94 *idols*: See above, note to verse 33.

164 *lead my gray hairs in sorrow to the underworld*: Compare Genesis 44:29.

167 *You are my every honor*: Compare Virgil, *Eclogues* 5.34.

193 *under a vaulted roof*: Compare Sallust's description of the Tullianum in Rome, where some of the Catilinarian conspirators were imprisoned (*Bellum Catilinae* 55.3–4): "est in carcere locus . . . circiter duodecim pedes humi depressus . . . atque insuper camera lapideis fornicibus iuncta; sed incultu tenebris odore foeda atque terribilis eius facies est" (there is in the prison a place . . . about twelve feet underground . . . and above it a room with a vaulted ceiling made of stone; but from disuse, darkness, and stench its appearance is foul and terrifying).

199 Most editors agree that there is a line missing in M after verse 199, because there is nothing to motivate the subjunctive verb in verse 200 *(gustassent).* Celtes, the first editor of Hrotsvit, composed a substitute line to fill the lacuna: "Qui cum vidissent vultum capti speciosum" (When they had seen the beautiful face of the captive); Conrad Celtes, ed., *Opera Hrosvite illustris virginis et monialis germane gente Saxonica orte* (Nuremberg, 1501).

224 *Caesar*: That is, the caliph.

248 *placating*: *Placantur* is used here with an active meaning (that is, as a deponent).

grass-covered altar: A *caespes* (plot of grass, bit of sod) was used as a primitive form of pagan altar; see Horace, *Odes* 3.8.4, and Juvenal, *Satires* 12.2.

280 *river*: The Guadalquivir.

283 *spouting such things to the breezes*: Compare Virgil, *Aeneid* 1.102, of Aeneas howling in a storm.

317–18 *suffer . . . heads*: Compare Acts 27:34.

323 *schools that wander the streams*: Compare Prudentius, *Cathemerinon* 3.46–47.

327 *for that place*: *Illic* here is equivalent to *illuc.*

341 *shekels*: *Seclis* is for *siclis,* from *siclus,* a Hebrew shekel.

The Fall and the Conversion of the Vicar Theophilus

title An early poetic version of the Faust legend, *Theophilus* recounts the story of a sixth- or seventh-century Greek cleric who sells his soul to the devil but is rescued after praying to the Virgin Mary. Various Greek versions of the legend of Theophilus are preserved. Hrotsvit's source was the Latin prose translation by Paulus Diaconus of Naples, who flourished around 875 CE; G. Henschenius, ed., *Acta sanctorum Februarii* (Antwerp, 1658), vol. 1, pp. 483–87. An English translation of that Latin legend is available in Philip Mason Palmer and Robert Pattison More, *The Sources of the Faust Tradition* (New York, 1965), 60–75.

Vicar: The term *vicedom(i)nus* does not refer to a specific office; when applied to clerics it might be rendered by "vicar," "administrator," "steward," "assistant (to a bishop)," or the like.

2 *Sicily*: A mistake for Cilicia. Either Hrotsvit or her scribes (or, perhaps, a corrupted version of her source text) confused the province of Cilicia, on the southern coast of Turkey, the region from which Theophilus hails, with Sicilia (Sicily).

5 *Theophilus*: The name is variously scanned by Hrotsvit, here with the second and third syllables long.

11 *with flourishing zeal*: Compare Boethius, *Consolatio Philosophiae,* book 1, metrum 1.1.

13 *sevenfold*: The three disciplines of the *trivium* (grammar, rheto-

ric, logic) and the four of the *quadrivium* (arithmetic, geometry, astronomy, and music).

17 *in the vernacular tongue the "vicariate"*: That is, in Old Saxon *(Altsächsich)*. See also the note above to the title of *Theophilus*. On the reading *vicedom* (for *Vitztum*), see Paul von Winterfeld, "Zu Hrotsvits Theophilus, v 17," *Zeitschrift für deutsches Altertum und deutsche Literatur* 43 (1899): 45–46.

22 *least of Christ's people*: Compare Matthew 25:40.

24–25 *distributed . . . homeless*: Compare Isaiah 58:7.

50 *tainted by many vices*: Compare Prudentius, *Praefatio operum* 9.

62 *Theophilus*: *Istec* is a contraction of *iste-ce* (this here [man], Theophilus).

73 *slight*: That is, his removal from his position as vicar.

135–36 There appear to be missing lines at this point; they would have described the restoration of Theophilus to his former office.

150 *death . . . of the guilty*: Compare Ezekiel 18:23, 33:11.

154 *this same man*: *Istec* contracts *iste-ce* (this here [man]).

160 *Avernus*: A volcanic crater in Italy near Cumae, where there was believed to be an entrance to hell; hence Avernus is an alternate name for hell.

164 *of my own choosing*: The phrase could also be rendered "of the vow I made."

170 *Erebus*: A primordial deity of darkness and a region of hell.

178 *even a just man can scarcely be saved*: Compare 1 Peter 4:18.

216 *my divine Son*: *Mis* is here equivalent to *mei* (my).

225–34 This passage is not in Hrotsvit's source.

238 *being captivated unjustly by an empty hope*: Compare Virgil, *Aeneid* 11.49.

245 *Ninevites . . . three days*: See Jonah 3:1–10. The reference to "three days" points to a Christian interpretation of the passage, linking the period of Jonah's preaching in Nineveh to the three days he spent in the belly of a whale. See, for example, Augustine, *De civitate Dei* 18.44; Ambrose, *Explanatio psalmorum xii,* Psalm 47, chapter 25.2.

250–57 *David*: See 2 Kings (2 Samuel) 11:2–12:13.

258–69 *Peter*: See Matthew 16:17–19 and 26:69–75.

279 *judge . . . fire*: See Isaiah 66:16.

296 *Theophilus*: *Istec* is a contraction of *iste-ce* (this here [man]).

305–10 *insults . . . cross*: Compare John 19:1–6 and Matthew 27:26–31.

308 *to drink*: *Potatus* here has a causative sense.

311–12 *shepherd . . . dying*: See John 10.11.

314 *Erebus*: A primordial deity of darkness, and a region of hell.

316–17 *of Tartarus . . . accompanied by no small throng*: Compare Aldhelm, *Carmina ecclesiastica* 6 *(In sancti Thomae apostoli)*, lines 7–8.

320 *third day . . . alive*: Compare Prudentius, *Apotheosis* 531.

327 *render . . . according to their merits*: See, for example, Matthew 16:27 and Romans 2:5–6.

336 *my sweet love*: *Mis* is here equivalent to *mei* (my).

345 This line was transposed by Strecker (followed by Homeyer and Berschin) because its placement after line 334 is suggested by the source text of Paulus Diaconus of Naples (see above, note to *Theophilus,* title).

350 *your sad heart*: *Tis* is here equivalent to *tui* (your).

362 *mother of long ago*: Eve.

383–84 *that holy day*: The Lord's Day (Sunday).

399–400 *death of a wicked man*: Compare Ezekiel 18:23 and 33:11.

448–55 This closing prayer, a table blessing, is separated from *Theophilus* only by an elaborate punctuation mark after *Amen* (verse 447). The presence of this table blessing here may be a relic of an earlier edition of Hrotsvit's hagiographic poems, one in which this was the end of the series (the remaining three poems being added only in a later edition). The poem's presence here may suggest that Hrotsvit's hagiographic poems were intended to be read in refectory (see also the note to *Gongolf* 1, "O merciful sower of light").

451 *first virgin*: Eve.

The Conversion of a Certain Desperate Young Man by Saint Basil the Bishop

title There are no original titles in M for the two introductory poems, nor is there one for *Basil* proper, and I have followed Walter Berschin, *Opera omnia* (Munich, 2001) (for Prologue 2) or the fifteenth-century rubrics in M (for the Preface and the poem proper) in supplying them. *Basil* is another version of the Faust theme treated in the preceding poem, this time altering the circumstances of the sinner and making it a love story, not one of frustrated ambition or pride. The victim this time is not a cleric, but a slave who has fallen for his master's daughter. He sells his soul to the devil in exchange for the devil's inflaming the girl with love. She marries him, in defiance of her father, then discovers what he has done. He repents and is saved by Basil, the fourth-century Church Father. Hrotsvit's source is an episode (chapter 8) in the *Life* of Saint Basil by Amphilochius, perhaps in the Latin translation tentatively attributed to Ursus, ed. *Florilegium Casinense,* in *Bibliotheca Casinensis* (Montecassino, 1873–1894), vol. 3, pp. 205–19, at 211–13 (BHL 1024). The version of this Latin translation edited in PL, vol. 73, cols. 302–5 (BHL 1022), cited by Homeyer, *Hrotsvithae opera,* 172, as Hrotsvit's source text, is not as close verbally to Hrotsvit as the version in *Bibliotheca Casinensis.* Ursus, however, refers in his preface (PL, vol. 73, col. 295) to a preexisting translation of this particular episode, and it is possible that this earlier translation was the text Hrotsvit knew. (If a separate manuscript version of this episode survives, it has not, so far as I know, been published.)

1–6 The presence before *Basil* of this second dedicatory address to Gerberga, in elegiac couplets, strengthens the implication of the closing prayer at the end of *Theophilus* that the first five poems of the present book 1 (*History of the Birth of Mary* through *Theophilus*) were originally a separately published book and that the remaining three poems were an addition to that original book, producing a later, expanded edition. It is, however, curious that in these dedicatory verses, Hrotsvit alludes (verse 3) only to *Basil* itself, not to the other two poems, *Denis* and *Agnes,* that follow.

7–16 A new address to the reader in a different meter (hexameters); it is separated from the preceding dedication to Gerberga and from the following poem proper, *Basil,* by blank lines in M (these lines were for rubrics that were not added until the fifteenth century). Like verses 1 to 6, these lines allude only to *Basil,* not to the last two poems in Book 1.

13 *does not want . . . life*: See Ezekiel 33:11.

15 *joyfully rejoice*: See Isaiah 61:10.

17 *At the time*: Basil was bishop of Caesarea in Cappadocia from 370 until 379 CE.

60–70 The text is disordered and perhaps lines are missing from M in this section.

71 *hellish ministers*: Compare Prudentius, *Hamartigenia* 958.

81 *growling . . . lion*: See 1 Peter 5:8.

134 *disgrace*: Manuscript M reads *Tu decus* (You the glory), which was corrected by Strecker to *Dedecus* (Disgrace). He is followed in this by Wiegand, "The Non-Dramatic Works of Hrotswitha," and Berschin, and approved by Homeyer. But the reading of M is defensible and would mean, "[You are] both the glory and the pain of the mother who bore you."

144 *a true believer*: Hrotsvit writes *catholicus,* but in this period before the split with the Eastern Orthodox Church—and long before the Protestant Reformation—the word means any orthodox Christian, a member of the universal Christian Church; it does not mean Catholic in the modern sense.

158 *black snare of death*: She means the eternal death of her soul. Had she died as an infant, still pure, she would have escaped eternal damnation.

162 *firm voice*: *Constanti* could instead be taken with *neganti,* and the passage would mean "She immediately responded to him while he persisted in denying."

176 *to him*: *Sibi* here means *ei.*

194 *deliberately*: The Latin suggests the choice is Basil's, but *sponte* could also mean that it is the sinner who is deliberately shut away in darkness to repent. Latin *sponte* is normally feminine, and usually appears with *sua* rather than *suo,* so we would expect *sponte sua* if the passage means "by his [the sinner's] choice."

his own dark chamber: Hrotsvit is flexible about the meanings of *suus* and *eius,* so it is not impossible she means "his [Basil's] own dark chamber."

220 *enter the battle*: Compare Prudentius, *Contra Symmachum* 1.644.

259 *out of the mouth of the . . . lion*: See 2 Timothy 4:17.

The Passion of Saint Denis, an Outstanding Martyr

title Denis (Latin, *Dionysius*), a third-century bishop martyred in Paris, is the patron saint of the city and was especially venerated by the Merovingian royal family. Some of the biographical accounts of Denis prior to Hrotsvit conflated him with a first-century figure, Dionysius the Areopagite, an early convert of Paul the Apostle, and Hrotsvit's account assumes the two are identical. Relics of Denis were given to Henry the Fowler (Gerberga's grandfather) and deposited at nearby Quedlinburg, where the church was dedicated to Saints Denis and Servatius, so the saint was known and important in Hrotsvit's wider circle. The principal source for Hrotsvit's poem is the *Passio sancti Dionysii* by Hilduin of Saint-Denis (BHL 2175). Hilduin (ca. 775–ca. 860) was abbot of Saint-Denis in Paris and later archbishop of Cologne. The Latin text with English translation of Hilduin's work is in Michael Lapidge, *Hilduin of Saint-Denis: The Passio S. Dionysii in Prose and Verse,* Mittellateinische Studien und Texte 51 (Leiden, 2017); the text can also be found in PL, vol. 106, cols. 23–50. It is possible that Hrotsvit was familiar as well with an earlier anonymous *Life* of Denis (BHL 2178), known by its opening words *Post beatam et gloriosam,* which is included along with an English translation as an appendix to the volume of Lapidge cited above, pp. 680–703, and is also edited in C. Byeus, ed., *Acta sanctorum Octobris* (Brussels, 1780), vol. 4, pp. 792–94.

1 *highest, lowest, and in between*: That is, the three regions of the world: heaven, earth, and the underworld (or, perhaps, air, land, and sea); compare Prudentius, *Apotheosis* 226.

7 *Memphis*: Hrotsvit means, generically, Egypt, but Memphis is especially associated with astrology or astronomy and with pagan worship. Hilduin places Denis's studies in the city of Heliopolis.

23–39 See Acts 17:15–34.

39 *Christian*: See above, note on *Basil* 144.

85 The lack of grammatical coherence indicates that a line or more has been omitted in M.

107 *Clement*: Saint Clement, bishop of Rome (88–99 CE).

123–24 *harvest . . . few*: See Matthew 9:37.

131 *the power of loosing . . . binding*: See Matthew 16:19.

133 *your instruction*: *Tui,* the possessive form of the personal pronoun; Classical Latin would use the possessive adjective *tuae.*

134 *pupil*: That is, Gaul.

156 *Domitian*: The Roman emperor Domitian (81–96 CE).

160 *Sisinnius*: The name of this prefect is in Hrotsvit's hagiographical sources, but he is not otherwise known.

179 *my dear man*: *Mis* is here used for *mei* (my).

187 *my mercy*: *Mei,* the possessive form of the personal pronoun; Classical Latin would use the possessive adjective *meae.*

190 *three martyrs*: That is, Denis with his two companions, Rusticus and Eleutherius. They are treated at length in Hrotsvit's source, but not earlier mentioned by her.

213 *secret of your mysteries*: *Tis* (your) is used for *tui,* the possessive form of the personal pronoun; Classical Latin would use the possessive adjective instead. *Tui* is to be construed with *secretum* (secret), not *mysteriorum* (mysteries).

261 *prize of double honor*: Compare Prudentius, *Peristephanon* 5.537–44.

The Passion of Saint Agnes the Virgin and Martyr

title Saint Agnes (ca. 291–304) was born into a noble Christian family in Rome and martyred at the age of twelve or thirteen under Diocletian. Hrotsvit's principal source was the pseudo-Ambrose *Vita,* also called pseudo-Ambrose, *Epistula* 1 (BHL 156), ed. G. Henschenius, *Acta sanctorum Ianuarii* (Antwerp, 1643), vol. 2, pp. 351–54; and PL, vol. 17, cols. 735–42. An English translation of the pseudo-Ambrose Life is in Michael Lapidge, *The Roman Martyrs: Introduction, Translations, and Commentary* (Oxford, 2018), 353–62.

43 *Simphronius*: There is no prefect of this name recorded under Diocletian. Hrotsvit sometimes calls him "prefect," sometimes "governor."

72 *surpasses all*: Compare Virgil, *Aeneid* 6.856, where Anchises describes Marcellus as the epitome of Roman greatness, who "surpasses all men" *(viros supereminet omnis)*. Hrotsvit makes Agnes even more eminent, surpassing everyone in heaven and on earth, and so outshining Marcellus.

97 *abundance of milk*: The listing of delectable food and drink, as well as the phrase *copia lactis,* seems to be borrowed from Virgil, *Eclogues* 1.82 (but he writes *pressi copia lactis,* "abundance of cheese").

115 *sank into his bed*: Compare Walafrid Strabo, *Visio Wettini* 944, and *Waltharius* 392.

129–33 The syntax is difficult. I follow von Winterfeld in taking *iunctum* (131) in the sense of *iniunctum* (literally, "believe it had been enjoined upon her").

202 *know him and am known by him*: See 1 Corinthians 13:12.

258 *radiating*: *Radiebat* is here equivalent to *radiabat.*

392 *threefold structure*: The earth, sea, and sky.

420 *clearly*: *Clarum* is adverbial, modifying *rutilante* (shining).

445 *lamb*: The lamb is Agnes's standard iconographic attribute, reflecting a supposed derivation of her name from Latin *agnus,* though in fact her name is Greek and means "holy" or "pure."

446 *to be respected*: *Venerari* is a deponent verb, but used here passively.

Book 2

Preface

1 *true Christians*: See above, note on *Basil* 144.

3 *Strong Voice*: Hrotsvit seems to have etymologized her name as a compound of Old Saxon *hrōth* (glory, rumor, fame) and *swīth* (strong), which she Latinized as *clamor validus.*

A Letter of the Same Woman to Certain Learned Patrons of This Book

title *Learned Patrons*: Hrotsvit addresses this *Letter* to a group of learned supporters who have read her earlier works, and encouraged her writing, but she does not name any of them. It is often assumed that Archbishop Bruno of Cologne (d. 965) was among them.

5 *testimony of three*: See Deuteronomy 19:15.

9 *thread . . . Philosophy*: See Boethius, *Consolatio Philosophiae* book 1, prosa 1.3–5.

to insert them: Hrotsvit is referring in particular to the learned discourses on music in *The Conversion of Thais* and on math in *The Passion of the Holy Virgins Faith, Hope, and Charity.*

10 *this only I know, that I know nothing*: Jerome, *Epistles* 53.9, ed. I. Hilberg, CSEL 54 (Vienna, 1910), 462.

11 *like a reed*: See Matthew 12:20, and Bede, *In Lucae evangelium expositio* 2.7: "quid per harundinem nisi carnalis animus designatur qui mox fauore uel detractione tangitur in partem quamlibet inclinatur" (what is signified by the reed unless the carnal spirit, which as soon as it is touched by favor or attraction bends in some direction).

The Conversion of Gallicanus 1

title The title of this play (and of all the others) is taken from the first words of the introductory paragraph that precedes it. The principal source for Hrotsvit's first play is a combined account of the *Acta* of Gallicanus (BHL 3236 or 3237) and the *Passio* of John and Paul (BHL 3238–42), who were martyred under Julian the Apostate. Versions of these texts are edited by J. Papebroch, *Acta sanctorum Iunii* (Antwerp, 1709), vol. 5, pp. 35–39 (Gallicanus), and vol. 5, pp. 158–61 (John and Paul). The two are found combined in some of the medieval manuscripts, including, probably, the one used by Hrotsvit. There are multiple versions and variants of each (see the entries in BHL for some of the divergences). It is unclear precisely which versions or variants Hrotsvit used since they are not all published in critical editions, but they are all fairly similar in content. English translations of BHL 3236, 3238, and 3242 are in Michael Lapidge, *Roman Martyrs,* 363–80. It is a modern convention to divide Hrotsvit's *Gallicanus 1* from *Gallicanus 2,* deriving from the division of the *Acta* and the *Passio* in the *Acta sanctorum* edition (which was done for liturgical purposes). In M the two parts are separated in the same way that acts or scenes are separated within a single play. Each of Hrotsvit's plays in M begins with an introduction which summarizes the plot, and *Gallicanus 2* has no separate summary, its contents being included in the summary to *Gallicanus 1*.

intro *Scythians*: The war is against the Goths, who in 323 occupied an area of Scythia.

Constance, emperor Constantine's daughter: Called Constantia by Hrotsvit, but actually named Constantina (b. after 307, d. 354), she was the eldest daughter of Constantine the Great (272–337, emperor 306–337) and his second wife, Fausta.

Julian the Apostate: Roman emperor (331/332–363, emperor 361–363).

1.3 *no*: *Si* is here equivalent to *non*. See note to *Gongolf* 392. So also at 1.6, 1.8, and 9.1.

3.1 *my venerable lord*: *Mis* = *mei* (my).

3.2 *Good luck!*: It is unclear whether this is meant ironically, as in, "Good luck with that!" or "Fat chance!" See Isidore, *Etymologies* 1.37.27: "Charientismos est tropos, quo dura dictu gratius proferuntur, uti cum interrogantibus, 'Numquid nos quaesierit aliquis?' respondetur: 'Bona Fortuna!' Vnde intellegitur neminem nos quaesisse." (Charientism is a figure of speech whereby a harsh expression is delivered more graciously, as when to those inquiring, "Did anyone ask after us?" the response is given, "Good luck!" And from that it is understood that no one asked after us.)

face is indeed the mirror of the mind: Jerome, *Epistles* 54.13, ed. Hilberg, CSEL 54, 479.

5.2 *leprosy*: In Hrotsvit's source text, the *Acta* of Gallicanus, ed. Papebroch, *Acta sanctorum Iunii,* vol. 5, p. 37, Constantia says she was cured of leprosy and led to take vows of chastity by the prayers of Saint Agnes.

5.4 *your grace will abound in us*: Compare 2 Corinthians 9:8.

5.6 *your every command*: *Tis* = *tui.*

12.6 *my dear*: *Mis* = *mei.*

12.8 *trust . . . confounded*: See Psalms 21(22):6.

12.10 *rush into your arms*: Hrotsvit's language (especially *irruere* and *amplexus*) suggests she has in mind the reunion of Jacob and his father in Genesis 46:29; so Gallicanus, the son-in-law to-be, returning from a foreign land, is embraced by his father.

The Conversion of Gallicanus 2

title See above, the note to the title of *The Conversion of Gallicanus 1*. *Julian the Emperor*: Julian the Apostate, Roman emperor 361 to 363.

1.2 *Whoever . . . disciple*: See Luke 14:33.

2.1 *propitious indeed!*: The soldiers' reply is ironic.

4 *Rautianus*: Not otherwise identifiable.

5.2 *predecessors*: Paul means only the Christian emperors, Constantine and his sons.

9.2 *and reigns . . . Amen*: Only the first words of the doxology are provided in the manuscripts.

The Passion of the Holy Virgins Agape, Chionia, and Hirena

title In modern scholarship, Hrotsvit's second play is often called by the name of its villain, *Dulcitius.* The title here follows the text of M. The play tells of the martyrdom under Diocletian of three sisters after they have mocked their jailers, Dulcitius and Sisinnius. Hrotsvit's source text is an abbreviated account of their martyrdom that forms part of a *Vita* of Saint Anastasia, with whom they were connected. The text is edited by G. Henschenius and D. Papebroch, *Acta sanctorum Aprilis* (Antwerp, 1675), vol. 1, pp. 248–50, and by H. Delehaye, *Étude sur le légendier romain* (Brussels, 1936), 227–35, the latter version being closer to the text used by Hrotsvit. But Hrotsvit follows her source only in its basic outline of the facts of the martyrdom; the comic elements and scenes are her own invention.

1.6 *royal chrism*: The oil with which she was anointed in baptism.

7 *you have become a laughingstock*: See Jeremiah 20:7.

11.1 *Soldiers*: There is no indication in M of a break between the last sentence (word) spoken by the soldiers in section 10 and the first in section 11.

We will not: *Si* is used here as equivalent to *non*. See note to *Gongolf* 392.

11.4 *Not for you, Lord, not for you*: This is modeled on Psalms 113:9(115:1).

The Raising from the Dead of Drusiana and Callimachus

title Called *Callimachus* in much modern scholarship, Hrotsvit's main source for *The Raising from the Dead of Drusiana and Callimachus* was a Latin translation of a section of the apocryphal acts of Saint John the Evangelist, in the version of the *Virtutes apostolorum* (BHL 4616) printed under the name of Abdias, often called pseudo-Abdias in modern studies. There is no critical edition of the work, which is usually cited from the inadequate edition of Johann Albert Fabricius, *Codex apocryphus Novi Testamenti* (Hamburg, 1702), in which the portion relevant to Hrotsvit's play is in vol. 2, pp. 542–57. See the studies on this text by Els Rose, "*Virtutes apostolorum*: Editorial Problems and Principles," *Apocrypha* 23 (2012): 11–45, and Els Rose, "*Virtutes apostolorum*: Origin, Aim, and Use," *Traditio* 68 (2013): 57–96.

2.2 *This description does not apply to only one thing*: Hrotsvit presents this discussion as a philosophical disputation, based on ideas and definitions explained in the pseudo-Augustinian *Decem categoriae,* chapter 9 (PL, vol. 32, cols. 1426–27). The humor of the passage comes, in part, from the contrast between the logical, rational, academic language and philosophical questioning of the friends, on the one hand, and the simple, brief, lovesick (which is to say, irrational) responses of Callimachus on the other.

2.2 *indivisible . . . one particular thing . . . prime essence*: The terms *atomus* (Greek, ἄτομος, "indivisible"), *enarithmus* (from Greek ἕν, "one," and ἀριθμός, "number"), and *ousia* (οὐσία, "essence") are found in the *Decem categoriae;* see previous note.

2.4 *Whoever dissimulates*: Compare *Disticha Catonis* 1.26.

2.5 *No doubt . . . Fates*: Compare Virgil, *Aeneid* 1.39.

3.5 *By the faith of gods and men*: Compare Terence, *Andria* 246.

4 Drusiana's self-blame is a stark reflection of the misogyny of her experience. Her predicament and her response to it call to mind the episode of Susanna and the Elders (Daniel 13), but it is also possible that Hrotsvit intends to describe Drusiana's actions and attitudes as a Christian parallel to Lucretia's.

9.6 *distinguish knowledgeably*: Compare Prudentius, *Psychomachia* 790.

9.7 *knot . . . unraveled*: Compare Boethius, *Commentaria in Topica Ciceronis* 1.8, ed. J. C. Orelli, *Ciceronis opera omnia* (Zurich, 1833), vol. 5.1, p. 285, line 40.

9.10 *drawing the breath of life:* Compare Virgil, *Aeneid* 1.387.

9.12 *triple misfortune*: Boethius, *Consolatio Philosophiae* book 4, prosa 4.5, states that the triply unfortunate are those who (1) wish to do wrong, (2) have the ability to do it, and (3) do actually perform it ("triplici infortunio . . . scelus velle, posse, perficere"). Callimachus says he had the wish, but not the ability.

9.23 *forgive another*: See Matthew 6:12.

9.26 *Divine . . . matter*: Compare Boethius, *De Trinitate* 2.30.

9.29 *evil tree*: See Matthew 7:17.

The Fall and Conversion of Mary, Niece of Abraham

title For this play (called *Abraham* in much modern scholarship), Hrotsvit's primary source was the Latin translation of a Greek *Vita* of Abraham, falsely attributed to Ephrem the Syrian (BHL 0012). The Greek text is edited by G. Henschenius and D. Papebroch, *Acta sanctorum Martii* (Antwerp, 1675), vol. 2, pp. 741–48 (the portion relevant to Hrotsvit's play starts with chapter 25, p. 745). A Latin translation was made in the sixth century and is printed in PL, vol. 73, cols. 281–92 and 651–60. The latter section of the Latin version concerns Mary, and it sometimes circulated separately in manuscript; details and bibliography in Homeyer, *Hrotsvithae opera,* 298n2.

1.1 *he would be there . . . name*: See Matthew 18:20.

1.2 *one heart and one soul*: See Acts 4:32.

1.3 *no criticizing*: *Si* = *non;* see note to *Gongolf* 392.

1.4 *two Olympiads*: An Olympiad is four years; if one year were added to her current age, she would be eight (twice four years). That is, she is seven years old.

2.1 *founder of virginity*: That is, the Blessed Virgin Mary.

2.3 *star of the sea*: See above, note to *History of the Birth of Mary* 276. Mary is associated through this etymology of her name with Polaris, the pole star: she is humans' guide toward Christ, just as the pole star guides sailors to safe harbor.

2.5 *and passing . . . paths*: This passage (*instabilemque . . . semitas,* in Latin) is not present in the Munich manuscript (M) but appears in the Cologne manuscript. The Latin is odd in several ways: for example, the placement of *et* (and) before *cursum* (course), even though *cursum* seems to govern *planetarum* (planets) as well as *solis* (sun); the lack of any clarifying modifier for *semitas* (paths); and the shift in word order, tense, and construction in the parallel phrases from *pertransies* (you will pass through) through *percurres* (you will run through). Perhaps some or all of the additional text in the Cologne manuscript represents intrusive glossing or some other corruption to the original; perhaps the Munich version is a later, cleaner revision of whatever the original version was.

2.6 *lives like an ass*: Boethius, *Consolatio Philosophiae* book 4, prosa 3.19, says that a man who is *segnis ac stupidus* (slow and stupid) lives like an ass.

deny my own self: See Mark 8:34.

3.3 *my dearest daughter*: *Mis* = *mei.*

twice two lustra: That is, twenty years (a *lustrum* is a five-year period).

3.4 *inspection*: Hrotsvit uses a term that can mean "a visit," but that also has a technical monastic sense of "official visit for inspection," that is, a visit by a higher authority intended to ensure that proper monastic rules are being followed in a monastic community.

3.8 *had my mind not been distracted*: Compare Virgil, *Eclogues* 1.16 and *Aeneid* 2.54.

3.11 *not without distress*: *Si = non;* see note to *Gongolf* 392.

7.6 *It is human . . . living in sin*: Similar sentiments appear in Augustine, *Sermones ad populum* 164, ed. S. Boodts, *Sermones de Novo Testamento (157–183): Sermones in epistolas apostolicas II,* CCSL 41Bb (Turnhout, 2016), p. 274, line 294; in Otloh of Saint Emmeran, *Liber proverbiorum* (PL, vol. 146, col. 313B); and elsewhere. See Meinolf Schumacher, "'. . . ist menschlich': Mittelalterliche Variationen einer antiken Sentenz," *Zeitschrift für deutsches Altertum und deutsche Literatur* 119 (1990): 163–70. Hrotsvit may have learned it from the widely circulated medieval Latin translation of John Chrysostom's *De reparatione lapsi,* ed. Jean Dumortier, *A Théodore,* Sources chrétiennes 117 (Paris, 1966), chapter 16, pp. 304–5, lines 79–80, where it follows shortly after a discussion of a fallen prostitute (chapter 14, pp. 295–98): "peccare namque humanum est, permanere autem in peccatis diabolicum" (to sin is indeed human, to remain in sin is diabolic).

7.15 *sheep*: See Luke 15:4–7.

shepherd: See John 10:11.

7.16 *Oh—what should I call you*: Compare Virgil, *Aeneid* 1.327.

9.5 *angelic hosts*: See Luke 15:10.

perseverance . . . unrighteous one: See Luke 15:7.

9.6 *return to her senses*: See 2 Timothy 2:26.

He does not want . . . perish: See Ezekiel 33:11.

The Conversion of Thais

title Called *Paphnutius* in much modern scholarship, *The Conversion of Thais* is a prostitute-conversion story, with various twists on the legends of Mary Magdalene, Pelagia, and Mary the niece of Abraham. In the eastern versions (Greek, Syriac, Arabic), the hermit or monk who converts Thais has various names, but he is regularly called Pafnutius in the Latin accounts. A Latin version of the Thais legend circulated in the West, perhaps as early as the sixth century, edited by H. Rosweyde, *Acta sanctorum Octobris* (Brussels, 1780), vol. 4, pp. 225–26 (BHL 8012).

Three different Latin texts were published by François Nau, *Histoire de Thaïs,* Annales du Musée Guimet 33, part 3 (Paris, 1903), 36–62. Among these, the one he refers to by the letter *l* is the closest to the text Hrotsvit used. The longest of Hrotsvit's plays, *The Conversion of Thais* is also the least dependent on its source text, much of the narrative being Hrotsvit's own creation, including the long dialogue between Paphnutius and his students about music, with which the play opens. There is some evidence to suggest that Hrotsvit's fifth and sixth plays, *The Conversion of Thais* and *The Passion of the Holy Virgins Faith, Hope, and Charity,* were a later supplement to her corpus, added in response to the reception her first four plays had gotten from her "learned patrons"; see Berschin, *Opera omnia,* xxiii–xxiv, and Stephen L. Wailes, "Hrotsvit's Plays," in *A Companion to Hrotsvit of Gandersheim (fl. 960),* ed. Phyllis R. Brown and Stephen L. Wailes (Leiden, 2013), 121–22. In the final two plays, she reworked the themes of two of her earlier plays *(The Passion of the Holy Virgins Agape, Chionia, and Hirena* and *The Fall and Conversion of Mary),* exploring the different effects created by varying the details in stock narratives—a technique she may have learned from her study of Terence, but which could equally have been gleaned from ancient and medieval hagiographical narratives.

intro *five years*: The text proper (section 9) speaks of three years.

1.3 *Certainly*: Latin *porro* here is equivalent to *certe* (certainly); this meaning is well attested in medieval glossaries but is absent from the standard modern dictionaries.

1.4 *four elements*: That is, earth, water, air, and fire; see Boethius, *De institutione musica* 1.2.

1.6 *because nothing . . . nature*: See Boethius, *De institutione arithmetica* 1.2.

1.8 *tiniest bit*: *Scrupulum* could, alternatively, mean "difficulty."

1.10 *There are said to be three*: Compare Boethius, *De institutione musica* 1.2.

1.13 *set of pitches*: I follow Calvin Bower, *Fundamentals of Music* (New Haven, 1989), 7n31, in rendering *modulatio* as "set of pitches," and, in general, I follow his translations for musical terms as closely as I can, both here and in *The Passion of the Holy Virgins Faith, Hope, and Charity*.

1.14 *diatesseron*: See Boethius, *De institutione arithmetica* 1.1 and 2.48.

1.20 *Apostle*: That is, Paul, in 1 Corinthians 1:27.

1.21 *God ordered all things . . . weight*: Wisdom 11:21.

1.23 *There is a certain indecent woman*: Hrotsvit begins from this point to follow her source text.

1.25 *precious possessions*: Compare Boethius, *Consolatio Philosophiae* book 2, prosa 5.23.

3.7 *wine of sorrow*: Psalms 59(60):5.

3.12 *Oh, how . . . changed*: Compare Virgil, *Aeneid* 2.274.

5.2 *to prescribe . . . with a pointer*: Hrotsvit writes *velut radio praescribere,* imitating Virgil, *Eclogues* 3.41 and *Aeneid* 6.850, or Boethius, *Consolatio Philosophiae* book 1, prosa 4.4, who is himself imitating Virgil. All of these passages refer to astronomical measurements made with an instrument of some kind (and all use the verb *describere,* not *praescribere*). Modern translators of these passages variously render them as "with a pointer," "with a rod," "with a compass," or the like. A surveyor's rod (sight rod), or a *dioptra,* which has a pointer, might have been familiar to Hrotsvit, and it is not impossible that she had some acquaintance with an astrolabe of some sort.

7.16 *captive*: Latin *captivus, -a,* could also be translated "poor wretched man/woman"; see A. Blaise, *Lexicon latinitatis medii aevi* (Turnhout, 1975).

10.4 *no small*: *Si = non;* see note to *Gongolf* 392.

11.1 *those who unite in prayer . . . everything*: See Matthew 21:22.

11.3 *captive*: See note above, at 7.16.

12.2 *If God will mark . . . it*: Psalms 129(130):3.

12.5 *persist in loving*: See 1 Timothy 2:15.

12.6 *heavenly host . . . seas*: Compare Psalms 148.

The Passion of the Holy Virgins Faith, Hope, and Charity

title Often called *Sapientia (Wisdom)* in modern scholarship, after the mother of the three virgins—who, like them, is an abstract concept personified as a Christian martyr, not a historical person—*The Passion of the Holy Virgins Faith, Hope, and Charity* has many similarities to *The Passion of the Holy Virgins Agape, Chionia, and Hirena,* and, like *The Conversion of Thais,* it begins with a lengthy pedagogical excursus, this time on abstract mathematics (perfect numbers). The names of the three virgins are those of the three gifts of the Holy Spirit. Their mother's name, Sapientia, is a Latin equivalent of Sophia, a saint especially venerated in the circle of the empress Theophanu. Otto II and Theophanu named one of their daughters Sophia (ca. 975–1039), and she was from childhood, at the latest from 979, raised in Gandersheim Abbey, where she became abbess in 1002. If Hrotsvit was still alive at the end of the 970s, she will have known the young Sophia. Hrotsvit's source for the legend of these holy virgins is an eighth-century Latin work, attributed to an otherwise unknown Milanese priest named Johannes. There are no critical editions of the Latin legends of Faith, Hope, and Charity, although they and their mother Wisdom were widely venerated in the West. The basic details of their martyrdom can be extracted from the early modern reworking of the text published by Boninus Mombritius in his *Sanctuarium seu vitae sanctorum* (Milan, before 1480), vol. 2, pp. ccv–ccx, more readily available in the edition of the monks of Solesmes (Paris, 1910), vol. 2, pp. 374–84. A medieval version, somewhat closer to Hrotsvit's text in some passages, is in *Florilegium Casinense,* in *Bibliotheca Casinensis* (Montecassino, 1873–1894), vol. 3, pp. 276–83. Details on various manuscript versions are given by Homeyer, *Hrotsvithae opera,* 351n9.

intro *Diocletian*: In the play itself, the emperor is called Hadrian (as in Hrotsvit's source text), perhaps suggesting that Hrotsvit wrote the plays and introductions at different times and never reconciled the differences; see discussion in Homeyer, *Hrotsvithae opera,* 350 and 357. Hadrian is not known to have presided over trials of Christians; Diocletian is the most notorious of the early Christian persecutors. Since the title characters are allegorical figures, not historical martyrs, the time, place, and other circumstances of their martyrdom are not historical questions.

fifth mile marker: Later (8.2) said to be at the third mile marker.

3.1 *A pronouncement of Christ's*: Mark 13:11: "And when they shall lead you and deliver you up, be not thoughtful beforehand what you shall speak; but whatsoever shall be given you in that hour, that speak ye. For it is not you that speak, but the Holy Ghost"; see also Luke 21:14–15.

3.2 *dress*: *Habitus* could also mean "bearing."

3.3 *tenderly and calmly*: Compare Prudentius, *Peristephanon* 2.63.

3.5 *Do not open*: The Latin expression *cor apponere* appears in Ecclesiastes 8:16 ("apposui cor meum ut scirem sapientiam," I committed my heart to learning wisdom) and also Proverbs 22:17 ("appone autem cor ad doctrinam meam," but devote your heart to my teaching).

3.6 *Italy*: Some of the Latin versions of Hrotsvit's source text explicitly name Italy as Wisdom's country of origin; all seem to name Milan as her home city. Conrad Celtes emended the text to "Greece" *(Grecie)*.

3.9 *deficient*: A "deficient" number is one of which the sum of the aliquot parts is less than the number itself. The aliquot parts (also called aliquot divisors, or proper divisors) of a number *N* are the whole numbers less than *N* by which *N* can be divided to produce a whole number. They are, then, the "factors" of *N*, excluding *N* itself. For example, 8 has a half, which is 4, a fourth, which is 2, and an eighth, which is 1. Added together, $4 + 2 + 1 = 7$, which is less than 8, so 8 is a "deficient" number (see Boethius, *De institutione arithmetica* 1.19).

evenly even: An evenly even number is one that can be divided into two equal parts, and then those parts can be continuously divided into equal parts until unity is reached. For example, 8 has a half of 4, which in turn has a half of 2, which in turn has a half of 1, and the unity cannot be further divided into a whole number, so 8 is an evenly even number (see Boethius, *De institutione arithmetica* 1.9). This definition, and all of the subsequent discussion here, in Hrotsvit's text and in my notes, assumes that we are talking only about natural numbers (not fractional or decimal numbers). Charity's age is 8; but 8 is not the only deficient, evenly even number; 4 is another example, and so is 16 (to mention only those deficient numbers that could possibly describe a young girl's age).

evenly odd: An evenly odd number is an even number, but one that cannot be divided into two equal, even numbers. For example, 10 is an even number, but when divided in half produces two odd numbers, namely, it produces two 5s; and 5 cannot be divided into equal, whole parts. Since 2 is an even number and 5 an odd number, and 2 × 5 = 10, by definition 10 is an evenly odd number (Boethius, *De institutione arithmetica* 1.10). The first deficient, evenly odd number is 10, the next is 14, then 22.

abundant: An abundant number is, in a sense, the opposite of a deficient number. An abundant number is one for which the sum of the aliquot parts is greater than the number itself. For example, 12 has a half (namely, 6), a third (4), a fourth (3), a sixth (2), and a twelfth (1). If we add them together, 6 + 4 + 3 + 2 + 1 = 16, which is greater than 12; therefore 12 is an abundant number (Boethius, *De institutione arithmetica* 1.19).

oddly even: An oddly even number falls in between evenly even and evenly odd: that is, it can be divided into two equal, even numbers (just like an evenly even number), but the division into equal parts cannot be continued all the way to unity, for at some point, the division into halves produces a pair of odd numbers. For example, 12 can be divided into two equal, even numbers, namely, into two 6s. But 6, when divided in half, produces two 3s, odd numbers (Boethius, *De institutione arithmetica* 1.11). The first "abundant, oddly even" number is 12, the next is 20.

3.11 *two Olympiads*: Eight years.

two lustra: Ten years.

three Olympiads: Twelve years.

3.19 *in that one only the lower extremity . . . divisor would be odd*: Wisdom's discussion (based on Boethius, *De institutione arithmetica* 1.9 and 1.10) assumes a series of numbers generated from the factors of a number. For example, 8 has the series 1, 2, 4, 8, while 10 has the series 1, 2, 5, 10. In the first sequence (based on the number 8, which is evenly even) only the lower extremity, 1, is indivisible. If we start with the greater extremity of this series, 8, the continuous sequence of numbers otherwise (8, 4, and 2) are all divisible. In the second sequence (based on the number 10, which is evenly odd), only the greater extremity, 10, is necessarily divisible; the middle terms, 2 and 5, must perforce include an odd number, so the middle terms are not all divisible (into whole numbers). In the first sequence (an evenly even sequence), all of the middle terms, 2 and 4 (the divisors and quotients), are themselves evenly even. In the second sequence, the middle terms, 2 and 5, are not all evenly even; for if 2 (an even number) is the divisor, 5 (an odd number) is the quotient; if 5 (odd) is the divisor, then 2 (even) is the quotient.

3.20 *divisor . . . quotient*: For example, in the number 10, if we talk about halves, 2 is the divisor; if we talk of fifths, 5 is the divisor. If 2 is the divisor, there are 5 of them in 10, so 5 is the quotient ($10 \div 2 = 5$), which describes how many instances of the divisor are present in 10. Likewise, if 5 is the divisor, there are 2 of them in 10, so 2 is the quotient: $10 \div 5 = 2$.

3.21 *oddly even*: See above, note to 3.9.

3.22 *arranged everything . . . weight*: Wisdom 11:21; by a nice touch, the character Wisdom here quotes the biblical book of the same name.

4.3 *mother-in-law*: Compare Jerome, *Epistles* 22.20, ed. Hilberg, CSEL 54, 170.

5.1 *captive*: See note to *Thais* 7.16.

5.8 *drenched in sweat*: Compare Prudentius, *Peristephanon* 10.456.

5.17 *hardness of your heart*: Compare Prudentius, *Peristephanon* 5.177.

5.20 *eyes raised upward*: See John 17:1.

5.22 *shape-shifting craftiness*: Compare Prudentius, *Apotheosis,* preface 26.

A command worthy of an emperor: The use of torture hooks *(ungulae)* is mentioned in the emperor Justinian's *Codex* 9.18.7, so their employment constitutes an imperial form of punishment.

5.23 *sundered scraps*: Compare Prudentius, *Peristephanon* 11.119.

5.29 *beneficial in the present*: Compare Prudentius, *Peristephanon* 10.541.

5.32 *Diana*: See Acts 19:27–34.

6.2 *three men*: Compare Daniel 3:23–24.

7.2 *protectress*: Compare Prudentius, *Peristephanon* 10.835.

8.2 *third milestone*: Contrast the introductory preface of this play, where it is the fifth mile marker.

9.8 *singing a new song*: See Psalms 97(98):1.

9.9 *above . . . below*: See above, note to *The Passion of Saint Denis* 1.

Let Him Say Amen

title This poem appears in M on a page by itself (fol. 129v), without any rubric or explanation, immediately after the end of *The Passion of the Holy Virgins Faith, Hope, and Charity.* It consists of four epanaleptic elegiac couplets (distichs in which the wording of the first half of the hexameter line is identical to the second half of the pentameter line) quoted from the conclusion of Bede's verses on virginity in praise of Queen Etheldreda (a poem embedded in the *Ecclesiastical History of the English People* 4.20).

10–11 *sweet-sounding*: This compound adjective modifies "lyre" in line 10 and "hymn" in line 11, but I have obscured this—and taken other liberties of word choice and word order—for the sake of reproducing the pattern of the epanaleptic elegiacs.

acrostic *Let him say amen . . . salvation*: The first letter of each of Bede's hexameter lines, on the left margin, when read vertically downward, forms an acrostic spelling *AMEN.* Above the Bedan verses are five lines, each blank except for a single capital letter, spelling *DICAT* (let him say) when read vertically downward, in a column aligned with the letters *AMEN.* It appears that Hrotsvit—if she had anything to do with this poem—may have intended to create an hexameter acrostic of her own, five lines in length (not five distichs in length), each line beginning with a successive letter of the word *DICAT.* Her five lines spelling out *DICAT* would conclude with the four distichs from Bede spelling out *AMEN.* There are also in the right margin, in capitals letters running upward, the following words: *QUICUMQUE VIAM CUPIT IRE SALUTIS* (whoever wishes to travel the road of salvation). These words stand alone; they are not integral to the verses next to which they appear (they do not make an acrostic from the final letters of the successive lines of verse); and they are written at a right angle to the verses, so the page must be rotated ninety degrees clockwise to read these words in proper orientation. The capital letters on the page, if read from top to bottom in the left margin, then from bottom to top in the right margin, form a hexameter verse: *Dicat amen, quicumque viam cupit ire salutis* (the short first syllable in *amen* is unusual, but not unparalleled in Christian poetry). Other than the single verse created by the capital letters, this figure poem (or acrostic, or whatever the poem was intended to be) is incomplete.

Von Winterfeld recognized the distichs as Bede's but included them in his edition *(Hrotsvithae opera,* 199). Strecker and Homeyer omitted them. Berschin struck a compromise by including them in his volume, but only as a photograph (*Opera omnia,* 268). It is clear that if Hrotsvit had composed six lines of her own and quoted one from Bede, we would consider the poem hers; likewise, if she had composed two or three lines and quoted two or three from Bede. Where the tipping point is, I do not know, but it seems that for Strecker and Homeyer, quoting six lines and writing one did not make the poem Hrotsvit's. I do not think it should be excluded either because of the percentage of original verses, or because of its incomplete state; but, in the end, I include the item primarily because it is discussed in current scholarship, and it will facilitate further discussion to have it here along with the rest of her work. Since Berschin does not print the work, I follow the text of von Winterfeld, where Hrotsvit's deviations from Bede are noted in the apparatus criticus. It is unclear whether Hrotsvit's deviations are intentional, are accidental mistakes, or are derived from a manuscript of Bede with the variants she employs.

John, or Inscriptions for the Book of the Apocalypse

title These thirty-five hexameter lines appear in M after the plays of book 2 (and after the poem *Let Him Say Amen*) and before the epics (and before the preface and prologues to the epics) of book 3. The lines describe passages from Revelation, and they appear to have been made as captions or titles *(tituli)* for illustrations—it is unclear whether for illustrations in a manuscript or elsewhere (murals, mosaics, bas-relief carvings, tapestries, panel paintings, or the like). Similar collections of epigrams were made by many Christian poets, including Prudentius, Venantius Fortunatus, Aldhelm, and others. Von Winterfeld, Strecker, and Berschin divide the lines into twelve segments; Homeyer into fourteen, adding additional breaks at verses 8 and 32 (see her discussion, *Hrotsvithae opera,* 377n6). Since these verses are not known except in M and are not explicitly attributed to Hrotsvit in M, some scholars have expressed hesitation about whether they are hers (see, for example, Berschin, *Opera omnia,* x–xi, who reserves judgment).

1.1–2 See Revelation 4:1–2.

1.3 See Revelation 4:4.

1.6 See Revelation 5:1.

1.8 See Revelation 5:2–3.

2.10 See Revelation 5:4–5.

3.12–13 See Revelation 5:6–9.

4.14–15 See Revelation 6:9–11.

5.16–17 See Revelation 7:2–3.

6.18 See Revelation 7:9.

7.20 See Revelation 8:1.

8.21 See Revelation 8:3.

9.23 See Revelation 12:1.

9.25–26 See Revelation 12:3–5.

9.27 See Revelation 12:9.

10.28 See Revelation 14:1.

10.29 *chaste*: Hrotsvit's *virgineus coetus* here does not mean virgin girls, but "they (masc.) who were not defiled by women" of Revelation 14:4; see Revelation 14:3–4.

11.30 See Revelation 13:1, 13:4, 13:7.

11.31 *True*: One of the heavenly riders who battle the dragon; see Revelation 19:11, 19:19.

11.32 See Revelation 19:20, 20:2.

12.33 See Revelation 20:12.

12.35 See Revelation 20:13.

Book 3

Preface to the Deeds of Otto

title Hrotsvit's epic on Otto I survives only in manuscript M, where it is defective, sixteen leaves being lost after verse 752 (a loss of 384 lines), and a further twelve leaves (288 lines) after verse 1184; by Berschin's calculations, of the original 1511 lines, 672 are lost (nearly forty-five percent of the poem). The poem is preceded by a preface and separate prologues to Otto I and Otto II. References within the poem indicate it was begun before October 965 and completed before March 968; the two prologues may have been added later.

1 *Gerberga*: Gerberga II, abbess of Gandersheim from 956 to 1001. Hrotsvit states in the Preface that she was instructed to write *The Deeds of Otto* by Abbess Gerberga and that she had no written sources on which to base her narrative. Her oral sources would have included members of the imperial family and court, including Gerberga herself. Hrotsvit often had to tread lightly, for example, when describing the revolts against Otto, especially when these revolts involved Otto's brother Henry I (919–955; duke of Bavaria, 948–955), the father of her abbess. Hrotsvit's poem falls somewhere between panegyric and historical epic. Her positive portrayal of the Ottonian rulers may reflect a desire—hers or Gerberga's—to elicit from them greater patronage for Gandersheim.

enlisted: Hrotsvit uses military language to describe the canonesses as "soldiers for Christ."

2 *not distress*: *Si = non;* see note to *Gongolf* 392.

3 *august emperor's*: Otto I, the Great, Holy Roman emperor from 962 to 973.

9 *not because of my presumption*: *Si = non;* see note to *Gongolf* 392.

10 *Archbishop William*: William, archbishop of Mainz from 954 to 968, son of Otto I and cousin of Gerberga II.

Prologue to Emperor Otto I

title *Otto I*: Otto I, "the Great" (912–973), duke of Saxony and king of Germany (936–973), Holy Roman emperor (962–973).

3 *emperors*: Hrotsvit uses the title/name Augustus (in the plural) to emphasize that Otto is not just another emperor, but a new Augustus. She employs forms derived from the Latin word *augustus* three times in this prologue (verses 3, 4, 24), highlighting the fact that Otto has been crowned emperor. This dates the poem after 962.

30–35 Hrotsvit's account covers the years when Otto was duke of Saxony and king of the Germans but stops with his imperial coronation in 962; she implies here that she would like to be asked to write an account of his later years as emperor (his "second scepter").

Prologue to Emperor Otto II

title *Otto II*: Otto II, co-emperor with his father from 967 to 973, and sole emperor after his father's death (973–983).

5 *writing*: Hrotsvit writes *textum*, "a weaving, a textile."

20 *Solomon*: Hrotsvit compares Otto I to King David as the warrior king, and Otto II to Solomon as the son who inherited the throne and peace.

29 *the conflict of the two women*: See 3 Kings (1 Kings) 3:16–28.

The Deeds of Otto

5 *rock*: The etymology of the name of the Saxons from the Latin word *saxum* (rock) is at least as old as Isidore of Seville (*Etymologies* 9.2.100).

6 *Oddo*: Oddo I, duke of Saxony (d. 912), a son of the Saxon Count Liudolf (d. 866) who founded the Liudolfinger dynasty. He was also called Otto, but throughout I refer to this man as Oddo, to avoid confusion with his grandson, the emperor Otto I. Oddo was the father of Duke Henry the Fowler, and grandfather of Emperor Otto I.

7 *Henry*: Henry I, "the Fowler" (876–936), duke of Saxony (912–936) and king of East Francia (919–936).

22 *Mathilda*: Saint Mathilda (ca. 892–968), daughter of the Saxon Count Dietrich and his wife Reinhild, second wife of Henry the Fowler, and founder of Quedlinburg Abbey.

27 *Henry*: Henry the Fowler; see above, note to *The Deeds of Otto* 7.

34 *Otto*: Otto I, "the Great" (912–973).

44 *fierce peoples*: Hrotsvit is thinking in particular of the Hungarians, with whom the Ottonians battled in the tenth century.

46 *Henry*: Henry I (919/921–955), duke of Bavaria (948–955); father of Abbess Gerberga II of Gandersheim.

53 *Bruno*: Born 925, archbishop of Cologne (953–965) and duke of Lorraine (954–965).

55 *Christian*: See above, note on *Basil* 144.

68 *Henry*: Henry the Fowler; see above, note to *The Deeds of Otto* 7.

77 *Edith*: Also called Eadgyth (910–946), daughter of the English king Edward the Elder (r. 899–924). As the wife of Otto I, Edith was queen of Germany from 936 till her death in 946.

79 *brother*: Edith's brother was Æthelstan, king of the Anglo-Saxons (924–927) and king of England (927–939), the successor to Edward the Elder.

80 *ignoble*: The mother of Æthelstan was Edward's first consort, Ecgwynn, who either died or was dismissed after 899.

86 *born*: The Latin *edita* is a pun on Edith's name.

96 *Oswald*: Saint Oswald, king of Northumbria (r. 634–641/642); he is celebrated, for example, by Bede (*Ecclesiastical History of the English People* 3.1–3, 3.6, and 3.9).

112 *Adiva*: It is unclear who precisely this sister was, or what became of her subsequently, but the story is also told in the late tenth-century *Chronicle of Æthelweard* (see Homeyer, *Hrotsvithae opera,* 410n112).

122 *Liudolf*: Born in 930 and died in 957, only son of Otto and Edith, duke of Swabia (950–954); not to be confused with his great-great-grandfather, Liudolf, duke of Saxony (d. 866). All references to a Liudolf in *The Deeds of Otto* are to Liudolf, duke of Swabia.

151–52 Hrotsvit alludes here to a battle in 936 against Boleslaus I, duke of Bohemia. Boleslaus attacked Otto's allies, the Thuringians, and defeated two of Otto's armies. A certain Ekkehard, in direct violation of Otto's orders, counterattacked, and he and his men were slaughtered. The incident is described by Widukind of Corvey, *Rerum gestarum Saxonicarum libri tres* 2.3–4, ed. P. Hirsch and H.-E. Lohmann, MGH, Scriptores rerum Germanicarum in usum scholarum 60 (Hannover, 1935), 68–71.

153 *Henry*: Henry I (919/21–955), duke of Bavaria (948–955); father of Abbess Gerberga II of Gandersheim.

157 *Arnulf*: Duke of Bavaria (d. 937).

158 *Judith*: Born in 925 and died after 985, duchess of Bavaria (947–955) and regent during the minority of her son, Henry II of Bavaria (951–995).

166 *ancient enemy*: The devil.

176 *Eberhard*: Duke of Franconia (r. 918–939).

181 *Belecke*: *Castellum Baduliki,* Belecke an der Möhne, a small town just north of Warstein (Kreis Soest) in Nordrhein-Westfalen.

188 *enemy*: Hrotsvit's use of the term *socius* here is peculiar; it normally means "friend," "associate," or "ally," but Eberhard is treating Henry as an enemy. Such a meaning is rare but is attested in DMLBS under the lemma *socius* 10.

192–93 *redeemed Lot*: See Genesis 14:14–16.

196 *royal*: Modifies *pompa* (procession) as well as *fratri* (brother).

209 *Gilbert*: Also called Giselbert, duke of Lorraine (d. 939); he was married to Otto I's sister, Gerberga of Saxony.

252–54 *who so many times . . . the kingdom*: See 1 Kings (1 Samuel) 18–24.

271–75 *Look, it is I. . . . the innocent*: See 2 Kings (2 Samuel) 24:17.

279 *aforementioned counts*: Eberhard and Gilbert.

283 *Udo*: Also called Odo, count of Wetterau (ca. 895–949).

296 *the example of David*: 2 Kings (2 Samuel) 1:11–27 describes David's lamentations, including the canticle "Jonathan's Bow."

302–4 *the just man . . . instead of him*: See Proverbs 11:8.

351 *royal city*: That is, Frankfurt.

378 *Avars*: That is, the Hungarians.

385 *against*: *Ad* is here equivalent to *adversus;* see Charlton T. Lewis and Charles Short, *A Latin Dictionary* (Oxford, 1975), under *ad* I.A.2.a.ζ.

421 *Liutgard*: Only daughter of Otto and Edith, born 932, died 953.

443 *realm*: Ludwig was duke of Swabia (950–957).

447 *Conrad*: Conrad the Red, duke of Lorraine (944–953).

455 *Ida*: Daughter of Herman I, duke of Swabia (d. 986).

467 *Lothar*: Also called Lothar of Arles, king of Italy (948–950).

471 *Rudolf*: Rudolf II (ca. 880–937), king of Burgundy from 912 and king of Arles from 933.

474 *Adelaide*: Also called Saint Adelaide (931–999); the name Adelaide means "noble."

484 *Berengar*: Berengar II (ca. 900–966), king of Italy (r. 950–961), also called Berengar of Ivrea.

487 *King Hugh*: Born in approximately 880 and died in 947, king of Italy from 926 to 947. Berengar I (ca. 845–924) was king of Italy from 887 until his death, and also Holy Roman emperor between 915 and 924. His grandson, Berengar II, was prevented from the succession when Hugh was crowned in 926 (around the time Berengar's father, Adalbert of Ivrea, died). Lothar succeeded Hugh in 947 and died in 950, at which point Berengar II finally succeeded to his grandfather's title.

512 *removed Peter from the chains*: See Acts 12:3–11.

516 *Adelhard*: Bishop of Reggio from 945 to 952.

520 *city*: That is, Reggio.

554 *sheaths of growing grain*: Literally, "sheaths of growing Ceres," the classical goddess of grain standing by metonymy for "grain."

575 *stalks of grain*: Literally, "culms of Ceres"; see previous note.

602–4 Berengar II led a revolt against King Hugo around 940 and had to flee to Germany and Otto's protection when that revolt failed.

614 *without warfare*: Literally, "without Mars," the god of war standing by metonymy for war.

621 *accompanied by no small crowd*: Compare Virgil, *Aeneid* 2.40.

632 *marching in step*: Compare Virgil, *Aeneid* 1.82.

665 The wedding took place in the fall of 951.

687 *Conrad*: That is, Conrad the Red, who married Otto's daughter Liutgard.

720 *had sold . . . people*: Berengar asserts that Otto sold his kingdom back to him, so he, Otto, was effectively selling to Berengar the noblemen themselves. The passage is discussed by Rudolf Köpke, *Ottonische Studien zur deutschen Geschichte im zehnten Jahrhundert,* vol. 2, *Hrotsuit von Gandersheim* (Berlin, 1869), 105–6.

753–1136 A quire of eight leaves (sixteen pages), carrying 384 verses, is lost following line 752 in the Munich manuscript (M); I follow Berschin's numbering of the lines, which differs from that of von Winterfeld, Strecker, and Homeyer (following this gap, they assign to Berschin's lines 1137–84 numbers four higher than Berschin has). In the missing lines, covering the years from 953 to 957, Hrotsvit would probably have treated Liudolf's revolt, his defeat and penance, the Hungarian campaigns of 953–955, and Liudolf's campaigns in Italy in 956/7.

1150 *kingdom*: Liudolf led another expedition into Italy in 956/7 and drove out Berengar but died of fever shortly thereafter.

1166 *at last*: *Quandoquidem* is here equivalent to *quandoque.*

1168 *and no burden . . . journey*: The construction of lines 1167–69 is difficult: Hrotsvit seems to shift from a purpose clause in verse 1167 (imperfect subjunctive in secondary sequence following *ut*) to a result clause in 1168 (perfect subjunctive following [*ut*] *non;* see *Allen and Greenough's New Latin Grammar* [Boston, 1903], paragraph 485c); both clauses depend on *iussit* (ordered) in verse 1169. But the lack of a connective between verses 1167 and 1168 and the lack of a repetition of *ut* in 1168 are problematic, particularly since both verses precede *iussit* in 1169. Von Winterfeld, *Hrotsvithae opera,* 545, and Homeyer, *Hrotsvithae opera,* 435, tentatively suggest emending *non* (the negative adverb) to *nec* (the negative conjunction), but the change addresses only one of the difficulties.

1185–1472 Six leaves (twelve pages), carrying 288 verses are lost after this verse in the Munich manuscript. The missing text would have covered the years 957–962, including Liudolf's death, Otto's second campaign in Italy, and his coronation in 962 as emperor by Pope John XII. Again, I follow Berschin's numbering, while that of von Winterfeld, Strecker, and Homeyer is six lines higher starting from Berschin's line 1473.

1473 The text resumes with the end of a description of the coronation of Adelaide as empress.

1477 *King*: Hrotsvit's account is of the deeds of *King* Otto; she stops at the point that he became emperor.

1483–87 *how in the hard struggle . . . Willa*: Hrotsvit is referring to Otto's battles against Berengar between 962 and 964.

1488–92 *and how, inspired . . . leader*: The deposed pope was John XII; his successor was Leo VIII (963–965).

1493–94 *and how, with the kingdom . . . Italy*: The reference is to Otto's campaign in Italy in 966 against Adalbert, the son of Berengar.

1495 *both his dominions*: That is, as king and as emperor.

1497 *king*: Otto II was crowned king in 961.

1498 *insignia of imperial honor*: Otto II was crowned emperor in Rome in 967.

Proem to the Origins of the Gandersheim Convent

title Hrotsvit's second epic is a history of the founding and early years of her convent at Gandersheim. It was written after December 968, when Otto II became co-emperor (see *Origins* 77–80), and after Hrotsvit had written the *Deeds of Otto* (see *Origins* 80–81). It may be her last work. It is the only major work of Hrotsvit's not preserved in the Munich manuscript (M), though it may have once been present there; it survives only in modern copies (from the seventeenth and eighteenth centuries; see Berschin, *Opera omnia,* xix–xxi). Hrotsvit mixes documentary sources with local legends and primarily focuses on the piety of the individual founders and benefactors of the convent, the Liudolfinger family. *The Origins of the Gandersheim Convent* is thus, to some extent, an expansion and continuation of *The Deeds of Otto,* memorializing his and his family's role in building and endowing Gandersheim.

5 *Liudolf*: Died 866, a count of Saxony and the founder of the Liudolfinger dynasty, called by some later writers, including Hrotsvit, duke of Saxony; not to be confused with his great-great-grandson, Liudolf, duke of Swabia (d. 957). All references to a Liudolf in *The Origins of the Gandersheim Convent* are to Liudolf, duke of Saxony.

6 *Oddo*: Otto I (830/840–912), duke of Saxony (880–912). Throughout I refer to this man as Oddo, to avoid confusion with his grandson the emperor. Oddo was the father of Henry the Fowler, and grandfather of Emperor Otto I.

The Origins of the Gandersheim Convent

13 *Louis*: Louis the German (806/810–876), son of Louis the Pious and grandson of Charlemagne, king of East Francia from 843 to 876.

21–24 *Oda . . . Billung . . . Aeda*: Oda is countess of Saxony (806–913), wife of Liudolf, and daughter of Billung (a member of a Saxon dynasty of the same name) and Aeda, his wife. Nothing further is known about Aeda or her husband Billung.

70 *Henry*: Henry the Fowler; see above, note to *The Deeds of Otto* 7.

71 *Otto*: Otto I, "the Great," king of Germany (936–973) and Holy Roman emperor (962–973).

75 *throne*: The term is used metaphorically for "sovereignty." The verse may be corrupt; see Homeyer, *Hrotsvithae opera,* 453; Strecker, *Hrotsvithae opera,* 252; and von Winterfeld, *Hrotsvithae opera,* 231.

77 *son*: Otto II, co-emperor with his father Otto I from 967 to 973; sole emperor, 973–983.

81–82 *The pages . . . describe them more fully*: Hrotsvit is referring to her poem *Gesta Ottonis.*

91 *prophecy*: For *monitus* with the meaning "omen, prophecy," see Lewis and Short, *A Latin Dictionary,* under 2 *monitus* II.

103 *a small church*: The small church across the river Gande was

called Brunshausen; the nuns lived there for several years while the abbey of Gandersheim was under construction.

109 *Hathumoda*: First abbess of Gandersheim (ca. 840–874), she was only twelve years old when appointed, so her parents sent her to study at Herford Abbey.

115 *Herford Abbey*: The oldest nunnery in the duchy of Saxony, a house of secular canonesses, founded in approximately 789.

119 *Louis*: Louis, the German (d. 876), mentioned above in verse 13.

121 *Holy Father*: Pope Sergius II (844–847); the journey of Liudolf and Oda occurred around 845.

151 *may be watched over*: Normally deponent, *tueri* is used here passively.

162–63 *Anastasius . . . Innocent*: Popes Anastasius I (399–402) and Innocent I (402–417), who were the subject of a lost work or works by Hrotsvit.

183 Sense and grammar indicate that there is a verse (or more) lost at this point.

231 *fauns*: Hrotsvit's mention of fauns and monsters indicates that she is modeling this miracle on the prophecies given to Latinus and his daughter in Virgil's *Aeneid* 7.58–106.

234 Sense and grammar indicate that there is a verse (or more) lost at this point.

272 *and to cut away . . . digging*: Two versions of this line, different in wording but nearly identical in sense, appear in the manuscripts (numbered 272a and 272b by modern editors); my translation follows the second (272b). They may both be authorial, one being a later reworking. The translation of 272a: "and cut the mass of earth by digging around."

288 *dukes mentioned above*: Hrotsvit mentioned only Oddo above (*Proem to the Origins of the Gandersheim Convent* 6), but Liudolf and Oda had at least one other surviving son, Bruno, duke of Saxony (r. 866–880). He is mentioned below, at verses 362–63.

297 *torments*: The manuscripts read *febres* or *febris;* other editors emend to *fines* (the limits) or *flores* (the flowering).

307 *Louis*: Louis the Younger, king of East Francia (d. 882), second son of Louis the German.

317 *dying*: Hathumoda died in 874.

318 *Gerberga*: Gerberga I, also called Gerberga the Elder, another daughter of Liudolf and Oda (d. 896).

362–63 *Bruno . . . enemies of the Lord*: Oldest son of Liudolf and Oda, died in 880 fighting the Normans (Vikings), not the Hungarians, as Hrotsvit mistakenly says. He is venerated as Saint Bruno of Saxony by the Catholic Church.

365 *bishops*: The bishops of Minden and Hildesheim died along with Bruno.

368 *Louis*: Louis the Younger, king of East Francia.

393 *Wigbert*: Bishop of Hildesheim (880–908).

448 *Liutgard*: Liutgard of Saxony, queen of East Francia as wife of Louis the Younger.

452 *Arnulf*: Arnulf of Carinthia (887–899), not Louis's immediate successor as king of East Francia, Charles the Fat having intervened.

464 Louis died in 882.

470 Liutgard died in 885.

475 Gerberga died in 896.

485 *Christina*: Another daughter of Liudolf and Oda, third abbess of Gandersheim (896–919).

531 Oddo died in 912.

564 *Henry . . . Otto*: These are Henry the Fowler and his son, the emperor Otto I, born just as his grandfather Oddo was dying.

576 Oda died in 913.

584 Christina died in 919/20.

595 *they might . . . divine odes*: The text breaks off at verse 594, with an incomplete sentence; verse 595 was supplied by Berschin, modeled on *The History of the Birth of Mary* 86 and *Ascension* 89 and 148.

Appendix

title This poem appears in a composite manuscript of sermons, Würzburg, Universitätsbibliothek, M.p.th.f. 34, fol. 79v, in a portion of the manuscript from the tenth or eleventh century. The poem was studied and attributed to Hrotsvit on linguistic, stylistic, and metrical grounds by Tino Licht, "Hrotsvitspuren in ottonischer Dichtung (nebst einem neuen Hrotsvitgedicht)," *Mittellateinisches Jahrbuch* 43 (2008): 347–53, at 351; it was earlier edited, without attribution, by Karl Strecker, MGH Poetae Latini aevi Carolini 5.1–2 (Leipzig, 1937), 393. For an image of the original, see Virtuelle Bibliothek Würzburg, http://vb.uni-wuerzburg.de/ub/mpthf34/pages/mpthf34/158.html.

Bibliography

Editions and Translations

Bergman, Mary Bernardine, trans. "The Establishment of the Monastery of Gandersheim." Edited by Thomas Head. In *Medieval Hagiography: An Anthology,* edited by Thomas Head, 237–54. New York, 2001.

———. "*Hrotsvithae liber tertius:* A Text with Translation, Introduction and Commentary." PhD diss., Saint Louis University, 1942.

Berschin, Walter, ed. *Hrotsvit. Opera omnia.* Munich, 2001.

Bonfante, Larissa, trans. *The Plays of Hrotswitha of Gandersheim.* With Alexandra Bonfante-Warren. New York, 1979. Second edition, Oak Park, IL, 1986.

———, trans. *The Plays of Hrotswitha of Gandersheim: Bilingual Edition.* Edited by Robert Chipok. Mundelein, IL, 2013.

Celtes, Conrad, ed. *Opera Hrosvite illustris virginis et monialis germane gente Saxonica orte.* Nuremberg, 1501.

Goullet, Monique, trans. *Œuvres poétiques.* Grenoble, 2000.

Homeyer, Helene, ed. *Hrotsvithae opera.* Munich, 1970.

———, trans. *Werke in deutscher Übertragung.* Munich, 1973.

St. John, Christopher [Christabel Marshall], trans. *The Plays of Roswitha.* London, 1923. Reprint, New York, 1966.

Strecker, Karl, ed. *Hrotsvithae opera.* Leipzig, 1906. Second edition, Leipzig, 1930.

Tillyard, H. J. W., trans. *The Plays of Roswitha.* Charing Cross, 1923.

Wiegand, Gonsalva. "The Non-Dramatic Works of Hrotswitha: Text, Translation, and Commentary." PhD diss., Saint Louis University, 1936.

Wilson, Katharina, trans. *The Dramas of Hrotsvit of Gandersheim.* Saskatoon, 1985. Revised edition, *The Plays of Hrotsvit of Gandersheim.* New York, 1989.

——, trans. *Hrotsvit of Gandersheim: A Florilegium of Her Works.* Cambridge, 1998.

Winterfeld, Paul von, ed. *Hrotsvithae opera.* MGH Scriptores rerum Germanicarum in usum scholarum 34. Berlin, 1902.

Zeydel, Edwin. "On the Two Minor Poems in the Hrotsvitha Codex." *Modern Language Notes* 60 (1945): 73–76.

Further Reading

Berschin, Walter. *Biographie und Epochenstil im lateinischen Mittelalter.* Vol. 4, *Ottonische Biographie: Das hohe Mittelalter 920–1120 n. Chr.* Part 1, *920–1070 n. Chr.* Stuttgart, 1999.

Bodarwé, Katrinette. *Sanctimoniales Litteratae: Schriftlichkeit und Bildung in den Ottonischen Frauenkommunitäten Gandersheim, Essen und Quedlinburg.* Münster, 2004.

Brown, Phyllis R., Linda A. McMillin, and Katharina Wilson. *Hrotsvit of Gandersheim: Contexts, Identities, Affinities, and Performances.* Toronto, 2004.

Brown, Phyllis R., and Stephen L. Wailes, eds. *A Companion to Hrotsvit of Gandersheim (fl. 960): Contextual and Interpretive Approaches.* Leiden, 2013. With extensive bibliography, pp. 363–79.

Hoffmann, Hartmut. *Schreibschulen und Buchmalerei: Handschriften und Texte des 9.–11. Jahrhunderts.* Schriften der Monumenta Germaniae historica 65. Hannover, 2012.

Licht, Tino. "Hrotsvitspuren in ottonischer Dichtung (nebst einem neuen Hrotsvitgedicht)." *Mittellateinisches Jahrbuch* 43 (2008): 347–53.

Newman, Eva May. *The Latinity of the Works of Hrotsvit of Gandersheim.* Chicago, 1939.

Rädle, Fidel. "Hrotsvit von Gandersheim." In *Die deutsche Literatur des Mittelalters: Verfasserlexikon,* 2nd ed., edited by Kurt Ruh, Gundolf Keil, Werner Schröder, Burghart Wachinger, and Franz Josef Worstbrock, vol. 4, pp. 196–210. Berlin, 1978–2008.

——. "Hrotsvit von Gandersheim: Von der poetischen Salvierung einer unheiligen Welt." In *Ambivalenzen des geistlichen Spiels: Revisionen von*

Texten und Methoden, edited by Jörn Bockmann and Regina Toepfer, 259–90. Gottingen, 2018.

Scheck, Helene. "The Whore as *Imago Dei:* Being and Abjection in Hrotsvit's Rewriting of Thais." In *Sexuality, Sociality, and Cosmology in Medieval Literary Texts,* edited by Jennifer N. Brown and Marla Segol, 7–32. New York, 2013.

Zeydel, Edwin H. "Were Hrotsvitha's Dramas Performed during Her Lifetime?" *Speculum* 20 (1945): 443–56.

Index